The Complete Alekhine

Batsford Chess Library

The Complete Alekhine

GRAHAM BURGESS

An Owl Book
Henry Holt and Company
New York

Library of Congress Catalog Card Number: 92-54265

ISBN 0-8050-2425-5 (An Owl Book: pbk.)

Henry Holt books are available at special discounts
for bulk purchases for sales promotions, premiums,
fund-raising, or educational use. Special editions
or book excerpts can also be created to specification.

For details contact: Special Sales Director,
Henry Holt and Company, Inc., 115 West 18th Street,
New York, New York 10011.

First American Edition—1992

Printed in the United Kingdom
Recognizing the importance of preserving
the written word, Henry Holt and Company, Inc.,
by policy, prints all of its first editions
on acid-free paper.∞

10 9 8 7 6 5 4 3 2 1

Advisor: R.D. Keene GM, OBE
Technical Editor: Andrew Kinsman

Contents

Bibliography

Books

Siebenhaar, Delnef and Ottstadt, *Die Aljechin Verteidigung* (Schachverlag Reinhold Dreier): vol. 1 (2 ♘c3, 3 ♘c3, Chase, Four Pawns) 1986, vol. 2 (4 Misc., Exchange, 4 ♘f3) 1989. Referred to as 'SDO', these colossal tomes are very complete reference works and contain large amounts of original analysis.

Bagirov, *Zashchita Alekhina* (Fizkultura i Sport 1987). Also published in German.

Alburt and Schiller, *The Alekhine for the Tournament Player* (Batsford 1985).

Encyclopaedia of Chess Openings, vol. B (Šahovski Informator 1984). The principal authors are Bagirov for the lines with 4 ♘f3 and Hort for the rest. However, much of the Exchange Variation has, for some reason, been neglected.

Hort, *Alekhine's Defence* (A. & C. Black 1981). Languageless.

Eales and Williams, *Alekhine's Defence* (Batsford 1973). An excellent book, well ahead of its time.

Schwarz, *Aljechin - und Nimzowitsch - Verteidigung* (Das Schach Archiv 1969).

Many other games collections, general works and tournament bulletins were also consulted.

Periodicals

Informator

New in Chess Yearbook

Skakhmaty v SSSR

Byulleten Ts.Sh.K. SSSR

Chess

Skakbladet

Modern Chess Theory

The New Chess Player

New in Chess Magazine

Shakhmatny Byulleten

Chess in the USSR

British Chess Magazine

Pergamon Chess

Schach Echo

The Chess Player

ChessBase Magazine

Acknowledgements

I would especially like to thank those who helped by supplying original source material: Orla and Lykke Christiansen, Michael and Edith Schlosser, Arne Andersen, Carsten Buch, Alex Easton, Mike Rabbitt and Rajko Vujatović, and the many people who gave valuable help with analysis. Batsford should also be thanked, for showing interest in this project, which is my third book.

Graham Burgess
Svendborg 1991.

Symbols

+	Check
++	Double check
#	Checkmate
$\pm$ ($\mp$)	Slight advantage to White (Black)
$\pm$ ($\mp$)	Clear advantage to White (Black)
+− (−+)	Winning advantage to White (Black)
=	Level position
∞	Unclear position
!	Good move
?	Bad move
!!	Outstanding move
??	Blunder
!?	Interesting move
?!	Dubious move
Ch	Championship
IZ	Interzonal
Z	Zonal
ol	Olympiad

Correspondence

The symbols for move evaluations tend to be used in a variety of ways. For instance !? may mean 'there are alternatives' or 'maybe good'. ?! is often used when an annotator does not trust a move, but suspects that it could possibly be made to work. Some players mark their moves !! if they are a good attempt to blow the opponent off the board, even if objectively a simpler approach may be preferable.

Introduction

Opening schemes range from those in which Black aims to develop methodically, carefully neutralising White's threats, to those in which Black attempts to meet fire with fire, entering into a full-scale battle for the initiative from the outset. Alekhine's Defence represents the latter strategy in its purest form.

In the nineteenth century, 1 ... ♘f6 was generally regarded as a mistake, the most notable 'prehistoric' items being two odds games Anderssen–Pearson, London 1862 (2 e5 ♘d5 3 ♗c4) and Stanley–Horne, Cambridge 1860 which reached the line 2 ♘c3 d5 3 ed by transposition. The real history of the defence began in Budapest 1921, when Alexander Alekhine's impressive victory over Steiner suggested that chasing the impudent knight might be a double-edged venture. The new opening quickly found followers, amongst the 'hypermoderns' and elsewhere, but this was largely due to the natural appeal of any brash new idea. Before the end of the decade, many players, uncertain of its objective merits, especially against the Four Pawns Attack, began to abandon the opening.

The idea, however, had been established, and, especially in the post-war Soviet Union, analysts painstakingly constructed a sound theoretical basis for the Alekhine, the popularity of which gradually increased during the 1950s and 1960s. Players such as Mecking, Hort, Ljubojević, Timman, Vaganian and Larsen demonstrated the opening's dynamic potential, but it was Fischer's successes which led to the Alekhine's boom of the early to mid-1970s. However, the main line with 4 ♘f3 began to be perceived as unpleasant for Black, on account of the lines 4 ... g6 5 ♗c4 ♘b6 6 ♗b3 ♗g7 7 ♘g5 d5 8 f4 and 4 ... ♗g4 5 ♗e2 e6 6 0-0 ♗e7 7 c4 ♘b6 8 ♘c3 0-0 9 ♗e3 d5 10 c5 ♗xf3 11 gf. With no leading player willing to defend the opening's honour, it again retreated to the theoretical sidelines.

The 1980s saw a great deal of regeneration, notably from Lev Alburt, and a new generation of

Soviets, following the continuing example of Vladimir Bagirov. Currently, the Alekhine's bad reputation persists, but this is in spite of its rather healthy theoretical status and respectable record in practice. In most lines, Black has a choice of a number of reasonably sound options in addition to a variety of obscure attempts to create chaos.

Generally in an introduction to an openings book, the reader expects to find some general guidance as to how the opening in question should be played. In the case of the Alekhine this is no simple matter, since, unlike such openings as the Benoni, Queen's Gambit Declined and, to a lesser extent, main line Sicilians, the pawn structure will be in a state of flux quite some way into the game. Therefore Black must decide how to attack White's centre and consider how the tension may eventually be resolved before committing his minor pieces. Indeed, in the battle for the initiative, development may have to be delayed in order to secure counterplay — it is all too easy, having provoked White's pawns forward, to develop modestly, only to find one's pieces have no scope. White, in turn, should look to develop flexibly and actively, ready to counter Black's attempts to destroy the white centre.

I have tried to squeeze as much relevant material as possible into this book, to provide the reader with a wide range of possible repertoires without sacrificing detail in the critical lines. Naturally, attention is focused on the more fashionable and theoretically important systems, but without crowding out secondary lines, especially when these seem capable of renovation, or exemplify important ideas which may be employed in related variations.

I am indebted to the efforts of previous authors, and have tried to be as accurate as possible in attributing analysis. When variations appear without attribution, this is due to the original source being unclear, the moves being self-evident, or the analysis being original.

To update, the reader should begin with *Informator 51*, *NIC Yearbook 20*, *NIC Magazine 91/5*, *Shakhmatny Byulleten* 91/1, and *ChessBase Magazine* 22. I would recommend that this be done in a critical manner: on the one hand new games do not necessarily supersede old theory, nor on the other should they be viewed primarily in the context of existing theory. For instance, a player may have come up with a refinement in the move order, rather than merely 'transposed', or perhaps not have 'missed a strong possibility to attack', having found in his home analysis the theoretical recommendation to be dubious.

Of course, one can have too

much theory. A player who is familiar with a few key positions and a number of important ideas is liable to have more success in practice than one who has memorised a large mass of theory. Is it any use during a game to know that in a particular position there are five viable continuations, but not remember which is best, or why? Generally, though, understanding goes hand in hand with knowledge, enabling a chessplayer to find/recall the correct plan at the board.

To finish, I would like to wish readers creative satisfaction, good results and maybe even a few brilliancies in their Alekhine's adventures.

1 White does not play 2 e5

The moves in this chapter are fairly popular, though perhaps this is due more to the committal nature of 2 e5 than their intrinsic merits.

2 d3 and 2 ♗c4 are both rather compromising, but 2 ♘c3 is a sensible developing move which holds out some hope of an advantage. Players well versed in the subtleties of the Vienna and the Four Knights' may very well consider 2 ... e5. After 2 ... d5, White's only critical continuation is 3 e5, whereupon 3 ... ♘e4 has emerged as the main choice for hard-core Alekhine players. This move remains experimental in character, though results are encouraging.

Todorčević–Tal
Marseille 1989

1	**e4**	**♘f6** *(1)*
2	**d3**	

2 ♗c4 is an extremely enterprising idea, but poses Black no real problems. 2 ... d5 3 ed ♘xd5 4 ♘c3 transposes to 2 ♘c3 d5 3 ed ♘xd5 4 ♗c4. A route to solid equality is 2 ... e6 3 ♘c3 d5, but Black has two ambitious ideas:

(a) 2 ... ♘xe4 3 ♗xf7+ ♔xf7 4 ♕h5+ ♔g8 (4 ... g6 5 ♕d5+ e6 6 ♕xe4 ♗g7 7 ♕f4+ ♗f6?! 8 ♘c3 d5 9 ♘f3 ♖f8 10 d4± was Meštrović–Vukić, Yugoslav Ch 1975, but simply 7 ... ♔e8 is a substantial improvement.) 5 ♕d5+ e6 6 ♕xe4 d5 7 ♕e2 c5 was judged good for Black by Euwe, due to Black's bishops and strong centre, but the weakness of e5 and Black's inability to castle seem no less relevant, e.g. 8 ♘f3 ♘c6 9 d3 ♗e7 10 ♗f4 ♗f6 11 c3 ♗d7 12 0–0 ♕b6 13 ♘bd2 ♖e8 14 ♘e5 ♘xe5 15 ♗xe5 h5 16 ♘f3 ♗c6 17 a4 h4 18 h3 ♕d8 19 d4± Sermek–H. Grünberg, Bled 1989.

(b) 2 ... b5!? 3 ♗b3 (3 ♗xb5 ♘xe4) 3 ... c5!? (3 ... ♗b7 4 d3 c5 5 ♘f3 e6!? 6 e5 ♘g8 7 0–0 ♘c6 8 c4?! b4 9 ♗f4 ♘ge7 10 d4!? [Ivanović–Kovačević, Sarajevo 1983] 10 ... ♘xd4! 11 ♘xd4 cd 12 ♛xd4 ♘f5 13 ♛d3 ♗c5 gives Black good prospects on the kingside. White should prefer 8 c3=) 4 e5 c4 5 ef gf 6 ♛f3 ♘c6 7 ♘e2 ♗b7 8 ♛g3 ♕a5 9 ♗xc4 bc 10 ♘a3 ♛d5 11 ♘c3 ♛e6+ 12 ♔d1 ♘e5 13 ♖e1 h5 14 f4 h4 15 ♛e3 ♗h6 16 ♖e2 ♛f5 17 ♘xc4 ♗xf4 18 ♛f2 ♛g4 19 d3 ♗xh2 20 ♘e3 ♛g3 21 ♛xg3 ♗xg3 22 d4 ♘f3!? 23 ♘f5 e6 24 ♘e4 ♗xe4 25 ♖xe4 ♘g5 26 ♗xg5 fg 27 ♘xg3 hg∓ Glavan–Dobren, Pula 1990.

2 ... e5

Black has plenty of feasible alternatives, but this is the simplest way to profit from White's insipid second move. Black is ideally placed to meet an attempt to reach a King's Indian Attack, so how is White to develop?

3 ♘f3

3 f4 is a logical attempt to justify 2 d3, but the moves do not blend well: 3 ... ♘c6! 4 ♘f3 (4 fe ♘xe5 5 ♘f3 ♘xf3+ 6 ♛xf3 d5 7 e5 ♛e7 8 d4 ♘e4 9 ♗d3 ♛h4+ 10 g3 ♛g4 11 ♘d2 ♛xf3 12 ♘xf3 ♗e7 13 ♗e3 ♗h3 14 ♗xe4 de 15 ♘d2 0–0–0 16 0–0–0 f6 17 ef ♗xf6 18 c3 ♖he8= Nimzowitsch–Alekhine, New York 1927) 4 ... d5 5 ed (5 fe de 6 ef ef 7 ♛xf3 ♘d4 8 ♛e4+ ♗e6 9 ♔d1!∓ Carr–Burgess, Cambridge 1989) 5 ... ♘xd5 6 fe ♗g4 7 ♗e2 (7 c3 ♘xe5 8 ♛e2 ♗d6 9 d4 ♗xf3 10 gf ♛h4+ 11 ♔d1 0–0–0 12 de ♖he8) 7 ... ♗xf3 8 ♗xf3 ♛h4+ 9 g3 (9 ♔f1? 0–0–0 10 ♘c3 ♗c5! 11 ♘e4 ♘e3+ 12 ♗xe3 ♗xe3 13 ♛e1 ♛h6 14 ♘g3 ♘d4!∓ Maroczy–Alekhine, New York 1924) 9 ... ♛d4 10 ♛e2 0–0–0 11 c3 ♛xe5 12 0–0 ♛xe2 13 ♗xe2 ♗e7, with ... ♗f6 to follow, was assessed as equal by Alekhine.

3 ... ♘c6
4 ♗e2

After **4 ♘bd2 d5**, White has a couple of independent ideas:

(a) **5 g3?! ♗c5!** (Logical when White fianchettoes.) 6 ♗g2 de 7 de 0–0 8 0–0 a5 9 a4 (9 c3 b6! took control of the a6–f1 diagonal in Rakić–Ciocaltea, Novi Sad 1973, since 10 ♛e2? fails to 10 ... ♗a6 11 ♘c4 a4!. There followed 10 ♘b3 ♗d6 11 ♗g5 h6 12 ♗xf6 ♛xf6 13 a4 ♗a6 14 ♖e1 ♘d8!∓) 9 ... ♛e7 10 c3 ♖d8 11 ♘h4? g6 12 h3 b6! 13 ♖e1 ♖d3! 14 ♘hf3 ♗xf2+! 15 ♔xf2 ♛c5+ 0–1 Todorčević–Kovačević, Ljubljana 1989.

(b) **5 c3** intends 5 ... ♗e7 6 b4 a6 7 a3 0–0 8 ♗b2 ♖e8 9 ♛c2. Black may as well prevent this with 5 ... a5, whilst 5 ... g6 is also logical, since b4 is less effective when Black has e5 well defended.

4 ... d5
5 ♘bd2 g6

5 ... ♗c5 exposes the bishop for no good reason here, e.g. 6 c3 de 7 de a5 8 0–0 0–0 9 ♛c2 ♖e8 10 ♘c4 ♛e7 11 ♗g5± Keres–Allen, Vancouver 1975.

By developing the bishop modestly, Black can maintain the central tension. The principal alternative to the text is **5 ... ♗e7** 6 0–0 (6 c3 a5 7 ♕c2 0–0 8 ♘f1 ♖e8 9 ♘g3 g6 10 0–0 ♕d6 11 b3 ♗f8 12 ♗b2 ♗g7= Csom–Lengyel, Hungarian Ch 1966) 6 ... 0–0 7 c3 a5. From this position, Marangunić–Flear, Bern Open 1991 continued 8 a4 (8 ♕c2 ♖e8 9 ♖e1 ♗f8 10 ♘f1 h6 11 ♗d1 b6 12 ♘g3 ♗a6 13 ♗e2 g6= Barcza–Pogats, Hungarian Ch 1959) 8 ... ♖e8 9 h3 ♗f8 10 ♖e1 h6 11 ♗f1 ♗e6 12 ♕c2 ♘d7! 13 ♘b3 f5 14 ed ♗xd5 15 ♘fd2 ♕f6 16 ♗e2 (16 ♘c4) 16 ... ♖ad8 17 ♗f3 (17 ♗h5) 17 ... ♕f7 18 ♗xd5 ♕xd5 19 ♘f1 f4!, when White was clearly in desperate trouble. After 20 d4 ed 21 ♖xe8 ♖xe8 22 ♗xf4 d3 23 ♕d1 ♘c5! 24 ♘xc5 ♗xc5 25 ♘e3 ♗xe3 26 ♗xe3 ♘e7! 27 c4 ♕e4 28 ♕h5 ♘f5 29 ♗d2 ♖e5! 30 ♕g4 ♕xg4 31 hg ♘d6 32 b3 ♖e2 33 ♖d1 ♘e4 34 ♗e3 d2 35 ♔f1 ♘g3+! Black obtained a won ending.

6 0–0

6 c3 ♗g7 (6 ... a5 7 ♕a4) 7 b4 (7 0–0 a5; 7 ♕c2 0–0 8 ♘f1?! b6! 9 ♘g3 ♗b7∓ Tartakower–Bogolyubov, London 1922) 7 ... 0–0 8 ♗b2 ♘h5 9 g3 ♗h3 crossed White's plans in Csom–Polgar, Hungarian Ch 1966.

6	...	♗g7
7	c3	a5!
8	a4	0–0
9	♖e1	♖e8

| 10 | ♗f1 | b6 *(2)* |

Often a useful move, especially when White has no pressure on the long diagonal.

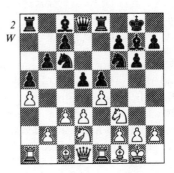

2
W

11	ed	♘xd5
12	♕b3	♘f4
13	♘e4	♗e6
14	♕c2	♘d5
15	g3	h6
16	♗g2	♕d7
17	♘ed2	♖ad8
18	♘c4	♘db4!

In trying to generate play against e5, White has allowed a devastating combination.

19	cb	♘xb4
20	♕c3	♕xd3
21	♘a3	e4

All is now clear. Black will have a won ending. 22 ♕xd3 ♘xd3 23 ♖xe4 ♘xc1 24 ♖xc1 ♗xb2 25 ♖xc7 ♖d1+ 26 ♖e1 ♖xe1+ 27 ♘xe1 ♗xa3 28 ♘d3 ♖d8 29 ♗f1 ♗f5 30 ♖c3 ♗b4 31 ♖b3 ♖d4 32 f3 ♗d7 33 ♔f2 ♗xa4 34 ♖b2 ♗e7 35 ♔e3 ♖d6 36 ♘e5 ♖d1 37 ♗c4 ♖e1+ 38 ♖e2 ♗c5+ 39 ♔d3 ♖xe2 40 ♔xe2 ♔g7 41 ♘xf7 ♗e7 42 ♘e5 ♗d6 0–1.

Gibbs–Schmid
Lugano 1968

1 e4 ♘f6 2 ♘c3 d5
3   ed   ♘xd5
4   ♘ge2

A related idea is **4 g3**, inviting transposition to a line of the Vienna, with 4 ... e5. This is considered satisfactory for Black, though far from simple to play. Black has two main methods of disrupting White's intended control of the long diagonal:

(a) **4 ... b6** 5 ♗g2 ♗b7 6 ♘f3 (Black's initial achievement is to keep this knight away from its ideal post on e2.) 6 ... e6 7 0–0 ♗e7 (7 ... ♘xc3 8 bc ♗e7 9 a4 a5 Darcyl–Hjorth, Dortmund 1980) 8 ♖e1 0–0 9 ♘e4 ♘d7 10 d3 ♘c5 11 ♘xc5 ♗xc5 12 ♘e5 ♕c8 13 ♗d2 f6= Westerinen–Timman, Tallinn 1973.

(b) **4 ... ♘xc3** 5 bc ♕d5 6 ♘f3 (6 ♕f3) 6 ... ♕e4+ 7 ♗e2 ♗h3 8 ♖g1. Clearly this is a major inconvenience for White, but Black must now back-pedal with care. Benkö–Martz, USA Ch (New York) 1972 continued 8 ... ♗g4 (8 ... ♗c8!?) 9 d3 ♕c6 10 c4 e6 11 ♖b1 ♗e7 12 ♘e5 (12 ♗b2!? ♗b4+ 13 ♘d2 ♗xe2 14 ♕xe2± Martz) 12 ... ♗xe2 13 ♕xe2 ♕a6 14 ♔f1 (After 14 ♕f3, Black can try 14 ... ♗f6 15 ♘g4 ♗c3+ or 14 ... 0–0 15 ♕xb7 ♕xa2 16 ♖b2 ♕a1 17 ♔e2 ♗a3 18 ♖e1 ♘a6) 14 ... ♘c6 15 ♘xc6 ♕xc6 16 ♗b2 0–0 17 ♕g4 and a

draw was agreed in view of 17 ... f6 18 ♖e1 e5 19 ♕e4.
    4 ♘xd5 is very insipid indeed. After **4 ... ♕xd5**, White has tried two moves.
    (a) **5 ♕f3 ♕c5** (5 ... e6 6 ♕xd5 ed 7 ♘f3 ♗f5 8 d3 ♘c6 9 ♗f4 ♔d7! 10 0–0–0 ♖e8 was quite pleasant for Black in Smyslov–Vaganian, Moscow TV 1987. Is this any way to use the white pieces?) 6 ♕b3 ♘c6 7 ♘f3 e5 8 ♗c4 f6 9 0–0 ♗d6 10 d4 ed 11 ♗g8 ♘e7 12 ♕f7+ ♔d7 13 b4 ♕xb4 14 ♗d2 ♕c5 15 ♖fe1 b6 16 ♕xg7 ♖xg8 17 ♖xe7+ ♗xe7 18 ♕xg8 ♗b7 19 ♕xh7 ♗xf3 20 ♕h3+ ♔c6 21 ♕xf3+ ♕d5∓ Razinkin–Aronin, USSR 1960.
    (b) **5 d4 ♘c6 6 ♘f3** (6 c3 e5; 6 ♗e3 e5 7 de ♕xe5 8 c3 ♗c5∓) and Black can break in the centre immediately, or develop a little first:
    (b1) **6 ... e5** 7 ♗e3 (7 ♘xe5 ♘xd4; 7 de ♕xd1+ 8 ♔xd1 ♗g4 9 ♗f4 ♗c5∓) 7 ... ♗g4 (7 ... ed 8 ♘xd4 ♗c5=) 8 de ♗xf3 9 ♕xf3 ♕xf3 10 gf ♘xe5 11 0–0–0 ♗d6 12 ♗b5+ ♔f8 13 ♗e2 h5! 14 ♖d5 ♘g6 15 ♗d3 b6 16 h3 ♖e8 17 ♖g1 ♖e6 18 ♔d1 ♖f6 19 ♗d4 ♖xf3 and Black had secured counterplay in Salazar–Alburt, Santiago 1981.
    (b2) **6 ... ♗g4** 7 ♗e2 0–0–0 8 c3 e5 9 0–0 ed 10 cd ♗d6 (10 ... ♘xd4? 11 ♘xd4 ♗xe2 12 ♕xe2 ♕xd4 13 ♗g5± ♕d3? 14 ♖ad1+−; 10 ... ♗xf3 11 ♗xf3 ♕xd4 12 ♕b3=) 11 ♗e3 ♔b8 12

h3 ♗d7 13 ♕c2?! (13 ♖c1=) 13 ... f6 14 a3 ♖de8 15 ♖fd1 ♘e7 16 ♕c4 ♗c6 17 ♕c1 g5 18 ♘e1 h5 19 ♗f3 ♕f5∓ Alburt–Vasiukov, Kharkov 1967.

4 d4 was met by **4 ... ♘c6** 5 ♗b5 (5 ♘xd5 transposes to 4 ♘xd5 ♕xd5 5 d4 above; 5 ♘f3) 5 ... ♘xc3 6 ♗xc6+ bc 7 bc ♕d5 8 ♕f3 ♗f5 9 ♕xd5 cd 10 ♗f4∓ in Factor–Alekhine, Pasadena 1932, whilst **4 ... ♗f5** is also good: 5 ♗d3 ♗xd3 6 ♕xd3 ♘c6 and White must defend against 7 ... ♘db4, and after 5 ♘xd5 ♕xd5, Black threatens to win a pawn with 6 ... ♕e4+. Also feasible is the forthright **4 ... ♘xc3** 5 bc g6, transposing to lines considered under 4 ♘f3 after 6 ♘f3 or 6 ♗c4 ♗g7 7 ♘f3.

4 ♘f3. Black has tried a number of approaches.

(a) **4 ... ♘c6** 5 d4 ♗f5 6 a3 g6 7 ♗c4 ♘b6 8 ♗a2 ♗g7 9 ♗e3 e5 10 ♕e2 0–0 11 de ♗g4 12 ♖d1 ♔e8= Yates–Nimzowitsch, Baden Baden 1925.

(b) **4 ... ♗g4** 5 d4 e6 6 ♘xd5 ♕xd5 7 ♗e2 is much less dynamic for Black than the line 4 ♘xd5 ♕xd5 5 d4 above, since Black no longer has an option of a quick ... e5.

(c) **4 ... ♗f5** 5 ♘h4?! (5 d4 ♘b4; 5 ♘xd5 ♕xd5 6 d4? ♕e4+; 5 ♗c4) 5 ... ♗g6 6 ♘xg6 hg 7 ♕f3 e6 8 ♗c4 ♖h5!? 9 g4?! ♖e5+ 10 ♘e2 ♘c6 11 c3 (11 ♕g3 ♗d6 12 f4 ♘xf4) 11 ... ♘b6 12 d4 ♘xc4 13 de ♘6xe5 14 ♕h3 (14 ♕xb7 c6

threatens 15 ... ♖b8, 16 ... ♕d5) 14 ... ♕d5 15 ♘g3 ♕d3 0–1 Fellegi–Glatt, Hungary 1974 was an amusing miniature.

(d) **4 ... ♘xc3 5 bc g6 6 d4 ♗g7** *(3)*. The position resembles an Exchange Grünfeld, but with the pawn on c2 instead of e4 — this can only be in Black's favour!

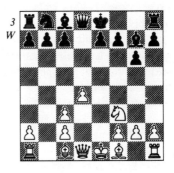

(d1) **7 ♗e3** c5 8 ♕d2 ♕a5 9 ♗c4 ♘c6∓ Mosionzhik–Bagirov, Novosibirsk 1962.

(d2) **7 ♗f4** 0–0 8 ♗e5 c5 9 ♗xg7 ♔xg7 10 ♕d2 ♕d6 11 dc ♕xd2+ (Hort considers the ending after 11 ... ♕xc5 12 ♕d4+ ♕xd4 13 cd marginally to favour White.) 12 ♘xd2 ♗e6 13 ♘b3 ♖c8 14 ♘d4 ♗d7 15 ♖b1 e5! 16 ♘b3 a5! 17 ♘d2 ♖xc5 18 ♖xb7 ♗c6 19 ♖b2 ♖xc3! 20 ♘c4 ♘d7 21 ♔d2 ♖h3 22 gh ♗xh1 23 ♖b5! ♖d8 24 ♖xa5 ♘b6+ 25 ♔e1 ♘d5 26 ♘e3 f5 27 ♘xd5 ♗xd5 28 c4 ♗f3 29 ♗e2 ♗xe2 30 ♔xe2 ♖d4 31 ♖c5 e4 and both player's fine manoeuvres had led to a balanced, though still sharp, rook ending in Kholmov–Alburt, USSR Ch 1972.

(d3) **7 ♗c4** 0–0 8 0–0 c5 9 ♗a3 (9 ♗e3 ♘c6; 9 ♕e2 ♘c6 10 ♗e3 ♗g4 11 ♖ab1 cd 12 cd ♘xd4 13 ♗xd4 ♗xf3 14 ♕xf3 ♕xd4 ½–½ Weidemann–Behrhorst, Bundesliga 1987/8) and now 9 ... b5!? 10 ♗d3 (10 ♗xb5 ♕a5 11 ♗d3 ♕xa3 12 ♗e4 ♗a6) 10 ... ♘d7 11 ♗xb5 ♕a5 12 ♗xd7 ♕xa3 is possibly a little speculative, whilst 9 ... ♘d7 is a solid, logical continuation. In Janetschek–Eslon, Barcelona 1975, Black opened lines rather too obligingly: 9 ... cd 10 cd ♘c6 11 c3 ♕a5 12 ♕b3 ♗g4 13 ♗d5 ♗f6 14 ♖fe1±.

4 ♕f3. Black now has a number of moves:

(a) **4 ... e6** 5 ♗c4 c6 6 ♗b3 ♗e7 7 ♘ge2 0–0 8 d4 ♘xc3 9 ♕xc3 b6 10 ♕f3 ♗b7 11 0–0 ♕c8 12 ♕g3 ♘d7 13 c3 c5 set up a strong defensive position in Meštrović–Cvitan, Zurich 1983. White now overpressed, to put it mildly: 14 ♗h6 ♗f6 15 ♗c2 ♖d8 16 ♘f4? ♔h8! 17 ♗g5 ♗xg5 18 ♕xg5 cd 19 ♕h5 ♘f6 20 ♕xf7 e5 21 ♘h3 ♗xg2! 0–1.

(b) **4 ... ♘b6** has generally been the recommended move, as ♗c4 is prevented. White can investigate the pawn sacrifices 5 d4 and 5 a4 a5 6 d4!?

(c) **4 ... c6** 5 ♗c4 ♗e6 gives White the choice between 6 ♘h3 ♘d7?! (6 ... ♘c7 7 ♗b3) 7 ♗xd5 ♘e5 8 ♕e2 ♗xd5 9 ♘f4!± Taimanov–Buchmann, Leningrad

1974, and 6 ♘ge2 ♘c7 7 ♗xe6 ♘xe6 8 d4!? ♘xd4 9 ♘xd4 ♕xd4 10 ♗e3 when White has good attacking chances.

(d) **4 ... ♘b4** is a sound route to equality. 5 ♗c4 e6 6 ♗b3 ♘8c6 7 ♘ge2 ♘a5 8 ♗a4+ (8 0–0? ♘xb3 9 cb ♕d3 10 ♕g4 h5 11 ♕g3 ♕xg3 12 hg ♘d3 13 ♘f4 ♘xf4 14 gf ♗d7 15 d4 0–0–0 16 d5 ed 17 ♘xd5 ♗c6 18 ♘c3 h4 19 f3 h3 20 ♗e3 ♖d3 21 ♔f2 ♖xe3 22 ♔xe3 ♗c5+ 23 ♔d3 hg 24 ♖fe1 ♗xf3 25 ♘e2 ♗xe2+ 0–1 Lapinski–Bagirov, Daugavpils 1990) 8 ... ♗d7 9 a3 ♘d5 10 ♘xd5 (10 ♗xd7+ ♕xd7 11 d3 c5 12 ♘xd5 ed= Elkin–Nosenko, Jurmala 1985) 10 ... ♗xa4 (10 ... ed? 11 ♕xd5 ♗xa4 12 ♕e4+) 11 ♘e3 ♗c6 12 ♕h5 b6 13 b4 ♕f6 14 ♖b1 ♘b7 15 ♗b2 ♕g6 16 ♕h4 ♗d6 17 ♘f4 ♗xf4 18 ♕xf4 ♘d6 19 d3 0–0 20h4 f6= Simagin–Bagirov, Moscow 1968.

4 ... ♘c6!

Black controls d4 while frustrating White's intention of a king's fianchetto, as we shall see. Less assertive, though also good, is **4 ... e6** 5 g3 ♘xc3 6 ♘xc3 ♗d7 (preparing to oppose the long diagonal) 7 ♗c4 c5 8 0–0 ♘c6 9 ♖e1 ♘b4 10 ♗d5 ♗c6 11 ♗xc6+ ♘xc6 12 d3 ♗e7 13 ♗e3 0–0 14 ♘e4 b6 ½–½ Keres–Marović, Erevan 1971. A direct method also gave reasonable play in Lisitsyn–Mikenas, Riga 1968: **4 ... ♗g4** 5 h3 ♘xc3 6 bc ♗xe2! 7 ♗xe2 c6 8 d4 e6 9 ♖b1 ♕c7 10

♗e3 ♘d7 11 c4 ♗e7 12 ♕d2
0–0 13 0–0 ♖ad8 14 c3 e5! 15 f4
ed 16 cd ♗f6 17 ♕c1 ♖fe8 18
♖d1 ♘f8 19 ♗f3 ♘g6∓.

5 g3?

5 d4?! ♘xc3 6 bc e5 makes the
knight on e2 look rather silly.
White's best is 5 ♘xd5 ♕xd5 6
♘c3 ♕d6!?, though Black's control of d4 guarantees equal play.

5 ... ♗g4
6 ♗g2 ♘d4! *(4)*

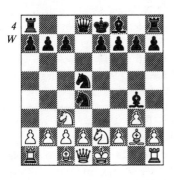

Curiously enough, the mirror-
image of this position can occur
in the English Opening: 1 c4 e5 2
♘c3 ♘c6 3 ♘f3 g6 4 d4 ed 5 ♘d5
♗g7 6 ♗g5 ♘ge7? (6 ... ♘ce7!)
7 ♘xd4! or 1 ♘f3 g6 2 c4 ♗g7 3
♘c3 e5 4 d4 ed 5 ♗g5!? ♘e7? (5
... f6 6 ♕xd4) 6 ♘d5 ♘bc6 7
♘xd4! Beaumont–Cooper, Bristol
League 1991.

7 ♗xd5?

This loses material, as does 7
♘xd4 ♗xd1 8 ♗xd5 e5!, but
White could battle on with 7 h3
♘xc3 8 dc ♘f3+ 9 ♗xf3 ♕xd1+
10 ♔xd1 ♗xf3∓ though with no

great prospect of eventual survival.

7 ... ♕xd5!
8 f3

With the result decided, White
may as well have allowed one of
the pretty mates: **8 ♘xd5 ♘f3+ 9
♔f1 ♗h3 #** or **8 0–0 ♘f3+ 9
♔h1 ♘g5+ 10 ♘xd5 ♗f3+ 11
♔g1 ♘h3 #.**

8 ... ♕xf3
9 ♖f1 ♕g2
0–1

Lein–Alburt
New York 1980

1 e4 ♘f6 2 ♘c3 d5 3 ed ♘xd5
4 ♗c4

This is the main attempt to
justify the exchange on d5. Black
does best to reply with simple
development, whilst bearing in
mind possibilities of hunting down
this bishop to reduce pressure on
f7.

4 ... ♘b6

4 ... ♘xc3 is just about playable: 5 ♕f3 e6 6 ♕xc3 ♘c6 (6 ...
♕g5?! 7 ♔f1! ♘c6 8 ♘f3; 6 ...
♘d7) 7 ♘f3 ♕f6 8 ♕xf6 gf 9 d4
♗d7 (9 ... ♖g8?! 10 ♗f4) and
White was only a little more
comfortable in Schultz–Prokes,
Bardyov 1926.

4 ... e6 has been played fre-
quently here. However, a computer pointed out that **5 ♗xd5**
(only a computer would consider
such an ugly move!) 5 ... ed 6
♕e2+ ♗e6 (6 ... ♗e7 7 ♕e5) 7
♕b5+ wins a pawn. After 7 ...

♘c6 8 ♕xb7 ♘b4 (8 ... ♘d4 9 ♘b5) 9 ♕b5+ ♗d7 10 ♕e2+ ♗e7 11 d3 0-0 12 a3 ♖e8 13 ♕d1!? real compensation for Black is not obvious.

Also interesting is **5 ♘ge2!?** ♗e7 6 d4 0-0 7 0-0 b6 8 ♖e1 ♗b7 9 ♘xd5± Liiva–Burgess, Võsu (Estonia) 1989.

As for queen moves, **5 ♕g4** ♘f6 6 ♕g3 ♗c5! 7 ♕xg7? ♖g8 8 ♕h6 ♗xf2+! is rather misguided, but **5 ♕f3** will transpose to other lines with ♕f3 (e.g. 5 ... ♘b4!? is considered under 4 ♕f3 ♘b4 5 ♗c4 e6).

5 ♘f3 ♗e7 6 0-0 0-0 is unlikely to cause Black any problems: **7 ♘e4?!** c5 8 c3 b6 9 d4 ♗b7 10 ♘g3 ♘d7∓ Vucinić–Kovačević, Yugoslav Ch 1985; **7 d4** b6 (7 ... ♘xc3 8 bc ♘d7= Keres) 8 ♘e4 ♗b7 9 ♕e2 ♘d7 10 ♖d1 c5 11 dc (11 ♗b5?! cd 12 ♘xd4 ♕c7∓ Bisguier–Keres, Tallinn 1971) 11 ... ♘xc5= Bagirov; **7 ♖e1** ♘xc3 (7 ... ♘f6 8 d4 ♘bd7 9 ♗f4 ♘b6) 8 bc ♘d7 9 d4 b6 10 a4 a6 11 ♕e2 ♗b7 12 ♗d3 c5 13 ♗f4 ♕c8 was comfortable for Black in Fedorov–Sandić, Belgrade GMA 1988.

5 ♗b3

5 ♗e2?! is rather insipid and illogical. 5 ... c5!? (5 ... e5) 6 ♘f3 ♘c6 7 0-0 e5 8 d3?! (8 ♗b5, despite the loss of tempi, is the only consistent continuation. As the game proceeds, White obtains the black side of a King's Indian gone wrong.) 8 ... ♗e7 9 ♖e1 0-0 10 ♗f1 f6 11 h3 ♗e6 12 a4 ♘d7 13 g3 ♖f7 14 ♗g2 ♘f8 15 ♗e3 ♕d7 16 ♔h2 g5∓ Maroczy–Flohr, Bled 1931.

5 ... ♘c6

There are a couple of inferior alternatives.

5 ... c5?! meets with a strong reply which activates White's queen and restricts the c8 bishop: 6 ♕h5! e6 (6 ... c4 7 ♗xc4 wins a pawn in return for some activity.) 7 d3 ♘c6 (7 ... ♗e7 8 ♘e4) 8 ♗g5! ♗e7 9 ♗xe7! ♕xe7 10 ♘e4 and White's forces gather for a kingside onslaught.

5 ... e5?! leaves f7 too weak: 6 d3 ♘c6 7 ♘f3 ♗g4 (7 ... ♗e7 8 ♘g5 ♗xg5 9 ♕h5±) 8 h3 ♗h5? (8 ... ♗xf3± is necessary, though an admission of failure.) 9 ♘xe5!! ♗xd1 10 ♗xf7+ ♔e7 11 ♗g5+ ♔d6 12 ♘e4+ ♔xe5 13 f4+ ♔d4 14 ♖xd1 has given White a mating attack in several games, the earliest of which was probably Imbaud–Strumilo, 1924.

6 ♘f3

White has a number of options:

(a) **6 f4?!** is dreadfully ugly. 6 ... ♘d4 7 ♘f3 ♘xb3 8 ab g6 left Black very comfortable in Dowden–Tomaszewski, Graz 1978.

(b) **6 ♕h5?!** g6 7 ♕f3 ♘e5 8 ♕f4 ♗g7 9 d4 ♘ec4∓.

(c) **6 ♘ge2** e5! is now perfectly feasible since White cannot play quickly against f7. 7 0-0 ♗e7 8 d3 0-0 9 ♔h1 a5 10 a3 ♘d4 11 ♘xd4 ed∓ W. Schmidt–Rührig, Germany 1977.

(d) **6 d3** is something of a waiting move. Weak is 6 ... e5?! 7 ♘f3! (see 5 ... e5?!), while on 6 ... ♗f5, White can hunt down the bishop, but this gives no more than equality: 7 ♘ge2 e6 8 ♘g3 ♗g6 9 ♗e3 ♗e7 10 ♕d2 ♘d4 11 ♘e2 ♘xb3= was Kostjoerin–Dietrich, Lugano 1968.

(e) **6 ♕f3** e6 7 ♘ge2 (7 ♕g3 ♘d4 8 ♘f3 ♘f5 9 ♕e5 ♗d6 10 ♕e4 0–0 11 d4 ♘d7 12 ♗g5 ♘f6 13 ♕d3 h6 was fine for Black in Stoll–Grün, 1981.) 7 ... ♘a5 8 ♕g3 ♗d7 9 d4 ♗c6 10 ♗f4 ♖c8 11 0–0 g6 12 ♗e5 ♗d6! 13 ♘f4 ♗xe5 14 de ♘xb3 15 ab a6 16 ♖ad1 ♕e7. Black's alert play has been exemplary. In Costigan–Ghizdavu, USA 1976, there followed 17 ♖d4 ♖d8 18 ♘ce2 ♖d7! 19 ♖fd1 ♔d8! 20 ♘d3 ♔c8 21 b4 ♗b5!∓ 22 ♘c5 ♗xe2 23 ♖xd7 ♘xd7 24 ♖xd7 ♖d8! leading to a won ending.

6   ...   ♗f5

This is the most common move, but a couple of alternatives should be noted: **6 ... ♘a5** 7 d4 ♘xb3 8 ab ♗g4 9 h3± ♗f5 10 ♕e2 c6 11 ♗g5!? h6 12 ♗h4 ♘d5 13 0–0 ♘f6 14 ♖fd1 g5 15 ♗g3 ♗g7 16 d5 Larsson–Smagin, Naestved 1988; **6 ... g6!?** 7 ♘g5 e6 8 d3 ♘d4 9 0–0 ♗g7 10 ♘ce4 h6 11 ♘f3 ♘xb3 equalised in Rozentalis–Bagirov, Vilnius 1985. Note that on **6 ... e5?!**, 7 d3 is still strong (see 5 ... e5?!).

7   d4

Three other ideas:

(a) **7 a4** is logical, but time-consuming. 7 ... ♘a5 8 ♗a2 e6 9 0–0 ♗e7 10 ♖e1 0–0 11 ♘e4 c5!? 12 ♘g3 ♗g6 13 d3 ♘c6! 14 ♗b3 c4 15 dc ♕xd1 16 ♖xd1 ♘a5 17 ♗f4 ♘bxc4 18 ♗xc4 ♘xc4 19 ♘e5 ♘xe5 20 ♗xe5 ♖fd8 21 c4 ♖ac8 and Black's fine play gave him a distinct plus in Epishin–Cs. Horvath, Leningrad 1989.

(b) **7 0–0** e6 8 ♖e1 (8 d3 and 8 d4 transpose to lines below.) 8 ... ♗e7 9 ♘e4 ♘a5! 10 ♘g3 ♗g6 11 ♘e5 ♘xb3 12 ab ♘d7 13 ♘xg6 hg 14 ♕f3 c6 15 d3 ♘f6 was equal in Barczay–Hazai, Hungary 1977. Note that Black did not rush to castle while the h-file was of potential use.

(c) **7 d3** e6 8 0–0 ♗e7 and three moves have been tried: 9 ♖e1 0–0 10 ♗f4?! (10 a3 ♖e8 followed by ... ♘d5.) 10 ... ♘a5 11 h3 ♘xb3 was pleasant for Black in Estrin–Hazai, Agaard 1976; 9 ♗f4 0–0 10 ♕d2 ♘d5 11 ♘xd5 ed 12 ♖fe1 ♗f6= Barle–Hazai, Pula 1975; 9 ♗d2 0–0?! (9 ... ♘a5=) 10 ♘e4 ruled out ... ♘a5, leaving White somewhat better in Winants–Stull, Lyon Z 1990.

7   ...   e6 *(5)*

8   ♗f4?!

8 0–0 ♗e7 9 d5 ed 10 ♘xd5 ♘xd5 11 ♗xd5 0–0= was an attempt to remove all dynamism in Taimanov–Tseshkovsky, USSR Ch 1976. There's not a great deal Black can do about it if White plays like this!

8 h3 ♘a5 9 ♕e2 ♘xb3 10 ab

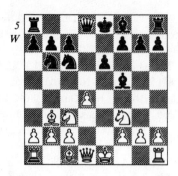

5
W

♗d6 11 0–0 c6 12 ♘e4 ♗xe4 13
♕xe4 ♘d7 14 c3 h6 (Black is
careful not to castle into an
attack.) 15 ♘d2 0–0 16 ♘c4 ♗c7
17 f4 ♘f6 18 ♕e2 ♖e8 19 ♗d2
♕d5∓ 20 b4 ♘e4 21 ♗e1 b6 22
♘d2 ♘xd2 23 ♗xd2 a5 24 ba ba
25 ♗e3 ♖eb8 gave Black pressure
on the queenside in Apicella–
Palatnik, Belgrade GMA 1988,
which White managed to survive.

The text puts the bishop on
rather a bad square; Byrne and
Mednis suggest it should have
gone to e3 (even on move 9, though
of course White is not playing for
advantage any more).

8	...	♗d6
9	♕d2?!	0–0
10	♗g3	♗g4!
11	0–0–0	

Lein 'castles into it' hoping to
justify his play, but more prudent
was damage limitation, e.g. 11
♗xd6 ♕xd6 12 ♘e4. But who
wants to be fighting for a draw
with White after eleven moves?

11	...	♘a5!
12	♖de1	♘xb3+
13	ab	a5!

14	♘e5	♗f5
15	♗f4	♗xe5!
16	♗xe5	a4
17	ba	♘xa4
18	g4	♗g6
19	h4	♘xc3
20	♕xc3	♖a6
21	♕e3	

The opposite-wing attacks have
not been much of a race. Byrne &
Mednis give the pretty variation
21 ♕xc7?! ♕a8 22 ♕e7 ♖c8 23
c3 ♖xc3+! 24 bc ♖a2 winning.
Instead, the game finished in more
mundane fashion (after 21 ♕e3) 21
... ♖c6 22 c3 ♕a8 23 ♔d1 ♕a4+
24 ♔e2 ♕b5+ 25 ♔f3 ♕xb2 26
♖c1 f6 27 ♗g3 ♗c2 28 c4 ♕b3
29 ♖xc2 ♕xc2 30 ♖c1 ♕a2 31
♔g2 ♖e8 32 c5 ♕d5+ 33 ♔h2
♖d8 34 ♖d1 e5 35 g5 ed 36 ♕f4
♕xc5 37 gf ♖xf6 38 ♕d2 ♖f7 39
♖c1 ♕h5 40 ♕d3 c5 41 ♕b5 d3
42 ♖e1 d2 0–1.

Bellón–Kovačević
Karlovac 1979

1 e4 ♘f6 2 ♘c3 d5

3	e5	♘fd7

3 ... d4 generally leads to rather
dreary positions, though a lively
option for White is **4 ♘ce2**, which
can be met by 4 ... d3!?, 4 ... ♗g8,
4 ... ♘e4 (transposing to 3 ... ♘e4
4 ♘ce2 d4), or 4 ... ♗g4 5 f4 ♘c6
(5 ... h5 6 h3 ♘h6 7 ♘f3 ♘f5 8
d3 c5 9 g3 ♘c6 Meštrović–Borgo,
Aosta 1990) 6 ♘f3 f6 7 h3 ♘h6 8
c3!?± Tal–Böhm, Wijk aan Zee
1976. White normally plays **4 ef**

dc 5 fg (5 bc ef 6 d4 ♗d6 7 ♗d3 0–0 8 ♕f3 c5 9 ♘e2 ♕c7 10 ♗f4 ♘c6= Lukin–Marinković, Leningrad 1989. 5 ♕h5 can be met by 5 ... cb 6 ♗xb2 ef 7 ♗c4 g6 8 ♕e2+ ♗e6 Konieczka–Behrhorst, Bundesliga 1986/7 or 5 ... ♕d6 6 dc ♕xf6 7 ♗e3 ♕f5 8 ♕e2 ♘c6 9 ♘f3 e5 10 0–0–0 ♗d6 Konieczka–Kavalek, Bundesliga 1987/8.) **5 ... cd+** and now:

(a) **6 ♗xd2 ♗xg7** 7 ♕f3 (7 ♕h5 is well met by 7 ... ♕d6 8 ♘f3 ♕g6 9 ♕c5 ♕b6 or 7 ... ♕d4!? 8 c3 ♕e4+ 9 ♗e3 ♘c6 10 ♘f3 ♕g6.) 7 ... ♗xb2 8 ♖d1 ♕d4 (8 ... ♕d6 9 ♗c4 ♗f6 10 ♘e2 ♘c6 11 ♗c3 ♗xc3+ 12 ♕xc3 ♕b4 13 ♗b5!∞ Balashov–Timoshenko, Moscow Ch 1989) 9 ♘e2 ♕g4 10 ♕b3 ♗f6?! (10 ... ♗g7; 10 ... ♗e5!? 11 ♗c3 ♗g7) 11 ♘f4 (11 ♗f4!?) 11 ... ♘c6 12 ♗e2 ♕f5 13 ♘d5 ♗e5 14 ♗c3 (14 f4!?) 14 ... ♖g8 15 f4! and now in Balashov–Alburt, USSR Ch (Leningrad) 1974, 15 ... ♗d6 16 0–0 ♗d7 was necessary.

(b) **6 ♕xd2 ♕xd2+ 7 ♗xd2 ♗xg7 8 0–0–0.** White has the simple plan ♘e2 and ♗c3, which seems to preserve some advantage:

(b1) **8 ... ♗g4** 9 f3 (9 ♖e1!? e6 10 f3 ♗f5 11 g4 ♗g6 12 ♘e2; 9 ♗e2 ♗xe2 10 ♘xe2±) 9 ... ♗f5 (9 ... ♗e6 10 ♘e2) 10 ♘e2 ♘c6 11 ♗c3 0–0 12 g4 ♗g6 13 h4 h6 14 h5 ♗h7 15 f4 ♗e4 16 ♖h3 ♖ad8 17 ♖e1 e6 18 ♖g3 ♘e7 19 f5 ef 20 ♗xg7 ♔xg7 21 ♘c3±

Taulbut–Iskov, Silkeborg 1980.

(b2) **8 ... ♗e6!?** 9 ♘e2.

(b3) **8 ... ♗f5** 9 ♘e2 ♘d7 10 ♘g3 (10 ♗c3 ♖g8 11 ♗xg7 ♖xg7 12 ♘g3 ♗d7=) 10 ... ♗g6 11 h4 h5 12 f4 e6 13 f5±.

(b4) **8 ... 0–0** 9 ♗c4 ♘d7 10 ♘f3 ♘b6 11 ♗d3 ♗g4 12 ♖de1 ♗xf3 13 gf e6 14 ♖hg1± Bisguier–Kreisman, US Open 1989.

(b5) **8 ... ♘c6** 9 ♗b5 (9 ♘e2 ♗d7 10 ♗c3 can be met by 10 ... ♖g8 11 g3 ♗g4= Machulsky–Palatnik, Kiev 1989, or 10 ... ♗xc3 11 ♘xc3 0–0–0 12 ♗e2 ♗f5 13 ♖xd8+ ♖xd8 14 ♖d1 ♖xd1+ 15 ♗xd1 ½–½ Kengis–Bagirov, Jurmala 1985.) 9 ... ♗d7 10 ♘e2 (10 ♘f3 0–0–0 11 ♖he1 e6 12 ♘g5 ♖df8 13 ♗e3 a6 14 ♗e2 h6 15 ♘e4 ♘e7 gave White only a small edge in Chekhov–Barlov, Tjentište 1975.) 10 ... a6 11 ♗a4 0–0–0 12 ♗c3 ♗xc3 (12 ... ♖hg8) 13 ♘xc3±.

4 e6

4 ♘xd5 ♘xe5 5 ♘e3 c5 (5 ... ♘bc6) 6 b3 ♘ec6! 7 ♗b2 e5=.

4 ♘f3 ought not to be very harmful, but 4 ... d4 (4 ... c5; 4 ... e6) 5 ♘e2 e6 6 ♘exd4 ♘xe5 7 ♘xe5 ♕xd4 8 ♘f3 ♕d6 9 d4 c5 10 ♗b5+ ♗d7 11 ♗xd7+ ♘xd7 12 0–0 was perhaps a shade better for White in Yanev–Donchev, Bulgarian Ch (Sofia) 1989.

4 f4 can easily transpose to a French Defence, but both sides have ways to avoid this:

(a) **4 ... d4?!** 5 ♘e4 e6 6 ♘f3 ♘c5 7 ♘xc5 ♗xc5 8 ♗d3!±

Gufeld–Vukić, USSR–Yugoslavia 1979.

(b) **4 ... ♘b6** 5 d4 h5 6 ♘f3 ♗f5 7 ♗e2 e6 8 0–0 ♘c6 9 a3 ♗g6 10 b3 ♘e7 11 ♘h4 ♘f5 gave Black reasonable prospects in Pirisi–Bagirov, Budapest 1983.

(c) **4 ... c5** 5 ♘f3 ♘c6 6 d4 cd!? 7 ♘b5 ♘db8! 8 c3?! ♗g4 9 ♗e2 dc 10 ♕xd5 ♕xd5 11 ♘c7+ ♔d7 12 ♘xd5 cb∓ Habershon–Shovel, British Ch (Edinburgh) 1985.

(d) **4 ... e6** 5 ♘f3 (5 d4 is a French.) **5 ... c5 6 g3 ♘c6 7 ♗g2 ♗e7 8 0–0.** Now Black can insert 8 ... a6 9 a4, but should probably not follow up with 9 ... ♕a5 10 d3 b5, since 11 f5! b4 12 fe fe 13 ♘e2 ♘dxe5?! 14 ♘xe5 ♘xe5 15 ♘f4 ♗f6 16 ♕h5+ g6 17 ♕e2 ♗g7 18 ♘xd5 ed 19 ♗h6! ♗g4 20 ♕e3 ♕c7 21 ♗xg7 ♕xg7 22 ♖ae1 gave White a winning position in Balashov–Schmidt, Riga 1975. After **8 ... 0–0**:

(d1) **9 d4** cd 10 ♘e2 b5?! 11 ♘exd4 ♘xd4 12 ♘xd4 b4 13 ♗e3 ♕b6 14 ♕g4± Horn–Landenbergue, Geneva 1986.

(d2) **9 ♔h1** b5?! 10 ♘xb5 ♗a6 11 a4 ♕a5 12 ♕e2 ♖ab8 13 d3 ♗xb5 14 ab ♕xb5 (14 ... ♕xa1 15 bc ♘b6 16 f5!) 15 f5! ef 16 e6± Kupreichik–Balashov, Kiev 1984.

(d3) **9 d3** f6 10 ef ♘xf6 11 ♕e2 ♖e8 12 ♗d2 (Alburt proposes that Black should seize on the weakness of e3, with 12 ... ♘b4 followed by ... d4, ... ♘bd5 and ... ♘g4.) 13 h3! h6 14 ♖ae1 e5? 15 fe ♘xe5 16 ♘xe5 ♖xe5 17

♕d1!± a6 18 ♗f4 ♖xe1 19 ♕xe1 ♗xf4 20 ♖xf4 d4 21 ♘d5 ♘xd5 22 ♗xd5+ ♔h8 23 ♕e5! 1–0 Balashov–Schmidt, Halle 1976.

4 d4 also invites a French, which would arise after 4 ... e6. An independent try is **4 ... c5**. Then 5 e6 fe is considered below (4 e6 fe 5 d4 c5), 5 ♘xd5?! cd 6 ♕xd4? ♘b6! drops a piece, 5 dc e6 6 ♘f3 ♘c6 is a harmless line of the French, 5 ♗b5?! ♘c6 (5 ... e6) 6 ♘f3 (6 ♘xd5?! ♘xd4) 6 ... e6 simply misplaces the bishop, whilst on 5 f4 cd 6 ♘b5 ♘c6 7 ♘f3, Shovel's 7 ... ♘db8!? is possible.

4 ... fe
5 d4 *(6)*

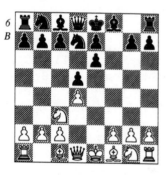

5 ... g6

5 ... c5 6 ♘f3 ♘c6 7 dc g6 (7 ... a6 8 ♗e3 ♘f6 9 ♗g5 ♕c7 10 g3±) 8 h4 ♘f6 9 ♗b5 (9 h5 gh 10 ♗e2 e5 11 ♘g5 ♗g4) 9 ... ♗g7 10 ♗f4 0–0 11 ♗xc6 ♘e4!? 12 ♗e5 ♗xe5 13 ♘xe4 ♗g7= Lyublinsky–Mikenas, Moscow 1949.

5 ... ♞f6 6 ♞f3 g6 7 ♞e5 (7 ♗f4!?) 7 ... ♗g7 8 h4 c5 9 h5 cd worked well for Black in Suttles–Mecking, Sousse IZ 1967.

6 h4 ♞f6?!

After **6 ... ♗g7 7 h5 ♞f8**, possible continuations are **8 ♗d3 ♞c6!** 9 hg hg 10 ♖xh8 ♗xh8 11 ♗e3 (11 ♗xg6+? ♞xg6 12 ♛h5 ♚f7 13 ♞f3 ♛g8!) 11 ... e5! 12 de d4 13 ♗h6 dc 14 ♛f3 ♗f5 15 ♗xf5 ♞xe5! which gave Black the initiative in Bobkov–Sokolov, corres. 1960, **8 ♞f3 c5!?**, **8 ♗f4 c5** 9 ♞b5 ♞a6 10 ♞f3 ♗d7 11 ♞e5 ♛a5+ 12 ♛d2 ♛xd2+ 13 ♚xd2 c4 Hector–Maus, Copenhagen Open 1990, and **8 h6 ♗f6** 9 g4 ♖g8 10 g5 ♗h8 11 ♞f3 e5 12 de (12 ♞xe5 ♗xe5 13 de c6) 12 ... c6 intending ... ♗g4 (Alburt).

7 h5! ♞xh5

No improvement was 7 ... ♖g8 8 hg hg 9 ♞f3 c5 10 ♞e5 ♞c6 11 ♗b5 ♗d7 12 ♗xc6 ♗xc6 13 ♗e3 ♛a5 14 ♛f3 ♛b4 15 0–0–0 c4 16 g4 g5 17 ♖h5 a5 18 ♖xg5 ♗g7 19 ♖xg7 ♖xg7 20 g5+ − in Hector–Schön, Malmo 1988.

8	**♖xh5!**	**gh**
9	**♛xh5+**	**♚d7**
10	**♞f3**	**♗g7**
11	**♗h6**	**♗f6**
12	**♞xd5!**	

More incisive than 12 g4 ♛e8 13 ♛h3. Black should now try 12 ... c6 13 ♞f4 ♚c7, though White's compensation is clearly excellent.

12	**...**	**ed?**
13	**♛xd5+**	**♚e8**
14	**♛h5+**	**♚d7**

15	**0–0–0**	**c6**

15 ... ♛g8 16 ♞e5+ ♚d8 17 ♞f7+ ♚d7 18 ♗c4! e6 19 ♗xe6+! ♚xe6 20 ♖e1+ ♚d7 21 ♛d5# is an example of the blunt nature of White's threats.

16	**♗f4**	**♛g8**

16 ... ♛e8 17 ♞e5+ ♚d8 18 ♞f7+ ♚d7 19 ♛f5+.

17	**♞e5+**	**♚d8**
18	**♞f7+**	**♚d7**
19	**♛f5+**	**♚e8**
20	**♛xc8+**	**♚xf7**
21	**♗c4+**	**1–0**

Vorotnikov–Kengis
Riga 1983

1 e4 ♞f6 2 ♞c3 d5 3 e5

3	**...**	**♞e4**
4	**♞ce2**	

This is the critical move, by which White aims to trap, or at least gain tempi on, the e4 knight. Plenty of other moves have been tried. Some of these give positions that can be reached via 2 e5 ♞d5 3 ♞c3 ♞xc3 4 dc (or 4 bc) 4 ... d5. Thus 4 ♛f3 ♞xc3 5 dc, 4 d4 ♞xc3 5 bc, 4 ♗d3 ♞xc3 5 dc, 4 g3 ♞xc3 5 dc and 4 ♞f3 ♞xc3 5 dc are considered in those sections.

(a) **4 ♞b1 d4 5 f4 ♞c6 6 ♞f3 e6 7 d3 ♞c5 8 c4 b6 9 ♞a3 ♗b7 10 ♞c2 a5 11 ♗e2 ♞b4** was fine for Black in Hartmann–Vogler, Mainz 1981.

(b) **4 ♞f3 ♗g4** (4 ... ♞xc3) **5 h3 ♗h5 6 g4 ♞xc3 7 bc ♗g6 8 d3 e6 9 ♗g2 c5 10 0–0 ♞c6 11 ♛e2 ♗e7 12 ♗f4 ♛a5** gave Black no problems in Brito–Alburt, Hastings 1980/1.

(c) **4 &d3 ♘c5!?**

(d) **4 ♕f3 ♘xc3** (4 ... ♘c6?! is no more than a cheap trap: 5 &b5 [5 ♘xe4? ♘d4] 5 ... ♘xc3 6 dc±) 5 ♕xc3?! (5 dc) 5 ... e6 6 ♘f3 c5 7 &b5+ ♘c6 8 d4 ♕b6 gave White a very silly position in Beutel–Spiegel, Lörzweiler 1986.

(e) **4 ♘xe4 de 5 d4 ed** (5 ... e6 transposes to an interesting and probably underestimated line of the French [6 &c4!?]. 5 ... &f5 is an attempt to avoid the drawish simplifications possible following the en passant capture: 6 ♘e2 ♘c6 [6 ... e6 7 &e3 c5 8 dc ♘d7 Klip–Bagirov, Dieren 1990] 7 c3 e6 8 ♘g3 &g6 9 h4 h5 [9 ... h6!?] 10 &e2 ♕d5 was Mirković–Siegel, Bela Crkva 1985. Now after 11 ♘xh5 Black's compensation is not clear: 11 ... ♘xe5? 12 ♘f4; 11 ... e3?! 12 ♘f4; 11 ... &xh5 12 &xh5 &e7 13 g3.) **6 &xd3** (6 ♕xd3 is extremely insipid. 6 ... ♕xd3 7 &xd3 ♘c6 8 &f4 h6!? 9 &b5 &d7 10 e6 &xe6 11 &xc6+ bc 12 &xc7 &d5 gave Black a very pleasant ending in Rucheva–Levitina, USSR 1985.) **6 ... ♘c6** and White has now tried a number of moves:

(e1) **7 ♕e2? ♘d4 8 ♕e4? &f5 9 ♕xb7 &xd3 10 cd ♖b8–+** was Kuzmin–Zukhin, Moscow 1984. Presumably White wasn't in a mood to play chess.

(e2) **7 f4 ♕d5!** is a powerful centralisation.

(e3) **7 &f4 ♕d5!** (Other moves fail to equalise.) 8 ♘f3 &g4 9 h3 (Since 9 &e2 ♕e4! is promising for Black, White steers the game towards a draw.) 9 ... &xf3 10 ♕xf3 ♕xf3 11 gf e6 12 &b5 0–0–0 13 &xc6 ½–½ Mordue–Burgess, Bristol Ch 1990.

(e4) **7 ♘f3 &g4 8 h3** (8 &f4 ♕d5!) 8 ... &xf3 9 ♕xf3 ♕d4 10 0–0 ♕xe5 11 &f4 ♕f6 12 ♖ad1 g5 13 &xc7 ♕xf3 14 gf &g7 and Black had a reasonable ending in Rõtov–Karpov, Leningrad 1969.

4 ...   f6

4 ... d4 is the other, and probably sounder, method of disrupting White's pawn centre. 5 d3 ♘c5 poses Black no problems: 6 b4?! ♘e6 7 ♘f3 c5! 8 bc ♘c6 9 &b2 b6! 10 c3 bc 11 ♖c1 ♖b8 12 &a1 ♕a5 13 ♕d2 g6 14 cd ♕xd2+ 15 ♘xd2 ♘b4∓ Filtser–Bronstein, Moscow 1959; 6 ♘g3 ♘c6 7 f4 e6 8 ♘f3 b6 9 &e2 &b7 10 0–0 &e7 11 &d2 a5 12 &e1 g5!? 13 fg &xg5 14 &d2 &e7 15 ♘h5 ♖g8 16 &h6 ♕d5 left Black's pieces rather better placed in Kurlenda–Lados, Slupsk 1989; 6 ♘f3 ♘c6 7 h3 (7 b4 ♘e6 achieves little after either 8 b5 ♘b8 9 &b2 c5 or 8 &b2 ♘xb4 9 ♘exd4 ♘xd4 10 ♘xd4 c5 11 ♘b3 g6!? ∞.) 7 ... g6 8 c3 &g7 9 ♘exd4 ♘xe5 10 ♘xe5 &xe5 11 ♘f3 &g7 12 d4 ♘e4= Dähr–Grzesik, Braunschweig 1983.

Therefore, White generally plays **5 c3!?** which practically forces Black to sacrifice a pawn, since 5 ... dc? is just a cheap trap (6 ♕a4+? ♘d7 7 ♕xe4 ♘c5), but not one suitable even for five-minute games since simply 6 bc gives Black a dreadful position. After **5 ... ♘c6** *(7)*, White has tried two moves:

(a) **6 ♘xd4 ♘xd4** (6 ... ♘xe5? 7 ♕e2 ♕d5 8 ♘b5!) 7 ♕a4+ c6 8 ♕xd4 ♕xd4 9 cd ♘g5 10 ♗c4 (10 d3 ♘e6 11 ♗e3 ♘c7 12 ♘f3 ♗g4 13 ♗e2 e6 14 a3 0-0-0) 10 ... ♘e6 (10 ... b5!? 11 ♗e2!? [11 ♗b3 ♗f5= Bagirov] 11 ... ♘e6 12 ♘f3 ♗d7 13 d3 0-0-0 14 ♗e3 ♗e8 15 ♖c1 f6 Pekárek) 11 ♘e2 ♘c7 12 a3 (12 d3 a5 13 a4 e6 14 ♗d2 ♘d5 15 ♘c3 ♘b4= Yako-vich–Kengis, USSR 1984) 12 ... ♗e6 13 d3 ♗d5 14 0-0 e6 15 ♗d2 0-0-0 16 ♖ac1 ♗e7 17 b4 ♔b8 18 ♗e3 ♖d7 19 ♘c3 ♖c8. This position illustrates well the type of compensation Black is aiming for. All the black pieces are on good squares, especially the 'bad' bishop on d5, while White's extra doubled pawn, firmly block-aded, will never provide any win-

ning chances. Indeed, after 20 ♘e4 b5 21 ♗xd5 ♘xd5 22 ♘c5 ♗xc5 23 ♖xc5 ♖b7 24 ♖fc1 ♖b6 25 ♖1c2 ♔b7 26 ♖e2 ♖a6 27 ♗c1 ♖a4 28 ♗b2 a5 it was Black who was playing for a win in Garcia Callejo–Bagirov, Amsterdam OHRA 1989.

(b) **6 cd ♘g5** gives a problematic position. White can either dog-gedly hang on to the pawn or look for a way to return it for some tempi.

(b1) **7 d5** ♕xd5 8 d4 ♘e4.

(b2) **7 g3** ♘e6 8 ♗g2 ♘exd4 9 ♕a4 and Black can choose between 9 ... ♕d7 and SDO's 9 ... b5!? 10 ♗xc6+ ♘xc6 11 ♕xb5 when 11 ... ♕d7 makes it difficult for White to keep the pawn in a satisfactory way.

(b3) **7 d3** ♘e6 8 ♘f3 ♘exd4 9 ♘exd4 ♘xd4 10 ♕a4+ ♘c6 11 d4 is a position that can be reached with 7 h4 or 7 f4, except that here White has done without these useful/weakening moves. Black can choose between 11 ... ♗e6 to place the bishop on d5, 11 ... ♕d5, and 11 ... e6 with ideas of an irritating check on b4 and ... ♗d7.

(b4) **7 f4** ♘e6 8 ♘f3 ♘exd4 9 ♘exd4 ♘xd4 10 ♕a4+ ♘c6 11 ♕e4?! (11 d4 can be met by 11 ... ♕d5, 11 ... ♗e6 or 11 ... e6) 11 ... ♗e6 12 ♗b5 ♗d5 13 ♕e2 e6∓ Harandi–Ogaard, Siegen ol 1970.

(b5) **7 h4** ♘e6 8 ♘f3 ♘exd4 (8 ... a6?! 9 d5 ♕xd5 10 d4 ♘ed8?!

11 ♘c3 ♕d7 12 d5 ♘a7 13 e6 ♕d6 14 ♕d4 c5 15 ♕a4+ b5 16 ♘xb5 was clearly a disaster in Shulman–Shabalov, Riga 1986, though 10 ... ♕e4 11 ♗e3! ♘ed8 12 ♘c3 ♕f5 is not much of an improvement.) 9 ♘fxd4 ♘xd4 10 ♕a4+ ♘c6= Bellón–Schmidt, Pula 1975.

(b6) **7 ♕a4** a6 8 f4 ♘e6 9 ♘f3 b5 10 ♕c2 ♗b7 11 ♕c3 g6. In return for a rather useless pawn, Black has some well-placed pieces. However, White has a space advantage and hopes of play against the black king. Wittmann–Herndl, Austrian Ch (Wolfsberg) 1985 continued 12 d3 ♕d5 13 ♗e3 ♗g7 14 h4 h5 15 ♖h3 and Black unwisely castled into it: 15 ... 0–0? 16 ♖g3 ♔h8 17 ♕d2 (threatening ♘c3) 17 ... b4 18 ♖c1 ♕xa2 19 f5! and White's attack was overwhelming. The black king is perfectly happy on e8, so Black should certainly prefer 15 ... ♗h6, pressuring f4 while waiting for White to reveal a plan.

It should also be mentioned that **4 ... ♘c5** 5 d4 ♘e6 gives Black little chance of equality. After 6 f4 g6 7 ♘f3 (7 ♗e3!?) 7 ... c5 8 c3 ♘c6 Black can hope for counterplay, but 6 ♗e3! hinders ... c5, while keeping options open as to which pawn should lead a kingside advance. Fomina–Alexandria, USSR Women's Ch (Tbilisi) 1976 continued 6 ... c5 7 dc ♘c6 (7 ... ♘a6 8 ♘c3!? d4 9 ♗b5+ ♗d7 10 ♗xa6 is intriguing, though 8 ♘f3 is certainly safer.) 8 ♘f3

♕a5+ 9 ♘c3 g6 10 ♕xd5 ♗g7 11 ♗e2 0–0 12 0–0 ♖d8 13 ♕c4 ♘xe5 14 ♘xe5 ♗xe5 15 ♘d5 ♖e8 16 c3± ♗g7 17 ♖ad1 ♖b8 18 f4 ♘d8 19 b4 ♕a4 20 ♘xe7+! and White won. In Chikovani–Mikadze, USSR 1976 Black opted for simple development but White had no difficulty in retaining a very pleasant position: 6 ... g6 7 ♘f3 ♗g7 8 h4 h5 9 c3 b6 10 ♘g5.

5 d3

5 ♘f3 is best met by 5 ... fe 6 d3 ♘d6 7 ♘xe5 ♘d7 8 ♘xd7 ♗xd7 9 ♘f4 c6 10 ♕e2 ♘f7 11 d4 g6 when Black has no serious problems. Smyslov–Alburt, USSR Ch 1977 continued 12 ♘e6 ♗xe6 13 ♕xe6 ♗g7 14 c3 ♕d6 15 ♕xd6 ♘xd6 16 f4 ♔d7 17 ♗d3 b5 18 a3 a5 19 ♔e2 b4 20 ♗d2 bc 21 bc a4 22 ♖hb1 ♖hb8 23 ♖b4 ♖xb4 24 ab e6 25 ♗c2 ♘c4 26 ♖xa4 ♖xa4 27 ♗xa4 ♘xd2 and the game was soon drawn.

5 ♘f4 has been tried by Chris Baker. Now **5 ... g6** 6 d3 ♘g5 transposes to 5 d3 ♘g5 6 ♘f4 g6 considered below. **5 ... e6** 6 d3 ♘g5 similarly transposes to 5 d3 ♘g5 6 ♘f4 e6, though White can try 6 ♕h5+ ♔d7 7 f3 (7 ♘g6?! hg 8 ♕xh8 ♘xf2!) 7 ... fe 8 fe ef 9 ed ♕e8 10 de+ ♕xe6+ which is rather murky.

5	...	♘g5 *(8)*
6	♗xg5	

Fairly harmless are **6 f4** ♘f7 and **6 ♘g3** ♘f7 7 ef ef 8 d4 ♘c6 9 c3 ♗e6 10 ♗d3 ♕d7 11 ♘1e2 ♘d6 12 ♕c2 g6= Dvoretsky–

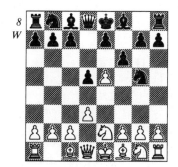

8
W

Schmidt, Tbilisi 1974.

6 ②f4 demands careful play from Black:

(a) **6 ... g6** is generally considered best: 7 h4 ②e6 8 h5 (8 ②f3 c5 9 d4 ②c6 10 dc ②xf4 11 ♗xf4 ♗g4 12 ef ef 13 ♕e2+ ♕e7 14 0-0-0 0-0-0 15 ♗d6 ♕xe2 16 ♗xe2 ♗xd6 17 cd ♖xd6 18 ♖he1 d4 was OK for Black in Zeidler-Dunworth, British Ch [Swansea] 1987.) 8 ... ②xf4 9 ♗xf4 g5 10 ♗g3 ②c6 11 d4 ♗h6 was very murky in Terentiev-Kengis, USSR 1983, but White prematurely released the central tension: 12 ef? ef 13 ♗b5 0-0 14 c3 ②e7∓.

(b) **6 ... e6** has been condemned on the basis of Burger-Alburt, New York 1980: 7 ef (7 ②f3!?) 7 ... ♕xf6 8 ♕g4 ♗b4+ 9 ♔d1 0-0 10 ②h5 ♕xf2 11 ②f3 ♖xf3 12 ♕xb4 ②c6 13 ♕d2 ♕xd2+? 14 ♗xd2 ♖f5 15 g4 ♖e5 16 ♗f4 ②f7 17 ♗xe5 ②fxe5 18 ♗e2 ②d4 19 c3 ②xe2 20 ♔xe2 ♗d7 21 ♖hf1 ♗b5 22 ♖ad1 and Black had insufficient compensation; however Benko pointed out that 13 ... h6 saves Black since after 14 h4

②h7 the knight will not hamper the rook's retreat.

6 ... fg

7 h4

7 ♕d2 e6 8 h4 forced open the h-file in Chekhlov-Kengis, Riga 1989, but Black used the tempo to build up his own attack: 9 ... gh, 9 ②f3 ♗e7 10 d4 c5 11 dc ②c6 12 0-0-0 0-0 13 ♔b1 b6! 14 cb ♕xb6 15 ②ed4 ♖b8 16 b3 ②xd4 17 ②xd4 a5 18 g3 a4 19 gh ab 20 cb ♗b4 21 ♕e3 ♖a8 22 ♖g1 ♗f7 23 f4 ♖c7 24 ♖g2 ♗c3 25 h5 ♖a4! 26 ②f5 d4! 27 ②xg7 ♖xa2! 0-1.

7 ②g3 seems insufficiently active. 7 ... e6 8 ♕g4 g6 9 h4 ②c6 10 ②f3 gh 11 ♖xh4 ♕e7 12 0-0-0 ♗d7 13 d4 0-0-0 14 ♔b1 ♕g7 15 ♖h1 h5 16 ♕h4 ♗e7 17 ②g5 ♖df8 18 f4 ♕h6 19 ②e2 ②d8∓ was Paoli-Alburt, Odessa 1976.

7 ... gh?!

The further course of the game demonstrates that Black must keep the h-file closed. Thus **7 ... g4 *(9)*** is necessary. There can follow:

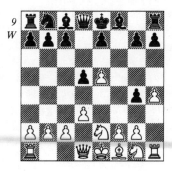

9
W

(a) **8 ♘f4** g6 9 d4 (9 h5?! ♗h6 10 ♘ge2?? g5) 9 ... ♗h6 (Rather too speculative was 9 ... c5?! 10 dc ♘c6 11 ♕xd5 ♕a5+ 12 c3 ♗h6 13 g3 ♗f5 14 ♗c4 ♖f8 15 b4!± C. Baker–Burgess, Bristol League 1991.) 10 ♘d3 ♘a6 11 ♗e2 (11 c3) 11 ... c5 12 ♗xg4 cd (Dunworth suggests 12 ... c4 followed by 13 ... ♕b6.) 13 h5 ♘c5 14 ♗xc8 ♖xc8 15 ♘f3 and now Dunworth's 15 ... ♕b6!? gives Black a reasonable game. Instead W. Watson–Dunworth, London (Lloyds Bank) 1987 continued sharply: 15 ... ♕a5+?! 16 ♔f1 ♘e4 17 hg hg 18 ♘xd4 ♔d7 19 g3 ♗e3! 20 ♕g4+ ♔c7 21 ♖xh8 ♖xh8 22 ♘b3 ♕b6?? (Time trouble; 22 ... ♘d2+.) 23 fe ♕xe3 24 ♔g2 ♘g5 25 ♖e1 1–0.

(b) **8 d4** c5 (8 ... g6?! 9 h5) 9 c3 (9 dc! is critical) 9 ... ♘c6 10 ♘f4 cd 11 cd g6 12 ♗d3 ♗h6 13 ♘ge2 (13 ♘fe2?! 0–0 14 h5 ♕a5+ 15 ♔f1 ♗e3!) 13 ... 0–0 (13 ... g3? 14 fg ♗g4 15 ♕b3) 14 g3 ♗xf4 15 gf (15 ♘xf4 ♘xd4 16 h5 g5) 15 ... ♗f5 16 h5 ♕b6 17 hg hg 18 ♗xf5 gf 19 ♖h5 and now a draw was agreed in C. Pedersen–Burgess, Assens (Rehau Cup) 1990, in view of the line 19 ... e6 20 ♔f1 ♔g7 21 ♔g2 ♖h8 22 ♕h1 ♘xd4 (22 ... ♕xb2!? 23 ♖b1 ♖xh5) 23 ♕h4 ♖xh5 24 ♕xh5 ♘xe2 25 ♕g5+ ♔f7 26 ♖h1 ♘xf4+ 27 ♕xf4 ♖g8 28 ♖h7+ ♖g7 29 ♕h6 ♖xh7 30 ♕xh7+ ♔e8 31 ♕g8+ ♔d7 32 ♕f7+ ♔c8 33 ♕e8+ with a draw.

8	♘f4	g6
9	♖xh4	♗g7
10	d4	c5
11	♗d3	♕a5+

11 ... c4 and 11 ... cd are both met by 12 ♖xh7!

12	♔f1	cd
13	♖xh7!	♖xh7
14	♗xg6+	♔d8
15	♗xh7	♗xe5
16	♕f3	♘c6

An attempted improvement over Polovodin–Palatnik, Moscow 1979, which continued 16 ... ♗xf4 17 ♕xf4 ♘c6 18 ♘f3 (18 ♕f8+ is also extremely strong.) 18 ... ♕c7 19 ♕f8+ ♔d7 20 ♖e1 ♕d6 21 ♗d3 a6 22 ♖e6! and White had a winning attack.

17	♘xd5	♗e6
18	♕f8+	♔d7
19	♕xa8	♕b5+
20	♗d3	♕xb2
21	♘b6+!	♕xb6
22	♘f3	♗b8

This is Black's imaginative idea, but it's not quite adequate. Kengis also mentions 21 ♖e1 ♗xd5 22 ♕f8±.

23	c3!	dc
24	♖b1	♕xb1+!
25	♗xb1	♔c7
26	♗e4?	

White should bring over his king to neutralise the c-pawn, winning fairly easily: 26 ♔e1! ♗d5 27 ♔d1! (Kengis). After the text, the passed pawn gives Black sufficient counterplay.

26	...	♗d5!
27	♗h7!	e6

28 ♘g5   ♘b4?!

Here Kengis could have obtained a small advantage with 28 ... ♘a5! 29 ♔e2 ♘c4 30 g4! ♘b6 31 ♕xb8+ ♔xb8 32 ♔d3∓, but in time trouble, let things slip. The game finished 29 ♔e2 b5 30 ♘xe6+! ♔c8 31 ♕xd5 ♘xd5 32 ♗f5 ♔d7? (32 ... ♔b7 33 ♗e4 ♔c6 34 ♘d4+ ♔c5 35 ♘b3+ ♔d6 was sufficient to draw since 35 ♘xb5? fails to 35 ... c2 36 ♔d2 ♘b4! threatening 37 ... ♗f4+.) 33 ♘d4+ ♔d6 34 ♘xb5+ ♔c5 35 ♘a3 ♘b4 36 ♗b1! ♗d6 37 g3 a6 38 f4 ♗c7 39 ♔f3 ♔d4 40 ♘c2+ ♘xc2 41 ♗xc2 a5 1-0.

2 2 e5 Miscellaneous

White has a number of ways to side-step main line theory. Some of these are peculiar, others simple development which fashion has passed by.

3 ♘c3 is the most respectable of these moves. White relies on free and rapid development at the cost of structure. Black's most solid, and possibly best, procedure is 4 ... d5 following the exchange on c3.

Kuijf–Bagirov
Amsterdam OHRA 1989

1 e4 ♘f6 2 e5 *(10)*

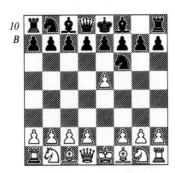

2 ...   ♘d5
2 ... ♘e4 has rather a shocking appearance. The conclusion of Fahrni's analysis in 1922 and Stefan Bücker's recent practical tests is that White should play to trap the e4 knight, rather than wildly fling pawns at it.

(a) **3 d3** ♘c5 4 d4 ♘e6 5 ♗e3 (5 d5 ♘c5 6 b4 ♘a4!? 7 c4 b5 gives a position best described as a mess after 8 c5 a6 or 8 cb ♘b6 9 ♘c3 d6!) 5 ... d6 6 ♘f3 g6 7 d5 ♘g7 8 ed ♕xd6! 9 ♘c3 ♘f5 10 ♗d4 ♗g7! 11 ♘b5 ♕d8 12 ♗xg7 ♘xg7 13 ♕d4 0–0 14 0–0–0 ♘d7 15 ♕f4 c6 16 ♘c3 ♕a5 17 g4 ♘f6 18 d6 ♘d5! 19 ♘xd5 cd 20 de ♖e8∓ Domont–Bücker, Biel 1984.

(b) **3 d4!** gives Black two ways to rescue the knight:

(b1) **3 ... e6.** Now White can win a pawn with 4 ♘h3!? h6 5 ♕g4 d5 6 f3 h5 7 ♕f4 g5 8 ♘xg5 ♘xg5 9 ♕xg5 ♗e7 though Black has some compensation; Bücker gives 10 ♕g7!? ♖f8 11 ♕h7 ♔d7 12 ♕xh5 c5. SDO analyses 4 ♗d3 d5 when Black might be OK: 5 h4 c5; 5 ♘e2 f6 6 ♘f4 fe 7 ♕h5+ ♔d7; 5 ♘h3 ♕h4 (5 ... f6) 6 0–0 f6 7 f3 ♘g5 8 ♘f4 fe 9 g3 ♕h6 10 ♘e2 ♕f6 11 de ♗c5+.

(b2) **3 ... f6** 4 ♗d3 d5 5 ♘c3!? (5 f3 ♘g5 6 ♗xg5 fg 7 f4 was recommended by Fahrni, but Keitlinghaus showed that things are far from clear after 7 ... c5 8 ♕h5+ g6 9 ♗xg6+ hg 10 ♕xh8 ♕b6, since White's pieces are uncoordinated.) 5 ... ♗f5 (5 ... ♘xc3 6 ♕h5+ ♔d7 7 bc e6 8 c4± Bücker) 6 ♕f3 e6 and now in Rausis–Bücker, Dortmund 1990, 7 ♘xe4?! de 8 ♗xe4 ♕xd4! 9 ♗xf5 (9 ♗xb7? ♗g4!) 9 ... ♕xe5+ 10 ♘e2 ♕xf5 11 ♕xb7 ♕d5 gave Black a decent position. Instead, 7 g4! ♗g6 8 ♘xe4 would have cut out the tactics and won a pawn: 8 ... ♗xe4 9 ♗xe4 fe 10 ♗d3 e4 11 ♗xe4 de 12 ♕xe4 ♕d5± or 8 ... de 9 ♗xe4 ♗xe4 (9 ... ♕xd4? 10 ♗xb7 c6 11 ♗xa8 ♗e4 12 ♕b3+ –) 10 ♕xe4 ♘c6 11 ef! ♕xf6 12 ♗e3± (Bücker).

2 ... ♘g8 is rather unenterprising, but objectively may have more merit than 2 ... ♘e4. Black can achieve a solid position, though White has no trouble maintaining a space and development advantage. A merit of the knight's retreat is possible access to e7, but White will not now have to play the weakening c4 advance to remove the irritating knight from the centre. Players are much too sensible these days to over-reach trying to smash flat such positions. After **3 d4** we have:

(a) **3 ... d5** 4 ♗d3 c5?! 5 dc± leaves Black a tempo down on a bad line of the Caro–Kann (1 e4 c6 2 d4 d5 3 e5 c5?! 4 dc). Instead, Cladouras–Steinbacher, Bundesliga 1989/90 was a rare example of over-ambitious play by White: 4 c4 ♗e6 5 ♘c3 c6 6 cd ♗xd5 7 ♘xd5 ♕xd5 8 ♘e2 e6 9 ♘c3 ♗b4 10 ♕g4 ♘e7 11 ♗d2 ♗xc3 12 bc c5 13 ♕xg7 ♖g8 14 ♕xh7 cd 15 f4 dc 16 ♗xc3 ♕c5 17 ♗d2 ♘bc6 and White was unable to organise this position.

(b) **3 ... d6**. White has two logical approaches:

(b1) **4 ed** ♕xd6 5 ♘c3 ♘f6 (5 ... c6 6 ♗c4 ♘f6 7 ♘ge2 ♗g4 8 f3 ♗f5±; 6 ♘f3) 6 ♘f3 ♗g4 (6 ... c6; 6 ... a6?! 7 ♗e3 ♘c6 8 ♕d2 ♗g4 9 ♘g5!± Karpov–Lutikov, USSR 1979) 7 h3 ♗h5 8 g4 ♗g6 9 ♘e5 c6 10 ♗f4 ♘d5 11 ♕d2 ♘xf4 12 ♕xf4 ♘d7 13 0-0-0 ♘xe5 14 de ♕c7 15 ♗d3 ♗xd3 16 ♖xd3 g6 17 ♘e4 f6 18 g5± Psakhis–Sygulski, Jurmala 1987.

(b2) **4 ♘f3** ♗g4 (4 ... c6; 4 ... de; 4 ... ♗f5 5 ♗d3; 4 ... h6 5 ♘c3 g5 6 h3 ♗g7 7 ♗e3 ♘c6 8 ed cd 9 d5± Unzicker–Bricard, Wildbad 1990) 5 h3! ♗h5 (5 ... ♗xf3 6 ♕xf3 c6 7 ed; 5 ... ♗f5 6 ♗d3 ♕d7 7 ed± Smejkal–Vesely, Czechoslovakia 1968) and now White can try 6 e6!?, but 6 g4 ♗g6 7 ♘c3 e6 8 ♗f4 d5 9 ♗d3 gave White a safe advantage in Ernst–Welling, Copenhagen Open 1988.

3 ♘f3

3 g3 d6 4 ed ♕xd6 5 ♗g2 g6 6 ♘e2 ♗g7 7 d4 ♘b6 8 0-0 0-0-0 9 ♗f4 ♕d8 10 ♘bc3 c6 11 ♘e4

♘8d7 12 c3 h6 13 h4 e5 gave Black a pleasant game in Zakhariev–Donchev, Bulgarian Ch (Sofia) 1989.

3 b3 is a well-intentioned move, but the idea of pressure on the long diagonal just doesn't work very well: 3 ... d6 4 ed ♕xd6 5 ♗b2 ♗f5 6 ♘f3 ♕e6+ 7 ♗e2 ♘f4 8 ♘d4 ♕e5∓ Gusev–Orev, Primorsko 1972 or **3 ... g6! 4 ♗b2 ♗g7**.

(a) **5 c4 ♘b4!?** (For 5 ... ♘b6 see the line 3 c4 ♘b6 4 b3 g6 5 ♗b2 ♗g7 below.) 6 a3 ♘4c6 7 d4 d6 8 f4 de 9 fe is an unusual type of Four Pawns Attack. Gipslis–Gutman, Latvian Ch (Riga) 1974 concluded 9 ... 0–0 10 ♕d2 ♕d7 11 ♗e2 ♖d8 12 ♘f3 f6 13 ef ef 14 d5 ♘e5 15 ♘xe5 fe 16 0–0 ♘c6 17 c5 ♘d4 18 ♗c4 b5 19 cb ab 20 ♕d1 b5 21 ♗d3 ♕xd5 22 ♘c3 ♕xb3 23 ♕xb3+ ♘xb3 24 ♖ad1 ♗g4 0–1.

(b) **5 ♘f3** is probably best met by 5 ... d6. An alternative approach was seen in Smyslov–Adorjan, Amsterdam 1971 (by transposition from 1 b3 ♘f6 2 ♗b2 g6 3 e4 ♗g7 4 e5 ♘d5 5 ♘f3): 5 ... c5 6 ♘c3 ♘f4?! 7 d4 ♘c6 8 g3 cd 9 ♘xd4 ♘xd4 10 ♕xd4 ♘e6 11 ♕e3 d6 12 f4 de 13 ♗b5+ ♔f8 14 fe ♕d4 15 ♕xd4 ♘xd4 16 0–0–0 ♗xe5 17 ♘d5 ♘xb5 18 ♗xe5 f6 19 ♘xf6! ef 20 ♖d8+ ♔g7 21 ♗xf6+ ♔xf6 22 ♖xh8 ♔g7 23 ♖d8 ♘c7 24 ♖e1 1–0.

3 c4 ♘b6 4 b3 is a similar idea to 3 b3 above; clearly transpositions are possible. After **4 ... g6 5 ♗b2** (5 ♘c3 d6 6 ed cd 7 ♗b2 ♗g7 8 ♗e2 ♘c6 9 ♘f3 ♗g4 10 d4 d5 11 c5 ♘c8 12 h3 ♗xf3 13 ♗xf3 e6 14 ♘e2 0–0 15 ♕d2 b6 16 b4 bc 17 dc ♖b8 18 ♗xg7 ♔xg7 19 ♖b1 ♕h4 gave Black good play in Frenkel–Hjorth, New York Open 1984.) **5 ... ♗g7**, White has a number of ways to try to justify this rather peculiar system of development:

(a) **6 d4** d6 7 ed and now 7 ... cd is a good version of the Exchange Variation for Black, while 7 ... ed 8 ♗d3 0–0 9 ♘e2 c5 10 ♘a3 d5 yielded good play in Steiner–Tartakower, 1934. Black can also try to keep more options open by delaying ... d6: 6 ... 0–0 7 ♘d2 d6 8 ♘gf3 ♘c6 9 h3 de 10 de ♗f5 11 ♕e2 ♕d7 12 ♘e4 ♖ad8 13 ♘c5 ♕c8 14 g4 ♘d7 15 ♘a4 ♗d3! with fine play in Gurgenidze–Kakageldiev, Daugavpils 1974.

(b) **6 ♕f3** e6 (Another, clearer, way of dealing with White's 7 c5 threat is 6 ... d6!? 7 e6 0–0) 7 d4 ♘c6 8 ♘d2 d6 with reasonable play for Black in a correspondence game Welling–Diepstraten.

3 ♕f3 looks like a dreadful move, but some care is needed from Black. 3 ... e6 4 ♗c4 (4 c3 c5 5 ♗c4 ♘c6 6 ♗xd5 ed and now White should prefer 7 ♕xd5 ♕g5 in spite of Black's excellent play, to 7 d4?! cd 8 ♘e2 dc 9 0–0 c2 10 ♘bc3 d6 11 ed ♗xd6 12

♘xd5 0–0∓ Rajković–Ljubojević, Yugoslavia 1974.) 4 ... ♘c6! (4 ... ♘b6 5 ♗b3 ♘c6 6 ♕g3 d6) 5 ♗xd5 ed 6 ♕xd5 ♕g5 and Black has no problems at all.

3 ♗c4 ♘b6 4 ♗b3 can be met by 4 ... d5 5 ed ed 6 d4 ♗e7 7 ♘f3 0–0 8 0–0 ♗g4 9 h3 ♗h5 10 c3 ♘c6 11 ♘bd2 a5 12 ♘e4 a4 13 ♗c2 a3 14 ba d5 15 ♘g3 ♗g6 16 ♗xg6 hg 17 ♔h2 ♗xa3 18 h4 ♘c4∞ Tatarintsev–Murashko, USSR 1982, but Black's most dynamic approach is 4 ... c5!? *(11)* threatening to trap the bishop, while controlling d4. Now White has four ways of meeting the ... c4 threat.

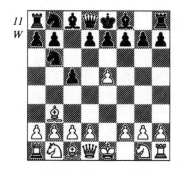

(a) 5 ♘a3 ♘c6 6 ♘f3 d5 7 ed e6 (7 ... ed!?) 8 ♘b5 ♗xd6 9 ♘xd6+ ♕xd6 gave Black pressure against White's sensitive squares on the d-file in Honfi–Sarkozy, Hungary 1950.

(b) 5 c3 c4 6 ♗c2 ♘c6 7 ♘f3 d6 8 ed ♕xd6 9 d4 cd 10 ♕xd3 ♕xd3 11 ♗xd3 ♗g4 12 ♗e2 e5∓ Johnstone–Browne, Saint

John 1988 (by transposition from a c3 Sicilian).

(c) 5 ♕e2 was the preferred move in the 1920s. 5 ... ♘c6 6 ♘f3 (6 c3 e6 7 ♘f3 d5 8 ed ♗xd6 9 0–0 0–0 10 d4 cd 11 cd ♗e7 12 ♖d1 ♗f6 gave White nothing in Seitz–Grünfeld, Debrecen 1925.) 6 ... d5 7 ed e6! 8 ♘c3 (8 c3) 8 ... ♗xd6 9 ♘e4 ♗e7 10 d3 ♘d5 11 0–0 0–0 12 ♗d2 b6 and White suffered due to the weakness of d4 in Yates–Rubinstein, Dresden 1926.

(d) 5 d3 ♘c6 6 ♘f3 gives Black two reasonable ways to handle the position:

(d1) 6 ... e6 7 ♘c3 d5 8 ed ♗xd6 9 ♘e4 ♗e7= Ivanović–Marović, Vršac 1977. White could play for c3 and d4.

(d2) 6 ... d5 7 ed ed (7 ... e6) 8 0–0 ♗g4 9 ♗g5 ♗xf3 10 ♗xf7+ ♔d7!! Apparently this was a shock for White in Bischoff–Kindermann, Dortmund 1989, which concluded 11 ♗e6+ ♔e8 12 ♗f7+ ♔d7 13 ♗e6+ ½–½. This variation has subsequently become a popular choice for 'grandmaster draws'.

> 3   ...   d6
> 4   ♗c4

4 ♘c3 ♘xc3 5 dc transposes to the line 3 ♘c3 ♘xc3 4 dc d6 5 ♘f3 having sidestepped the solid 4 ... d5 line. 4 ... e6 is viable, but presumably the reason for the unpopularity of this move order is 4 ... de! 5 ♘xe5 ♘xc3 when White has nothing better than 6 bc ♘d7 since 6 ♗c4? ♘d5 7 ♕f3 ♗e6

and 6 ♕f3? f6 7 ♗c4 e6 8 ♕h5+ g6 are ineffective.

4 ...   ♘b6

The potential of the line with 3 ♘f3 and 4 ♗c4 was first shown by Keres. A good example was Keres–Grigorian, USSR 1970: 4 ... c6 5 0–0 (5 d4 ♗g4 6 h3 ♗xf3 7 ♕xf3 de 8 de e6 is a line of the Panov Variation; 5 ♘c3?! ♘xc3 6 bc d5 7 ♗e2 ♗g4 8 ♖b1 ♕c7∓ Speelman–Suba, Hastings 1978/9) 5 ... g6 (5 ... ♗g4) 6 ♘c3 ♘b6 (... g6 and ... ♘xc3 do not fit together very well.) 7 ♗b3 ♗g7 8 ed ♕xd6 9 ♘e4 ♕c7 10 d4 0–0 11 ♖e1 a5 12 a4 ♘a6 13 ♗g5 ♘d5 14 ♕d2 ♗e6 15 ♗h6+ ♖ad8 16 ♗xg7 ♔xg7 17 ♗c4 ♘b8 18 h3 ♗c8 19 ♘g3 h6 20 h4 c5 21 ♗xd5 ♖xd5 22 c4 ♖dd8 23 d5 e6 24 ♕c3+ f6 25 de ♖de8 26 h5 1–0.

5 ♗b3

5 ♗xf7+? ♔xf7 6 ♘g5+ forces Black to find just a few accurate moves: 6 ... ♔g8 7 e6 (7 ♕f3 ♕e8) 7 ... ♕e8 8 ♕f3 g6! 9 d4 ♘c6 10 c3 ♘d8. Black is simply material up. Amusing alternatives are 7 ... h6? 8 ♕f3 hg? 9 ♕f7+ ♔h7 10 h4 g4 11 h5 ♗xe6 12 ♕g6+ ♔g8 13 ♕xe6+ ♔h7 14 ♕f7 and 15 h6 wins (Bronstein) and 6 ... ♔g6? 7 ♕f3! ♔xg5 (7 ... ♕e8 8 e6!) 8 ♕f7! g6 9 d4+ ♔h5 10 ♕f4 h6 11 h3 g5 12 ♕f7+ 1–0 Nordijk–Landau, Rotterdam 1927.

5 ...   d5

This is not the only move:

(a) **5 ... ♘c6** can transpose to 3 d4 d6 4 ♗c4 ♘b6 5 ♗b3 ♘c6, though after 6 e6 Black can contemplate 6 ... ♗xe6, while after 6 ... fe, 7 ♘g5 is an option. 6 ed cd (6 ... ed) 7 0–0 g6 gives White little.

(b) **5 ... ♗f5** is strongly recommended by Alburt. The position after 6 d4 is considered under the move order 3 d4 d6 4 ♗c4 ♘b6 5 ♗b3 ♗f5 6 ♘f3.

(c) **5 ... c5!?** is quite possibly the best move. 6 a4 (6 d3 d5 7 c3 ♘c6 8 h3 ♗f5 9 0–0 e6 10 ♖e1 ♗e7 11 ♗c2 ♕c7 12 ♗f4 ♖c8∓ Fershter–Alburt, Kiev 1970) 6 ... ♘c6 7 ♕e2 (7 a5 c4∞) 7 ... d5 8 c3 ♗f5 9 a5 c4 10 ab cb 11 ba ♕b6 12 0–0 ♗xb1 13 ♖xb1 e6 Zhelyandinov–Mikenas, Vitebsk 1970.

6 d4   ♗g4
7 h3   ♗xf3

Black has no objection to this exchange, which is just as well since 7 ... ♗h5? 8 e6 fe 9 g4 ♗f7 10 ♘e5 is very unpleasant.

8 ♕xf3   e6
9 0–0

9 ♕g3!? is worth comparing with Zhelyandinov–Bagirov below, but with the bishop still on f8, ♕g3 seems less logical. If Black wishes to play analogously to our main game, then 9 ... g6 could be tried. In Sax–Polgar, Budapest 1972, after 9 ... c5 10 dc ♘6d7 11 ♘c3 ♘c6 12 0–0 ♕a5, Black's intention of 13 ... ♘xc5 encouraged White to sacrifice: 13 ♗xd5!? ed 14 ♘xd5 ♘xc5 15 c4

♘e6 16 ♗e3 0-0-0 though this looked rather speculative.

9 ... c5
10 dc ♗xc5

An improvement over 10 ... ♘6d7 11 ♗f4 ♘c6 12 ♘c3 ♗xc5 13 ♕g3± g6 14 ♖ad1 0-0 15 ♘xd5!? ed 16 ♖xd5 ♘d4 17 ♕g4 h5 18 ♕d1 ♕c8 19 ♖xd4 ♗xd4 20 ♕xd4 ♘c5 Zhelyandinov-Bagirov, Gomel 1968. This position is not so bad for Black, but White's sacrifice was not compulsory.

11 ♕g3 g6!
12 ♗h6

Stops Black castling in the hope that pins on the a4-e8 diagonal will be a major nuisance. However Black can evict the bishop before this causes any real problems.

12 ... ♘c6
13 ♘c3

13 c3 ♘d7 14 ♗a4 a6 15 ♗xc6 bc 16 ♘bd2 ♗f8! is considered unclear by Bagirov.

13 ... ♘d4!
14 ♕d3?!

Bagirov gives two superior, unclear, options for White: 14 ♖ad1!? ♘f5 15 ♕f4 ♘xh6 16 ♘e4! ♘f5 17 ♘xc5 ♕e7 and 14 ♗g5 ♘f5 15 ♕f4 ♗e7 16 ♗xe7 ♕xe7 17 ♘b5 0-0.

14 ... ♘f5!
15 ♕b5+ ♘d7
16 ♗a4 ♕c7!

Black is now somewhat better, which encourages White to try desperate measures, leading to a rapid defeat: 17 ♗e3 ♘xe3 18 fe

♖d8 19 ♔h1 0-0 20 e4 ♕xe5 21 ♕e2 d4 22 ♗xd7 dc 0-1.

Radulov-Stefanov
Elenite Festival 1986

1 e4 ♘f6 2 e5 ♘d5
3 ♘c3 ♘xc3

3 ... e6 4 ♗c4!? ♘b6 (4 ... ♘xc3) 5 ♗b3 d5 6 ed cd 7 d4 ♗e7 offers White some advantage, due to Black's constricted queenside. Kislov gives 8 ♕h5 ♘c6 9 ♘f3 d5 10 h4 as an ambitious method. Instead, more traditional approaches have also succeeded in casting doubt on 3 ... e6:

(a) **4 ♘xd5** ed 5 d4 (5 f4 d6 6 ♘f3 ♗e7; 5 ♕f3 c6 and now 6 ♕g3 d6 7 d4 de 8 de ♗f5 9 c3 ♘d7 10 ♘f3 ♕b6! and 6 c4 ♕e7! 7 ♕e3 dc 8 ♗xc4 d5 gives White nothing.) 5 ... d6 6 ♘f3 ♘c6 7 ♗f4 (7 ♗g5 ♗e7 8 ♗xe7 ♘xe7! Bagirov; 7 ♗b5!? ♗d7 8 0-0 ♗e7 9 ed Radulov-Liliedahl, Skopje ol 1972; 7 ♗e2 ♗e7 8 ♗f4 0-0 9 0-0 f6! 10 ef ♗xf6= Sämisch-Alekhine, Budapest 1921) 7 ... ♗e7 (7 ... de 8 de ♗c5 9 ♕d2 ♘e7 10 0-0-0 c6 11 ♗e3 was pleasant for White in Byrne-Jansson, Skopje ol 1972.) and now 8 ♗e2 is Sämisch-Alekhine, whilst Sax-Cafferty, Teesside 1972 continued 8 ♗b5 0-0 9 0-0 ♗g4 (9 ... f6!?) 10 ♗e2 ♕d7 11 ♕d2 ♖ad8 12 c3 ♖fe8=.

(b) **4 d4!**. Now if Black captures on c3, the move ... e6 will have had little point, while it is hard for Black to play otherwise. 4 ... d6 5

♘f3 de (5 ... ♘c6 6 ♗b5 ♘xc3 7 bc de 8 ♘xe5 ♗d7 9 ♘xd7 ♕xd7 10 0-0 gave White a space advantage and prospects of an attack against the black king in Byvshev–Aronin, Leningrad 1956; 5 ... ♗e7 6 ed ♗xd6 7 ♘e4±) 6 ♘xe5 ♘xc3 7 bc ♘d7 8 ♗f4 and Black must now accept a lasting inferiority, e.g. 8 ... ♗e7 9 ♗d3 ♘xe5 10 ♗xe5 ♗f6 11 ♕e2 Andersson–Kraidman, Siegen ol 1970, since 8 ... c5? fails to 9 ♗b5: 9 ... ♗e7 10 ♗xd7+ ♗xd7 11 ♕f3!; 9 ... a6 10 ♗xd7+ ♗xd7 11 ♕f3! ♕e7 (11 ... ♗e7 12 ♘xf7; 11 ... f6 12 ♕h5+ Flückiger–Borner, Switzerland 1984) 12 ♕xb7 ♖d8 13 ♕xa6 cd 14 0-0 ♕a3 15 ♕b7 ♕a8 16 ♖ab1+– Finnlaugsson–Jonsson, corres. 1988; 9 ... ♕a5 10 ♕d3!±.

3 ... c6 4 ♗c4 (4 d4 d6 5 f4 ♗f5 6 ♘xd5 cd 7 ♘f3 ♘c6 8 ♗d3 ♗xd3 9 ♕xd3± Zaitsev–Westerinen, Moscow 1982) 4 ... ♘xc3 5 dc d5 6 ♗d3 c5 7 ♗f4 ♘c6 8 ♕d2 ♗g4?! (8 ... ♗e6!? 9 ♘f3 h6 10 h4 ♕d7 11 0-0-0 0-0-0 12 ♖he1 g6 is judged ± by Kislov, but Black could try 11 ... ♗g4.) 9 h3 ♗h5?! 10 g4 ♗g6 11 e6! ♕c8 (11 ... fe 12 ♗xg6+ hg 13 ♘f3±; 11 ... ♗xd3 12 ♕xd3! fe 13 ♘f3 ♕d7 14 0-0-0 0-0-0 15 ♖he1±) 12 ef+ ♗xf7 13 0-0-0 c4 14 ♗f1 b5?! (14 ... e6 15 ♗g2 ♗e7 16 ♘e2 0-0 17 ♗g5 ♗xg5 18 ♕xg5 b5 19 f4 ♕a6 20 ♔b1 b4 21 f5!± Kislov) 15 ♗g2 ♕a6? (15 ... e6 was necessary, as now White has a very strong queen sacrifice.) 16 ♗xd5! 0-0-0 17 ♗xf7 ♖xd2 18 ♗e6+! ♔b7 19 ♖xd2 ♘b8 (19 ... ♕xa2 20 ♖d7+ ♔a8 21 ♗d5+–) 20 ♗d5+ ♔c8 21 ♘f3 e6 (21 ... ♕xa2 22 ♗e6+ ♔b7 23 ♖d8 ♕a1+ 24 ♔d2 ♕xh1 25 ♖xb8+ ♔a6 26 ♗c8+ ♔a5 27 ♗c7+ ♔a4 28 ♖a8+–) 22 ♖e1! ed 23 ♖e8+ ♔d7 24 ♖xb8 ♗d6 25 ♗xd6 ♖xb8 26 ♗xd8 ♕xa2 27 ♖xd5+ ♔c6 28 ♖g5 a6 29 ♖xg7 ♕a1+ 30 ♔d2 ♕xb2 31 ♘d4+ ♔b6 32 ♗c7+ 1-0 Kislov–Tsarëv, Moscow 1989.

4 dc
4 bc gives Black the standard choice between 4 ... d6 and 4 ... d5. 4 ... c5 can also be tried, keeping transpositional options open, e.g. 5 f4 ♘c6 6 ♘f3 d5. Black can try to keep White guessing with 5 f4 d6 6 ♘f3 ♘c6!?, e.g. 7 d4 e6 8 ♗e2 ♗e7 9 0-0 0-0 10 ♗e3 ♕a5 11 ♗d3 de 12 fe ♕xc3 Zotkin–Nikolenko, Moscow 1983. Probably best is 7 ♖b1!?, holding back d4 to avoid giving Black a target (7 ... de?! 8 ♘xe5!±).

Another transpositional possibility is 4 ... d6 5 ♗c4!? d5 (5 ... de 6 ♕h5) 6 ♗e2, which can lead to the standard 4 ... d5 lines.

4 ... d6 5 f4:
(a) **5 ... de 6 fe ♕d5** (6 ... ♗f5 7 ♕f3 ♕c8 8 ♘e2! ♗xc2 9 ♘d4 ♗g6 10 e6!± Keres; 6 ... c5 7 ♘f3 ♘c6 8 ♗e2 g6) **7 ♘f3** gives Black two options:

(a1) **7 ... c5** 8 d4 ♘c6 9 ♗e2

♗g4 10 0–0 cd (10 ... e6 11 ♖b1!; 10 ... 0–0–0 11 ♘g5! ♗xe2 12 ♕xe2 f6 13 c4!±) 11 cd e6 (11 ... ♗xf3? 12 ♗xf3 ♕xd4+ 13 ♕xd4 ♘xd4 14 ♗xb7 ♖b8 15 ♖b1+ –; 11 ... 0–0–0 12 c3 f6 13 ♕a4!± Dückstein–Kavalek, Sarajevo 1967) 12 ♖b1 ♕d7 13 ♘g5!± Tal–Podgaets, Sochi 1970.

(a2) **7 ... ♘c6** 8 d4 ♗g4 (8 ... ♕e4+?! 9 ♔f2!±) 9 ♗e2 e6 10 0–0 ♗e7 11 ♘g5!? (11 ♖b1!?) 11 ... ♗xe2 12 ♕xe2 0–0 13 ♕h5 (13 ♕g4 f5!?) 13 ... ♗xg5 14 ♕xg5 ♕e4 15 ♗a3 ♖fd8 16 ♖f2 ♖d7 17 ♖af1 ♘a5 was Bilek–Larsen, Sousse 1967. The most incisive was then 18 ♖f3! ♘c4 (18 ... ♔h8 19 ♖g3 ♖g8 20 ♗f8! ♕g6 21 ♕h4) 19 ♖g3 ♕g6 (19 ... g6 20 ♗e7) 20 ♕h4 ♕xc2 21 ♕f6 g6 22 ♗c1 ♘d2 23 ♕f2+ –.

(b) **5 ... g6 6 ♘f3 ♗g7 7 d4 0–0** *(12)* (7 ... f6 8 ♗d3±).

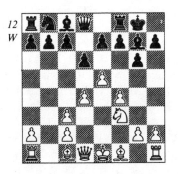

12
W

(b1) **8 ♗d3** c5 9 0–0 de! (9 ... ♕c7 10 ♗e3) 10 de! (10 fe?! ♘c6 11 ♗e3 ♗g4∓) 10 ... ♗f5 (10 ... ♘c6 11 ♗e3 b6) 11 ♗e3 b6 12

♕e2 and now Black should prefer 12 ... ♗xd3 or 12 ... ♘c6 to 12 ... e6 13 ♖ad1 ♕c7 14 ♘g5 when the plan ♘e4, ♗f2–h4 gives White the advantage, according to Keres.

(b2) **8 ♗c4** ♘c6! (8 ... c5 9 0–0 cd 10 cd ♗g4 11 ♗e3 de 12 fe ♘c6 13 ♗b3 ♖c8 14 ♕f2!? ♘a5 15 h3 ♗xf3 16 ♕xf3 ♘xb3 17 ab ♖c3 18 ♕e4± ♕b6 19 ♗d2 ♖cc8 20 d5 ♕c7 21 ♗f4 a6 22 c4 and Black was soon squashed in Nikolac–Grzesik, Bundesliga 1986/7.) 9 0–0 ♘a5 10 ♗d3 c5 11 ♕e2 b6= Pavlenko–Bagirov, Baku 1966.

(b3) **8 ♗e2** c5 9 0–0 de (9 ... cd?! 10 cd de 11 fe ♘c6 12 c3 b6 13 ♕e1 ♗b7 14 ♕h4 ♖c8 15 ♘g5 h6 16 ♘f3 e6?! 17 ♗g5! ♕d5 18 ♗xh6 ♗xh6 19 ♕xh6 ♘e7 20 ♗d3 ♖xc3 21 ♖f2!+ – was Zotkin–Bartovsky, Leningrad–Moscow 1985; after 16 ... ♔h7 17 h3! intending ♘h2–g4, White has a strong attack.) 10 fe ♘c6 (10 ... ♕a5?! 11 ♗d2 ♘c6?! 12 e6! fe 13 ♘g5± Beckemeyer–Grzesik, Bundesliga 1987/8) 11 ♗e3 ♕a5 12 ♕e1 ♗f5 left Black with no problems in Widera–Van der Tak, corres. 1977.

4 ... d5!

(a) **5 ♕f3?!** c5 6 c4?! ♘c6! 7 cd? ♘d4 8 ♕e4 f5! 9 ef ♗f5– + Benko–Guimard, Argentina 1939.

(b) **5 ♗a3!?** prevents an immediate ... c5, but Black has resources: 5 ... b6! (5 ... ♘d7!?; 5 ... ♗f5?! 6 ♘f3 ♘d7 7 ♘d4±

Tal–Eversole, USA Open 1988) 6
d4 c5 7 f4 (7 dc e6; 7 ♗b5+ ♗d7
8 ♗d3 ♘c6 9 ♘f3 c4 10 ♗e2
♗g4= 11 ♘g1 ♗xe2 12 ♘xe2
e6 13 ♗xf8 ♖xf8 Vorotnikov–
Agzamov, USSR 1974) 7 … e6 8
♘f3 ♕d7 9 ♖b1 ♗a6 10 ♗xa6
♘xa6 11 0–0 g6 (11 … ♕a4 12
f5! ♕xa3 13 ♘g5) 12 ♕e2 ♕a4∓
Haïk–Torre, Athens 1971.
   (c) 5 f4 c5 (5 … d4!? 6 ♗b2 dc
7 ♗xc3 ♗f5! 8 ♘f3 e6 is OK for
Black, e.g. 9 d4 c5, 9 ♖b1 b6 or 9
♗e2 c5 10 0–0 ♘c6 11 d3 ♗e7.)
6 ♘f3 ♘c6 (6 … ♗g4?! 7 h3 ♗xf3
8 ♕xf3 e6 9 ♗b5+ ♘c6 10 c4±
Saariluoma–Enigl, Teesside 1974)
7 ♗e2 (7 c4 ♗g4 8 ♖b1 ♖b8 9
♗e2 e6 10 0–0 transposes.) 7 …
♗g4 (7 … e6 8 d4 ♗e7 9 0–0
♗d7 10 ♔h1 ♕c7 11 c4 dc 12 d5
ed 13 ♕xd5 ♗e6 14 ♕e4 0–0–0
15 ♗xc4 ♘d4 16 ♗xe6+ fe=
Zotkin–Safarov, Moscow 1984) 8
♖b1 ♖b8 9 0–0 e6 10 c4 dc 11 h3
♗xf3!? (11 … ♗h5 12 g4 ♗g6
13 ♗xc4 h5 14 d3 hg 15 hg ♘d4
16 c3 ♘xf3+ 17 ♕xf3 ♕h4 18
♖b2± Upton–Dunworth, British
Ch [Swansea] 1987) 12 ♗xf3 ♕d7
13 ♕e2 b5 14 ♗e4 ♘d4 15 ♕f2
♗e7 16 c3 ♘c6 17 ♕f3 ♘d8 18
♖d1 ♕c7 19 d3 cd 20 ♕xd3 c4 21
♕f3 0–0 22 ♗e3 f5 23 ef ♗xf6
24 ♖bc1 ♘f7 25 ♕g4 ♖fe8 26 f5
e5 27 ♗d5 ♔h8 28 ♗e6 gave
White reasonable compensation
in Dückstein–Hölzl, Austrian Ch
1989 (by transposition from 4 …
c5 5 f4 ♘c6 6 ♘f3 d5).
   (d) 5 d4 c5 6 ♘f3 ♘c6 (13)

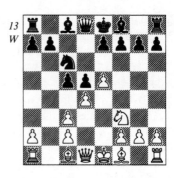

(d1) 7 h3?! e6 8 ♗d3 cd 9
cd ♘b4!∓ I. Zaitsev–Vasiukov,
USSR Ch (Alma Ata) 1968.
   (d2) 7 ♗d3 ♗g4 (7 … cd 8 cd
♘b4) 8 ♖b1 (8 h3 ♗xf3 9 ♕xf3 e6
10 ♖b1 ♕c7 11 0–0 c4= Mecking–
Bobotsov, Palma 1969) 8 … c4! 9
♗e2 ♕d7 10 h3 ♗xf3 11 ♗xf3
e6 12 0–0 0–0–0 and now 13 g3
f6 14 ef gf 15 ♗g2 is equal, but in
Zaitsev–Bagirov, Minsk 1983, 13
g4? f6 14 ef gf 15 ♗g2 h5 allowed
Black to win by a direct attack.
   (d3) 7 ♗e2 ♗g4 8 0–0 e6 9 ♖b1
♖b8 (9 … ♕d7 10 h3 ♗xf3=; 9
… ♕c7?! allowed the interesting
thrust 10 c4! dc 11 d5! ed 12 ♕xd5
♗e6 13 ♕e4 0–0–0 14 ♗xc4 in
Bohosian–Schmidt, Tbilisi 1974.)
10 h3 ♗h5 11 ♗g5 (11 ♗d3 c4
with queenside play to follow.) 11
… ♗e7 12 ♗xe7 ♕xe7 13 ♖b5
♗xf3 14 ♗xf3 0–0 15 ♕d3 (15
♖xc5 ♘xe5∓) 15 … a6 16 ♖bb1
b5 17 ♕e3 ♕a7 18 ♖fd1 b4∓
Vaisman–Alburt, Bucharest 1978.

4 …   d6

4 … d5 may well be Black's best
here. Note that this line can be
reached from 2 ♘c3 d5 3 e5 ♘e4

followed by 4 ... ♘xc3 5 dc.

Minor options for White: **5 g3?!** ♘c6 6 f4 ♗f5 7 ♘f3 e6 8 ♗e3 ♘a5 9 ♔f2 c5 10 b4 ♘c6 11 ♖b1 d4∓ Blatny–Bagirov, USSR 1984; **5 f4** ♗f5=; **5 ♗e3** ♗f5 6 ♗d3 ♗xd3 7 ♕xd3 e6=; **5 ♗g5** c6 6 ♗d3 ♘d7 7 ♕e2 (7 e6 ♘e5) 7 ... ♘c5 8 0-0-0 ♕a5 9 ♔b1 e6 10 h4 ♘a4 11 ♗c1 b5 12 ♕g4 ♖b8 13 a3 c5 14 ♖b3 b4 gave Black a decisive attack in Zhuravlev–Vasiukov, Riga 1968; **5 ♘f3** ♗g4 6 h3 ♗xf3 7 ♕xf3 e6 8 ♗e3 c5 9 0-0-0 ♘c6 10 ♕g3 ♕c7 11 f4 0-0-0= Radulov–Flatow, Skopje 1972.

More significant are the following:

(a) **5 ♕f3** g6 6 ♗f4 (6 ♗g5 ♗g7 7 0-0-0 c6 8 ♕e3 ♕b6 9 ♖d4 ♘d7 10 ♘f3 ♘f8 11 ♗f6 ♘e6 12 ♗xg7 ♘xg7 13 ♕e1 ♗f5= Christensen–Burgess, Gausdal 1991.) 6 ... ♗g7 7 0-0-0 c6 8 h4 (8 c4 ♗e6) 8 ... h5 9 ♕e3 ♕b6 10 ♕d2 ♗g4 (10 ... ♗f5 is best met by 11 ♘e2, since 11 ♘f3 ♗g4 12 ♗e2 ♗xf3 13 ♗xf3 e6 14 g4 hg 15 ♗xg4 ♘d7 gives Black the edge, according to Bagirov.) 11 f3 ♗e6 12 ♘h3 ♗xh3 13 ♖xh3 e6 14 c4! and now 14 ... ♘d7?! 15 ♗e3! ♕c7 16 f4 a6 17 cd cd 18 ♗d4 ♖c8 19 ♖c3 ♕d8 20 ♖xc8 ♕xc8 21 ♕e3 gave Black problems in Arapović–Bagirov, Moscow 1985. Instead, 14 ... ♕c7 15 cd cd maintains reasonable chances.

(b) **5 ♗d3** c5 6 f4 (6 ♗f4 ♘c6 and now 7 ♘f3 ♗g4 8 h3 ♗xf3 9 ♕xf3 e6= was Platonov–Palatnik, Kiev 1978; instead 7 ♕d2!? transposes to Kislov–Tsarëv — see 3 ... c6.) 6 ... ♘c6 7 ♘f3 ♗g4 8 h3 (8 0-0 e6 9 h3 ♗xf3 10 ♕xf3 c4 was quite all right for Black in Kosten–Brameld, British Ch [Southport] 1983, but 11 ♗e2 ♗c5+ 12 ♔h1 b5? 13 a4 a6 14 ♗e3! ♕b6 15 ♗xc5 ♕xc5 16 ab ♕xb5 17 b3± was rather an unfortunate follow-up.) 8 ... ♗xf3 9 ♕xf3 e6 10 ♕g3?! g6 11 ♗e3 (11 c4 ♘b4) 11 ... c4 12 ♗e2 ♘e7 13 ♕f2 ♘f5!? 14 ♗xa7 ♘g3! 15 ♖g1 ♕a5! 16 ♗d4 ♘f5 17 ♗b6?! ♕b5 18 a4? (18 b3) 18 ... ♕xb2 19 ♔d2 d4! 20 ♗xd4 ♗b4! 21 ♖gc1 (21 ♖gb1 ♗xc3+! 22 ♗xc3 ♖d8+ 23 ♗d3 ♖xd3+!) 21 ... ♘xd4 22 ♕xd4 ♗xc3+! 23 ♕xc3 ♖d8+ 24 ♗d3 ♖xd3+ 0-1 S. Nikolić–Orev, Kislovodsk 1968.

(c) **5 c4 c6** (5 ... d4?! 6 f4 ♗f5 7 ♘e2! ♘c6 8 ♘g3 e6 9 ♘xf5 ef 10 ♗d3 g6 11 a3 a5 12 ♕f3± Ghizdavu–Torre, Niš 1972; 5 ... ♗e6 is playable, provided Black meets 6 ♘f3 not with 6 ... dc? or 6 ... ♕d7?, but 6 ... ♘c6!) and White has been unable to achieve much from this position:

(c1) **6 ♗e3** ♕a5+ 7 ♕d2 ♕xd2+ 8 ♗xd2 ♗f5= Radulov–Vukić, Uljma 1975.

(c2) **6 f4** ♗f5 7 ♗e3 e6 (7 ... ♕a5+!?=) 8 ♕d2 ♗e7 9 0-0-0 ♘d7 10 ♗e2 and White was perhaps very marginally more comfortable in Povah–Cafferty, Birmingham 1977.

(c3) **6 ♘f3 ♗g4 7 h3 ♗xf3 8 ♕xf3 e6** gives Black at least equality. 9 cd (9 ♗d2?! ♘d7 10 ♗c3 ♕b6 11 cd cd 12 0-0-0 ♗c5 13 ♕g4 0-0 14 f4 ♖fc8∓ Simons-Burgess, Weymouth 1989) 9 ... ♕xd5 10 ♕xd5 cd 11 c4 ♗b4+ 12 ♗d2 ♗xd2+ 13 ♔xd2 ♘c6 14 f4 0-0-0 15 ♔e3 h6 16 ♖d1 ♘e7= Kuzmin-Alburt, Leningrad 1974.

5 ♘f3

5 ed?! ♕xd6! 6 ♕xd6 cd 7 g3 ♘c6 8 ♗e3 g6 9 ♘f3 ♗g7 10 ♗g2 0-0 11 ♘d4 ♗d7 12 0-0 ♖fc8 led to a minority attack and an endgame win for Black in Kolste-Réti, Baden Baden 1925.

5 ♗c4?! ♘c6 6 ♘f3 (6 ♗f4? de 7 ♕xd8+ ♔xd8) 6 ... de 7 ♕e2 (7 ♕xd8+ ♘xd8 8 ♘xe5 f6 9 ♘d3 e5 10 0-0 ♗e6 11 ♗b3 ♗d6 12 ♖e1 g5∓ Nezhmetdinov-Spassky, Tbilisi 1959) 7 ... f6 8 ♗e3 (8 ♗d2 e6 9 0-0-0 ♗d6 10 ♘h4 ♕e7) 8 ... e6 9 ♘h4 g6 10 f4 ♗d6 11 0-0 ♕e7∓ Green-Williams, Coventry 1970.

5 ♗f4 ♘c6 (Keres considered 5 ... de 6 ♕xd8+ ♔xd8 7 0-0-0+ ♗d7 8 ♗xe5 f6 9 ♗g3 e5 10 f4 to give White some advantage.) 6 ♘f3 (6 ♗b5 ♗d7 7 ♕e2 a6 8 ♗c4 e6 9 ♘f3 is considered under 7 ... a6 in the note to 7 ... e6 below.) 6 ... de 7 ♕xd8+ (7 ♘xe5 ♕xd1+ 8 ♖xd1 ♘xe5 9 ♗xe5 c6= Tatai-Gheorghiu, Las Palmas 1972) 7 ... ♘xd8 8 ♗xe5 (8 ♘xe5 c6 9 0-0-0 f6 10 ♘c4 ♘f7 11 ♗g3 e5 12 ♘d2 g6 13 ♗c4 ♘d6 14 ♗b3 ♗h6 15 f3 ♗f5 16 ♔b1 0-0-0 17 ♗f2 ♔c7 18 g4 ♗c8 19 h3 ♗f4 20 c4 ♘f7 21 ♘e4 f5 led to a win for Black in Filipowicz-Chekhov, Warsaw 1990.) 8 ... c6 9 0-0-0 (9 ♘d2 f6 10 ♗g3 ♘f7 11 0-0-0 ♗d7 12 ♗c4 ♘d6 13 ♗xd6 ed 14 ♖he1+ ♔d8 15 ♗e6 ♗xe6 16 ♖xe6 ♔d7 17 ♖de1 d5 18 c4 dc 19 ♘xc4 b5 20 ♘d2 ♗d6= Lein-Martz, Chicago 1982) 9 ... f6 10 ♗g3 e5 (10 ... ♗e6) 11 ♗c4 and here Boleslavsky gave 11 ... ♗e7=. Instead in Roos-Schmidt, Bagneux 1978, Black allowed a pulverising blow: 11 ... ♘f7?! 12 ♖he1 g6? 13 ♗xe5! 1-0.

5 ... ♘c6

5 ... de 6 ♕xd8+ ♔xd8 7 ♘xe5 ♔e8

(a) **8 ♗c4 e6 9 ♗f4** (9 0-0 ♗d6 10 ♖e1 ♘d7; 9 ♗e3 ♗d6 10 ♘d3 ♗d7 11 0-0-0 ♗c6 12 f3 ♘d7 14 ♘b4 ♘b6 14 ♗e2 was Radulov-Jansa, Örebro 1966; 14 ... ♘e5! would have maintained equality.) 9 ... ♗d6 10 0-0-0 ♘d7 11 ♖he1 ♘xe5 12 ♗xe5 ♗xe5 13 ♖xe5 ♔e7 14 ♖c5! c6 15 f4 marginally favoured White in Pfleger-Schmidt, Polanica Zdroj 1971.

(b) **8 ♗e3 f6** (8 ... ♘d7 9 ♘d3!? Keres) 9 ♘f3 (9 ♘d3 e5 10 f4 e4) 9 ... e5 10 ♘d2!? ♗e6 11 f4 ♘d7 12 0-0-0 ♗d6 (12 ... ♗e7 13 ♗d3 with f5 and ♘e4 to follow.) 13 ♘e4 ♔e7 14 ♘xd6 cd 15 g3 gave White a substantial advantage in Hübner-Ghizdavu, Graz 1972.

6   ♗b5   ♗d7 *(14)*

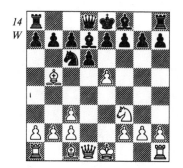

Other moves have been tried:

6 ... e6 7 ♗f4 ♗e7 8 ♕e2 0–0 9 0–0–0 a6 10 ♗d3 ♗d7 11 h4 and suddenly Black was faced with an overwhelming attack in Makarychev–A. Petrosian, USSR 1969.

A forthright approach gave Black a decent game in Torre–Réti, Baden Baden 1925: **6 ... a6** 7 ♗xc6+ bc 8 ♗f4 ♖b8 9 b3 e6 10 ♕d3 d5 11 0–0 ♕d7 12 ♖ad1 a5 13 ♖fe1 ♖a8 14 ♘g5 h6 15 ♘h3 ♗a6 16 ♕g3 g6. This game attained notoriety when Réti later tried to castle queenside.

6 ... g6!? 7 ♗f4 ♗g7 8 0–0 0–0 gave Black an excellent ending in Mack–Hennigan, British Ch (Blackpool) 1988 after 9 ♖e1?! de 10 ♘xe5 ♘xe5 11 ♗xe5 ♕xd1 12 ♖axd1 ♗xe5 13 ♖xe5 ♗e6!∓, but White should try 9 ed cd 10 ♕d2.

7   ♕e2   e6

7 ... ♘xe5 8 ♘xe5 de 9 ♕xe5 f6 (9 ... c6 10 ♗c4 and now 10 ... f6 11 ♕e2 leaves Black only a little worse. Instead 10 ... ♕b8 11 ♕e4 e6 12 ♗g5! h6 13 ♗h4 put Black in a permanent bind in Keres–Schmid, Zurich 1961, on account of 13 ... g5? 14 ♖d1 gh 15 ♕d4!+−) 10 ♕h5+ (10 ♔e2 e5 11 ♗c4± Keres) 10 ... g6 11 ♕e2 e5 12 ♗e3 (12 ♗c4!?; 12 0–0 ♗d6 13 ♗h6?!! ♕e7 14 ♗xd7+ ♕xd7 15 ♕f3 ♔f7 16 ♖ad1 ♕e6 17 ♖fe1 c6∓ Ottavi–Palatnik, Rome 1990) 12 ... ♗d6 13 0–0–0 b6 14 f4 0–0 15 fe ♗xb5 16 ♕xb5 fe 17 ♗h6± Markland–Korchnoi, Bath 1973.

7 ... a6 8 ♗c4 e6 (8 ... de) 9 ♗f4 de 10 ♗xe5 (10 ♘xe5 ♗d6 11 ♗g3 ♘xe5 12 ♗xe5 ♗xe5 13 ♕xe5 ♕f6= Hug–Schmidt, Pula 1975) 10 ... ♗d6 (10 ... ♘xe5 11 ♘xe5 ♗d6= Lechtynsky–Schmidt, Brno 1975) 11 ♗xg7 ♖g8 12 ♗e5 ♘xe5 13 ♘xe5 ♗xe5 14 ♕xe5 ♖xg2∞ Shamkovich–Bronstein, Moscow 1961.

8   ♗f4   ♗e7

After this, Black has serious problems. 8 ... a6 9 ♗d3 (9 ♗c4) 9 ... de 10 ♘xe5 ♗d6 11 ♖d1 ♕f6=   Schroeder–Jürgensen, Hamburg 1981.

9   0–0–0   d5
10   c4   a6
11   ♗a4   dc

Already Black has no satisfactory continuation.

12   ♗xc6   bc
13   ♕xc4   ♖b8
14   ♖xd7!

The defenders are systematically stripped from the black king.

The denouement is impressive: 14 ... ♛xd7 15 ♖d1 ♛c8 16 ♛xc6+ ♚f8 17 ♗g5 f6 18 ef gf 19 ♘e5! h6 20 ♘d7+ ♚f7 21 ♗xf6 ♗xf6 22 ♛f3 ♛d8 23 ♘e5+ ♚g7 24 ♖xd8 ♖hxd8 25 ♛g4+ ♗g5+ 26 f4 ♖b4 27 g3 ♖e4 28 ♘d3 ♖ed4 29 h4 1–0.

3 Chase Variation

The idea of pushing the pawn to c5 costs White no tempi, but is highly double-edged. The pawn is undeniably weak, but White hopes that it will turn out to be a thorn in Black's side: capturing it costs tempi, while exchanging it opens lines. The character of the Chase Variation is very much that of a gambit — in many lines the main task facing Black is to find the most palatable way to digest a pawn.

Dishman–Burgess
Birmingham (BUCA) 1990

1 e4 ♘f6 2 e5 ♘d5 3 c4 ♘b6 4 c5 ♘d5 *(15)*

5 ♘c3
5 d4 d6 6 cd ed (6 ... cd leads to a line of the c3 Sicilian.) 7 ♘f3 and Black can choose between 7 ... ♗e7 8 ♘c3 de 9 ♘xe5 ♗e6 10 ♗d3 ♘d7= (Sveshnikov) and 7 ... de!? 8 ♘xe5 ♗b4+ 9 ♗d2 0–0 10 ♗c4 ♗xd2+ 11 ♕xd2 f6 12 ♘c3 c6 13 ♘f3 ♖e8 14 ♘e2 ♗g4 15 0–0 ♘d7 with at least equality in Szeles–Knežević, Keszthely 1981.

5 ...   c6
After **5 ... ♘xc3 6 dc**, Black's d-pawn should probably not advance: **6 ... d5** (6 ... d6 7 cd) 7 cd ed 8 ♗f4!± (8 ♗c4 ♘c6=) 8 ... d5 (8 ... ♘c6 9 ed ♗xd6 10 ♗xd6 ♕xd6 11 ♕xd6 cd 12 0–0–0±) 9 ♗d3 ♗e6 10 ♘f3 ♗e7 11 ♘d4 g6?! (11 ... ♕d7) 12 ♘xe6 fe 13 h4 ♘c6 14 h5 g5 15 ♗g3 ♕d7 16 ♕c2± ♗f8 17 h6 ♕f7 18 0–0–0 ♘e7 19 ♕a4+! c6 20 c4 left Black's king with little prospect of safety in Sveshnikov–Palatnik, Belgrade GMA 1988.

Instead, Bagirov's idea **6 ... ♘c6** 7 ♘f3 e6 8 ♗e3 b6 seems playable. 9 ♕a4 (Black's position was the better organised after 9 cb ab 10

a3 f5 11 ef ♕xf6 12 ♗g5 ♕f7 13
♗d3 ♗a6 14 c4 ♗d6 15 ♕c2
♕h5 in Fogarasi–Bagirov, Budapest 1989.) 9 ... ♗xc5 10 ♗xc5
bc 11 0–0–0 f6! (The e-pawn must
be removed: 11 ... 0–0 12 ♗d3
f5 13 g4!) 12 ♗b5 ♘xe5 (12 ...
♗b7 13 ef gf 14 ♖he1!) 13 ♖he1
0–0 14 ♘xe5 fe 15 ♗xd7 ♕g5+
16 ♔b1 ♗xd7 17 ♕xd7 ♕g6+
18 ♔a1 ♖xf2 19 ♕xc7! h6! left
Black no worse in Capello–Bagirov, Tunis 1979.

5 ... e6 is, naturally, playable. 6
♗c4 is considered under the move
order 5 ♗c4 e6 6 ♘c3, while for
6 ♘xd5 ed 7 d4 d6 8 cd cd see the
next note. Independent options:

(a) **6 ♕g4** h5!? 7 ♕c4 d6!? (7 ...
♘xc3=) 8 cd cd 9 ♘xd5 ed 10
♕xd5 ♘c6 11 ♗b5 ♗d7 12 ed
♖h6 13 ♗c4 ♖e6+ 14 ♔f1 ♕f6
gave Black good chances in
reward for his imaginative play in
Õim–Mikenas, Palanga 1961.

(b) **6 ♘xd5** ed 7 d4 b6 8 ♗e3
(8 cb ab 9 ♘f3 ♗e7 10 ♗d3
♗a6; 8 ♘f3 bc 9 dc c6) 8 ... bc 9
dc c6 10 ♗d3 ♘a6 (10 ... ♗a6
11 b4!±; 10 ... ♕a5+ 11 ♕d2
♕xd2+ 12 ♔xd2 ♘a6 13 ♖c1
♖b8 may improve.) 11 ♖c1 ♕a5+
12 ♗d2! ♕xa2 13 ♖a1 ♕xb2 14
♗xa6 ♗xa6 15 ♖xa6 ♕xe5+ 16
♘e2 ♗xc5 17 0–0 0–0 18 ♘f4 was
Hennings–Smejkal, Kapfenberg
1970. White's attacking chances
are probably slightly more relevant than Black's pawns.

(c) **6 d4**:

(c1) **6 ... d6** 7 cd cd 8 ♘f3

can also arise from a c3 Sicilian.
Black's most robust defence is 8
... ♘c6 9 ed (9 ♗g5 ♘xc3 10 bc
♕a5; 9 ♗b5 ♘xc3 10 bc ♗d7 11
ed ♗xd6 12 0–0 0–0=; 9 ♗d3
de 10 de ♘db4=; 9 ♕b3 ♗e7!?
is best met by 10 ed ♕xd6=, since
10 ♘xd5 ed 11 ♕xd5 ♗e6 12 ♕e4
de 13 de ♗d5! is unpromising.) 9
... ♗xd6 10 ♗d3 ♘f4 11 ♗xf4
♗xf4. White appears to have no
advantage, e.g. 12 0–0 0–0 13
♖e1 g6 14 ♗f1 ♗h6 15 ♕a4
(Ozsvath–Csom, Budapest 1967)
15 ... ♗d7, or 12 ♕e2
(Damjanović–Buljovčić, Belgrade 1966) 12 ... ♘b4 13 ♗b5+
(13 ♗b1 ♘d5) 13 ... ♗d7 14 d5
0–0 15 ♗xd7 ♕xd7 16 de ♕xe6!
which Bagirov assesses as equal.

(c2) **6 ... ♘xc3** 7 bc b6 8 ♕g4
(8 ♕f3; 8 cb ab 9 ♕g4?! c5! 10
dc ♕c7!∓ Lein–Zelčić, Belgrade
GMA 1988) 8 ... f5 (The ♗g5
threat must be met.) 9 ef ♕xf6 10
♗d3 bc 11 ♘f3 ♘c6 12 0–0 gave
White a pleasant position in Ings–
Baier, corres. 1978.

6 ♗c4

6 ♘xd5 cd 7 d4 d6 8 cd ed *(16)*
fails to pose Black any problems:

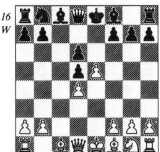

(a) **9 f4?** ♘c6 (After 9 ... de!? neither 10 de ♗c5 nor 10 fe ♕h4+ can satisfy White.) 10 ♘f3 ♗g4 11 ♗e3 de 12 fe ♗b4+ 13 ♔f2 0–0 14 ♗e2 f6! 15 ef ♕xf6 16 ♖f1 ♖ae8! 17 ♕b3 ♕e6 18 ♗b5 ♗xf3 19 gf ♖xf3+! 20 ♔xf3 ♕h3+ 0–1 Molnar–Tartakower, Paris 1955.

(b) **9 ed?** ♗xd6 leaves White trying to equalise.

(c) **9 ♘f3** ♘c6 (9 ... ♗e7 10 ♕b3 ♘c6) 10 ♗e2 (10 ♗d3?! ♗g4) 10 ... de (10 ... ♗e7 11 0–0 0–0 12 ♕b3!?) 11 de (After 11 ♘xe5, 11 ... ♗b4+ 12 ♗d2 ♕b6 13 ♘xc6 bc 14 ♗xb4 ♕xb4+ 15 ♕d2 ♖b8 equalised comfortably in Voskanin–Schmidt, Riga 1975, whilst 11 ... ♗d6 12 ♕a4 0–0 13 ♘xc6 bc 14 ♕xc6 ♗b4+ 15 ♔f1 ♖b8 16 ♗f4 ♖b6 17 ♕a4 ♖e8 18 ♗d3 ♗d7 19 ♕xa7 ♖be6 20 f3 ♕h4 21 ♗g3 ♕e7 22 a3 ♗b5 23 ab ♗xd3+ 24 ♔g1 ♕xb4 25 h3 ♗f5 26 ♔h2 ♗xh3! proved effective in Pazos–Anand, Dubai ol 1986.) 11 ... ♗b4+ (11 ... ♗c5?! 12 0–0 0–0 13 ♗g5 ♕b6 14 ♕xd5 ♘d4 15 ♘xd4 ♗xd4 16 ♗d3! ♖e8 17 ♖ae1 ♗xb2 18 ♗f6! ♕d4 19 ♗xh7+ gave White a winning attack in Siaperas–Czerniak, Zagreb 1969.) 12 ♗d2 ♕a5 13 a3 (13 ♗xb4 ♕xb4+ 14 ♕d2 ♕xd2+ 15 ♔xd2 ♗g4 16 ♖ac1 ♔e7=) 13 ... ♗xd2+ 14 ♕xd2 ♕xd2+ 15 ♔xd2 ♗g4 16 ♗b5 ♗xf3 17 gf ♔d7 (17 ... 0–0 18 ♗xc6 bc 19 ♖ac1 ♖fb8 20 ♖xc6 ♖xb2+ 21 ♔e3 ♖b3+ was also level in Siaperas–Flatow,

Lugano ol 1968.) 18 f4 a6 19 ♗xc6+ bc 20 b4 a5 21 f5 g6 was an unbalanced, but equal, ending in Zier–Herndl, Vienna Open 1986.

6 d4 d6 7 cd ed is fine for Black. 8 ♘xd5 cd transposes to the lines above; Sveshnikov–Bracken, Budapest Open 1989 continued sharply with 8 ♘f3 ♘xc3 9 bc ♗g4!? 10 h3 ♗xf3 11 ♕xf3 de 12 ♗c4 ♕f6 13 ♕e2 ♘d7 14 f4 ♕h4+ 15 ♔d1 f6 16 ♔c2 0–0–0.

6 ♘f3 d6 7 ♘xd5 cd 8 cd ed 9 ♕b3?! (9 d4) 9 ... ♘c6 10 ♗b5 ♗e7 11 ♕xd5 0–0 left White seriously under-developed in Sikora–Alburt, Decin 1977.

6 ♕b3 d6 7 cd ed 8 ♗c4 transposes to 7 cd ed 8 ♕b3 below.

6 ...   d6

The unbelievable **6 ... b6** 7 ♘xd5 cd 8 ♗xd5 ♘c6 9 cb ♕xb6 10 ♕b3 ♕a5 11 ♗xf7+ ♔d8 12 ♕d5 ♕c7 13 ♘f3 ♖b8 gave Black some compensation in Woda–Timmermans, Val Thorens 1988.

6 ... e6 7 ♘e4 (7 d4 b6 8 cb ab 9 ♘ge2 ♗a6 10 ♗b3 d6 11 ♘xd5 ½–½ Rozentalis–Kengis, Daugavpils 1989) 7 ... b6 8 ♘d6+ ♗xd6 9 cd 0–0 (9 ... ♕g5?! 10 ♘f3!?) 10 d4 (10 ♕h5 ♗a6 11 d3 f6 12 ♘f3 ♘b4 13 ef ♕xf6 14 ♗g5 ♕f5 0–1 S. Wolff–Kengis, Luxembourg 1990) 10 ... ♗a6 11 b3 f6∞ Szabolcsi–Kneževic, Budapest 1981.

7   ♕b3

Instead, **7 ♘xd5?** cd 8 ♗xd5 e6

(8 ... de? 9 ♕b3∞) 9 ♗f3 de 10 b4 e4∓ (Kopylov) is weak, whilst **7 ed** ♘xc3! 8 dc ed 9 cd ♗xd6 allows easy equality. A couple of serious alternatives:

(a) **7 ♕f3** led to fascinating play in Chekhov–K. Grigorian, Moscow Ch 1979: 7 ... ♘d7 8 ♗xd5 (8 ed?! ♘e5 9 ♕e4 ♘xc4 10 ♕xc4 ed 11 ♘xd5 ♗e6!∓) 8 ... ♘xe5 9 ♗xf7+ ♔xf7 10 d4 g6 11 cd ♕xd6 12 ♘ge2 ♗g7 13 ♗f4 ♕b4 14 0–0 0–0 15 ♕e3 ♖e8 16 a3 ♕xb2 17 ♖fb1 ♕c2 18 ♘g3 g5 and Black's extra pawn was reasonably sound. Play continued 19 ♗e5 ♘xe5 20 de ♕g6 21 ♖b4 b6 22 h4 g4 23 ♖e1 ♗e6 24 h5 ♕h6 25 ♕e4 c5 26 ♖bb1 ♖ad8 27 ♘b5 ♖d7 28 ♖bd1 ♖f8 29 ♖xd7 ♗xd7 30 ♘xa7 ♕e6 31 ♕b7 ♗h6 32 ♘e4 ♗a4 33 ♕a6 ♗b3 34 ♘b5 ♕xe5 35 ♕xb6 g3 36 fg ♗d2 37 ♕xc5 ♕xc5+ 38 ♘xc5 ♗xe1 39 ♘xb3 ♗xg3 40 ♘5d4 e5 41 ♘e2 ♗f2+ 42 ♔h2 ♖a8 43 ♘d2 ♖xa3 44 ♘e4 ♖e3 45 ♘xf2 ♖xe2 and Black won.

(b) **7 cd ed** fails to improve White's prospects.

(b1) **8 ♘f3** ♗e7 9 0–0 ♘xc3! is a timely exchange approved by Alburt. 10 dc 0–0 is equal, whilst 10 bc followed by d4 can be met by ... c5 and queenside play.

(b2) **8 ♘xd5** cd 9 ♗xd5 de 10 ♕b3 transposes to (b3).

(b3) **8 ♕b3** de 9 ♘xd5 cd 10 ♗xd5 ♕c7 11 ♘f3 ♗d6 and now 12 0–0 0–0 13 d3 ♘d7 (13 ... ♘c6) 14 ♗e3 ♘f6 15 ♖ac1 ♕e7 16

♗g5 h6 was no problem for Black in Dubinin–Kopylov, Leningrad 1946. A more violent approach was tried in Vuksanović– Tradardi, Rome Open 1990: 12 ♘g5 0–0 13 ♕d3 g6 14 ♕e4 (14 ♕g3 ♘c6) 14 ... ♔g7 (14 ... ♘c6!?) 15 d3 ♕e7? 16 h4 ♗b4+?! 17 ♔f1 ♗f5 18 ♕e3 ♗c5 19 ♕g3 ♘c6 20 h5+ –. Instead both 15 ... h6 and 15 ... ♗f5 are perfectly adequate.

| 7 | ... | ♘d7 |

7 ... de is also just about playable. 8 ♘xd5 cd 9 ♗xd5 e6 10 ♗xb7 ♗xb7 11 ♕xb7 ♕d5! 12 ♕c8+ ♔e7 (12 ... ♕d8 Sveshnikov) 13 ♕c7+ ♔f6 14 d4 ♘c6 15 ♘f3 and now Palatnik's suggestion is 15 ... ed 16 ♕f4+ ♔e7 17 0–0 f6∞. Instead in Sveshnikov– Palatnik, Chelyabinsk 1974, after 15 ... ♘xd4?! 16 ♗g5+ ♔g6 17 ♘xe5+ ♔xg5 18 0–0! ♕xc5 19 f4+ ♔h6! 20 ♘xf7+ ♔h5 21 ♕b7 ♗e7, White had at his disposal the strong 22 b4! ♕xb4 23 g4+!

8 ♘xd5

8 cd?! ♘xe5! is complicated, but, as Hort demonstrated, promising for Black: 9 ♘xd5 cd 10 ♗xd5 e6!? 11 ♗xb7 (11 d4 ♘c6 12 ♗xc6+ bc and ... ♗a6 ideas give the white king some problems.) 11 ... ♖b8 12 ♕a4+ ♗d7 13 ♕xa7 ♖xb7!? (13 ... ♗xd6) 14 ♕xb7 ♗c6 15 d7+ ♔e7 16 ♕b4+ ♔xd7 17 ♕d4+ ♗d6 and White has serious problems.

| 8 | ... | ♘xc5 |

8 ... cd? 9 ♗xd5 e6 10 ♗xe6! fe

11 ♕xe6+ ♕e7 12 ♕xe7+ ♔xe7
13 cd+ ♔f7 14 d4 ♘b6 15 f4 was
very good for White in Sveshnikov–Knežević, Dubna 1979.

9 ♘c7+   ♔d7

9 ... ♕xc7?! 10 ♗xf7+ ♔d8
11 ♕c2? g6 12 ♕c3 ♗g7! 13 ed
ed 14 ♕xg7 ♖e8+ 15 ♔f1 ♕e7
was good for Black in Binci–Pisa,
Buenos Aires 1985, but 11 ♕e3 is
an obvious improvement.

10 ♕e3   ♔xc7
11 d4

11 ♗xf7? ♗f5 12 ♗c4 d5 13
♗e2 d4∓. After 11 d4, 11 ... ♗e6
12 ♗e2? ♘d7 13 ♘f3 ♗d5 14
0–0 e6 left Black a sound pawn
up in Kislova–Levitina, Togliatti
1974, but 12 b3 d5 13 ♗e2 ♘d7
14 f4 gives White rather good
compensation, as Black's minor
pieces are uncoordinated.

11 ...   d5!
12 ♗e2   ♘e6 *(17)*

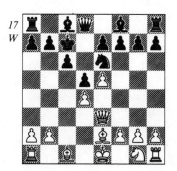

A strange sight. It appears that
Black has forgotten how the long-
range pieces move, but the black
pieces have good prospects of an
harmonious development, whilst

their king is in no imminent
danger. White must work hard to
demonstrate compensation.

13 f4   g6

13 ... g5!? 14 fg h6 is a reasonable way to return the pawn.

14 g4   h5
15 gh   gh
16 ♘f3

16 f5 is met not by 16 ... ♗h6?!
17 ♕f2, but by 16 ... ♘g7 when
the white pawns are in trouble.

16 ...   ♗h6
17 ♘g5   ♗xg5
18 fg   ♔b8
19 ♗d2

Necessary, to stop 19 ... ♕b6
winning a pawn. Now Black
should consider trying to seize the
initiative with 19 ... c5 20 dc d4.
The resulting position is chaotic,
unclear and with little prospect of
safety for either king.

19 ...   h4
20 ♖f1   ♖g8
21 ♖xf7   ♘xg5
22 ♕xg5!?

A fully reasonable queen sacrifice, since Black's only active
pieces are removed, lines towards
to black king become opened, and
also White lacks a purposeful
alternative.

22 ...   ♖xg5
23 ♗xg5   ♗e6

In time trouble I found a reasonable defence. Were Black satisfied
with a draw, 23 ... ♕g8 24 ♗xe7
a5 25 ♗d6+ ♔a7 26 ♗c5+
♔b8 would be suitable.

The game continued: 24 ♗xe7

♕a5+ 25 b4 ♕a3 26 ♖f3! ♕b2 27
♖d1 ♔c7 28 ♗xh4 ♖g8 29 ♗g3
♕xb4+ 30 ♔f2 ♔c8?! (With both
players seriously short of time, the
play becomes a little illogical, 30
... ♔d7 would be normal.) 31 ♖f6
♖f8 32 ♔e3 ♖xf6 33 ef c5 34
♗e5 ♕c3+ 35 ♔f2 ♕b2 36 ♖g1
cd? (36 ... c4 37 h4!? c3 38 ♗f4
♕b6 was established afterwards as
a probable draw. After 36 ... cd?,
White has the strong 37 ♖g3!
when Black is stuck for a plan.) 37
♖g7? ♕d2 38 ♖g3 ♗g4! 39 ♖xg4
d3 40 f7 ♕xe2+ 41 ♔g3 ♕xe5+
42 ♖f4 (The dust has cleared,
leaving an ending where the white
f-pawn ties down the queen and,
together with the h-pawn, constitutes enough play to save the half-
point.) 42 ... ♕g7+ 43 ♔f3 ♕f8
44 h4 ♔d7 45 h5 ♔e7 46 ♔e3
b5 47 ♔xd3 a5 48 h6 ♕xh6 ½-½.
In view of White's threat of 49 h7,
the line 48 ... ♕xh6 49 f8♕+ ♕xf8
50 ♖xf8 ♔xf8 51 ♔d4 b4 52
♔xd5 a4 53 ♔c4= is inevitable.

Langschmidt–Zeh
Correspondence 1988

**1 e4 ♘f6 2 e5 ♘d5 3 c4 ♘b6 4 c5
♘d5**

    5   ♗c4   e6
    6   d4

6 ♕g4 has been tried, without
success, by Radojević:

(a) **6 ... d6** 7 cd cd 8 d4 ♕c7 9
♘d2 (9 ♕e2? de 10 de ♘d7 11 ♘d2
♘f4! 12 ♕e4 ♘xe5 0–1 Radojević–
Pribyl, Hradec Kralove 1973/4) 9
... de 10 ♘gf3 ♘d7!∓ Radojević–

Hloušek, Hradec Kralove 1973/4.
(b) **6 ... ♘b4!?** 7 ♘a3 (7 ♗xe6?
♘d3+) 7 ... b6 8 d4 ♗a6 9 ♕e4
♘8c6 (9 ... ♗xc4 10 ♘xc4 ♘c6)
10 ♗xa6 ♘xa6∓ 11 ♕d3? ♘ab4
12 ♕c4 bc 13 dc ♘xe5! 0–1 Radojević–Bagirov, Trinec 1973.

6 ♘c3 has been the subject of
considerable theoretical and
practical debate. The move can
lead to great complications, in
which Black must judge carefully
how much greed is appropriate.
However, Black's resources
appear fully adequate, so the line
is not much seen nowadays. 6 ...
♘f4?! invites White to fall for 7
♕g4? ♕h4!–+, while 7 d4 ♘xg2+
8 ♔f1 ♘h4 9 ♘f3 ♘f5! is far from
clear, but 7 g3 ♘g6 8 d4 d6 9 h4
de 10 h5 ♘e7 11 h6 ♕xd4 12 ♕e2
♘f5 13 ♘e4 ♗xc5 14 hg ♘xg7 15
♘f6+ ♔e7 16 ♗e3 ♕d6 17 ♗g5
♕c6 18 ♘f3 h6 19 ♘d5++ 1–0
Khatset–Shiryaev, Moscow 1961,
may be the way to punish Black's
extravagance. Black's best is **6 ...
♘xc3 7 dc** (7 bc d5 8 cd cd 9 ed
♗xd6 10 d4 0–0 11 ♘f3 ♕c7! 12
♕d3 ♘d7 13 0–0 b6 14 ♗b3 ♗b7
15 h3 e5!∓ Sergeant–Tartakower,
Hastings 1945/6). Now 7 ... b6 is
playable: 8 ♕g4 (8 cb ab and now
9 ♕g4 ♗b7 10 ♗f4 ♘e7 or 9 ♘f3
d5 10 ed cd 11 0–0 ♗e7 12 ♘d4
0–0= 13 f4 d5 14 ♗d3 ♗a6!
Sveshnikov–Bagirov, USSR Ch
[Kharkov] 1967) 8 ... ♘c6 9 ♘f3
♗b7 (9 ... bc 10 ♗g5 ♘e7 11
0–0–0 h6 12 ♗h4 g5 13 ♗xe6!
Lerner–Dzhalilov, USSR 1981) 10

♗f4 ♘e7!? 11 cb ab 12 0–0 ♘f5 13 ♘d4 (13 ♖fd1 ♗e7 with ... h6 and ... g5 to follow) 13 ... h5! 14 ♕h3 was Barber–Depasquale, Australian Ch (Melbourne) 1987. Rogers gives 14 ... ♕h4! 15 ♘xf5 (15 ♕h4 ♘xh4 16 f3 ♘g6∓) 15 ... ♕xh3 16 gh (16 ♘xg7+? ♗xg7 17 gh ♖g8∓) 16 ... ef∓. However, the main continuation is 7 ... ♘c6 8 ♗f4:

(a) 8 ... ♕h4 tries to make the most of the threat of taking on c5, though Black should be very wary of actually grabbing the pawn. 9 g3 (9 ♕d2? ♘xe5! 10 ♗e2 ♘g6 11 ♗xc7 ♗xc5 12 ♗g3 ♕a4 13 h4 h5 14 ♘f3 d5 15 b4 ♗b6 16 ♘d4 a6 17 ♗d1 ♕d7 18 ♗b3 ♘e7∓ Angelov–Suba, Varna 1975) 9 ... ♕e7 10 ♘f3 (10 ♕e2 g5! 11 ♗d2 ♕xc5 12 ♗xg5 ♕xe5! 13 ♕xe5 ♘xe5 14 ♗f6 ♘xc4 15 ♗xh8 ♘xb2∓ Hölzl–Speelman, Hastings 1971/2) 10 ... h6 (10 ... ♕xc5?! 11 ♕e2) 11 ♗e3 (11 ♕e2!? g5!?; 11 h4 b6 12 cb ab 13 0–0 ♗b7 14 ♕e2 g5 15 hg hg 16 ♗xg5 ♕xg5! 17 ♘xg5 ♘d4∓ Rohland–Unger, Fort Worth 1984) 11 ... b6! (11 ... g5? 12 ♗b5!) 12 cb ab 13 ♕e2 ♗b7 14 0–0?! (14 0–0–0∞) 14 ... g5 15 ♘d4?! (15 ♘d2 ♘xe5 16 ♗d4 ♘xc4 17 ♗xh8 ♘xd2 18 ♕xd2 f6 can hardly be bad for Black.) 15 ... ♘xe5 16 ♗xg5 hg 17 ♕xe5 ♖xh2!–+ Hegedus–Grünberg, Romanian Ch (Bucharest) 1985. 18 ♔xh2 is met by 18 ... f6!.

(b) 8 ... ♗xc5 9 ♕g4 g5 is one of the more peculiar lines in opening theory. Black gives away this pawn in order to set up a pin on the g-file. 10 ♗xg5 (10 ♕xg5?! ♕xg5 11 ♗xg5 ♘xe5 12 ♗f6 ♗xf2+!? 13 ♔e2 ♘xc4 14 ♗xh8 ♗xg1 15 ♖hxg1 ♘xb2 16 ♖gf1 b6∓ Domino–Delander, Berlin 1952) 10 ... ♖g8 *(18)* (10 ... ♘xe5? 11 ♕h4+ –). Now:

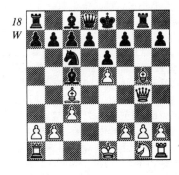

(b1) 11 ♘f3? loses material to 11 ... ♘xe5! 12 ♗xd8 ♖xg4 13 ♘xe5 ♖e4+.

(b2) 11 f4?! ♘xe5 12 ♕h4 ♖xg5 13 fg ♘xc4 14 ♕xc4 ♕xg5 15 ♘e2 and now 15 ... ♕xg2? 16 0–0–0 d6 17 ♖hg1! ♗xg1 18 ♖xg1 ♕xh2 19 ♕xc7 was a disaster in Gulko–Spitsyn, Moscow 1963, but Bagirov's 15 ... d6! is more than adequate for Black.

(b3) 11 ♗xd8 ♖xg4 12 ♗e2 ♖xg2 (12 ... ♘xe5? 13 ♗xc7! ♖e4 14 f3!± Van der Tak) 13 ♗xc7 b6! (13 ... ♖xf2!? 14 ♘f3 b6 15 ♖g1 ♘e7 16 ♗d6 ♗a6!∞ Sauermann) 14 ♘h3 (14 b4!? ♗xf2+ 15 ♔f1 ♖xg1+ 16 ♔xf2 ♖g6

17 ♖hg1 ♗b7 18 ♗h5 ♘e7 19 ♗xg6 hg∞ ½–½ Trapl–Neckař, Hradec Kralove 1972) 14 ... ♗b7 15 ♗f3 ♖g8 16 0–0–0 ♘a5!? (16 ... ♖c8 17 ♗d6) 17 ♖hg1 ♔e7! 18 ♗d6+ ♗xd6 19 ed+ ♔f6 20 ♗g4!? h5! 21 ♗e2 (21 ♗xh5 ♖xg1 22 ♖xg2 ♖h8∓ Nederkoorn) 21 ... ♖xg1 22 ♖xg1 ♗c6 23 ♘f4 ♔e5 24 ♘xh5 ♔xd6 gave Black an excellent ending in Kling–Nederkoorn, corres. 1981/2.

(b4) **11 ♘h3** ♗e7 12 f4 (12 ♗xe7 ♖xg4 13 ♗xd8 can be met by 13 ... ♖xc4 14 ♗xc7 ♘xe5!= or 13 ... ♔xd8 14 f4 ♖xg2 15 0–0–0 ♔e7! 16 ♖dg1 ♖g6 17 ♘g5 h6 18 ♘f3 ♖xg1 19 ♖xg1 d6∓ Gertsch–Rosell, corres. 1984.) 12 ... ♘xe5 13 fe ♗xg5 14 ♕h5 ♖g7 15 0–0 ♕e7! (15 ... b6? 16 ♖xf7!; 15 ... h6?! 16 ♗d3! ♕e7 17 ♖f3 ♔f8 18 ♖af1 ♔g8 19 ♘f2 d6 20 ♘g4 de 21 ♘f6+! gave White a strong attack in Sokolov–Kuuksmaa, USSR 1977. It is due to this manoeuvre that Black's queen's bishop should be ready to cover f1.) 16 ♖f3 (16 ♗d3 b6 17 ♗e4 c6 18 ♗xh7 ♗a6 19 ♖fe1 0–0–0 20 ♗e4 f5∓ Angelov–Popov, Sofia 1972) 16 ... b6 (16 ... h6?! 17 ♗d3) 17 ♖g3 h6 18 ♘f2 ♕c5 19 ♕e2 d6 20 ed cd 21 ♖d1 ♗b7∓ Angelov–Orev, Sofia 1971.

     6 ...   b6

6 ... d6 7 cd cd transposes to a line of the c3 Sicilian.

     7 ♕g4

7 ♗xd5 ed 8 cb (8 ♗e3? bc 9 dc c6 10 ♘c3 ♘a6∓ Kononenko–Bagirov, Baku 1969) 8 ... ab is fine for Black, who has the plan of ... c6 followed by ... ♘a6–c7–e6.

7 cb ab. Now in practice White has tried three knight moves:

(a) **8 ♕g4** gives a position that has been reached via the move order 6 ♕g4 b6?! 7 cb ab 8 d4. Black should try 8 ... f5!?, since 8 ... ♗a6 9 ♗xd5 ed 10 ♘c3 ♘c6 11 ♘ge2± (SDO) and 8 ... ♗b7 9 ♗g5 ♕c8 10 ♘c3 ♗b4 11 ♖c1 (Radojević–Schmidt, Lublin 1971) are unpromising.

(b) **8 ♘e2** ♗a6 9 ♗xd5 ed 10 ♘bc3 c6 11 0–0 ♗e7 12 ♖e1 0–0 13 ♘g3 d6 14 ♘h5 f5!∞ Semeniuk–Mikhalchishin, Chelyabinsk 1975.

(c) **8 ♘c3** ♗b7 (8 ... ♘xc3 9 bc d5 10 ♗d3 ♗a6 11 ♗xa6 ♖xa6∓ Machulsky–Agzamov, Lvov 1974) 9 ♘xd5 ed 10 ♗d3 d6 11 ♘e2 de 12 de ♘d7∓ 13 e6?! fe 14 ♘f4 ♗b4+ 15 ♔f1 ♕f6 16 ♕e2 e5 17 ♗b5 c6 18 ♘xd5 cd 19 ♗xd7+ ♔xd7 20 ♕b5+ ♔c7 21 ♕xb4 d4 22 ♗d2 ♖hf8 23 ♗e1 ♕g5 24 f3 ♗xf3 25 ♗g3 ♗h5+ 0–1 Rausis–Shirov, Latvian Ch (Riga) 1986.

(d) **8 ♘f3** ♗a6 *(19)*

(d1) **9 b3** ♗b4+ 10 ♗d2 ♘c6 11 0–0 ♗xd2 12 ♕xd2 ♘ce7 13 ♖e1 h6 14 ♕e2 ♗b7 15 a4 ♘f4∓ Machulsky–Bagirov, Kirovabad 1973.

(d2) **9 ♘bd2** ♗e7 10 0–0 0–0 11 ♖e1 d6 12 ♗b3 ♘d7 13 ♘c4

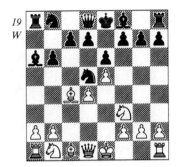

gave White a pleasant edge in Kuksov–Baburin, RSFSR Ch 1986, but Black should stir up trouble with 9 ... ♗b4, e.g. 10 0–0 ♗xd2 11 ♘xd2 ♕h4.

(d3) **9 ♗xa6 ♗b4+!?** (9 ... ♘xa6 10 0–0 ♗e7 with ... ♘ab4 and ... f5 to follow, is also fine.) 10 ♗d2 ♗xd2+ 11 ♘bxd2 ♖xa6 12 0–0 ♘c6 13 a3 0–0 14 ♘e4 f5 15 ef gf! (15 ... ♘xf6 16 ♘xf6+ ♕xf6 17 d5) 16 ♕d2 ♕e8 17 ♘c3 ♘ce7 18 ♘xd5 ♘xd5 gave Black good play and a clear structural superiority in Gonzales Mestres–Marović, Spain 1977.

7	...	bc

7 ... d6?! 8 cd cd 9 ♘f3 ♗b7 10 0–0 ♘d7 11 ♗g5 ♗e7 12 ♗d2 de 13 de ♔f8 14 ♘c3 h5 15 ♕g3 h4 16 ♕g4 h3 17 ♗xd5 gave White a very useful advantage in Wolff–Hennigan, Oakham 1986.

8	♗xd5	ed
9	♗g5	♗e7
10	♗xe7	♕xe7
11	♕xg7	♕f8
12	♕f6	cd

Black could well try **12 ... ♖g8**, which looks rather promising.

13	♘e2	♕b4+
14	♘bc3	♖g8
15	a3	♕xb2
16	♖b1	♕xa3
17	♘xd5	♕a5+
18	♘ec3	♘c6
19	♖b5	♕a1+
20	♘b1	a6
21	♘xc7+	♔f8
22	♕d6+	♘e7
23	♘d5	ab
24	♕xe7+	♔g7

White now has a draw by perpetual check, but rejects this possibility. This allows Black a powerful regrouping, culminating in a devastating counter-attack: 25 0–0 ♖a6 26 ♘f6 ♖e6 27 ♘h5+ ♔h8 28 ♕xf7 ♕a8! 29 g3 ♗a6 30 ♕xd7 ♕e8 31 ♕d5 ♗b7 32 ♕xb7 ♕xh5 33 f4 ♕e2 34 ♖f2 ♕d1+ 35 ♖f1 ♕d3 36 ♕g2 ♕e3+ 37 ♔h1 ♖h6 38 ♖g1 ♖h4! 0–1.

Shirazi–Alburt
US Ch (Berkeley) 1984

1 e4 ♘f6 2 e5 ♘d5 3 c4 ♘d5 4 c5 ♘d5

5	♗c4	c6
6	♕e2	

6 d4 b6 is very adequate for Black, whilst 6 ♘c3 is considered under 5 ♘c3 c6 6 ♗c4.

6	...	e6

Two other moves have been tried.

(a) **6 ... ♕a5** is rather greedy:

(a1) 7 ♘c3 ♕xc5 8 ♘e4 ♕a5 9 ♕f3 e6 (9 ... d6!?) 10 ♘h3 ♘b6 11 ♘hg5 ♘xc4 12 ♕xf7+ ♔d8 13 0–0 ♕xe5 gave White a powerful initiative for the material in Jäckle–Jürgensen, Hamburg 1986.

(a2) 7 ♘f3 ♕xc5 (7 ... e6 8 0–0 ♗xc5 9 d4 ♗e7 10 ♗g5 ♕d8 11 ♗xe7 ♕xe7 12 ♘bd2 f5 13 ef gf 14 ♖ac1 0–0 15 ♗xd5 cd 16 ♘h4 ♘c6 is probably a better way to capture the pawn, though also gave White good compensation in Gurgenidze–Breitman, USSR 1968.) 8 d4 ♕b4+ 9 ♘bd2 d6 10 0–0 ♗g4 11 h3 ♗xf3 12 ♘xf3 e6 was Makarychev–Alburt, Ashkhabad 1978; now 13 ♗d2! ♕b6 14 ♘g5 de 15 ♘xe6! fe 16 ♕xe5 would have been promising for White.

(b) 6 ... b6 7 ♘c3 ♘xc3 (Safer is 7 ... bc 8 ♘xd5 cd 9 ♗xd5 ♘c6 10 ♘f3±) 8 dc bc 9 ♘f3 e6 10 ♘g5 f5 (10 ... f6 11 ♘e4) 11 ♗f4 ♗e7 and White put his development advantage to immediate use in Shirazi–Alburt, Lone Pine 1981: 12 h4 ♕a5 13 g4! h6 14 ♘xe6! de 15 gf. White has too many avenues to the black king; the game concluded 15 ... h5 16 ♖g1 ♔f8 17 fe ♗a6 18 ♗g5 ♗xg5 19 ♖xg5 ♕c7 (19 ... ♗xc4 20 ♕f3+) 20 0–0–0 ♗xc4 21 ♕xc4 ♔e8 22 ♕d3 1–0 (22 ... ♖h6 23 ♖xg7!).

	7	**d4**		**b6**
	8	**cb**		**ab**
	9	**♘f3** *(20)*		

Soltis–Alburt, New York Open 1988 continued with the unnatural **9 ♘h3**. This move avoids obstructing the queen and the f-pawn, but as would be expected, Black has an effective counter. 9 ... ♗a6 10

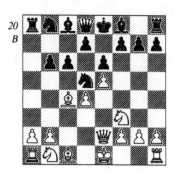

♗xa6 ♗b4+! (10 ... ♖xa6 11 0–0, meeting 11 ... ♗e7?! with 12 ♕g4 0–0? 13 ♗h6, illustrates White's ideas. The *zwischenzug* frustrates this.) 11 ♗d2 (11 ♘d2 ♖xa6 Alburt) 11 ... ♘xa6 12 0–0 0–0 13 ♘c3 ♘ac7 14 ♘e4 ♗xd2 15 ♕xd2 f5! 16 ♘d6 ♘e8! gave White little compensation for his structural inferiority. Black went on to win an interesting and thematic ending: 17 ♘xe8 ♖xe8 18 a4 ♕e7 19 ♖fc1 ♖a7 20 b3 ♖ea8 21 ♖ab1 h6 22 f3 ♖a5 23 ♘f2 ♕b4 24 ♕xb4 ♘xb4 25 ♖c4 ♘d5 26 ♘d3 ♔f7 27 ♖c2 ♔e7 28 ♔f2 ♖b8 29 ♖a1 ♖a7 30 ♔e2 g5 31 ♔d2 f4 32 ♖ca2 ♘e3 33 ♔c3 ♖a5 34 g3?! (The start of a plan which gives White too many weaknesses. Alburt recommends 34 b4∓) 34 ... ♖f8 35 gf? ♘d5+ 36 ♔d2 ♘xf4 37 ♘xf4 ♖xf4–+ 38 b4 ♖xd4+! 39 ♔c3 ♖ad5 40 a5 ♖d3+ 41 ♔c2 ♖xf3 42 a6 ♖f8 43 ♖e1 ♖a8 44 ♔c3 ♖a7 45 ♖e3 h5 46 h3 ♔d8 47 ♔b3 ♔c7 48 ♔c2 b5 0–1.

A suggestion of Hort's is **9 ♘c3** ♗a6 (9 ... ♗b4!?) 10 ♗xa6 ♘xa6

11 ♘xd5 ed 12 ♘h3 but his assessment ± (presumably based on 12 ... ♗e7 13 ♕g4) seems dubious on account of 12 ... ♕h4 or 12 ... ♗b4+ 13 ♗d2 ♕h4. Instead 12 ♘f3 ♗e7 intending ... 0-0, ... ♘c7-e6 and maybe ... f5 gives Black reasonable play.

9 ...   ♗e7

9 ... ♗a6 is liable to transpose. A couple of independent options:

(a) An attempt to keep Black's queenside bottled up is **10 b3!?** ♗e7 (10 ... ♗b4+ is met not by 11 ♘bd2? ♘c3 12 ♕d3 ♗xc4 13 ♕xc4 ♖xa2 14 ♕xb4? ♘d5!, but 11 ♗d2 ♗xd2+ 12 ♕xd2.) 11 0-0 0-0 12 ♘bd2?! and now 12 ... ♗xc4 is fine for Black since 13 bc?! loses a pawn to 13 ... ♖xa2!? 14 cd ♖xa1 15 d6 ♗g5 16 ♘xg5 ♕xg5 17 ♘b3 ♖xc1 or 13 ... ♘c3 14 ♕e3 ♘xa2, though neither of these lines is utterly clear. Instead Dannevig–Burgess, Gausdal Peer Gynt 1990 continued 12 ... f5?! 13 ef ♘xf6 14 ♖e1 ♔h8 15 ♘e5± ♕e8 16 a4 ♕h5 17 ♕d3?? b5!–+ 18 ab cb 19 ♘xd7 bc 20 ♘xf6 ♗xf6 21 ♕e4 ♗b7 0-1.

(b) **10 0-0** ♗e7 11 ♘c3 ♘xc3 (11 ... 0-0 12 ♗xa6 ♘xa6 13 ♘xd5 ed followed by ... ♘c7-e6 is OK.) 12 bc ♗xc4 13 ♕xc4 b5 14 ♕d3 ♖a4 (14 ... ♘a6 15 a4) 15 ♘d2 d5?! (15 ... ♘a6 aiming for d5.) 16 ed ♕xd6 17 ♖e1± ♘d7?! 18 ♘e4 ♕d5 19 ♕g3 gave Black

grave difficulties in Maier–Rührig, W. German Ch (Bad Neuenahr) 1987.

10   0-0

10 ♘bd2 ♗a6 11 ♗xa6 ♘xa6 12 ♘e4 f5 13 ef ♘xf6 14 ♘xf6+ ♗xf6 15 ♗f4 0-0 was fine for Black in Shabalov–Schmidt, Riga 1983.

10 ...   0-0
11 ♘bd2   ♗a6

Alburt considers the game to be level. Note that 12 b3?! transposes to Dannevig–Burgess above (12 ... ♗xc4!).

12	♘e4	♗xc4
13	♕xc4	f5
14	ef	gf
15	♗h6	♖f7
16	a3	♔h8
17	♘c3	b5
18	♕d3	♘b6
19	♖ae1	♕g8
20	d5?!	

Black has a clear structural superiority, but this attempt to solve White's problems ends up highlighting them, thanks to a few tactical nuances: 20 ... ♘xd5 21 ♘xd5 cd 22 ♕c3 b4! 23 ab ♘c6 24 b5 ♗b4 25 ♕e3 ♘e7 26 ♖a1 ♘f5 27 ♕b3 ♗d6 28 ♖xa8 ♕xa8 29 ♗d2 ♗c5 30 ♕c3 ♗b6 31 ♗e3 ♘xe3 32 fe ♔g8 33 ♘d4 f5 34 ♖f3 f4! 35 ♔f1 ♕a1+ 36 ♔e2 ♗a5 37 ♘b3 ♕g1 38 ♕c8+ ♖f8 39 ♕xd7 ♕e1+ 0-1.

4 Unusual Fourth Moves for White

The moves in this chapter are not White's most critical tries for advantage, but are very far from feeble.

4 f4 is a related idea to the Four Pawns. White hopes to profit by holding back the c-pawn, but the possibility of answering a subsequent c4 with ... ♘b4 gives Black some useful extra options.

4 ♗e2 is surprisingly promising. It is quite possible that 4 ... de is not quite sufficient for equality, so 4 ... g6 may be preferable.

4 ♗c4 was popular in the 1970s. It is still a sharp move, but Black has a number of reliable methods.

Kupreichik–Kengis
Podolsk 1990

1 e4 ♘f6 2 e5 ♘d5 3 d4 d6 *(21)*
4 f4

Very rarely seen but of historical interest is **4 ♗g5**. This rather peculiar move has the merits of pinning the e-pawn, aiming at the black king and avoiding a pin with ... ♗g4. A good illustration of

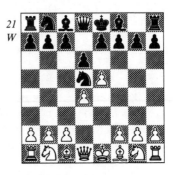

these ideas was Shofman–Gavrikov, Moldavia 1974: **4 ... h6** 5 ♗h4 de 6 de c6 7 ♘d2 ♗f5 8 ♘b3 ♕b6 (8 ... ♘b4 9 ♕xd8+ ♔xd8 10 0-0-0+ ♘d7 11 ♘d4) 9 ♘f3 e6 10 ♗e2 (10 ♘bd4? ♗b4+ 11 c3 ♘xc3!) 10 ... a5?! (10 ... ♘d7) 11 0-0 ♘d7 12 ♘bd4 ♗g6 13 ♗d3 ♗h5? 14 ♘xe6! fe 15 ♘d4! ♗f7 (15 ... ♘7f6 16 ♕d2) 16 ♘xe6! ♘xe5 (16 ... ♗xe6 17 ♗g6+ ♗f7 18 ♕h5 ♘xe5 19 ♕xe5+ ♗e7 20 ♕xg7) 17 ♖e1 ♗d6 (17 ... ♗xe6 18 ♖xe5 ♔d7 19 ♖xe6 ♔xe6 20 ♕g4+ with a king hunt.) 18 ♘xg7+ ♔d7 19 ♘f5 ♕c5 20 ♘xd6 ♕xd6 21 ♗g3

♖ae8 22 c4 ♘b4 23 ♗f5+ ♔c7
24 ♕xd6+ ♔xd6 25 ♖ad1+ ♘d5
26 cd ♗xd5 27 ♗g6 ♖e6 28 ♖xe5
♖xe5 29 ♖e1 1–0.

Steiner–Alekhine, Budapest
1921, the first outing of the then
new opening, saw a more successful approach: **4 ... de** 5 de ♘c6 6
♗b5 (6 ♘f3 ♗g4 7 ♗b5 h6 8
♗d2 e6 9 0–0 ♘de7 10 h3 ♗h5 11
♖e1 a6 12 ♗e2 ♕d7= Lutikov–
Kopylov, corres. 1968) 6 ... ♗f5
7 ♘f3 ♘db4! 8 ♘a3 ♕xd1+ 9
♖xd1 ♘xc2+ 10 ♘xc2 ♗xc2 11
♖c1 ♗e4 12 ♘d4 (12 e6 f6) 12 ...
♗xg2 13 ♖g1 0–0–0! 14 ♘xc6
♗xc6 15 ♗xc6 bc 16 ♖xc6 ♖d5
17 ♗f4 e6 18 ♔e2 ♗c5! (The
only way to retain winning
chances.) 19 b4! ♗xb4 20 ♖xg7
♖d7 21 ♗e3 a5! (Black must play
very accurately to limit the activity
of the white rooks.) 22 ♖c4 h5 23
♖h4 ♗c3! 24 ♖g5 ♖d5 25 f4 f6!
and Black went on to win.

4 ... de

After **4 ... g6**, White should
transpose to the Four Pawns with
5 c4!, since 5 ♗d3?! ♘b4 is pleasant for Black.

The main alternative to the text
is **4 ... ♗f5**. Then 5 ♗d3?! ♗xd3 6
♕xd3 de gives White some tactical
problems: 7 ♕b5+ (7 fe – see 4
... de 5 de ♗f5 6 ♗d3? below.) 7
...♘c6 8 de ♘db4! 9 ♘a3 a6 10 ♕e2
e6 11 ♗e3 ♘d4 12 ♕c4 ♘f5 13
♗f2 ♕d5! 14 ♕xd5 ♘xd5 15 ♘e2
♘fe3∓ Mnatsakanian–Mikenas,
Tallinn 1968. The attempt to
transpose to a Four Pawns, **5 c4**,

can be met by 5 ... ♘b4!? 6 ♕a4+
♘8c6 7 d5?! ♘c2+, e.g. 8 ♔f2 (8
♔e2? b5!; 8 ♔d2 ♘xa1 9 ♘a3
de) 8 ... ♘xa1 9 ♘a3 (9 dc? b5!) 9
... ♘c2 10 dc b5 11 ♘xb5 de. Thus
White normally continues **5 ♘f3**
e6 6 ♗d3 ♗xd3 7 ♕xd3 c5 8
c3 (8 dc ♕a5+ 9 ♗d2 ♕xc5=
Bokhosian–Orev, Pernik 1975) 8
... cd 9 cd when Black can choose
between 9 ... ♕a5+ 10 ♘c3 ♘xc3
11 bc ♕a6= 12 ♕xa6 ♘xa6 13
♗a3 d5 14 ♗xf8 ♖xf8 15 ♔d2
♘b8 16 f5 ♘c6 17 fe fe 18 ♘g5
♔e7 19 ♘xh7 ♖f5 Nun–Alburt,
Decin 1976 and 9 ... ♘c6 10 ♘c3?!
♘db4 11 ♕e4 de∓ Sznapik–
Maciejewski, Lodz 1975.

5 fe

Rather illogical is 5 de?! ♗f5 6
c4 ♘b4 7 ♕xd8+ ♔xd8 8 ♘a3
e6∓.

5 ... c5!?

This is the most consistent continuation: Black exchanged on e5
to weaken White's pawns, not just
to open the f-file for White's rooks!

(a) **5 ... ♘c6** invites transposition to a Four Pawns with 6
c4 ♘b6, though White has good
alternatives:

(a1) 6 ♘f3 ♗g4 7 ♗e2 e6 8
0–0 ♗e7 9 c3 0–0 10 ♘e1!? ♗xe2
(10 ... ♗f5?! 11 ♗d3!) 11 ♕xe2
♕d7 12 ♘d2 f6! 13 ef ♘xf6 14
♘d3± Zapata–Kovačević, Zenica
1986.

(a2) 6 c3 ♗f5 7 ♘f3! (7 ♗d3
♗xd3 8 ♕xd3 f6! 9 ♘f3 fe 10 de
♘b6!∓ Nun–C. Chandler, corres.
1986) 7 ... e6 8 ♗d3 ♗xd3 9

Qxd3 Qd7 (9 ... Be7 10 0-0 0-0 11 Nbd2 Qd7 12 Ne4 f6) 10 0-0 0-0-0 11 b4! f6 12 b5! Na5 13 Nbd2 c5 14 c4 Nf4 15 Qe4 Ng6 16 Bb2 was pleasant for White in Vitoliņš–Kengis, Riga 1978.

(b) **5 ... Bf5!?** retains the option of ... c5.

(b1) **6 Bd3?** Bxd3 7 Qxd3 Nb4 8 Qe4 Qxd4 9 Qxb7 Nxc2+!? (9 ... Qd5=) 10 Ke2 Qc4+! 11 Kd1 (11 Kf2 Qa6; 11 Kd2 Qb4+) 11 ... Qd3+ 12 Nd2 Ne3+ 13 Ke1 Qd5 14 Qc8+ Qd8 15 Qb7 c6∓.

(b2) **6 Nf3** e6 7 Bd3 (7 c3 c5 8 Bb5+ Nc6 9 Bg5 Qb6 10 Qa4 a6 Meijer–Diepstraten, Baahn 1980; 7 a3 Nb6!? 8 b4?! a5 9 b5 c5 10 bc bc 11 Be3 Be7 12 c4 0-0 13 Nc3 N8d7 14 Bd3? Bxd3 15 Qxd3 Nc5 16 Qe2 Nb3 17 Rb1 a4 18 c5 Nd5 19 Nxa4? Qa5+ 0-1 Formanek–Dunning, Las Vegas 1973.) 7 ... Bxd3 8 Qxd3 c5 9 0-0 h6! 10 Kh1 Nc6 11 c4?! Ndb4 12 Qe4 Nxd4 13 Nxd4 cd 14 Qxb7 Be7 15 Qe4 Rc8 was good for Black in Lazaridis–Hansen, Groningen 1982.

6 Nf3

Three other moves have been seen:

6 c4? is an attempt to transpose to the Four Pawns, Argunov Variation. However, instead of 6 ... Nb6, Black has 6 ... Nb4!∓ when White is struggling to survive. 7 d5 (7 a3 N4c6) 7 ... Bf5 8 Na3 e6 (Threatens 9 ... Qh4+) 9 Qa4+ Qd7 10 Qxd7+ Nxd7 11 Nf3 (11 de Nxe5 12 ef+ Kxf7 13 Nf3 Nxf3+ 14 gf g6! Tal) 11 ... ed 12 cd Nxd5 13 Bc4 N7b6 14 Bb5+ Bd7 15 0-0 Bxb5 16 Nxb5 a6 17 Nc3! h6! 18 Ne4 Be7 19 b3 0-0 20 Ba3 Nb4 21 Bxb4 cb 22 Rad1 Rad8 23 Nd6 Rd7 24 Rd4 Nc8!! enabled Black to consolidate the extra pawn in Zapata–Tal, Subotica IZ 1987.

6 c3 Nc6 7 Nf3 Bg4 8 Be2 e6 9 0-0 Be7 10 Kh1 0-0 11 h3 Bxf3 12 Bxf3 Rc8 13 a3 was insufficiently active to give White any advantage in Nun–Ambroz, Czechoslovakia 1987.

6 Bb5+ Bd7 7 Bxd7+ Qxd7 8 Nf3 cd 9 Qxd4 e6 (9 ... Nc6) 10 0-0 h6. Provided White's pressure on the f-file comes to nothing, the weakness of e5 will become the crux of the position, so Black cuts out Ng5. After 11 a3, Bagirov prefers the natural) 11 ... Nc6 to 11 ... Qc6 12 Qd3 Nd7 13 c4 N5b6 14 Nbd2 a5 (14 ... Nxe5 is risky.) 15 b3 Be7 16 Bb2 Nc5 17 Qe2 0-0 18 Nd4 when Black was under a little pressure in Vitoliņš–Bagirov, Frunze 1979.

6 ...   cd
7 Qxd4   Nc6
8 Bb5

8 Qe4?! e6 9 c4 Bb4+ is rather disruptive. At first sight the text hardly looks playable, but there lurks a subtle tactical point.

8 ...   Qa5+

Kengis proposes 8 ... Bf5 and ... e6 as a route to equality.

9 Nc3   Nxc3

10	♗xc6+	bc
11	♗d2!	*(22)*

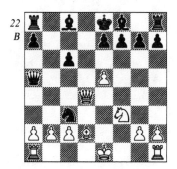

This is the move which makes sense of White's play; it would now be very easy for Black's lack of development to become acute.

11	...	♘b5!?
12	♗xa5	♘xd4
13	♘xd4	e6!
14	0-0-0	

After 14 ♘xc6, the black bishops spring into action: 14 ... ♗b7 15 ♘d4 ♗c5!? 16 ♘f3 0-0 17 0-0-0 ♗d5 and ... f6 will break open the position.

14	...	♗d7
15	♖d3!	c5
16	♖hd1	♗a4!

16 ... cd 17 ♖xd4 ♗c6 18 ♖d8+ ♖xd8 19 ♖xd8+ ♔e7 20 ♖c8 ♗e8 21 ♖c7+ ♗d7 22 ♖xa7± (Kengis) highlights Black's need to develop.

17	♖a3	♗d7
18	♘f3	♗c6
19	c4	♗e7
20	♗c7	g5!

21	♗d6	g4
22	♗xe7	

White did not have to hurry with this exchange.

22	...	♔xe7
23	♘e1	a5!

Kengis now assessed the position as unclear, though Black has rather the more weaknesses to defend: 24 ♖d6 ♖hc8 25 ♖g3 h5 26 ♘d3 ♖c7 27 ♘f4 ♖g8 28 h4 ♖h8 29 ♖b3 ♗d7 30 g3 a4 31 ♖bb6 ♖a7 32 ♔c2 ♖c7 33 ♔c3 ♖a7 34 ♖a6 ♖b7 35 ♖db6 ♖c7 36 ♖a5 ♖h7 37 ♖a8 ♗c6 38 ♖g8 ♗e4 39 ♖bb8 ♗c6 40 ♖g5 ♗e4.

Presumably in some time trouble, Black's position has become very disorganised. The remainder is largely a technical task, as White chooses how to pick off the pawns.

41 ♖gg8 ♗c6 42 ♔d2 ♖d7+ 43 ♔e3 ♖d4 44 ♖bc8 ♖e4+ 45 ♔d3 ♖d4+ 46 ♔c3 ♗d7 47 ♖xc5 ♖d1 48 ♖c7 f6 49 ef+ ♔xf6 50 ♖g6+ ♔f5 51 ♖c5+ ♔e4 52 ♘xh5 ♔f3 53 ♘f6 ♖h8 54 ♘xg4 ♖b8 55 b4 ab 56 ab ♖b1 57 ♔d4 ♖d1+ 58 ♔e5 ♖xb3 59 ♔f6 ♔g2 60 ♖e5 ♔g1 61 ♖e3 ♖f1+ 62 ♔e7 ♖b7 63 ♘e5 ♗a4+ 64 ♔xe6 ♗c2 65 ♖g5 ♖f8 66 ♖e2 ♗h7 67 ♖a2 ♖e8+ 68 ♔d5 ♖d8+ 69 ♔c5 ♖c8+ 70 ♔d4 ♖b3 71 ♖a7 ♖d8+ 72 ♔c5 ♗e4 73 ♖d7 ♖a8 74 ♔d4 ♗b1 75 h5 ♔g2 76 g4 ♖b2 77 ♖gg7 ♖e2 78 ♖ge7 ♖g8 79 h6 ♖g5 80 ♖d5 ♖xg4 81 ♘xg4 ♖xe7 82 ♘f6 ♖f7 83 ♖d6 1-0.

Kupreichik–Palatnik
Kislovodsk 1982

1 e4 ♘f6 2 e5 ♘d5 3 d4 d6

4   ♗e2

Behind this unassuming little move, a favourite of Romanishin and Kupreichik, lie a number of cunning ideas. Firstly, White keeps open the option of playing f4, while preventing ... ♗g4 for the time being. Against Black's most natural system of development, as in our main game here, White has the c3, ♕a4 deployment which poses some unusual problems. At any rate, 4 ♗e2 has scored very well in practice, so is well worth investigating in some depth.

4   ...   de

The main alternative is **4 ... g6**, inviting transposition to the Exchange Variation, with 5 c4 ♘b6 6 ed. Instead:

(a) **5 c4** ♘b6 6 f4 de 7 fe c5 8 d5 (8 dc ♕xd1+ 9 ♔xd1 ♘a4) 8 ... ♗g7 is a line of the Four Pawns in which ♗e2 is a little inappropriate, e.g. 9 ♗f4 0–0 10 ♘c3 e6.

(b) **5 f4** *(23)* gives Black an interesting choice.

(b1) **5 ... ♗g7** 6 ♘f3 0–0 7 0–0 de 8 fe c5 9 c4 ♘b6 (9 ... ♘b4?! 10 d5 ♗f5 11 ♘c3 ♘d7 12 ♗f4 ♗g4 13 a3 ♘a6 14 ♘g5! Romanishin–Konopka, Erevan 1986) 10 d5 e6!? (10 ... ♗g4? 11 ♘g5 ♗f5 12 ♖xf5! gf 13 e6+ Andonov–Kuczynski, Camaguey 1987) 11 ♘c3 ed 12 cd ♗g4 (SDO)

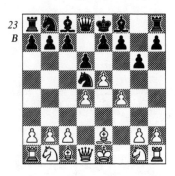

and White's centre is under pressure.

(b2) **5 ... c5!?** aims to leave the f4 pawn to obstruct the white forces. 6 ♘f3 ♗g7 7 c4 ♘b4 8 d5 ♗f5 9 0–0 ♘d7 10 a3 ♘a6 11 ed ed 12 ♗d3 ♗g4 13 ♕e1+ ♔f8 14 ♘c3 ♘c7 15 ♘g5 h6 16 ♘ge4 ♗f5 17 ♗d2 ♘f6 18 ♘f2 ♕d7 19 ♕b1 b5 gave Black counterplay in Kupreichik–Kengis, Minsk 1985.

(b3) **5 ... ♗h6!?** is a remarkable idea. Bishops overshooting a queen's fianchetto have become a common sight, but the mirror image is very rare. In any case, White was confused in Pirttimäki–Chekhov, Lvov 1983: 6 ♗f3 de 7 c4?? (7 fe ♘e3) 7 ... ♘xf4! 8 ♘a3 (8 g3 ♘d3+) 8 ... ♗g7 9 g3 ♘e6 0–1.

5 de   ♘c6

Romanishin–Bagirov, Jurmala 1987 featured a safe plan for Black: 5 ... ♗f5 6 c3 c6! 7 ♘f3 e6 8 0–0 ♘d7 9 ♘bd2 ♘7b6 10 ♘d4 ♗g6 11 ♘2f3 ♗e7 12 c4 ♘c7 13 ♗e3 0–0 14 ♕c1 c5 15 ♘c2 ♘a6 16 ♖d1 ♕b8 17 ♘ce1 ♖d8 18 ♘d3 ♕c7 19 a3 ♖d7 20 ♕c3 ♖ad8 with roughly level chances and a tough battle in prospect. White can also sacrifice the c-pawn for some compensation: 6 ♘f3 ♘b4 7 ♕xd8+ ♔xd8 8 ♘a3 ♘xc2+ 9 ♘xc2 ♗xc2 10 0–0 e6 11 ♗g5+ as in Klundt–Kindl, Bundesliga 1985.

6 ♘f3 ♗g4

A logical alternative is 6 ... ♘db4 7 ♕xd8+ ♘xd8 8 ♘a3 ♗g4 9 0–0 ♘e6 10 ♗d2 ♘c6 11 ♘c4 0–0–0 12 ♗e3 g6 13 c3 ♗g7 14 ♖fe1 when White's advantage was of a marginal nature in Tal–Fernandez, Seville 1987.

7 c3

7 h3 is a rather less subtle way of encouraging the exchange on f3. 7 ... ♗xf3 8 ♗xf3 e6 9 0–0 ♗c5 10 c3 ♘xe5 11 c4 (The pin is harmless after 11 ♗xd5? ♕xd5 12 ♕xd5 ed 13 ♖e1 f6) 11 ... ♘b4 12 ♗xb7 ♕xd1 13 ♖xd1 ♖b8 14 ♗e4 f5 15 a3 fe 16 ab ♖xb4 17 ♖a5 ♖xc4 18 ♘d2 0–0! 19 ♘xe4! ♖d4 20 ♖f1 ♖xe4 21 ♖xc5 ♘d3= Romanishin–Palatnik, Kislovodsk 1982.

7 ♘g5 is comfortably met by 7 ... ♗xe2 8 ♕xe2 h6 9 ♘f3 e6 10 0–0 g5 11 ♖d1 ♕e7 Nevednichy-Nosenko, USSR 1985.

The main alternative to the text is the natural **7 0–0 e6**. Best now seems to be 8 c3, but there are alternatives.

(a) **8 ♖e1** ♗e7 9 a3 (9 ♘bd2?! ♘f4! gives White nothing better than 10 ♗b5 0–0 11 ♗xc6 bc∓ since 10 ♗f1?! ♘d4 11 c3 ♘h3+! is disaster, as analysed by Euwe.)

9 ... 0–0 10 ♗d2 ♕d7 11 ♘c3 ♖ad8 12 ♘xd5 ♕xd5= Jackson-Ady, London 1985.

(b) **8 c4** (Perenyi) 8 ... ♘b6 9 ♘bd2 ♗e7 10 h3 ♗xf3 11 ♘xf3 0–0= SDO.

(c) **8 ♘bd2 ♘f4.**

(d) **8 c3!** ♗e7 9 ♕a4. The cunning point of White's move order is that the e7 square is unavailable to the black knights. 9 ... ♗xf3 10 ♗xf3 0–0 11 ♖e1 (11 ♕e4 ♗g5 12 ♘a3 ♗xc1 13 ♖axc1 ♕g5 equalised in Chiburdanidze-Stadler, Belgrade 1979.) 11 ... ♗g5 12 ♘d2 ♖b8 (12 ... ♘b6) 13 ♘f1 b5 14 ♕g4 ♗xc1 15 ♖axc1 ♘ce7 16 ♘g3 ♘g6 17 ♕d4 ♘b6 18 b3 ♕e7 19 ♕b4! c5 20 ♕xb5 ♘bd7 21 ♕e2 ♘gxe5 22 ♗e4. Black has removed the e5 pawn, but in return for some structural weaknesses. Now 22 ... ♕h4 looks best, but Romanishin–Palatnik, Kherson 1989 continued 22 ... f5?! 23 f4! fe 24 fe ♘xe5 25 ♕xe4 and White won a pawn.

7 ... e6

After **7 ... ♕d7 8 0–0** (8 h3 ♗xf3 9 ♗xf3 0–0–0 10 ♕e2) **8 ... 0–0–0 9 ♖e1** Black has tried two moves:

(a) **9 ... e6** 10 ♗b5 ♗c5 11 ♘bd2 and now 11 ... a6? allowed 12 ♕a4 ♗h5 (12 ... ♘xc3 13 bc ♗xf3 14 ♘xf3 ab 15 ♕xb5 gives White a powerful initiative) 13 ♗xc6 seriously weakening Black's pawn structure in Klundt–D. Werner, Bundesliga 1983. Instead 11 ... ♗xf3 12 ♘xf3 a6 is fairly reasonable for Black.

(b) **9 ... ♕f5!?** equalised comfortably in Nonnenmacher–Behrhorst, Bundesliga 1985: 10 ♘h4 ♗xe2 11 ♕xe2 ♕d7 12 ♘a3 e6 13 ♘c2 h6 14 ♘f3 ♗c5.

7 ... ♘b6 was played in Romanishin–Agzamov, Frunze 1985, but White maintained some advantage with 8 ♘bd2 e6 9 0–0 ♗e7 10 a4 a5 11 ♖e1 0–0 12 ♕b3 ♕d5 13 ♕b5! ♖fd8 14 ♘f1 ♕e4 15 ♗e3 ♖d5 16 ♕b3 since on 16 ... ♘xe5 there followed 17 ♗xb6 ♗xf3 18 ♘g3 ♕g6 19 ♗xc7 winning a pawn.

8   ♕a4

8 0–0!? is considered under 7 0–0 e6 8 c3 above.

8   ...   ♗xf3

A point of White's last two moves is to force this exchange, since 8 ... ♗h5? 9 ♗b5 is clearly miserable for Black.

9   ♗xf3   ♕d7
10   ♕e4   ♘de7

Instead **10 ... g6** 11 ♗d1 ♗g7 12 f4 gives White a comfortable, though small, advantage. Rather more assertive is Bagirov's **10 ... g5!?** which prevents White supporting e5, though Black will have to pursue the initiative with great vigour to justify such a structural weakening.

11   ♗f4   ♘g6
12   ♘d2

Preserving the f4 bishop from the exchange would lose time and be illogical, as it is not an especially good piece.

12   ...   0–0–0
13   0–0–0   ♕d3
14   ♕a4!   ♕f5?

Rather surprisingly, this move appears to lose by force. Since **14 ... ♕a6?!** 15 ♕xa6 ba 16 ♗g5 ♗e7 17 ♗xe7 ♘gxe7 18 ♘c4 is just a different variety of agony, the startling counterattacking shot **14 ... ♗a3!** *(24)* was necessary.

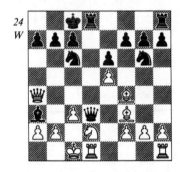

24
W

Kupreichik then analysed 15 ♘c4 ♕xc3+ 16 ♔b1 ♕b4 17 ♗xc6 bc 18 ♕xc6 ♘xf4 19 ♕a8+ ♕b8! – a classic example that connecting one's rooks is sometimes of more than just aesthetic value.

15   ♗xc6   ♘xf4

15 ... ♕xf4 16 ♕xa7 bc 17 g3! ♕h6 18 f4! leaves the black king terminally stranded.

16   ♗e4!

Much stronger than 16 ♘e4?! ♘d5!, as White is now targeting both the king and the queen, e.g. 16 ... ♘e2+ 17 ♔c2 ♕xf2 fails to 18 ♖hf1 ♕c5 (18 ... ♕e3 19 ♖f3) 19 ♘b3.

16   ...   ♕xe5
17   ♘f3!   ♕f6

18	♖xd8+	♕xd8
19	♘e5!	

With a choice of tempting options, Kupreichik simply creates far more threats than Black can defend.

19	...	♗c5
20	♖d1	♘d5

20 ... ♕g5 21 ♗xb7+ ♔b8 22 ♘d7+ ♔xb7 23 ♕b5+ mates or wins a queen.

21	♗xd5	1-0

In view of 21 ... ed 22 ♕g4+ ♔b8 23 ♘d7+.

Avshalumov–Agzamov
USSR Ch (Sevastopol) 1986

1 e4 ♘f6 2 e5 ♘d5 3 d4 d6

4	♗c4

White aims to compromise Black's development by means of threats to f7.

4	...	♘b6

4 ... c6 5 ♕e2 (5 ♘f3 ♗g4 6 h3 ♗xf3 7 ♕xf3 de 8 de e6 transposes to a line of the Panov Variation.) 5 ... de (5 ... g6 6 h3 ♗g7 7 ♘f3 is considered under 4 ♘f3 g6 5 ♗c4 c6) 6 de ♗f5 (6 ... g6 fails to equalise: 7 h3 ♗g7 8 ♘f3 0–0 9 0–0 ♕c7 10 ♖e1 a5 11 a4 ♘a6 12 ♘bd2 ♘b6 13 ♗xa6! ♘xa6 14 c4± Matulović–Kovačević, Krk 1976 or 7 ♗d2 ♗g7 8 ♘c3 ♕c7 9 ♘f3 ♘xc3 10 ♗xc3 0–0 11 0–0± b5 12 ♗b3 c5 13 ♗d5 ♗b7 14 ♗xb7 ♕xb7 15 e6 ♗xc3 16 bc ♘c6 17 ♖ab1 ♖ab8 18 a4 a6 19 h4 f6 20 h5± Kuchukhidze–Minasian, USSR 1990.) 7 ♘f3 (7 h3!?) 7 ... e6 8 0–0 ♗g4 (8 ...

♘d7 9 h3 ♗e7 10 a3 0–0 11 ♗a2 ♕c7 12 c4 ♘5b6 13 ♘c3 should offer White some advantage, though 13 ... ♘c5 14 ♖d1 ♖fd8 keeps it to a minimum.) 9 ♘bd2 ♘d7 10 ♗b3 (10 a3!? prepares a more comfortable retreat square for the bishop.) 10 ... ♘c5! 11 ♘e4 ♘xe4 12 ♕xe4 ♗xf3 13 ♕xf3 ♕c7 14 ♖e1 ♘e7! 15 ♗g5! (15 ♗f4?! ♘g6 16 ♗g3 h5!) 15 ... ♘g6 16 ♖ad1 was Mestel–Popov, Malta ol 1980. Popov gives 16 ... ♗c5! 17 ♕g3 0–0 18 h4 ♘e7 19 h5 ♘f5 20 ♕g4 h6 21 ♗f4 ♖ad8 22 c3 ♖xd1 23 ♖xd1 ♖d8 24 ♖xd8+ ♕xd8 25 ♗c2 ♕d7 as Black's clearest route to equality.

5	♗b3

5 e6? ♘xc4 6 ef+ is just reckless. It is far from clear that White has adequate play after 6 ... ♔d7, but the simplest answer is 6 ... ♔xf7 7 ♕f3+ ♔e8 8 ♕h5+ g6 9 ♕b5+ ♕d7 10 ♕xc4 ♕g4! when White can hardly hope to survive, e.g. 11 ♕d5 e6.

5	...	de

If undisturbed, White will continue with ♕e2, ♘f3, 0–0 and maybe c3, whilst closing the centre gives White a pleasant space advantage: **5 ... d5** 6 ♕e2 (6 ♘f3 ♗g4, considered under 3 ♘f3 d6 4 ♗c4 ♘b6 5 ♗b3 d5 6 d4 ♗g4, allows Black good play; 6 a4 e6 7 ♘f3 c5 8 c3 ♘c6 9 0–0 cd 10 cd ♗e7 11 ♘c3 ♘b4 12 ♕e2 a6 13 ♗f4 ♗d7 14 ♘d1 ♘c8 15 ♘d2 h5 16 ♘f3 ♘a7 17 ♕d2 ♘ac6 18 ♗g5 f6∞ Hickl–Bischoff, Dortmund 1987.) 6 ... a5 (6 ... e6 intending 7 ... c5.) 7 c3 ♗f5 8 a4 e6 9 0–0 c5 10 dc ♗xc5 11 ♘d4± Tal–Spiridonov, Sochi 1973.

After **5 ... g6**, White need not transpose to 4 ♘f3 g6 5 ♗c4 ♘b6 6 ♗b3: Yudovich–Bezrikov, USSR 1983 continued 6 ♕f3 d5 7 ♘c3 c6 8 h4 h5 9 ♘h3 ♗g4 10 ♕g3 ♗xh3 11 ♖xh3 ♕d7 12 ♗e3 ♕g4 13 ♕h2±.

A move very much in the provocative spirit of the opening is **5 ... ♘c6!? 6 e6** (6 ♘f3 de 7 d5!? can be met by 7 ... e4!? or 7 ... ♘a5 8 c4 ♘xb3; 6 ed cd 7 ♘f3 d5=) **6 ... fe 7 ♘f3 e5!?** *(25)* (For 7 ... g6 see 4 ♘f3 g6 5 ♗c4 ♘b6 6 ♗b3 ♘c6 7 e6 fe.) is a position thoroughly analysed by Kovačević and by Olafsson:

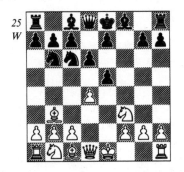

25
W

(a) **8 ♘g5** e6 9 ♗xe6 (9 ♘xe6? ♗xe6; 9 de d5!) 9 ... ♗xe6 10 ♘xe6 ♕e7 11 d5 (11 ♘xf8? ed+) 11 ... ♘d4! 12 ♗g5 ♕f7∓.

(b) **8 d5** ♘a5 (8 ... ♘d4) 9 ♘g5 ♘xb3 10 ab (10 ♕f3? ♘d4–+) 10 ... ♕d7 11 0–0 (11 ♘e6? ♘xd5 12 ♘xf8 ♕c6!–+; 11 ♗e3 ♕g4∓)

11 ... ♕f5 12 f4 (12 ♘c3 h6 13 ♘ge4 e6∞) 12 ... ef 13 ♖xf4 ♕xd5 14 ♕e2 e5 15 ♘c3 ♕c6∞.

(c) **8 de** d5! 9 ♘c3 (9 ♗e3 e6 10 0–0 ♘a5 11 ♘bd2 ♗e7 12 c3 ♘xb3 13 ab c5 14 ♖a5 ♘d7 15 ♖a4 0–0 16 ♖g4 ♔h8 17 ♖e1 ♖f5 18 ♖f4 ½–½ Matulović–Begovac, Sombor 1978) 9 ... ♗g4! 10 ♘xd5 e6! 11 ♘xb6 ♕xd1+ 12 ♔xd1 ab 13 ♔e1 ♗xf3 14 gf ♘d4! (14 ... ♘xe5?! 15 ♗e3! ♔d7! 16 ♔e2 ♗d6 17 ♖ag1± Parma–Kovačević, Yugoslavia 1978.) 15 ♗e3 ♗c5 16 f4 ♖f8 17 ♖d1 ♘xb3 18 ab ♖a2 19 ♖b1 ♖f5! 20 h4 g6 21 ♔e2 ♗e7= Matulović–Kovačević, Yugoslavia 1976.

6 ♕h5

6 ♕f3?! e6 7 de a5 8 c3?! (8 a4 ♘8d7 9 ♕g3 ♘c5 10 ♘c3 ♗d7 11 ♘f3 ♘xb3 12 ab ♗c6 13 0–0 ♕d3 14 ♖d1 ♕g6∓ Gross–Biehler, St. Ingbert 1987) 8 ... a4 9 ♗c2 ♗d7! 10 ♕g3 ♗b5 11 ♗g5 ♕d5 12 ♘a3 (12 ♘d2 ♘c6 13 f4 ♘c4 left Black well on top in Gufeld–Vasiukov, Kislovodsk 1968.) 12 ... ♗xa3 13 ♖d1 ♗xb2 14 ♖xd5 ♘xd5∓ Estrin.

6	...		e6
7	de		a5

7 ... c5 8 ♕e2 ♗d7 9 ♘f3 ♗c6 10 ♘bd2 (10 c3) 10 ... ♕c7 10 c3 (11 0–0? ♗xf3 Wolf–Appel, Miesenbach 1988) gives White the freer game.

8 a4

8 ♘c3!? a4 9 ♗g5 ♗e7 10 ♖d1 ♗d7! 11 ♗xe6 g6 12 ♗xd7+ ♘8xd7 13 ♗xe7 ♕xe7= as

analysed by Haag, is rather too forcing, while just plain bad are 8 c3? ♕d3 and 8 a3? a4 9 ♗a2 ♘c6 10 ♘f3 ♘d4 11 ♘xd4 ♕xd4∓ 12 ♕e2 (12 0–0 ♖a5 Hohler–Ghizdavu, Bath 1973) 12 ... ♖a5! 13 f4 ♘d5 14 c3 ♕a7 (Bagirov).

8 ... ♘c6

8 ... ♘a6 targets the a-pawn, but this turns out to be rather poisoned:

(a) **9 ♘c3 ♘c5 10 ♗a2!?** (10 ♗g5 ♗e7 11 ♖d1 ♗d7 12 ♗e3 ♘xb3 13 cb 0–0 14 ♘f3 ♕e8! 15 0–0 f5!? 16 ♕xe8 ♗xe8 17 ♗xb6 cb 18 ♘d4 ♗h5 19 f3 ♔f7 led to a good ending for Black in Soltis–Fernandez Garcia, New York Open 1987.) 10 ... ♘bxa4?! (10 ... ♗d7 11 ♘f3 is Sax–Ghinda below.) 11 ♗g5 ♗e7 12 ♖d1 ♗d7 13 ♘xa4 g6 (13 ... ♘xa4 14 ♗xe6) 14 ♕h6 ♘xa4 15 ♕g7 ♖f8 16 ♗h6+– ♘xb2 17 ♖d2 ♕c8 18 ♘f3 ♗b5 19 ♘g5 ♘c4 20 ♗xc4 ♗xc4 21 ♘xh7 ♗d5 22 c4 ♗b4 23 0–0 ♗xd2 24 ♕xf8+ ♔d7 25 ♕xf7+ ♔c6 26 cd+ 1–0 Radosavljević–Widermann, Balatonbereny 1988.

(b) **9 ♘f3 ♘c5 10 ♗a2!** presents Black with a choice:

(b1) **10 ... ♘cxa4** 11 0–0 ♗e7 12 ♘c3 (12 ♕g4) 12 ... ♘xc3 13 bc ♗d7?! (13 ... 0–0) 14 ♖d1± Prizant–Giulian, British Ch 1977.

(b2) **10 ... ♘bxa4** 11 0–0 g6 (11 ... ♗e7 12 ♕g4 g6 13 ♗h6!) 12 ♕g4 h5 (12 ... ♗g7 13 ♗e3) 13 ♕c4 ♘b6 14 ♕e2± Olafsson.

(b3) **10 ... ♗d7** 11 ♘c3 ♘bxa4

(11 ... ♗c6 12 ♗e3 ♗e7 13 ♖d1 ♕c8 14 ♘g5 g6 15 ♕h6 ♗f8 16 ♕h4± Olafsson; 11 ... g6 12 ♕g4 h5 13 ♕g3 ♗e7 14 ♗e3 h4 15 ♕f4 ♖h5 16 0–0–0 ♘bxa4 17 ♘xa4 ♘xa4 18 g4± Bryson–Oakley, corres. 1984) 12 ♗g5 ♗e7 (12 ... ♕c8!? 13 ♘xa4 ♗xa4 14 0–0–0∞ Adorjan) 13 ♘xa4 ♗xa4 14 ♖d1 ♘c5 (14 ... ♘xb2? 15 ♗xe6!) 15 ♗e3 0–0 16 c3! ♕e8 (16 ... a4 17 ♗b1!) 17 ♗xc5! (17 ♗b1 f5!) 17 ... ♗xc5 18 ♘g5 h6 19 ♘e4 ♗e7 20 ♘f6+! gave White a decisive attack in Sax–Ghinda, Bath 1973.

9 ♘f3 *(26)*

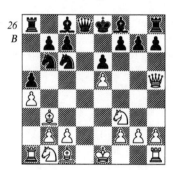

26
B

9 ... ♘d4

9 ... ♘d7 10 ♗g5 (10 ♗xe6 ♘dxe5 11 ♘xe5 ♗xe6 12 ♘xc6 bc=) 10 ... ♗e7 11 ♗xe7 (11 ♗xe6 ♘dxe5 12 ♘xe5 ♗xe6 13 ♗xe7 ♕xe7 14 ♘xc6 bc= Sax–Hazai, Hungary 1974) 11 ... ♕xe7 12 0–0 b6 13 ♘c3 ♗b7 14 ♖fe1 0–0–0 15 ♖ad1 h6 16 ♘b5 g6 17 ♕g4 g5 18 c3 ♕c5 19 ♕g3 ♖dg8? 20 ♘fd4 ♘cxe5? 21 ♘xe6 fe 22 ♗xe6+– Nun–Grün, Trnava 1984.

Ghizdavu's suggestion 9 ... ♗b4+!? may be of great importance, but remains untried. 10 ♘bd2 (10 c3 ♕d3!∓; 10 ♗d2 ♘d4∓) 10 ... ♘d4 11 ♘xd4 ♗xd2+! 12 ♗xd2 ♕xd4 leaves White with some weak pawns, while the exchanges have reduced White's attacking potential.

10 ♘xd4

10 0–0?! ♘e2+ 11 ♔h1 ♘xc1 12 ♖xc1 g6 13 ♕g4 ♗g7 14 ♘c3 0–0 ∓ Commons–Kent, USA 1975.

10	...	♕xd4
11	♘c3!?	

11 0–0 g6 12 ♕g5 (12 ♕e2 ♗g7 13 ♖e1 ♘d7 14 ♘c3 Nun–Hlousek, Hradec Kralove 1975) 12 ... ♗g7 13 ♖e1 ♘d7 14 ♗d2 gave White a small, but pleasant advantage in Kruszynski–Szymczak, Poland 1978.

11	...	♘d5!?
12	♘xd5	ed
13	0–0	c6
14	h3	♗e7
15	c3	♕e4
16	♗d2	♗e6
17	f4	♗c5+
18	♔h2	0–0–0

With both sides now developed, the play can be assessed as balanced. Neither king is particularly safe, so a sharp battle ensued: 19 ♕d1 ♕g6 20 ♕e1 ♗b6 21 ♗e3 c5 22 ♖c1 ♗f5 23 ♕f2 ♕c6 24 ♗d1 ♔b8 25 ♗e2 ♗e4 26 ♗b5 ♕c7 27 ♕g1 f5!? 28 b4 ab 29 cb d4 30 ♗f2 ♕e7 31 bc ♗xc5 32 ♖fd1 ♗a3 33 ♖c4 d3 34 ♗a7+

♔a8 35 ♗b6 ♖d5 36 ♕e3 ♗b4 37 ♖c7 ♕e6 38 ♗c4 ♕g6 39 g3 ♖dd8 40 ♗c5 ♗a5 41 ♖e7 ♕c6 42 g4? g6 43 ♗b5 ♕d5 44 ♔g3 h5 45 ♖g7 hg 46 h4 (46 hg ♗g2!) 46 ... ♖c8 47 ♗xd3 ♗xd3 48 ♖xd3 ♕h1 0–1.

Arnason–Alburt
Lone Pine 1980

1 e4 ♘f6 2 e5 ♘d5 3 d4 d6 4 ♗c4 ♘b6

5	♗b3	♗f5!?

Black simply places the bishop on the available square and challenges White to attack f7 (otherwise, what is the bishop doing on b3?). Bagirov and Alburt support this move, with which they have both achieved excellent results.

6 ♕f3

6 ♘f3 e6 7 0–0 ♗e7 8 a4!? (8 ♕e2 d5 9 ♗e3 ♘8d7 10 ♘bd2 0–0 11 ♖ac1 ♔h8 12 ♖fe1 g5 13 ♔h1 ♖g8 14 ♖g1 g4 15 ♘e1 f6 gave Black very interesting play on the kingside in Mihaljčišin–Filipović, Banja Luka 1981.) 8 ... de?! (8 ... 0–0!) 9 ♘xe5 and now Black should play 9 ... 0–0. Instead, in J. Fries Nielsen–C. Hansen, Esbjerg 1981, White was allowed to produce a superb combination: 9 ... ♘6d7? 10 ♘xf7! ♔xf7 11 ♕f3 ♔e8 12 ♕xb7 ♘b6 13 a5 ♕c8 14 ♕f3 ♘d5 15 c4 ♖f8 16 cd ♗xb1 17 ♕e2 ♗f5 18 de ♕b7 19 ♗a4+ ♔d8 20 d5 ♕b4 21 ♗d2 ♕d4 22 ♗c3 ♕d3 23 ♕e5 ♕e4 24 ♕xg7 ♕g4 25 d6! cd 26 a6!! ♕xg7 27 ♗a5+ ♔c8 28 ♖ac1+ ♘c6

29 ⃞xc6+ ⃝b8 30 ⃝c7+ ⃝c8 31 ⃝xd6+ ⃝d8 and 1–0.

6 ...   ♛c8

Sacrificing the b-pawn with **6 ... e6** 7 ♛xb7 d5 worked well in Gerbert–Hjorth, World Junior (Dortmund) 1980: **8 ♘c3 ♝b4** 9 ♘e2 0–0 10 0–0 a5! 11 ♝a4 ♛c8 12 ♛xc8 ⃞xc8 13 a3 ♝f8 14 ♝e3 ♘xa4 15 ♘xa4 ♝xc2∓, but **8 ♝a4+** is a better attempt to disrupt Black's plans.

7 ♘h3 (27)

Harmless alternatives are **7 ♝xf7+?!** ♝xf7 8 g4 ♘c6 9 c3 de∓, **7 g4 ♝e6** 8 ♝xe6 ♛xe6 9 ♛xb7 de, **7 ed?!** cd 8 ♘h3 (8 ♝xf7+?! ♝xf7 9 g4 ♛xc2 10 ♛xf5+ ♛xf5 11 gf ♝f6!∓ Mražik–Neckař, Prague 1989) 8 ... ♘c6 9 c3? ♘xd4∓ Kovačević–Prins, corres. 1985, and **7 ♛g3 c5!** 8 dc dc 9 c3 c4 10 ♝d1 ♘c6 11 ♘f3 ♝d3 12 ♝e3 ♘d5∓ 13 ♘d4 e6 14 ♘d2 ♘xe3 15 ♛xe3 ♝c5 16 ♝a4 0–0 17 ♘xc6 ♝xe3 18 ♘e7+ ♝h8 19 ♘xc8 ♝xd2+ 20 ♝xd2 ⃞axc8 which gave Black a big endgame advantage in Striković–Alburt, New York Open 1988.

A good and relatively unexplored alternative is **7 ♘e2**; if threats to f7 achieve nothing, then e2 is a better square than h3. 7 ... e6 (7 ... ♘c6 and 7 ... c5 are well worth considering.) 8 ♘bc3 (8 ♝f4 de 9 de c5; Hort likes 8 g4 ♝g6 9 ♘f4 ♘c6 10 ♛e3, but then 10 ... de 11 de ♘d7 looks rather pleasant for Black.) 8 ... de 9 de ♘8d7= 10 ♝f4 ♘c5 (10 ... c5!?) 11 ♛g3

a5 12 a4 h5!? 13 ♝g5 ♘bd7 14 ♝c4 h4 15 ♛e3 h3 16 g3 ♝xc2∞ Soltis–Blocker, New York 1980.

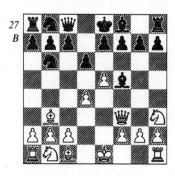

27
B

7 ...   ♘c6

There are three fascinating alternatives:

7 ... c5!? led to a short, sharp fight in Arnason–C. Hansen, World Junior (Dortmund) 1980: 8 dc dc 9 ♝xf7+ ♝xf7 10 g4 g6 11 ♘g5+ ♝e8 12 gf ♛xf5 13 ♛xb7 ♛xe5+ 14 ♛e4 ♘c6 15 ♝e3 ♛xe4 16 ♘xe4 ♘c4 17 ♝xc5 ♘xb2 18 ♘bc3 ♘c4 19 ⃞b1 ♝h6 20 ♝e2 ♝f7 21 ⃞b7 ⃞hb8 22 ⃞hb1 ♝f4 23 ♝xe7 ⃞xb7 24 ⃞xb7 ⃞b8 ½–½.

7 ... e6 8 ♘g5 ♝e7 9 ♘xf7 ⃞f8! (White wins after 9 ... 0–0? 10 ♛xf5!) 10 ♘g5 ♝xc2 (An unusual way to exchange pawns!) 11 ♛h5+ (11 ♝xe6 ⃞xf3 12 ♝xc8 ⃞d3!) 11 ... ♝g6 12 ♛h3 ♝xg5 13 ♝xg5 (13 ♝xe6? ♝f5!–+) 13 ... d5. A forced sequence has led to an unbalanced, but fairly equal position. In Šibarević–Bagirov, Banja Luka 1976 some manoeuvring followed: 14 0–0 ♘c6 15 ♛c3

&f7 16 a4 a5 17 ♘a3 &g8 18
♖ac1 ♘d7 19 ♘b5 ♘db8 20 f4
♘a6 and Black managed to
restrain the kingside majority.

7 ... d5!? is a rather surprising
move, but **8 ♗xd5 ♘xd5 9 ♕xd5
♘c6** is clearly unpromising for
White. Kengis–Bagirov, Jurmala
1987 saw Black set up a very
satisfactory position after **8 ♘f4
e6 9 0–0 c5 10 c3 ♘c6 11 ♗e3 c4**
(11 ... ♘a5!? 12 ♗d1 ♘bc4 13
♗c1 cd 14 cd ♘c6∞ Bagirov) 12
♗d1 ♕d7 13 ♘d2 h6 14 g4 ♗h7
15 b4 a5! 16 b5 ♘e7 17 a4 0–0–0.

8 c3 e6!

Neglecting f7 is a fatal error: 8
... de? 9 ♘g5 e6 10 ♘xf7!

9 ♘g5 ♗e7
10 ♕g3

A familiar theme from Šibarević–Bagirov is 10 ♘xf7?! ♖f8!
11 ♘g5 ♗xb1 12 ♗xe6 ♖xf3
13 ♗xc8 ♖xc8 14 ♘xf3 ♗e4∓.
White may consider exchanging
on d6 which would avoid later
difficulties with the e5 pawn and
the d-file.

10 ... ♕d7
11 0–0 de
12 de ♕d3
13 ♘f3 0–0–0 *(28)*

Black has free development and
hopes of showing the e5 pawn
to be weak: the main aims of
Alekhine's Defence.

14 ♖e1 h6
15 ♗e3 ♘d5
16 ♘bd2 g5
17 ♘c4 ♗h7

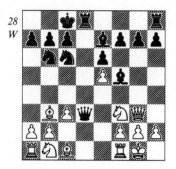

28
W

18	**♖ad1**	**♕f5**
19	**♗a4**	**g4**
20	**♘d4**	**♘xd4**
21	**♗xd4**	**♕f4**
22	**♘e3!**	**♕xg3**
23	**hg**	**h5**
24	**♗b3?!**	

**24 ♗xa7 b6 25 ♘xd5 ♖xd5 26
♖xd5 ed 27 ♗c6 ♗e4 28 b4∞**
should have been ventured. Now
Black gradually takes over.

**24 ... ♘b6! 25 ♘c4 ♘d7 26 ♖d2
♗g6 27 ♗d1?! ♗g5 28 ♗e3
♗xe3 29 ♖xe3 b5! 30 ♘a3 ♘b6
31 ♖xd8+?** (Presumably in time
trouble, White misses a few subtleties. 31 ♖ee2 gives prospects of
survival.) **31 ... ♖xd8 32 ♗b3 a6!**
(The advance of the c-pawn is
more than White's fragile position
can stand.) **33 ♖e2 c5 34 &h2
&c7 35 ♗c2 ♗d3 36 ♖d2 ♗xc2
37 ♖xc2** (37 ♖xd8 &xd8 38 ♘xc2
♘a4) **37 ... ♖d1 38 ♖e2 ♖a1
b3 ♘d5 40 c4** (40 ♖c2 &b6! puts
White in zugzwang.) **40 ... ♘c3 41
♖b2 b4 42 ♘c2 ♖xa2 43 ♖xa2
♘xa2 44 f3 ♘c1 45 fg hg 0–1.**

5 Exchange Variation

The Exchange Variation is a very sensible idea. White secures a small but solid space advantage, which may be increased later. Black's counterplay is generally based on the ... d5 advance, which is best delayed to cause White the maximum inconvenience, but not for so long that White's pawn can itself advance safely to d5.

Initially, Black must decide how to recapture. 5 ... ed is the solid move, avoiding an imbalanced pawn position. Often both sides end up playing on the same side of the board, so Black must be particularly accurate to ensure adequate counterplay.

5 ... cd is the dynamic, and consequently more popular approach. The pawn structure dictates that queenside play is in order for White, while Black will look to the centre and kingside, alert to any opportunities to disrupt White's queenside activities. Some of the traditional main lines for White have hit hard times, but to make up for this there has been a stream of new ideas and refinements.

Serper–Dreev
Sochi Junior 1986

1 e4 ♘f6 2 e5 ♘d5 3 d4 d6
    4   c4   ♘b6
    5   ed *(29)*

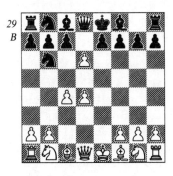

    5   ...   ed
    6   ♘c3

6 ♗d3 ♘c6 gives White nothing in view of ... ♘b4 possibilities.

After **6 ♘f3**, there are obvious transpositional possibilities to lines below (especially after 6 ... ♗e7), but **6 ... ♗g4** can lead to independent lines:

    7 b3 ♗e7 8 ♗b2 ♗f6=.

    7 ♗e2 c6 (7 ... ♗e7) is the exchange line of the Flohr–Agzamov variation.

7 ♗e3 c6!? 8 ♘c3 ♘8d7 9 ♗d3 ♗e7 10 0–0 ♘f6 11 ♖e1 0–0 12 b3 ♖e8 13 ♗c2 d5= Laitinen–Mira, Thessaloniki ol 1984.

7 h3 ♗h5 (7 … ♗xf3!? 8 ♕xf3 ♘c6) 8 ♗e2 (8 ♕b3?! ♘c6 9 d5 ♕e7+! 10 ♗e3 ♗xf3 11 gf ♘d4 12 ♕d1 ♘f5∓) 8 ♗e2 and White has gained from the insertion of h3 and … ♗h5, since 8 … ♗e7 9 0–0 0–0 10 ♘c3 ♘c6 11 b3 ♗f6 12 ♗e3 d5 (12 … ♖e8!? 13 ♕d2 h6 14 ♖ad1 a5) 13 c5 ♘c8 is a line in which Black would meet h3 with … ♗e6, were it not already on h5. After 14 ♕d2 ♗g6 15 ♘h2 (15 ♖ad1) 15 … b6 16 cb ab 17 f4! the kingside advance causes Black problems.

6 … ♗e7

6 … g6 7 ♘f3

(a) 7 … ♗g4 8 h3 (8 ♕e2+ ♕e7 9 ♘e4 ♗xf3 10 gf h6 is far from clear, whilst 8 ♗e2 ♗g7 9 ♗e3 0–0 10 0–0 ♘c6 11 b3 ♘e7 is comfortable for Black.) 8 … ♗xf3 9 ♕xf3 ♘c6 10 ♗e3 ♗g7 11 0–0–0 ♕f6!? (11 … 0–0?! 12 h4 f5 13 c5! ♘d7 14 ♗c4+ ♔h8 15 h5! gives White a very strong attack.) 12 ♕g3 h5 was a postal game Wikström–Nordström, in which Black was allowed to equalise with 13 ♗g5?! ♕xg5+! 14 ♕xg5 ♗h6.

(b) 7 … ♗g7 8 ♗g5 f6 9 ♗e3 ♘c6 (9 … c6?! 10 a4 ♗g4 11 a5 ♘c8 12 ♕b3± Ragozin–Sefc, Prague 1956; 9 … 0–0?! 10 c5! ♘6d7 11 ♗c4+ ♔h8 12 h4 dc 13 h5 gh 14 ♖xh5 ♕e8 15 g4 cd 16 ♕xd4 f5 17 ♕f4 ♘f6 18 ♖h4

♘xg4 19 0–0–0 ♕g6 20 ♖dh1 ♘d7 21 ♕g5! ♘h6 22 ♕xg6 hg 23 ♗xh6 ♗xh6+ 24 ♖xh6+ 1–0 was Franzen–Kneževič, Tatra Cup 1981, whilst 10 … dc 11 dc ♘6d7 12 ♕d5+ ♔h8 13 0–0–0 ♘c6 14 h4! is no improvement.) 10 ♗e2 0–0 transposes to Zsofia Polgar–C. Hansen, Åbenrå rapid 1989, which Black won quickly: 11 0–0 ♔h8!? 12 a4 ♗g4 13 a5? ♗xf3 14 gf ♘d7 15 f4 a6 16 ♗d3 f5 17 d5 ♘d4 18 ♗b1 ♕f6 19 ♖a3 c5 20 ♘a4 ♕h4 21 ♔h1 ♖ae8 22 b4 ♘f6 23 f3 ♘h5 24 ♗f2 ♕h3 0–1.

The provocative 6 … ♘c6 was tried in Hausner–Graf, Bundesliga 1989/90. After 7 h3 ♗e7 8 ♘f3 0–0 9 ♗e3 ♗f5 10 d5!? ♘e5 11 ♘xe5 de 12 ♗e2 ♘d7 13 0–0 a5 14 ♖c1 ♗c5 15 ♕d2 ♕e7, Black had everything in order.

7 h3

White can try placing the bishops on e3 and d3. Against this plan, Black does best to delay castling a little, as 7 ♗e3 0–0 8 ♗d3 ♘c6 9 g3!? ♗g5?! 10 ♕h5! h6 11 ♘f3 ♗xe3 12 fe ♕e8 13 ♔f2 gave White a strong attack in Skachkov–Donchenko, Kiev 1987. Therefore:

(a) 7 ♗e3 ♘c6 8 ♖c1 (8 ♘ge2 0–0 9 ♘f4 ♗f6 10 ♗e2 ♘e7=) 8 … 0–0 9 h4?! ♗f6 10 g4 ♖e8 11 ♗e2 ♗xg4! 12 ♗xg4 ♘xc4 13 ♘d5 ♘xe3 14 ♘xe3 ♘xd4 15 ♔f1 c6 gave Black good play in Suttles–Korchnoi, Sousse IZ 1967.

(b) **7 ♗d3 ♘c6** and now:

(b1) **8 ♘ge2** can be met by **8 ... ♗g4 9 f3 ♗h5 10 0-0 ♗g6 11 b3 d5 12 c5 ♘c8 13 ♗xg6 hg 14 ♘f4 ♗f6 15 ♖e1+ ♘8e7 16 ♘fxd5 ♗xd4+ 17 ♗e3=** De Loman–Schiffer, Amsterdam 1980 or **8 ... 0-0 9 0-0 (9 h3 ♗f6 10 ♗b1 g6 11 b3 d5 12 c5 ♘d7 13 ♘xd5?! ♘xc5!) 9 ... ♖e8 10 a3?! ♗f6 11 ♗e3 g6!? 12 ♕c2 ♘e7 13 ♘g3 d5 14 c5 ♘d7 15 b4 ♘f8 16 b5 h5∓** Atkinson–Fogarasi, Groningen 1989.

(b2) **8 ♗e3 ♗f6 9 ♘ge2 0-0 10 0-0 ♗g4 (10 ... ♖e8!?) 11 f3 ♗h5 12 b3 ♖e8 13 ♕d2 ♗g6 14 ♖ae1 d5 15 c5 ♘c8 16 f4 ♗xd3 17 ♕xd3** (Ilyin Zhenevsky–Rabinovich, Tbilisi 1937) **17 ... ♘b4 18 ♕d2 ♖xe3=**.

7 ♘f3 ♗g4 8 ♗e2 ♘c6 (8 ... 0-0 9 b3 ♘c6?! gives White the advantage after **10 h3 ♗xf3 11 ♗xf3 ♗f6 12 ♗e3 ♗g5 13 ♗xg5 ♕xg5 14 0-0 ♖fe8 15 ♗xc6! bc 16 ♕f3 ♕a5 17 ♖fe1 d5 18 cd!**, as in Sigurjonsson–Bischoff, Reykjavik 1982.) **9 d5!? (9 b3 ♗f6!?) 9 ... ♗xf3 10 ♗xf3 ♘e5 11 ♗e2 0-0 12 b3 ♗f6 13 ♗b2** was Dvoiris–Kengis, Barnaul 1988. Kimelfeld analysed **13 ... a5! 14 a4 (14 0-0 a4 15 f4 a3!; 14 a3 a4 15 f4 ♘g6!) 14 ... ♘d7** followed by ... ♘c5 as adequate for Black.

The most popular line is **7 ♗e2 0-0 8 ♘f3 ♗g4 9 0-0 (9 b3 c5 10 ♗e3 ♘c6 11 ♖c1 f5 12 dc dc= 13 ♘d5 ♘xd5 14 cd ♘b4 15 a3 f4 16**

♗xc5 ♗xc5 17 ♖xc5 ♗xf3 18 gf ♘a6 19 ♖c3 ♕f6 20 ♖d2∞ Minić–Smyslov, Palma IZ 1970) **9 ... ♘c6 10 b3**.

(a) **10 ... d5 11 c5 ♘c8 12 h3 ♗xf3!? 13 ♗xf3 ♗f6 14 ♗e3 (14 ♘xd5 ♗xd4 15 ♗f4 ♗e5!) 14 ... ♘8e7 15 g4 g6 16 ♗g2 (16 ♖c1 ♗g7 17 a3 ♖e8± Tatai–Ciocaltea, Reggio Emilia 1967/8) 16 ... ♗g7 17 f4?! (17 ♖c1) 17 ... f5 18 g5 b6! 19 ♖c1 bc 20 ♘e2 ♕d7! 21 ♕d2 cd 22 ♘xd4 ♘d8! 23 ♖c2 c6** and Black managed to convert the extra pawn in Adorjan–Larsen, Las Palmas 1977.

(b) **10 ... ♗f6 11 ♗e3 d5 12 c5 ♘c8 13 h3** (13 b4? is simply a bad plan, since White does not have a queenside majority here; the weakened squares are more important. 13 ... ♘8e7 14 b5 ♘a5 15 h3 ♗xf3 16 ♗xf3 c6 17 ♕d3 ♘c4∓ Gipslis–Larsen, Sousse 1967. Note that 14 h3? fails to 14 ... ♗xf3 15 ♗xf3 ♘xb4 16 ♖b1 ♘a6 17 ♖xb7 ♘xc5!) **13 ... ♗e6** *(30)*. Other squares are grossly inferior, as White's kingside pawns are liable to advance.

Black's play must now be very circumspect, striking the right balance between breaking up White's eventual queenside push, and some sort of action on the kingside.

(b1) **14 ♘e1 ♘8e7 15 g4 g5! (15 ... g6!?) 16 h4 h6 17 ♘g2 ♘g6** secured counterplay in Ćirić–Knežević, Titograd 1965.

(b2) **14 g4 g6 15 ♘e1 ♖e8 16**

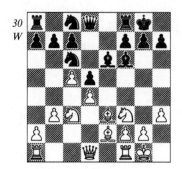

30
W

♘g2 ♗g7 17 ♕d2 ♘8e7 18 ♘f4 ♕d7 19 ♘xe6 ♕xe6∓ Z. Berg–Wessendorf, San Bernardino 1986.

(b3) **14 ♗b5** ♘8e7 15 ♗g5 ♗xg5 16 ♘xg5 ♘f5 17 ♘f3 f6 18 ♖e1 ♕d7 19 b4 ♘fe7 20 ♗a4 a6= Browne–Marović, Rovinj Zagreb 1970.

(b4) **14 b4** a6 (14 ... ♘xb4? 15 ♖b1 ♘a6 16 ♗xa6±) 15 b5 (15 ♖b1 ♘8e7 16 g4 h6 17 ♗d3 g5! 18 a4 ♗g7 19 b5 ab 20 ab ♘a5∓ Pedersen–Jansa, Athens 1970) 15 ... ab 16 ♘xb5 ♘8a7!? (16 ... ♘a5 17 ♗f4 c6 18 ♘c7 ♖a7 19 ♘xe6 fe) 17 a4 b6 18 ♖c1 ♘xb5 19 ab ♘a5 20 cb cb 21 ♘e5 ♕d6 (21 ... ♗xe5?! 22 de ♘c4 23 ♗d4± Hansen) 22 ♗d3 was Sznapik–C. Hansen, Copenhagen Open 1982. Hansen gives 22 ... ♗xe5 23 de ♕xe5 24 ♗xb6 ♘c4 25 ♗d4 ♕f4 as Black's best. Instead there followed 22 ... ♖fc8?! 23 ♘g4 ♗xg4 24 ♕xg4 ♘c4 25 ♗f4!±.

(b5) **14 ♕d2** has been the most popular. Black could well try **14 ... g6**, since 15 g4 ♗g7 16 ♘e1 f5 (Eales, Williams) gives Black counterplay. Another logical approach, leading to complicated play is **14 ... b6!?** 15 ♘a4 ♘8e7 16 g4 ♘g6 17 ♖ac1 ♗d7 18 ♘c3 bc 19 ♘xd5 ♗xd4 20 ♗xd4 cd 21 ♘xd4 ♘xd4 22 ♕xd4 ♗e6 ½–½ Mortensen–C. Hansen, Esbjerg 1984. The 'normal' move, **14 ... h6** seems to imply an inappropriate amount of activity on the kingside, given that White has wasted no time on the other wing: 15 ♗d3! ♘8e7 16 g4 g5 17 ♘e2 ♗g7 18 ♘h2! gave White a strong attack in Armas–Graf, W. Germany 1989. After 18 ... ♘g6 (18 ... f5 19 f4 gf 20 ♘xf4 ♘xd4 21 ♘h5) 19 f4 gf 20 ♘xf4 ♘xf4 21 ♖xf4 Black's position was clearly deficient.

7	...	0–0
8	♘f3	♖e8
9	♗e2	♗f5

9 ... ♗f6 10 0–0 ♘c6 gives White's queen's bishop a choice of squares:

(a) **11 ♗f4** ♗f5 12 ♖c1 (After 12 b3?! ♗e4! 13 ♘xe4 ♖xe4 14 ♗e3 d5 15 c5 ♘d7, White suffered due to the weakness of his d-pawn in Ostojić–Schmidt, Monte Carlo 1969.) 12 ... h6 (12 ... ♗e4 can now be met by 13 d5.) 13 b3 (13 d5 ♘e5 14 ♘d4 ♗h7 15 b3 ♘bd7 gave Black a good position in Kuznetsov–Shovel, Oakham 1986.) 13 ... d5!? (13 ... ♗g6!? is a useful waiting move, with possible ideas of ... a5–a4; 13 ... ♖e7 14 ♕d2 ♕d7 15 ♖fd1 ♖ae8∞ Matanović–Larsen, Palma 1968.) 14 c5 ♘c8 15 ♗b5 ♘8e7. Now 16 g4 is met by 16 ... ♗e4!?, whilst

16 ♘e5?! ♘g6! 17 ♗g3 ♗xe5 18 de d4 gave Black the advantage in Moors–Fleck, Bundesliga 1985/6.

(b) 11 ♗e3 ♗f5 12 ♖c1 (12 b3 h6 13 ♖c1 ♖e7 14 ♕d2 ♕d7 15 ♖fd1 ♖ae8 was level in Suetin–Vukić, Odessa 1975, but 13 ♕d2 retains more flexibility with the rook's position) 12 ... h6 (12 ... d5? 13 c5 ♘c4 15 ♘xd5!) 13 d5 ♘e5 14 ♘d4 ♗h7 15 b3 ♘bd7 16 ♘a4 ♘c5 was roughly equal in Brodsky–A. G. Panchenko, Ukrainian Ch (Simferopol) 1990.

10 0-0 ♘8d7!?

10 ... ♘c6 leads to the lines in the previous note.

With the bishop denied the g4 square, Black's pressure on the centre is less, so the ... d5 push is best delayed a little to avoid White pushing forward on the kingside. Dreev's move is therefore logical, as it keeps the knight more flexible, with ideas of manoeuvring to useful squares on the kingside.

11	♗f4	♘f8
12	b3	♘g6
13	♗h2	c6
14	♕d2	♗f6
15	♖fe1	a5! *(31)*

Now White has run out of useful non-committal moves, while the possibility of ... a4 is rather irritating. A kingside push will simply give Black's minor pieces some good squares, so Serper's decision to exchange some pieces is understandable.

| 16 | ♗d3 | ♖xe1+ |
| 17 | ♖xe1 | ♗xd3 |

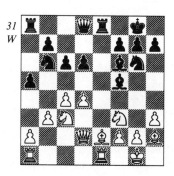

| 18 | ♕xd3 | d5 |

Having caused maximum inconvenience by delaying this push, Black fixes to pawns to suit his bishop.

| 19 | c5 | ♘d7 |
| 20 | ♗d6 | ♘gf8 |

Black, with counterplay against d4, can claim full equality.

21	♘e5	♗xe5
22	♗xe5	♘xe5
23	♖xe5	♘e6
24	♘e2	♕f6
25	♕e3	a4
26	b4	♕g6?

This, however, is simply a blunder, as Black's back rank now proves a fatal weakness. 26 ... a3 with ideas of ... ♖a4 was necessary.

The rest is straightforward: 27 ♘f4! ♕b1+ 28 ♔h2 ♘f8 29 ♖e7 ♕xa2 30 ♕f3!. White has an overwhelming attack and need only prevent the black queen returning to defend. 30 ... ♕c2 31 ♘d3 f6 32 ♕g4 g6 33 ♕h4 ♕d2 34 f4! 1-0.

Meiers–Kengis

Riga 1989

1 e4 ♘f6 2 e5 ♘d5 3 d4 d6 4 c4 ♘b6 5 ed

5 ... cd

6 ♗e3

6 d5 is best met by 6 ... e5 ensuring Black a fair share of the centre, with possible kingside expansion to follow.

6 ♗d3 e5 7 ♘e2 ♘c6 8 d5 ♘b4 9 ♘bc3 f5 10 ♗b1 a5 11 0–0 ♗e7 12 f4 0–0 13 b3 ♗f6 gave Black perfectly reasonable chances in Sigurjonsson–Hort, Hastings 1974. More standard play with 6 ... ♘c6 7 ♘e2 g6 is also feasible.

6 ♗g5 g6 7 ♕d2 can transpose to the game after 7 ... ♗g7 8 0–0, whilst Buljovčić–Ivkov, Yugoslavia 1965 demonstrated a good alternative: 7 ... h6 8 ♗e3 ♗g7 9 ♘c3 ♗f5 10 h3 g5 11 g4 ♗g6 12 h4 ♘c6∓.

6 ... g6

In Hartston–Schmid, Menorca 1974, Black was able to justify some very unusual play: 6 ... ♗f5 7 ♘c3 e6 8 ♘f3 ♗e7 9 ♗e2 0–0 10 0–0 ♘a6!? 11 ♕b3 ♕b8 12 ♗f4 ♘c7 13 ♖ac1 ♖d8 14 h3 h6! 15 ♖fd1 ♘d7 16 ♗g3 a6 17 ♘d2 ♕a7=.

7 ♕d2

7 a4 hopes for 7 ... a5?! 8 ♕d2 ♘c6 9 d5. Instead 7 ... d5 8 c5 ♘c4 9 ♗xc4 dc 10 ♘f3 ♘c6 11 0–0 ♗g7 12 ♘a3 ♗g4!? 13 ♘xc4 would have been fine for Black in Kapengut–Kupreichik, USSR

1969, had he chosen 13 ... ♕d5! rather than 13 ... ♗xd4? 14 ♗xd4 ♗xf3 15 ♘d6+!.

7 d5 ♗g7 8 ♗d4 ♗xd4 9 ♕xd4 0–0 10 ♘c3 e5 gives Black fine play. Black's compensation after **11 de** ♘c6!? (11 ... ♗xe6 12 0–0–0 ♘c6 13 ♕xd6 ♕g5+ 14 f4 ♕a5 Bagirov) 12 ef+ (12 ♕d2 ♗xe6∓) 12 ... ♖xf7 13 ♕d2 ♕e8+ 14 ♔d1 ♗e6 15 ♘d5 ♘e5 16 b3 ♖c8 was superb in Dobkin–Weil, Tel Aviv 1936. On the other hand, **11 ♕d2** f5 12 ♘f3 (12 h4 ♕f6 13 h5 g5 14 h6 ♔h8) 12 ... ♘8d7 13 0–0–0 (13 ♕h6 ♕e7 14 ♘g5 e4 15 ♘e6 ♖f6 16 ♘b5 ♘e5 17 ♘bc7 ♖b8 18 b3 ♘a8!∓ Orton–Martz, US Open 1973) 13 ... ♕f6 14 ♕h6 ♕e7 15 ♖e1 e4 16 ♘d2 (16 h4) 16 ... ♘e5 17 h3?! (After 17 f3, Black will be happy to meet fe with ... f4 – a typical King's Indian blockading sacrifice.) 17 ... ♘bd7 18 ♕e3 ♕h4 19 g3 ♕f6 20 ♔b1 ♘c5 allowed the black forces domination in Suttles–Fischer, Palma IZ 1970.

7 h4 is an old idea of Hartston's recently tested by Davies. After **7 ... h5** 8 d5, White has a substantially improved version of the 7 d5 line, though 8 ... ♘8d7 9 ♗d4 ♘f6 10 ♗d3 ♗g7 11 ♘h3 0–0 (11 ... ♘bd7?! 12 ♘c3 ♘c5 13 ♗c2± Hartston–Williams, England 1973) 12 ♘g5 e5 13 de ♗xe6 14 ♘xe6 ♖e8 15 0–0 ♖xe6 16 ♘d2 ♘g4 gave Black counterplay in Hartston–Bryson, British Ch (Edinburgh) 1985. It is also possible to ignore the h-pawn with **7 ... ♗g7!?** 8 h5 ♘c6 9 ♘c3 when Black should prefer **9 ... 0-0** 10 hg fg∞, as analysed by Westerinen and Jansa, to justifying White's play with **9 ... d5?** 10 c5 ♘c4 11 ♗xc4 dc 12 ♘ge2± ♕a5 13 h6 ♗f6 14 0-0 0-0 15 d5 ♘b4 16 ♘e4! ♗h8 17 ♗d4! Davies–Westerinen, Oslo 1988.

7 ♗d3 ♗g7 8 ♘e2 ♘c6 9 0-0 ♗g4 10 f3 ♗f5 11 b3 ♗xd3 12 ♕xd3 0-0 13 ♘bc3 d5 led, in Hartston–Alexandria, Sinaia 1970, to positions considered under 6 ♘c3 g6 7 ♗e3 ♗g7 8 ♗d3 0-0 9 ♘ge2.

7 ... ♗g7

7 ... ♘c6 is rather an over-reaction to White's idea (8 ♗h6? ♗xh6 9 ♕xh6 ♗f5∓), since 8 d5 ♘e5 9 h3 leaves the knight embarrassed for a decent square.

8 ♗h6 0-0

8 ... ♗f6 9 ♘c3 ♘c6 10 d5 ♘e5 11 ♘e4 (11 b3!?) 11 ... ♘exc4 12 ♗xc4 ♘xc4 13 ♕e2 ♕a5+ 14 ♔f1 ♗xb2 15 ♖b1 ♕xa2 16 ♖c1 b5 17 ♖e1 ♕a3! was very messy in Kapengut–Polikarpov, Minsk 1970.

8 ... ♗xh6 9 ♕xh6 ♘c6 has been tried by the author. 10 ♕g7 ♖f8 11 ♘f3 ♗g4 12 ♘g5 ♘a4 13 ♘xh7 ♕a5+ 14 ♘d2 0-0-0 15 ♘xf8 e5 gives strong play for the rook, whilst 10 ♘f3?! ♗g4 11 ♕g7 ♔d7! 12 ♕xf7?! ♖f8 13 ♕xh7 ♗xf3 14 gf ♖xd4 15 ♕xg6 ♘xf3+ 16 ♔d1 ♘a4 17 ♗h3+ ♔c7 18 b3 ♘b2+ (18 ... ♖f4! 19 ba ♕h8

20 ♕e6 ♖af8−+) 19 ♔c2 ♘e5 20 ♕g3 ♖f3 21 ♕h4 ♘bd3 22 ♖f1 ♘f4! led to a rout in Kennaugh–Burgess, Liverpool Open 1988. However, 10 ♘c3 ♗f5 11 ♕g7 ♖f8 was unclear in Waller–Burgess, Vienna Open 1990.

9	**h4**	**e5**
10	**d5**	**♗xh6**
11	**♕xh6**	**♘a6**
12	**♘c3**	**♕e7**
13	**0-0-0**	**♗d7**
14	**♘f3**	**f6** *(32)*

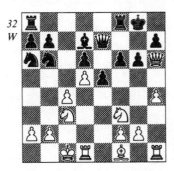

White's play now appears rather naïve, since the h-file play has clearly come to nothing, whilst the white king can expect little safety.

15	**♗e2**	**♖ac8**
16	**♘d2**	**f5**
17	**f4**	**ef**
18	**♕xf4**	**♘c5**
19	**♔b1**	**♘ba4**
20	**♘xa4**	**♘xa4**

Suddenly White is faced with the loss of a piece in view of the threat of 21 ... ♕g7. The game concluded 21 ♔a1 ♕xe2 22 ♕xd6 ♖f7 23 ♖he1 ♕f2 24 h5 ♕d4 25

♕b4 ♕b6 26 ♕a3 ♕c5 27 hg hg
28 ♕b3 ♕b6 29 ♕a3 a5 30 ♘f3
♕b4 31 ♕xb4 ab 32 ♘e5 ♖g7 33
♖c1 ♘c5 34 b3 f4 35 ♖cd1 ♖a8
36 ♔b2 ♗f5 37 d6 b6 38 ♖d5
♖ga7 39 a4 ba+ 40 ♔a2 ♖e8 41
♖ed1 ♗c2 42 b4 ♗xd1 43 bc
♗b3+ 44 ♔xb3 a2 45 ♖d1 bc
46 ♘c6 a1♕ 47 ♖xa1 ♖xa1 48 d7
♖e3+ 0–1.

Johansen–L. Schmidt
Malaysia Z 1990

**1 e4 ♘f6 2 e5 ♘d5 3 d4 d6 4 c4
♘b6 5 ed cd**

   6   ♘c3   g6

6 ... ♘c6!? 7 d5 ♘e5 8 ♗e3 g6
9 ♗d4 ♗h6 10 h4 0–0 11 h5
♗g7 12 f4 ♘g4 13 ♗xg7 ♔xg7
14 ♕d4+ f6 15 ♘f3 e5 16 de ♗xe6
17 0–0–0 ♖e8 18 hg hg 19 ♘g5
♗g8 20 ♘ge4 d5 21 cd ♖c8 22 d6
♘d5 23 ♔b1 ♘ge3∞ Semënova–
Lelchuk Popova, USSR Women's
Ch (Volzhsky) 1989 was an excellent example of imaginative play
leading to a total mess.

   7   ♗d3

7 b3 ♗g7 8 ♗b2 0–0 9 ♘ge2
♘c6 (9 ... d5!?) 10 d5 ♘e5 11 ♘d4
e6 12 de fe 13 ♗e2 ♖f4 14 ♘db5
♗d7!? 15 ♕d2 ♕f6 16 0–0 (16
0–0–0 d5!) 16 ... ♗c6 17 ♖ad1
♖f8 18 f3 ♗h6 19 ♘xd6. Now,
in Granda–Howell, World U-16
(Guayaquil) 1982, 19 ... ♘g4!
would have given Black excellent
winning prospects.

7 h4 is best met by **7 ... h5**,
whereupon White has tried in a
variety of ways to profit from the
insertion of these moves.

(a) **8 b3?!** ♗g7 9 ♗e3 ♘c6 10
♘f3 ♗g4 11 ♗e2 d5 12 c5 ♘c8
13 b4 a6 14 ♕a4?! ♖a7! 15 ♘e5
♗xe5 16 ♗xg4 ♗g7 17 ♗xc8?
♕xc8 18 ♘xd5 ♕g4! 19 ♘c7+
♔d8 20 ♘d5 ♕xg2 0–1 Wadding-
ham–Vareille, Hastings Challengers 1985/6.

(b) **8 ♗g5** ♗g7 9 ♖c1 ♘c6
10 d5 ♘e5 11 b3 0–0∓ Baljon–
Palatnik, Teesside 1974.

(c) **8 ♗e3 ♗g7** and now Kurajica has tried some interesting
ideas:

(c1) **9 ♗d3** ♘c6 10 ♘ge2 0–0
(10 ... ♗g4!?) 11 ♕b3 (11 ♕d2
♘b4!=; 11 a3? d5 12 c5 ♘c4∓; 11
b3 d5 12 c5 ♘d7 13 ♗g5? ♘xd4!
14 ♘xd5 ♖e8 15 ♖c1 ♘e5 16 ♗e4
f5 17 ♕xd4 fe 18 ♘xe7+? ♕xe7!
19 ♗xe7 ♘d3+ 0–1 Ortel–Hazai,
Hungary 1973) 11 ... e5 12 d5
♘d4 13 ♗xd4 ed 14 ♘b5 ♖e8
15 ♔f1 ♗g4 16 ♘bxd4 ♖c8∓
Kadrev–Orev, Sofia 1963.

(c2) **9 ♕d2** ♘c6 10 0–0–0? ♗f5
11 ♗d3 ♗xd3 12 ♕xd3 ♖c8 13
b3 ♘b4 14 ♕d2 ♘xc4! 15 bc ♖xc4
16 ♘ge2 ♕a5 17 ♔b2 0–0 18
♗h6 ♗xh6 19 ♕xh6 ♖fc8 20
♕d2 ♘xa2! 21 ♖h3 ♖b4+ 22
♔c2 ♕b5 0–1 Girling–D. Clarke,
corres. 1987.

(c3) **9 ♗e2** ♘c6 (9 ... 0–0
10 g4) 10 d5 ♗xc3+ 11 bc ♘a5
12 ♕d4 ♖g8 13 ♖d1 ♘a4 14
♘f3 ♗g4∞ Kurajica–Bagirov,
Erevan 1971.

(c4) **9 c5!?** dc 10 dc should
be met by 10 ... ♘6d7, since 10

♗xc3+?! 11 bc ♕xd1+ 12 ♖xd1 ♘6d7 13 f3 ♘c6 14 ♗c4 ♘de5 15 ♗b3 0–0 16 ♘e2 ♔g7 17 ♔f2 ♗d7 18 ♖d2 gave White some advantage in Listengarten–Dzhalilov, Baku 1972.

(c5) **9 ♕b3!?** ♘c6 10 ♖d1 (10 0–0–0 0–0 11 ♗e2 e5 12 de ♘xe5 13 ♕b4 ♗e6 14 ♖xd6 ♕c8 15 c5 ♘bc4 showed the weakness of the white king in Kurajica–Hecht, Montilla 1972.) 10 ... 0–0 11 ♗e2 e5 (Safer and probably sounder was 11 ... ♗d7!? 12 ♘f3 ♘a5 13 ♕b4 ♘c6 14 ♕a3 ♗g4 15 b3 d5 16 c5 ♘c8 17 ♘xg5 ♗xe2 18 ♘xe2 e6 19 b4 ♘8e7 in Kurajica–Bagirov, Banja Luka 1976.) 12 ♘f3 ed 13 ♘xd4 ♕e7 14 ♗g5 (14 ♘db5!?) 14 ... ♕e5 15 ♘f3 ♕e8 16 ♗e3 ♗e6 17 ♕b5 ♘e5 18 ♘xe5 ♗xe5= Kurajica–Hecht, Wijk aan Zee 1973.

After **7 ♗e3 ♗g7**, White has tried a number of ideas:

(a) **8 ♖c1!?** 0–0 9 b3 ♘c6 10 ♗e2 e5 (10 ... d5 11 c5 e5 12 ♘f3 ed 13 ♘xd4 ♘d7 14 0–0 ♘de5) 11 ♘f3 ♗g4 12 de de 13 0–0 f5 14 ♗c5 ♖e8 15 ♔h1!? ♗xf3 16 ♗xf3 e4= Houston–Burgess, London (Lloyds Bank) 1990.

(b) **8 c5** dc 9 dc ♘6d7 10 ♘f3 ♘c6 (10 ... ♕a5) 11 ♕a4 0–0 12 ♗e2 ♘de5 13 ♘xe5 ♗xe5 14 ♖d1 ♕a5= Fette–Grün, Bundesliga 1983.

(c) **8 ♕d2** is comfortably met by either 8 ... 0–0 (compare Meiers–Kengis) or 8 ... ♘c6 9 ♖c1 (9 ♘f3?! ♗g4) 9 ... d5.

(d) **8 h4** can transpose to lines considered above after 8 ... h5, or after 8 ... ♘c6 9 h5 to 6 ♗e3 g6 7 h4 ♗g7 8 h5 ♘c6 9 ♘c3.

7 ♗e3 ♗g7 8 ♗d3 0–0 (8 ... ♘c6 9 ♘ge2 ♗g4 is best met by 10 f3 ♗f5 11 b3, transposing.) **9 ♘ge2 ♘c6 10 0–0** *(33)* (Slower methods allow Black more counterplay in the centre: 10 b3?! d5 11 c5 ♘d7 12 ♗b5 e5! 13 0–0 ♘xc5 14 de d4 15 ♘xd4 ♘xe5 16 h3 ♘e6 17 ♘xe6 ♗xe6 18 f4? ♕a5!∓ Minić–Fischer, Palma IZ 1970; 10 a3? ♗g4 11 f3 ♗f5 12 b3 ♗xd3 13 ♕xd3 d5 14 c5 ♘d7 15 0–0 e5 16 b4 a5! 17 ♖ab1 ab 18 ab ed 19 ♘xd4 ♘de5∓ Twine–Burgess, Bristol League 1990; 10 ♕d2? e5 11 d5 ♘b4 was good for Black in Patterson–Ghizdavu, USA 1975, since ♕d1–d2xd3 involves a loss of tempo.)

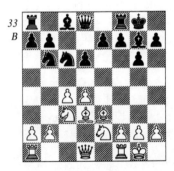

33
B

Now Black generally chooses between the two moves below. Lesser alternatives are: **10 ... e6** 11 b3 ♗d7 12 ♕d2 d5 13 c5 ♘c8 14 a3 ♘8e7 (Minić–Planinc,

Yugoslavia 1970) 15 b4±; **10 ... d5** 11 c5 ♘c4 12 ♗xc4 dc 13 ♕a4±; **10 ... ♘b4** 11 b3 d5 (11 ... ♘xd3 12 ♕xd3±) 12 c5 ♘d7 13 a3 (13 ♗b1!?) 13 ... ♘xd3 14 ♕xd3 ♘f6 15 ♘g3± Ilyin Zhenevsky–Eremin, USSR 1931.

(a) **10 ... e5 11 d5** (11 de de 12 c5 ♘d7 13 a3 a5 14 ♗b5 ♘f6 15 ♕a4 ♕c7= Buza–Grünberg, Romania 1977) **11 ... ♘b4** (11 ... ♘e7?! 12 b3 ♘d7 13 ♘e4 ♘f5 14 ♗g5 f6 15 ♗d2± Fischer–Berliner, US Ch [New York] 1960/1) **12 b3 ♘xd3** (12 ... a5 13 ♖c1 ♘xd3) **13 ♕xd3** and now:

(a1) **13 ... ♘d7** 14 ♕d2 f5 15 f4! b6 (15 ... g5!?) 16 ♖ad1 ♘f6? (16 ... ♖e8) 17 fe de 18 ♗g5± Fischer–Berliner, US Ch (New York) 1962/3.

(a2) **13 ... ♖e8!?** is very logical, as White's f4 is not positionally justifiable until Black has played ... f5. Jhunjunwala–Timman, Teesside 1974 was not really a test of the idea: 14 ♖ac1?! ♘d7 15 b4?! a5 16 ♘b5?! e4! 17 ♕d2 ♘e5 18 ♘f4 ab∓.

(a3) **13 ... f5** 14 f4 ♘d7 15 ♖ad1 (15 ♕d2 is a1.) 15 ... g5!? 16 g3 (16 fg f4 17 ♗f2 ♕xg5 18 ♘e4 ♕g6 19 ♘2c3 ♖f7 20 ♘b5 ♗f8∞ SDO; 18 ... ♕h6!?) 16 ... gf 17 gf ♘f6 18 ♖f2 (18 ♗f2? ♘e4!∓; 18 fe? de 19 d6 ♗d7 20 ♘d5 ♘xd5 21 ♕xd5+ ♔h8 22 ♕xb7 f4! 23 ♗xa7 ♖xa7! 24 ♕xa7 ♕g5+ punishes White's greed with a decisive attack, as analysed by Smith; 18 h3 ♔h8 19 ♔h2 ♘h5 20 c5 dc

21 ♗xc5 ♖g8 22 ♕f3 ♘xf4 23 ♘xf4 ♕c7!–+ Levy–Torre, Reggio Emilia 1972/3.) 18 ... ♔h8 19 ♖g2 (19 c5!?) 19 ... b6 20 ♖f1 ♗d7 21 ♗d2 ♕e7 22 h3?! ♘e4 23 ♘xe4 fe 24 ♕xe4 ♗xh3 25 ♖h2 ♗f5 26 ♕e3 ♖f7 27 ♘g3 ♖af8∓ 28 ♘xf5 ♖xf5 29 ♕h3 h6 30 ♖e1 ♖8f6! 31 fe ♖xe5–+ 32 ♖xe5 ♕xe5 33 ♖g2 ♕a1+ 34 ♔h2 ♖f1 35 ♕c8+ ♔h7 36 ♕d7 ♕e5+ 0–1 Jones–Smith, corres. 1985.

(b) **10 ... ♗g4** is based on a little trick, and constitutes Black's soundest defence. 11 h3 ♗xe2 gives Black full equality after either 12 ♗xe2 e5 or 12 ♘xe2 ♘b4 (12 ... d5 13 c5 ♘d7) 13 b3 ♘xd3 14 ♕xd3 d5, so **11 f3 ♗f5! 12 b3** (12 ♗xf5?! ♘xc4) **12 ... ♗xd3 13 ♕xd3** has normally been played.

(b1) **13 ... e6!** attempts to profit from delaying ... d5. 14 ♖ac1 (14 ♖ab1 ♖e8!?) 14 ... d5 15 c5 ♘c8 16 ♕d2 ♖e8 17 ♗h6 ♗h8 18 ♗g5 ♕d7 ½–½ Minić–Gipslis, Erevan 1971.

(b2) **13 ... d5** 14 c5 ♘c8 15 ♖ab1 (15 ♕d2 ♖e8 16 ♖fd1 e6 17 ♗h6 ♗h8 18 ♗g5 ♕d7 19 ♖ab1 ♘8e7 20 ♘b5 ♘f5∓ Hartston–Alexandria, Vrnjacka Banja 1971) 15 ... e6 16 b4 (16 ♕d2 ♖e8 17 b4 a6) and now Black should probably play 16 ... a6, rather than 16 ... ♘8e7 17 b5 ♘a5 18 ♗f2 ♘c4 19 ♖fd1 ♘f5 20 ♘g3 ♘h4 21 ♘f1 ♕g5 22 g3 h5 23 f4 ♕g4 24 ♔h1 ♘f5 25 ♕e2 ♕h3 26 ♖d3 ♖ae8 27

♘d2 ♘xd2 28 ♕xd2 ♘e7 29 ♕e2
♕f5 30 ♖e1, as in Ivell–Bryson,
British Ch (Edinburgh) 1985,
though Black eventually prepared
... e5 and reached a tenable
ending.

| | 7 | ... | ♗g7 |
| | 8 | ♘ge2 | 0–0 |

8 ... ♘c6 provoked a self-
destruct in De Sousa–N. Regan,
Hastings Chalengers 1990/1: 9 d5
(9 ♗e3 0–0 transposes to lines
given above.) 9 ... ♘e5 10 b3?!
♗g4 11 f3?? (11 0–0? ♗xe2; 11
♗b2 ♕d7!? prepares to meet 12
f3 with 12 ... ♗f5, while 12 0–0
♘f3+ 13 ♔h1 ♗e5, though not
strictly necessary, is very interesting.) 11 ... ♘xf3+! and Black won.
White should play 10 0–0, when
Black has more tactical possibilities than in our main game, e.g. 10
... ♗g4 11 f3 ♘xd3 12 ♕xd3 ♗f5
13 ♕d1 or 10 ... ♘xd3 11 ♕xd3
♗f5 12 ♕d1 0–0 (12 ... a5!? 13
♘d4 ♕c8) 13 b3 ♘d7.

| | 9 | 0–0 | ♘c6 *(34)* |

9 ... e5 may prove effective as
a means of avoiding the problems
caused by White's next move. 10
♗e3 ♘c6 leads to variations considered above (7 ♗e3 ♗g7 8
♗d3 0–0 9 ♘ge2 0–0 10 0–0 e5);
alternatives appear harmless.

| | 10 | d5!? | ♘e5 |

10 ... ♘b4 11 ♗b1 e6 12 a3
♘a6 13 b3 ed 14 cd ♘c5 15 ♖a2!?
was Johansen–Wohl, Canberra
1981. Black's play has been very
logical, but Johansen claims a
slight edge, as it is not so easy for

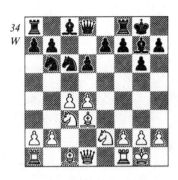

Black to find counterplay.

| | 11 | b3 | ♘xd3 |

11 ... ♘bd7 12 ♗c2! left White
slightly for preference in
Johansen–Depasquale, Adelaide
1980 due to the awkward position
of the e5 knight.

| | 12 | ♕xd3 | ♘d7 |

Instead, **12 ... e5?!** 13 de and 14
♗a3 illustrates one advantage of
leaving the bishop on c1, whilst **12
... ♗f5** is comfortably met by 13
♕d2 with ♗b2 and ♘d4 to follow,
with a small advantage for White
according to Johansen.

	13	♗e3	♘c5
	14	♕d2	a6
	15	♗d4!	♗d7
	16	♗xg7	♔xg7
	17	♘d4	

Black now tries for counterplay
on the queenside. Given that this
fails, 17 ... ♖e8 or 17 ... ♔g8
could be considered, but Black's
position is clearly very passive and
unpleasant.

	17	...	♖b8
	18	♖fe1	b5?!
	19	b4!	♘a4
	20	♘xa4	ba

21	a3	♖c8
22	♖ac1	♖e8
23	c5	♗b5?

Abject, but 23 ... dc 24 bc e5 25 ♘e2 and 23 ... e5 24 de ♗xe6 25 cd are also rather unpalatable.

24	c6	♖c7
25	♖c3	

White embarks on a mating attack, against which Black is in no position to defend: 25 ... ♕c8 (25 ... ♔h8; 25 ... h6) 26 ♖h3 ♖h8 (26...h5 27 ♖xh5!) 27 ♕h6+ ♔g8 28 ♖f3! (Threatens 29 ♘f5, while preventing 28 ... ♕f8 due to 29 ♕xf8+ ♔xf8 30 ♘e6+) 28 ... ♗c4 29 ♘f5 ♕f8 30 ♕h4 ♗xd5 31 ♖xe7! ♖xc6 (31 ... ♗xf3 32 ♖xc7) 32 ♘h6+ ♔g7 33 ♕d4+ (33 ♕f6+ is a little quicker, but presumably the text seemed more amusing to Johansen.) 1–0.

Perović–Begovac
Yugoslavia 1985

1 e4 ♘f6 2 e5 ♘d5 3 d4 d6 4 c4 ♘b6 5 ed cd 6 ♘c3 g6

7 a4!?

This is Nona Alexandria's idea, which aims to compromise Black's queenside. Also ♖a3 is prepared, whereupon ... ♗xc3 (after White plays d5) will not cripple White's, pawn structure.

7 ... a5

It is logical to halt White's pawn-pushing, but 7 ... ♗g7 8 a5 ♘6d7 9 ♘f3 0–0 (9 ... ♘c6?! 10 d5! ♘xa5 11 ♖a3! b6 12 b4 ♘b7 13 ♘d4± Alexandria) 10 ♖a3 d5!? 11 ♘xd5 ♘c6, attempting to profit

from White's lack of development, is interesting. Instead, Black should certainly avoid 10 ... ♘f6?! 11 d5 when White had a very solid space advantage in Alexandria–Gipslis, Tbilisi/Sukhumi 1977.

Note that 7 ... ♘c6? is really asking for trouble: 8 a5 ♘d7 9 d5 ♘b4 10 ♗e3 ♗g7 11 ♘f3 0–0 12 ♗e2 ♘f6 13 0–0 left Black with a thoroughly unpleasant position in Ardiansyah–Tan, Auckland 1977.

8 c5

Nigel Davies has adopted an alternative approach, based on simple development. The insertion of a4 and a5 provides White with some extra possibilities. After **8 ♘f3** Black has tried:

(a) **8 ... ♗g4?!** 9 ♗e3 ♘c6 10 d5 ♗xf3 11 gf ♘b4 12 ♗d4 ♖g8 13 c5 dc 14 ♗b5+ ♘d7 15 ♗xc5 ♗g7 16 0–0 and Black has no real prospects of organising much of a position. Davies–C. Hansen, Graested 1990 concluded 16 ... b6 17 ♗e3 ♔f8 18 ♕e2 ♗f6 19 ♖ad1 ♔g7 20 ♘e4 ♗e5 21 d6 ♘c5 22 ♗g5 ♘e6 23 ♗xe7 ♘f4 24 ♕c4 ♕b8 25 ♘g5 ♖f8 26 ♖fe1 h6 27 ♖xe5 hg 28 ♗xf8+ ♕xf8 29 d7 ♕h8 30 ♖e7 ♖f8 31 ♕d4+ 1–0.

(b) **8 ... ♗g7** 9 ♗e3 0–0 10 ♗e2 ♘c6 (10 ... d5) 11 d5 (In the standard lines, this would be strongly met by ... ♘a5.) 11 ... ♘e5 12 ♘xe5 ♗xe5 13 0–0 ♘d7 14 ♖a3 ♘c5 15 ♗d4 ♗xd4 16 ♕xd4 ♗d7 17 ♘b5 b6 18 ♖e1

♜e8 19 ♝g4 f5 20 ♝f3 ♜c8
21 ♞c3 ♜f8 22 ♝d1 ♜f7 ½–½
Davies–Chekhov, Gausdal International 1990.

8	...	dc
9	♝b5+	♞6d7
10	♝f4!	♝g7
11	♞d5	e5! *(35)*

This is clearly the only move, since 11 ... 0–0? 12 ♝c7 ♕e8 13 ♞b6 ♜a6 14 dc was a catastrophe in Alexandria–Stadler, Belgrade 1982.

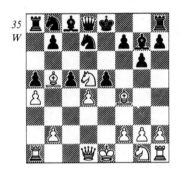

35
W

12 de

Perović analyses 12 ♝xe5 ♝xe5 13 de 0–0 14 ♞f3 ♞c6 15 ♝xc6 bc 16 ♞e3 ♝a6, which is clearly rather awkward for White.

12	...	0–0
13	♞f3	♞c6

13 ... ♞b6 14 ♞c3?! (14 ♞xb6 ♕xb6 15 0–0 ♞c6 16 h3 and White can aim for play against c5.) 14 ... ♝e6 15 ♞e4 ♞d5 16 ♝g5 ♕c7 17 ♜c1 b6 18 0–0 ♞d7 19 ♝xd7 ♕xd7 20 ♞f6+ ♞xf6 was pleasant for Black in Högn–Diaz, Limburg 1988.

14 ♝g5!

As in the note to White's 12th, 14 ♝xc6 bc 15 ♞e3 ♝a6 is troublesome, so White disrupts the black kingside.

14	...	f6
15	♞xf6+	

15 ef is well met by 15 ... ♞xf6.

15	...	♞xf6
16	♝xc6	♕xd1+
17	♜xd1	bc
18	ef	♝xf6
19	♝xf6	♜xf6
20	♜d8+	

A fairly forced sequence has led to a sharp ending. White's king must be activated; for this purpose 20 0–0 ♝g4 is clearly no good.

20	...	♜f8
21	♜xf8+	♔xf8
22	♔d2	♜b8
23	♔c3	♝e6
24	♜e1	

Perović proposes ♞g5, now or on the next move, as more ambitious, though rather less prudent.

24	...	♝d5
25	♞d2	c4

½–½

Grzesik–G. Hartmann
Bundesliga 1985

1 e4 ♞f6 2 e5 ♞d5 3 d4 d6 4 c4 ♞b6 5 ed cd 6 ♞c3 g6

7	h3	♝g7
8	♞f3	0–0
9	♝e3	

In the main line of the Exchange Variation, one is accustomed to seeing the manoeuvre ♝f1–e2xc4, the loss of tempo in which is clear.

Here White leaves the bishop at home, anticipating ... d5, c5 ♘c4, whereupon the bishop can take the knight directly.

9 ... ♘c6
10 ♖c1

Other moves are inconsistent: **10 d5?!** ♘a5 11 ♗d4 e5! 12 de ♗xe6 13 ♗xg7 ♔xg7 14 ♕d4+ ♕f6 15 b3 d5!∓ 16 c5 ♘d7 17 ♕xf6+ ♘xf6! 18 0-0-0 ♖ac8 19 b4 ♘c6 20 a3 a5∓ Mikac-Khmelnitsky, Šibenik 1989; **10 ♕d2** d5 11 c5 ♘c4 12 ♗xc4 dc 13 0-0 ♗f5 is fine for Black since, although White has gained a tempo over normal lines, it has been used to put the queen on a bad square.

After 10 ♖c1, over-protecting c3, White is ready to seize a useful space advantage with 11 d5.

10 ... e5

After **10 ... d5 11 c5 ♘c4 12 ♗xc4 dc 13 0-0** Black cannot equalise:

(a) **13 ... ♗f5** 14 b3! (Makes good use of the rook on c1; alternatively, 14 ♕a4 gives a normal exchange variation where the rook's improved position is moderately helpful.) 14 ... ♗d3 15 ♖e1 ♘xd4 16 ♘xd4 ♗xd4 17 bc ♗xe3 18 ♖xe3 ♗xc4 19 ♕xd8 ♖fxd8 20 ♖xe7 ♗a6 21 ♖ce1 ♔f8 22 ♖c7 ♖ac8 23 ♖ee7 ♖xc7 24 ♖xc7 gave White a very pleasant ending in Gipslis-Ciocaltea, Bucharest 1968.

(b) **13 ... b6** 14 ♕a4 ♘xd4 (14 ... ♘a5 15 ♖fd1±) 15 ♗xd4

♗xd4 16 ♘xd4 ♕xd4 17 cb ♕xb6 18 ♘d5±.

(c) **13 ... e5** 14 d5 ♘b4 15 b3 ♘d3 16 ♖c2 cb (16 ... e4 17 ♘xe4 ♕xd5 18 ♖xc4) and now, rather than 17 ♖d2? ba!∓ Grzesik-Paulsen, Bundesliga 1985/6, White should play the simple 17 ab ♘b4 18 ♖d2 with some advantage.

11 de

(a) **11 c5??** ed and Black won a pawn in Cording-Hawes, corres. 1979.

(b) **11 d5** ♘d4 (11 ... ♘e7 is less logical when this centralising move is available.) 12 ♘xd4 (12 ♗xd4 ed 13 ♘xd4 ♖e8+ and now 14 ♗e2 drops the c-pawn, whilst 14 ♘ce2? is strongly met by 14 ... ♕f6 or 14 ... ♕h4.) 12 ... ed 13 ♗xd4 ♗h6 (13 ... ♖e8+ 14 ♘e2!?; for 14 ♗e2 see 11 ♗e2) 14 ♖a1 (14 ♖b1 ♖e8+ 15 ♗e2 ♗f5; 14 ♗e2 ♖e8!? or 14 ... ♗xc1) 14 ... ♖e8+ 15 ♗e2 ♘xc4.

(c) **11 ♗e2 ♖e8!?** (11 ... f5 12 d5 ♘e7 is again less logical) gives White two principal options:

(c1) **12 d5** ♘d4 13 ♘xd4 ed 14 ♗xd4 ♗h6 (14 ... ♘xc4?! 15 ♗xg7 ♔xg7 16 ♕d4+ ♘e5 17 f4 ♕h4+ 18 g3 ♕xg3+ 19 ♔d1 ♕h4) 15 0-0 (15 ♖a1 ♘xc4; 15 ♖b1 ♗f5 or 15 ... ♘xc4) 15 ... ♕g5!? 16 ♕d3 ♗f5 17 ♕f3 ♕d2 18 ♗xb6 ab. White's pieces resemble a house of cards.

(c2) **12 de** de 13 c5 e4!? 14 ♘g5 ♗xc3+ 15 ♖xc3 ♘d5 16 ♗c4 ♘xe3 (16 ... ♘xc3) 17 ♗xf7+ (17 ♕xd8 ♘xg2+ 18 ♔f1 ♘xd8∓)

17 ... ♔g7 18 ♕xd8 (18 ♖xe3
♕xd1+ 19 ♔xd1 ♖e5−+) 18 ...
♘xg2+ 19 ♔f1 ♖xd8 20 ♔xg2
h6 21 ♘e6+ ♔xf7 22 ♘xd8+
♘xd8−+.

11 ... de

12 c5 ♘d7

12 ... e4 13 ♗g5 (13 ♘xe4 ♘d5;
13 ♕xd8 ♖xd8 14 ♘d2) 13 ...
♗xc3+ 14 bc ♘d5 15 ♘xe4 ♘xe3
16 ♕xd8 ♘xg2+ 17 ♗xg2.
White's pawns are a mess, but
Black is under some pressure.

13 ♗c4 ♘d4! *(36)*

An alternative plan, involving
a kingside advance, was tried in
Modr−Neckař, Prague 1983: 13
... h6 14 0−0 ♔h7 15 ♘e4 f5.
Now White's sacrifice was over-
zealous: 16 ♘eg5+? hg 17 ♘xg5+
♔h8 18 ♘e6 ♕e7 19 ♘xf8 ♕xf8∓.
Instead, 16 ♘d6 ♘f6 17 ♕a4
would have given White good
prospects.

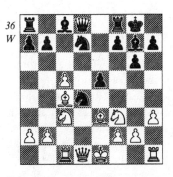

14 ♘e4

14 ♘xd4 ed 15 ♗xd4 ♕e7+
(15 ... ♖e8+ 16 ♘e2 ♕a5+) 16
♘e2 ♗xd4 17 ♕xd4 ♘e5 18 ♕e3
½−½ Kienast−Spiegel, Ingelheim

1989. A possible continuation is
18 ... ♖e8 19 ♗b3 ♗f5 20 0−0
♘d3 21 ♖c3 ♕f8!

14 ... b6

The plan with 14 ... h6 is again
a little cumbersome, leaving f7
rather weak: 15 0−0 ♔h7 16 ♘d6
♕f6 17 ♗xd4 ed 18 b4±.

15 ♗g5

15 ♗d5? ♘xc5 16 ♖xc5 (16
♗xa8 ♘xf3+ 17 ♕xf3 ♘d3+) 16
... bc 17 ♗xa8 ♗a6∓.

15 ... ♕c7

16 ♗e7 ♗b7!

17 c6

17 ♗xf8 ♗xe4 gives Black
reasonable compensation.

17 ... ♕xc6

18 ♘eg5

18 ♗xf7+? ♖xf7 19 ♖xc6 wins
the queen for too much material.

18 ... ♔h8

19 ♗d3?

19 ♘xf7+? ♖xf7 20 ♗xf7 loses
to 20 ... ♕e4+ 21 ♔f1 ♗a6+ 22
♔g1 ♘e2+ 23 ♔h2 ♕f4+, whilst
two messy lines are **19 ♗xf7**
♘xf3+ (19 ... ♘c5) 20 gf and **19
♗xf8 ♖xf8 20 0−0 ♗h6!?**
The text allows the exchange
sacrifice in overwhelming circumstances.

19 ... ♘c5

20 ♗e4 ♕b5!

21 ♗xf8 ♖xf8

White can now only prolong
the struggle by desperate measures
(♖xc5), but instead opts for a
quick and violent finish: 22 ♗xb7
♘d3+ 23 ♔d2 ♘xf2 24 ♘xd4
♕d3+ 25 ♔e1 ♘xd1 26 ♖xd1

♕e3+ 27 ♘e2 ♕xg5 28 ♖f1 f5
0–1.

Klovan–Bagirov
USSR Ch (Alma Ata) 1969

**1 e4 ♘f6 2 e5 ♘d5 3 d4 d6 4 c4
♘b6 5 ed cd 6 ♘f3 g6 7 ♗e2 ♗g7
8 0–0**

8 ♗e3 0–0 9 ♘bd2!? (9 ♘c3
♗g4!? 10 h3 ♗xf3 11 ♗xf3 ♘c6
12 b3 f5! 13 ♕d2 e5 14 de de 15
♗xc6 bc 16 ♕xd8 ♖axd8 17 ♖d1
e4 18 ♘e2 ♖d7! was fine for Black
in Klovan–Vasiukov, USSR Ch
1966.) 9 ... ♗f5 (9 ... ♘c6 10 d5!?)
10 a3 (10 0–0 e5) 10 ... e5 11 d5
♘8d7 12 0–0 ♖c8 13 h3 h5 14
♖c1 ♘c5 15 ♘b3 e4 16 ♘fd4 ♗d7
17 ♕d2 f5 18 ♘xc5 dc 19 ♘b5
♗xb5 20 cb ♕d6 21 ♗f4 ♕f6 22
♖c2 ♔h7 23 ♖d1 ♖f7 24 b4 c4
25 d6 c3 26 ♕e3 ♕e6 gave Black
good play in Gobleja–Kengis,
Daugava Club Ch 1989.

**8 ... 0–0
9 ♗e3**

9 b3 ♘c6 10 ♗b2 is rather a
peculiar idea. 10 ... ♗g4 (10 ...
d5 11 c5 ♘d7 12 ♘c3 e5 13 de
♘dxe5 14 ♘xe5 ♗xe5 15 ♗f3
♗e6∞ SDO) 11 ♕d2 (11 ♘a3 e6
12 h3 ♗xf3 13 ♗xf3 d5 14 ♕d2
♕h4 15 ♖fd1 dc 16 ♗xc6 bc 17
♘xc4 ♘xc4 18 bc ♖fd8∓ Novak–
Pytel, Poland 1971) 11 ... e6 (A
nuance of move order; after the
immediate 11 ... d5, 12 c5 ♘c8 13
b4 could follow, rather than the
knight being ostracised to a3.) 12
♘a3 d5! 13 ♖fd1 (13 c5 ♘c8) 13
... dc 14 ♘xc4 ♘xc4 15 bc ♕b6

16 ♖ab1 ♗f5 17 ♗d3 ♗xd3 18
♕xd3 ♖fd8∓ Karpov–Vaganian,
Leningrad 1969.

**9 ... ♘c6
10 ♘c3**

10 ♘bd2 bolsters the f3 knight,
but is rather a passive move. This
suggests Black should strike in the
centre without delay.

(a) **10 ... ♗g4?!** 11 d5 ♘e5 12
♘xe5 ♗xe2 13 ♕xe2 ♗xe5 14
♘f3 ♗g7 15 ♖ad1 ♘d7 16 b3±
Bronstein–Bagirov, Leningrad
1963.

(b) **10 ... ♗f5?!** 11 d5 ♘b4 (11
... ♘e5!?) 12 ♗d4 ♗h6 13 ♗c3
♗c2 14 ♕c1 ♗d3 (Gipslis–Vasiukov, Leningrad 1968) 15 ♗xd3
♘xd3 16 ♕c2±.

(c) **10 ... e5!?** 11 de (11 d5 ♘d4)
11 ... de 12 ♗c5 ♖e8 13 ♘e4
♕xd1! 14 ♖axd1 ♘d4! 15 ♘xd4 ed
16 ♗f3 ♘xc4 17 ♗xd4 ♘xb2∞
Klovan–Ovanesian, Tallinn 1968.

(d) **10 ... d5 11 c5 ♘d7 12 ♕b3**
(12 ♘b3 e5 13 de ♘dxe5=) and
Black must now decide how far to
push the e-pawn.

(d1) **12 ... e6** poses White the
problems of finding a plan. Probably ♖ac1, ♖fd1 is the right way
to begin, since the knights then
have more flexibility. The queen,
rather awkwardly placed on b3, is
still discouraging ... e6–e5. Here
are two examples of how White
should not proceed: 13 ♗b5 h6
14 ♗xc6 bc 15 ♗f4 ♖e8 16 ♖fe1
f6 17 ♕c2 g5 18 ♗e3 ♘f8 19 ♘b3
e5 20 h3 e4 21 ♘h2 f5 with an
overwhelming position for Black,

Hultqvist–Hjorth, corres.; 13 ♖fe1
h6 14 ♖ad1 g5 15 h3 ♘f6 16 ♘h2
♗d7 17 a3 b6 18 cb ab 19 ♖c1
♕b8 20 ♗b5 ♖c8∓ Hasan–
Hecht, Nice ol 1974.

(d2) **12 ... e5** seems most logical,
but is perhaps a little drawish. 13
de (13 ♕xd5 ed 14 ♘xd4 ♘xd4 15
♗xd4 ♘xc5!) 13 ... ♘dxe5 14
♘xe5 ♘xe5 15 ♖fd1 (15 ♗d4
♖e8) 15 ... ♘g4 (Maybe best is 15
... d4!? 16 ♘f3 and now either 16
... ♘xf3+ 17 ♗xf3 ♗e6 or 16 ...
♘c6!?) 16 ♗xg4 ♗xg4 17 f3 ♗e6
18 ♕xb7 ♖b8 (18 ... ♕c8!? 19
♕xc8 ♖fxc8 20 ♖ac1 ♗xb2 21
♗c2 ♗g7∞ Hultqvist–
Lundgren, corres. 1981) 19 ♕xa7
♖xb2 20 ♘b3? (20 ♖ab1 d4!; 20
c6! ♕h4!? may offer White some
advantage.) 20 ... ♕h4 21 ♕c7
♗h6! 22 ♗d4 (22 ♕e5 ♖e2 23 f4
♗g7) 22 ... ♗f4 23 ♕xf4 ♖xg2+
24 ♔xg2 ♗h3+ 25 ♔g1 ♕xf4
26 ♖d2 ♖e8 27 c6 ♕xf3 28 c7
♖e4 0–1 Ničevski–Jansa, Athens
1969.

| 10 | ... | ♗g4 |
| 11 | b3 | d5 |

11 ... e6, to meet 12 ♕d2 d5 13
c5 not with 13 ... ♘d7 14 ♖ac1
♗xf3 15 ♗xf3 f5 16 ♘e2±, but
13 ... ♘c8!, is a good idea, except
that White can take advantage of
the situation with **12 h3!** ♗xf3 13
♗xf3 d5 (13 ... ♕f6 14 ♘e2 d5
15 c5) 14 cd!. Black then has
problems after either 14 ... ♘xd5
15 ♘xd5 ed 16 ♖c1± Marić–
Hulak, Novi Sad 1974, or 14 ...
ed 15 a4 a5 16 ♘b5± Minić–

Kovačević, Zagreb 1974.
   11 ... e5 12 d5 ♗xf3 (12 ... ♘e7
13 ♖c1 ♘f5 14 ♗g5±) 13 ♗xf3
♘d4 14 ♗e2 is quite pleasant for
White, since ... f5 will be strongly
met by f4.

| 12 | c5 | ♘c8 *(37)* |

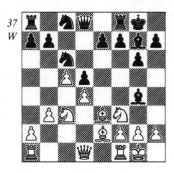

37
W

13 b4
13 h3 is rather illogical. 13 ...
♗xf3 14 ♗xf3 e6 15 ♖c1 (15
♖b1 ♘8e7 16 g4 e5!; 15 b4 a6 16
b5?! ab 17 ♘xb5 ♘8e7 18 ♗g5
♕a5 19 ♗xe7 ♘xe7 20 ♕d3 ♘c6
21 a4 b6!∓ 22 cb? ♕xb6 Toran–
Korchnoi, Uppsala 1956; 15 ♕d2
♘8e7 16 ♘b5?! ♘f5! 17 ♗g4 a6
18 ♗xf5 ab 19 ♗c2 and now
Browne–Fischer, Rovinj Zagreb
1970, became unclear after 19 ...
♖a3? 20 b4!; instead 19 ... b4! was
positionally winning, as Fischer
realised, presumably a little too
late.) 15 ... ♘8e7 16 ♘e2 ♘f5=
Schmidt–Jansa, Marianske Lazne
1962.
   13 ♖c1 e6 14 ♕d2 ♗xf3 15
♗xf3 ♘8e7 16 ♘e2 b5!? 17 a4 b4
18 ♗h6?! ♗xh6 19 ♕xh6 ♘f5 20
♕f4 h5 21 g3 ♕f6 22 ♖fd1 was

Roski–Nikolaiczuk, Porz Open 1986. Black could now have struck with 22 ... ♘cxd4! 23 ♘xd4 e5 24 ♕d2 ♘xd4 25 ♗xd5 ♖ad8 26 ♗g2 ♘f3+ 27 ♗xf3 ♖xd2 28 ♖xd2 ♕xf3 29 c6 ♖c8 30 c7 ♕b7–+.

13 ♕d2 e6 14 ♖ad1 ♘8e7 15 ♘h4 ♗xe2 16 ♘xe2 b6! White has d4 well protected, but cannot reply with b5 here: swings and roundabouts! Kuijpers–Kavalek, Beverwijk 1967, continued 17 ♖c1 ♖c8 18 b4 bc∓ 19 ♖xc5 (19 dc d4; 19 bc ♘a5) 19 ... ♕b6 20 a3 ♘b8! 21 ♗g5 f6 22 ♗e3 ♘d7 23 ♖xc8 ♖xc8 24 ♖c1 ♕a6 25 ♖xc8+ ♘xc8 and White's weaknesses were acute.

13 ♘e1 ♗xe2 14 ♘xe2 b6! 15 ♖c1 e6 16 ♕d2 bc 17 ♖xc5 ♕b6 gave Black satisfactory play in Hübner–Timman, Sarajevo (2) 1991: 18 ♕c3 ♘b4 19 ♘d3 ♘a6 20 ♖c6 ♕b7 21 ♕c2 ♘e7 22 ♖c3 ♖fc8 23 ♖c1 ♖xc3 24 ♕xc3 ♖c8 25 ♕d2 ♖xc1+ 26 ♕xc1 ♕c6 27 ♕d2 ♘f5 28 g4 ♘h4 29 ♘e1 ♗f8 30 ♗g5 ♗b4 31 ♕e3 ♗xe1 32 ♗xh4 ♗b4 33 ♘f4 ♗f8 34 ♘h5 gh 35 ♕g5+ ♔h8 36 ♕f6+ ½–½.

13 ...   a6

An interesting new idea in Moroz–Palatnik, Kherson 1989, was to omit ... a6, possibly to play it with greater effect later (e.g. when a knight on a4 interferes with the support of the b-pawn): **13 ... ♗xf3** 14 ♗xf3 e6 15 b5 (15 ♖b1 invites transposition to the main line, but more consistent

with Black's idea is 15 ... b6!? 16 b5 ♘a5 and now 17 c6 gives Black the d6 square, whilst 17 ♘a4?! allows 17 ... a6!, breaking up White's pawns.) 15 ... ♘a5 16 ♗e2 b6 17 ♕d2 (In view of the threat of 17 ... bc, White must make one concession or another.) 17 ... a6 (Good, now that 18 a4 drops an exchange. Instead 17 ... bc 18 dc d4 19 ♖ad1 e5 20 ♘e4 gives Black rather a cumbersome pawn centre.) 18 ♖ac1 bc 19 dc ab 20 ♘xb5 ♘c6 21 ♘d6 ♘6e7 22 ♘xc8 ♕xc8 23 c6 ♕c7 24 ♗c5 ♗e5 25 g3 ♗d6 26 ♗b5 ♖fc8 27 ♗e3 ♖a3 28 ♖c2 ♖b8 29 ♗d3 e5 30 ♖fc1 d4 31 ♗g5 ♘d5 32 ♗e4 ♘c3 33 ♗g2 ♖ba8 34 ♗f6 ♖xa2 35 h4 ♖xc2 36 ♖xc2 ♗e7 37 ♗xe7 ♕xe7 38 ♖b2 ♖c8 39 ♖b7 ♕e6 40 ♕b2 ♔g7 (40 ... e4 41 ♖d7) 41 ♔h2 ♘d5 42 ♗h3 ♕xc6 43 ♗xc8 ♕xc8 and an ending resulted which White was able to survive.

The immediate **13 ... e6?!** gives White the advantage after 14 b5 ♘a5 (14 ... ♗xf3?? 15 bc ♗xe2 16 cb+–) 15 ♘d2!

Note that the b-pawn is defended tactically: **13 ... ♘xb4?!** 14 ♖b1 ♘a6 15 ♗xa6±. 13 ... a6 has the point that 14 a4? fails to 14 ... ♘xb4 15 ♖b1 a5, so White must defend the b-pawn directly in order to advance further.

14   ♖b1

14 ♕d2 e6 15 ♖fd1 ♘8e7 16 ♘e1 ♗xe2 17 ♘xe2 ♘f5 18 ♘f3 h6 19 a4 ♖e8 20 b5 ♘a5 21 ♕c3

♘c4 22 ♘d2 ♘cxe3 23 fe e5!∓
was an excellent demonstration
of Black's optimum strategy in
Westerinen–Hort, Leningrad
1967.

14 ♕b3 e6 **15 ♖fd1** ♘8e7 **16** b5
♘a5 **17 ♕b4** ab **18 ♘xb5** ♘ec6 **19
♕e1** ♘c4∓ Zuidema–Hort,
Örebro 1966.

14 ... e6
15 a4 ♘8e7

15 ... b6!? 16 b5 ab 17 ab ♘a5
18 ♘a4 (18 c6 is very double-
edged, since Black's knights then
have superb prospects.) 18 ... ♘c4
19 ♗f4 ♗xf3 20 ♗xf3 ♕h4 21
g3 ♕f6 gave Black good counterplay in Janošević–Knežević, Kral-
jevo 1967.

16 b5 ab
17 ab ♗xf3

17 ... ♘a5!? is best met by 18
♘e5 ♗xe2 19 ♕xe2 ♗xe5 20 de
♘f5 with unclear play. Instead
Van Baarle–Van der Tak, Ghent
1986 continued 18 ♖b4?! ♘f5 19
♖e1 (19 ♗g5) 19 ... ♗xf3 20
♗xf3 ♘c4 21 b6 ♘a5! 22 ♘b5
♘c6 23 ♖a4 ♕f6 and the d-pawn
was doomed.

18 ♗xf3 ♘a5
19 ♗e2

19 ♗g5 h6 20 ♗xe7 ♕xe7 21
♘a4 (21 ♕d3 ♕g5 22 ♖b4 ♘c4
23 ♖xc4 dc 24 ♕xc4 ♖ad8 25
♖d1 ♕f4 was an intriguing, but
unconvincing exchange sacrifice in
Janošević–Gheorghiu, Skopje
1968) 21 ... ♘c4 22 ♖b4 ♖a5 23
♗e2 ♖d8 24 b6 ♕h4 25 c6 bc 26
♘c5 ♖b5 27 ♖xb5 cb 28 b7 ♖b8!∓

is old analysis of Boleslavsky's.

19 ... ♘f5
20 ♕d2 h6

20 ... ♘c4 21 ♗xc4 dc 22
♕e2 ♗xd4 23 ♖fd1 e5 24 ♗xd4
followed by 25 ♕xc4 is promising
for White, but a decent alternative
is **20 ... ♘xe3** 21 fe ♗h6 22 ♖f3
(22 ♖b4!?) 22 ... f5 23 ♖b4 g5 24
♘a4 g4 25 ♖f1 ♕g5 26 ♖f4 ♕e7
27 ♖f1 ♕g5 repeating, as in
Krzyszton–Ekström, corres. 1972.

21 ♖fd1 ♖e8
22 b6 *(38)*

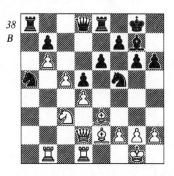

38
B

22 ♖b4 is an alternative
approach, intending ♘a4–b6.
Fienisch–Matthey, corres. 1982
continued 22 ... e5 23 de d4 24
♗xd4 ♘xd4 25 ♖xd4 ♕c7 26 f4
♘b3 27 ♕e3 ♘xd4 28 ♕xd4 ♖ed8
29 ♘d5 and White had more than
enough for the exchange.

After **22 b6**, White threatens
♘b5–c7, so Black must hit back
in the centre. After **22 ... e5 23 ♘b5**
Black has two ways to capture on
d4:

(a) **23 ... ed** 24 ♗f4 ♗e5!? (24

... ♘c4 25 ♕c2 ♘a3 26 ♘xa3
♖xa3 27 ♗c7 ♕g5 28 ♗b5 ♖c3
29 ♕e2 ♘h4 30 ♗g3 ♖c8 31 c6±)
25 ♗xe5 ♖xe5 26 ♘c7 ♖c8 27
♕xa5 ♖xe2 28 ♕b5 ♖c2 29 ♖bc1
has generally been given as good
for White, but 29 ... ♖xc1 30 ♖xc1
♕g5 threatens ... ♘h4, e.g. 31
♖e1? ♘h4 32 ♖e8+ ♔h7! 33
g3 ♖xe8 34 ♘xe8 ♕c1+ 35 ♕f1
♘f3+ 36 ♔g2 ♘e1+ 37 ♔h1
d3−+.

(b) 23 ... ♘xd4 24 ♗xd4 (24
♘c7 ♘ac6 25 ♗b5 ♘xb5 26 ♖xb5
d4 27 ♗xh6 ♖e7 28 ♗xg7 ♔xg7
29 ♘xa8 ♕xa8 gave White an
unimportant material advantage
in Wagner–Packroff, corres. 1982)
24 ... ed 25 ♘c7 ♘c4! 26 ♗xc4
(26 ♕e1 ♘b2!? 27 ♖xb2 d3 28
♘xe8? ♕xe8 29 ♖bb1 de∓ was a
postal game Mende–Demian, but
28 ♖xd3 improves.) 26 ... dc as
analysed by Boleslavsky, gives
Black fine compensation.

However, Klovan and Bagirov
found a simpler solution to the
problems of this complicated position.

½–½

Geller–Vaganian
Moscow 1985

**1 e4 ♘f6 2 e5 ♘d5 3 d4 d6 4 ♘f3
g6 5 ♗e2 ♗g7 6 0-0 0-0 7 c4
♘b6 8 ed cd**

A rather unusual, though perfectly feasible move order. White
could now play 9 h3 ♘c6 10 ♘c3
to avoid 9 ... ♗g4, but Geller,

apparently, was not too concerned
about this possibility.

9   ♘c3   ♘c6
10   h3   ♗f5
11   ♗f4   h6

With this move, Black prepares
12 ... e5, by preventing ♗g5 in
reply. Naturally, Black has other
options.

(a) **11 ... d5?** is ineffective here
since 12 c5 ♘c4 does not hit a
bishop on e3. Karpov–McKay,
Stockholm 1969 continued 13 b3
♘4a5 14 ♖c1 b6 15 cb ab 16 ♕d2
♘b7 17 ♘b5 ♖c8 18 ♖c3 ♕d7 19
♖fc1 f6 20 ♗c7!+−.

(b) **11 ... ♖e8** 12 ♖c1 e5 (Else
13 d5) 13 ♗g5 ♕b8 (13 ... ♗f6
14 ♗xf6 ♕xf6 15 de de 16 c5 is
very comfortable for White.) 14 d5
(14 de?! de 15 c5 ♘c8 16 ♘d5 e4∓
Buchner–Paulsen,   Bundesliga
1980) 14 ... ♘d4 15 ♘xd4 cd 16
♘b5 and White wins a pawn.

(c) **11 ... ♖c8** 12 ♖c1 e5 13 de
(13 ♗g5!?) 13 ... de 14 ♗g5 f6
15 ♗e3 ♗e6 16 ♘b5 e4 17 ♘fd4
♘xd4 18 ♕xd4 f5= Archvadze–
Suetin, Novosibirsk 1971.

(d) **11 ... e5** 12 ♗g5 ♕c8!? 13
♗e3?! (13 de) 13 ... ♘b4 14 de
♘xc4 15 ♗xc4 ♕xc4 16 ♕xd6
♖fd8 17 ♕c5 ♕xc5 18 ♗xc5
♘d3∓ 19 ♗a3 a6 20 g4 ♗e6 21
♖ab1 ♘f4 22 ♔h2 ♖d3 23 ♔g3
♗xe5 24 ♖be1 ♗c7 25 ♖d1
♖ad8 26 ♖xd3 ♖xd3 27 ♖d1 b5
0–1 L. Cooper–Mortazavi, Oakham 1990.

12   ♖c1

Vaganian suggests the pawn

sacrifice **12 d5** ♘a5 13 ♘d4 ♘axc4 14 b3 ♘e5 15 ♘xf5 gf 16 ♕d2, though no one has been sufficiently convinced to try this out in practice.

12 ♕d2 g5 13 ♗e3 (13 ♗g3?! d5 14 c5 ♘c4 15 ♕c1 e6! 16 b3 ♘4a5 17 ♖d1 b6∓ 18 ♕a3 bc 19 ♕xc5 ♖e8! 20 ♘b5 ♗f8∓ Ghinda–Ghizdavu, Timişoara 1972) 13 ... d5 14 c5 (14 ♘xd5?! ♘xd5 15 cd ♕xd5 16 ♖ac1 ♖fd8! 17 ♗c4 ♕e4!∓ (threatening ... ♗xh3) L. Å. Schneider–Alburt, Reykjavik Open 1982) 14 ... ♘c4 15 ♗xc4 dc 16 d5 (16 ♖fd1) 16 ... ♘b4 17 h4 (17 ♗d4 f6 18 ♗e3 ♗d3∓ Faibisovich–Bagirov, Kiev 1970) 17 ... ♗d3 18 hg! hg 19 ♗xg5 ♘xd5!∓ 20 ♖fe1 f6 21 ♗h6 ♘xc3 22 ♗xg7 ♔xg7 23 ♕xc3 ♖h8 24 ♘d4 ½–½ (24 ... ♔f7 25 ♘e6 ♕d5 provides strong threats on the h-file.) Adorjan–Eales, Groningen 1970.

12 ... e5

Having defended the c3 knight, White was threatening 13 d5 (13 ... ♘a5? 14 b3).

13 ♗e3

The illogical 13 de?! de 14 ♗e3 ♘d4 gives Black the advantage.

13 ... e4
14 ♘d2 d5 *(39)*

Varying from **14 ... ♖e8** which brought him success in Karpov–Vaganian, Leningrad 1969. 15 ♘b3?! d5 16 cd ♘b4!∓ 17 ♕d2 ♘4xd5 18 ♘c5 ♘xe3 19 fe ♕g5 20 ♔h1 ♖ad8 21 ♖c2 ♕g3 22 ♕c1 ♘d5 23 ♘xd5 ♖xd5 24 ♗b5 ♖c8

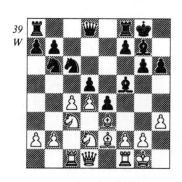

25 ♗a4 b6 26 ♘xe4 ♗xe4 27 ♖xc8+ ♔h7 28 ♖c2 ♖h5 29 ♔g1 ♖xh3 30 ♖xf7 ♕h2+ 31 ♔f1 ♕h1+ 32 ♔e2 ♕xg2+ 33 ♖f2 ♕g4+ 34 ♔d2 ♖h1 0–1. 15 g4 is certainly an improvement, when Black must go 'all-in' with 15 ... ♕h4 16 gf (16 ♔h2 ♘xd4 17 ♗xd4 ♗xd4 18 gf ♗e5+) 16 ... gf! 17 ♘b3 f4.

According to Vaganian, also pleasant for Black is **14 ... ♘xd4** 15 ♘dxe4 ♘xe2+ 16 ♕xe2 ♖e8.

15 cd ♘xd5
16 ♘xd5 ♕xd5
17 ♗c4 ♕d8

The more active 17 ... ♕d7? fails to 18 g4 ♗e6 19 d5 ♗xd5 20 ♘xe4.

18 d5?

Although very risky, 18 g4 was essential. 18 ... ♗c8!? 19 ♘xe4 ♘a5! 20 ♗e2 f5 21 ♘c5 ♕h4 followed by 22 ... b6 gives Black a strong attack for just one pawn.

18 ... ♘e5
19 ♗c5 ♖e8
20 ♗b5 ♘d3!
21 ♗xe8 ♕xe8
22 ♖c2 ♘xc5

23	♖xc5	e3
24	♕c1	

24 ♖e1 and 24 ♕e2 both lose on the spot to 24 ... ♗d4!

24	...	ed
25	♕xd2	♕e5!

Two bishops generally overpower rook and pawn, especially here where coupled with a centralised queen aiming at the white king. The game finished 26 ♖e1 ♕d6 27 ♖cc1 ♖d8 28 ♕a5 ♗d4 29 ♖cd1 ♗c5 30 ♕a4 ♕g3 31 ♖e8+ ♖xe8 32 ♕xe8+ ♔g7 33 ♖d2 ♗xh3 34 ♕e4 ♗f5 35 ♕c4 ♕d6 36 a3 ♗b6 37 ♕c3+ ♔h7 38 b4 h5 39 g3 ♗e4 0–1.

Sigurjonsson–Alburt
Reykjavik 1982

1 e4 ♘f6 2 e5 ♘d5 3 d4 d6 4 c4 ♘b6 5 ed cd 6 ♘c3 g6 7 h3 ♗g7 8 ♘f3 0–0 9 ♗e2 ♘c6 10 0–0 ♗f5

11	♗e3	d5
12	c5	

12 g4?! ♗e4! 13 ♘g5 h6! 14 ♘gxe4 de 15 c5 ♘d5 16 ♘xe4 f5 17 gf gf 18 ♘c3 f4 19 ♗c4 e6 20 ♕xg4 fe 21 ♕xe6+ ♔h8 22 ♘xd5 ef+ 23 ♖xf2 ♖xf2 24 ♔xf2 ♕g5!∓ E. Holland–Burgess, Muswell Hill 1989.

12	...	♘c4
13	♗xc4	

13 ♗c1 does not work with Black's pawn on h7: 13 ... b6 14 g4?! ♗c8 15 b3 bc! 16 bc cd 17 ♘xd5 d3∓ Janošević–Hort, Skopje 1969.

13	...	dc
14	♕a4 (40)	

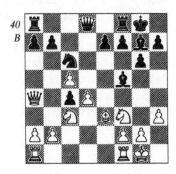

40
B

14	...	e5!?

This excellent move has caused this line's popularity to plummet, since White seems barely able to obtain equality. The older move **14 ... ♗d3** is probably adequate, though Black must play with extreme care: **15 ♖fd1 ♕a5** (15 ... ♘xd4? 16 ♘xd4 ♗xd4 17 ♖xd3!; 15 ... f5 16 d5 ♘e5 17 ♘e1 f4 18 ♗d4 ♕c8 19 ♘xd3 cd 20 ♗xe5 ♗xe5 21 ♕c4±; 15 ... e5 16 d5 ♘d4 17 ♘e1!±; 15 ... ♕e8!?) **16 ♕xa5 ♘xa5 17 ♘e1** (17 b4!? ♘c6 18 b5 ♘b4) **17 ... ♗f5** and now:

(a) **18 ♖ac1** ♘c6 19 g4 ♗d7 20 d5 ♘b4 21 b3 cb (21 ... ♘xa2!? 22 ♘xa2 cb∞ Dvoretsky–Bagirov, Tbilisi 1973) 22 ab e6!= Bagirov.

(b) **18 d5** h5 (18 ... b5!?) 19 ♖ac1 ♖ac8 20 f3 ♖fd8 21 g4 hg 22 hg ♗d7 23 ♔f2 f5!= 24 g5 e6! 25 c6?! bc 26 de ♗xe6 27 ♗xa7 ♖xd1 28 ♖xd1 c5! turned out well for Black in Pritchett–Schmidt, Pula 1975.

(c) **18 g4** ♗d7 **19 f4** (Alburt's recommendation 19 d5 can be met by 19 ... e6 or 19 ... f5!?) 19 ... f5 20 g5 e6 21 ♘f3 ♖fd8 22 d5!? ed 23 ♗d4 ♗e6 24 ♘b5 gave White good compensation in Conoval–Balendo, corres. 1979.

15 ♖fd1

At first sight it appears that **15 ♕xc4** is simply good for White, but after 15 ... ed 16 ♖fd1 ♗e6! the queen has no especially good square. 17 ♕a4 (or 17 ♕b5) is strongly met by the easily over-looked 17 ... ♗d7!. Therefore the queen cannot remain in touch with d4; on 17 ♕e2 (or 17 ♕f1) Black's most incisive move is 17 ... b6, since 18 cb? ♕xb6 is no good for White.

A more obviously harmless move is **15 de**. After 15 ... ♗d3, 16 ♗g5 f6 17 ef ♗xf6 18 ♗h6 ♗g7 19 ♗xg7 ♔xg7 20 ♖fe1 ♖xf3! shattered White's king position in Vujaković–Begovac, Oberwart 1981, whilst 16 ♖fd1 ♘xe5 17 ♘xe5 ♗xe5 18 ♖ac1 ♕e8! (Bagirov) clearly gives White nothing.

More intriguing is the piece sacrifice **15 d5** ♘d4 16 ♘e1 (16 ♘d2 ♗d3) 16 ... b5! 17 ♘xb5 (17 cb ♕xb6) 17 ... ♘xb5 18 ♕xc4 (18 ♕xb5 ♕xd5) 18 ... ♖b8 19 ♘f3 ♕f6 though Black's kingside play is rather quicker than White's pawn roller.

15 ... ♘xd4
16 ♘xd4 ed
17 ♗xd4 ♗xd4!

18 ♕xc4 ♗xf2+!

In this way Black maintains material equality and ensures counterplay against the white king.

19 ♔xf2 ♕f6

The most ambitious, though 19 ... ♕g5 is perfectly adequate, an important tactical point being 20 ♖d6 ♖fe8 21 ♕d4 ♗e4!= Stoica–Hazai, Hungary 1976.

20 ♕d4 ♕xd4+
21 ♖xd4 ♖ac8

Probably the correct rook, despite leaving the a-pawn un-defended, since Black wishes to control the d-file in some lines.

22 b4

22 ♖b4 ♖fd8 23 ♖d1 ♖xd1 24 ♘xd1 ♖xc5 25 ♖xb7 ♖c2+ gives Black at least enough play.

22 ... b6
23 ♘d5 bc
24 ♘e7+

Black has rather the better of a highly tactical ending. Now 24 ... ♔h8 would avoid the possibility of 25 ♘xf5+, but leave the king further from the action.

24 ... ♔g7
25 ♘xc8

Naturally 25 ♘xf5+ gf 26 bc ♖xc5 is unpleasant for White, but is a reasonable drawing attempt.

25 ... cd
26 ♘xa7 ♖d8!
27 b5 d3
28 a4!?

28 b6 d2! 29 ♖d1 ♗c2 30 b7 ♗xd1 31 ♘c6 ♗f3! 32 ♘xd8 d1♕ and Black, a tempo ahead, wins.

28	...	d2
29	♖d1!	

29 b6 ♖d6! breaks the coordination of White's pawns with the knight: 30 a5 d1♕ 31 ♖xd1 ♖xd1 32 b7 ♖b1 33 a6 ♗e4 34 ♘c8 ♗xb7−+.

29	...	♗c2
30	♔e2	♗xa4?

Here Alburt missed a probable win with 30 ... ♖e8+!, giving up the d-pawn to stop ♘c6 gaining a tempo on the rook: 31 ♔xd2 ♗xd1 32 ♔xd1 ♔f6 33 b6 ♔e6 34 a5 ♔d6 35 a6 ♔c5 36 b7 ♔b6 and Black stops the pawns.

After the text the game finished 31 ♖xd2 ♖xd2+ 32 ♔xd2 ♗b3 33 ♔d3 ♗d5 34 g3 ♗g2 35 b6 ♔f6 36 ♔d4 ♔e6 37 ♔c5 ♔d7 38 ♘b5 g5 39 ♘d6 f5 40 ♘xf5 ♗xh3 41 ♘h6 ♗e6 42 ♔d4 ♔c6 43 ♔e5 ♗b3 44 ♔f6 ♔xb6 45 ♔xg5 ♔c5 46 ♔f6 ♔d4 47 ♔g7 ½−½.

Khmelnitsky–Palatnik
Ukrainian Ch (Kherson) 1989

1 e4 ♘f6 2 e5 ♘d5 3 d4 d6 4 c4 ♘b6 5 ed cd

6	h3

There are many move orders which reach the main-line position after ten moves, all with their subtleties. 6 h3 cuts out any ... ♗g4 ideas, but makes a plan without a kingside fianchetto feasible for Black: 6 ... ♘c6 7 ♘c3 ♗f5 8 ♗e3 e6 9 ♘f3 ♗e7 10 ♗e2 0-0 11 0-0 d5 12 c5 ♘c4 13 ♗xc4 dc 14 ♕a4 ♗d3 15 ♖fd1 ♗f6 16

♖ac1 ♕a5 is OK for Black. After 6 ♘c3, however, 6 ... ♗f5 is brutally treated: 7 ♕f3! ♕c8 (7 ... ♕d7 8 c5) 8 c5 dc 9 dc ♕xc5 10 ♕xb7 (or 10 ♗e3!?) guarantees White some advantage.

6	...	g6
7	♘f3	♗g7
8	♗e2	0-0
9	0-0	♘c6
10	♘c3	♗f5
11	♗g5	

This move aims to provoke ... h6 before dropping the bishop back to e3, but gives Black fewer options than 11 ♗f4.

11	...	h6
12	♗e3	

Instead 12 ♗h4 is unimpressive. After 12 ... g5 13 ♗g3 e5 14 de (14 d5 ♘a5!?) 14 ... de 15 ♖c1 e4 16 ♘d2 ♖e8 17 c5 ♘d5 18 ♘xd5 ♕xd5 19 ♘c4 ♕xd1 20 ♖fxd1 ♘d4 Black stood well in Cuasnicu–Darcyl, Buenos Aires 1983.

12	...	d5
13	c5	

Karpov's original idea in playing 11 ♗f4 h6 12 ♗e3 was to maintain a pawn on c4, using the weakness of h6 to gain a tempo in some lines. However, this plan brought only limited success. **13 b3 dc 14 bc ♖c8** (14 ... e5 15 d5 e4 16 ♘d4; 14 ... ♘a5 15 c5 ♘d5 16 ♘xd5 ♕xd5 17 ♕d2 ♘c6 should just about equalise.) **15 ♖c1 ♘a5 16 c5 ♘bc4 17 ♗f4** and Black has two good methods: **17 ... g5 18 ♗g3 b6** (18 ... ♕d7

19 ♖e1!? intending ♘e5) 19 ♗xc4 ♘xc4 and now Karpov–A. Petrosian, Rostov-on-Don 1971 finished 20 ♕e2? bc! 21 d5 (21 ♕xc4? cd) 21 ... ♗xc3 22 ♖xc3 ♘b6∓ ½–½. Instead 20 cb is roughly level.

17 ... e5 was Boleslavsky's idea, to undermine the c5 pawn (now we see the reason for 14 ... ♖c8) 18 ♘xe5 ♘xe5 19 ♗xe5 ♗xe5 20 de ♖xc5 21 f4 (21 ♕a4?! ♕b6 22 ♕f4 ♕b2 23 ♕e3 ♖fc8 and White was getting pushed around in Beliavsky–Jansa, Sukhumi 1972.) 21 ... ♕b6 22 ♕d4 ♖d8 23 ♕e3 ♖c6 24 ♕xb6 ♖xb6 25 ♖fd1 just about maintained the balance in Domankusiv–Fauth, corres. 1986.

In this line Black can dismantle the pawn centre quite easily and one feels that it is White who is trying to equalise.

| 13 | ... | ♘c4 |
| 14 | ♗c1 | |

This is the new idea from the Ukraine! After the natural 14 ♗xc4 dc, the move ... h6 turns out to be fairly useful. 15 ♕d2 does exploit the weakness, but puts the queen on a bad square: 15 ... ♗d3 16 ♖fe1 g5 17 b3 f5 18 bc ♗xc4 Sher–Schmidt, Riga 1976. After **15 ♕a4**, as in the line after 11 ♗e3, Black can try 15 ... ♗d3 or 15 ... e5.

(a) **15 ... ♗d3** 16 ♖fd1 ♕a5 17 ♕xa5 ♘xa5 18 ♘e1 (18 b4!?) 18 ... ♗f5 19 ♖d2 (19 g4!?) 19 ... g5 gave the bishop some squares in Stean–Timman, Islington 1970. There followed 20 ♖ad1 ♖fd8 21

d5 ♖d7 22 ♘c2 ♖ad8 23 ♘b4 e6 24 g4 ♗d3 25 d6 ♖c8 26 ♘a4 ♗e4 27 ♗d4 ♘c6 28 ♗xg7 ♔xg7 29 ♖e1 f5 30 ♘xc6 ♖xc6 and Black won by creeping in on the queenside.

(b) **15 ... e5** 16 ♖fd1 (16 de ♘xe5 17 ♘xe5 ♗xe5 18 ♗xh6 ♕h4 gives Black a useful attack; 16 ♕xc4 ed 17 ♖fd1 ♗e6 18 ♕a4?! ♗d7!) 16 ... ed 17 ♘xd4 ♘xd4 18 ♗xd4 ♗xd4 19 ♕xc4 ♗xf2+ 20 ♔xf2. Now 20 ... ♕f6 is Sigurjonsson–Alburt, with some useful extra room for the black king, whilst 20 ... ♕g5 21 ♖d6 ♖ae8 22 ♕d4 ♗e4 23 ♘xe4 ♕f4+ was also perfectly satisfactory in Dvoretsky–Arkhipov, Moscow 1979.

| 14 | ... | b6 |
| 15 | b3 | bc!? |

Black logically blows open the long diagonal. The safer, but less ambitious 15 ... ♘4a5 was played in Brodsky–Palatnik in a later round at Kherson 1989. With accurate play Black survived, though after 16 cb ab 17 ♗e3 ♗e4 18 ♖c1 ♗xf3 19 ♗xf3 e6 20 ♘b5 ♕d7 21 ♗e2 ♖fc8 22 ♕d2 h5 23 ♗f4 ♗f8 24 ♖c2 ♗b4 25 ♕e3 ♘e7 26 ♖xc8+ ♖xc8 27 g4 hg 28 hg ♘ec6 29 ♔g2 ♗f8 30 ♗h6 ♕e7 31 ♖h1 White still maintained pressure.

16	bc	cd
17	♘xd5	*(41)*
17	...	e6

The first tactical point is that **17 ... d3** fails due to the weakness of Black's kingside: **18 ♗xd3**

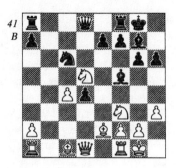

41
B

♗xd3 19 ♕xd3 ♗xa1 20 ♗xh6
♗g7. With a pawn at h7, White
would have insufficient compensation; without it, Black seems lost.
One strong possibility is 21 ♗g5!?
intending ♖e1 or ♕e4–h4 (21 ...
f6? 22 ♕xg6!+−), but Khmelnitsky's preference has been 21 ♗xg7
♔xg7 22 ♕c3+ and now:

(a) 22 ... ♔g8 23 ♖e1! (Threatens 24 ♖xe7) 23 ... ♕a5 (23 ...
♖e8 24 ♘g5 e5 25 ♕f3 ♕xg5
26 ♘f6+ wins.) 24 ♕e3 ♕xa2?
(Khmelnitsky analysed 24 ... ♔g7
25 ♘d4 ♖ac8 26 ♘xc6 ♖xc6 27
♕d4+ f6 28 ♖xe7+ ♖f7 29 ♖e8
with ♕h4 and a devastating attack
to follow.) 25 ♕h6 ♕b2 26 ♖e5!
1–0 Khmelnitsky–S. Kozlov,
Naberezhnye Chelny 1988.

(b) 22 ... f6 23 ♘g5 ♕d6 24
♘c7! ♔g8 25 ♘ge6 ♖fc8 26 c5!
♕d7 27 ♕c2! ♘e5! 28 ♖d1 ♕c6
29 f4 ♖xc7 30 ♘xc7 ♕xc7 31 fe
and Black had survived, but only
to a hopeless ending, in Khmelnitsky–Pesotsky, Kiev 1989.

18   ♗a3!?
Brodsky–Khmelnitsky, Kharkov 1988 featured the less strong

18 ♗b2?! ed 19 ♘xd4 ♘xd4 20
♗xd4 ♗xd4 21 ♕xd4 dc and a
draw was agreed.

18   ...   ♖e8
18 ... d3 fails to the simple 19
♗xd3 ♗xa1 20 ♗xf8 ♗xd3 21
♕xd3 ed 22 cd ♔xf8 23 ♖xa1
♘b4? 24 ♕d4+−; 18 ... ed 19
♗xf8 ♗xf8 20 cd ♕xd5 21
♗d3± Palatnik.

19   ♘f4   e5
19 ... ♕a5 lacks appeal due to
20 g4!? ♗e4 21 ♗d6 and 20 ♗d6
e5 21 ♘d5 e4 21 ♘h2.

20   ♘d5   d3!
21   ♗xd3   ♗xd3
Black is correct to take off the
light-square bishops: 21 ... e4 22
♗e2 ef 23 ♗xf3 ♕a5 (23 ...
♗xa1?! 24 ♕xa1 ♘e5 25 ♔h1!±
Khmelnitsky) 24 ♗d6 ♘e5.

22   ♕xd3   e4
23   ♕e3   ef
24   ♕xf3   ♘e5!
24 ... ♗xa1? 25 ♖xa1 ♘e5 26
♕f4 (Khmelnitsky) leaves Black
helpless.

25   ♕b3
25 ♕e2 ♖c8 26 ♖ac1 ♖e6 (26
... ♘xc4? 27 ♘e7+!) 27 ♘e3 ♕a5!?
is fine for Black.

25	...	♖b8!
26	♕a4	♖c8
27	♖ac1	♕h4!
28	♖fe1	♖e6
29	♕xa7	♖xc4
30	♘e7+	♔h7 *(42)*
31	♕b8?	

A serious mistake in mutual
time trouble. 31 ♕a8! h5 32 ♕g8+
transposes to the game. However,

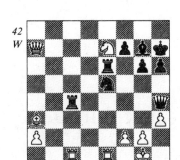

Black could now play 31 ... ♖xe7! 32 ♗xe7 (32 ♖xc4 loses to 32 ... ♘f3+ or 32 ... ♘xc4.) 32 ... ♖xc1! with the point that 33 ♗xh4? ♖xe1+ 34 ♔h2 ♘f3+ 35 gf

♗e5+ picks up the queen.

31	...	h5?
32	♕g8+	♔h6
33	♖e3	♖xe7
34	♖xc4	♕xc4
35	♗xe7	1-0 on time

After 35 ... ♕c1+ 36 ♔h2 ♕c7 37 f4 (37 g3? ♕e7 38 f4 ♘f3+!−+ and not 38 ... ♘g4+? 39 hg ♕xe3 40 g5 #) 37 ... ♕xe7 38 fe, Black can secure a draw with 38 ... ♕g5 followed by 39 ... ♗xe5+ (Palatnik) or 38 ... ♗xe5+ 39 ♔h1 ♕c5! 40 ♖e1 ♕f2, since 41 ♕f8+ ♔h7 42 ♕b4 ♕g3 43 ♔g1?? allows 43 ... ♗c3−+.

6 Four Pawns Attack without 6 ... ♘c6

The Four Pawns Attack is White's most ambitious system against the Alekhine. White sets up a large pawn centre, claiming a substantial spatial plus. Once developed, White intends that this will provide cover for an attack.

Black's play must therefore be extremely purposeful. Two main courses of action suggest themselves: to attack the pawn centre immediately, or to restrain the pawns while preparing to chip away at them, generally with f6, to reduce White's space advantage.

The second method is generally introduced by 5 ... de 6 fe ♘c6, considered in the next chapter.

The immediate assault on the centre generally involves ... c5. The subject of the last three games of this chapter is 5 ... de 6 fe c5, which leads immediately to immense tactical complications.

But first we deal with unusual lines for Black, and the attempt to place bishops on f5 and b4, before striking with ... c5.

Pisa Ferrer–Bagirov
Barcelona 1984

1 e4 ♘f6 2 e5 ♘d5 3 d4 d6 4 c4 ♘b6 5 f4 *(43)*

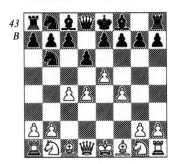

43
B

| 5 | ... | ♗f5 |

5 ... g5?! is something of a curiosity, but some of the better-publicised 'refutations' are not so clear.

6 ♕h5!? de (6 ... gf 7 d5 or 7 ♗xf4!?) 7 c5! ♘d5 (7 ... ♕xd4!?) 8 fe ♘f4 (8 ... ♘b4) 9 ♗xf4 gf 10 ♗c4 e6 11 ♘e2 ♘c6 12 ♘bc3 with an assault on f7 in Durão–Pomar, Madrid 1982.

6 ed ♕xd6!? (6 ... gf?! 7 dc!

♕xc7 8 ♘c3 e5 9 de ♘c6 10 ♗xf4
♗e6 11 ♘e4! ♗b4+ 12 ♔f2±
Tringov–Planinc, Varna 1970) 7
♘c3 (7 c5?! ♕e6+ 8 ♕e2 ♘d5 9
fg ♗g7 is roughly level due to the
weakness of d4; 7 ♗e2 c5 8 ♘c3
♕xd4 9 ♕b3 ♘c6 10 ♘f3 ♕d8
11 fg ♗f5 12 0–0 ♘b4 13 ♘e1
♕d4+∞ Blackstock–Trangmar,
Oxford 1970) 7 ... gf (7 ... ♘c6) 8
♗e2 c5 9 ♘b5 should be good for
White.

5 ... g6 6 ♘c3 ♗g7 7 ♗e3
0–0 (7 ... de 8 de!?±; 7 ... f6?! 8
ed ed 9 c5! ♘6d7 10 ♗c4 c6 11
f5!± P. Bücker–Westerinen, Bundesliga 1985) 8 c5! (8 ♘f3 ♗e6!?)
8 ... dc (8 ... ♘6d7 9 ♘f3 e6 10
h4 dc 11 dc ♕e7 12 h5 ♖d8 13
♕c2 b6 14 ♘g5 ♗a6 15 ♘xh7!
♔xh7 16 hg++ ♔g8 17 gf+
♕xf7 18 0–0–0 ♗xf1 19 ♕h7+
♔f8 20 f5! ♗xg2 21 fe ♕xe6 22
♖hf1+ ♗xf1 23 ♖xf1+ ♘f6 24
♗h6 ♗xh6+ 25 ♕xh6+ ♔e8 26
♖xf6 ♕g4 27 e6 ♕g1+ 28 ♔c2
♕g2+ 29 ♔b3 ♘d7 30 ♕h5+
1–0 Minasian–Gukasian, Armen-
ian Ch 1987) 9 dc ♘6d7 (9 ...
♕xd1+? 10 ♖xd1 ♘6d7 11
♘d5+ −) 10 h4! c6 (10 ... h5
11 e6!) 11 h5 ♕a5. Here Rogers
recommends 12 ♕a4! ♕xa4 13
♘xa4±. Instead Rogers–Depasquale, Australian Ch 1985 continued 12 a3?! ♖d8! 13 ♕a4 ♕xa4
14 ♘xa4 ♘f8!? 15 h6 ♗h8 16
♘f3±.

5 ... de 6 fe g6 7 ♘c3 ♗g7 *(44)*.
White has three reasonable tries
for advantage:

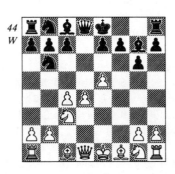

(a) **8 ♘f3** should probably be
met by 8 ... c5 9 d5 (9 dc!?) 9 ...
♗g4 (compare 6 ... c5 7 d5 g6).
Instead 8 ... ♗g4 9 c5 ♘d5 10
♗c4 e6 11 0–0 ♘xc3 12 bc 0–0
13 ♕e1 is assessed as ± by Nunn,
e.g. 13 ... ♘c6 14 ♗g5 ♕d7 15
♕h4 h5? 16 h3 ♗xf3 17 ♖xf3 b6
18 ♗b5 ♕d5 19 ♗xc6 ♕xc6 20
♗e7 ♖fc8 21 ♖af1 ♕e8 22 g4
1–0 Vajs–Marinković, corres.
1977.

(b) **8 c5** ♘d5 9 ♗c4 c6 (9 ...
♘xc3 10 bc 0–0 11 ♘f3 ♘c6 12
0–0 ♘a5 13 ♗d3 b6 14 ♗a3 ♗e6
15 ♕e2 ♕d7 16 ♘g5± Suetin–
Ledger, Hastings Challengers
1990/1) 10 ♘f3 0–0 11 0–0 b6 12
♕b3 e6 13 ♗g5 ♕c7 14 ♘e4
♗a6 15 ♗xd5 ♗xf1 16 ♗xe6∞
Spassky–Graf, Bundesliga 1989/90.

(c) **8 ♗e3** 0–0 (8 ... c5!? 9 dc
♕xd1+ [9 ... ♘6d7!? 10 e6 fe
11 ♘f3 ♕a5 Zvara–S. Bücker,
Prague 1991] 10 ♖xd1 ♘6d7 11
♘b5 ♘a6 12 e6 fe 13 b4 0–0
14 a3 e5∞ Larsson–Nordström,
corres. 1976) 9 ♘f3 (9 h4 h5) 9 ...
c5?! (9 ... ♘c6 10 ♖c1 ♗g4 11 h3
♗xf3 12 gf e6 13 h4 h5 14 ♘e4

♘d7∞ Bergström–Nordström, corres. 1976) 10 dc ♘6d7 11 e6 fe 12 ♗e2! (12 ♕c2 ♕a5∞) 12 ... ♕a5 13 0–0! ♘xc5 14 ♕e1! ♗f6 (14 ... ♘c6 15 ♕h4) 15 ♖d1 ♘c6 16 ♘g5! ♔g7 17 ♕h4 ♖h8 18 ♖xf6! ef 19 ♘ge4 ♘xe4 20 ♕h6+ ♔f7 21 ♘xe4 ♕c7 22 ♘xf6 ♘e7 23 ♖f1 ♘f5 24 ♘xh7 ♗d7 25 ♖xf5+ 1–0 Van der Kleij–Hoekstra, corres. 1984.

5 ... ♗f5 is an idea generally attributed to Trifunović. In our main game Bagirov uses it as a transpositional tool to reach the line 5 ... de 6 fe ♗f5 7 ♘c3 e6 8 ♘f3 ♗b4 9 ♗e3, while avoiding the unpleasant possibility of 9 ♗d3!.

6 ♘c3

6 ♗d3 ♗xd3 7 ♕xd3 de 8 fe c5! is fine for Black: 9 d5? e6 10 ♘c3 ♕h4+; 9 ♘f3 e6 10 ♘c3 (10 0–0) 10 ... cd 11 ♘e4 ♕c7 12 b3 ♘c6 13 0–0 ♘d7= Orev–Kupka, Albena 1971.

6 ... e6
7 ♗e3

7 ♘f3 would thwart Black's intentions, since on **7 ... de 8 fe ♗b4, 9 ♗d3** would follow:

9 ... c5 10 0–0! cd 11 ♘e4 ♘c6 (11 ... 0–0 12 ♗g5±) 12 ♗g5 ♕c7 13 a3! ♗f8 (13 ... h6!?) 14 c5 ♗xe4 15 cb ♗xf3 16 ♕xf3 ab 17 ♖ac1 h6 18 ♗d2 ♖c8 19 ♕h5!± Honfi–Hazai, Hungarian Ch 1974.

9 ... ♗g4 10 0–0 ♘c6 (10 ... c5 11 ♘e4!) 11 c5! ♗xc3 (11 ... ♘d5 12 ♘e2!) 12 bc ♘d5 13 ♕e1 ♘de7

(13 ... 0–0? 14 ♗g5 ♕d7 15 ♗xh7+!) 14 ♖b1 ♖b8 15 ♘g5 ♗f5 16 ♗xf5 ♘xf5 17 ♕e4 ♕d7 18 d5!± Velimirović–Martz, Vrnjacka Banja 1973.

9 ... ♗xd3 10 ♕xd3 c5 11 0–0! cd (11 ... h6 12 ♘e4!; 11 ... ♗xc3 12 bc h6 13 ♘d2! ♘8d7 ♘e4 0–0 15 ♘f6+ gf 16 ef ♘xf6 17 ♗xh6+ − Lutovinov–Kuuksmaa, corres. 1975) 12 ♘e4 ♘6d7 (12 ... 0–0 13 ♘eg5 g6 14 ♘xh7! ♔xh7 15 ♘g5+ ♔g7 16 ♕h3 ♖h8 17 ♖xf7+ ♔g8 18 ♖h7!+−; 12 ... ♘c6 13 c5 ♘c8 14 ♘fg5 ♘xe5 15 ♕b5+ +−; 12 ... h6 13 c5 ♘c8 14 ♕b5+ ♘c6 15 ♕xb7+−; 12 ... ♘8d7 13 a3 ♘c5 14 ♘xc5 ♗xc5 15 ♘g5± Vetemaa–Tseitlin, Pärnu 1973) 13 ♘fg5 ♘xe5 14 ♕g3 ♘bd7 15 ♗f4 ♕b6 (15 ... ♘g6 16 ♘xf7!) 16 ♗xe5 f6 17 ♗d6! fg 18 ♗xb4 ♕xb4 19 ♘d6+ ♔e7 20 ♖f7+ ♔d8 21 ♕xg5+ ♔c7 22 ♘b5+ ♔c8 23 ♖af1 b6 24 ♖xd7 ♔xd7 25 ♕xg7+ 1–0 Ivkov–Timman, Amsterdam 1974.

However, the point of Black's move order is that **7 ... ♘a6** is possible: **8 ♗e3** (8 ed ♗b4!?) **8 ... c5 9 ♗e2** (9 ♖c1 de; 9 d5 ♘b4 10 ♖c1 de 11 ♘xe5 f6; 9 dc dc 10 a3 ♗e7) **9 ... ♗e7** and now:

(a) **10 0–0** 0–0 11 dc (11 ♕d3 cd!; 11 d5 ♘c7; 11 ♖c1 de 12 fe?! cd 13 ♘xd4 ♗g6 14 ♘cb5? ♘d7! 15 ♗f4 ♘ac5! 16 ♘c3 ♕b6!∓ Urzica–Hazai, Pula 1975) 11 ... dc 12 ♕e1 ♕e8 13 ♕f2 ♘a4 14 ♘d1 ♖d8 15 b3 ♘b6 16 ♘c3

♘c8 17 ♘e1 f6= Milev–Schmid, Moscow 1956.

(b) **10 dc** dc 11 a3 0–0 12 ♕b3 ♕d7 13 0–0 ♖ad8 14 ♖fd1 ♕c7= 15 h3 ♘c8 16 ♘d2 ♘b8 17 g4 ♗g6 18 ♘d5?! ed 19 cd ♗d6! 20 ♗f3 ♗xe5 21 fe ♕xe5 22 ♗g2 ♗c2!∓ Yudasin–Barkovsky, Leningrad 1984.

7 ... de

7 ... ♘a6 8 ed! cd (8 ... ♘b4? 9 c5 ♘c2+ 10 ♔f2 ♘xa1 11 dc+ —) 9 ♘f3 ♗e7 10 ♗e2 0–0 11 ♖c1! (11 0–0 ♖c8 12 b3 ♘d5!) 11 ... ♘d7 12 b3 ♘c7 13 0–0 d5 14 c5 ♘b8 15 b4 a6 16 a4 was good for White in Gašić–Mihaljčišin, Sarajevo 1970.

7 ... ♗e7 8 ♘f3 0–0 9 ♗d3!± leaves White's central superiority unchallenged.

8 fe ♗b4
9 ♘f3

9 a3? ♗xc3+ 10 bc ♕h4+ 11 ♗f2 ♕e4+ wins a pawn in view of 12 ♕e2 ♘xc4! 13 ♕xe4 ♗xe4 14 ♗xc4 ♗xg2 and 12 ♗e2 ♕xg2! 13 ♗f3 ♕g6 14 ♗xb7 ♗e4.

9 ♕b3 can be met by 9 ... a5, since 10 a3? a4 11 ♕xb4? (11 ♕d1 ♗xc3+ 12 bc ♕h4+) 11 ... ♘c6 12 ♕c5 ♘d7 traps the queen.

9 ♗e2 c5 10 dc ♘6d7 11 ♕d6 ♘c6 12 ♘f3 ♕a5 13 ♘d4 ♘xd4 14 ♗xd4 ♖c8∓ Ugolik–Bagirov, Sochi 1971.

9 ♗d3?! ♗xd3 10 ♕xd3 c5 11 0–0–0 cd 12 ♗xd4 ♘c6∓ Bagirov.

9 ... c5 (45)

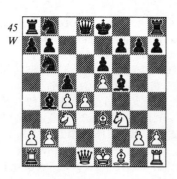

10 ♕b3

10 a3 can be met by 10 ... ♗xc3+ 11 bc ♘c6 12 ♗e2 0–0 13 0–0 ♘a5 14 ♘d2 ♗g6, when 15 ♖f4! ♖c8 (15 ... f6) 16 h4 h6 17 h5 ♗h7 18 ♖g4 ♔h8 19 ♕c1! is recommended by Bagirov. More ambitious is **10 ... cd!?**:

(a) **11 ab?!** de! 12 ♕xd8+ (12 ♘b5!? ♘c6 13 ♘d6+ ♔f8 14 ♗d3 ♘xe5 15 ♗xf5 ♘xf3+ 16 ♕xf3 ♕xd6 17 0–0 ef 18 c5 ♕d4∓ Bagirov) 12 ... ♔xd8 13 0–0–0+ ♔e7 14 c5 a5!—+ 15 cb ab 16 ♗d3 ♗xd3 17 ♖xd3 ♖a1+ 18 ♘b1 ♖c8+ 0–1 Miulescu–Ghizdavu, Romania 1972.

(b) **11 ♗xd4** ♗xc3+ 12 ♗xc3 ♕xd1+ 13 ♖xd1 ♘a4! 14 ♖c1 ♘c6 15 ♗e2 ♔e7!∓ Ghizdavu.

(c) **11 ♕xd4** ♕xd4 12 ♗xd4 ♗xc3+ 13 ♗xc3 (13 bc?! ♘6d7) 13 ... ♘a4 14 ♗b4 ♘xb2 (14 ... ♘c6?! 15 0–0–0!) 15 ♘d4 and now rather than **15 ... ♘d3+?!** 16 ♗xd3 ♗xd3 17 ♘b5± or **15 ... ♘c6** 16 ♘xc6 bc 17 ♗d6± Ostojić–Marović, Yugoslav Ch (Umag) 1972, SDO's **15 ... a5!**, breaking the coordination of White's minor pieces, looks fine: 16 ♘xf5 ab; 16 ♗d6 ♗g6 17 ♘b5 ♘a6; 16 ♗c5 ♗g6 17 ♘b5 ♘a6 18 ♘d6+ ♔e7; 16 ♘b5 ♔d7; 16 ♗c3 ♘a4; 16 ♗d2 ♗g6 17 ♘b5 0–0 18 ♘c7 ♖a7 19 ♗e3 b6 20 ♗xb6 ♖b7 21 c5 ♘d7.

10 ♗e2 ♘c6 11 0–0. Now:

(a) **11 ... ♗xc3?** 12 bc 0–0 13 ♕e1 gives White the advantage after either 13 ... ♖c8 14 dc! ♘d7 15 ♘d4! or 13 ... ♗g6 14 ♖d1 cd 15 cd ♘e7 16 ♕b4 ♗e4?! (Parma–Hecht, Berlin 1971) 17 d5!+ −.

(b) **11 ... 0–0!?** 12 dc ♘d7 (12 ... ♗xc3!?) 13 ♘a4 ♘dxe5 14 ♘xe5 ♘xe5 15 ♕b3 ♗g4! 16 ♖ad1 ♕a5 17 ♗xg4 ♘xg4 18 a3 ♕c7 19 ♖f4 ♘xe3 20 ♕xe3 ♕c6!= Krasnov–Kimelfeld, Moscow 1972.

(c) **11 ... cd** 12 ♘xd4 ♘xd4 (12 ... ♗g6 13 ♘xc6 bc 14 ♕c1!?) 13 ♗xd4 (13 ♕xd4?! ♕xd4 14 ♗xd4 0–0–0∓) 13 ... ♗c2! 14 ♕d2 ♖c8 (14 ... ♘a4 15 ♕f4) 15 ♔h1 (15 b3 ♗c5; 15 ♕f4) 15 ... 0–0 (15 ... ♘xc4?? 16 ♕xc2 ♕xd4 17 ♕a4+) 16 b3 ♗c5 17 ♘b5 ♗xd4 18 ♘xd4 (18 ♕xd4 ♕xd4 19 ♘xd4 ♗e4!=) 18 ♘xd4 ♗g6! (18 ... a6? 19 ♗f3±) 19 ♗f3 (19 ♕e3) 19 ... ♖c7 20 ♕e3 ♖d7 21 ♖ad1 a6 22 ♗e4 ♘c8! 23 ♗xg6 hg 24 ♖d3 ♕b6= Pritchett–Williams, Caorle 1972.

10   ...   ♘c6
10 ... cd 11 ♘xd4 (11 ♗xd4 ♘c6 12 0–0–0 0–0) 11 ... ♕h4+ 12 g3 (12 ♗f2 ♕e4+) 12 ... ♕e4

13 ♔f2 ♗xc3 14 ♗g2 ♕xd4 15 ♗xd4 ♗xd4+ 16 ♔e2 ♘8d7 17 ♖he1 ♗xe5 was also promising for Black in Marjan–Suba, Novi Sad 1974. Keene also gave **10 ... ♘a6.**

11	**dc**	**♘d7**
12	**0–0–0**	**0–0!**
13	**g4?!**	

13 ♗d3!?∞ is a better try.

13	**...**	**♗xg4**
14	**♗e2**	**♗xf3!**

An improvement over Tal's analysis, which ran 14 ... ♗xc5 15 ♘e4 ♗xe3+ 16 ♕xe3 ♗xf3 17 ♖xd7! ♕xd7 18 ♘f6+!+ −.

15	**♗xf3**	**♗xc5**
16	**♘e4**	**♗xe3+**
17	**♕xe3**	**♘cxe5**
18	**♖hg1**	**♕e7**
19	**♘d6**	**♘xf3!**

The point: Black's queen will cost White dearly. White has nothing better than the following combination, as 20 ♕xf3 ♘e5 and 20 ♘f5 ♕f6 21 ♖xg7+ ♔h8 are no good.

20	**♖xg7+**	**♔xg7**
21	**♘f5+**	**ef**
22	**♕xe7**	**♘de5**

Black need only coordinate his pieces and avoid threats to his king. 23 ♕xb7 ♖fb8 24 ♕e7 ♖e8 25 ♕a3 ♘xh2 26 ♕h3 ♘hg4 27 ♕h5 ♘g6 28 ♖h1 ♔f6!∓ 29 ♖f1 ♘e3 30 ♖g1 ♖ad8 31 b3 a5 32 ♕h2 ♘g4 33 ♕c2 ♔g5 34 ♕c3 ♖e5 35 a3 ♘f4 36 ♔b1 f6 37 ♕c1 ♖d3 38 ♖f1 ♖ee3 39 ♔a2 ♖xb3 40 c5 ♖bc3 0–1.

Vetemaa–Shabalov

Haapsalu 1986

1 e4 ♘f6 2 e5 ♘d5 3 d4 d6 4 c4 ♘b6 5 f4 de 6 fe

    6 ...   c5

Without further ado Black strikes at the weakest point of White's pawn centre. This logical idea was first investigated by Argunov in the 1920s, but for much of the time since has been considered refuted. Ljubojević helped clarify various lines in the 1970s, but only recent investigations by Latvian players have given the line an air of respectability.

Clearly the Argunov Variation does not allow for half-measures. Matters come to a head very quickly, and both sides must play with the utmost vigour to prove their case.

    7 d5

7 dc?! ♕xd1+ **8** ♔xd1 ♘a4! gives Black the advantage, since 9 b4 a5 10 a3 ab 11 ab fails to 11 ... ♘c3+.

7 ♘f3 has been tried, rather surprisingly, by Velimirović. **7 ... cd 8** ♕xd4 (8 ♘xd4 e6) **8 ... ♕xd4** (8 ... ♘c6 9 ♕xd8+ ♘xd8 10 ♘c3 intends c5 and ♘b5 [Bagirov].) **9 ♘xd4** and now Velimirović–Bagirov, Palma GMA 1989 continued **9 ... ♘c6 10 ♘b5!** ♔d8 11 ♘1c3! ♘xe5 (11 ... a6?! 12 ♗e3 ♘d7 13 0–0–0±) 12 ♗f4 ♘bd7 (12 ... ♘exc4? 13 ♗c7+! ♔d7 14 ♗xb6 ♘xb6 15 0–0–0+ ♔c6 16

♗e2+ –) 13 0–0–0 f6 14 ♗e2 e6 15 ♗xe5 fe 16 ♗f3 a6 17 ♘d6 ♗xd6 18 ♖xd6 ♔e7 19 ♖hd1 ♖b8 20 ♘e4 ♖f8 21 ♘g5 ♘f6 22 ♖b6 h6 23 ♘e4 ♘xe4 24 ♗xe4 and Black was quite lucky to survive the ensuing ending. Instead, **9 ... e6** seems better, e.g. 10 ♘b5 ♘a6 11 ♗e3 ♗b4+ 12 ♘d2 0–0 13 ♘xa7 ♘d7 14 ♘xc8 (14 ♘b5 ♘ac5) 14 ... ♖fxc8.

    7 ...   e6

An intriguing alternative is **7 ... g6**. Black intends to castle and then attack White's centre. After **8 ♘c3 ♗g7 9 ♗f4** (9 ♘f3?! ♗g4 gives all of Black's pieces activity; 9 ♗e3 0–0!? is fine for Black after either 10 ♗xc5 ♘8d7 11 ♗xb6?! ♕xb6 or 10 ♘f3 ♗g4 11 ♗xc5 ♘6d7.) **9 ... 0–0 10 ♕d2 e6**, White must make an important decision.

(a) **11 0–0–0 ed 12 cd ♗g4 13 ♖e1** (13 ♗e2 ♗xe2 14 ♕xe2) 13 ... c4 14 h3 ♗f5 15 g4 ♗d3 16 ♗xd3 cd 17 ♕xd3 ♘a6 18 d6 ♖c8 19 ♔b1 ♘c5 20 ♕e2 ♘e6 21 ♗g3 ♘c4 22 ♘f3 ♕a5 23 ♖c1 ♗h6 24 g5 ♗xg5 25 ♘xg5 ♘xg5 26 ♖hd1 ♖c5 27 h4 ♘e6 28 ♘e4 ♕b5 29 ♕h2 ♖c6 30 h5 ♘e3 31 ♘f6+ ♔g7 32 hg ♖xc1+ 33 ♖xc1 ♕d3+ 34 ♔a1 ♕xg6∓ 35 a3 ♘d4 36 ♖g1 ♘f3 37 d7 ♘xh2 38 ♘e8+ (38 ♗xh2 ♖d8) 38 ... ♔h8 39 ♗xh2 ♘c2+ 40 ♔b1 ♘xa3++ 41 ♔a2 ♕e6+ 42 ♔xa3 ♖xe8 43 de♕+ ♕xe8 44 ♗f4 ♕e6 0–1 Ilincić–Marinković, Vrnjacka Banja 1989. A spectacular game, though not, of course, conclusive.

(b) **11 d6** ♘c6 **12 ♘f3** ♘d7 **13 ♕e3** f6 **14 0-0-0** fe **15 ♗h6** (15 ♗g5!?) 15 ... ♘d4 **16 ♗xg7** ♔xg7 **17 ♘xe5** ♘f5 **18 ♕e1** ♕g5+ **19 ♖d2** and now 19 ... ♘d4 leaves the game unclear; instead Klinger–Bischoff, Zug 1985 continued 19 ... ♕e3?! **20 ♕xe3** ♘xe3 **21 ♘f3** ♘b6 **22 ♘e4** ♖f5 **23 ♗d3** ♗d7 **24 ♘eg5** h6 **25 ♖e2** hg **26 ♖xe3** ♖f4 **27 ♘xg5** ♘xc4? **28 ♖xe6** ♗e8 **29 ♖xe8!** 1-0.

7 ... g6 is a very logical and ambitious idea, though there is much analytical work to be done before any definite conclusions can be reached.

8 ♘c3

8 d6? is a blunder, but after 8 ... ♕h4+ **9 g3** ♕e4+ **10 ♕e2** ♕xh1 **11 ♘f3**, Black's knights must co-ordinate properly to extricate the queen: 11 ... ♘c6! **12 ♘bd2** ♘d7! **13 ♔f2** ♘dxe5! **14 ♘xe5** ♕xh2+ **15 ♗g2** ♘d4! **16 ♕d1** ♗xd6 **17 ♘f1** ♕xg2+ **18 ♔xg2** ♗xe5 and Black had much more than enough material for the queen in Nekrasov and Tokar–Argunov and Yudin, Orenburg consultation 1931.

8 ... ed

8 ... ♕h4+ **9 g3** ♕d4 **10 ♗d2!** ♕xe5+ **11 ♗e2** ed **12 ♘f3** gives White a powerful initiative, e.g. 12 ... ♕e6?! **13 0-0** ♗e7 **14 ♖e1** 0-0 **15 cd**; 12 ... ♕d6 **13 ♗f4** ♕d8 **14 0-0** d4 **15 ♘b5** ♘a6 **16 ♘g5** Meszaros–Blatny, Czechoslovakia 1952; 12 ... ♕e7 **13 cd ♗h3** **14 ♘g5** Heiny–Vendl.

9 cd c4 *(46)*

9 ... ♕h4+ **10 g3** ♕d4 is insufficient, though White must react with great vigour. **11 ♗b5+** (11 ♗f4 g5 **12 ♗xg5** ♕xe5+ **13 ♕e2** also gives Black problems.) **11 ... ♗d7 12 ♕e2** ♘xd5 (12 ... a6?! **13 e6** fe **14 ♕xe6+** ♗e7 **15 ♗g5** left Black in a hopeless mess in Konovalov–Ignatenko, corres. 1948.) **13 e6 fe** (13 ... ♗xb5 **14 ♘xb5** ♕b4+ **15 ♗d2** ♕xb2 **16 ef++ ♔xf7 17 ♕h5+ ♔e6 18 ♘f3** ♕xa1+ **19 ♔f2** and White wins [Panov, Estrin].) **14 ♕xe6+** (After 14 ♘f3, the queen sacrifice 14 ... ♘xc3! leaves the game very unclear.) **14 ... ♘e7 15 ♘f3** and Black has no adequate defence:

(a) **15 ... ♕b4 16 ♘e5!** (16 a3 ♕xb5!; 16 ♕e2 ♗xb5; 16 ♗xd7+?! ♘xd7 **17 ♘g5** 0-0-0! **18 ♘f7** ♘c6 **19 ♘xh8?!** (19 ♘xd8 ♘xd8) 19 ... ♘d4! and the black pieces swarmed in on the white king in Dragomiretsky–Kaev, Sverdlovsk 1934.) 16 ... ♗xb5 (16 ... ♘c6 **17 ♗g5** ♕xb2 **18 ♗xc6+** bc **19 0-0+ −**; 16 ... ♕d4 **17 ♗g5** ♘c6 **18 ♗xc6** ♗xc6 **19 ♘xc6** bc **20 ♖d1** ♕b4 **21 0-0+ −**) **17 ♗g5** ♕xb2 (else 0-0-0 and ♕f7+ ideas win easily.) **18 ♘xb5** ♕xa1+ (18 ... ♕xb5 **19 0-0-0+ −**) **19 ♔f2** ♕xh1 (19 ... ♕b2+ **20 ♔e3** ♕xb5 **21 ♖d1+ −**) **20 ♕c8+** ♘xc8 **21 ♘c7 mate!** (analysis by Bryson).

(b) **15 ... ♕f6 16 ♕e2!** ♗xb5 (16 ... a6 **17 ♘d5** ♕d6 **18 ♗c4±**; 16 ... ♘bc6 **17 ♘e4** ♕e6 **18 ♗c4** ♕g6 **19 ♘h4** ♗g4 **20 ♘xg6** ♗xe2

21 ♘d6+!+ — Ljubojević–Mozes, Dresden 1969.) 17 ♘xb5 ♘a6 18 ♗g5 ♕b6 19 0-0-0! ♖d8 20 ♖xd8+ ♔xd8 21 ♖d1+ ♔c8 22 ♗f4 1-0 Balashov–K. Grigorian, Riga 1967.

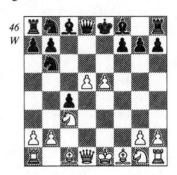

10   a3?!

The main moves are 10 d6 and 10 ♘f3, which are covered in subsequent games. There are a few miscellaneous moves, most of which are unimpressive.

(a) **10 ♗xc4??** ♕h4+.

(b) **10 g3?!** ♗c5 11 ♗xc4? (11 ♘f3 ♗g4 12 ♗g2) 11 ... ♘xc4 12 ♕a4+ ♘d7 13 ♕xc4 ♘xe5 14 ♕e4 0-0 15 ♔f1 ♖e8 was horrible for White in Türk–Giersiepen, Hamburg 1970.

(c) **10 ♗f4?!** ♗b4! 11 ♗xc4 ♘xc4 12 ♕a4+ ♘c6! 13 dc ♘xb2 (makes use of the bishop's absence from c1) 14 cb+ ♘xa4 and Black wins.

(d) **10 ♕d4?!** ♘c6 11 ♕e4 ♘b4 12 a3 (12 d6?! g6! 13 ♘b5 ♗f5 14 ♕xb7 ♕h4+ 15 ♔e2 ♗e4! 16 ♘f3 ♕g4 17 ♘c7+ ♔d7 18 ♘d5+ ♔e6 19 ♘c7+ ♔f5! [J. Adams] and the king is quite safe, so Black

wins!) 12 ... ♘4xd5 13 ♘xd5 ♕xd5 14 ♕xd5 ♘xd5 15 ♗xc4 ♘c7 16 ♗e3 ♗e6 and Black's position was the more pleasant in Ciocaltea–Ljubojević, Málaga 1971.

(e) **10 e6** is an interesting attempt to expose the black king. 10 ... ♗b4?! 11 ef+ ♔xf7 12 ♘f3 ♖e8+ 13 ♗e2 ♕xd5 14 ♕xd5 ♘xd5 15 0-0 ♘b6, as in Levin–Chernin, Philadelphia 1982, gave White the strong option of 16 ♘g5+! ♔g8 17 ♗h5 g6 18 ♗f3, when f6 is particularly sensitive. Instead Black is advised to investigate **10 ... fe** 11 ♕h5+ g6 12 ♕e5 ♖g8 13 de (13 ♘f3 ♗g7; 13 ♗g5) 13 ... ♘c6 or **10 ... ♗c5** 11 ef+ ♔xf7 12 ♘f3 ♖e8+ 13 ♗e2 ♗g4, which both look fine for Black.

(f) **10 ♗e3!?** is a radical way to remove the threat to the d5 pawn. 10 ... ♗b4 11 ♗xb6 ♕xb6 12 ♕d2 0-0 13 ♘f3 ♗g4 14 h3 (How else to defend the e-pawn?!) 14 ... ♗xf3 15 gf ♘d7 16 f4 ♘c5 17 0-0-0 ♘e4 18 ♕d4 ♘xc3 19 ♕xb6 ♘xa2+ 20 ♔b1 ab 21 ♗xc4 ♘c3+ 22 bc ♗xc3 23 d6 ♖a4 24 e6! gave Black problems in Aleksandrov–Shabalov, Riga 1987. Van der Tak suggests that instead **19 ... ab** 20 bc ♗xc3 21 ♔c2 ♖a3 gives Black good play, noting that 22 ♗xc4? ♖c8 23 d6 ♖xc4 24 d7 ♗d4+ 25 ♔d2 ♖a8 26 ♔d3 b5 is no good. More logical is **22 d6** b5 23 ♖d5 b4 24 ♗xc4 ♗xe5 25 fe ♖c3+ 26 ♔b2 ♖xc4 27 ♖c1 ♖xc1 28 ♔xc1 ♖d8 29 ♔c2 ♔f8 30 ♔b3 ♔e8 31

♔xb4 ♔d7 with a likely draw. Another possible improvement over the game is **21 ... g5!?** to break up White's pawns (22 fg ♗d6; 22 f5 ♗d6), since 22 ♖hg1 ♔h8 23 ♖xg5 allows 23 ... ♗e7.

10	...	♗c5
11	♘f3	0–0

11 ... ♗g4 12 ♗e2 ♘8d7 (12 ... 0–0) 13 ♗f4 (13 ♘d4? ♘xe5 14 ♗xg4 ♕h4+; 13 e6 fe 14 ♘g5 ♗f5 15 ♖f1 ♗g6; 13 ♗g5 f6 14 e6 ♗xf3 15 ed+ ♘xd7 16 ♗xf3 fg 17 ♕e2+ [SDO] is roughly level.) 13 ... 0–0 14 ♕c2 ♗xf3 15 gf and now the simple 15 ... ♖e8 leaves Black on top. Instead Al Kindji–Wians, World Junior Ch 1985 continued 15 ... ♕h4+ 16 ♗g3 ♕h6 17 f4 ♖fe8 18 ♕d2 ♖ad8∞, though Black won in the end.

12	♗e2?!	♗f5
13	♗g5	♕d7
14	♕d2	h6
15	♗f4	♘a6
16	0–0–0	♖ac8
17	h3	♘a4
18	♘d4	♗xd4
19	♕xd4	♘6c5
20	♗xc4	♕b5!! *(47)*

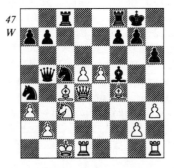

47
W

Devastating. The queen is immune, as either capture is met by 21 ... ♘b3 #.

21	♖d2	♘xc3
	0–1	

I. Clark–Burgess
Weymouth Open 1989

1 e4 ♘f6 2 e5 ♘d5 3 d4 d6 4 c4 ♘b6 5 f4 de 6 fe c5 7 d5 e6 8 ♘c3 ed 9 cd c4

10	d6

A well-founded move. White blocks the development of Black's kingside and menaces both ♘b5–c7+ and ♘f3, ♗g5. The dark side of 10 d6 is equally clear: White makes yet another pawn move while undeveloped, loses control of c6 and e6 and leaves the central pawn duo less flexible. These considerations guarantee play of the utmost violence!

10	...	♘c6

The most critical continuation, using the conceded c6 square to hit e5, but other moves are possible.

(a) **10 ... ♗f5** 11 ♘f3 ♘c6 12 ♗e2 ♕d7 13 0–0 0–0–0 14 ♗e3 ♗g4 15 ♗xb6 ab 16 ♘d5 ♔b8 17 ♘xb6 ♕e6 (Blau–Vogler, 1981) 18 ♗xc4+–.

(b) **10 ... ♗e6** prepares to meet 11 ♘b5 with 11 ... ♘d5 threatening a queen check on a5 or h4. Instead simply 11 ♘f3 ♘a6 is quite pleasant for White.

(c) **10 ... g6** 11 ♘f3 ♗g7 12 ♗g5 f6 13 ef ♗xf6 14 ♗xf6 ♕xf6 15 ♗xc4 ♘xc4 16 ♕a4+ ♘c6 17 ♕xc4 ♗e6 (17 ... ♕xd6 18 0–0 leaves the black king in trouble: 18 ... ♗e6 19 ♖fe1+ −) 18 ♕c5 0–0 19 0–0 ♖ad8 20 ♖ad1 allowed White to keep the extra pawn in Zude–Rührig, W. German Ch (Bad Neuenahr) 1987.

11 ♗f4

Alternatives:

(a) **11 ♘f3 ♗g4 12 ♗f4 g5!** 13 ♗xg5 (After 13 ♘e4?!, Black should not resign, but play 13 ... gf! 14 ♘f6+ ♕xf6 15 ef 0–0–0 and slaughter White on the centre files, as in T. Paunović–Mršević, Yugoslavia 1982; 13 ♗g3 ♗g7 14 ♕e2 ♘d7 15 0–0–0 0–0 [SDO] gives rather a messy position in which White's collapsing centre and more exposed king ensure reasonable play for Black.) 13 ... ♕xg5 14 ♘xg5 ♗xd1 15 ♖xd1 ♘xe5 16 ♘b5 0–0–0 17 ♘xa7+ ♔b8. Black has good play.

(b) **11 ♘b5 ♕h4+** (Bronstein proposed 11 ... ♘xe5 12 ♘c7+ ♔d7 in 1973.) 12 g3 (King walks are a bad idea, e.g. 12 ♔d2? ♕f4+ 13 ♔c2 ♗f5+ or 12 ♔e2? ♕e4+ and now 13 ♔f2 ♘xe5 or 13 ♗e3 ♗g4+ 14 ♘f3 ♘xe5 15 ♘c7+ ♔d8 16 ♘xa8 ♘xf3.) 12 ... ♕e4+ 13 ♕e2 (13 ♔f2? is met not by 13 ... ♕xh1? 14 ♘c7+!+−, but 13 ... ♘xe5! when 14 ♗g2 ♘d3+ 15 ♔f1 ♕f5+ picks up the knight, whilst on 14 ♘c7+ ♔d8 15 ♗g2 ♘d3+ 16 ♔f1 ♕d4 17 ♕e2 ♗xd6 18 ♘xa8 ♖e8 19 ♗g5+ f6 20 ♕f3 ♗g4 Black wins.) 13 ... ♕xh1 (13 ... ♕xe5?! only gives Black one pawn for the exchange: 14 ♘c7+

♔d8 15 ♕xe5 ♘xe5 16 ♘xa8 ♘xa8 17 ♗f4 ♗xd6 18 0–0–0 [SDO].) 14 ♗g5 (14 ♘c7+?! ♔d8 15 ♗g5+ ♗e7! gives White no real compensation for the rook after 16 de+ ♔xc7 or 16 ♗xe7+ ♘xe7 17 de+ ♔xc7.) 14 ... f6 and now 15 ef+ ♔f7 or 15 ♘c7+ ♔f7 16 e6+ ♔g6 with a remarkably unclear mess of a position in either case.

11 ... g5

Jepsen's idea 11 ... ♗e6 has the point that 12 ♘b5?! ♘d5 defends c7 with gain of tempo. 12 ♘f3 h6 intends 13 ... g5. After 13 ♘d4 ♘xd4 14 ♕xd4 g5 15 ♗g3 ♗g7, Black has managed to develop, but the white centre remains intact to provide cover for a kingside attack.

12 ♘e4

Instead 12 ♗g3 ♗g7 leaves White's centre crumbling, but 12 ♘b5 ♗g7 13 ♘c7+ ♔f8 14 ♘xa8 gf 15 ♘xb6 ♕xb6!? 16 d7 ♕b4+! is interesting. After 17 ♕d2 ♗xd7 18 ♕xb4+ ♘xb4 19 ♖c1 b5 Black will have two good pawns for an exchange. A sharper line is 17 ♔f2 ♕xb2+ (17 ... ♕c5+ 18 ♔e1 ♕b4+ repeats moves; 18 ... ♗xd7!?? 19 ♕xd7 ♗xe5 is an interesting attempt to expose the white king.) 18 ♗e2 (18 ♘e2 ♕b6+ 19 ♔e1 ♗xd7! 20 ♕xd7 ♘xe5) 18 ... ♗xd7 19 ♕xd7 ♕xa1 20 ♕c8+ ♔e7 21 ♕xb7+ ♔d8 22 ♕xc6 ♕d4+.

The most radical method against 12 ♘b5 is the queen sacri-

fice **12 ... gf** 13 ♘c7+ ♛xc7 14
dc ♗b4+. Compared with the
continuation below, the white king
is less comfortable, but the c7
pawn is a nuisance as it takes two
tempi to round up. There can
follow 15 ♔f2 ♗c5+ 16 ♔e1
♗e6 intending 17 ... ♘d5 (instead
16 ... ♗b4+ repeats) or 15 ♔e2
♗e6 again followed by 16 ... ♘d5.
Black's chances appear rather
good.

12	...	gf
13	♘f6+	♛xf6
14	ef	♗e6 *(48)*

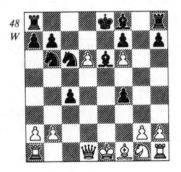

Black has succeeded in the stra-
tegic aim of destroying the white
centre, at the cost of some
material. Queen versus pieces' positions are always very finely balanced: the queen is very strong
at exploiting looseness, but if the
minor pieces remain compact and
well coordinated, the queen can
end up flailing around uselessly.

15 ♘f3?

A natural developing move, in
a position which calls for more
radical measures. **15 ♘e2?** 0-0-0

16 ♘xf4? ♗xd6 is worse still, but
15 ♛h5! is critical. There can then
follow **15 ... ♗xd6 16 0-0-0
0-0-0 17 ♘f3** and now:

(a) **17 ... ♖hg8?** 18 ♘g5 ♖g6 19
♘xe6 fe 20 f7 ♖f6 21 ♛xh7 ♗e7
22 ♖xd8+ ♘xd8 23 ♛e4 and
Black's position has disintegrated
in Zude–S. Bücker, W. German
Ch (Bad Neuenahr) 1987.

(b) **17 ... ♘b4?** invites 18 ♖xd6?
♘xa2+ 19 ♔b1 ♖xd6 20 ♔xa2
♖d5!, but fails to 18 ♘d4±.

(c) **17 ... c3!?**.

(d) **17 ... ♔b8!?** removes the
king from some irritating checks
and vacates c8 for a rook to aim
at the white king. An important
point is 18 ♘g5?! ♗f5 when Black
is on top after both 19 ♘xf7 ♗g6
20 ♘xd8 ♗xh5 21 ♘xc6+ ♔c7
and 19 ♛xf7 ♘b4. Instead 18
♗e2 c3! leaves the position
genuinely unclear.

| 15 | ... | 0-0-0 |
| 16 | ♗e2 | |

The white king will come under
pressure if he flees to the queenside: 16 ♛c2 ♗xd6 17 0-0-0 ♘b4.

| 16 | ... | ♗xd6 |
| 17 | a3 | |

17 ♔f1? ♘d5. The text invites
17 ... ♗b4+? 18 ab ♖xd1 19
♖xd1 with 20 0-0 and 21 ♘g5 to
follow.

17	...	♖hg8
18	♛c2	♗c5
19	♖d1	♖xd1+

19 ... ♖de8?! 20 b4∞. Now
White should recapture with the
bishop, though Black has excellent

play, e.g. 20 ♗xd1 ♘d5!? 21 ♕xc4 ♗b6. After the knight reaches e3 'free of charge' White's position is grim.

20	♔xd1?!	♘d5
21	♕c1	♘e3
22	♕e4	♖xg2
23	♖e1	

23 ♗d1 c3 24 b4 ♖a2 25 bc ♖a1+ 26 ♕b1 ♖xb1+ 27 ♔xb1 ♗d5−+.

| 23 | ... | ♘a5 |
| 24 | ♘d2? | |

24 ♕e5 ♘b3+ 25 ♔b1 ♖xe2?! 26 ♖xe2 ♗f5+ 27 ♔a2 ♘c1+ is only a draw, but 25 ... b6 keeps the pressure on; it's hard to find a move for White. As played, a beautiful mate arises.

24	...	c3
25	b4	cd+
26	♔xd2	♘b3+
27	♔c3	♗d4+
28	♔d3!?	♗c4 # *(49)*

0−1

49
W

Minasian–Shabalov
Minsk 1990

1 e4 ♘f6 2 e5 ♘d5 3 c4 ♘b6 4 d4 d6 5 f4 de 6 fe c5 7 d5 e6 8 ♘c3 ed 9 cd c4

10 ♘f3

The standard move, posing Black the problem of which knight to pin.

10 ... ♗b4!

Until recently, **10 ... ♗g4** was automatically played here, but this gives White a number of continuations which make Black's survival problematical.

11 ♗xc4 ♘xc4 12 ♕a4+ ♘d7 13 ♕xc4 ♗xf3 14 gf ♘xe5 15 ♕e2 (15 ♕e4 ♕h4+) and now Black should play neither 15 ... ♕e7? 16 0-0!± Browne–Ničevski, Skopje 1970, nor 15 ... ♕h4+ 16 ♔d1 ♕d4+?! (16 ... ♗d6) 17 ♔c2, but 15 ... ♗d6!? 16 f4 ♕h4+ 17 ♔d1 0-0 18 fe ♖ae8 19 ♕e4 ♕h5+ 20 ♔c2 ♖xe5 21 ♕d3 ♗b4 22 ♗d2 ♖c8 23 ♔b3 ♗xc3 24 ♗xc3 ♖xd5 25 ♕e4 ♖b5+ 26 ♔c2 ♖e5 27 ♕d3 ♖d5 28 ♕e4 ♖e5 29 ♕d3 ♖d5 ½-½ Velimirović–Barlov, Arandjelovac 1980.

11 ♕d4!? ♗xf3 12 gf ♗b4 13 ♗xc4 0-0 (The alternatives are less logical: 13 ... ♘8d7?! 14 ♗b5 and 13 ... ♘c6?! 14 ♕e4± fail to help Black, whilst the compensation Black obtained after 13 ... ♗xc3+ 14 bc ♘xc4 15 ♕xc4 0-0 16 ♕d4?! ♘d7 17 0-0 ♘b6 18 ♖d1 ♖c8 in Toledo–Segal, Fortaleza 1975 was mainly due to White's 16th.) **14 ♖g1!** (14 ♗e3 ♘c6 15 dc ♕xd4 16 ♗xd4 ♘xc4 17 cb ♖ab8 18 0-0-0 ♖xb7∞; 14 ♗h6!? ♘xc4! 15 ♕g4 g6 16 ♕xc4 ♗xc3+ 17 bc ♖e8 18 ♕d4 ♕f6!= Birtwistle–Burgess, Muswell Hill

1989) **14 ... g6** (14 ... ♕c7? 15 e6
f6 16 ♗h6 ♕xc4 17 ♖xg7+ ♔h8
18 ♖g8+! ♔xg8 19 ♕g1+ 1–0
Ljubojević–Honfi, Čačak 1970; 14
... ♖e8 15 ♗h6 g6 16 0–0–0 ♕c7
17 ♗b3 ♗xc3 18 bc ♖ac8 19
♔b2 ♘a6 20 d6 ♕c5 21 e6 ♕xd4
22 ef+ ♔h8 23 ♖xd4+ – SDO.)
15 ♗g5 (15 ♗b3? ♘c6 16 ♕e4
♘xe5; 15 ♗h6? ♘c6 16 ♕e4
♘xe5!? 17 ♗xf8 ♕xf8 18 ♗b5
♕c5!∓ Gibbs–Stuart, corres.
1971) **15 ... ♕c7** (15 ... ♕c8? 16
♗b3 ♗c5 17 ♕h4!) **16 ♗b3 ♗c5
17 ♕f4** is a well-known position,
the assessment of which has
changed greatly over the years. It
seems that capturing the rook is
fatal for Black, who therefore
stands somewhat worse:

(a) **17 ... ♗xg1 18 d6** (18 ♔e2?
♕c5!– + 19 ♖xg1 ♕xg1 20 ♗f6
♕g2+! 21 ♔e3 ♕xb2 22 ♔d3
♘8d7 23 ♘e4 ♖ac8 24 ♕h6
♘xe5+ 25 ♔e3 ♖c3+! 0–1
Gheorghiu–Ljubojević, Manila
1973; 18 0–0–0?! ♘8d7 19 ♖xg1
♕xe5 20 ♕xe5 ♘xe5 21 ♖d1
♘xf3∓ Grünfeld–Letzelter, Buenos
Aires ol 1978) and now:

(a1) **18 ... ♕c8** 19 0–0–0 ♗c5
20 e6! fe 21 ♕e5 ♖e8 22 ♗h6
♕d7 23 ♘e4 ♘c6 24 ♘f6+ wins,
as analysed by Bronstein.

(a2) **18 ... ♕c6** 19 0–0–0 transposes to (c) after 19 ... ♘8d7,
whilst SDO gives 19 ... ♗c5 20 e6
♘8d7 21 e7 when White regains
the rook with an excellent position.

(a3) **18 ... ♕c5 19 ♘e4 ♕d4** (19

... ♕b4+ 20 ♔f1 + –; 19 ... ♕e3+
20 ♕xe3 ♗xe3 21 ♗xe3 gives
White far too much for the
exchange.) **20 ♖d1 ♕xb2 21 ♘f6+**
(21 e6? ♘8d7 22 e7 ♕xh2∓ Grünfeld–Ljubojević, Riga 1979) **21 ...
♔h8 22 ♖d2** (50) and no matter
which square the queen chooses,
Black can only avoid mate at the
cost of too much material:

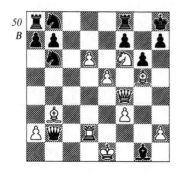

(a31) **22 ... ♕b1+** 23 ♔e2 ♘8d7
(23 ... ♕f5 24 ♕h4 ♕xe5+ 25 ♔f1
♕b5+ 26 ♔xg1 ♕c5+ 27 ♔h1
♕c1+ 28 ♗d1) 24 ♕h4 h5 25
♘xh5+ – Moura–Rinaldi, corres.
1983.

(a32) **22 ... ♕c1+** 23 ♔e2 (23
♗d1? ♕c4!) 23 ... ♕c5 24 ♔f1
♕c1+ 25 ♗d1! ♘8d7 (25 ...
♕c4+ 26 ♔xg1±) 26 ♔xg1
♕c5+ 27 ♔h1 ♕xe5 28 ♕h4 h5
29 ♘xh5 gh 30 ♕xh5+ ♔g8 31
♖g2+ – SDO.

(a33) **22 ... ♕a1+** was a startling
success in Grünfeld–Wiemer,
Tecklenburg 1984 which continued 23 ♔e2? ♘c6! 24 ♕h4
h5∞, but Weidemann's **23 ♗d1!**

leaves Black defenceless, e.g. 23 ... ♘8d7 24 ♕h4 ♕xe5+ 25 ♔f1 h5 26 ♘xh5 gh 27 ♕xh5+ ♔g8 28 ♖g2 etc.

(b) **17 ... ♖e8** 18 ♗f6 ♘8d7 19 ♘e4! (19 d6 ♘xe5! 20 ♔f1 ♗xd6 21 ♘b5 ♕c6 22 ♘xd6 ♕xd6 23 ♖d1 ♕c6 24 ♗xe5 ♕b5+ was equal in a game I. Zaitsev–Shashin.) 19 ... ♖xe5 (19 ... ♘xe5? 20 ♖xg6+!+ −) 20 ♗xe5 ♘xe5 21 ♔e2! ♗d6 and now in Bonaventure–Renaud, Le Havre 1977, White's 22 ♕h6? was rather reckless. Natural play with 22 ♖ac1 makes it hard for Black to demonstrate compensation.

(c) **17 ... ♘8d7** 18 d6 ♕c6 (18 ... ♕c8 19 0-0-0) 19 0-0-0! ♗xg1 20 ♖xg1 gives White rather too much compensation after either 20 ... ♘c5 21 ♗c2 or 20 ... ♕c5 21 ♖e1 ♖ae8 22 e6.

11 ♗e2! ♗c5 (11 ... ♗b4 12 0-0 gives Black the unpleasant choice between 12 ... ♗xc3 13 bc ♕xd5 14 ♕xd5 ♘xd5 15 ♗xc4+ ♘b6 16 ♗b3 h6 17 ♘d4 ♗h5 18 e6+ − Boudre–Werner, Royan Open 1988 and 12 ... 0-0 13 ♘g5!? ♗xe2 14 ♕xe2 h6 15 e6! which gave White a large advantage in Silakov–Bagirov, Baku 1969, since 15 ... hg 16 ef+ ♖xf7 17 ♖xf7 ♔xf7 18 ♕e6+ ♔f8 19 ♗xg5 wins for White.) **12 ♘g5! ♗f5** (12 ... ♗xe2 13 ♕xe2 0-0+) **13 ♖f1!** (13 ♗h5 g6 14 ♕f3∞) **13 ... ♗g6 14 h4 h6** (14 ... h5 15 ♗f4+ secures White's centre in preparation for further advances:

15 ... ♘a6 16 a3; 15 ... 0-0 16 ♗xh5 ♗d3 17 ♗e2! or 15 ... ♘8d7 16 e6 ♘f6 17 d6.) **15 h5 ♗d3** (15 ... ♗h7 16 ♖xf7! ♘8d7 17 ♖xg7 ♘xe5 18 ♘xh7 ♖xh7! 19 ♖g8+! ♗f8 20 ♗f4+ Foisor.) **16 ♗xd3 cd** was S. Bücker–Fleck, Bunde 1985, which became unclear after 17 ♕f3? 0-0 18 ♘xf7 ♕h4+ 19 g3 (19 ♔d1 ♘8d7) 19 ... ♕h2 20 e6. Instead, Foisor proposed a sacrificial method of stripping the pawn cover from Black's king while introducing the white queen into the attack: **17 ♖xf7!** hg (17 ... ♘xd5 18 ♕xd3!; 17 ... ♘8d7 18 ♕g4 ♘xe5 19 ♕e6+ ♗e7 20 ♖xg7+) 18 ♖xg7 ♘xd5 (Neither 18 ... ♔f8 19 ♗xg5 ♕e8 20 ♕f3+ ♔xg7 21 ♗f6+ nor 18 ... ♘8d7 19 ♗xg5 ♕b8 20 d6 ♘xe5 21 h6! gives Black much hope.) 19 ♕f3 ♘e7 20 ♕f7+ ♔d7 21 ♕d5+ and White even emerges with extra material.

11 ♗xc4

11 ♗g5 was Timman's recommendation. **11 ... f6?** 12 ef gf 13 ♕e2+ is clearly bad. Black cannot get by without the exchange on c3: **11 ... ♕xd5** 12 ♕xd5 ♘xd5 13 0-0-0 ♘e7 (13 ... ♗xc3? 14 ♖xd5+ −) 14 ♘b5 ♘a6 15 a3 ♗c5 16 ♗xc4 0-0 17 b4 h6 18 bc hg 19 ♘xg5 ♘xc5 20 ♘c7 ♖b8 21 ♘xf7+ −.

Instead, after **11 ... ♗xc3+ 12 bc ♕xd5** play is sharp, but Black appears to survive. **13 ♕xd5** (13 ♗xc4?! ♕xd1+ 14 ♖xd1 0-0) **13 ... ♘xd5 14 0-0-0 ♘e7** *(51)* and now White has two principal courses of action:

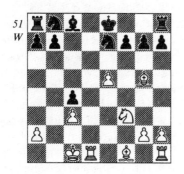

51
W

(a) **15 ♗xe7 ♔xe7 16 ♗xc4 ♗g4** (16 ... ♘c6 17 ♘g5 ♖d8 18 ♘xf7 ♖xd1+ 19 ♖xd1 ♗e6 20 ♗xe6 ♔xe6 21 ♘g5+ ♔xe5 22 ♖d7 won a pawn in Delnef–Jung, St. Ingbert 1985.)

(a1) Black survives after **17 e6 ♗xe6 18 ♗xe6** (18 ♖de1 ♘d7 19 ♗xe6 fe 20 ♘g5 ♘c5 21 ♖hf1 ♖af8) 18 ... fe 19 ♖he1 (19 ♘e5 ♖f8 20 ♖he1 ♖f5) 19 ... ♘a6 20 ♘d4 ♘c7 21 ♘f5+ ♔f6 22 ♖d7 ♘d5 (SDO).

(a2) **17 ♖hf1 ♘c6.** Now SDO analyses extensively the rook sacrifice 18 ♘g5 ♗xd1 19 ♖xf7+ ♔e8 20 ♖xb7 (20 ♔xd1? ♖d8+ and 21 ... ♖d7; 20 ♖c7?! ♗g4 21 ♖xb7 ♖f8 22 ♗b5 ♖c8 23 ♖xg7 ♔d8) but it's not much of a winning attempt. 20 ... ♗a4 (Necessary, since the knight was threatened.) 21 ♘e6 (21 ♘f7 ♖f8 22 e6 ♘e7 23 ♘d6+ ♔d8 24 ♘f7+) and now the safest for Black is 21 ... ♖b8, when 22 ♘xg7+ draws.

Instead 21 ... ♘a5 22 ♘xg7+ ♔d8 23 ♘e6+ ♔c8 (23 ... ♔e8=) 24 ♖c7+ ♔b8 25 ♗d5 ♖e8 26 ♖c5 ♘b7 27 ♖c4 ♗b5 28 ♖b4 a6 29 a4 ♖xe6 30 ♗xe6 ♗c6 (SDO) is a rather unclear ending.

(b) **15 ♗xc4 ♘bc6 16 ♖hf1 ♗g4 17 h3** (17 ♗xe7 ♔xe7 transposes to (a2) above; 17 ♖de1 ♗e6! blocks out e6 ideas and leaves Black with no problems.) 17 ... ♗xf3 18 ♖xf3 ♘xe5 19 ♗xf7+ ♘xf7 20 ♗xe7 ♔xe7 21 ♖e1+ ♘e5! 22 ♖xe5+ ♔d6 23 ♖fe3 ♖ad8 intending ... ♖d7 fully equalised in Bryson–Burgess, Edinburgh 1990.

11 ... ♗xc3+!
Before Ree and Timman pointed out this move, theory condemned 10 ... ♗b4 on the basis of 11 ... ♘xc4? 12 ♕a4+ ♘c6 13 dc ♗xc3+ 14 bc b5 ♕b4 (15 ♕xb5 is also strong.) 15 ... a5 16 ♕c5 ♕d3 17 ♗g5 (Boleslavsky).

12	bc	♘xc4
13	♕a4+	♘d7
14	♕xc4	♘b6
15	♕b5+	

SDO's main line is 15 ♕f4 ♕xd5! (15 ... ♘xd5?! 16 ♕g3 0–0 [16 ... ♘xc3 17 ♕xg7] 17 ♗h6) 16 0–0 (16 ♗a3 ♕d3) 16 ... 0–0 17 ♗a3 ♖d8! (Black is prepared to give up the queen for two rooks in answer to 18 ♖ad1, so White must lose a tempo to gain the d-file.) 18 ♗e7 ♖e8 19 ♖ad1 ♕e6 20 ♗b4 ♕f5 (Gaining more time, since a queen exchange clearly favours Black.) 21 ♕h4 ♗e6 22

♘g5 ♕g6 23 ♖d6 ♘c4 and Black is at least OK.

15	...	♕d7
16	♕xd7+	

Other moves can be tried:

(a) **16 ♕c5** ♕xd5 17 ♗a3 ♕xc5 18 ♗xc5 ♗e6 ½–½ Klundt–Migl, Bundesliga 1987/8 was very insipid. Black could well have played on.

(b) **16 ♕b1!?** (Coleman) 16 ... ♕xd5 (16 ... ♘xd5) 17 0–0 (17 ♗a3 ♘c4) 17 ... ♗g4 18 ♗a3 0–0–0 (18 ... ♘c4) 19 ♗d6 ♘c4 (19 ... ♗xf3?! 20 ♕f5+) 20 ♖d1 (20 ♘g5? ♘xd6) 20 ... ♕c6 21 ♘d4 ♕b6.

(c) **16 ♕e2!?** has features in common with 15 ♕f4 above. **16 ... ♕xd5 17 0–0** (17 ♗a3 ♕c4) **17 ... 0–0 18 ♗a3 ♖e8**:

(c1) **19 ♘g5?!** ♖xe5 20 ♕f2 (20 ♖xf7? ♗e6) 20 ... ♖xg5 21 ♖ad1 ♖xg2+! 22 ♕xg2 ♕xg2+ 23 ♔xg2 ♗e6.

(c2) **19 ♖ad1** ♕c4 20 ♕c2 ♕g4 21 ♖d4 ♕g6 22 ♕f2 (22 ♕e2!?) 22 ... ♗e6 23 ♘h4 ♕h5 24 ♗d6 ♖ac8 25 ♕g3 ♖c4 26 h3 and now 26 ... h6! preparing 27 ... ♖ec8 leaves Black on top. Instead in Rigo–Burgess, Århus 1990, after 26 ... ♖ec8? 27 ♗e7! (threatening 28 ♗f6+ −) 27 ... ♖xd4 28 cd ♔h8 things were rather unclear.

(c3) **19 ♕c2!?** h6 (To prevent 20 ♘g5) 20 ♖ad1 ♕e6 21 ♗d6 ♕f5 22 ♕e2 ♗e6 23 ♘d4 ♕g4 24 ♕f2 (24 ♕xg4 ♗xg4 25 ♖d3 ♘c4) 24 ... ♗c4 25 h3 (25 ♖fe1 ♘d5) 25 ... ♕g5!? 26 ♖fe1 ♘d5 27 ♘f3 (27

♖c1 ♘f4; 27 e6 fe 28 ♘xe6 ♖xe6 29 ♖xe6 ♘xc3) 27 ... ♕f5 28 ♖d4 ♖ac8 29 ♕d2 ♘b6 left Black well-developed and structurally superior in Coleman–Burgess, Hastings Challengers 1990/1.

After the exchange of queens there results an interesting semi-ending with an extra pawn for White. Black has excellent counterplay against White's four weak pawns, aided by the opposite-colour bishops.

16	...	♗xd7
17	d6	♖c8 (52)

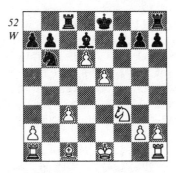

52
W

18	♗e3

18 ♗d2 keeps the extra pawn for a while, but is rather passive. It seems that Black's knight should go to c4.

(a) **18 ... ♘a4** 19 ♖c1 (19 ♖b1!? b5) 19 ... ♗b5 and now White should avoid 20 ♔f2 ♗c4 21 ♖b1 b5 22 ♖he1 a6 23 a3 ♗d5 24 ♖e3 ♔d7 25 ♗e1 ♖c5 26 ♖d1 ♖hc8∓ (the centre pawns simply drop off) Verney–Burgess, Hastings Challengers 1989/90 and 20 ♘d4 ♗c4 21 ♘b3 ♗xb3 (21 ... ♘c5!?) 22 ab ♘c5∓ (SDO) in favour of 20 ♖b1! a6 (20 ... ♗a6!?) 21 ♘d4 ♖c5 22 ♘xb5 ♖xe5+ 23 ♔f2 ♖f5+ (23 ... ab?! 24 ♖e1) 24 ♔g3 ab 25 ♖e1+ when Black has some problems.

(b) **18 ... ♘c4!** 19 0-0 ♘xd2 20 ♘xd2 0-0 (Black should not regain the pawn at the cost of the initiative: 20 ... ♖xc3?! 21 ♖ac1±) 21 ♖f3 ♗c5 22 ♖e3 ♖fc8 23 ♖c1 b5 24 a3 ♖d5 25 ♘b3 ♖c4 26 ♖f1 h6 27 ♘d4 ♖c8 28 ♖ef3 ♖xe5 29 ♖xf7 ♖d8 ½-½ Durão–Bagirov, Kuşadasi 1990.

| 18 | ... | ♖xc3 |
| 19 | ♗xb6 | |

After **19 ♔d2** Shabalov recommends **19 ... ♘d5!** as a little better for Black. Instead, **19 ... ♖a3** 20 ♗xb6 ab 21 ♖hb1 ♗c6 22 ♖xb6 ♔d7 23 ♘d4 ♗xg2 24 ♖g1 ♖xa2+ 25 ♔e3 ♖a3+ 26 ♔d2 ♖a2+ ½-½ was Shirov–Shabalov, Riga 1986.

| 19 | ... | ab |
| 20 | ♔d2 | ♖c5 |

20 ... ♖a3= transposes to Shirov–Shabalov in the previous note; Shabalov mentions 20 ... ♖c6!?.

| 21 | ♖hb1 | b5 |

After 21 ... ♗c6 22 ♖xb6 ♔d7 23 ♖ab1, the b7 pawn is vulnerable.

22	a4	0-0!
23	ab	f6
24	♖a7	♗f5?

Black plays for some clever tactics which turn out not to work. Necessary was **24 ... ♖b8** (playable next move also, but then Black is fighting for a draw) 25 ef gf, and ... ♖d5–d6 completes the destruction of White's centre, whereupon Black has all the chances.

25	♖b3	fe?
26	♖xb7	♖c2+
27	♔e3	♗e6
28	♖d3!	

White avoids 28 ♖a3? ♗c4 29 ♘xe5 ♖e2+ 30 ♔d4 ♖f4+ when Black wins. After 28 ♖d3!, Black's best practical chance was probably 28 ... e4!? when White must find some precise moves: 29 ♖d2! ef! 30 ♖xc2 ♗d5! 31 ♖e7! (Note that 31 ♖bc7? fg 32 ♖xg2 ♗xg2 33 d7 ♗h3 34 b6 ♖d8 35 b7 ♗xd7 36 ♖xd7 ♖xd7 37 b8♕+ ♔f7 does not win, since Black will have a fortress when the rook reaches f6 or h6.) 31 ... fg 32 ♖xg2!! ♗xg2 33 d7 ♗h3 34 b6 and White wins.

Instead, in the game, White was obliged to play a very strong exchange sacrifice: 28 ... ♗c4 29 ♘xe5! ♗xd3 30 ♔xd3 ♖xg2 31 d7 ♖xh2 32 ♖c7 ♖h1 33 b6 h5 34 ♖c8 ♖d1+ 35 ♔c2 ♖xd7 36 ♖xf8+ ♔xf8 37 ♘xd7+ ♔e7 38 b7 1-0.

7 Four Pawns Attack with 6 ... ♞c6

In this chapter we consider lines in which Black aims to co-exist with the white pawns. Piece pressure is used to restrain the pawns, whereafter one strategy is to increase pressure on d4 with the aim of provoking some weakening to provide footholds for the black pieces. This is characterised by the moves 9 ... ♛d7 and 9 ... ♝g4, the latter also aiming to disturb White's king position.

In the main line, Black, with 9 ... ♝e7, prepares kingside castling to be followed by ... f6. After the exchange on f6, Black will aim to show that e6 is no more of a weakness than White's d-pawn. The most popular option for White is to pre-empt this with 10 d5. However, this exposes White's king just as much as Black's, and gives rise to positions in which it appears that a set has been thrown randomly onto the board. Chances appear roughly balanced, but much painstaking analytical work is still needed.

Gdanski–Hellers
Champigny Junior 1984

1 e4 ♞f6 2 e5 ♞d5 3 d4 d6 4 c4 ♞b6 5 f4 de 6 fe

6 ...   ♞c6 *(53)*

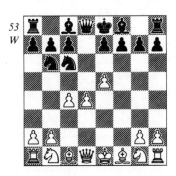

7 ♝e3

7 ♞f3?! ♝g4 (7 ... ♝f5? 8 d5 ♞b4 9 ♞d4) 8 e6 (Otherwise Black has simply gained a tempo over the 9 ... ♝g4 line.) 8 ... fe 9 c5 (9 ♝e2 ♛d7! 10 c5 ♞d5 11 0–0 e5) 9 ... ♞d5! 10 ♝b5 ♛d7! 11 0–0 (11 ♞bd2 g6 12 ♛a4 ♝g7 13 ♞e5 ♝xe5 14 de ♞e3!∓ 15 ♛e4 0–0! 16 ♛xe3 ♞b4!–+) 11 ... g6 12

♕a4 (12 ♘bd2 ♗g7 13 ♕a4
♗xf3! 14 ♘xf3 0–0 15 ♘e5 ♗xe5
16 de a6∓ Hort) 12 ... ♗xf3
13 ♖xf3 ♗g7 14 ♔h1 ♖f8 15
♖xf8+ ♔xf8 16 ♘c3 a6 17 ♗d2
♖b8∓ Kalantar–Bagirov, Batumi
1961.

7   ...   ♗f5

Rohde's 7 ... h5 is liable to lead,
after 8 ♘c3 ♗g4 9 ♘f3 e6, to a
standard position with the extra
move ... h5. It is not clear how
this can help Black.

8   ♘c3   e6

8 ... f6 is rather an outrageous
move, probably best met by the
pawn sacrifice 9 e6 ♘b4 10 ♖c1
♗xe6 11 a3.

The simplest reply to **8 ... ♘b4**
9 ♖c1 c5 is 10 ♘f3 e6 11 ♗e2,
considered under 9 ... ♘b4 below.

9   ♘f3

This move brings us to the
traditional main line position of
the Four Pawns Attack. 9 ... ♗b4,
the popular 9 ... ♗g4 and 9 ...
♗e7, the main line, are dealt with
in subsequent games.

9   ...   ♕d7

9 ... ♘b4 was one of Alekhine's
ideas. After extensive practical
trials and analysis, it seems that
Black cannot equalise. 10 ♖c1 (10
♗g5?! ♗e7 11 ♗xe7 ♔xe7! 12
♖c1 c5 13 a3 cd 14 ♘xd4 ♘d3+!∓
Marjanović–Agzamov, Belgrade
1982) **10 ... c5 11 ♗e2!** (11 ♗g5?!
♗e7 12 ♗xe7 ♔xe7!; 11 d5?!
ed 12 cd ♘4xd5 gives Black the
advantage after 13 ♗g5 ♗e7 14
♗b5+ ♔f8! or 13 ♗b5+ ♗d7
14 ♗g5 ♘xc3! 15 ♖xc3 ♗e7;

11 a3) gives Black three principal
options:

(a) **11 ... ♗g4** 12 0–0! (12 ♗g5
♗e7 13 ♗xe7 ♕xe7 14 ♘e4
0–0∞) 12 ... ♗xf3 13 ♗xf3 ♘xc4
14 ♗f2 ♘xb2 (14 ... ♕d7 15 ♘e4)
15 ♕b3 ♘bd3 16 a3!± is Bagirov's
recommendation, after which
Black's queenside in particular is
faced with collapse, e.g. 16 ... ♘xc1
17 ♗xc1 or 16 ... ♘xf2 17 ♖xf2
cd 18 ab dc 19 ♗xb7.

(b) **11 ... cd** 12 ♘xd4 ♗g6 (12
... ♕c7? 13 c5!; 12 ... ♘c6?! 13
0–0!? and now 13 ... ♘xe5 14 c5!
♘bd7 15 ♗xf5 ef 16 ♘d5± is less
disastrous than 13 ... ♘d7? 14
♘xf5 ef 15 ♖xf5 g6? 16 ♖xf7!!
♔xf7 17 e6+ ♔xe6 18 ♕d5+
♔e7 19 ♖f1+− Mikhalchishin–
Agzamov, USSR Ch [Frunze]
1981.) 13 c5! (Other moves are
possible, but this recommendation
of Levenfish's seems by far the
simplest and strongest.) 13 ... ♘d7
(13 ... ♗xc5 14 ♗b5+ ♔f8 15
♘xe6+) 14 ♕a4 ♘d3+ 15 ♗xd3
♗xd3 16 ♖d1 ♗g6 17 c6 with a
large advantage.

(c) **11 ... ♗e7** 12 0–0 *(54)* gives
Black two dismal options:

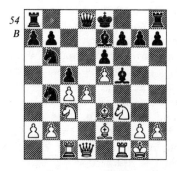

54
B

(c1) **12 ... cd** 13 ♘xd4 ♗g6 14 a3 (14 ♘db5 0–0) 14 ... ♘c6 15 ♘xc6 bc 16 ♕xd8+ ♖xd8 (16 ... ♔xd8 17 b4!) 17 ♖fd1! 0–0 18 b4 ♘d7 19 ♗f4 c5 20 b5 ♘b8 21 ♗e3 ♖c8 22 ♖d2 left Black with a dreadful ending in Penrose–Mecking, Palma 1969.

(c2) **12 ... 0–0** 13 dc! (13 a3) 13 ... ♘d7 14 a3 ♘c6 15 b4 ♘dxe5 (15 ... ♘cxe5 16 ♘b5 ♗e4 17 ♘d6 ♗xf3 18 gf± Veröci–Stadler, Subotica 1974) 16 ♘b5! (16 ♘xe5 ♘xe5 17 ♘b5 ♗g5 18 ♖c3! also gave White the advantage in Hort–Knežević, Slanchev Briag 1974.) 16 ... ♗d3 (16 ... ♘g4 17 ♗f4 e5 18 ♘xe5± Mikhalchishin) 17 ♘xe5 ♘xe5. Now in Mikhalchishin–Karsa, Lvov 1983, 18 ♗f4 ♗xe2 19 ♕xe2 ♘d3 20 ♖cd1 ♘xf4 21 ♖xf4 left White better, but Mikhalchishin pointed out the even stronger 18 ♗d4! ♗xe2 19 ♕xe2 ♘c6 20 ♗c3 when in addition to the queenside majority White has pressure on the black kingside.

10 ♗e2

10 d5?! is tricky, but seems to be bad: 10 ... ed 11 cd ♘b4 12 ♘d4 ♘6xd5 (12 ... a6? 13 a3! denies Black the vital check on b4: 13 ... ♘4xd5 14 ♘xd5 ♕xd5 15 ♘xf5 ♕xe5 16 ♕c2±) 13 ♘xd5 (13 ♘xf5 ♕xf5 14 ♘xd5 0–0–0) 13 ... ♘xd5 14 ♘xf5 0–0–0! (14 ... ♗b4+?! 15 ♔e2∞) 15 ♕d3 (15 ♘d6+? ♗xd6 16 ♕xd5? ♗b4+; 15 ♗e2? ♗b4+; 15 ♕f3? ♘xe3) 15 ... g6 and now Bullockus–Oakley, corres. 1984 concluded 16

♘d6+? ♗xd6 17 ed ♘xe3 0–1. Instead 16 ♘g3 ♘xe3 (16 ... ♗b4+!?) 17 ♕xe3 ♗c5 18 ♕f4 ♖he8 19 ♔e2 ♕d5 is very unpleasant for White.

10 a3? is just a loss of time: 10 ... ♗g4 11 ♗e2 ♗xf3 12 gf ♗e7 13 ♕d2 ♗h4+ 14 ♔f1 f6 15 ♘e4 fe 16 ♘c5 ♕f7 17 ♘xb7 0–0 18 d5 ♘xc4!!–+ Moore–Foote, Michigan 1983.

Also illogical is **10 ♖c1?!** 0–0–0 11 h3 f6 12 ef gf 13 ♗e2 ♖g8 14 g4 ♗g6∓ when White's king came under attack in Yuferov–Nekrasov, Minsk 1984.

10 ♕d2 ♘b4 (10 ... f6) 11 ♖d1 (11 ♖c1 c5) 11 ... 0–0–0 12 ♗e2 ♘c2+ 13 ♔f2 f6∓ Bakulin–Aronin, Moscow 1961.

10 ...   ♖d8

10 ... 0–0–0 is the relatively solid main line. 11 d5? ed 12 ♗xb6 d4!∓ gives White problems, whilst 11 ♕d2 f6 (11 ... ♘a5!?) 12 ef (12 0–0–0) 12 ... gf 13 0–0 (13 0–0–0? ♘a5! 14 c5 ♘bc4 15 ♗xc4 ♘xc4 16 ♕e2 ♘xe3 17 ♕xe3 h5!∓ Hudson–Hoppe, 1959) 13 ... ♖g8 with ideas of ... ♕g7 and ... ♘e5 gives Black good play.

Therefore, White generally replies with **11 0–0**, when Black must watch out for tactics on the h3–c8 diagonal:

(a) **11 ... ♗e7?!** should be met not by 12 ♕d2 f6! 13 c5?! ♘d5 14 ♗b5 ♖hg8 15 ♗f2 ♗g4 16 ♗g3 f5 17 ♘e2 g5, as in Pavlov–Panov, Moscow 1927, but 12 d5! ed (12 ... ♘b4 13 ♘d4) 13 ♗xb6 ab 14 cd ♘b4 (14 ... ♗c5+ 15 ♔h1 and now 15 ... ♘e7 16 ♘h4!? ♔b8 17 ♘b5 ♗g6 18 ♕a4 ♘c8 19 b4! ♗e7 20 ♖f3 or 15 ... ♘b4 16 ♘g5! ♔b8 17 a3! ♘c2 18 ♘xf7±) 15 ♘d4! g6 (15 ... ♗c5 16 ♖xf5!) 16 ♘xf5 gf 17 ♖xf5! ♗c5+ 18 ♔h1 ♘xd5 19 e6! fe 20 ♖xd5!+−, as analysed by Ernst Grünfeld.

(b) **11 ... f6?!** 12 d5! ♘xe5 (12 ... ed?! 13 ♗xb6; 12 ... ♕e8?! 13 ♗xb6 ab 14 ♕a4 gives White a strong attack, e.g. 14 ... ♘b8 15 ♕a8 fe 16 ♘xe5 ♗d6 17 c5 ♗xc5 18 ♔h1 ♗d6 19 ♗b5 ♕h5 20 ♗c6+−) 13 ♘xe5 fe 14 a4 a5 (14 ... ♔b8 15 a5 ♘c8 16 ♕b3± Teschner–Maier, 1962) 15 ♘b5 ♗b4 16 d6 c5 17 ♗g5! (17 ♗d2?! ♕xd6!?; 17 ♕c1 intending 18 ♗d2 is also strong.) 17 ... ♖df8 18 ♗d2 ♔b8 19 ♗xb4 cb 20 ♕d2 ♕c6 21 ♕e3 e4 22 ♖fd1 e5 23 d7! ♕h6 24 ♕c5 ♕c6 25 ♕xe5+ ♔a8 26 d8♕+ 1-0 Erlandsson–Arnesson, corres. 1976.

(c) **11 ... ♗g4 12 c5** (12 ♘g5 ♘xc4 13 ♖xf7 ♕e8 14 ♗f2 h6 15 ♗xg4 hg 16 ♖xf8 ♖xf8 17 ♕e2 ♘b6∞ SDO) **12 ... ♘d5 13 ♘xd5 ♕xd5** *(55)*

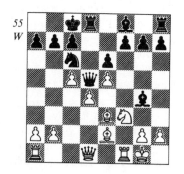

(c1) **14 ♗f2** f6=.

(c2) Nunn analysed **14 h3 ♕e4** 15 ♕b3 ♘xd4! 16 ♘xd4 ♗xe2 17 ♖f4 ♕d3 18 ♘xe2 ♕xe2 19 ♖xf7 ♖d5 20 ♖af1 ♕xe3+ with equality.

(c3) **14 b4 ♕e4** 15 ♕b3 ♘xd4 16 ♘xd4 ♗xe2 17 ♖f4 ♕xe5 18 ♖e1 g5 19 ♖f2 ♗h5 20 ♖d2 ♗g7 21 ♕a4 was Platonov–Kupreichik, USSR Ch 1969, when Petrosian's 21 ... ♖xd4! 22 ♖xd4 ♕xe3+ 23 ♖xe3 ♗xd4 would have been more than adequate.

(c4) Martz suggested **14 ♖e1!?** with the ideas 14 ... ♕e4 15 ♗d3, 14 ... ♕d7 15 ♕b3 and 14 ... ♗e7 15 b4.

(c5) **14 ♘g5 ♗xe2** 15 ♕xe2 ♘xd4 16 ♗xd4 ♕xd4 17 ♔h1 ♕d2! (17 ... ♕b4? 18 ♘xf7 ♖d2 19 ♖ad1!+−; 17 ... ♖d5 18 ♖ad1 ♕xc5 19 ♖xd5 ed 20 ♖xf7±) 18 ♕xd2 ♖xd2 is an ending where Black must be a little careful, but should have no real problems. 19 ♖xf7 (19 c6!? h6! 20 ♘xf7 ♖g8= Watson) 19 ... ♗xc5 20 ♘xe6 ♗d4! (20 ... ♗b6 21 ♖c1±) 21 ♘xd4! (21 ♖xc7+ ♔b8 22 ♖d7 ♗xb2 and 21 ♖c1 ♗xe5 22 ♘xc7 ♖xb2! are good for Black.) 21 ... ♖xd4 22 ♖xg7 (22 ♖af1 ♖d7 23 ♖xd7 ♔xd7 24 ♖xf7+ ♔e6 25 ♖xc7 ♖d8 26 ♔g1 ♖d7 ½-½ Gipslis–Kengis, Jurmala 1983) 22 ... ♖e4 (22 ... ♖e8 Alburt; 22 ... h5?! 23 ♖c1 c6 24 h3! intending ♖c3 is ± according to Gipslis) 23 ♖c1 c6 24 ♖f1 h5! 25 h3 (25 ♖g5 a5!) 25 ... ♖xe5 26 ♖ff7 ♖b5= 27 b3 a5! 28 ♔g1 ♔b8 29 g4 hg

½–½ Ligterink–Gipslis, Amsterdam 1976.

11 ♕d2

11 0-0 ♗g4

(a) **12 c5** ♘d5 (12 ... ♗xf3 13 ♖xf3 ♘d5 14 ♗f2 ♗e7± 15 ♗c4? ♘xc3 16 ♖xc3 ♘xe5∓ Hellers–Bjarnehag, Stockholm 1983) 13 ♘xd5 ♕xd5 14 ♕e1 (After 14 ♘g5 ♗xe2 15 ♕xe2 ♖d7 16 ♕f2 ♘d8, Black has everything in order.) 14 ... ♘e7 15 ♔h1 ♘f5 16 ♗g1 h5 17 h3 ♕d7 18 ♕d1 c6 19 ♗f2 ♗xf3 20 ♗xf3 g6 21 ♗e4 ♗h6 22 ♗h4 ♘e3 led to an equal ending in Heim–Timmer, Bern 1988.

(b) **12 ♘g5**

(b1) **12 ... ♗xe2** 13 ♕xe2 (13 ♘xe2 ♘xc4 14 ♖xf7 ♘xe3 gives Black the advantage after 15 ♕b3?! ♗e7 16 ♘xe6 ♔xf7! 17 ♘xd8++ ♔e8 18 ♘f7 ♘xd4!∓, but White should play 15 ♖xd7 ♘xd1 16 ♖xd8+) 13 ... ♘xd4 14 ♗xd4 ♕xd4+ 15 ♔h1 ♖d7 and now instead of Hellers' 16 ♖ad1 ♕xc4 17 ♕f3 ♗b4! 18 ♖xd7 ♔xd7 19 ♕xf7+ ♔c8∓, SDO recommends 16 ♕f3!?.

(b2) **12 ... ♘xc4** 13 ♗f2 (13 ♖xf7 ♘xe3 14 ♖xd7 ♘xd1 15 ♖xd8+ ♘xd8 16 ♗xg4 ♘e3∞ Posch–Klinger, Leutasch 1984) 13 ... ♗e7! (13 ... ♗xe2?! 14 ♕xe2 ♗e7 15 ♕h5!± Estrin–Oakley, corres. 1962) 14 ♘xf7 ♗xe2 15 ♕xe2 ♔xf7 16 ♗e3+!? (16 ♕xc4 ♖hf8) 16 ... ♗e8 17 ♕xc4 leaves the black king rather unhappy after either 17 ... ♖f8 or 17 ... ♘b4.

11 ...   ♘b4?!

Since this should give White the advantage, Hellers' suggestion **11 ... ♘a5!?** 12 b3 ♗b4 13 0-0 0-0 14 ♖ad1 c5 15 ♕b2 should be tried. Instead **11 ... f6** is nonsense with Black's king still in the centre, whilst **11 ... ♗e7** 12 0-0 0-0 13 ♖ad1 f6 14 ef ♗xf6 15 ♕c1 is a position which can be reached via 9 ... ♗e7 10 ♗e2 0-0 11 0-0 f6 12 ef ♗xf6 13 ♕d2 ♕d7?! 14 ♖ad1 ♖ad8 15 ♕c1. Black's queen is not ideally placed on d7, and repositioning will involve a loss of time. 15 ... ♗g4 16 ♘e4 does not help Black.

12	0-0	c5
13	d5!	ed
14	cd	♘6xd5
15	♗b5	♘c6
16	♖ad1?!	

16 ♘xd5! ♕xd5 17 ♕xd5 ♖xd5 18 ♗c4 ♖d7 19 ♘g5 ♗g6 20 e6 fe 21 ♘xe6± (Hellers) is the logical continuation of White's central breakthrough.

16	...	♘xc3
17	♕xc3	♕xd1
18	♖xd1	♖xd1+
19	♔f2	♗e7
20	♗xc5?!	

After this, Black can claim an advantage. 20 ♗xc6+ bc 21 ♗xc5 ♖d5 22 ♗xe7 ♔xe7 23 ♕a3+ c5 24 ♕xa7+ ♗d7 would maintain mutual chances.

20	...	0-0!
21	♗xc6	♗xc5+
22	♕xc5	bc
23	♕xa7	♖b1
24	♕b6	c5

25	a4	c4
26	♘d2?	

26 ♕b4 was essential. There now follows an amusing finish (though not of course for Gdanski).

26	...	c3!

After 27 ♘xb1 c2, the pawn promotes.

0–1

Minasian–Kengis
Frunze Otborochniy 1989

1 e4 ♘f6 2 e5 ♘d5 3 d4 d6 4 c4 ♘b6 5 f4 de 6 fe ♘c6 7 ♗e3 ♗f5 8 ♘c3 e6 9 ♘f3

9	...	♗g4

Despite the loss of tempo clearly inherent in this move, it is based on sound concrete considerations: Black disrupts White's king position, while stepping up the pressure on d4.

10	♗e2	♗xf3

Black must exchange before White can castle, else the following queen manoeuvre will not be possible. Now, after 11 ♗xf3?! ♘xc4, White can regain the pawn, but Black will have a very pleasant position.

11	gf	♕h4+
12	♗f2	♕f4
13	c5	

13 ♕c1 is a reasonable and popular alternative. 13 ... ♕xc1+ 14 ♖xc1 0–0–0 15 ♖d1 (15 c5 ♘d5! 16 ♘xd5 ♖xd5 17 ♖c4 ♖d7 18 f4 ♘e7= Bagirov. For 15 ... ♘d7, see the note to White's 14th move.) 15 ... ♗b4 (15 ... g6?! 16 a3 ♗h6 17 b4 ♖d7 18 ♘e4 ♖hd8 19 c5 ♘d5 20 b5 ♘ce7?! 21 c6!± bc 22 bc!? ♘xc6 23 ♗b5 ♘de7?? 24 ♗a6+ 1–0 Valvo–Alburt, Philadelphia 1988; 15 ... ♗e7 16 f4 g5 17 c5 ♘d5 18 ♘xd5 ♖xd5 19 ♗h5 f6 20 ♗g4 f5 21 ♗e2 ♖dd8 22 ♗c4 ♔d7 23 fg ♗xg5 24 ♖g1 ♖hg8 25 ♔e2 ♖g6 26 h4 ♗h6 27 h5 ♖xg1 28 ♖xg1 ♘e7= Bottema–Visser, Dieren Open 1988; 15 ... ♘a5 16 c5 ♘d5 17 ♘xd5 ♖xd5 18 ♗d3 ♗e7 19 ♗e4 ♖dd8 20 b4 ♘c6 21 a3 a6 22 f4 f6 23 ♔e2 g5= Eremin–Mikenas, Gorki 1955) 16 a3 ♗xc3+ 17 bc ♘a5 18 c5 ♘d5 19 ♔d2 f6! 20 ♗g3 ♖hf8= Prins–Tartakower, Hastings 1945/6.

13	...	♘d7

13 ... ♘d5?! 14 ♘xd5 ed 15 ♕d2 gives White a distinct advantage, e.g. 15 ... ♕f5 16 ♕d3 ♕d7 17 f4 ♘e7 18 ♖g1 h5 19 ♗f1! g6 20 ♗h3 ♕a4 (Bogdanović–Vukić, Yugoslavia 1973) 21 b3± Bukić.

14	♘e4	(56)

After 14 ♕c1 Black has little choice but to exchange queens; the only question is: on c1 or b1?

(a) 14 ... ♕f5 15 ♕b1 ♕xb1+ (15 ... ♕f4? 16 ♕e4±) 16 ♖xb1 0–0–0 17 f4 (17 0–0 ♗e7 18 b4 ♘f8 19 ♖fd1 ♗g5 20 b5 ♘e7 21 c6 ♘f5= Platonov–Bobotsov, Beverwijk 1970) 17 ... ♗e7 (17 ... ♘e7!?) 18 ♖d1 g5 (18 ... ♘f8 19 d5) 19 fg ♗xg5 was Valvo–Deep Thought, UNIX Mail Match 1988/9. Valvo's analysis continues 20 ♘e4! ♗f4 (20 ... ♗e7 21 a3 f6 22 ef ♘xf6 23 ♘g5) 21 a3 ♖hg8 22 b4±.

(b) 14 ... ♕xc1+ 15 ♖xc1 0-0-0 16 f4 (16 0-0 ♗e7 17 ♖fd1 f6; 16 ♘e4 ♘db8! 17 ♘g5 ♖d7 18 ♗b5 h6 19 ♘e4 g6 20 0-0 ♗g7∓ Byrne–Alburt, Berkeley 1984) 16 ... ♘e7 17 ♗f3 ♘b8 18 0-0 ♘bc6 19 ♖fd1 ♘b4 20 ♗h4 h6 (20 ... c6? 21 ♘e4) 21 a3 ♘bc6 (21 ... ♘bd5 22 ♘xd5 ed 23 f5!±) 22 d5 ed 23 ♗xe7! (23 ♘xd5 g5! 24 ♗g3 gf 25 ♗h4 ♖d7!∓ Bagirov) 23 ... ♗xe7 24 ♘xd5 and now Bagirov gives 24 ... f5! 25 b4 ♗h4 26 b5 (26 ♘e3 ♘d4!) 26 ... ♘e7 27 ♘e3 ♘g6 28 ♘g2 ♗e7=. Instead Murey–Bagirov, Belgrade GMA 1988 concluded abruptly: 24 ... ♖he8?! 25 b4 ♗h4 26 b5 ♘e7 27 ♘e3! ♘g6 28 ♘f5 ♗e7? 29 ♘d6+!!+− ♔b8 (29 ... cd 30 cd+ ♔b8 31 ♖c7) 30 ♘xe8 ♖xe8 31 ♖c4 b6 32 cb ab 33 ♖a4 1-0.

14 ♗b5!? aims to disrupt Black's plans of castling queen-side. Black should try 14 ... ♗e7 or 14 ... f6. Instead in Melton–Bullockus, corres. 1975, Black demanded to see the proof: 14 ... 0-0-0? 15 ♗xc6 bc 16 ♕e2 f6? 17 ♕a6+ ♔b8 18 ♕xc6! fe 19 ♘b5 e4 20 0-0 1-0.

14 ♕d2 ♕xd2+ 15 ♔xd2 0-0-0 16 ♔c2 ♘db8 17 ♖ad1 ♘e7 18 b4 ♘bc6 19 ♔b3 ♘f5 20 ♔c4 g6 21 ♖d3 ♗h6 22 b5 ♘ce7 23 a4 ♗f4 24 a5 ♘d5 25 ♘xd5 ♖xd5 26 h3 ♖hd8 27 ♖b1 ♔d7 28 b6 ab 29 ab c6 30 ♖a1 ♔e8= Poulsen–Nikolajsen, Denmark

1978 featured a standard manoeuvre for Black.

14 ♕d3 ♗e7 (14 ... f6) 15 ♖d1 ♗h4 16 0-0 ♗xf2+ 17 ♖xf2 0-0-0= Böhm–Schmidt, Wijk aan Zee 1975.

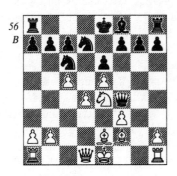

56 B

14 ...   ♗e7

14 ... 0-0-0 15 ♕a4 ♘db8 (15 ... f6 may well be an improvement, though 16 d5!? ♘cxe5 17 de is very messy.) 16 ♖d1 (16 d5? ♘xe5 17 ♘d6+ ♗xd6 18 ♕xf4 ♘d3+) 16 ... ♗e7 17 0-0 f5 (The universally recommended 17 ... ♗h4?? loses a piece to 18 d5 or 18 ♗xh4 ♕xh4 19 d5.) 18 ef gf 19 ♗c4 ♖d5 20 ♗g3 ♕f5 21 ♗xd5 ed 22 ♘c3 h5 23 ♘e2 ♖e8 24 ♖d2 ♕g5! 25 f4 ♕g4 26 ♔h1 h4 27 ♗e1 ♗xc5! 28 ♕b3! and now, rather than the 28 ... ♖xe2?! 29 ♖xe2 ♕xe2 30 ♕h3+ ♘d7 31 dc± of Kupreichik–Alburt, Daugavpils 1974, Suetin analysed 28 ... ♗b4 29 ♘c3 h3 30 ♗g3 ♗xc3 as unclear, though the burden of proof is on Black.

15   ♕b3   0-0-0
16   ♖d1

White cannot afford to prevent the bishop reaching h4: 16 h4 f5! 17 ♗e3 ♖xd4!∓.

16	...	♗h4!
17	♘g3	f6
18	♕xe6	♔b8

Kengis gives the variation 18 ... fe 19 d5 ♖he8 20 ♕h3 ♘d4 21 c6 bc 22 dc+ −, but this seems far from clear: 22 ... ♘xc6 23 ♗a6+ ♔b8 24 ♖xd7 ♗xg3 25 hg (25 ♖xd8+? ♖xd8 26 hg ♕c1+ 27 ♔e2 ♖d2+ 28 ♔e3 ♖d1+) 25 ... ♕c1+ 26 ♔e2 ♘d4+! 27 ♗xd4 ed+ 28 ♔f2 ♕xb2+ 29 ♔g1 ♖e1+ 30 ♗f1 ♖xf1+ 31 ♔xf1 ♕c1+ 32 ♔f2 ♕d2+ 33 ♔g1 ♖e8! and Black wins.

19 ef?!

19 ♕g4 ♕xg4 20 fg fe 21 de ♘dxe5 22 0–0 maintains equality.

19 ... ♘xf6

19 ... ♖he8!? 20 ♕g4 ♕xg4 21 fg ♘xf6 22 ♔f1 ♗xg3!? 23 hg ♘e4 would give Black slightly the better of a complex position.

20 ♕e3 ♘d5

The tricky 20 ... g5 gives White a pleasant ending after 21 ♕xf4! gf 22 ♘f5 ♗xf2+ 23 ♔xf2 ♖d5 24 ♗d3 ♘xd4 25 ♘xd4 ♖xd4 26 ♖he1!

21	♕xf4	♘xf4
22	♗b5	♘b4!
23	a3	♘c2+
24	♔f1	♗f6
25	♘f5	♘h3

25 ... g6?! 26 ♗a4 ♘xa3? 27 ♘e3!+ − would be rather embarrassing for Black.

After the text, the game headed towards a draw: 26 d5 g6 27 ♗a4! gf 28 ♗xc2 ♘xf2 29 ♔xf2 ♗xb2 30 ♖d3 ♗e5 31 ♖d2! ½–½.

Hübner–Hort
Biel 1987

1 e4 ♘f6 2 e5 ♘d5 3 d4 d6 4 c4 ♘b6 5 f4 de 6 fe ♘c6 7 ♗e3 ♗f5 8 ♘c3 e6 9 ♘f3 ♗g4

10 ♕d2

Though generally considered the main line, this queen move allows Black very interesting counterplay in a variety of lines and has achieved a miserable score in practice.

10 ... ♗b4

This cunning bishop move aims to provoke a weakening of White's queenside pawn formation, to give the knights some footholds.

10 ... ♕d7 11 ♗e2 (11 0–0–0 ♗b4 12 a3 ♗e7; 11 h3 ♗h5 12 g4 ♗g6 13 ♘h4 0–0–0 14 ♘xg6 hg 15 0–0–0 ♗b4 16 ♗e2 ♘a5 17 b3 c5 18 ♕c2 cd 19 ♖xd4 ♕c6 20 ♖xd8+ ♖xd8 21 ♖f1 ♗c5 22 ♗g5 ♖d7 23 ♘b5 ♕g2 24 ♘xa7+ ♔b8 25 ♘b5 ♘c6 26 a3 ♗xa3+ 0–1 Borm–Haïk, London 1978) 11 ... 0–0–0 12 c5! (12 ♖d1?! ♗xf3 13 gf f6 is good for Black due to 14 f4 g5! and 14 ef gf 15 0–0 ♕f7 16 ♕e1 f5 Maciejewski–Popov, Bucharest 1974; 12 0–0–0 ♗e2 13 ♖hf1 f6! 14 ef ♗xf6 15 ♘e4 ♗e7 16 ♕c3 ♘b4 17 ♕b3 ♗f5 18 ♘e5 ♕a4 19 ♕xa4 ♘xa4 20 ♘c3 ♘c2 gave Black fine play in Mestel–Kuligowski, Tjentište 1975.) 12 ... ♗xf3 (12 ... ♘d5 13

Nxd5 Qxd5 14 b4 a6 15 a4±) 13 cb (13 gf Nd5∓) 13 ... Bxg2! (13 ... Bxe2 14 ba Nxa7 15 Qxe2±) 14 Bb5! a6 (14 ... Bxh1? 15 ba+−) 15 Qxg2 ab and now Shabalov gives 16 a4! b4 17 bc Qxc7 18 Nb5 Qd7 19 0-0 as good for White. Instead, in Shabalov–Kengis, Riga 1989, he did not secure the b5 square and found himself at a disadvantage: 16 bc? Qxc7 17 0-0 b4 18 Ne4 f5! 19 Ng5 Qd7 20 Rac1 Kb8 21 Rfd1 and now 21 ... Ne7!! 22 Nf7 Nd5 23 Bg5 Be7 24 Nxh8 Rxh8 would have given Black excellent prospects, according to Shabalov.

10 ... Be7 11 0-0-0 (11 Be2? Bxf3 12 gf Bh4+ 13 Kf1 f6 14 f4 0-0∓) and Black has now tried various moves:

(a) **11 ... a5?** 12 h3 Bh5 13 g4 Bg6 14 d5! ed 15 cd Nb4 16 Bxb6 cb 17 d6 1-0 Bet–Cibin, corres. 1977.

(b) **11 ... 0-0?!** 12 h3 Bh5 13 g4 Bg6 14 h4 Nb4 (14 ... f6 15 ef Bxf6 16 h5 Be8 17 g5 Be7 18 Qg2± Adam–Tepenag, corres. 1963) 15 Qg2! (Frees d2 for the rook; 15 h5 Bc2 16 Re1 a5 17 d5 Na4 18 Nd4 Nxc3 19 bc Be4 20 Rh2 Na6∞ Shiyanovsky–Spassky, Tallinn 1959) 15 ... Bc2 16 Rd2 Ba4 17 Nxa4 Nxa4 18 a3 gave White a strong attack in Pekker–Golbin, Vilnius 1975.

(c) **11 ... f6!?** 12 ef Bxf6 13 Ne4 0-0 14 Be2 Qe8 15 Nfg5 Bf5 16 g4 Bxg5 17 Nxg5 Bg6 18 h4 h5 19 gh Bf5 20 Rhg1 a5 21 h6 Nb4

22 b3 Rf6 23 hg Qe7 24 Rdf1 a4 was Schenstok–Timman, Netherlands 1968. Black's kingside has disintegrated, but the white king turns out to be the one in trouble.

(d) **11 ... Qd7** 12 h3 (12 d5? Bxf3) 12 ... Bf5 (12 ... Bxf3 13 gf 0-0-0 14 f4 Bb4 15 Qc2 Kb8 16 a3 Bxc3 17 Qxc3 Ne7 and now rather than 18 Bg2?! Qa4! Durão–Bobotsov, Praia da Rocha 1969, Bagirov gives 18 Bd3! as offering White marginally the better of a messy position.) 13 d5? Na5 14 Bxb6 (14 c5 Nbc4 15 de Qxe6∓ Kirov–Popov, Sofia 1973) 14 ... ab 15 Qf4 Bb4 16 de? Nb3+ 0-1 Andreev–Khmelnitsky, Naberezhnye Chelny 1988. Instead, White should play 13 g4 Bg6 14 h4 Nb4 15 h5 (15 Qg2? Nxa2+! 16 Nxa2 Qa4) 15 ... Bc2 16 Re1 — compare Shiyanovsky–Spassky in (b) above, though 16 ... Na4 looks fine for Black.

11   a3

11 0-0-0 Na4 puts pressure on White's king, whilst **11 Be2 Bxf3** 12 gf gives Black a host of playable options: 12 ... Qh4+, 12 ... Na4, 12 ... Qd7 or **12 ... Na5**, as in Urzica–Ghizdavu, Romanian Ch 1973, which continued 13 b3 c5 14 dc Nd7 15 0-0-0 Qe7 16 Kb2 Nxc5 17 Bg5! Qc7 18 Qe3 a6 19 Rd6 and now Black went wrong with **19 ... Rc8?** 20 Rhd1 0-0? 21 Bf6!+− Nxc4+ 22 Bxc4 Bxc3+ 23 Kb1! 1-0. Instead **19 ... Nd7** 20 Rhd1! would give White compensation, but Ghizda-

vu's preference is **19 ... h6!?** 20
♗h4 ♖c8 21 ♖hd1 g5 22 ♗g3
(22 ♗e1!?) 22 ... b5! since 23 cb?
fails to 23 ... ♗xc3+.

| **11** | **...** | **♗e7** |

Now White must take pre-
cautions against the threat of 12
... ♘a5.

| **12** | **♘e4** |

12 ♖d1 f6 13 ef ♗xf6 14 ♘e4
♕e7 15 ♗e2 ♗xf3 16 gf 0–0–0
17 ♘xf6 gf 18 0–0 ♖d7 19 ♕c3
♖hd8 20 ♔h1 f5 21 ♖g1 f4 22
♗xf4 ♘xd4 23 ♖xd4 ♖xd4 24
♗g5 ♕f7 25 ♗xd8 ♖xd8 26 c5
♘d5 27 ♕e5 ♕f5 gave Black a
good ending in Pazos–Alburt,
Portland Open 1987.

12 b4 (An attempt to profit from
the move 11 a3.) 12 ... ♗xf3 13
gf ♗h4+ 14 ♔d1 and now in
Kremenietsky–Vaganian, Moscow 1981, **14 ... a5?!** 15 b5 ♘e7
16 ♔c2 ♘f5 17 ♖d1 f6 18 ♗d3!
fe 19 de 0–0 20 c5! gave Black
problems. Instead **14 ... f6!** 15 f4
g5! with fully-fledged counterplay
should be preferred.

| **12** | **...** | **♕d7** |

12 ... a5 intending ... a4 and ...
♘a5 is a reasonable alternative,
e.g. 13 ♗e2 ♗xf3 14 gf ♗h4+
Messing–Ghizdavu, Varna 1973.

| **13** | **♗e2** | **0–0–0** |
| **14** | **0–0–0** |

14 ♖d1 avoids the trouble in
which the white king soon finds
itself, but in such a position neither
king can expect much long-term
safety.

| **14** | **...** | **♗f5** |

| **15** | **♘g3** | **♗g6** |
| **16** | **h4?** |

Presumably Hübner had over-
looked Black's startling reply, but
after 16 ♗d3, Black's counterplay
is fully adequate: 16 ... ♗xd3 17
♕xd3 ♘a5 18 c5 ♘d5 19 b4 or 16
... ♘xd4 17 ♘xd4 ♗xd3 18 ♕xd3
c5 19 ♕c2 cd 20 ♗xd4=.

| **16** | **...** | **♘b4!** *(57)* |

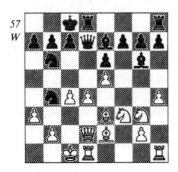

| **17** | **b3** |

The knight is immune: 17 ab
♕a4 18 ♗d3 ♘xc4–+.

| **17** | **...** | **♘c2** |
| **18** | **c5** | **♕c6!** |

A key move in the combination,
threatening ... ♗xc5.

| **19** | **♗d3** | **♘xe3** |

Hort gives 19 ... ♘xa3! 20 ♔b2
♗xd3 21 ♕xd3 ♗xc5 as more
decisive. Instead, White is given a
chance to organise some sort of
position.

| **20** | **♕xe3** | **♘d5** |
| **21** | **♕f2** |

21 ♕d2?! fails to 21 ... ♗xc5!

21	**...**	**♗xd3**
22	**♖xd3**	**♕a6**
23	**♖hd1**	**♕xa3+**

24 ♕b2 ♕xb2+
25 ♔xb2 f5

Black faces a hard battle to convert the extra a-pawn. 26 ♘e2 h6 27 h5 g5 28 hg ♖dg8 29 ♖h1 ♖xg6 30 g3 h5 31 ♖h3 ♖g4 32 ♘c3 ♘xc3 (32 ... ♘b4!?) 33 ♔xc3 ♔d7 34 b4 c6 35 ♘d2 b5! 36 ♔c2! ♔c7 37 ♔d1 f4 (37 ... ♗d8! intending ... ♔b7 and ... a5 is better. Now White has some chances of saving the half-point.) 38 gf ♖xf4 39 ♔e2 h4 40 ♔e3 ♖g4 41 ♘e4 ♖g1! 42 ♖a3 ♔b8 43 ♖h2 ♖f8! 44 ♖aa2 ♖b1 45 ♘f6? (45 ♖ab2!∓) 45 ... ♗xf6 46 ef ♖xf6 47 ♖xh4 ♖f7!−+ 48 ♔e4 ♖d7 49 ♔e5 ♖xb4 50 ♖d2 a5 51 ♔xe6 ♔c7 52 ♔e5 ♖e7+ 53 ♔f6 ♖d7 54 ♔e5 a4 55 ♔e4 ♖c4 0–1.

Timman–Marović
Banja Luka 1974

1 e4 ♘f6 2 e5 ♘d5 3 d4 d6 4 c4 ♘b6 5 f4 de 6 fe ♘c6 7 ♗e3 ♗f5 8 ♘c3 e6 9 ♘f3

9 ... ♗e7

9 ... ♗b4 is an alternative posting for the bishop. The move has a poor reputation, though this is mainly since Black often exchanges voluntarily on c3, rather than waiting to be provoked.

(a) **10 ♖c1 ♗g4!?** has similar ideas to 9 ... ♗g4, but the long-term destination of White's king is more of a problem here.

(b) **10 a3?! ♗xc3+ 11 bc ♕d7 12 ♗e2 ♘a5 13 ♘d2 ♕c6 14 0–0!**
(14 ♗f3? ♕a4 15 c5 ♕xd1+ 16 ♖xd1 ♘d5 17 ♗xd5 ed 18 0–0 ♗g6! 19 ♖de1 ♔d7!∓ Faibisovich–Bagirov, Baku 1969) 14 ... ♘axc4 15 ♘xc4 ♘xc4 16 d5! ♘xe3 17 dc ♘xd1 18 cb ♖b8 19 ♗b5+ ♔f8 20 ♖axd1 ♖xb7 21 ♖d8+ ♔e7 22 ♖xh8 ♖xb5∞ Bagirov.

(c) **10 ♗e2 0–0** (10 ... ♘a5!? 11 c5 ♘d5 12 ♗d2 ♘c6 13 0–0 0–0 14 ♗g5± Rohde–Shamkovich, New York 1976). Now:

(c1) **11 a3!? ♗xc3+ 12 bc ♘a5 13 ♘d2 c5 14 0–0 ♗g6 15 ♖f4 ♖c8 16 ♕f1 ♘a4 17 ♖c1 ♕e7 18 h4∞** Koch–Stull, Lyon Z 1990.

(c2) **11 0–0**

(c21) **11 ... ♗xc3?!** 12 bc ♘a5 13 ♘d2 ♕d7 14 ♖f4 (14 ♖f3 ♕a4!? 15 ♕f1 ♗g6 16 c5± Alburt) 14 ... ♗g6 (14 ... f6) 15 ♕f1 c5 16 h4! gives White a strong kingside attack. The plan is simply to advance the h- and g-pawns.

(c22) **11 ... ♘a5!?** 12 ♘d2 (12 c5 ♗xc3! is fine for Black after 13 bc ♘bc4 14 ♗g5 ♕d5! or 13 cb ♗b4 14 ♕a4 ♘c6 15 bc ♕xc7 16 d5 ed 17 ♘d4 ♗d7! 18 ♘xc6 a5!.) 12 ... ♗g6 13 ♕e1 c5 14 a3 (14 ♖f4 cd 15 ♗xd4 ♖c8 16 a3 ♘c6 17 ab ♘xd4 18 ♖xa7 ♘c2 19 ♕c1 ♕c7 20 c5 ♘xb4! 21 cb ♕xb6+ 22 ♔h1 ♕xa7 23 ♖xb4 ♕e3!∓ Mundra–Pötzsch, corres. 1985) 14 ... ♗xc3 15 bc ♖c8 16 ♖c1 ♕e7. Now White should try 17 ♖f3!?, supporting a3 while preparing a kingside attack. Instead 17 h4 cd 18 cd ♕xa3 and 17 ♕g3? cd 18 cd ♕xa3 19 ♖a1 ♕b4 20 h4 ♘axc4

21 ♘xc4 ♘xc4 22 h5 ♘xe3 23 ♛xe3 ♖c3∓ Goldenberg–Ghizdavu, Graz 1972, are less good.

(c3) **11 ♖c1!?** could well be White's best line. **11 ... ♛d7** 12 a3 ♗xc3+ 13 ♖xc3 ♖ad8 14 0–0 ♗g4 15 ♔h1! ♗xf3 (15 ... h6 16 b4! ♗xf3 17 ♗xf3 ♘xd4? 18 ♖d3) 16 ♗xf3 ♘xd4 17 ♗g5! is unpleasant for Black, e.g. 17 ... ♖b8 18 ♗e4 ♘f5 19 ♛h5 g6 20 ♛e2 (Bagirov). **11 ... ♘a5** 12 ♗g5 (12 ♘d2?! c5) 12 ... ♛d7 (12 ... ♗e7±) 13 c5 ♘a4 (13 ... ♘d5!? 14 ♗d2 b6) 14 ♛d2 b6 15 0–0 ♘xc3 (15 ... bc 16 ♗b5!) 16 bc ♗a3 17 ♖cd1 bc 18 ♘h4 ♗g6 19 ♘xg6 fg 20 ♗f3± Bohak–Preo, corres. 1983.

10 d5

10 ♗e2 leads to positions of a completely different character, with both sides developing calmly. **10 ... 0–0 11 0–0 f6 12 ef** (12 ♛b3 a6! 13 a3 fe 14 de ♘d7 15 ♖ad1 ♛c8∓ De Graaf–Prins, Holland 1987; 12 ♘h4 fe 13 ♘xf5 ef 14 d5 ♘d4! 15 ♗xd4 ed 16 ♛xd4 ♘d7!; 12 ♛e1 fe 13 de ♘d7! 14 ♖d1 ♛e8 15 ♛g3 ♗c5 16 ♗xc5 ♘xc5 17 ♘h4 ♘e4= Sarink–Van der Tak, corres. 1982) **12 ... ♗xf6 13 ♛d2** (13 h3 ♛e8! 14 g4 ♛g6 15 ♔h1 ♗e4 16 ♘xe4 ♛xe4∓) **13 ... ♛e7** (13 ... ♖f7 14 ♖ad1 ♖d7 15 c5! ♘d5 16 ♘xd5 ed 17 ♘e5!±; 13 ... ♛e8 14 ♗g5! ♖d8 15 ♗xf6 ♖xf6 16 ♖ad1 ♗g4 17 ♘e4 ♖f5 18 ♛e3 ♗xf3 19 ♖xf3 ♖xf3 20 gf! ♛g6+ 21 ♔h1 ♛h6 22 f4! ♖e8 23 ♘g5± Ignatiev–Larsen, Moscow 1962)

14 ♖ad1 (14 ♖ae1 ♔h8 15 ♔h1 ♖ad8 16 ♗g1 ♛b4!?; 14 c5 ♘d5 15 ♘xd5 ed 16 ♖ae1 ♗e4 17 b4 a6 18 a4 ♖ae8) **14 ... ♖ad8 15 ♛c1** *(58)* (15 c5?! ♘d5 16 ♘xd5 ed∓). Black now has two principal options:

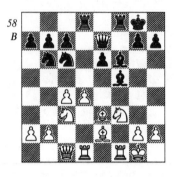

(a) **15 ... e5** 16 d5 ♘d4 17 ♗xd4 (17 ♘xd4 ed 18 ♗xd4 ♗g5 19 ♛a1 c5!? 20 ♗f2 ♗c2∞ Alburt) 17 ... ed 18 ♘xd4 ♗g5 19 ♛a1 ♗d7. Black has compensation.

(b) **15 ... h6** 16 ♔h1 ♔h8 17 h3 ♗h7 18 ♗g1 (18 ♖fe1?! ♛f7 19 ♖f1 ♛g8 20 b3 ♖fe8 21 c5?! ♘d5 22 ♗b5 ♘xc3 23 ♛xc3 ♗e4∓ Jovčić–Kovačević, Titovo Užice 1978) 18 ... ♖fe8 19 ♖fe1 ♛f7 20 ♛f4!? (20 c5 ♘d5 21 ♗b5 ♘db4 22 a3 a6 23 ab ab 24 ♘xb5 ♘xb4 25 ♛c4 ♘c6 26 ♗h2 ♖d7= Hecht–Timman, Wijk aan Zee 1971) and now 20 ... g5 followed by ... ♛g7 is probably best. Instead Klundt–Grzesik, Bundesliga 1985 continued 20 ... ♖e7 21 ♗f1 ♛e8 22 ♛g3 ♖dd7 23 ♘e4±.

Note that the attempt to avoid the complications following 10 d5, by means of the move order **6 ... ♗f5 7 ♘c3 e6 8 ♘f3 ♗e7 9 ♗e3 0-0?!** fails to **10 ♗d3!**:

10 ... ♗g6 11 h4!?

10 ... ♘c6 11 ♗xf5 ef 12 b3! ♕e8 12 c5± Lazarević–Alexandria, 1971.

10 ... ♗xd3 11 ♕xd3 ♘c6 12 ♖d1 f6 13 ef ♗xf6 14 0-0 ♕e8 15 b3 ♖ad8 16 ♕e4!± Velimirović–Hloušek, Kapfenburg 1970.

10 ... ♗g4 (This would be more than adequate if 9 ... ♘c6 had been played.) 11 0-0 ♘c6 12 h3 ♗xf3 (12 ... ♗h5 13 ♗xh7+! ♔xh7 14 ♘g5+ ♗xg5 15 ♕xh5+ ♗h6 16 ♖f6+ −) 13 ♕xf3 ♗g5 (13 ... ♘xd4? 14 ♕e4; 13 ... f6? 14 ef ♗xf6 15 ♕e4; 13 ... ♘xe5 14 ♗xh7+ ♔xh7 15 de ♕d3 16 ♖ad1± Velimirović–Marović, Yugoslav Ch 1972) 14 ♖ad1 f5 (14 ... f6? 15 ♗xg5 fg 16 ♕e3!± Morgado–Svenningson, corres. 1984) 15 ef ♖xf6 16 ♕e4 ♗xe3+ 17 ♕xe3 ♖xf1+ 18 ♗xf1 ♕e7 19 ♘e4. White has a clear positional advantage.

10 ... ♘b4

Black hopes to profit by leaving the pawn on c4 to limit the scope of White's king's bishop, but Black's knights' lack of access to d5 turns out to be no less important.

11 ♖c1

11 ♘d4 ♗g6 12 a3 (12 de c5! 13 ef+ ♔xf7!) **12 ... c5 13 ♘xe6** (13 ab cd and now 14 ♕xd4 ♗xb4 15 de 0-0!= Uitumen–Jansa, La Hababa 1967, or 14 ♗xd4?! ♗xb4 15 ♗e2 0-0 16 d6 ♕h4+

17 ♗f2 ♕g5 18 ♗g3 ♕e3 19 ♕d2 ♘xc4∓) **13 ... fe 14 ab cb**. White has two squares for the knight:

(a) **15 ♘b5** 0-0 16 ♖xa7 (16 ♘d4 ♗c5 17 ♗d3?? ♗xd4 0-1 Collado–Smejkal, Barcelona 1973; 16 d6?! ♗g5 17 ♗d4 ♗e3!∓ Kokkoris–Marović, Greece 1970) 16 ... ♖xa7 17 ♘xa7 ed 18 cd ♘xd5 19 ♗c4 ♗f7 20 ♗f2 ♕c7 21 ♕d4 ♘f4= Alburt.

(b) **15 ♘a4** 0-0 (Gipslis' 15 ... ♘d7 is considered to be refuted by 16 ♕d4 ♕a5 17 d6 ♗d8 18 c5 b5 19 b3! 0-0 20 ♘b6 ♕xa1+ 21 ♕xa1 ab 22 ♕b2! ♘xe5 23 ♕xe5! ♗f6 24 ♕xe6+ ♔h8 and now Ermenkov's 25 c6!) 16 ♘xb6 ab 17 ♖xa8 ♕xa8 18 d6 ♗d8 19 ♗e2 b3! (19 ... ♕a2 20 ♗d4 b5) 20 ♖f1 ♕a5+ 21 ♕d2 ♕xe5 22 ♖xf8+ ♔xf8 23 ♗f4 ♕a5 24 d7 ♗e4 25 ♗d6+! ♔f7 26 ♗b4! ♕e5 27 ♕e3 ♕f5 28 ♕xb3 ♗xg2∞ is generally considered best play.

11 ... ed

11 ... 0-0? 12 a3 ♘a6 13 ♗d3! is obviously bad, whilst **11 ... f6?** 12 a3 ♘a6 13 g4! ♗xg4 14 ♖g1 gave White an overwhelming kingside initiative in Velimirović–Gipslis, Havana 1971.

12 a3 c5

12 ... ♘xc4 13 ♗xc4 dc 14 ab ♕xd1+ 15 ♖xd1 (15 ♘xd1 ♗xb4+ 16 ♗d2±) 15 ... ♗xb4 16 0-0± was Kostro–Hloušek, Luhačovice 1971. The three pawns are nearly worth the piece.

13 ab d4

| 14 | ♗xd4 | cd *(59)* |

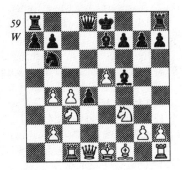

| 15 | ♛xd4 |

15 ♘xd4. Now 15 ... ♗g6 16 c5! is good for White after either 16 ... ♗g5 17 ♖a1! or 16 ... 0–0!? 17 ♘f3! ♘d7 18 ♗b5! ♘b8 (18 ... ♗g5 19 ♖a1 ♘xe5 20 ♘xe5 ♛f6 21 ♘f3 ♖ad8 22 ♛b3 denied Black compensation in Uitumen–Vaganian, Dubna 1973.) 19 ♛xd8 ♖xd8 20 ♔e2 a5 21 ♖hd1 ab 22 ♘d5 Stanciu–Bagirov, Wroclaw 1975. Therefore **15 ... ♛b8** is normal:

(a) **16 ♛e2 ♗g6** (16 ... ♗e6!? is quite possibly an improvement.) 17 c5 ♘d7 18 c6!? (18 e6 ♘e5 19 ♛b5+ ♔f8 20 ef a6 21 ♛e8+∞; 18 ♘d5 ♗g5!? 19 c6 0–0 20 cd ♗xc1 21 e6∞ Nunn) 18 ... ♘xe5 (18 ... bc 19 ♘xc6 ♛b7 20 ♘d5± Nunn) 19 ♘d5. Now 19 ... ♗h4+ 20 g3 0–0 21 c7 ♛c8 22 gh ♖e8 23 ♔d1 ♛d7 24 ♗g2 was good for White in Nielsen–Gouverneur, corres. 1975.

(b) **16 ♘xf5 ♛xe5+** 17 ♗e2 ♛xf5 18 c5 ♘d7 (18 ... ♖d8 19

♛c2!) 19 ♘d5 (19 ♛d5 ♛f4! 20 ♖d1 0–0–0!; 19 ♗g4 ♛e5+ 20 ♛e2 ♛xe2+ 21 ♔xe2 ♘e5) 19 ... ♗d8 20 ♖c3 0–0 21 ♘e3 (21 ♗g4 ♖e8+) 21 ... ♛e6 22 ♗g4 (22 0–0±) 22 ... f5 23 ♗f3 ♘f6 24 0–0 (24 ♗xb7 ♖b8 25 ♗d5 ♘xd5 26 ♛xd5 ♖e8!) 24 ... ♘e4 25 ♗xe4 led to a good ending for White in Velimirović–Marović, Yugoslavia 1977.

| 15 | ... | ♗xb4 |
| 16 | c5 |

16 ♛f4 is an untried suggestion of Timman's.

| 16 | ... | ♘d5 |

After **16 ... ♗xc3+!? 17 ♖xc3** (17 bc ♘d7 18 ♛d6 ♛e7) **17 ... ♘d5 18 ♗b5+,** Timman gave **18 ... ♔f8 19 ♖a3±,** but SDO's **18 ... ♗d7** is clearly a better try, e.g. 19 c6 bc 20 ♖xc6 ♘c7, 19 ♗xd7+ ♛xd7 20 ♖d3 ♖d8 21 0–0 0–0 22 ♖fd1∞, or 19 ♛xd5 ♗xb5 20 ♛xb7 ♖b8 21 ♛xa7 (21 ♛e4) 21 ... 0–0 22 ♔f2 ♗c6∞.

| 17 | ♗b5+ | ♗d7 |
| 18 | ♛xd5? |

18 ♗xd7+! ♛xd7 19 0–0 ♘xc3 (19 ... ♗xc3 20 bc 0–0–0 21 ♘g5±) 20 bc ♛xd4+ 21 cd ♖d8 22 ♖c4 a5 23 ♔f2± Vrabec–Jurek, Czechoslovakia 1976.

18	...	♗xb5
19	♛xb7	♖b8
20	♛e4	a5
21	♔f2	♗xc5+
22	♔g3	0–0
23	♖hd1

23 ♘d5 fails to 23 ... f5! 24 ef ♛d6+, but 23 ♘xb5 ♖xb5 24 ♛c6

♕b6 25 ♕xb6 ♗xb6 26 ♖c2 ♖d8
gives Black just a small advantage.

23	...	♕b6
24	♘g5?	♗f2+
25	♔f3	f5!
26	ef	♕xf6+
27	♔g4	h5+

0–1

Velimirović–Kovačević
Pula 1978

1 e4 ♘f6 2 e5 ♘d5 3 d4 d6 4 c4
♘b6 5 f4 de 6 fe ♘c6 7 ♗e3 ♗f5
8 ♘c3 e6 9 ♘f3 ♗e7

10	d5	ed
11	cd	

11 ♗xb6 ab 12 cd ♘b4 13 ♘d4
is an interesting idea, but one
would not expect that this
exchange of pieces should enhance
White's attacking prospects. Black
should avoid **13 ... ♕d7?** 14 a3
♘xd5 15 ♘xf5+–, **13 ... ♗d7?**
14 a3 ♗c5 15 ♘f3 ♘a6 16 b4±
and **13 ... ♗c8?** 14 a3 ♘xd5 15
♗b5+ ♔f8 16 ♕f3! ♗c5 17
♖f1! f6 18 0–0–0+– Velimirović–
Kovačević, Yugoslav Ch (Pula)
1981, but may experiment with
Cafferty's **13 ... ♗e4!?** 14 ♘xe4
(14 d6 ♗h4+; 14 ♗b5+ c6 and
now 15 ♘xc6 bc 16 ♘xe4 cb 17
d6 0–0! 18 0–0 ♗g5∓ or 15 dc
bc 16 ♘xe4 ♕xd4 17 ♕xd4 ♘c2+
18 ♔d2 ♘xd4 19 ♗c4 ♖a5∓)
14 ... ♕xd5 15 ♗b5+ (15 ♘c3?
♕xd4) 15 ... c6 16 ♘d6+ ♗xd6
17 ed∞ 0–0 (17 ... ♕xd4? 18
♕e2+) 18 0–0 cb 19 ♘f5 ♕xd1 20
♖axd1.

The most reliable move is **13 ...
♗g6** *(60)*

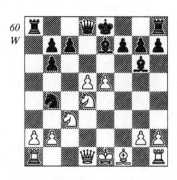

(a) **14 ♗b5+** c6 15 dc 0–0! 16
cb ♖b8 17 ♘c6 ♘xc6 18 ♗xc6
♕c7 19 ♘d5 ♗h4+! 20 g3 ♕xc6
21 gh ♕xb7 22 ♕f3 ♖fe8 23 0–0
♖xe5 24 ♘c3 ♕e7 25 ♕g3 ♖e8 26
♖f4 ♗h5 27 ♖af1 h6∓ Murey–
Palatnik, Palma GMA 1989.

(b) **14 d6**. Black is really spoilt
for choice:

(b1) **14 ... ♗xd6** 15 ed 0–0 16
dc ♕xc7 17 ♗b5 ♖ad8 18 0–0
♘c2 19 ♕xc2 ♗xc2 20 ♘xc2
♖d2∓ Majerić–Rogulj, Zagreb
1981.

(b2) **14 ... 0–0** 15 a3 (15 de
♕xe7) 15 ... cd 16 ab ♖xa1 17
♕xa1 de 18 ♘f3 ♗xb4 19 ♕d1
(19 ♗e2 e4 20 ♘e5 ♕d4 21 ♘xg6
hg∓) 19 ... ♕f6 20 ♕b3 ♕f4 21
♗e2 occurred in Chandler–
Kengis, Jurmala 1983. 21 ... ♕c1+
22 ♗d1 ♕e3+ 23 ♗e2 ♗c5 24
♖f1 ♖d8! intending ... e4 would
then have been extremely strong.

(b3) **14 ... ♗h4+** 15 g3 0–0
16 a3 (16 gh? ♕xh4+ 17 ♔e2

♗d3+) 16 ... ♕g5! (16 ... c5 17
♞f3 ♞c2+ 18 ♔f2 ♗g5 19 ♗d3
♞xa1 20 ♗xg6 hg 21 ♕xa1 ♗h6
22 ♕a2 ♕d7 23 ♕d5 and now in
Murey–Kovačević, Hastings
1981/2, 23 ... ♖ae8!∓ was possible.) 17 ♔f2 (17 gh ♕e3+; 17 ab
♗xg3+ 18 hg ♕xg3+ 19 ♔e2
♕xe5+ 20 ♔f2 ♖xa1–+) 17 ...
♕xe5 18 ♞f3 (18 gh? ♞d3+ 19
♗xd3 ♕xd4+ 20 ♔e2? ♗h5+)
18 ... ♕c5+ 19 ♕d4 (19 ♔g2
♞c2) 19 ... ♕xd4+ 20 ♞xd4 ♗f6
21 ♖d1 ♞d3+ left Black pawns
up in Carlsson–Kuhnrich, corres.
1985.

11	...	♞b4
12	♞d4	♗d7
13	♕f3	

13 ♞f3 is a rather peculiar idea,
inviting a repetition of moves with
13 ... ♗f5 14 ♞d4. Geller–Vaganian, Sochi 1986 continued instead
13 ... ♗g4 14 ♗xb6 ab 15 ♗e2
♗c5 16 a3 ♗xf3 17 ♗xf3 ♕h4+
18 g3 ♕d4 19 ♕xd4 ♞c2+ 20
♔d2 ♞xd4 21 ♗d1 c6 22 ♔d3
b5 with equality.

A major alternative is **13 ♕b3**.
Then 13 ... a5? fails to 14 d6! cd
15 e6 fe 16 ♗b5!±, so normal is
13 ... c5 14 dc (14 ♞f3?! c4 15
♗xc4 ♞xc4 16 ♕xc4 ♞c2+ 17
♔f2 ♞xa1 18 ♖xa1 ♖c8 19 ♕e4
♗c5 20 ♖e1 was reckoned by
O'Kelly to give White compensation; 14 ♞db5 ½–½ Grünfeld–
Fernandez Garcia, New York
Open 1987 failed to shed much
light on this particular idea.) **14 ...
bc** and now White has generally

placed the rook on d1 one way or
another.

(a) **15 ♖d1** ♕b8!? (15 ... ♞4d5?
16 ♞xc6! ♗xc6 17 ♗b5!±; 15 ...
♞6d5 16 ♞xd5 ♞xd5 17 ♗c4
♖b8 18 ♕d3 ♞xe3 19 ♕xe3 ♕a5+
20 ♖d2! ♗b4! 21 ♗xf7+! ♔e7!?
22 ♕g5+ ♔xf7 23 0–0+ ♔g8 24
♞f5 ♗xf5 25 ♕xf5 was Timman–
Kovačević, Wijk aan Zee 1980.
Now 25 ... h6! would have left
White with nothing better than to
take the perpetual.) 16 e6 fe 17
♞f3 (17 ♞xe6? ♕e5) 17 ... a5 18
♞e4 ♞6d5 19 ♗c5 ♗xc5 20 ♞xc5
♞xa2!∓ Polajzer–Kovačević,
Maribor 1980.

(b) **15 0–0–0**. Now 15 ... ♞4d5?
fails to 16 ♞xc6 ♗xc6 17 ♗xb6
♗g5+ 18 ♔c2±, so Black has
tried:

(b1) **15 ... ♞6d5** 16 ♗c4 and
rather than 16 ... ♞xe3? 17
♗xf7+ ♔f8 18 ♞e6+ or 16 ...
0–0?! 17 ♞xc6 ♗xc6 18 ♞xd5
♗xd5 19 ♗xd5 ♕c7+ 20 ♕c3!
♕a5 21 ♔b1 ♖ac8 22 ♕b3 ♖cd8
23 ♗c4 ♕xe5 24 ♖xd8 ♖xd8?!
(Ljubojević–Rogulj, Yugoslav Ch
1977) when 25 ♗xf7+ ♔h8 26
♕e6 would simply have won a
pawn, best is 16 ... ♖b8! 17 ♞xd5
♞xd5 18 ♗xd5 ♖xb3 19 ♗xb3
♗g5! when Black's chances are
preferable.

(b2) **15 ... ♕c7** 16 ♗c4?! (16 e6
fe 17 ♞xe6 ♕e5 18 ♖xd7!?∞ is
given by Palatnik.) 16 ... ♞xc4 17
♕xc4 ♕xe5! 18 ♖he1 0–0∓ 19 a3
(19 ♗d2 ♕c5; 19 ♞f3 ♕e6; 19
♗g1 ♕g5+) 19 ... ♞d5 20 ♞xc6

♗xc6 21 ♘xd5 ♗xa3!!−+ 22 ba
(22 ♘c3 ♖fc8) 22 ... ♖fc8 23 ♗c5
(23 ♔b1 ♗xd5 and 24 ... ♖ab8+)
23 ... ♗xd5 24 ♖xe5 ♗xc4 25
♔b2 f6 0–1 Tsarëv–Palatnik,
Kiev 1989. The rook will be chased
away from the defence of the
bishop.

13 ... c5

Alburt suggested 13 ... 0–0 14
a3 c5 15 ab cd 16 ♗xd4 ♗xb4.

14 dc

14 ♘b3!? ♘c2+ 15 ♔f2 ♘xa1
16 ♘xa1 0–0 17 ♗d3 f5 gave
White interesting compensation in
Rigo–Schroll, Vienna 1987.
Instead, **14 e6** is comfortably met
by 14 ... 0–0.

14 ... bc

14... ♘xc6? failed rather drastically in Ligterink–Böhm, Amsterdam 1974: 15 e6! fe 16 ♗d3
♗h4+ 17 g3 ♗f6 18 ♕h5+ and
a massacre followed, but **14 ...
♗xc6** 15 ♘xc6 bc might be playable.

15 e6

15 a3 was played in Ljubojević–
Hartston, Las Palmas 1974, in
which **15 ... ♘4d5?!** 16 ♘xd5
♘xd5 17 ♗c4 ♕a5+ 18 ♗d2
(18 ♔f2? ♘xe3!∓) 18 ... ♕c5 19
♗xd5 ♕xd5 20 ♕xd5 cd 21 ♖c1
a5! just about held the balance.
Instead, Hartston gave **15 ... c5!**
16 ab cd 17 ♗xd4 0–0 as equal.

15 0–0–0?! 0–0 16 ♘f5 ♘6d5 17
♘xe7+ ♕xe7 18 ♘xd5 cd! 19 a3
♖fc8+ 20 ♔b1 ♘c2 21 ♗c1
♖ab8−+ Trkalyanov–Kova-
čević, Stip 1979.

15 ... fe

Black's position collapses after
15 ... ♗xe6? 16 a3 ♘4d5 17 ♘xc6.

16 0–0–0

16 a3?! ♘4d5 17 ♗d3 (17 ♗f2
♘xc3 followed by 18 ... ♗f6 is
very pleasant for Black.) 17 ...
♘xe3 18 ♕xe3 (18 ♕h5+? g6 19
♗xg6+ ♔f8 20 ♔e2 ♔g7!−+)
18 ... 0–0 19 ♕e4 (19 ♘xe6 ♗xe6
20 ♕xe6+ ♔h8 21 0–0–0 ♖b8!∓
and it turns out that it is White's
king that is in danger.) 19 ... g6
20 h4?! (20 ♘xe6 ♗xe6 21 ♕xe6+
♔g7 22 0–0–0 ♖b8!∓) 20 ...
e5!−+ 21 ♘f3 ♗f5 22 ♗c4+
♔g7 23 ♕e2 ♘xc4 24 ♕xc4 ♕b6
25 0–0–0 ♖ab8 26 ♖d2 ♗xa3 27
♔d1 ♕b3+ 28 ♕xb3 ♖xb3 29 ba
♖xc3 30 ♘xe5 ♖xa3 31 ♖e1 ♖e8!
32 ♖de2 ♖d8+ 33 ♔c1 ♖b3 0–1
Velimirović–Kovačević, Yugoslav
Ch 1979.

16 ... ♘6d5
17 a3 ♘xc3
18 ♘xe6!? *(61)*

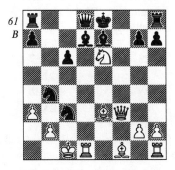

18 ... ♕a5

18 ... ♕c8?? allows mate in
three, but Cafferty pointed out the

queen sacrifice **18 ... ♘ca2+!** 19 ♔b1 ♗xe6 20 ♖xd8+ ♖xd8. Black already has a reasonable amount of material for the queen, has maintained a knight on b4 and so can reckon on creating some strong threats against the white king.

19	**♘xg7+**	**♔d8**
20	**♖xd7+!?**	**♔xd7**
21	**♕g4+**	**♔c7**
22	**ab**	**♘a2+?**

After this, White's king becomes surprisingly safe. Necessary and good is **22 ... ♕a1+** 23 ♔c2 ♘d5 when White may have nothing better than 24 ♘e6+ ♔b7 25 ♘c5+ ♗xc5 26 ♕d7+ ♘c7 27 ♗b5 cb 28 ♖xa1 ♗xe3 which gives Black more than enough for the queen.

23	**♔b1**	**♘xb4**
24	**♗c4!**	**♔b7**
25	**♕d7+**	**♕c7**
26	**♖d1**	

With the devastating threat of 27 ♘e6. 26 ... ♘d5? 27 ♖xd5 is no defence, so Black must return the exchange.

26	**...**	**♖ad8**
27	**♕xc7+**	**♔xc7**
28	**♘e6+**	**♔b7**
29	**♘xd8+**	**♖xd8**
30	**♖xd8**	**♗xd8**
31	**g4!**	

The ending is highly favourable for White due to the weakness of Black's kingside and the lack of coordination between the knight and bishop: 31 ... ♘d5 32 ♗c1 ♗h4 33 ♗d3 ♘f6 34 g5 ♘g4 35 h3 ♘f2 36 ♗f5! (The adventures of Black's knight have resulted only in it being trapped.) 36 ... ♔c7 37 ♗f4+ ♔d8 38 ♔c2 ♔e7 39 ♔d2 ♔f7 40 ♔e2 ♔g7 41 ♗e3 ♘h1 42 ♔f3 ♘g3 43 ♗d3 1–0.

Velimirović–Kovačević
Yugoslav Ch 1984

1 e4 ♘f6 2 e5 ♘d5 3 d4 d6 4 c4 ♘b6 5 f4 de 6 fe ♘c6 7 ♗e3 ♗f5 8 ♘c3 e6 9 ♘f3 ♗e7 10 d5 ed 11 cd ♘b4 12 ♘d4 ♗d7

13	**e6**	**fe**
14	**de**	**♗c6**
15	**♕g4**	

Other moves give little:

15 ♘xc6 ♕xd1+ 16 ♖xd1 (16 ♔xd1 ♘xc6 17 ♗b5 0–0–0+) 16 ... ♘c2+ 17 ♔d2 ♘xe3 18 ♔xe3 bc 19 ♗e2 (19 ♗a6 0–0= Urzica–Grünberg, Romanian Ch 1974) 19 ... 0–0 20 ♖hf1 ♗f6 21 ♗g4 ♘c4+ 22 ♔e2 ♖ab8 23 b3 ♘d6 Hort–Biehler, Lugano 1987.

15 a3 ♘4d5 16 ♕f3 ♗h4+ (16 ... ♖f8? 17 ♕h5+ g6 18 ♕xh7+ — Laine–Rantanen, corres. 1977; 16 ... ♗f6 Nunn) 17 ♗f2 ♗xf2+ 18 ♕xf2 ♕f6 19 ♕xf6 ♘xf6 20 ♘xc6 bc 21 ♗a6 ♖d8= Riedel–Grzesik, Bundesliga 1987/8.

15 ♕h5+ g6. White hopes to profit from the weakening of Black's kingside, but White's knight being denied access to f5 gives Black extra possibilities. 16 ♕h6 (16 ♗e2? ♗f6∓) 16 ... ♗f6 (16 ... ♗h4+!? 17 g3 ♗f6) 17

0–0–0 ♕e7! 18 a3 ᘯ4d5 19 ᘯxc6
bc 20 ᘯxd5 ᘯxd5 21 ♖xd5! cd 22
♗b5+ ♔d8 23 ♖f1 (23 ♗c6?
d4! is unpromising, so White targets the h4–d8 diagonal.) 23 ...
♖f8 24 ♖xf6 ♖xf6 25 ♗g5 ♖b8
and in Filipenko–Gleizerov,
USSR 1987, it turned out that a
perpetual was inevitable: 26 ♗d7
(26 a4 ♖b6!) 26 ... ♕c5+ 27 ♔b1
♖xb2+!.

  15 ...   ♗h4+
  16 g3   ♗xh1 *(62)*
  16 ... ᘯ6d5? is met by 17
♗h6!!+ –, whilst **16 ... ♗f6?** 17
0–0–0! ♗xh1 18 ᘯf5! gives White
a winning attack: 18 ... ♕xd1+ 19
♕xd1 ♗c6 20 ᘯxg7+! Martin-
Rivas, Málaga 1981, or 18 ...
ᘯ6d5 19 ᘯxg7+ ♗xg7 20 ♕h5+
♔e7 21 ♗c5+ ♔xe6 22 ♗h3+
1–0 Williams–Cafferty, British Ch
(Blackpool) 1971.

62
W

  17   ♗b5+
The main line is **17 0–0–0 ♕f6
18 gh 0–0**, though permutations
of these moves are feasible: 17
0–0–0 0–0 18 gh ♕f6, or 17 gh 0–0
18 0–0–0 ♕f6. The consequences

were first analysed thoroughly by
players at Cambridge University in
the early 1970s. White has generally
chosen a bishop move.

  19 ♗h3? ♗f3 20 ᘯxf3 ♕xf3
21 ♕xf3 ♖xf3 22 ♗xb6 ab 23 e7
♔f7! 24 ♖d8 ♔xe7 25 ♖xa8
♖xh3–+.

  19 ♗g5?! ♕xf1! 20 ♖xf1 (20 e7?
ᘯxa2+ 21 ᘯxa2 ♕c4+ 22 ᘯc3
♖f1∓ Kupreichik–Alburt, Odessa
1974) 20 ... ♖xf1+ 21 ᘯd1 (21
♔d2 ᘯc4+ 22 ♔e2 ♖af8 23 ᘯd1
ᘯc2!– +) 21 ... ᘯd3+ 22 ♔c2
ᘯe1+ and now White must allow
the perpetual with 23 ♔c1 ᘯd3+,
since after 23 ♔c3? ᘯd5+! 24
♔c4 ᘯf3 25 ᘯxf3 ♗xf3 26 ♕h3
♗e2+ 27 ♔xd5 ♖xd1+ the
queen was no match for the black
rooks in Rinaldi–Nederkoorn,
corres. 1985.

  19 ♗e2 gives Black two principal options (19 ... ♗c6? 20 ♗g5
♕e5 21 e7 ♖f2 22 ᘯxc6 ᘯxc6 23
♖d8+ is bad):

  (a) **19 ... c5** 20 ♗g5 (20 ♖xh1
cd 21 ♗xd4 ♕h6+ 22 ♔b1 ♖f4
23 ♗xg7 ♖xg4 24 ♗xh6 ♖g6∓)
20 ... ♕e5 (20 ... ♕f2 21 ♗h6
and now not 21 ... ♕f6? 22 ᘯf5!±,
but 21 ... ♕g2!?) 21 e7 (21 ᘯdb5!?
♗d5 22 e7 ♖fe8! 23 ᘯxd5 ᘯ4xd5
24 ♗c4 ♔h8 25 ♗xd5 ᘯxd5 26
♕c4! a6! was Botterill–Williams,
British Ch (Eastbourne) 1973; 27
ᘯd6! ♕xd6 28 ♖xd5 ♕xh2 29
♖d8 ♕g1+ would then have been
a draw.) 21 ... cd 22 ef♕+ ♖xf8
23 ♕xd4 (23 ♖xd4? h5!) 23 ...
♕xd4 24 ♖xd4 ᘯc6 25 ♖f4 ᘯe5

(25 ... ♖xf4; 25 ... h6) 26 ♖xf8+
♔xf8 27 ♗f4 gave White a slight
edge in Gaprindashvili–Alexandria, Women's World Ch (Pit-
sunda) 1975, which 27 ... ♘bd7
would have kept to a minimum.

(b) **19 ... ♗d5 20 ♗g5** (20
♖g1?! ♕g6 21 ♕h3 ♘d3+; 20 a3
♘a2+ 21 ♘xa2 ♗xa2 22 ♖g1
♘d5 23 ♗g5 ♕g6! Palaty–Hlous-
kovi, Czech Ch 1983) **20 ... ♕e5
21 e7** gives Black three viable
options:

(b1) **21 ... ♖fe8** 22 ♘xd5 (22
♘f5 ♗e6) 22 ... ♘4xd5!? (22 ...
♕xd5!? 23 ♘f5 ♕c5+) 23 ♘f5
♔h8 (Boleslavsky analysed 23 ...
g6 24 ♘h6+ ♔g7 25 ♖f1 ♖xe7
26 ♘f5+ gf 27 ♖xf5 ♕xf5 28 ♕xf5
♖xe2 29 ♕g5 ♖ee8 30 ♗d8+
with a perpetual.) 24 ♗d3 ♘xe7!
25 ♘xe7 ♖xe7 26 ♗xe7 ♕xe7 27
h5 ♘d5= Korman–Alburt, Lund
1976.

(b2) **21 ... ♖f7** 22 a3 (22 ♘f3?
♘xa2+!∓) 22 ... ♘c6 23 ♘xd5
♘xd5 24 ♗c4 ♘cxe7 25 ♘f3 (25
♗xe7 ♖xe7 26 ♘f5 c6 27 ♘xe7+
♕xe7=) 25 ... ♖xf3 26 ♕xf3 c6
27 ♖f1 h6 28 ♕f7+ ♔h8 29
♗d3 ♕d6! gave White sufficient
compensation only to regain the
pawn in Hübener–Sprenger, corres. 1983/4.

(b3) **21 ... ♖f2** 22 a3 c5! 23
ab cd 24 ♖xd4 h5! with at least
equality in Marjanović–Čičo-
vački, Sombor 1978.

19 ♗b5!? c5! (19 ... c6 leads to
positions considered in the note
to Black's 19th move in the main

game; 19 ... ♗f3? 20 ♘xf3 ♕xf3
21 ♕xf3 ♖xf3 22 ♗xb6 ab 23
e7+−; 19 ... ♗c6?! 20 ♗g5! ♕e5
21 e7 ♖fe8 22 ♘f5!± Marjanović–
Rogulj, Yugoslavia 1975; 19 ...
♕e5 just gives White an extra
option besides transposing to the
main line with 20 ♗g5 c5, viz. 20
♗h6!? c5 21 ♖g1 and now Black
should try 21 ... g6, since after 21
... cd 22 ♕xg7+! ♕xg7 23 ♗xg7
♖f2 24 ♗xd4+ ♖g2 25 ♖xh1
♘c6 26 ♗c5 ♖e8 27 e7! ♘d7 28
♗d6 a6 29 ♗c4+ ♔g7, 30 ♖e1!
intending ♘d5–c7 would have
given White some advantage in
Kveinis–Panchenko, Daugavpils
1979.) **20 ♗g5** (20 ♖xh1 ♘6d5 21
♗g5 ♕xd4 22 ♕xd4 cd 23 ♘xd5
♖ac8+ 24 ♔b1 ♘xd5 25 e7=
SDO) **20 ... ♕e5** (20 ... ♗f3?
21 ♘xf3 ♕xf3 22 ♕xf3 ♖xf3 23
e7+−; 20 ... ♕f2 with the ideas
21 e7 cd and 21 ♗h6 ♕f6 22 ♘f5
♗f3! may well be playable.) **21 e7
cd 22 ef♕+ ♖xf8 23 ♖xh1** *(63)*
(After 23 ♕xd4?!, Black has 23
... ♘xa2+!, based on 24 ♘xa2?
♕xb5∓ 25 ♖xh1? ♕c6+. Weide-
man–Hübner, Bundesliga 1983
continued instead 24 ♔c2 ♕f5+
25 ♗d3 ♕f2+ 26 ♕xf2 ♖xf2+
27 ♔b3 ♘xc3 28 bc ♖xh2 29
♗d8 and the grandmaster was
subsequently held to a draw.) Now
Black must choose carefully:

(a) **23 ... a5?** 24 ♕e2! (24 ♕e4?
♘xa2+!∞) 24 ... ♕c7 25 ♕e6+
♔h8 26 ♖f1!+− ♖xf1+ (26 ...
♖g8 27 ♗e7! ♕c8 28 ♕xb6
♘xa2+ 29 ♔b1 ♘xc3+ 30 bc

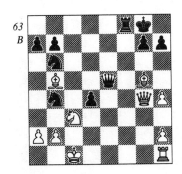

♕xc3 31 ♕e6 h6 32 ♗c4 1–0
Renet–Darcyl, Belfort 1983) 27
♗xf1 h6 28 ♕e8+ ♔h7 29 ♕e4+
♔h8 was Strenzwilk–Ladzinski,
Baltimore 1981; the plan 30 ♗f4
♕c5 31 ♗g2 ♘d7 32 ♕e8+ ♘f8
33 ♕b5 ♘xa2+ 34 ♔c2 ♘b4+
35 ♔b3 ♕c8 36 ♕xb7 was
sufficient to give White a winning
ending.

(b) **23 ... ♖c8?** 24 ♔b1 dc 25
♕xb4 c2+ 26 ♔c1 +– SDO.

(c) **23 ... h6!?** 24 ♗xh6 dc and
now 25 ♖g1 ♖f7 (25 ... cb+!?
SDO) 26 ♕xb4 ♕xh2, as given by
Wall and McCambridge, is rather
unclear. SDO analyses 25 ♕xb4
cb+ 26 ♔b1 ♕f5+ 27 ♔xb2
♕f6+, when Black has all the
chances.

(d) **23 ... a6!?** is reasonable. 24
♕e2 ♕xe2 25 ♗xe2 (25 ♘xe2? ab
26 ♘xd4 ♖f2!∓ is SDO's improvement on Boleslavsky's analysis.)
and now 25 ... ♘4d5= (Boleslavsky) and 25 ... dc 26 ♗e7 ♖e8 27
♗xb4 ♖xe2 28 ♗xc3 (SDO) are
both adequate for Black.

(e) **23 ... dc!?** is the simplest for
Black. 24 ♕xb4 cb+ (24 ... h6!?

drew comfortably in Murey–
Alburt, Beersheva 1980.) 25 ♔b1
♘d5! 26 ♕c4 (26 ♗c4 ♕e4+ 27
♔xb2 ♖f2+ 28 ♔a3 ♖f3+ is a
perpetual, since 29 ♔a4?? fails to
29 ... a6.) 26 ... ♖f2 (Threatens
27 ... ♕e4+!) 27 ♕c8+ ♔f7 28
♕xb7+ ♔g8 29 ♕c8+ ♖f8 30
♕c4 ♖f2 31 ♕c8+ ½–½ Krantz–
Nederkoorn, corres. 1977. Black
must keep re-installing the threat,
so White must keep checking.

17 ...   c6

17 ... ♗c6?! 18 0-0-0 ♕f6 19
gh 0-0 is a bad line for Black: 20
♗g5 ♕e5 21 e7 ♖fe8 22 ♘f5!±.

18   0-0-0   0-0

18 ... ♘4d5? 19 ♘xc6! bc 20
♕xg7+ –.

19   gh

Now 19 ♘xc6? ♘xc6 20 ♖xd8
♗xd8 leaves Black material up.

19 ...   h5!

Bad are **19 ... cb?** 20 ♘f5 ♕f6
21 ♗d4+ – and **19 ... ♘6d5?!** 20
♗c4! ♔h8 21 ♗g5 ♕a5 (21 ...
♕e8 22 ♖xh1) 22 e7 ♖fe8 23 ♘f5
♘xc3 24 ♗h6+ –, as analysed by
Kovačević. Here are two alternatives that, at least, are unrefuted:

(a) **19 ... ♘4d5** 20 ♘xd5 ♕xd5
(20 ... ♘xd5 21 ♗c4; 20 ... ♗xd5
21 ♗d3 ♕f6 22 ♖g1) and now
Roth's 21 e7!? may be investigated,
if White does not want a perpetual
with 21 ♖g1 g6 22 ♗d3 ♗f3! 23
♕xg6+.

(b) **19 ... ♕f6** 20 ♗g5:

(b1) **20 ... ♕e5?** 21 e7 ♖fe8 (21
... ♖f7 22 ♘f5! ♗d5 23 ♘h6+
Wall; 21 ... cb 22 ef♕+ ♖xf8

23 ♖xh1 ♘d3+ 24 ♔c2 ♘f2 25
♕e6+ ♕xe6 26 ♘xe6 ♘xh1 27
♘xf8 ♔xf8 28 ♗e3+− Bottlik)
22 ♘f5 h5 23 ♖xb4± Wall.

(b2) **20 ... ♕f2!?** is recommended by SDO. 21 e7 gives Black
the choice between 21 ... cb 22
ef♕+ ♖xf8 23 ♕e2 (23 a3 ♘c6;
23 ♗e7!? ♕e3+; 23 ♘de2 ♗f3
24 ♕e6+ ♔h8 25 ♕f5!?) 23 ...
♕xe2 24 ♘dxe2 ♗f3 25 ♗e7 ♖e8
26 ♗xb4 ♗xe2 27 ♖e1 ♗h5 28
♘xb5= and 21 ... ♖fe8 22 ♖f1
(22 ♗e2!?) 22 ... ♕g2 23 ♕f5!?
(23 ♕f4 h6; 23 ♕e6+ ♔h8 24 ♕f7
h6) 23 ... h6 24 ♘e6 (24 ♗e2!?)
24 ... ♕c2+ 25 ♕xc2 ♘xc2 26
♘c7. White could try 21 ♗e2,
preserving the bishop while cutting out Black's threats to c2 and
d3.

20   ♕g3

The only way to keep control
of g7 and f5 loses the initiative: 20
♕g6 cb 21 ♖xh1 ♕c7!.

20   ...   cb
21   ♗g5

21 ♘f5? fails to the typical queen
sacrifice 21 ... ♖xf5 22 ♖xd8+
♖xd8, whilst after **21 ♖g1?**,
White's king becomes the centre
of attention: 21 ... ♕f6 22 ♘f5
♘xa2+!! 23 ♘xa2 ♖ac8+ 24 ♔d1
♗f3+ 25 ♕xf3 ♕xf5−+.

21   ...   ♕b8
22   e7   ♖e8 *(64)*
23   ♖xh1?!

After this White is in some
trouble. After **23 ♕xb8!?** ♖axb8
24 ♖xh1 ♖bc8 25 ♔b1 a6 26
♖g1, White has the g-file for active

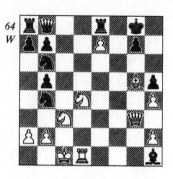

operations. Together with the e-
pawn, this ensures that White is
at least no worse.

23   ...   ♕xg3
24   hg   ♖ac8!
25   ♔b1   a6
26   ♖e4   ♖c7
27   ♘f5   ♘c8!
28   ♖c1   ♖xc1+?

Black is looking for a good
way to remove the e-pawn, but
in complicated endings, even a
specialist like Kovačević can go
astray. He later demonstrated the
correct method: **28 ... ♘d5** 29
♖xc7 ♘xc7 30 ♔c2 (30 ♘ed6?!
♖xd6 31 ♘xd6 ♖b8−+) 30 ... g6!
31 ♘fd6 (31 ♘f6+ ♔f7 32 ♘xe8
♘xe8 33 ♘e3 ♘xe7∓) 31 ... ♘xd6
32 ♘xd6 ♖b8 33 ♔d3 ♘e8 34
♘xe8 ♖xe8 35 ♔d4 ♖c8 36 ♔d5
♔f7 and Black wins.

After the text, the game finished
29 ♔xc1 ♘d5 30 ♘ed6 ♘xd6 31
♘xd6 ♖xe7 32 ♗xe7 ♘xe7 33
♔d2 (Now Black must be careful.)
33 ... b6 34 ♔e3 g6 35 ♔f4 ♔g7
36 ♔g5 ♘d5 37 ♘e8+ ♔f7 38
♘d6+ ♔g7 39 ♘e8+ ♔f7 40
♘d6+ ♔g7 ½-½.

8   4 ♘f3 Introduction

4 ♘f3 is the most popular line against the Alekhine. White develops in the most natural manner, supporting the e5 pawn. The principal replies, 4 ... g6 and 4 ... ♗g4 are the subject of the next three chapters.

Here we investigate the consequences of other moves, which range from rather passive to blatantly provocative. The most reliable of these ideas is 4 ... de 5 ♘xe5 g6, as played many times by Kengis.

Christiansen–Alburt
US Ch (South Bend) 1981

**1 e4 ♘f6 2 e5 ♘d5 3 d4 d6
4   ♘f3** *(65)*

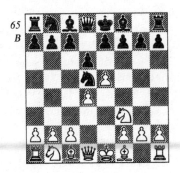

4   ...   ♘b6

This is a fairly solid move, preventing ♗c4 while preparing ... ♘c6 and/or ... g6. However, voluntarily withdrawing the knight from its central post is not an especially logical idea. White can certainly keep a slight edge, or try more ambitious methods.

4 ... c6 5 c4 ♘c7 6 h3 (6 ed ♕xd6 7 ♘c3 g6 8 ♗e3 ♗g7 9 ♕d2 ♗g4?! 10 ♘g5! ♘ba6?! 11 h3 ♗c8 12 ♖d1 ♗f5? 13 g4 ♗e6? 14 d5! cd 15 cd 0-0-0? 16 de ♕c6 17 ♕d7+!! 1-0 Hort–S. Bücker, W. German Ch [Bad Neuenahr] 1987; 6 ... ed) and now:

(a) **6 ... g6** 7 ed ed 8 ♘c3 ♗g7 9 ♗g5 ♕d7 10 ♕d2 0-0 11 ♗e2 f6 12 ♗h6 d5 13 ♗xg7 ♔xg7 14 0-0 ♕f7 15 cd ♘xd5 16 ♗c4 ♗e6 17 ♖fe1 ♘d7 18 ♘e4 ♘7b6 19 ♗b3 ♕c7 20 ♘c5 ♗f7 21 ♕a5± Spraggett–Suba, Szirak 1986.

(b) **6 ... de** 7 ♘xe5 ♘d7 8 ♘f3 g6 9 ♘c3 ♗g7 10 ♗e2 0-0 11 ♗f4 ♘e6 12 ♗e3 ♕c7 13 ♕c1 c5 14 dc ♘dxc5 15 0-0 ♗xc3 16 ♕xc3 ♘f4. Now Anand recommends 17 ♖fe1!? ♘xe2+ 18 ♖xe2±. Instead Anand–Suba,

Palma GMA 1989 continued 17 ♗d1 f6?! (17 ... ♘cd3!? 18 ♘e1±; 17 ... ♖d8 18 ♘d4 ♕e5∞) 18 ♘d4! a6 19 ♗f3! g5 20 ♖ad1 e5 21 ♘b3±.

4 ... ♗f5?! 5 ♗d3 ♕d7 (5 ... ♗xd3 6 ♕xd3 e6 7 0–0 de 8 de±; 5 ... ♗g6 6 ♗xg6 hg 7 c4 ♘b6 8 e6±) 6 0–0 ♘c6 (6 ... ♘b4 7 ♗xf5 ♕xf5 8 c3! ♘c2?! 9 ♘h4 ♕e4 10 ♘d2 ♕d3 11 ♖b1 de 12 ♘df3!± Kavalek–Ljubojević, Lanzarote 1973) 7 c4 (7 ed; 7 ♗xf5 ♕xf5 8 c4 ♘b6 9 ed ed 10 ♖e1+ ♗e7± Timman–Ljubojević, Hilversum 1973) 7 ... ♘b6 (7 ... ♗xd3 8 ♕xd3 ♘b6 9 ed ed 10 ♖e1+ ♗e7 11 d5 ♘d8 12 ♕e2±) 8 ed cd 9 b3 ♗xd3 10 ♕xd3 e6 (10 ... g6) 11 ♗a3! ♗e7 12 ♘c3 0–0 13 d5!± Rivas–Ochoa, Spanish Ch 1978.

5   a4

5 ♘c3 g6 (5 ... ♗g4?! 6 h3!?) **6** ♗f4 (6 ♗e2 ♗g7 7 a4 a5 8 0–0 ♘c6 9 ed cd 10 d5 ♘b4 11 ♗e3 0–0 12 ♕d2 ♗g4 was relatively harmless in Prandstetter–Neckař, Prague 1983.) **6 ... ♗g7** (6 ... ♗g4 7 h3 ♗xf3 8 ♕xf3 ♘c6 9 0–0–0 ♗g7 10 ♗b5 was good for White in Gobet–Landenbergue, Bern 1989.) **7 ♕d2 ♗g4** (7 ... 0–0?! 8 h4 h5 9 ♗h6 de 10 ♗xg7 ♔xg7 11 ♘xe5 ♘8d7 12 ♕g5 ♘xe5 13 ♕xe5+ ± Ambroz–Neckař, Prague 1983; 8 h3!?) **8 ♗h6** (8 ♕e3?! ♘c6 9 0–0–0 0–0 10 ♗e2 ♕c8 11 ♖he1 ♖d8 was fine for Black in Mnatsakanian–Konopka, Erevan 1986.) **8 ... 0–0**

(66) (8 ... ♗xh6?! 9 ♕xh6 ♗xf3 10 gf!). Now:

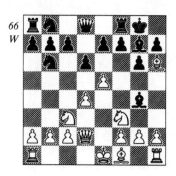

(a) **9 h4** ♗xf3 10 h5 ♗xh5!. This line was considered strong for White, but Honfi pointed out this natural defence. 11 ♖xh5 (11 ♗xg7 ♔xg7 12 g4 de) 11 ... ♗xh6 and now 12 ♖xh6 ♘8d7 (12 ... de 13 ♖h4!?) 13 ♖h3 ♖e8 gives Black a sound extra pawn, whilst the rook sacrifice 12 ♕xh6 gh is insufficient after 13 ♗d3 f5 14 ef ♖f7 or 13 ♘e4 f6 14 e6 ♕e8 15 ♗d3 f5.

(b) **9 ♗xg7** ♔xg7 10 ♗e2 de (10 ... ♘c6 11 0–0–0 de 12 ♘xe5 ♘xe5 13 ♕f4! Schlosser) 11 ♘xe5 ♗xe2 12 ♘xe2 ♘8d7 13 ♕a5!? ½–½ M. Schlosser–Honfi, Vienna 1990. White has a very small edge.

5 ♗e2 g6 6 0–0 ♗g7 7 ♗f4 (7 ed cd 8 a4 0–0! 9 a5 ♘d5 10 c4 ♘f6 11 h3 d5= Honfi–Schmid, Monte Carlo 1970) 7 ... ♘c6 8 c3 0–0 9 ♘bd2 ♗f5 10 ♖e1 ♕d7 11 ♗f1 ♖ad8= Kupper–Schmid, Krefeld 1967.

5 ♗d3 ♗g4 (5 ... ♘c6 6 ed ed!= Kengis) 6 h3 ♗xf3 (6 ...

♗h5?! 7 g4 ♗g6 8 e6!±) 7 ♕xf3 ♘c6 8 e6!? (Kengis' suggestion 8 ♗b5 de 9 de ♕d5± may be preferred.) 8 ... fe 9 ♕h5+ ♔d7 10 c3 ♕e8. Now 11 ♕g4! should be tried, since 11 ♕e2 g6 12 0–0 ♗g7 13 a4! a5 14 ♘d2 e5 15 ♘f3 ♔c8 16 ♘g5 ♘d8 17 de ♗xe5 was unclear in Vitolinš–Kengis, USSR 1986.

5 ...   a5
5 ... c6 6 a5 ♘d5 7 ♗e2 g6 8 0–0 ♗g7 9 c4 ♘c7 10 ed!? ♕xd6 11 ♘c3 0–0 12 ♗e3 ♘ba6 13 ♕c1 ♗g4 14 ♖d1± Sigurjonsson–Larsen, Ljubljana–Portorož 1977.

5 ... ♗g4 6 a5 ♘6d7 7 h3 ♗h5 8 e6 fe 9 g4± Matanović.

6   ♘c3
6 ♗b5+ c6 (White's idea is that Black's knight is robbed of the c6 square.) 7 ♗e2 (7 ♗d3 g6 8 0–0 ♗g7 9 ed ♕xd6 10 ♘bd2 0–0 11 c3 ♘8d7 12 ♘e4± Lukin–Ragialis, Tbilisi 1973) 7 ... g6 (7 ... de 8 ♘xe5 ♘8d7±; 7 ... ♗g4 8 ♘bd2 ♘8d7 9 ♘g5 is an improved version for White of the line 4 ... ♗g4 5 ♗e2 c6 6 c4 ♘b6 7 ♘bd2 ♘8d7 8 ♘g5.) 8 h3 (8 0–0 ♗g7 9 ed ♕xd6 10 ♘bd2 0–0 11 ♖e1 ♗f5 12 c3 ♘8d7= Anand–Konopka, Frunze 1987) 8 ... ♗g7 9 0–0 0–0 10 ♗f4± Ciocaltea–Hecht, Dortmund 1973.

6 ed is best met by 6 ... ed. Instead 6 ... cd 7 ♗b5+ ♗d7 8 d5! g6?! 9 ♕d4 ♖g8 10 0–0 ♗xb5 11 ab ♘8d7 12 ♖e1 ♗g7 13 ♕d1± was Hjartarson–Wolf, Bundesliga 1989/90.

6 ...   ♗g4
After **6 ... g6**, the violent approach works better thanks to the inclusion of a4 a5: 7 ♗f4 ♗g7 8 ♕d2 ♗g4 9 ♗h6 0–0 10 h4 ♗xf3 11 h5 ♗xh5 12 ♖xh5 ♗xh6 13 ♕xh6 gh 14 ♘e4! f6 15 e6 (15 ♖a3) 15 ... ♕e8 16 ♖a3! with a murderous attack. Therefore Black should play less ambitiously, e.g. 8 ... 0–0 or 9 ... ♗xh6, but with little hope of equality.

7 h3   ♗h5
7 ... ♗xf3 8 ♕xf3 d5 9 e6! fe 10 ♕h5+ ♔d7 11 ♗f4 g6 12 ♕e5! ♖g8 13 h4 ♗g7 14 ♕e3 intends g3 and ♗h3 with devastation.

8 e6!   fe
9 ♗e2   ♗xf3?!
9 ... ♘c6 10 ♘g5 ♗xe2 11 ♘xe2 ♕d7 12 ♘f4 ♘xd4! 13 ♗e3! e5 14 ♕h5+ g6 15 ♘xg6 ♘xc2+ 16 ♔e2 hg 17 ♕xg6+ ♔d8 18 ♘e6+! ♔c8 19 ♖hc1!±.

10	**♗xf3**	**c6**
11	**♕e2**	**g6**
12	**♘e4**	**♘a6**
13	**♘g5**	**♘c7**
14	**♗g4**	**♗h6**
15	**♘xe6!**	**♘xe6**
16	**♗xe6**	**♗xc1**
17	**♖xc1**	**♘xa4**
18	**0–0**	**d5**
19	**b3**	**♘b6**
20	**♕e5**	**♖f8**
21	**♕g7**	**♕d6**
22	**♖ce1**	**♕f4**

White's grip on the position cannot be shaken by 22 ... a4 23 c4! or 22 ... ♘d7 23 ♕xh7. Black's actual choice allows an excellent sacrifice.

23   ♗d7+!   ♔xd7
24   ♖xe7+   ♔d8

24 ... ♔c8 fails to 25 g3 ♕f6 26 ♖e8+.

25   ♖xb7   ♖a6

Instead 25 ... ♖e8 26 ♖xb6 ♕c7 27 ♖b7 ♕xg7 28 ♖xg7 ♖e7 29 ♖g8+ ♖e8 30 ♖xe8+ ♔xe8 31 ♖a1! gives White a won ending. The move in the game caves in immediately: 26 ♕e7+ ♔c8 27 g3 ♕f7 28 ♕xf7 ♖xf7 29 ♖xf7 a4 30 ♖e1 ♔d8 31 ba ♖xa4 32 ♖b1 ♖a6 33 ♖xh7 1–0.

I. Marinković–V. Bagirov
Leningrad 1989

1 e4 ♘f6 2 e5 ♘d5 3 d4 d6 4 ♘f3
4   ...   ♘c6

This is an immensely risky and ambitious line. Following the e6 pawn sacrifice, White has a number of lines which come very close to winning by force. However, Black's defensive and counter-attacking resources are quite considerable — in particular, the black king is surprisingly capable of looking after himself in hand-to-hand combat.

5   c4

Two other moves are less harmful:

5 ♗e2 de 6 ♘xe5 (6 de transposes to 4 ♗e2 de 5 de ♘c6 6 ♘f3) 6 ... ♘xe5 7 de ♗f5 8 a3 e6 9 0–0 a5 10 ♗f3 c6 11 ♘d2 ♗e7 12 ♘e4 0–0 13 c4 ♘b6 14 ♕b3 ♗xe4 (14 ... ♘d7 15 ♕c3 ♘c5 16 ♘xc5 ♗xc5 17 ♖d1 ♕b6 18 ♗e3! ♖fd8 19 ♖d6! Kengis–Grigorian, Togliatti 1985) 15 ♗xe4 ♕d4 16 ♖e1 a4=.

5 ♗b5 a6 6 ♗xc6+ (6 ♗a4 ♘b6) 6 ... bc 7 0–0 (7 h3 ♗f5 8 ♘a3 e6 9 ♘c4 ♗e7 10 ♕e2 0–0 11 0–0 ♕d7 12 ♘a5 ♖fb8 13 a3 c5!? 14 c4 ♕a4! 15 ♗d2 ♘f4! 16 ♕e3 ♘d3 17 b4 ♕d7 18 ed cd 19 ♖ab1 ♗d8!∓ Oll–Komarov, USSR 1984) 7 ... e6 (7 ... ♗g4 8 h3 ♗h5 9 ♘bd2 e6 10 ♘c4 ♗e7 11 ♘a5 ♕d7 12 c4 ♘b6 13 ♕b3 ♖b8 14 ed cd 15 c5± Lobron–Kindl, Berlin 1984) 8 ♘bd2 ♗e7 9 ♘c4 a5! 10 ♖e1 a4 11 ♗d2 ♗d7 12 ♕c1 0–0 13 ♘g5 ♕b8= Shamkovich–Larsen, Moscow 1962.

5   ...   ♘b6
6   e6

A very important alternative approach is **6 ed**. Then **6 ... cd?!** is bad: 7 d5 (7 h3!? g6 8 d5 ♘e5 9 ♘c3 ♘xf3+?! 10 ♕xf3 ♗g7 11 a4± Rogulj–Verrascina, Rome 1990) 7 ... ♘e5 (7 ... ♘b8 8 ♘c3 ♗g4 9 ♗e2 ♘8d7 10 b3 ♗xf3 11 ♗xf3 g6 12 ♗g5 ♗g7 13 ♖c1± Kots–Alburt, Kiev 1970) 8 ♘d4! ♘exc4 9 a4! ♘e5 10 ♘c3 a5 11 ♗b5+ ♗d7 12 f4 ♗xb5 13 fe ♗c4 14 e6!± Adorjan–Polgar, Budapest 1973.

After **6 ... ed**, play can transpose to the Exchange Variation, or White can try an early advance to d5: **7 d5** ♘e5 8 ♘d4 (8 ♘xe5 de 9 ♗d3 ♗b4+ 10 ♘c3 0–0 11 0–0

f5 12 ♕b3 ♗e7 13 ♘b5 ♘d7=
Przewoznik–Böhm; Polanica
Zdroj 1980) 8 ... c5! (After 8 ...
♗e7, Pogorelov recommends 9
f4!? ♘g4 10 ♗e2 ♘f6 11 ♘c3±;
since 9 ♗e2 0–0 10 b3 c5! brought
equality in V. Gurevich–Pogorelov, USSR 1988.) 9 dc ♘xc6, with
... d5 to follow, should equalise
according to Pogorelov. If White
wishes to exchange on e5, it is
better to do so with the bishop
already committed to e7, i.e. 7
♗e2 ♗e7 and now 8 d5 ♘e5 9
♘xe5 or 8 ♘c3 0–0 9 d5 ♘e5 10
♘xe5, but this is not troublesome
for Black. A line to avoid is 7 ♗e2
♗e7 8 ♘c3 ♗g4 9 b3 0–0?! (9 ...
♗f6) 10 h3 which transposed to
a good line for White of the
Exchange Variation in Sigurjonsson–Bischoff, Reykjavik 1982.

6   ...   fe
7   h4

7 ♘g5 is generally met by 7 ...
e5. The natural 7 ... ♕d7? is bad
due to 8 ♗d3 g6 9 ♘xh7 ♖xh7
10 ♗xg6+ ♖f7 11 ♗xf7+ ♔xf7
12 ♕h5+ ♔g8 13 h4+–, whilst
7 ... g6?! is very risky, e.g. 8 d5 ed
9 cd ♘e5 10 f4 ♘f7 11 ♗b5+
♗d7 12 ♘e6 ♕c8 13 ♗xd7+
♕xd7 14 ♘c3 c6 15 0–0 ♘xd5 16
♘xd5 cd 17 f5! gf 18 ♕xd5 ♘d8
19 ♘xd8 ♖xd8 20 ♗g5 ♗g7
21 ♖xf5± J. Polgar–Orev, Varna
1988. However, the apparently
suicidal 7 ... h6 might be playable:
8 ♕h5+ ♔d7 9 ♘f7 (9 ♘xe6!?
may give no more than a draw.) 9
... ♕e8 and now 10 ♕g6? ♖g8 11

♗d3 ♘d8 12 ♕h7 ♕xf7 13 ♗g6
♖h8! 14 ♕xh8 ♕xg6 15 ♕xf8
♕xg2 16 ♖f1 ♕e4+ was good
for Black in I. Gurevich–Hadjadj,
World U-14 (Mendoza) 1985.
Instead 10 ♗d3 ♘d8 11 ♗g6
♘xf7 12 ♗xf7 ♕d8 13 d5 c6 (13
... c5!?) 14 de+ ♔c7 15 c5 ♘d5
and 10 ♗e2 ♖g8 11 d5 ♘d4 just
seem unclear.

After 7 ... e5 White has tried
three moves:

(a) **8 ♕f3 ♘d4 9 ♕f7+ ♔d7 10
♗e3 h6!** (10 ... ♘c2+? 11 ♔d2
wins: 11 ... ♘xe3 12 fe ♕e8 13 c5!
or 11 ... ♘xa1 12 ♘e6 ♕e8 13
♕xe8+ ♔xe8 14 ♘xc7+ ♔d7 15
♗xb6 ab 16 ♘xa8 ♔c6 17 ♗d3.)
11 ♗xd4 hg 12 ♗xe5! ♕e8! 13
♕f3 ♔d8 and now 14 ♘c3? de 15
c5 ♘d7 16 c6 bc was a natural,
but incorrect sacrifice in Bondar–
Komarov, Kirovabad 1984.
Komarov considered 14 ♗c3
unclear.

(b) **8 d5 ♘d4 9 ♗d3** (9 ♗e3?!
♗f5; 9 ♘xh7? ♗f5):

(b1) **9 ... ♗f5 10 ♗xf5 ♘xf5
11 ♗e3!** (Blatny's improvement
over 11 ♘e6, maintaining control
over f7.) 11 ... ♕d7?! (11 ... g6 12
g4 ♘g7 13 ♕f3 ♕d7 14 ♘d2 e6
15 0–0–0 ed 16 cd c6? 17 ♘de4±
Haba–Freisler, Czech Ch 1987; 16
... h6 was necessary.) 12 g4 ♘xe3
13 fe 0–0–0 (13 ... ♘xc4 14 ♕e2!
♘b6 15 ♘c3±) 14 ♘d2! (14 ♘f7
♘xc4∞) 14 ... ♖e8 15 ♘e6 g5 16
a4± c6?! (16 ... h5 17 a5 ♘a8 18
♘e4 hg) 17 a5 ♘a8 18 ♘e4 h6 19
♕b3 ♔b8? (19 ... ♘c7 20 ♘4c5!)

20 ♘4c5! dc 21 ♘xc5 ♕c7 22 ♘a6+ 1–0 Blatny–Horn, Groningen Junior 1985.

(b2) **9 ... g6** 10 h4 (10 ♘xh7? ♗f5 11 ♗xf5 gf 12 ♕h5+ ♔d7 13 ♗e3 ♕e8∓ Rausch–Schlemermeyer, Bundesliga 1981/2) 10 ... ♗g7 11 ♘xh7? (11 h5 ♗f5) 11 ... ♗f5 12 ♗xf5 gf 13 ♕h5+ ♔d7 14 ♗e3 ♕e8 15 ♕xe8+ ♖axe8 16 ♗xd4 ed 17 ♘xg5 ♘xc4 18 ♘d2 ♘b6 19 ♘e6 ♖eg8 0–1 Eichler–Horn, corres. 1985.

(c) **8 ♗d3 ♘xd4** *(67)* (8 ... g6 can be met by 9 h4 or 9 ♘xh7 ♗f5 10 ♗xf5 gf 11 ♘xf8) and now 9 ♘xh7? ♗e6∓ is bad, but White has two good tries:

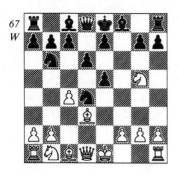

(c1) **9 ♕h5+!?** g6 10 ♗xg6+ hg 11 ♕xg6+ (11 ♕xh8? ♘c2+ 12 ♔d1 ♗f5!∓) 11 ... ♔d7 12 ♘f7 ♕e8 13 ♘xh8 ♕xg6 14 ♘xg6 ♘c2+ (14 ... ♗g7? 15 ♘a3 ♘xc4 16 ♘xc4! ♘c2+ 17 ♔d1 ♘xa1 18 ♗g5 ♔e8 19 ♘e3! e4 20 ♔c1+ – Marcinkiewicz–Kretschmar, corres. 1988/9) 15 ♔d1 ♘xa1 16 ♘xf8+ ♔e8 17 ♗h6 ♗f5 (17 ... ♘xc4∞ SDO) 18 ♘a3 d5 19 ♔d2

♘xc4+ (19 ... ♘c2) 20 ♘xc4 dc 21 ♖xa1 ♖d8+ and Black regains the piece.

(c2) **9 ♗xh7** ♖xh7 10 ♘xh7 ♗f5 11 ♘a3 ♘xc4 (11 ... e6!? 12 ♘xf8 ♔xf8 13 0–0 c5∞ Komarov) 12 ♘xc4! (12 0–0? ♘xa3 13 ba ♗c2! 14 ♕h5 g6∓; 12 ♕a4+ is well met by 12 ... b5 13 ♘xb5 ♗d7 14 ♕xc4 ♗xb5 15 ♕g8 ♔d7 or 12 ... ♕d7 13 ♕xc4 ♗xh7.) 12 ... ♘c2+ 13 ♔f1 ♘xa1 14 ♘xf8 ♔xf8 15 ♘e3! ♕d7 16 ♗d2! (16 ♕f3? g6 17 g4 ♕c6!! 18 ♔g2 ♕xf3+ 19 ♔xf3 ♗e6 20 ♗d2 ♘c2!–+ Völfl–Podgorny, corres. 1974) 16 ... ♗d3+ (16 ... ♘c2 17 ♘xc2 ♕a4 18 ♘e3 ♗d3+ 19 ♔g1 ♕xa2) 17 ♔g1 d5 18 ♕xa1 d4 19 ♘f1 e4 (19 ... ♕e6 20 h4 ♔f7 21 ♖h3 ♗f5 22 ♖f3 ♔e8 23 ♘g3 g6 24 ♘xf5 gf 25 ♕f1 a6 26 h5 ♔d7 27 h6 ♖h8 28 ♕d3+ – Winsnes–Åstrom, Sweden 1984) 20 h4 ♔g8 21 h5 ♖f8 22 h6 e3 23 ♘xe3 de 24 ♗xe3 ♖f7 25 b3± ♗e4 26 ♖h4 ♗f5 27 ♗d4 gh 28 ♕c1 ♖h7 29 ♕f4 a6 30 ♕g3+ ♔f8 31 ♕e5 e6 32 ♖f4 ♔g8 33 g4 ♗g6 34 ♖f6 ♗f7 35 ♖xh6 1–0 Winsnes–Zetterborg, Sweden 1986.

7 ♘c3 is a slightly calmer move.

(a) **7 ... e5** 8 d5 ♘d4 9 ♘xd4 ed 10 ♕xd4 e5 11 de (11 ♕d1!?) 11 ... ♗xe6 12 ♗e2 ♕f6= Vogt–Böhm, Polanica Zdroj 1980.

(b) **7 ... ♘d7** 8 d5!? (8 ♗d3 ♘f6) 8 ... ed 9 cd ♘ce5 10 ♘d4 ♘f6 11 f4 ♘f7 12 ♕b3± A. Kuzmin–Pogorelov, Budapest 1989.

(c) **7 ... g6 8 h4 ♗g7** and now:

(c1) **9 ♗e3 d5!** 10 c5 ♘d7 (10
... ♘c4? 11 ♗xc4 dc 12 ♕a4±
Nunn–Vaganian, London 1986)
11 h5 (11 ♗b5) 11 ... e5 12 h6
♗f6 13 ♘xd5 ed 14 ♘xf6+ ef 15
♘xd4 is assessed as unclear by
Nunn after either 15 ... ♕e7 or 15
... ♘de5.

(c2) **9 h5 e5 10 d5 ♘d4 11 hg**
♗g4! 12 gh (12 ♘xd4 ♗xd1 13
♘e6 ♗c2!= Fleck) 12 ... ♕d7 (12
... e6!? 13 ♗d3 ♕f6∞) 13 ♗d3
0–0–0 14 ♗e3 ♖df8 15 ♗xd4 ed
16 ♘e4 ♗xf3 (16 ... c6!?) 17 gf e6
18 de ♕xe6 19 ♕e2 and now Fleck
recommends 19 ... ♘d7, since after
19 ... d5? 20 c5!! de 21 cb ♕xb6
22 ♗xe4 d3! 23 ♕xd3 ♖d8 24
♕c4 ♕xb2 25 0–0! it was only by
a miracle that Black survived in
Kindermann–Fleck, W. Germany
1983.

7 ♗e3 is really quite vicious.

(a) **7 ... g6?!** 8 h4 ♗g7 9 h5 e5
(9 ... ♘d7 10 ♘g5 ♘f8 11 ♕f3!
♗f6 12 hg ♘xg6 13 ♘xh7 ♗xd4
14 ♗xd4 ♘xd4 15 ♕g4 ♘c2+ 16
♔d2 ♘xa1 17 ♕xg6+ ♔d7 18
♘f6+!± Gallagher–Landen-
bergue, Geneva 1987) 10 d5! e4 11
♘g5 ♗xb2 (11 ... ♘e5) 12 ♘d2
♗xa1 13 ♕xa1 ♘e5 14 ♘dxe4
♖g8 15 hg hg (Lau–Fleck, Bundesliga 1985/6) 16 f4! ♘bxc4 (16
... ♘exc4 17 ♗xb6 ♘a3 18 ♕c3
ab 19 ♖h8 ♖xh8 20 ♕xh8+ ♔d7
21 ♕g7+– and 16 ... ♘g4 17
♖h8 ♔d7 18 ♘e6 ♖xh8 19 ♘xd8
♖xd8 20 ♕g7+– are lines
analysed by Fleck.) 17 ♗d4! b5

18 fe de 19 ♗xc4 bc 20 ♗c5!
leaves Black in no position to
defend against ♖h7.

(b) **7 ... e5?!** 8 d5 e4 (8 ... ♘d4
9 ♘xd4 ed 10 ♗xd4 e5 11 de
♗xe6 12 ♗d3 ♕d7 13 0–0 gives
White a safe edge.) 9 ♘g5 ♘e5 10
♘xe4 ♕d7 11 ♘bd2 e6 12 f4±
Popov–Peshina, Riga 1968.

(c) **7 ... ♘d7 8 ♘c3 ♘f6** (68)
and now:

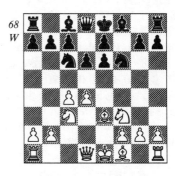

(c1) **9 ♗d3 g6 10 h4 ♗g7 11**
♘g5 e5 (11 ... 0–0? 12 h5) 12 d5
♘d4 13 h5 gh!? (13 ... ♗g4 14
f3±; 13 ... ♘xh5? 14 ♖xh5) 14
♗xd4 ed 15 ♘e2 (15 ♘ce4 ♗g4
16 ♕c2± Plachetka) 15 ... c6 16
♘xd4 (16 ♘f4) 16 ... ♕a5+ 17
♔f1 ♗g4 18 f3 0–0 19 ♕c2 ♘xd5!
20 cd ♗xd4 21 ♗xh7+ ♔h8 22
♗g6 (22 ♗g8? ♗f5–+) 22 ...
♕xd5 23 ♗xh5 ♕b5+ 24 ♕e2
(24 ♔e1 ♕e5+ 25 ♔d1 ♗f5 26
♗g6+ ♔g8 27 ♗h7+ ♔g7 28
♗xf5 ♖xf5 29 ♖e1 ♕f6 30 ♘e6+
♔f7 31 ♕c4 ♗xb2∓ Vogt) 24
... ♕xe2+ 25 ♔xe2 ½–½ Vogt–
Cibulka, Trenčianske, Teplice
1974.

(c2) **9 h4** ♖g8!? 10 ♗d3 g6 11
h5 ♘xh5 12 ♖xh5 gh 13 d5 ed 14
cd ♘b8 15 ♘g5 ♗g4 16 f3 e5!∓
Zeltner–Schoppmeyer, corres.
1984.

7 ♗d3 can be met by **7 ... e5**,
when 8 ♘g5 transposes to 7 ♘g5
e5 8 ♗d3. 8 de ♗g4 and 8 d5
♘b4 9 ♘g5 ♘xd3+ 10 ♕xd3 e6!
11 ♘xh7 ♕e7∞ Letelier–Penrose,
Moscow 1956 are less harmful.
Also possible is **7 ... ♘b4** 8 ♗e2
(8 ♘g5 ♘xd3+ 9 ♕xd3 ♕d7! 10
♘xh7 ♕c6 11 ♕g6+ ♔d7∞
Lehmann–Bogolyubov, Munich
1950) 8 ... g6 9 a3 ♘c6 10 b4 ♗g7
11 ♗b2 0–0 12 0–0 ♕e8 13 b5
♘d8 when White's space advantage slightly outweighed the pawn
minus in Vogt–Rogulj, Trenčianske Teplice 1979.

7	...	e5
8	d5	♘d4
9	♘xd4	ed
10	♕xd4	

Tal–Larsen, Eersel 1969 continued **10 ♗d3** ♕d7! 11 ♗g5 h6
12 ♗d2 ♕g4 13 ♗e2 ♕e4 14 0–0
♗f5 15 ♘a3 and now 15 ... g6 or
15 ... g5!? should have been tried,
instead of 15 ... ♕xh4?! 16 ♘b5!
d3 17 ♘xc7+! ♔d8 18 ♘xa8 de
19 ♕xe2 ♘xa8 20 c5! which gave
White a strong attack.

10 ♗g5 ♗f5 11 ♕xd4 h6 12
♗e3 ♕d7 13 ♘c3 e5 14 ♕d2 ♗e7
15 ♗e2 c5 gave Black reasonable
play in Amrov–Bryson, Dubai ol
1986. The move ... h6 is fairly
useful.

10	...	♕d7

10 ... e5 is reasonable:

(a) **11 de** ♗xe6 12 ♗g5 (12
♕e4?! ♕d7 13 ♕xb7 ♗e7) 12 ...
♕d7 13 ♗e2 ♔f7 (13 ... ♕f7) 14
0–0 (14 ♗h5+?! ♔g8) 14 ... h6 15
♗e3 ♗e7 16 ♘c3 ♖hf8 (Honfi–
Westerinen, Wijk aan Zee 1969)
17 ♕e4 with an edge for White
according to Bagirov.

(b) **11 ♕d1** ♗f5 12 ♘c3 (12
♗d3 e4 13 ♕e2 ♗e7 14 ♗xe4
♗xe4 15 ♕xe4 0–0 as analysed
by Herbrechtsmeier, gives Black
compensation due to White's
untidy development.) 12 ... ♕d7
13 ♗e3 (13 ♗d3 e4 14 ♘xe4
♘xc4=) 13 ... ♗e7 14 ♗e2 h6
15 a4 ♗f6 16 g4 ♗g6 17 a5 ♘c8
18 ♕b3 c5 19 ♔d2 ♗d8 20 ♗f1
0–0 21 ♗h3 ♖f3 22 g5 ♖xh3 23
♖xh3 ♘e7 was a good exchange
sacrifice in Garbarino–Hansen,
Copenhagen 1982.

10 ... ♗f5 11 ♘c3 ♕d7 12 ♗e2
e5 13 ♕d1 ♕f7?! (13 ... h6) 14 g4
♗d7 15 ♗e3 ♗e7 16 a4± P.
Cramling–Behrhorst, Lugano
1983.

11	♗e2

11 ♖h3 ♕g4 12 ♗f4 c5 13 dc
e5 gives Black adequate play.

11	...	e5
12	de	♕xe6
13	♖h3!	

13 ♗g5 c5 (13 ... ♕e5) 14 ♕d3
(14 ♕c3 d5) 14 ... ♕e5 15 ♘c3
♗f5 16 ♕e3 ♕xe3 17 ♗xe3
0–0–0 is comfortable for Black.

13	...	c5
14	♕c3	

14 ♕f4 ♕f5 15 ♖e3+ ♗e7 16

♕xd6 allows the startling 16 ...
♕xf2+!∓.

| 14 | ... | ♗e7! |
| 15 | ♖e3 | |

15 ♕xg7? ♖g8 16 ♕xh7 ♖xg2∓.

| 15 | ... | ♕f7 |
| 16 | ♗h5! | |

This looks devastating, but, as
often happens in the Alekhine,
Black's king leads a remarkable
counter-offensive.

16	...	♕xh5
17	♕xg7	♕xh4
18	♕xh8+	

18 g3? ♕h1+ 19 ♔e2 ♗g4+!

| 18 | ... | ♔f7 |
| 19 | ♖f3+ | |

19 ♘d2? ♗f5! 20 ♕c3 ♗f6∓.

| 19 | ... | ♗f5! |
| 20 | ♖xf5+ | *(69)* |

20 ♕c3? ♗f6 is good for Black
since 21 ♖xf5 can be met by 21
... ♕e4+.

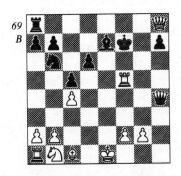

69
B

20	...	♔g6
21	♕c3	♔xf5
22	♘d2	♔e6

White has some development
problems, so decides to liquidate
to a tenable ending: 23 ♕h3+

♕xh3 24 gh ♗f6 25 a4 d5 26 cd+
♘xd5 27 ♖a3 ♘b4 28 ♔e2 ♔d5
29 ♖f3 ♖e8+ 30 ♔d1 ♖e6 31 b3
♔c6 32 ♘c4 b6 33 ♗d2 ♘d5 34
♔c2 a6 35 ♖f5 ♗d4 ½–½.

N. De Firmian–M. Rohde
US Ch (Long Beach) 1989

1 e4 ♘f6 2 e5 ♘d5 3 d4 d6 4 ♘f3

| 4 | ... | de |
| 5 | ♘xe5 | |

5 de is less ambitious, e.g. 5 ...
g6 6 ♗c4 c6 7 0–0 ♗g7 8 ♗b3
0–0 9 ♖e1 ♗e6 10 ♘bd2 ♘d7 11
♘d4 ♘c7 ½–½ Dautov–Kengis,
Baden Baden 1990.

| 5 | ... | ♘d7 |

5 ... ♘d7 is a highly risky and
provocative move, which, despite
being more than thirty years old,
is still controversial. The sacrifice
on f7 is certainly good enough for
an instant draw, but trying for
more leads to bizarre positions.

5 ... e6, on the other hand, is
just too insipid: 6 ♕f3! ♕f6 (6 ...
♘f6 7 ♗e3±) 7 ♕g3 h6 8 ♘c3
♘b4 9 ♗b5+ c6 10 ♗a4 ♘d7.
Now Tal recommends 11 ♘e4!
♕f5 12 f3 ♘xe5 13 de ♗d7 14 a3
♘d5 15 c4 ♘b6 16 ♗c2 with a
solid advantage, though in Tal–
Larsen, Bled (6) 1965, 11 0–0 ♘xe5
12 de ♕g6 13 ♕f3 ♕f5?! 14 ♕e2
♗e7 15 a3 ♘d5 16 ♘b5! also
proved effective.

| 6 | ♘xf7!? | |

6 ♗c4 e6 (6 ... ♘xe5 7 de c6 8
♕f3 ♕c7! was analysed by Van
der Wiel: 9 0–0?! ♕xe5 10 ♘c3
♗e6 11 ♗e3 ♘xe3 12 ♗xe6

♛xe6 13 ♖fe1 ♛f5∓, 9 ♗xd5 ♛xe5+ 10 ♗e4 f5 11 ♘c3 fe 12 ♛xe4 ♛xe4+ 13 ♘xe4 ♗f5=, or 9 ♗f4 g5!? 10 ♗g3 h5 11 ♘c3! ♗e6 12 h4 and now 12 ... ♘f4!? or 12 ... g4 13 ♘xd5±.) 7 ♛g4 h5 8 ♛e2 ♘xe5 9 de ♗d7 10 0-0 (Tal-Larsen, Bled 1965) 10 ... ♛h4!=.

6 ♘f3 e6 (6 ... g6 7 c4 ♘5f6 8 ♘c3 ♗g7 9 g3 0-0 10 ♗g2 ♘b6 11 b3 e5 12 de ♛xd1+ 13 ♘xd1 ♘g4 14 ♗b2± Byrne-Rohde, New York 1989) 7 g3!? ♗e7 8 ♗g2 (Jansa recommends 8 c4 as preserving some advantage, though this is certainly not terrifying for Black.) 8 ... 0-0 (8 ... b5) 9 0-0 b5!? 10 ♖e1 (10 ♛e2 a5) 10 ... ♗b7 11 ♛e2 and now in Jansa-Martin, Gausdal 1990, 11 ... a6 12 a4! gave White some useful queenside play. 11 ... b4 was best.

	6 ...	♔xf7
	7 ♛h5+	♔e6
	8 c4	

8 g3!? b5 (8 ... ♘7f6 9 ♗h3+ ♔d6 10 ♛e5+ ♔c6 11 ♗g2 b5 12 a4 b4 13 c4 bc 14 bc ♗a6 15 ♘d2 e6 16 c4 ♗d6 17 ♛xe6!!+-) 9 a4 (9 b3 b4 10 a3 ♘7f6 11 ♗h3+ ♔d6 12 ♛e5+ ♔c6 13 ♗g2 should, in Angelov-Orev, corres. 1961, have been met by 13 ... ♛d6.) 9 ... c6 10 ♗h3+ (10 ab g6 11 ♛e2+ ♔f7 12 bc∞) 10 ... ♔d6 11 ab (11 ♛e2 ♘7f6) 11 ... cb (11 ... ♔c7?! 12 ♗g2! ♘7f6 13 ♛e2 ♗g4 14 ♛c4 ♛d7 15 0-0 e6 16 ♖a6! ♘b6 17 ♖xb6!+- Bozić) 12 ♘d2 ♘7f6!? 13 ♛e5+ ♔c6 14

♗g2 e6 (14 ... ♛d6 15 b3! b4 16 ♛e2) 15 0-0 ♗d6 16 ♛e2 a6 17 c4!? bc 18 ♘xc4 ♔d7 19 ♘e5+!? ♗xe5 (19 ... ♔e8 20 ♗g5) 20 de gave White enduring compensation and attacking chances in Todorović-Bodiroga, Palić Junior 1988. The game finished 20 ... ♘e8 21 ♛g4 ♗b7 22 ♗g5 h5! 23 ♛h4 ♛b6 24 ♖ac1 ♘ec7 25 ♛a4+ ♗c6 26 ♛a3! ♘b5 27 ♛d3 ♖af8 28 ♛g6 ♖hg8 29 ♗e3! ♛b7 30 ♗c5 ♖e8 31 ♖fd1 ♘c7 32 ♗d6 ♘b5 33 ♗c5 ♘c7 34 ♖d2 a5 35 ♖dc2 ♗a4 36 ♖c3 ♗c6 37 ♗d6! 1-0.

White may also take an immediate draw with 8 ♛h3+ ♔f7 9 ♛h5+ etc.

	8 ...	♘5f6
	9 d5+	♔d6
	10 ♛f7	(70)

Other moves have been tried:

10 ♛f5?! ♘c5 11 ♗f4+ e5 12 ♗xe5+ (12 de+ ♔c6; 12 ♛xe5+ ♔d7 13 g3 ♗e7) 12 ... ♔e7 13 ♗xf6+ gf 14 ♛f3 ♔f7 15 ♘c3 ♛e7+ 16 ♗e2 ♛e5 17 0-0 ♗d6 18 g3 h5-+ Chandler-Sowray, Harrow (Aaronson Masters) 1979.

10 ♗f4+? e5 11 c5+ (11 de+ ♔xe6-+) 11 ... ♔e7 12 ♗g5 ♛e8 13 ♛h4 ♔f7∓ Andreev-Kharlamov, USSR 1981.

10 ♛h3 ♘c5 11 ♛a3 e5 12 ♗e3 b6 13 b4 (13 ♘c3 ♔e7 14 b4 ♘cd7∞ ECO) 13 ... ♘cd7 14 c5+ ♔e7 15 ♘c3 bc 16 bc ♔f7 17 ♗c4 ♘b6! Sowray.

10 ♛e2 e5 (10 ... ♘b8 11 ♗f4+ ♔d7 Sowray) 11 de ♘c5 12 ♘c3

(12 ♗f4+?! ♔e7 13 ♘c3 ♘xe6 14
♖d1 ♕e8 15 ♘d5+ ♔f7 16 ♘xf6
♗b4+!−+ Sowray) 12 ... ♘xe6?!
(12 ... ♔e7) 13 ♗g5 ♘d4? 14
0–0–0 c5 15 ♖xd4+ cd 16 c5+
♔d7 17 ♕b5+ ♔e7 18 ♗c4+−
Neulinger–Achs, Austria 1987.

**10 c5+ ♘xc5 11 ♗f4+ ♔d7
12 ♗b5+ c6 13 dc+ bc 14 ♕xc5**
(14 ♕d1+ ♔e8 15 ♗xc6+ ♗d7
16 ♗xa8 ♕xa8) 14 ... ♕b6! 15
♕xb6 ab 16 ♗e2 ♗a6 17 ♗f3?
e5 18 ♗e3 ♘d5 19 ♘d2 (19 ♗xd5
cd 20 ♗xb6 ♖b8∓) 19 ... ♗b4
20 0–0–0 ♗d3 21 ♘b1 (21 a3
♖xa3!) 21 ... e4 22 ♗g4+ ♔c7
23 a3 ♘xe3 24 fe ♗c5 25 ♖he1
♖hf8 26 ♖d2 ♖f6 27 g3 b5 28 ♘c3
b4 0–1 Bastow–Sowray, Islington
1978.

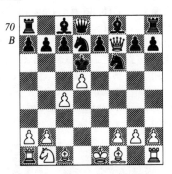

10 ... ♘e5
10 ... ♘c5? 11 b4! ♘ce4 12
f3+− and **10 ... ♘b6?** 11 ♘c3
♕e8 12 ♗f4+ ♔d7 13 ♕e6+
♔d8 14 ♕e5 ♕d7 15 0–0–0 (Intending 16 c5+−) 15 ... ♘e8 16
♗d3! ♘d6 17 c5 ♘f7 18 ♕e3 g5
19 ♗g3 ♗g7 20 ♗b5! ♕f5 21
♖he1 ♕f6 22 cb ab 23 d6!+− are
not real alternatives.

10 ... ♘b8!? 11 c5+! (11 ♘c3?
♗f5!; 11 ♗f4+? e5 12 c5+ ♔xc5
13 b4+ ♔d6 14 ♗e3 b6−+
Kupper–Popov, Enschede Z 1963)
11 ... ♔d7! (11 ... ♔xc5? 12
♗e3+ ♔d6 13 ♘a3! a6 14 ♘c4+
♔d7 15 d6± Kapengut; 11 ...
♔e5? 12 f4+ ♔d4 13 d6 ♔xc5
14 ♘c3+− Kirsauks–Hansaid,
corres. 1967) **12 ♗b5+** (12 c6+?!
bc 13 dc+ ♘xc6 14 ♗b5 ♕e8 15
♕c4 ♗b7 16 0–0 e5 17 ♗e3
♕e6! 18 ♕c2 ♘d5 19 ♖d1 ♔c8∓
Kirov–Orev, Bulgaria 1978) **12 ...
c6 13 dc+ bc** (13 ... ♘xc6? 14
0–0+−) **14 0–0** and now:

(a) **14 ... ♕e8?** is a standard idea
in the 10 ... ♘b8 line, but fails in
this instance: 15 ♖d1+ ♔c7 16
♗f4+ ♔b7 17 ♗a6+! 1–0
Ochsner–T. Sorensen, Århus 1985.

(b) **14 ... ♔c7** 15 ♗f4+ ♔b7.
Now 16 ♗a6+ ♔xa6 17 ♕c4+
♔b7 18 ♕b4+ ♔a6 19 ♕c4+ ½–½
was Ragialis–Kaunas, Vilnius
1979, but ECO gives 16 ♕b3! ♘fd7
(16 ... ♗g4 17 ♗e2+ ♔c8 18
♖d1) 17 ♗xc6++ ♔xc6 18
♕f3+ ♔xc5 19 ♖c1+ ♔b6 20
♕b3+ ♔a6 21 ♕c4+ ♔b7 22
♕d5+ ♔a6 23 ♗c7±.

(c) **14 ... ♕a5!?** 15 ♖d1+ ♔c7∞
Ernst–Lindberg, Swedish Ch
1982.

11 ♗f4 c5
12 ♘c3
12 ♘d2 g5! 13 ♗g3 g4 (13 ...
♗h6 14 ♘f3 ♖f8 15 ♘xe5! ♕a5+
16 ♔d1 ♖xf7 17 ♘c6+ gives
White a sound extra pawn.) 14
0–0–0 ♗h6 (14 ... ♖g8 15 ♖e1

and now after 15 ... ♖g5? 16 ♗d3 ♗h6 17. ♔c2! a disaster on e5 follows, whilst 15 ... ♖g7 16 ♗xe5+ ♔d7 17 ♕e6+ ♔e8 gives White a slightly improved version of the game, since Black has less control over f6. Horvath's analysis continues 18 ♗xc7! ♗xe6 19 ♗xd8 ♗xd5 20 ♗a5 ♗c6 21 f3±.) 15 ♖e1 ♖f8 16 ♗xe5+ ♔d7 17 ♕e6+ ♔e8 18 ♕d6! (After 18 ♕xf6? ♖xf6 19 ♗xf6 ♔f7! White does not have enough for the queen.) 18 ... ed 19 ♗xf6+ ♔d7 20 ♗xd8 ♔xd8. Bagirov gave this position as equal, due to the weakness of f2. Kallai–Cs. Horvath, Budapest 1990 concluded 21 ♗d3 (21 ♖e2 ♗f5) 21 ... ♖xf2 22 ♖e2 ♖xe2 23 ♗xe2 ♗d7 24 ♗d3 ½–½.

12 ... a6
13 0–0–0?

This fails due to Black's reply, threatening to win White's queen by a pin on the c1–h6 diagonal. With this problem in mind, Yudasin suggested **13 ♖d1!?** The move 13 b4 has been subjected to much analysis, but remains largely untested in practice.

13 b4:

(a) **13 ... cb?!** 14 c5+ ♔xc5 15 ♘a4+ ♔d6 16 ♘b2± Keres.

(b) **13 ... b6?** 14 ♖b1 g5 (14 ... cb 15 ♖xb4 ♔c5 16 ♖b1! ♘xf7 17 ♘a4+ ♔d4 18 f3!+ – Bagirov) 15 ♗g3 ♗h6 16 bc+ bc 17 ♖b7!! ♗d7 18 ♗d3 ♕e8 (Wolff analysed 18 ... ♖b8 19 ♖xb8 ♕xb8 20 ♘b5+! ab 21 ♗xe5+

♗xe5 22 ♕xe7+ ♔d4 23 ♕e3+ ♔c3 24 ♗e2+ ♔b4 25 ♕d2+ when White mates.) 19 ♗f5! ♖b8 (19 ... ♕xf7 20 ♘e4+ ♘xe4 21 ♖xd7#) and now Crum pointed out 20 ♕xe8! with decisive material gain due to the standard mating idea.

(c) **13 ... ♕c7?** 14 0–0–0 ♘fg4 (14 ... g6 15 ♗xe5+ ♔xe5 16 d6 ♗h6+ 17 f4+!+ – Bartek) 15 ♗e2 ♔d7 16 ♗xg4+ ♔d8 17 d6+ – Votava–Šarközy, Czechoslovakia 1988.

(d) **13 ... ♕b6** 14 bc+ ♕xc5 15 ♖d1 g5! 16 ♗xe5+ (16 ♗g3 ♕a3! 17 ♖d3 ♕c1+ 18 ♘d1 and now 18 ... ♘e4 or 18 ... ♘fg4 — Šarközy) **16 ... ♔xe5 17 ♗e2 ♗h6!** (17 ... ♔d6 18 0–0 ♗h6! 19 ♕xf6+) **18 d6** (In view of the threat ... ♖f8, White must act quickly.) **18 ... ♗e6** (18 ... ♖e8?! 19 d7! ♗xd7 20 ♖xd7 ♘xd7 21 ♗g4) **19 ♕xe7 ♖hf8** *(71)* and now, in addition to 20 ♗h5 ♕xc4!, Horvath analysed two possibilities:

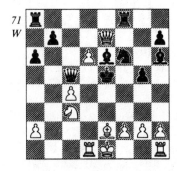

71
W

(d1) **20 ♕xb7.** The main lines of Horvath's analysis illustrate

Black's resources: 20 ... ♘d5 21 ♘xd5 (21 cd ♕xf2+!; 21 ♘e4 ♕b4+) 21 ... ♕xf2+ 22 ♔d2 ♕d4+ (22 ... g4 23 ♔c3!) 23 ♔e1 (23 ♔c2 ♗f5+) 23 ... ♕f2+ or 20 ... ♖ab8 21 ♕f3 (21 ♕xa6? ♘d5) 21 ... g4 22 ♕g3+ ♗f4 23 ♕h4 ♗xc4!? (23 ... h6 24 0–0 ♗g5 25 ♕g3+ ♗f4=) 24 g3! ♗e3! 25 0–0!∞ ♗xe2 26 ♘xe2 ♖b2 27 ♖de1 ♔xd6 28 fe ♕xe3+ 29 ♔h1 ♕e4+ 30 ♔g1=.

(d2) **20 0–0!** ♖f7 21 ♖fe1 ♖xe7 22 de. Black has an enormous material advantage, most of which will have to be returned, even for short-term survival.

13	...	g6!
14	♗xe5+	♔xe5
15	d6	♗h6+
16	♔c2	♕e8!
17	♖d5+	♘xd5
18	♕xd5+	♔f6

Thus the king escapes. White played a few more moves before acknowledging that Black is simply a rook up: 19 ♘e4+ ♔g7 20 ♕e5+ ♔f7 21 ♗d3 (21 de ♗f5) 21 ... ♗f5 22 g4 ♗xe4 23 ♗xe4 e6 24 ♖e1 ♕a4+ 25 ♔d3 ♖he8 26 h4 0–1.

Vitolinš–Kengis
Latvian Ch 1990

1 e4 ♘f6 2 e5 ♘d5 3 d4 d6 4 ♘f3 de 5 ♘xe5

| 5 | ... | g6 |
| 6 | c4 | |

6 ♕f3 can, and probably should, be met by **6 ... f6!?**. It has yet to be demonstrated that **6 ... ♗e6**

7 c4!? ♘b4 8 ♕xb7 gives Black adequate play:

(a) **8 ... ♕xd4** 9 ♕xa8 ♘c2+ 10 ♔e2 ♕xe5+ 11 ♔d1 ♕e1+ 12 ♔xc2 ♗f5 13 ♗d3 ♕e2+ 14 ♔b3 ♕xd3+ 15 ♘c3 ♕c2+ 16 ♔b4 e5+ 17 ♔a5 ♗b4+ 18 ♔xb4 0–0 19 ♔a3 ♘d7 20 ♕f3 ♘b6 21 ♕e2+ – Trepp–Bischoff, Südlohn 1981.

(b) **8 ... ♘c2+** 9 ♔d1 ♘xa1 10 ♕xa8 ♗g7 11 ♗d2 0–0 12 ♕xa7 gives White two extra pawns for compensation which is not apparent. 12 ... ♗f5 13 ♘a3 ♗e4 14 f3 ♘c6 15 ♘xc6 ♗xc6 16 ♗e3± was Halasz–Orev, Kecskemet 1985.

6 g3 ♗g7 7 c3 0–0 8 ♗g2 c6 9 0–0 ♘d7 10 ♘d3 e5 11 de ♘xe5 12 ♘xe5 ♗xe5 13 ♗h6 ♖e8! 14 ♖e1 ♗f5 15 ♘d2 ♕c7! 16 ♘c4 ♗f6 17 ♖xe8+ ♖xe8 18 ♗xd5 cd 19 ♘e3 ♗e4! equalises, since in Marjanović–Donchev, Kastel Stari 1988 there followed 20 f3?! g5!! stranding the h6 bishop and making a pin on the a7–g1 diagonal a potent idea.

6 ♘d2 ♗g7 7 ♘df3 0–0 (7 ... ♘d7? 8 ♘xf7) 8 ♗c4 c6 9 c3 ♘d7 (9 ... ♗f5) 10 ♘d3 is a modest idea; White simply maintains control of the e5. Hebden–Marinković, Vrnjacka Banja 1989 continued 10 ... a5 11 a4 ♘7f6 12 0–0 ♗g4 13 h3 ♗xf3 14 ♕xf3 h6 15 ♖e1±. A likely improvement is 11 ... ♘7b6 followed by 12 ... ♗f5, to exchange the more active white knight.

6 ♗e2 ♗g7 7 0–0 0–0 (7 ...
♘d7 8 ♘f3 c6 9 c4! ♘5f6 10 ♘c3
0–0 11 h3 ♘b6 12 a4 ♗f5 13 ♗f4
♘c8 14 ♕b3± was a good example
of how Black should not play,
in J. Polgar–Visser, Amsterdam
1990.) 8 ♗f3 c6 9 ♕e2 ♗e6 10
♖d1 ♘d7 11 ♘xd7 ♕xd7 12 c4
♘b6 13 ♘a3 ♖ad8= Meshkov–
Bagirov, Podolsk 1990.

6 ... ♘b6

7 ♘c3

**7 ♗e3 ♗g7 8 f4 c5 9 dc ♕xd1+
10 ♔xd1 ♘6d7 11 ♘d3 ♘a6 12
♘c3 0–0 13 ♗e2 ♖d8 14 ♔e1 e5
15 fe ♘xe5 16 ♘xe5 ♗xe5 17
♔f2 ♗e6 18 ♖ac1 ♖ac8 19 ♘d5
♔g7 20 b4 ♗xd5 21 cd ♘xb4 22
d6 ♘d5 23 ♗f3 ♘xe3 24 ♗xb7
♘g4+ 25 ♔f3 ♘xh2+ 26 ♔e4
♖xc5 27 ♖xc5 ♗xd6 28 ♖c8 ♖d7
29 ♗c6 ♖e7 30 ♔d5 ♗g3 31
♖e8 ♖xe8 32 ♗xe8 ♘g4 33 ♗b5
h5 34 ♔c6 f5 35 a4 h4 36 ♔b7
♗f2 37 a5 ♔f6 38 ♖c1 ♘e5 39
♖c2 ♗g1 40 ♖c1 ½–½** Aseev–
Kengis, Podolsk 1990.

7 ♗e2 ♗g7 8 ♗f4 (8 0–0 c5!?)
8 ... ♘8d7 9 ♘c3 ♘xe5 10 ♗xe5
♗xe5 11 de ♕xd1+, as given by
Chandler, more or less equalises.

**7 c5?! ♘6d7 8 ♗c4 ♘xe5 9 de
♕xd1+ 10 ♔xd1 ♘d7** was good
for Black in a computer game in
the USSR in 1984.

7 ... ♗g7

8 ♗e3

8 ♗f4 0–0 9 ♗e2 c6 (Black
opted for an unusual plan in
Dvoiris–Kengis, Tallinn 1981: 9
... f6 10 ♘f3 g5 11 ♗e3 g4 12

♘d2 f5 13 c5 f4 14 cb fe 15 fe.
Now capturing on b6 drops the
g4 pawn, so Kengis tried 15 ...
♘c6 16 bc ♕xc7 17 ♘de4 ♗h6
18 ♗c4+ ♔h8 19 ♕e2 ♗d7 with
rather nebulous compensation.) 10
0–0 ♗e6 11 b3 ♘8d7 12 ♘f3
♗g4 13 c5 ♗xf3 14 ♗xf3 e5! 15
♗xe5 ♘xe5 16 de ♘d7 17 ♘e4
♘xe5 18 ♖c1 ♕a5 left White having to play carefully to hold the
balance in King–Kengis, Jurmala
1985.

8 ... c5 *(72)*

This direct move gives rather
better chances than 8 ... ♗e6 9
f4 c6 10 b3 ♘8d7 11 ♗e2 f6 12
♘f3! ♘c8 (12 ... ♗f7!?) 13 d5 cd
14 ♘d4 ♗f7 15 cd f5 16 0–0 ♘d6
17 ♖c1 0–0 18 ♘e6 ♗xe6 19 de
♘f6 20 ♘d5 ♘xd5 21 ♕xd5 ♖c8!±
as in an earlier game Vitolinš–
Kengis, USSR 1988.

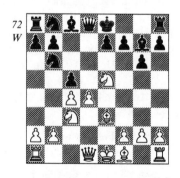

72
W

9	**dc**	**♕xd1+**	
10	**♔xd1**	**♗xe5**	
11	**cb**	**♗xc3**	
12	**bc**	**ab**	
13	**♗xb6**	**♗f5**	

Black's compensation is rather good, as the white bishops are obstructed by the weak c-pawns.

14	ⵌd2	ⵎc6
15	ⵌd3	ⵍa4!
16	ⵍhb1	ⵌxd3
17	ⵌxd3	ⵌd7
18	f4	ⵍha8
19	ⵍb2	e5!
20	g3	f5
21	ⵌc5	e4+
22	ⵌc2	ⵎa5

Black intentions become clear. The attack on the queenside pawns, together with the strong passed e-pawn, is more than White can stand. A pleasing tactical ending ensued: 23 ⵍb6 ⵎxc4 24 ⵍf6 ⵌc7 25 ⵍf7+ ⵌc6 26 ⵌe7 ⵍxa2+ 27 ⵍxa2 ⵍxa2+ 28 ⵌb3 (Has Black blundered?) 28 ... e3! (The key move, which enables Black to reach a won ending.) 29 ⵌh4 ⵎd6 30 ⵍe7 ⵍxh2 31 ⵍxe3 ⵎe4 32 ⵌc4 h6 (The rest is straightforward.) 33 ⵌe7 ⵍg2 34 ⵌd4 ⵍxg3 35 ⵍxg3 ⵎxg3 36 ⵌe5 ⵌd7 37 ⵌh4 ⵎe2 38 ⵌe1 ⵌc6 39 ⵌd2 h5 40 ⵌe1 ⵌc5 41 ⵌh4 b5 42 ⵌf6 ⵌd5 43 ⵌxg6 ⵌe4 44 ⵌxh5 ⵎxc3 0–1.

Kudrin–Kengis
Boston 1989

1 e4 ⵎf6 2 e5 ⵎd5 3 d4 d6 4 ⵎf3 de 5 ⵎxe5 g6
          6   ⵌc4   c6
6 ... ⵌe6?! 7 ⵎc3! ⵌg7 (7 ... ⵎxc3? 8 ⵌxe6; 7 ... f6? 8 ⵟe2!; 7 ... c6!? can be met by 8 ⵎe4 ⵎc7

9 ⵌb3± or 8 ⵟf3!? ⵌg7 9 ⵎe4! ⵎd7!?) 8 ⵎe4 ⵌxe5 (8 ... 0–0 9 ⵎg5±) 9 de ⵎc6 is an old idea of Larsen's. Rather than 10 ⵌb5? ⵎdb4! or 10 ⵎc5 ⵎe3!! with approximate equality, 10 b3! seems very strong, defending the bishop while preparing play on the long diagonal. Vlasak–Platanek, corres. 1990 continued 10 ... ⵎxe5 (10 ... 0–0 11 ⵌh6 ⵍe8 12 ⵎc5) 11 ⵌb2 f6 12 ⵌxe5 fe 13 ⵎc5! ⵌf7 14 ⵎxb7 ⵟd7 15 0–0! ⵟc6 16 ⵎa5 ⵟc5 17 ⵌxd5! ⵌxd5 (17 ... ⵟxd5 18 ⵟxd5 ⵌxd5 19 c4 ⵌe6 20 ⵍfe1+ –) 18 b4 ⵟd6 (18 ... ⵟb5 19 a4 ⵟd7 20 c4) 19 c4 ⵌe4 (19 ... ⵌe6 20 ⵟf3 ⵍb8 21 ⵍfd1 ⵟb6 22 c5) 20 ⵟe2 ⵌf5 21 c5 ⵟf6 22 ⵍae1 e4 23 f3! ef 24 ⵍxf3 ⵟd4+ 25 ⵌh1 0–0 26 ⵎc6 1–0.

The text has been played with considerable success by Kengis. There are obvious similarities with the line 4 ... g6 5 ⵌc4 c6 6 0–0 ⵌg7 7 ed ⵟxd6. Black is thinking in the long term of a queenside advance, and in the short term of play against the e5 knight.

          7   0–0
7 ⵎc3 ⵌg7 8 ⵎxd5 (8 ⵎe4 0–0 9 0–0 ⵌf5! 10 ⵎg3 ⵌe6 11 ⵟe2 ⵎd7 12 ⵎxd7 ⵟxd7 13 c3 f5!? 14 ⵍe1 ⵌf7 15 ⵌxd5 ⵟxd5 16 ⵌf4 c5 17 dc e5 18 ⵌxe5 ⵍfe8 19 f4 ⵌxe5 20 fe ⵟxc5+ 21 ⵟf2 ⵟxf2+ 22 ⵌxf2 ⵍad8 was more than OK for Black in Kamber–Kengis, Bern 1990.) 8 ... cd 9 ⵌb5+ (9 ⵟf3?? ⵌxe5 10 ⵌxd5 ⵌf6– +) 9

... ♘d7 10 ♕f3 ♗xe5! 11 ♗xd7+ ♗xd7= .McKay.

7 ♘d2 ♘d7 **8 ♘df3** ♘xe5 **9 ♘xe5** ♗g7 ½–½ Van Riemsdijk–Bagirov, Dieren 1990.

7 ...   ♗g7

8 ♖e1

8 ♘d2 0–0 **9 ♘df3** ♘d7 (9 ... ♗f5?! 10 ♖e1 ♘d7 11 c3 ♘xe5 12 ♘xe5 ♕d6 13 ♗b3 ♖ad8 14 ♗g5! ♗e6 15 ♘d3± Mainka–C. Horvath, Budapest 1990) 10 ♖e1 (10 ♘d3 a5! 11 a4 ♘7b6 12 ♗b3 ♗f5 13 ♖e1 ♗xd3 14 ♕xd3 e6 15 ♗g5 ♕c7 16 ♕e4 ♘c8 17 c4 ♘d6 18 ♕e2 ♘b4 19 ♖ad1 ♖fe8 20 ♕d2 ♘f5 21 g4 ♘e7 22 ♗f4 ♕d8 23 ♗e5 b5 24 ♕f4 bc 25 ♗xg7 ♔xg7 26 ♘g5 ♖f8 27 ♕e5+ ♔g8 28 ♗xc4 ♘ed5 29 ♘e4 ♕b8 30 ♘f6+ ½–½ Arnason–Kengis, Jurmala 1987) 10 ... ♘xe5 11 ♘xe5 (11 de ♗g4 12 h3 ♗xf3 13 ♕xf3 e6 14 ♗b3 ♕c7 15 ♕e4 ♖ad8 16 ♗g5 ♖d7 17 c3 h6 18 ♗h4 ♘e7= Magomedov–Kengis, Frunze Otborochniy 1989) 11 ... ♗e6 12 ♗b3 (12 ♗f1 ♕c8 13 ♗d2 ♖d8 14 c3 a5 15 ♕f3 a4 16 ♕g3 ♘f6= Conquest–Maus, Copenhagen Open 1990) 12 ... a5 13 c3 ♕c8 14 ♗d2 (14 ♘d3 ♖e8 15 ♘f4 ♘xf4 16 ♗xf4 ♗d5 17 h3 ♕d7 18 ♗e5 f6 19 ♗g3 b5 20 ♕e2 e6 21 ♗c2 a4= Kuzmin–Kengis, Moscow 1986) 14 ... ♖d8 15 ♖c1 c5 16 ♕f3 a4 17 ♗c4 ♕c7 18 ♘g4 ♗xg4 19 ♕xg4 cd 20 cd ♕d7 21 ♕xd7 ♖xd7 22 ♗xd5 ½–½ Smirin–Kengis, Daugavpils 1989.

8 ♗b3 0–0 **9 ♕e2** is a little too committal. 9 ... a5!? (9 ... ♗f5 10 ♖d1 ♘d7) 10 a3 (10 c3) 10 ... ♕b6 11 ♖d1 ♘d7 12 ♘f3 ♘7f6 13 ♘bd2 ♗f5 14 ♘c4 ♕a6 15 ♘fe5 ♖ac8 16 ♘d3 ♕a7 17 c3 ♘e4 gave Black a comfortable game in Liberzon–McKay, Nice ol 1974.

8 ...   0–0

8 ... ♘d7 9 ♘f3 ♘7b6 10 ♗f1 ♗g4 11 c3 0–0 12 ♘bd2 ♕c7 13 h3 ♗xf3 14 ♘xf3 e6 15 g3! ♖ad8 16 ♗g5± ♗f6 17 h4 ♗xg5 18 hg c5 19 dc ♕xc5 20 ♕c2 ♘b4 21 ♕e4 ♘c6 22 ♖ad1 led to an ending in which White's queenside majority proved strong in Arnason–Vaganian, Moscow GMA 1990.

9 h3

9 c3 ♗e6 10 ♘d2 ♘d7 11 ♘ef3 (11 ♘xd7 ♕xd7 12 ♗b3 ♖ad8 13 ♘f3 ♕c7 14 ♕e2 ♖fe8 15 ♗d2 ♗g4 16 h3 ♗xf3 17 ♕xf3 e6 18 ♖ad1 b5 19 ♗g5 ♖d7 20 h4 a5 21 a3 ♖c8 22 h5 h6 23 ♗c1 g5 24 g4 b4 25 ab ab 26 c4 ♘f4 27 ♗xf4 ♕xf4∓ Panbukchian–Kengis, Pula 1990) 11 ... ♗g4 (11 ... ♘c7 12 ♗f1! c5 13 ♘b3± A. Ivanov–Schmidt, Riga 1982) 12 h3 ♗xf3 13 ♘xf3 e6 14 ♗g5 ♕c7 15 ♕d2 ♖fe8 16 ♖ad1 b5 (Compare Arnason–Vaganian above. The difference between a minority attack and a queenside minority is tempi.) 17 ♗b3 a5 18 a3 ♘7b6 19 ♗h6 ♖ad8 20 ♘e5 c5 21 ♗xg7 ♔xg7 22 dc ♕xc5 23 ♗xd5 ♘xd5 24 ♘g4 f6 25 ♕h6+ ♔h8 26 ♖d4 ♕e7 27 ♕d2 ♖d7 28 ♖d1 ♖ed8 29 ♘e3 ♘b6 30 ♖xd7 ½–½ Klovan–Kengis, Latvian Ch 1990.

9 ♗b3 ♗e6 *(73)* is possibly the most critical:

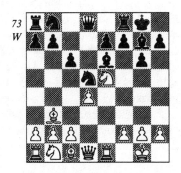

73
W

(a) **10 c3 ♘d7 11 ♘f3** (11 ♘d3 ♗f5 12 ♗g5 ♖e8= Sideif Zade–Kengis, USSR 1979) 11 ... ♘c7 (11 ... ♗g4!?) 12 ♗xe6 ♘xe6 13 ♕b3 ♕b6 14 ♕c4 c5 15 d5 ♘c7 16 ♖xe7 ♕d6 17 ♖e1 ♕xd5?! (17 ... ♘xd5= Bagirov) 18 ♘a3± Tseshkovsky–Kengis, Riga 1981.

(b) **10 ♘d2 ♘d7** (10 ... ♘c7 11 ♘df3 ♗xb3 12 ab ♘d7 13 ♘g4 h5 14 ♘e3 ♘b6 15 ♘c4 ♘e6 16 c3± De Firmian–Alburt, Reykjavik Open 1984) 11 ♘df3 ♘xe5 12 de (12 ♘xe5 can transpose to the lines following 8 ♘d2.) 12 ... a5 13 c3 ♕c7?! (13 ... ♕c8) 14 h3 ♖d8 15 ♘d4 ♗c8 16 e6 f5 17 ♕f3 a4 18 ♗xd5 ♖xd5 19 ♗f4 ♕d8 20 ♖ad1 ♗xd4 21 cd ♖a6 22 b4!? was De Firmian–Tal, Moscow GMA 1990, in which Black's attempt to break out failed: 22 ... c5 23 dc ♗xe6 24 ♗h6 ♗f7 25 ♕c3 ♖f6 26 ♖xd5 ♗xd5 27 ♖d1 ♖f7 28 ♕e5 e6 29 ♕xe6 1–0. Black may well try **13 ... a4!?**, e.g. 14 ♗xa4 ♘b6 15 ♗c2 (15 ♗b3

♕xd1) 15 ... ♕xd1 16 ♖xd1 ♗d5 17 ♖e1 ♖fd8, or 14 ♗c2 a3 15 ♘d4 ab 16 ♗xb2 ♕b6.

9	...	♘d7
10	♘f3	e6
11	c3	b5!

11 ... b6?! 12 ♗g5 ♕c7 13 ♗h4 ♗b7 14 ♗g3 ♕d8 15 ♘bd2 ♘5f6 16 ♕e2 c5 (Kudrin–Kengis, Philadelphia 1989) 17 ♗d6! ♖e8 18 ♘e5±. Black needs breathing room on the queenside.

12	♗f1	a6
13	a4	♗b7
14	♘bd2	♕b6
15	c4	

Kengis suggests 15 ♕b3!?.

15	...	bc
16	♘xc4	♕a7
17	♘a5	c5! *(74)*

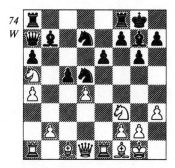

74
W

18	♘e5?

This looks strong, but Black's surprising reply leaves White's position hanging. White should bale out with **18 ♘xb7=**.

18	...	♗c8!!
19	♘ac6	♕c7
20	♗c4	♘7b6
21	♘a5	cd

22	♛xd4	♘d7
23	♘ac6	♗b7
24	♗xd5	♘xe5

Not 24 ... ♗xc6?! 25 ♗xc6
♘xe5 26 ♗f4 ♘xc6 27 ♛xg7+.

25	♘xe5	♗xd5
26	♖a3	♖ad8
27	♛e3	♛b7
28	♛g3	♖c8!
29	h4?!	♖c2
30	h5	♖fc8
31	♘d3	♖xc1!

This exchange sacrifice destroys

White's queenside. Even after the better 32 ♘xc1, White would be struggling. The game finished: 32 ♖xc1 ♖xc1+ 33 ♘xc1 ♛xb2 34 ♛e3 ♗d4! 35 ♘d3 ♗xe3 36 ♘xb2 ♗c1−+ 37 hg hg 38 ♘c4 ♗xa3 39 ♘xa3 ♔f8 40 a5 ♔e7 41 ♘c2 ♔d6 42 ♘b4 ♗c4 43 f4 e5 44 fe+ ♔xe5 45 ♔f2 ♔d4 46 g4 ♔c5 47 ♘c2 ♗b3 48 ♘e1 ♔b4 49 ♔e3 ♔xa5 50 g5 ♔b5 51 ♔d4 a5 52 ♘d3 ♗e6 0−1.

9 Alburt Variation: 4 ♘f3 g6

Lev Alburt has greatly enriched the theory of many variations of Alekhine's Defence, but it is in this line that his contribution has been the most significant. 4 ... g6 prepares kingside development while maintaining the flexibility of the queenside pieces. White can transpose to the Exchange Variation, but will normally attempt to profit from the weakness of f7. The blunt 5 ♘g5 does not seem an effective method, so the main move is 5 ♗c4. After 5 ... ♘b6 6 ♗b3 ♗g7, White may either continue with development, or attack f7 with 7 ♘g5, whereupon Alburt has shown 7 ... e6 to be playable, despite White's possibilities of invading on f6.

An extremely popular idea for White is to try to insert 7 a4 a5. It appears that White benefits slightly more than Black from this, so the search is on for other replies to 7 a4. If Khmelnitsky's 7 ... de 8 a5 ♘6d7 holds up to analysis, the Alburt Variation is alive and kicking; if not, it is just alive.

Ljubojević–Tal
Brussels World Cup 1988

1 e4 ♘f6 2 e5 ♘d5 3 d4 d6 4 ♘f3
4 ... g6 *(75)*

75
W

5 ♘g5

A few miscellaneous moves:

(a) **5 ♗e2 ♗g7 6 c4** (After 6 0–0 0–0, weak is 7 ♗g5 h6 8 c4 hg∓ Suer–Jansa, Athens 1969, but a very solid approach was seen in Malevinsky–Lopokhin, RSFSR Ch 1986: 7 ♖e1 ♘c6 8 ed cd 9 c3 h6 10 ♕b3 ♘b6 11 ♘bd2 e5 12 de de 13 ♘e4 ♗e6 14 ♕a3 and although White went on to win, Black's position at this point was not to blame.) **6 ... ♘b6** and now:

(a1) **7 ♗e3?!** de 8 ♘xe5 ♗xe5!
9 de ♕xd1+ 10 ♔xd1 ♘c6∓ 11
♘d2 (Ivanović–Alburt, Reykjavik
1982) 11 ... ♗f5! (Threatens 12
... ♘b4 to provoke a weakness.)
12 g4 ♗e6 13 f4 0-0-0 14 b3
♘d4! 15 ♗xd4 (15 h3 h5!) 15
... ♖xd4 gives Black a winning
advantage, as Alburt analysed.

(a2) **7 ed** ed is a way for Black
to refuse a normal Exchange Variation. Zso. Polgar–C. Hansen,
Åbenrå rapid 1989 continued 8
♗g5 f6 9 ♗e3 0-0 10 ♘c3 ♘c6
11 0-0 ♔h8 12 a4 ♗g4 13 a5?
♗xf3∓.

(b) **5 c4** ♘b6 6 ♘c3 (6 h4?! ♗g4
7 ♗e2 de!? 8 c5 e4 9 cb ef 10
♗xf3 ♗xf3 11 ♕xf3 ♘c6 12 d5
♘d4 13 ♕c3 ♕xd5 14 bc ♖c8) 6
... ♗g7 7 ♗e3 (7 ♗f4 ♗g4 or
7 ... 0-0) 7 ... 0-0 (7 ... ♘c6?! 8
e6; 7 ... ♗g4!?) 8 ed cd is a line
of the Exchange Variation.

(c) **5 b3?!** ♗g7 6 ♗b2 0-0 7 c4
♘b4!? (7 ... ♘b6) 8 a3 ♘4c6 9
♗e2 ♘d7 10 e6?! fe 11 ♘g5 ♘f6
12 0-0 e5 13 d5 h6 14 ♘f3 ♘b8 15
♘bd2 e6∓ Z. Rahman–Hennigan,
London (Lloyds Bank) 1989.

(d) **5 h3** is a loss of tempo unless
White is allowed to transpose to
the Exchange Variation (5 ... de!?).

5   ...   c6

5 ... de 6 de ♗g7 (6 ... ♘c6?!
7 ♗b5 h6 8 c4; 6 ... h6? 7 ♗xf7
♔xf7 8 c4 c6 9 ♘c3±) 7 ♗c4 (7
c4? ♘b4 8 ♕xd8+ ♔xd8 9 ♘xf7+
♔e8 10 ♘xh8 ♘xc2+ 11 ♔d1
♘xa1 12 ♘xg6 hg ♗d3 ♗f5

14 ♗xf5 gf 15 f4 ♘c6 16 ♘a3
♖d8+ 17 ♗d2 ♘b4 rescues the
knight, as Berliner discovered.) 7
... c6 8 e6 ♗xe6 9 ♘xe6 fe 10
♘d2 is rather a safe pawn sacrifice
for White. Black has continuing
problems after either 10 ... ♕d6
11 0-0 ♘d7 12 ♘e4 ♕b4 13 ♕e2
h6 14 a4 ♘e5 15 ♗b3 0-0 16
♗d2 Panchenko–A. Petrosian,
Riga 1973 or 10 ... ♘d7 11 0-0
♕b6 12 ♕e2 (12 ♕g4? ♘e5! Penrose–Cafferty, British Ch 1968.) 12
... ♘e5 (12 ... e5?! 13 ♘e4 0-0-0
14 ♘g5) 13 ♘e4.

5 ... f6 can lead to some amaz-
ing complications, but unfortun-
ately it seems that simple play by
White keeps an edge.

(a) **6 c4 ♘b6 7 e6 fg 8 d5 ♗g7
9 a4** *(76)* is regarded as almost a
refutation, but gives White no
more than unclear play, provided
Black chooses a good moment to
return the piece:

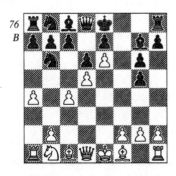

(a1) **9 ... a5** 10 h4 ♗xe6!? is
David Peel's idea, also analysed
by Cafferty: 11 de ♕c8 12 ♕g4 (12
♕e2 ♘c6) 12 ... ♘c6 13 hg (13

♗d3 ♘e5; 13 ♖a3 ♘e5; 13 c5 dc 14 ♗b5 0–0 15 ♗xc6 bc 16 hg ♖f5! 17 ♕h3 ♕xe6+ 18 ♗e3 ♘c4∓) 13 ... ♘d4 14 ♗d3 (14 ♖a3 ♕xe6+ 15 ♕xe6 ♘xe6 16 ♖ah3 ♘f8) 14 ... ♕xe6+ ♘xe6 16 ♖xh7 ♖xh7 17 ♗xg6+ ♔d7 18 ♗xh7 ♘xc4∓.

(a2) **9 ... 0–0!?** is an idea of the French postal player J. Hamar. **10 a5** c6 11 h4 (11 ab ♕xb6) 11 ... ♘xc4! 12 ♗xc4 cd 13 ♗xd5 g4 14 ♕xg4 ♕c7 15 ♗e3 ♗xb2 16 ♖a2 ♗c1 17 ♔e2 ♗xe3 18 fe ♘c6 19 h5 ♘e5∞ and **10 h4** ♖f5 11 hg ♖e5+ 12 ♗e3 c6 13 ♘c3 cd 14 cd ♘xd5 15 ♘xd5 ♕a5+ 16 ♘c3 ♖xe3+! 17 fe ♕xg5 18 ♘d5 ♗xe6 19 ♘f4 ♗f7 20 ♕c2 ♘c6∓ were the consequences in two of his games.

(b) **6 ef** ef 7 ♗c4 (7 ♘f3) 7 ... ♕e7+! 8 ♔d2! ♗h6 9 ♗xd5 ♗xg5+ 10 ♔c3 ♔d8 11 ♖e1 ♕g7∞ Boleslavsky.

(c) **6 ♗c4!** de (6 ... c6?! 7 ef ef 8 ♕e2+ ♕e7 9 ♘e4± Kosikov–Kutin, USSR 1989; 6 ... fg 7 ♗xd5 e6 8 ♗e4 de 9 de ♕xd1+ 10 ♔xd1 ♗g7 11 ♗xg5 ♗xe5 12 ♘c3±) 7 de c6 (7 ... fg 8 ♕xd5 ♕xd5 9 ♗xd5 c6 10 ♗b3 ♗g7 11 ♗xg5 ♗xg5 12 ♘c3± Listengarten–Ovanesian, Baku 1970) 8 ef ef 9 ♕e2+ ♕e7 10 ♘e4 ♗g7 11 ♘d6+ ♔d7 12 ♕xe7+ ♔xe7 13 ♘xc8+ ♖xc8 14 0–0 ♘d7 15 ♘d2 f5 gave White a pleasant ending in McKay–Basman, Lugano 1968.

6   c4

6 f4!? ♗g7 has been tried in two Kosikov–Khmelnitsky games. At Kiev 1989 there followed **7 ♗c4** 0–0 8 0–0 ♘a6!? 9 ♗b3 ♘ac7 10 c4 ♘b6 11 ♘c3 de 12 fe and now instead of 12 ... c5? 13 dc ♕xd1 14 ♖xd1 ♘d7 15 e6±, 12 ... f6!∞ would have been in order. At Voroshvilovgrad 1989, White was less successful: **7 c4** ♘c7 8 ♘c3 0–0 9 ♗e2 f6! 10 ef ef 11 ♘f3 d5 12 0–0 ♗e6 13 c5 ♗g4!∓ 14 ♕b3 ♕c8 15 ♗e3 ♖e8 16 ♗f2 ♘e6 17 g3 ♘d7 18 ♖fe1 ♕c7 19 ♔g2 ♔h8! 20 h3 ♗xf3+ 21 ♗xf3 f5! 22 ♖ad1 ♘f6 23 ♕c2 ♖ad8 24 b4 a6 25 a4 ♕d7! 26 ♖e2 g5! 27 ♔h1?! gf 28 ♕xf5 fg 29 ♗xg3 ♘xd4! 30 ♕xd7 ♘xd7 31 ♖xe8+ ♖xe8 32 ♗g4 ♘f6 33 ♗f2 ♘c2 0–1.

Bogdanović–Kavalek, Sarajevo 1967 was a fine demonstration of the latent dynamism in Black's position: **6 ♕e2** h6 7 ♘e4 (7 ♘f3 ♗g7 8 c4 ♘c7 9 ♗f4 ♘e6) 7 ... ♗g7 8 f4 (8 ed 0–0!?) 8 ... 0–0 9 ♘bc3 ♘xc3 10 ♘xc3 c5 11 d5 (11 dc de 12 fe ♘c6 13 ♗f4 ♕d4 14 ♕e3 ♗f5∓) 11 ... e6! 12 ♗e3 ed 13 ♘xd5 ♘c6 14 0–0–0 ♘d4∓.

The insipid **6 ed** ed (6 ... ♕xd6) 7 ♗c4?! quickly gave Black the upper hand in Qi Jingxuan–Timman, Taxco IZ 1985: 7 ... ♕e7+ 8 ♔e2 ♕xe2+ 9 ♗xe2 h6 10 ♘f3 ♘b4 11 ♘a3 ♗f5 12 ♔d1 ♘d7 13 ♘e1 ♖b6 14 c3 ♘4d5 15 ♘c4 ♘xc4 16 ♗xc4 ♗e6 17 ♗d3 ♗g7 18 ♘c2 0–0 19 ♗d2 c5. White was eventually suffocated.

The peculiar **6 h4** organises a retreat square for the knight: 6 ... de 7 de ♕c7 (7 ... f6!? Alburt) 8 ♕e2 (8 f4 f6!) 8 ... h6 9 ♘h3 ♗g7 10 f4 ♗e6 11 ♘a3 ♘d7 12 ♗d2 0–0–0∞ Barczay–Böhm, Wijk aan Zee 1977.

6 ♕f3 f6 7 ef (7 c4; 7 e6? ♕a5+ 8 ♗d2 ♕b6∓) 7 ... ef 8 ♘h3 ♗f5= Rohri–Wallner, Austrian Ch 1977.

6 ♗c4 de (Alburt reckons there's nothing to be gained by delaying this exchange, except perhaps to encourage White to short-circuit: 6 ... ♗g7 7 ♕f3?! 0–0 8 ♘c3 h6 9 ♘ge4 de 10 de ♘d7 11 e6? ♘e5∓ Choobak–Alburt, New York Open 1985.) 7 de h6! 8 ♘f3 ♗g7 9 ♕e2 0–0 10 0–0 ♗g4 11 ♘bd2 ♕c7 12 h3 ♗xf3 13 ♘xf3 e6 is given by Bagirov. Both sides' positions have pleasant features, and play is roughly balanced.

6 ... ♘c7
7 ♕f3

7 ♗d3 ♗g7 8 f4 de 9 de ♘e6= Bogdanović–Knežević, Yugoslav Ch 1965; **7 ed** ♕xd6 8 ♘c3 ♗g7 9 ♗e3 0–0 10 ♕d2 ♗f5 11 ♗e2 b5!? (Watzka–Jansa, Vrnjacka Banja 1967) left the knight's purpose on g5 rather unclear.

7 ... f6
8 ef ef
9 ♕e3+

9 ♘e4 f5 (9 ... ♗g7!? 10 ♗f4 0–0! is adequate for Black: 11 ♘bc3 ♘e6 12 0–0–0 f5 13 ♘g3 ♘xd4 Jansa–Jakobsen, Helsinki 1961) 10 ♘ec3 ♗g7! 11 d5 0–0 12

h4 ♘d7 13 ♗f4 ♘e5 14 ♕g3 ♕e8∓ Blatny–Kupka, Luhacovice 1969.

9 ...   ♗e7

9 ... ♕e7 10 ♘e4 d5 (10 ... ♔f7 11 c5±) fails not to 11 ♘xf6+?? ♔f7–+, but 11 ♘d6+!±. After the text, 10 ♘e4 is comfortably met by 10 ... 0–0.

10	**♘f3**	**0–0**
11	**♗d3**	**♖e8**
12	**0–0**	**d5**

12 ... ♗f8 13 ♕d2! ♗g4 (13 ... d5) 14 ♕f4 f5!? 15 d5 (Tal) leads to more unbalanced play, though probably favours White.

13	**♘c3**	**♗f8**
14	**♕d2**	**dc**
15	**♗xc4+**	**♗e6**
16	**♕d3**	**♘ba6?**

16 ... ♘d7! leads to equality, since White must liquidate the d-pawn before it becomes a weakness: 17 d5 (17 ♗f4 ♘b6 18 ♗xc7 ♗xc4∓; 17 ♗xe6+ ♖xe6! 18 ♗f4 ♘b6 19 ♗xc7 ♕xc7∓) 17 ... ♘xd5 (17 ... ♘c5 18 de ♕xd3) 18 ♘xd5 ♘c5 (Tal).

17	**a3**	**♗xc4**
18	**♕xc4+**	**♘d5**
19	**♗f4!**	**♕d7**
20	**♖ac1!**	

The badly placed knight on a6 and White's control of the c-file give Black serious problems. However, thanks to mutual time-trouble, Tal wriggled out: 20 ... ♖e6 21 ♘xd5 cd (21 ... ♕xd5 22 ♕xd5 cd 23 b4) 22 ♕d3 ♖ae8 23 ♖c2 ♗d6 24 ♗xd6 ♕xd6 25 ♖fc1 ♘b8 26 g3 (26 ♕b5 ♘c6 27 ♕xb7

♘xd4!) 26 ... ♘c6 27 b4 (27 ♖c5!?) 27 ... ♖6e7 28 ♖c5 (Tal recommended 28 h4 to secure White's kingside.) 28 ... ♖d7 29 ♕d2 a6 30 a4 ♘d8 31 ♖c8 ♖de7 32 b5 ab 33 ab ♘e6 34 ♕a5! ♕d7 35 ♖xe8+? (35 ♖8c3! ♕d6 and now quiet moves such as h4 and ♔g2 preserve White's advantage. Instead Tal is presented with a tactical opportunity.) 35 ... ♖xe8+ 36 b6 ♘f4!= 37 ♖e1 ♘e2+ 38 ♔g2 (38 ♔h1?! ♕f5) 38 ... ♘f4+ 39 ♔h1 ♖xe1+ 40 ♘xe1 ♘e6 41 ♘c2 ♔f7 42 ♕b4 ½-½.

Christiansen–Vaganian
New York Open 1990

1 e4 ♘f6 2 e5 ♘d5 3 d4 d6 4 ♘f3 g6

5 ♗c4   c6

This is a fairly popular alternative to 5 ... ♘b6. A couple of inferior methods of supporting the knight have been tried:

5 ... ♗e6?! 6 ♘g5 de 7 ♘xe6 fe 8 de ♗g7 9 f4 (9 ♕e2? 0–0 10 0–0 ♘c6 11 f4? ♘xf4! 12 ♖xf4 ♖xf4 13 ♗xe6+ ♔h8 14 ♗xf4 ♕d4+ 15 ♕e3 ♕d1+! 16 ♔f2 ♖f8–+ Himmel–Thal, E. Germany 1985) 9 ... 0–0 10 0–0 c6 (10 ... ♘c6 11 ♘c3!) 11 ♕e2 and with the tactics cut out, Black's position makes no sense.

5 ... de?! 6 de! c6 7 ♘c3! ♗e6 8 ♘g5 ♗g7 9 f4 ♘d7 10 ♗xd5! cd 11 ♗e3 ♘b6 12 ♘xe6 fe 13 ♗d4 ♘c4 14 b3 ♘a3 15 0–0 ♖c8 16 ♖f2 ♕a5 17 ♕d3 b5 18 ♖c1

b4 19 ♘e2 ♘b5 20 c3 bc 21 a4 ♘xd4 22 ♘xd4 was positionally winning for White in P. Cramling–Alburt, Reykjavik 1984.

6 0–0

6 h3 de!? (6 ... ♗g7) 7 de ♗g7 8 0–0 ♗e6= Balinas–Vaganian, Malta 1980.

6 ...   ♗g7

6 ... ♗g4?! 7 ed ♕xd6 8 h3 ♗xf3 9 ♕xf3 ♗g7 10 ♘c3! is strong, due to the weakness of f7.

7 ed

7 ♘c3 ♘xc3 8 bc d5 9 ♗d3 ♗g4 Frolov–Panchenko, USSR 1988.

7 h3 0–0 (7 ... de 8 ♘xe5 0–0 and 9 ... ♘d7 is reasonable for Black.) and now:

(a) **8 ♕e2** should probably be met by 8 ... ♗f5 9 ♖e1 (9 c3?! de 10 de a5 11 ♖d1 e6∓ Balenović–Wohl, Biel 1985) 9 ... de 10 de ♘b6, rather than 8 ... a5 9 ♖e1 (9 a4 ♘a6 10 ♖e1 ♘ac7= Mihaljčišin–Vukić, Banja Luka 1976) 9 ... de 10 de ♘a6 11 ♗xd5 cd 12 ♘c3 ♗e6 13 ♗e3± Lobron–Marinković, Amsterdam 1987.

(b) **8 ♖e1** de (8 ... h6?! 9 ♗b3 de 10 de ♘a6 11 ♕d4± Lanc–Pribyl, Brno 1975; 9 ... ♗e6!?) 9 de (9 ♘xe5 ♘d7) 9 ... a5 (9 ... ♘b6!?) 10 ♘bd2 (10 ♕e2!?) 10 ... ♕c7 11 ♘f1 ♖d8 12 ♕e2 ♘a6 13 a3 ♘c5= Matanović–Knežević, Ohrid 1972.

7 ...   ♕xd6
8 ♘bd2

After **8 ♗b3** 0–0 9 c4? ♘c7

(Mannion–Depasquale, Commonwealth Ch 1986) the d-pawn is a serious weakness.

8 ♖e1 is the main alternative to the text:

(a) **8 ... ♗g4 9 h3!?** (9 ♗g5!?; After 9 ♘bd2 0–0 10 h3 ♗xf3 11 ♘xf3, 11 ... e6 12 ♗f1 b5!= was Nunn–Vaganian, London 1984, whilst in Gažik–Palatnik, Kiev 1989, 11 ... ♘d7 12 ♗g5 e6 13 ♗b3 b5 14 ♕d2 a5 15 a4 b4 transposed to the main game, whereupon a draw was agreed.) 9 ... ♗xf3 10 ♕xf3 e6 (10 ... ♗xd4 11 ♘c3!) 11 ♘c3 0–0 12 ♗g5 ♘d7 (12 ... ♗xd4?! 13 ♗xd5 cd 14 ♘b5 ♕b6 15 ♘xd4 ♕xd4 16 ♗h6 ♖c8 17 ♖ad1! ♕h8 18 c4!± Chandler; 12 ... ♘xc3) 13 ♘e4± ♕c7 14 ♖ad1 b5 15 ♗b3 a5 16 a3 ♖fe8 17 h4 h6 18 ♗c1 b4 19 c4! Chandler–Vaganian, London 1984.

(b) **8 ... 0–0**

(b1) **9 h3 b5!?** (9 ... h6 10 ♘bd2 b6 11 ♗b3 ♘d7 was Ernst–Alburt, Subotica IZ 1987; Ernst gives 12 ♘c4 ♕c7 13 ♘ce5 ♘xe5 14 ♘xe5 ♗f5 as the safest way to keep an edge.) 10 ♗f1 ♗f5 11 c3 ♘d7 12 ♘bd2 h6 (12 ... ♖fe8? 13 g4±) 13 ♘e4 ♗xe4 14 ♖xe4 ♖fe8 15 ♖e1 (15 ♖h4!?) 15 ... ♖ad8 16 a4 a6 gave Black, able to choose between ... c5 and ... e5 as appropriate, adequate play in Prandstetter–Ambroz, Prague 1986.

(b2) **9 ♗g5!? ♗g4** (9 ... ♗e6 10 ♗b3 ♘a6 11 c4± Smyslov–Hort, Moscow 1966; 10 ... a5!?)

10 ♘bd2 ♖e8 (10 ... h6 11 ♗h4 e6 12 c3 ♕c7 13 ♗g3 ♕e7 14 ♕b3± Smyslov–Menvielle, Las Palmas 1972) 11 ♗b3 h6 12 ♗h4 ♘d7 13 c4 (13 h3) 13 ... ♘f4 14 c5 ♕xd4 15 ♖e4! ♗xf3 16 gf ♘h3+ 17 ♔g2 ♕xc5! 18 ♔xh3 ♕h5 (18 ... ♘f6! gives better chances.) 19 ♘f1 ♘e5 20 ♔g2!± Tal–Ljubojević, Wijk aan Zee 1973.

8 ...   ♗g4

8 ... 0–0 9 h3 (9 ♗b3 ♗g4 10 c3 ♘d7 11 h3 ♗xf3 12 ♕xf3 b5! 13 ♖e1 e6 14 ♘e4 ♕c7 15 ♗g5 f5 16 ♘d2 ♖ae8 17 ♗h4 ♘7b6 18 ♗g3 f4 19 ♗h2 e5!∓ Short–Vaganian, Lvov 1984) 9 ... ♗f5 (9 ... h6) 10 ♗b3 ♘d7 11 ♖e1 and now 11 ... b5!? should be preferred to 11 ... h6 12 ♘h4!± Kavalek–Böhm, Wijk aan Zee 1977.

9   h3

9 c3 0–0 10 ♘e4 ♕c7 11 h3 ♗xf3 12 ♕xf3 ♘d7 13 ♗b3 e5 14 de ♘xe5 15 ♕g3 ♘e7 16 ♕h4 ♘f5 17 ♘f6+ ♗xf6 18 ♕xf6 ♘d3 19 ♗c2 ½–½ Kontić–Marinković, Vrnjacka Banja 1989.

9 ♖e1 is considered under 8 ♖e1 ♗g4 9 ♘bd2.

9 ...   ♗xf3
10   ♘xf3

10 ♕xf3 0–0 11 c3 ♘d7 12 ♗b3 b5 13 a4 a6 14 ♖e1 ♖ae8 15 ab ab 16 ♖a6 ♘7f6 17 c4? ♘b4∓ Messa–Kengis, Albena 1986.

10 ...   ♘d7
11 ♗b3   0–0

Black should consider 11 ... b5

to avoid the next note, although 12 ... a6 is not available as a reply to 12 a4.

12   ♖e1

12 c4 ♘5f6 (12 ... ♘c7?? 13 c5 ♕f6 14 ♗g5+ −) 13 ♗e3 gives White a useful space advantage.

12   ...   e6

Now with e7 available for the knight, 13 c4 is not a problem.

13   ♗g5   b5

13 ... h6 forces the bishop towards a comfortable post on g3.

14   a4   b4?!

Now Black becomes a little over-extended. **14 ... a6** followed by ... ♘7b6 and ... c5 would more or less equalise.

15   ♕d2   a5 *(77)*

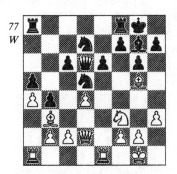

16   ♖ad1   ♖fe8
17   ♗h6   ♘7b6?

17 ... ♕f8! 18 ♗xg7 ♕xg7 19 ♘e5± Christiansen.

18   ♘e5   c5?

This caves in immediately, but White has a very strong attack after 18 ... ♖a7!? or 18 ... ♖ad8 19 ♖e4.

19   ♗xg7   ♔xg7

20   ♕h6+!   ♔g8
21   dc   ♕xc5
22   ♘xf7!

Having introduced the queen into the attack free of charge, it is no surprise that White has further resources. Now 22 ... ♖f8 23 ♘g5 ♕xf2+ does nothing to solve Black's problems.

22   ...   ♔xf7
23   ♕xh7+   ♔f6
24   ♖d3   ♘f4
25   ♖f3   ♕f5

25 ... g5 26 g3 ♕c6 27 ♕h6+! ♔f7 28 ♖dd3+ − Dlugy.

26   ♕c7!

White now regains the sacrificed piece. There followed 26 ... g5 27 ♕xb6 ♔g6 28 ♖fe3 ♕f6 29 ♖e5 ♖ad8 30 ♕e3 ♖d6 31 ♖xa5 ♕xb2 32 ♕e4+ ♔f6 33 ♕h7 1–0.

Kapengut–Sinanović
Pula Open 1990

1 e4 ♘f6 2 e5 ♘d5 3 d4 d6 4 ♘f3 g6 5 ♗c4

5   ...   ♘b6
6   ♗b3

The peculiar 6 ♗b5+ c6 7 ♗e2 was seen in Faibisovich–Khmelnitsky, Berlin 1989. 7 ... de 8 ♘xe5 ♗g7 9 0–0 0–0 was then the simplest route to equality, whilst 7 ... ♗g7 8 ed ed can hardly be bad.

6   ...   ♗g7

6 ... a5 can be met by 7 ♘g5 d5 (7 ... e6? 8 ♕f3) 8 a4 or **7 a4** ♗g7, both considered under 7 a4 a5. The sharp **7 e6!?** is not totally clear: 7 ... ♗xe6 (7 ... f6? 8 ♘g5!

c6 9 ♘f7+− ♕c7 10 ♘xh8!? a4
11 ♘xg6! hg 12 ♕g4 ab 13 ♕xg6+
♔d8 14 ♕f7 ♘8d7 15 ed ♘xd7
16 ♕xb3) 8 ♗xe6 fe 9 ♘g5 ♘c6
(9 ... ♗h6? 10 ♘xe6 ♕d7 11
♘xc7+ won a pawn in Beliavsky–
Menvielle, Las Palmas 1974.) 10
♘xe6 ♕d7 11 ♕e2. Now 11 ...
♘d8?! 12 ♘xf8 ♖xf8 13 ♘c3 ♘c6
14 ♗h6! ♖f5 (14 ... ♖f7) 15
0-0-0± d5 16 h4 0-0-0 17 g4
♖f7 18 f4 gave White a useful
advantage in Kapengut–Palatnik,
Beltsy 1977, but Alburt's recommendation 11 ... ♔f7 12 ♘g5+
♔g8 makes more sense. Quite
often in the Alekhine, ... ♔f7 is
a good way to remove a knight
from e6.

6... ♘c6 is a sensible developing
move. White can try:

(a) **7 ♘g5** e6 8 ♕f3 (8 ed cd 9
0-0 h6 10 ♘f3 ♗g7 11 d5 ♘xd5
12 ♗xd5 ed 13 ♖e1+ ♗e6 14
♘c3 0-0 15 ♘xd5 ♕a5 16 ♘e3 d5
17 c3 d4∓ Damjanović–Neckař,
Prague 1988) 8 ... ♕e7 9 ♘e4 (9
ed) 9 ... h6 10 ♗f4 de 11 ♗xe5
♘xe5 12 ♘f6+ ♔d8 13 de ♕c5
14 ♕d3+ ♔e7∞ Wedberg–Wes-
terinen, Gausdal 1983.

(b) **7 e6 fe**. Now 8 h4 is well met
by either 8 ... e5 9 de ♗g4 J.
Polgar–C. Hansen, Åbenrå rapid
1989, or 8 ... ♗g7 9 h5 e5 10 hg
(10 ♘g5?! d5 11 ♕f3 ♗f5 12 hg
♘xd4−+   Tukmakov–Stein,
Leningrad 1962) 10 ... hg 11
♖xh8+ ♗xh8 12 ♘h4 (12 d5
♘d4) 12 ... ♘xd4 13 ♘xg6 ♗f6
14 ♕h5 ♔d7∓ Postovsky–Pod-

gorny, corres. 1982/3. Therefore **8
♘g5 ♗g7 9 ♗xe6 ♖f8** is normal:

(b1) **10 c3** h6 11 ♕d3 ♖f6=
Vonthron–Kopp,   Bundesliga
1987/8.

(b2) **10 d5** ♘d4 11 c3 (11 h4; 11
0-0 ♘xe6 12 de h6 13 ♕d3 ♖f6 14
♘f7 ♖xf7∞ Binham–Rantanen,
Helsinki 1981) 11 ... ♘xe6 12 de
♖f6 (12 ... c6 13 0-0 ♖f6 14 ♕g4!)
13 ♘xh7 ♖xe6+ 14 ♗e3 ♕d7 15
0-0 ♕b5 16 ♘d2 ♗d7 17 ♘f3
♖xe3!? 18 fe ♕xb2 left White's
position rather uncoordinated in
Carleton–Podgorny, corres. 1986.

(c) **7 ed! cd** (7 ... ♕xd6 8 ♘c3
♗g7 9 ♘e4 ♕d8 10 c3 0-0 11 0-0
♗g4 12 h3 ♗xf3 13 ♕xf3 ♘a5
14 ♗c2 e5 15 de ♗xe5 16 ♗g5
f6 17 ♗h4 ♕e7 18 ♖fe1 ♔g7 19
♖e2 ♘d5 20 ♘g3 c6 21 ♕g4 ♕f7
22 ♖ae1 ♖ae8 23 b4± Winsnes–
Wesslén, Sweden 1987) **8 d5** (78)
and Black has a choice of evils:

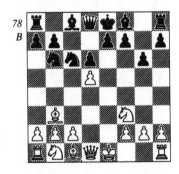

78
B

(c1) **8 ... ♘a5** 9 ♕d4 ♖g8 (9 ...
♘xb3 10 ab ♖g8 11 c4 ♗g7 12
♕f4 ♘d7 13 0-0 ♘f6 14 ♘c3 a6 15
♖e1± Penrose–Cafferty, British
Ch (Portsmouth) 1977; 9 ... f6 10

Bd2 Nxb3 11 ab Bg7 12 Ba5
Bf5 13 c4 0–0 14 0–0± Kuporo-
sov–Baburin, Gorky 1988) 10
Ba4+ Bd7 11 Bxd7+ Qxd7 12
Nc3 Rc8 13 0–0 Bg7 14 Qd3
Nac4 15 Re1 Bxc3 16 Qxc3
Nxd5 17 Qd4 Ncb6 18 c3 Kd8
19 Qd1 Nc7 20 a4 Ne6 21 a5 Na8
22 Be3 b6 23 Qb3 b5 24 Ne5+ −
Winsnes–Wesslén, Sweden 1986.

(c2) **8 ... Ne5** 9 Nxe5 de 10 Be3
(10 0–0 Bg7 11 a4 0–0 12 a5 Nd7
13 Be3 Nf6 14 h3 Ne8 15 Nd2
Nd6 16 Nc4± Mortensen–Hölzl,
Randers 1982) 10 ... Bg7 11 Qd2
0–0 12 Nc3 Bf5 13 Bh6 Rc8 14
Bxg7 Kxg7 15 Qe2 f6 16 g4
Bd7 17 h4 Qc7 18 0–0–0 Nc4 19
Ne4 a5 20 f3 Nd6 21 Nxd6 ed 22
a3 was Kavalek–Ernst, Subotica
IZ 1987. White's attack came first
in the game, but clearly Black is
not without chances.

7 Qe2

7 ed is rather harmless without
Black's queenside weakened by a4
a5. 7 ... cd 8 a4 (8 0–0 0–0 9 Re1
Bg4) 8 ... 0–0 9 0–0 (9 a5?! N6d7
10 0–0 Nc6 11 a6?! ba 12 Re1
Rb8∓ Robatsch–Ljubojević,
Amsterdam 1972) 9 ... Nc6 10
h3 Bf5 11 a5 Nc8 12 Qd2. In
Speelman–Peters, Hastings
1978/9, Black had problems after
12 ... d5 13 Ne5!? Nxe5 14 de
Bxe5 15 Re1 Bc7? 16 Bxd5
Qd6 17 g3 Rb8 18 Nc3 Bxh3 19
Qh6, but 12 ... Be4!? and 15 ...
Bf6 both improve.

After **7 0–0 0–0**, White does best
to transpose to the main line with

8 Qe2. Instead 8 a4 can be met by
8 ... de or 8 ... a5 (see 7 a4 a5),
whilst 8 Re1 Bg4 9 h3 Bxf3
10 Qxf3 Nc6∓ Iosif–Hennigan,
Oakham 1990 and 8 Bf4 Nc6 9
h3 Na5 10 Nbd2 Nxb3 11 ab f6∓
Maciejewski–Ghizdavu, Bucharest 1974, are harmless.

7 Nbd2?! 0–0 8 h3?! a5 9 a4?!
de 10 de Na6! 11 0–0 Nc5 12 Qe2
Qe8! won the a-pawn for no real
compensation in Spassky–
Fischer, Reykjavik (13) 1972.

7 ... 0–0

7 ... d5 is insufficiently challenging, and is therefore no longer
played, e.g. 8 0–0 0–0 9 Bf4 Bg4
10 Nbd2 Nc6 11 Qe3!? Na5 12 h3
Bf5 13 Qc3!± Geller–Ghinda,
Bath 1973.

7 ... Nc6 8 0–0 (8 h3; 8 c3 de 9
Nxe5 Nxe5 10 de Bf5=) and
now:

(a) **8 ... de** 9 de Nd4 10 Nxd4
Qxd4 11 e6 Bxe6 12 Bxe6 fe 13
Nd2 (13 Qxe6?! Qc4∓ Maciejew-
ski–Chekhov, Potsdam 1987) 13
... Qe5 (13 ... 0–0?! 14 Qxe6+
Kh8 15 c3 Qd6 16 Qe2 Nd5 17
Ne4± Geller–Alburt, USSR Ch
1975) 14 Qxe5 Bxe5 15 Re1±.

(b) **8 ... 0–0** 9 c3 (9 h3 transposes
to the main line.) 9 ... Bg4 10
Bf4 and now Black can try 10 ...
Qd7 11 Nbd2 Qf5 12 Bg3 Bh6
or 10 ... Bxf3 11 Qxf3 de 12 de
Nxe5 13 Qxb7 Qc8 14 Qe4 Qf5
15 Qxf5 gf 16 Na3 Nd3∞ Ernst–
Westerinen, Copenhagen 1985.

8 h3

8 e6 has been recommended as

good for White, but it's hard to see why. At any rate, no one, Alburt included, seems worried by this.

8 0–0 ♗g4!? 9 e6 (9 ♗f4 ♘c6; 9 ♘bd2 ♘c6) 9 ... d5 10 ef+ ♖xf7 11 ♘bd2 ♘c6 12 ♕e3 ♕d6 13 ♘g5 ♖f8 14 c3 e5 15 ♕g3 ♗f5 16 ♘de4 ♕e7 17 de ♘xe5∓ Fedorowicz–Alburt, US Ch (Estes Park) 1985.

8 ... ♘c6
9 0–0 *(79)*

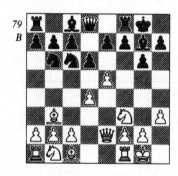

79
B

9 ... ♘a5

9 ... ♗f5 10 a4 de 11 de ♘d7 12 e6 ♗xe6 13 ♗xe6 fe 14 ♕xe6+ ♔h8 15 ♘bd2 ♘c5 16 ♕c4 ♕d6 gave Black a playable game in Fleck–Hartmann, Bundesliga 1987/8.

9 ... de is also possible (compare the lines with 7 a4 a5 inserted).

10 ♗g5!?

10 e6 ♘xb3 11 ef+ ♖xf7 12 ab h6 13 ♘c3 c6 14 ♗e3 a6 15 ♖fe1 ♗f5 16 ♖ad1 g5 17 d5 ♘xd5 18 ♘xd5 cd 19 h4 g4 20 ♘h2 e6 gave Black good play in De Firmian–Alburt, US Ch (Estes Park) 1986, but **10 ♘c3** ♘xb3 11 ab ♗f5 12

♗f4 f6 13 ed ed 14 d5! turned out well for White in Kapengut–Bartovsky, Minsk 1984.

10 ... ♘xb3
11 ab f6
12 ♗d2 ♗f5
13 ♘a3 g5

This unnatural move leads to a difficult position for Black. 13 ... fe 14 de d5 is a possible improvement.

14 e6!± h6

14 ... d5 15 c4 ♗e4 16 c5 ♘c8 17 ♘h2±.

15 c4 ♗g6
16 ♗c3 d5
17 c5 ♘c8
18 ♘h2! f5
19 f4! a6
20 ♘f3! ♗h5

20 ... g5 21 ♘h4 ♕e8 22 ♖xf4±.

21 fg hg
22 g4! fg
23 ♘xg5

White has ripped the defences from the black king at no material cost. The game finished 23 ... ♖f6 24 ♖xf6 ♗xf6 25 hg ♗g6 26 ♘f7! ♗xf7 27 ef+ ♔xf7 28 g5! ♕g8 29 ♕h5+ ♔e6 30 ♕g4+ ♔f7 31 ♘b5!+ – ♕xg5 32 ♕xg5 ♗xg5 33 ♘xc7 ♖b8 34 ♖f1+ ♔g8 35 ♖f3 ♗h6 36 ♘xd5 ♗f8 37 ♘c7 ♘a7 38 d5 ♘b5 39 ♘e6 ♖c8 40 ♗e5 ♗h6 41 ♖h3 1–0.

Christiansen–Alburt
US Ch (Jacksonville) 1990

1 e4 ♘f6 2 e5 ♘d5 3 d4 d6 4 ♘f3 g6 5 ♗c4 ♘b6 6 ♗b3 ♗g7
7 a4 de!?

Another rare, but much less radical idea is **7 ... c6**, which after 8 a5 ⒩d5 is the same as the line 5 ♗c4 c6, except that White has played a4–a5 'for free', but has used a tempo committing the bishop to b3 rather earlier than might normally be done. The largest point in Black's favour is that after a c4 advance, White cannot drive the knight from b4 with the a-pawn.

8 0–0 d5 gives Black a somewhat improved version of the line 7 ... d5. Vujadinović–Khmelnitsky, Šibenik 1989 continued 9 h3 0–0 10 ♕e2 a5 11 ♗f4?! ⒩a6! 12 ⒩bd2 c5 13 c3 ♗f5 14 g4 ♗d7 15 ♖fe1 ♕e8!∓ and suddenly White's a-pawn had become a terrible weakness.

8 ed ed 9 ♗g5 f6 10 ♗f4 ♕e7+ 11 ♔d2 d5 12 ♖e1 ♗e6 13 ♔e2 ♔f7 14 ♔f1, while one of the more startling examples of castling by hand in contemporary chess, was not very effective in Kudrin–Alburt, US Ch (Cambridge Springs) 1988. Black obtained a comfortable position and gradually assumed the advantage: 14 ... ♕d7 15 ⒩bd2 a5 16 ♖e3 ⒩a6 17 h3 ♖he8 18 ♕e2 ♔g8 19 c3 ♗f7 20 ♗c2 ⒩c7 21 ⒩h2 ⒩c4 22 ⒩xc4 dc 23 ♖e1 ⒩d5. Black won the ensuing ending by advancing on the queenside.

8 a5 ⒩d5 9 h3 0–0 10 0–0 de 11 ⒩xe5 ⒩d7 12 ⒩f3 e5 13 ♖e1 ♖e8 14 ⒩c3 ed 15 ⒩xd5 ♖xe1+ 16 ♕xe1 cd 17 ♗g5 ⒩f6 18 ⒩xd4

h6 19 ♗e3 a6 20 c3 ♕c7 gave White the more pleasant position in A. Ivanov–Alburt, San Mateo rapid 1989.

7 ... d5 8 a5 ⒩c4 is a peculiar idea of Alburt's that has been justified neither by practical results nor by theoretical investigations. Now **9 ⒩c3!?** c6 10 ♗xc4 dc 11 ♕e2 ♗e6 12 ⒩g5 ♗d5 13 e6 gave White some advantage in A. Ivanov–Alburt, US Ch (Long Beach) 1989, but the most popular has been **9 ⒩bd2**:

(a) **9 ... c5?** 10 ♗xc4! dc 11 ⒩xc4 cd 12 ♕xd4 0–0 13 ♕h4 ♕c7 14 0–0 ⒩c6 15 ♗f4 ♕d7 16 e6+ − Kudrin–Alburt, US Ch (Long Beach) 1989.

(b) **9 ... b5** 10 ab ⒩xb6 11 0–0 0–0 12 ♖e1 e6 (12 ... ♗a6 13 c3 ♗b5?! 13 e6± Short–Alburt, Foxboro [5] 1985) 13 ⒩f1. White intends ♗g5 and ♕d2 with a grip on Black's kingside, so De Firmian–Alburt, US Ch (Cambridge Springs) 1988 continued 13 ... h6 14 ⒩e3 ♔h7 15 ⒩g4 (Threatens 16 ♕d2+ −) 15 ... ♖h8 16 ♗e3 ⒩c6 17 ♕d2 ♕f8 18 ♖a3 (18 h4 a5 19 h5 gh 20 ⒩gh2 a4 21 ♗a2 ⒩a5∞ Dlugy) and now Black had to try 18 ... a5, intending counterplay after 19 ♖ea1 a4 20 ♗a2 ⒩a5. Instead 18 ... ⒩e7?! 19 ⒩f6+!? (19 h4!? ⒩f5 20 h5±) 19 ... ♗xf6 20 ef ⒩f5 21 ♗f4 ⒩d6 22 ♕c1 ⒩d7 23 ♗e5 left Black in a real mess.

(c) **9 ... ⒩xd2 10 ♗xd2 0–0 11 0–0 ♗g4** (Short–Alburt, Foxboro

[7] 1985 proceeded 11 ... c5 12 dc
♘c6 13 ♗c3 e6, when 14 ♗a2!
would have given White a great
advantage due to 14 ... ♘xa5 15
♗xd5.) **12 h3 ♗xf3 13 ♕xf3 e6
14 ♗b4** (14 ♕g4 c5 15 c3 ♘c6;
14 ♗a4 c5 15 dc ♗xe5∞ C.
Hansen–Alburt, Reykjavik 1986)
14 ... ♖e8 15 ♗a4 c6 *(80)* and
now:

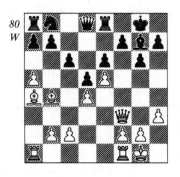

(c1) **16 c3** f6 (16 ... ♗f8; 16 ...
b5; 16 ... ♘d7 17 ♕e3 ♖c8 18
♗d6 ♗f8 Pirrot–Hartmann,
Bundesliga 1989/90) 17 ef ♗xf6
18 ♖e1 ♘d7 19 ♖e2 e5 20 c4!±
Zapata–Alburt, New York Open
1988.

(c2) **16 ♕e2** b5 17 ♗b3 ♘d7 18
♗d2 f5 19 c3 a6 20 g4! gave White
a solid advantage in Khalifman–
Marinković, Leningrad 1989. The
rest of the game illustrates well
where White's chances lie: 20 ...
♕h4 21 ♔g2 c5 22 f4 ♕e7 23 ♖g1
cd 24 cd ♖ac8 25 ♔h2 ♔h8 26
♖g2 ♘b8 27 gf gf 28 ♖ag1 ♖g8
29 ♕h5 ♘c6 30 ♗e3 ♕e8 31 ♕h4
♘xa5 32 ♗d1 ♘c4 33 ♗f2 ♖c7

34 ♗h5 ♕e7 35 ♕f6 h6 36 ♗h4
♕f8 37 ♕xe6 ♘e3 38 ♖e2 ♕b4 39
♖xe3 ♕xd4 40 ♖eg3 ♕xf4 41 ♗f6
♖c2+ 42 ♔h1 1–0.

Fedorowicz suggests that **7 ...
0–0** may be playable: 8 a5 ♘6d7
9 e6 fe 10 ♗xe6+ ♔h8 11 0–0±.

8   a5

8 ♘xe5 ♗xe5 9 de ♕xd1+ 10
♔xd1 ♘c6 11 a5 ♘d7 12 e6 fe 13
♗xe6 ♘f6 14 ♗xc8 ♖xc8 15 c3
0–0 16 ♔e2 a6 was comfortable
for Black in Meshkov–Kakageldiev, Kaluga 1981.

8   ...   ♘6d7

8 ... ♘d5 is much less ambitious.
9 de c6 10 0–0 (10 c4 ♘b4 11
♕xd8+ ♔xd8 12 0–0 ♗g4 13
♗f4 ♘d7=; 10 h3 0–0 11 0–0
♘a6 12 ♕d4 ♘dc7 13 ♕h4 ♘c5
14 ♗h6 ♘xb3 15 cb f6 exposed
White's attacking plans as rather
cumbersome in Düster–Kindl,
Remagen 1981.) 10 ... 0–0 (10 ...
♗g4 is a likely improvement.) 11
♕e2 ♕c7 12 ♖a4 b5 13 ♖h4 and
Black had done much to encourage a strong white attack in
Fichtl–Schonpol, Trinec 1972.
Note also that 8 ... e4?? loses to
9 ab ef 10 ♖xa7.

9   ♗xf7+

9 ♘g5 e6 10 ♗xe6 0–0 11 0–0
ed simply left Black a pawn to
the good in Gavrić–Khmelnitsky,
Pula Open 1990. The Ukrainian
consolidated comfortably: 12
♗a2 ♘e5 13 f4 h6 14 ♘f3 ♘ec6
15 ♘bd2 ♘a6 16 ♘e4 ♘e7 17 ♘e5
♘b4 18 ♗b3 ♘bc6 19 ♗d2 ♗f5
20 ♕e1 ♕c8 21 h3 ♗e6–+.

9 ♕e2 0–0 10 de ♘c5∓ is noted by Christiansen.

9 de ♘xe5 10 ♕xd8+ ♚xd8 11 ♘g5 (11 ♘xe5 ♗xe5 12 0–0!?) 11 ... ♚e8 12 ♘c3 h6 13 ♘ge4 ♘a6 14 ♗e3 ♘g4 15 0–0–0 ♘xe3 16 fe f5 17 ♘f2 c6 18 ♘d3 e5∓ Nicholson–Khmelnitsky, Budapest 1990.

9	**...**	**♚xf7**
10	**♘g5+**	**♚g8**
11	**♘e6**	**♕e8**
12	**♘xc7**	**♕d8!**

12 ... ♕f7 avoids a draw by repetition, but fails to trap the knight: 13 ♘xa8 ed 14 0–0 ♘a6 (14 ... h6 15 c3 ♚h7 16 cd) 15 c3 h6 16 cd ♚h7 17 b4 (analysis by Winsnes).

13 ♘xa8

13 ♘e6 ♕e8 14 ♘c7 repeats, though Black can still avoid a draw with 14 ... ♕f7.

13 ... ed *(81)*

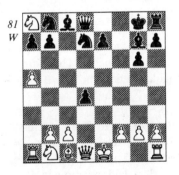

White's position looks grim: no development, no pawn centre, and material down as soon as the a8 knight is rounded up. However, the game is far from decided: the black king is somewhat exposed and the a8 knight is of some use, as it ties down the black forces to keeping it trapped and to spending some time actually capturing it in such a way as to maintain control of the centre.

Christiansen notes that White may now consider 14 0–0. His actual choice attacks the centre immediately, but allows Black to latch on to the b3 square.

14	**c3**	**♘c5!**
15	**cd**	

15 0–0 is feasible, but **15 b4** ♘e4 16 ♕b3+ e6 17 cd is inadequate, provided Black avoids the tempting 17 ... ♘xf2?! 18 0–0 ♕xd4 19 ♖a2! ♘d3+ 20 ♚h1 ♘c6 21 ♘c7! in favour of 17 ... ♘c6! intending 18 ... ♗d7 (Dlugy).

15	**...**	**♗xd4**
16	**0–0**	**e5**

Black may try to hold this move in reserve, e.g. 16 ... ♘ba6 17 ♘c3 ♗f5 18 ♘b5 ♗d3 19 ♘xd4 ♗xf1 20 b4!? or 16 ... ♘c6!? 17 ♘c3 ♗f5.

17 ♗e3?!

Christiansen claims some advantage for White after **17 ♘c3!** ♗f5 18 ♘b5 ♗d3 19 ♘xd4 ed 20 ♗f4!

17 ... ♘ba6

Dlugy proposes the more centralising 17 ... ♘c6!?.

18	**♘c3**	**♗f5**
19	**♖c1?!**	

Christiansen analysed **19 ♘b5!** ♗d3! as leading to equality: 20 ♗xd4 ed 21 b4!! ♗xf1! (21 ...

♘xb4 22 ♖c1! ♗xf1 23 ♖xc5 ♗xb5 24 ♕b3+ ±) 22 bc ♗xb5 23 ♕b3+ ♔g7 24 ♕xb5 ♕xa8 (24 ... ♕e7 25 c6=) 25 ♕d7+. Black's next move in the game intends ... ♕d7 and ... ♖xa8, rounding up the knight while maintaining control of d4.

19	...	♔g7!
20	♗xd4	♕xd4!
21	b4	

After 21 ♕xd4 ed 22 ♘b5 White should not lose.

21	...	♘d3
22	♘e2	

22 ♘b5! ♕d7 23 ♘ac7 ♘xc1 24 ♕xd7+ ♗xd7 25 ♖xc1 should survive.

22	...	♕d7
23	♖c3?	

White's last chance was 23 b5 ♘xc1 24 ♕xc1 ♕xb5 25 ♘g3∞.

23	...	♖xa8
24	g4	♘b2!

As if by magic the tactics favour Black, and a won ending results.

25	♕c1	♗d3
26	♕xb2	♕xg4+
27	♘g3	♗xf1
28	♔xf1	♕d4!

This move emphasises that the white pieces are rather badly coordinated. White can hardly avoid the loss of a second pawn.

29	♕c1?!	♖f8
30	♕e3	♕xe3
31	♖xe3	♘xb4
32	♖b3	

32 ♖xe5 does not win back a pawn in view of 32 ... ♖xf2+.

32	...	♖f4
33	♖c3	♖a6!
34	♖e3	♘c5!

The same knight fork trick as before defends the e-pawn, while with the knight more securely placed the ending becomes a fairly simple technical task. 35 ♖c3 b6 36 ab ab 37 ♔e1 h5! 38 h3 ♖b4 39 ♔e2 ♔f6 40 ♖c2 ♔g5 41 ♖d2 ♘e6 42 ♔e3 ♘f4 43 ♘e4+ ♔f5 44 ♘d6+ ♔e6 45 ♘c8 ♖b3+ 46 ♔e4 ♘d5! 0–1.

Kuijf–Blees
Dutch Ch (Hilversum) 1990

1 e4 ♘f6 2 e5 ♘d5 3 d4 d6 4 ♘f3 g6 5 ♗c4 ♘b6 6 ♗b3 ♗g7

7	a4	a5

These moves help White in that ... ♘a5 is impossible, b5 is weak, and the b6 knight is less securely defended. Similarly, Black can hope to benefit from the weakness of b4, White's inability to play ♗a4, and the potentially undefended bishop on b3. When both sides have weaknesses, whoever has the initiative benefits. Therefore particularly energetic play is in order.

8	♘g5

8 ♗f4 0–0 (8 ... ♘c6 9 ♕e2 de 10 ♗xe5 ♗xe5?! 11 de ♘d4 12 ♘xd4 ♕xd4 13 c3 ♕g4 14 f3 ♕h4+ 15 g3 ♕h3 16 ♘d2 gave Black a bad position in Ermenkov–Santo Roman, Novi Sad ol 1990.) 9 ♕e2 ♘c6 10 c3 (10 ♘bd2 de 11 ♗xe5 ♘xe5 12 de ♗g4) 10 ... ♗g4 11 ♘bd2 ♕d7!? 12 h3 13 de ♗e6 14 ♗c2 ♘d5 15 ♗h2

f6∓ Valkesalmi–Raaste, Jarven-
pää 1985.

8 0–0 0–0 9 h3 is best met by 9
... ♘c6. Then 10 ♕e2 leads to·
lines below, whilst 10 ♗f4 de 11
de ♗e6! 12 ♘bd2 ♗xb3 13 ♘xb3
♕xd1 14 ♖fxd1 ♘c4 15 ♖d7 ♖ac8
gave Black a very pleasant advantage in T. Wall–Hennigan, British
Ch (Plymouth) 1989.

8 ed was Keres' idea when he
introduced 7 a4 in 1970. With b5
and b6 weakened, this exchange
has more bite. **8 ... ♕xd6** is possible, while A. Ivanov–Alburt,
New York 1989 saw Black achieve
a decent position with **8 ... ed** 9
0–0 (9 ♗g5) 9 ... 0–0 10 ♖e1 d5
11 ♗f4 ♗e6 12 ♗e5 ♗h6 13
♘c3 ♖e8 14 h3 f6, but generally
preferred is **8 ... cd 9 0–0 0–0**:

(a) **10 ♘c3 ♗g4** 11 ♘b5 ♘c6 12
c3 d5!= Eretova–Nikolau, Skopje
1972.

(b) **10 ♗g5 ♗g4** 11 c3 h6 12
♗h4 ♘c6 13 ♘bd2 d5! 14 h3
♗xf3 15 ♘xf3 ♕d7= Ree–Palatnik, Kiev 1978.

(c) **10 h3!** ♘c6 11 ♘c3 d5 12
♗f4 ♗e6 (12 ... ♘xd4?! 13 ♘xd4
e5 14 ♗e3 ed 15 ♗xd4 ♘c4? 16
♘xd5) 13 ♘b5 ♖c8 14 c3 (14
♖e1 makes Black's position a little
difficult to organise.) 14 ... f6 15
♖e1 ♗f7 16 ♖e2 ♕d7 17 ♗g3
♖fe8 18 ♕e1 ♗h6 19 ♖d1 ♘d8
and Black went on to draw in
Adorjan–Smejkal, Wijk aan Zee
1972, but most players would
rather be White here. Alburt may
well be right to capture with the
e-pawn.

8 ♕e2 is the most popular alternative to 8 ♘g5. An important
point is then whether Black need
fear 9 e6 in reply to 8 ... 0–0 (a
move played by Alburt several
times); if not, then Black has more
flexibility vis-à-vis move order.

(a) **8 ... ♘c6 9 0–0** (9 ♘bd2 0–0
10 h3 is a position from Kovalëv–
Blees, Kecskemet 1989, in which
10 ... ♗f5 11 0–0 ♕d7 12 ♖e1 de
13 de ♗e6 14 ♘c4 ♗xc4 15
♗xc4 ♘d4 16 ♘xd4 ♕xd4 17
♗b3 e6 gave Black a playable
game.) Now:

(a1) **9 ... de** 10 de ♘d4 11 ♘xd4
♕xd4 12 e6 (12 ♖e1 ♗g4 13 ♗e3
♗xe2 14 ♗xd4 ♗c4 15 ♘d2
should not have given Black any
real problems in Kindermann–
Neckař, Prague 1988.) 12 ...
♗xe6 13 ♗xe6 fe 14 ♘a3?! (14
♕xe6 ♕c4!=; 14 ♘d2!?) 14 ... ♕e5
15 ♕f3 ♕d5 16 ♕g3 0–0∓ C.
Horvath–Chekhov, Halle 1987.

(a2) **9 ... 0–0** 10 ♖d1 ♗g4 11
h3 (11 ♘c3 ♕c8 12 h3 ♗xf3 13
♕xf3 de 14 de ♘xe5 15 ♕e2 gave
White enough for the pawn in
King–Nijboer, Lucerne 1989.) 11
... ♗xf3 12 ♕xf3 ♕d7 13 ♗f4 de
14 de ♕f5 15 g4 ♘xe5 16 ♕g3 ♕f6
17 ♘c3 g5 18 ♗e3 h6 19 f4 gf
20 ♗xf4 ♘g6 21 ♗e3 ♕e5=
Nijboer–Blees, Dutch Ch (Hilversum) 1990.

(b) **8 ... 0–0 9 h3** (9 0–0 ♗g4!?
10 e6?! d5!∓ Benjamin) **9 ... ♘c6
10 0–0** *(82)*. Now Black has tried
three ideas:

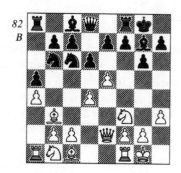

(b1) **10 ... d5** 11 ♘c3 ♗e6 12 ♗f4 ♕d7 13 ♖ad1 leaves White's space advantage unchallenged. Keres gave 13 ... ♘d8 14 ♕b5 ♕xb5 15 ♘xb5 c6± as Black's best.

(b2) **10 ... ♗f5** has been tried recently by Alburt, with a distinct lack of success.

(b21) **11 ♖e1 ♕c8** (After 11 ... ♕d7 12 ♘bd2 ♖ad8 13 ♘e4 ♕c8 14 ♘g3 ♗e6 15 c4, Byrne and Mednis suggest 15 ... d5 16 c5 ♘d7 followed by ... ♘db8–a6–b4. Instead De Firmian–Alburt, US Ch (Long Beach) 1989 proceeded 15 ... ♘b4 16 ♗g5 ♖de8 17 d5 whereupon 17 ... ♗f5 18 ♘xf5 ♕xf5 19 ed cd would have kept White's advantage small.) 12 ♘c3 de 13 de ♘d7 (13 ... ♗e6 14 ♗xe6 ♕xe6 15 ♘b5 ♖ac8 16 b3± Fedorowicz) 14 e6 ♗xe6 15 ♗xe6 fe 16 ♕xe6+ ♔h8 17 ♕e2 (17 ♘b5 ♘de5 18 ♘g5±) 17 ... ♘f6 18 ♘b5 ♘d5 19 c3 ♕f5 gave White a small, but very clear advantage in Fedorowicz–Alburt, US Ch (Long Beach) 1989.

(b22) **11 ♘c3!? ♔h8!?** 12 ♗f4

♘b4 13 ♖fe1 (13 ♖ad1 d5! restricts White to a tiny edge.) 13 ... ♕c8 (13 ... f6?! 14 e6; 13 ... d5 14 ♘d1!?) 14 ♘e4 f6 15 ♗h2 fe 16 de ♗xe4 17 ♕xe4 d5 18 ♕h4 e6 19 c3 occurred in Benjamin–Alburt, Philadelphia 1990. If the knight retreats, White has a strong attack with easy moves, so Alburt embarked on tactics: 19 ... ♘d3 20 ♖e2 ♕d8 (20 ... c5 21 ♗c2 c4 22 ♕d4!) 21 ♕d4 ♖xf3 22 gf ♘c1! 23 ♖xc1 ♕g5+ 24 ♕g4 ♕xc1+ 25 ♔g2. Sadly, Black's very clever idea has left his king defenceless. There followed 25 ... ♖e8 26 ♗f4 ♕b1 27 ♗c2 ♕a2 28 b3! ♕a3 29 h4! ♕f8 30 h5 ♗h6 31 ♗xh6 ♕xh6 32 hg hg 33 ♖e1! ♔g8 34 ♖h1 ♕g7 35 ♗xg6 ♖e7 36 ♖h7! ♕f8 27 ♕h4! 1–0.

(b3) **10 ... de** 11 de ♘d4 12 ♘xd4 ♕xd4 13 ♖e1. Now Minev–Alburt, Bucharest 1978 was agreed drawn after **13 ... ♘d7**, but White could certainly try 14 e6. **13 ... e6** 14 ♘d2 ♗d7 (14 ... ♘d5 15 ♘f3 ♕c5 16 ♕e4 ♕b4 17 ♗c4! ♘b6 18 b3± Short–Timman, Tilburg 1991) 15 c3 (15 ♘f3 ♕b4 16 ♗d2 ♕e7 17 ♗g5 ♕e8 18 ♕e4± Dončević–Palatnik, Rome 1990) 15 ... ♕c5 16 ♘f3 ♗c6 17 ♗e3 ♕e7 18 ♗g5 ♕c5 19 ♘d4 ♗d5 20 ♗xd5 ♕xd5 21 f4 ♕c4 22 ♕xc4 ♘xc4 23 b3 ♘b6 24 c4 ♖fc8 25 ♖ad1 ♗f8 26 ♘b5± Short–Hennigan, British Ch (Swansea) 1987. In view of the miserable nature of this line, Black should investigate **13 ... ♗e6!?**, since an open f-file

could be useful to Black. Bildat–
Gabriel, Vienna 1990 continued
14 c3?! ♕h4 15 ♗c2? f6 16 ef ♖xf6·
17 ♗e3 ♘d5 18 ♗b3? ♘xe3 19
♗xe6+ ♖xe6 20 fe ♗h6–+.

8   ...   e6

After **8 ... d5**, Kasparov recommends **9 0–0 0–0** (9 ... h6 10 ♘f3
♗g4 11 ♘bd2 ♘a6 12 h3 ♗f5 13
♖e1± Lanka–Bartovsky, corres.
1986) 10 ♖e1 ♘c6 11 c3 f6 12 ef
ef 13 ♘e6±, since after **9 f4 f6 10
♘f3** and an eventual exchange
of c-pawns, the b4 square could
become a weakness:

(a) **10 ... 0–0** 11 0–0 ♘a6 12
♗e3 (12 ♘c3 ♗g4 13 h3 ♗xf3
14 ♖xf3 e6 15 ♘b5± Sanchez
Almeyra–Hennigan, Rome 1990)
12 ... ♘c4 13 ♗xc4 dc 14 ♘a3
♕d5 (14 ... ♗e6 15 ♕e2 ♕d5
16 ♘d2 ♕c6∞ Ulmanis–Miller,
corres. 1983) 15 ♘d2 fe 16 de ♗d7
17 ♘axc4 ♗c6 18 ♕e2 ♕b4 19
♘f3 ♗h6! 20 ♘d4 ♗xf4! 21 ♘xc6
½–½ W. Watson–Hennigan, London (Lloyds Bank) 1985.

(b) **10 ... ♗g4** 11 ♘bd2 (11 0–0)
11 ... ♘a6 12 c3 fe 13 fe (13 de
♘c5! 14 ♗c2 0–0 15 h3 ♗f5∞)
13 ... 0–0 14 0–0 c5 15 ♕e1 (15
h3 ♗f5) 15 ... e6 16 ♕g3 ♗f5! 17
♘h4 cd 18 ♘xf5 (18 cd ♘b4) 18
... ♖xf5 19 ♖xf5 ef! 20 cd ♘b4
21 ♘f3 ♘c4∓ Pridome–Bagirov,
Cappelle la Grande 1988.

9   f4

9 ♕f3 ♕e7 (9 ... ♕d7 appears
no less viable than without a4 and
a5.) **10 ♘e4** *(83)* gives Black two
intriguing possibilities:

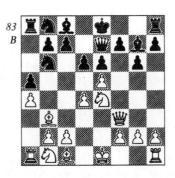

83
B

(a) **10 ... de 11 ♗g5 ♕b4+ 12
♘bd2** and now:

(a1) **12 ... ♕xd4?!** 13 0–0–0.

(a2) **12 ... ed?!** 13 ♘f6+ ♔f8 14
c3! ♕c5 (14 ... dc 15 bc ♕c5 16
♘de4 gives White an overwhelming attack after both 16 ... ♕c6
17 ♗c1! and 16 ... ♕f5 17 ♕e3!)
15 ♘de4 ♕f5 16 ♕e2 ♘d5?! (16 ...
h5 17 h4!? dc 18 ♘g3 ♕c5 19
♖c1!) 17 g4 ♕e5 18 f4! ♘xf4 19
♕f3 ♘d5 (19 ... ♘h3!? 20 ♗h4!
g5 21 ♖f1! Harley) 20 0–0 ♗xf6
21 ♗xd5 ed 22 ♗h6+! ♔e7
23 ♘xf6 ♗e6 and now 24 ♗f4!
would have been immediately
decisive in Harley–Buckmaster,
Southampton 1986.

(a3) **12 ... 0–0** 13 0–0–0.

(a4) **12 ... f5** 13 ♘f6+ ♔f7 14
c3 ♕d6 and now White should
certainly try SDO's 15 ♘fe4 ♕c6
16 g4, since 15 ♘de4 ♕c6 16 de
♘8d7 17 ♕f4 h6 18 ♗h4 ♗xf6∓
19 ♘xf6? ♘c5 20 ♗c2 g5 21
♗xg5 ♕xg2 0–1 was Kujawski–
Carnstam, corres. 1988.

(b) **10 ... d5** 11 ♘f6+ (11 ♘c5
♘8d7) 11 ... ♗xf6 12 ♕xf6 (12

ef!? ♕b4+ 13 ♘c3 is worth trying:
13 ... ♕xd4?! 14 0–0 or 13 ... ♘c6!
14 ♕g3!∞) 12 ... ♕xf6 13 ef c5!
14 ♘c3 (14 dc ♘6d7∞) 14 ... c4
15 ♗a2 ♗d7! 16 b3 ♘a6 17 ♗a3
(17 bc?! ♘b4) 17 ... ♖c8 (17 ...
♘b4) 18 ♔d2 ♘b4 19 ♘d1 0–0!?
(19 ... ♘xc2!? 20 ♔xc2 cb++ 21
♔xb3 ♗xa4+ 22 ♔b2 ♖c2+ 23
♔b1 ♖d2∞ Pushkin) and now
White should play 20 ♗b1, since
20 c3? ♘xa2 21 ♗xf8 cb! 22
♗e7 ♘c4+ left White in desperate
trouble in Kuznetsov–Pushkin,
USSR 1988.

	9	...	de
	10	fe	c5
	11	0–0	

Kasparov recommends **11 c3** cd
12 0–0 0–0 13 cd as more accurate,
since Black could now try **11 ...
♕xd4+** 12 ♕xd4 cd 13 ♖xf7 (13
♘xf7 0–0 14 ♘d6 ♖xf1+ 15 ♔xf1
♗d7 16 ♘xb7 ♘c6!) 13 ... ♗xe5
14 ♖f1 ♘c6.

| | 11 | ... | 0–0 |
| | 12 | c3 | cd |

12 ... ♘c6? gave White too free
a hand on the kingside in the
famous game Kasparov–Palatnik,
Daugavpils 1978: 13 ♘e4! ♘d7
(13 ... cd 14 ♗g5! and now 14 ...
♕c7 15 cd or 14 ... ♕d7 15 ♘f6+
♗xf6 16 ♗xf6 dc 17 ♕c1) 14
♗e3! (14 ♗g5 ♕b6!) 14 ... ♘e7 (14
... ♕b6 15 ♘a3 cd 16 ♘c4) 15
♗g5! cd (15 ... h6 16 ♗h4 g5 17
♗xg5!) 16 cd h6 17 ♗h4 g5 18
♗f2 (18 ♗xg5? hg 19 ♕h5 ♘xe5!)
18 ... ♘g6 19 ♘bc3 ♕e7 20 ♗c2
b6 21 ♗e3 ♗a6 22 ♖f2 ♘h8

23 ♗xg5! (Apparently, nowadays
Kasparov would prefer the
straightforward 23 h4! gh 24 ♕g4!
f5 25 ef ♘xf6 26 ♘xf6+ ♖xf6 27
♖xf6 ♕xf6 28 ♕e4! ♖d8 29 ♕h7+
♔f8 30 ♘b5!.) 23 ... hg 24 ♕h5
f5! 25 ♘xg5 ♖f7! 26 ♗xf5!! ♖xf5
27 ♖xf5 ef 28 ♘d5 ♕e8 29 ♕h7+
♔f8 30 ♕xf5+ ♔g8 31 ♕h7+
♔f8 32 ♖a3! ♖c8 33 ♖f3+ ♘f6
34 h3! ♕g6 35 ♖xf6+ ♗xf6 36
♘e6+ ♔e8 37 ♘xf6+ 1–0.

| | 13 | cd | ♘c6 |
| | 14 | ♘f3 | f6 *(84)* |

Black must attack the centre
immediately, or face a powerful
kingside attack.

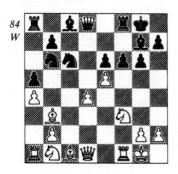

84
W

| | 15 | ♘c3 | |

15 ef ♕xf6 16 ♗e3 ♘d5 17
♗f2 ♘f4 is analogous to the main
line without the insertion of 7 a4
a5. The most important difference
made by these moves here is the
undefended state of the b3 bishop:

(a) **18 ♘bd2** ♕f5 19 ♔h1 (19
♗c2!?) 19 ... ♕g4 20 ♗g3 ♘h5?
(20 ... ♗d7=) 21 ♗d6 ♖fe8 22
♘c4 ♖a6 23 d5± Kavalek–
Alburt, US Ch (South Bend) 1981.

(b) **18 ᐤc3 ᐤh3+ 19 gh ♕xf3
20 ♕xf3 ♖xf3 21 d5** (21 ♔g2
ᐤxd4 22 ♗xd4 ♖xf1) 21 ... ᐤd4
22 ♗xd4 (22 ♗c4 ♖f4!? Pushkin)
22 ... ♗xd4+ 23 ♔g2 ♖xf1 24
♖xf1 ♗xc3 (24 ... ed 25 ♗xd5+
♔g7 26 ♖f7+ ♔h6 27 ᐤe4
♗f5= Kuijf–Blees, Dutch Ch
[Hilversum] 1989) 25 de ♗b4! 26
e7+ ♔g7 27 ♖f8 ♗xh3+ ½–½
Shlepnëv–Pushkin, corres. 1990.

15	**...**	**fe**
16	**♗g5**	**♕d7**

White also has compensation
after 16 ... ♕e8 17 de ᐤxe5 18
ᐤxe5 ♖xf1+ 19 ♕xf1 ♗xe5 20
♖e1 ♗d4+ 21 ♔h1 (Kasparov).

17	**de**	**ᐤxe5**
18	**ᐤxe5**	**♖xf1+**

The alternatives are 18 ... ♗xe5
and 18 ... ♕xd1.

19	**♕xf1**	**♕d4+**
20	**♔h1**	**♕xe5**
21	**♗d8!**	

An excellent way to exploit the
undefended knight on b6. Now 21
... ♖a6 is strongly met by 22 ♕b5!.

21	**...**	**♕c5**
22	**ᐤe4!**	**♕c6**

22 ... ♕b4 23 ᐤg5+ –.

23	**ᐤg5**	**ᐤd5**
24	**♕f7+**	**♔h8**
25	**♖f1**	**ᐤe3**

25 ... ♗d7 fails to 26 ♗xd5
and ♗f6.

26	**♖g1**	**ᐤg4?**

26 ... ᐤd5 is the only chance.

27	**♕f4**	**h5**
28	**h3**	**ᐤh6**
29	**♗f6**	**♕c5**
30	**ᐤxe6!**	**1–0**

Kuzhanov–Pushkin
Correspondence 1987

**1 e4 ᐤf6 2 e5 ᐤd5 3 d4 d6 4 ᐤf3
g6 5 ♗c4 ᐤb6 6 ♗b3 ♗g7**

7	**ᐤg5**	**e6**

7...d5 provides Black with fewer
possibilities for counterplay, and
consequently is out of fashion.
Fairly harmless are then 8 c3 f6 9
ef ef 10 ♕e2+ ♕e7= Hebden–
Hennigan, British Ch (Southampton) 1986 and 8 0–0 0–0 9 ♖e1
ᐤc6 10 c3 f6 11 ef ef 12 ᐤe6 ♗xe6
13 ♖xe6 Parma–Gheorghiu,
Skopje 1968, though White may
have a small edge here. White does
best to maintain a pawn at e5, viz
8 f4 f6 (8 ... 0–0 9 0–0 f6 has little
independent significance, except
for cutting out some options for
Black.) **9 ᐤf3.** Now Black has a
choice:

(a) 9 ... 0–0 10 0–0 ᐤa6!? 11 c3
(11 a4?! c5 12 c3 cd 13 cd ♗e6 14
♕e1? ᐤc4 15 ♗c2 ♖c8 16 ᐤc3
ᐤb4 17 ♗b1 ᐤc6 18 b3 ᐤ4a5 19
♗c2 ᐤb4 20 ♗d1 ᐤd3 21 ♕d2
ᐤxf4!– + Zso. Polgar–Hennigan,
London [Duncan Lawrie] 1988)
11 ... c5 12 ef ♗xf6 (12 ... ef) 13
ᐤe5 cd 14 cd ᐤb4 15 ᐤc3 ♗f5
16 a3 ᐤc6 17 g4 and White
embarked on a vigorous kingside
assault in Agnos–Hennigan, British Ch (Swansea) 1987.

(b) 9 ... a5 10 c3 (10 a4 is more
obliging — see 7 a4 a5 8 ᐤg5 d5.)
10 ... ᐤa6 11 0–0 (11 ♕e2!? 0–0
12 ♗e3) 11 ... 0–0 12 ♗c2 c5 13
ef (13 dc ᐤxc5 14 ♗e3 ᐤe6 15

♘a3 fe 16 fe ♗d7= Motwani–
Hennigan, British Ch [Sou-
thampton] 1986) 13 ... ♖xf6 14
dc ♘xc5 15 ♗e3 ♘e6 16 ♘e5
♕d6 17 g3 ♘d7 18 ♘f3 ♖f8 19
♘a3 ♘c7 20 ♘d4 e5 21 fe ♘xe5=
Unzicker–Chekhov, Moscow
1982.

(c) **9 ... ♘c6 10 c3** (10 ♗e3
♘a5!=). Black can insert ... 0–0,
0–0 and/or ... fe, fe, but loses
nothing by delaying these.

(c1) **10 ... ♗g4** 11 ♘bd2 0–0
(11 ... fe 12 fe ♗h6 13 h3 ♗f5 14
♘f1 ♗xc1 15 ♕xc1 e6 16 ♘e3
♕e7 17 ♘g4± Foigel–Balendo,
USSR 1979) 12 0–0 ♕d7 13 h3
♗xf3 14 ♘xf3 gives White a
pleasant space advantage. Grefe–
Dunning, Las Vegas 1974 continued 14 ... ♘d8 15 ♗c2 f5 (15
... ♘e6?! 16 f5!) 16 ♘g5 ♘e6 17
♘xe6 ♕xe6 18 g4! ♖ac8 19 ♖f2
♔h8 20 ♔h1 and White pro-
ceeded to attack down the g-file.

(c2) **10 ... ♗f5** *(85)*. White
has two approaches, which can
transpose:

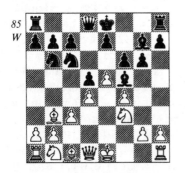

(c21) **11 ♘h4 ♗xb1** (11 ...
♗e4?! 12 ♘d2 ♗d3 13 ♕f3 ♗a6

14 f5) 12 ♖xb1 f5 (12 ... 0–0
transposes to c22, but White has
avoided 11 ... ♘a5.) 13 ♗c2 e6
14 ♘f3 ♕d7 (14 ... 0–0?! 15 g4!
fg?! 16 ♘g5 h6 17 ♘xe6 ♕h4+
18 ♔e2± Yudasin; in Mestel–
Alburt, Hastings 1983/4, 14 ...
♕e7 15 b3 ♘d8 16 0–0 ♗f8 was
met by a4–a5–a6). Now Yudasin
suggests 15 ♗d3 with ideas of
opening a new front on the queenside, whilst 15 0–0, to bring the
knight round to c5, was sufficient
for an advantage in Yudasin–
Kakageldiev, Ivano-Frankovsk
1982.

(c22) **11 0–0 0–0** (11 ... ♕d7?!
12 ♘bd2 fe 13 fe 0–0 14 ♖f2! ♘a5
15 ♗c2 ♗xc2 16 ♕xc2 ♕f5 17
♕d1 only succeeded in exposing
the black queen in Karpov–Torre,
Leningrad IZ 1973; 11 ... ♘a5!?
12 ♗c2 ♗xc2 13 ♕xc2 ♕d7 14
♘bd2 f5 15 ♘e1 gave White only
a small edge in Matanović–Martz,
Málaga 1973.) 12 ♘h4 (12 a4; 12
♘bd2; 12 ♖f2) 12 ... ♗xb1 13
♖xb1 fe 14 fe ♖xf1+ 15 ♕xf1±
♕d7 16 ♕e2 ♖f8 17 ♗c2 e6 18
b3 ♘c8 19 ♗d2 ♘8e7 20 ♘f3
♘d8 21 ♖f1 b6 22 ♗d3 ♘f7
23 ♗e3 c5 ½–½ Donchev–Pribyl,
Bratislava 1983.

8 f4

White avoids the intricate
tactics following 8 ♕f3 (see subsequent games). Black must
adopt an active approach, braving
the consequences of an open f-file.
Dismal was 8 ... h6 9 ♘f3 ♘c6 10
c3 ♘e7 11 0–0 ♗d7 12 a4 a5

13 c4± Panchenko–Fokin, Kursk 1987.

8	**...**	**de**
9	**fe**	

Completely harmless is 9 de?! ♕xd1+ 10 ♔xd1 ♘c6 11 ♘c3 ♗d7 12 ♗e3 ♘a5∓ Bisguier–Alburt, USA 1984.

9	**...**	**c5**
10	**0–0**	**0–0**
11	**c3**	**cd**
12	**cd**	**♘c6**
13	**♘f3**	**f6**
14	**ef**	

14 ♘c3!? fe 15 ♗g5 ♕d7 16 de ♘xe5 17 ♘xe5 ♖xf1+!? 18 ♕xf1 ♕d4+ 19 ♔h1 ♕xe5 20 ♗e7 ♗d7 21 ♖e1 ♕f5 22 ♕e2 ♖e8 23 ♗d6 ♕f6 gave Black adequate defensive resources in Pupols–Alburt, Portland 1987.

14	**...**	**♕xf6**
15	**♗e3**	**♘d5**
16	**♗f2**	**♘f4**

Black can contemplate 16 ... ♔h8 17 ♘c3 ♘xc3 18 bc e5 (18 ... ♗d7? 19 ♗g3± Hardicsay–Honfi, Hungary 1978) 19 d5 e4.

17   ♘c3

An important decision. At first this move was rejected due to the shattering of White's kingside pawns, but it has since been realised that Black's development problems, particularly with the c8 bishop, are at least as relevant.

17 ♘bd2 ♕f5 18 ♗e3 (18 ♗c2 ♕b5; 18 ♔h1 ♕g4) 18 ... ♕d3∓ 19 ♖e1 ♘xd4 20 ♗c4 ♘xf3+ 21 ♕xf3 ♕f5 22 ♗xf4 ♕xf4 23 ♕xf4 ♖xf4 24 ♘e4!? gave White enough

activity to scrape a draw in Shamkovich–Alburt, Reykjavik Open 1984.

17 ♔h1 b6 (17 ... ♕f5 does not work terribly well after 18 ♘c3.) 18 ♗e3 (18 ♘c3 is best met by 18 ... ♗a6. Instead 18 ... ♗b7 19 ♘e4 ♕e7 20 ♖e1 ♘a5 21 ♗c2 ♕b4 22 ♖b1 ♖ad8 23 ♗h4 ♖c8 24 a3 ♕b5 25 ♗e7 ♖f7 26 ♗d6 ♘xg2 was rather speculative in Arnason–Alburt, Reykjavik Open 1984) 18 ... ♗a6 19 ♔f2 ♖ad8 20 ♘c3 ♔h8 21 ♘e4 ♕e7 22 ♕c1 ♘d3 23 ♕xc6 ♗b7 24 ♕xe6 ♕xe6 25 ♗xe6 ♗xe4 26 ♖d2 h6 gave White an extra pawn of no great use in Kudrin–Alburt, New York 1985.

17   ...   ♘h3+

17 ... ♔h8 is rather illogical here, since ... e5 is unlikely to be a useful option. 18 ♗e3 ♕e7 19 ♕d2 ♘d5 20 ♘xd5 ed 21 ♗xd5 ♘b4 22 ♗b3 ♗f5 23 a3 ♘d3 24 ♗h6 ♖ac8 25 ♗xg7+ ♔xg7 26 ♔h1 ♕d6 27 ♘e1! denied Black compensation in Voormans–Blees, Dieren 1988.

18	**gh**	**♕xf3**
19	**♕xf3**	

19 d5 ♕xd1 20 ♖axd1 is less accurate, as capturing gives Black a comfortable game: 20 ... ed 21 ♗xd5+ ♔h8 22 ♔g2 ♗f5 23 ♖fe1? (23 ♗g3) 23 ... ♗xh3+ won a pawn in Zapata–Timman, Amsterdam OHRA 1987.

19	**...**	**♖xf3** *(86)*
20	**d5**	

20 ♔g2?! ♘xd4 21 ♗xd4 (21

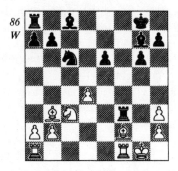

86
W

♖ad1 ♖f4) 21 ... ♖xf1 22 ♖xf1
♗xd4 leaves White fighting for a
draw.

20 ♘b5 poses more complicated
problems:

(a) **20 ... ♔h8?** was played in the
game Sokolov–Timman, Tilburg
1987?. **21 ♘c7 ♖b8 22 ♔g2** was
now possible, but the game continuation was also strong: **21 ♔g2
♖d3 22 ♖ad1 ♖xd1 23 ♖xd1
♗d7 24 ♘c7 ♖c8 25 ♘xe6 ♘a5
26 ♘c5! ♗f5!** (26 ... ♗c6+ 27 d5
♘xb3 28 ab ♗b5 29 ♘xb7 ♖c2
30 d6 ♗c6+ 31 ♔g1 ♗xb7 32 d7
♗f6 33 ♗d4+ −) and as Sokolov
analysed, decisive action was possible, thanks to the strength of the
passed pawn and the weakness of
Black's back rank: 27 ♗e6! ♖xc5
28 dc ♗xe6 29 b4 ♘c6 (29 ... ♘c4
30 ♖d8+ ♗g8 31 b5 ♗f6 32
c6!+ −) 30 b5 ♘e5 31 ♖d8+ ♗g8
32 ♗d4 h5 33 a3! ♔h7 34 ♗xe5
♗xe5 35 c6 and this pawn can
only be stopped at the cost of one
of Black's unfortunately-placed
bishops. Instead, in the game 27
♗d5?! b6 28 ♗e6 ♖c6! allowed
Black to put up resistance.

(b) **20 ... ♖xf2!?** is advocated
by Pushkin, who is clearly a great
fan of exchange sacrifices. Black
has compensation, or at least is
unlikely to lose, after either **21
♔xf2 ♗d7 22 d5 ♖f8+ 23 ♔g3
♗e5+ 24 ♔h4 ♖xf1 25 ♖xf1
♘a5 26 ♘c3 ♘xb3 27 ab ed** or **21
♖xf2 ♘xd4 22 ♘c7 ♖b8 23 ♔g2
♗d7 24 ♖e1 ♘xb3 25 ab e5**
Vasiliev–Pushkin, USSR 1987.

(c) **20 ... ♗d7!?** 21 d5 (21 ♔g2?
♖af8; 21 ♘c7? ♘xd4! 22 ♘xa8
♘e2+ 23 ♔g2 ♖xb3! 24 ab??
♗c6 # — apparently it was miss-
ing this that led to Timman reject-
ing 20 ... ♗d7.) 21 ... ♘a5 22
♘c7 ♘xb3 23 ab ♖c8! (23 ...
♖af8?!) 24 ♘xe6 ♗xe6 25 de
♖xb3 (25 ... ♗xb2 26 ♖ad1±)
and instead of 26 ♖xa7? when
White has a bad ending, Pushkin
recommends 26 e7! intending
♖ad1 as giving White a slight
edge.

20	...	♘a5
21	♘b5	♘xb3
22	ab	ed

22 ... ♗d7 23 ♘c7 transposes
to line (c) in the note to White's
20th move. The continuation in
the game looks safer.

| 23 | ♘c7 | ♖xf2 |
| 24 | ♖xf2 | |

Capturing the inactive rook is
illogical: 24 ♘xa8? ♖xb2∓.

24	...	♖b8
25	♖d1	d4
26	♘e8!	♗e5!

A common mistake after sacrificing an exchange is to be in too

much of a hurry to regain the material: 26 ... ♗h6? 27 ♖xd4 ♗e3 28 ♖d8±.

27	♖e1	♗h8
28	♘f6+	♗xf6
29	♖xf6	♗xh3!

29 ... ♗f5?! 30 ♖d6! d3 31 ♖e7 ♖f8 32 ♔g2! ♖f7 33 ♖xf7 ♔xf7 34 h4! gives White real winning chances.

30	♖d6	♖f8
31	♖xd4	♖f7
32	♖ed1	♔g7
33	♖4d3	♗f5
34	♖c3	♗e4!
35	♖e3	♗c6

With the bishop cemented on this excellent square, White's advantage is of a purely symbolic nature. In the following play, the only real danger to either side is trying too hard to win. 36 ♖f1 ♖d7 37 ♖fe1 ♖d2 38 ♖1e2 ♖d1+ 39 ♔f2 ♖h1 40 ♔g3 ♖g1+ 41 ♔f2 (41 ♔h4?? g5+ 42 ♔h5 ♗d5 would be dreadfully embarrassing.) 41 ... ♖h1 42 ♖h3 h5 43 ♔e3 ♖g1 44 ♖g3 ♖xg3+ 45 hg ♔h6 46 ♔f4 ♗d7 47 ♖e7 ♗c6 48 g4 hg 49 ♔xg4 a6! 50 b4 ♗d5 51 ♖e2 ♗c6 52 ♖h2+ ♔g7 53 ♔g5 ♔f7! (White must now be careful that the black king does not wreak havoc on the queenside.) 54 ♖h7+ ♔e6 55 ♖h4 ♔d6 56 ♔xg6 ♔c7 57 ♖g4 ♔b6 58 ♖g5 ♗b5 59 ♔f5 ♗c6 60 ♔f4 ♗b5 61 ♔e4 ♗c6+ 62 ♔d4 ♗b5 63 ♖g6+ ♗c6 64 ♔c4 ♔a7 65 ♔c5 ♗b5 66 ♖b6 ♗e2 67 b5 ♗xb5 (Not falling for 67 ...

ab? 68 ♖e6 ♗c4 69 ♖e1, when White wins.) ½–½.

Van der Wiel–A. Blees
Dutch Ch (Hilversum) 1990

1 e4 ♘f6 2 e5 ♘d5 3 d4 d6 4 ♘f3 g6 5 ♗c4 ♘b6 6 ♗b3 ♗g7 7 ♘g5 e6

8	♕f3	♕e7

8 ... ♕d7!? is Pushkin's idea, which has also been tried by Alburt.

(a) 9 d5?! ed 10 ed (10 e6? fe 11 0–0 h6 12 ♘h3 ♕f7–+) 10 ... h6! 11 dc (11 ♕e2+? ♔d8 12 dc+ ♕xc7 13 ♘f3 ♖e8–+) 11 ... ♕xc7 12 ♘h3 ♕e7+ gives Black the advantage, as analysed by Pushkin.

(b) 9 ed!? leads to unclear play in a variety of lines given by Pushkin:

(b1) 9 ... cd 10 ♘e4 (10 d5 e5 11 ♘e4 f5 12 ♘g5 ♕e7) 10 ... ♗xd4 11 ♘f6+ (11 ♗h6 d5; 11 ♗g5 f5 12 ♘f6+ ♗xf6 13 ♗xf6 ♖f8) 11 ... ♗xf6 12 ♕xf6 ♖g8.

(b2) 9 ... ♘c6!? 10 c3 (10 d5 ♘d4 11 ♕e4 ♘xb3 12 de fe 13 ab cd; 10 dc ♘xd4 11 ♕g3 ♘xb3 12 ab ♘d5) 10 ... h6! (10 ... cd?! 11 d5±) 11 ♘e4 f5 12 ♘c5 ♕xd6. Now 13 ♗f4? e5 and 13 0–0? ♗xd4! illustrate White's need for caution.

(c) 9 ♘e4 de. In practice White has always opted for the immediate knight check:

(c1) 10 ♗g5 can be met by 10 ... f5 11 ♘f6+ ♗xf6 12 ♗xf6 ♖f8 (12 ... e4!? 13 ♕f4) 13 de ♕f7 intending ... ♘8d7, or 10 ... ed

11 ♘f6+ (11 ♗f6 0–0 12 ♗xg7
♔xg7 13 ♕f6+ ♔g8 14 ♕e5 f5
15 ♘f6+ ♖xf6 16 ♕xf6 c5∓) 11 ...
♗xf6 12 ♗xf6 ♖g8∞ (Pushkin).

(c2) **10 ♘f6+ ♗xf6 11 ♕xf6
♖g8** *(87)* and now:

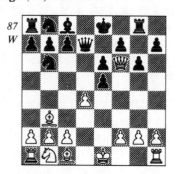

87
W

(c21) **12 de ♕d4!** 13 f4 (13 ♗g5?
♘c6; 13 ♕f4 ♕xf4 14 ♗xf4 g5! 15
♗g3 was Konchevsky–Pushkin,
USSR 1989. 15 ... ♗d7 intending
... ♗c6 and ... ♘8d7–f8–g6
would then have been promising
for Black.) 13 ... ♘8d7 (13 ... c5)
14 ♕g5 ♘c5 15 ♘c3 a5 16 a3 a4
17 ♗a2 ♘e4 18 ♘xe4 ♕xe4+ 19
♔d1 ♗d7 20 ♗d2 h6 21 ♕g3
♗c6 22 ♖e1 ♕xg2 gave Black a
clear extra pawn in Ljubojević–
Alburt, New York rapid 1990.

(c22) **12 ♗g5 ed** (12 ... ♘c6?!
13 ♘c3! ♕xd4 14 ♗a4! ♕d6 15
♖d1 ♘d5 16 ♘xd5 ed 17 ♖xd5
♕xf6 18 ♗xf6 ♗d7 19 0–0 g5 20
♖fd1 ♖g6 21 ♖xd7 ♖xf6 22 ♖xc7
was very grim for Black in Verin–
Pushkin, corres. 1990.) 13 ♘c3 (13
♘d2 ♘c6 and 13 0–0 are both
considered unclear by Pushkin.)
13 ... h6! 14 ♗h4 g5 (14 ... dc 15
♖d1 g5 16 ♖xd7 ♘8xd7 17 ♕xc3

gh) 15 ♘e4 gh (15 ... ♖g6 16 ♕xg6
fg 17 ♘f6+ ♔e7 18 ♘xd7 ♘8xd7
19 ♗g3 c5) 16 ♕xh6 ♖g6 17
♕h8+ ♔e7 18 ♕xh4+ with a
draw by repetition.

Another, rather more dubious,
possibility is **8 ... 0–0 9 ♕h3 h6**.
The knight then has two squares:

(a) **10 ♘f3 de 11 de ♘c6! 12
♗xh6 ♘xe5! 13 ♘g5** (13 ♘xe5
♗xe5 and now 14 ♗xf8 ♗xb2
15 ♗a3 ♗xa1 16 c3 ♕f6! 17
0–0 a5!∓ frees the bishop, whilst
14 ♘c3 ♖e8 15 ♖d1 ♕f6 16 ♘e4
♕h8 17 c3 ♗d7 18 0–0 ♗c6
19 f4?! ♗g7 20 ♗xg7 ♕xh3! 21
♘f6+ ♔xg7 22 ♘xe8+ ♖xe8 23
gh ♖h8 gave Black excellent compensation in Shamkovich–Alburt,
US Ch [South Bend] 1981).
Black's best may well be **13 ...
♕d4!?** 14 ♗xg7 ♔xg7, since 15
♕h7+?! ♔f6 leaves the black king
surprisingly safe. Instead **13 ...
♕f6** 14 ♘d2! ♗xh6 (14 ... ♕f5±)
15 ♕xh6 ♕xf2?! (15 ... ♕h8±) 16
♔d1 ♖d8 17 ♘e4 ♘g4 18 ♕g5
♖xd2+ 19 ♔xd2 ♘e3+ 20 ♔c1
♕xd2+ 21 ♔xd2 ♘xg2 22 h4!±
was Wahls–Hartmann, Bundesliga 1986/7.

(b) **10 ♘e4! de** (10 ... g5? 11 f4;
10 ... ♔h7? 11 ♘f6+ ♗xf6 12
♗xh6+ −; 10 ... d5?! 11 ♘c5±
Dzhindzhichashvili–Alburt, New
York Open 1984) **11 ♗xh6 ed** (11
... ♕xd4? 12 ♘bc3) **12 ♘g5!** (12
♗g5 f6) and White has a strong
attack: **12 ... e5** is met by 13 g4!
when Black has only managed to
expose f7; **12 ... ♘d5** 13 ♗xg7

♔xg7 14 ♕h7+ ♔f6 15 ♕h6 gave Black's king continuing problems in Ernst–NN, Göteborg Open 1986; **12 ... ♕f6** 13 ♘d2 (13 ♘h7 ♕e5+) 13 ... ♗xh6 14 ♕xh6 ♕g7 15 ♕h4 ♘8d7 16 ♘de4 c5 17 ♘xe6! fe 18 ♗xe6+ ♖f7 19 ♕e7 ♕f8 20 ♕g5 ♔g7 21 ♗xf7 ♕xf7 22 0–0 ♘d5 23 ♖e1 led, in Mandl–Hartmann, Bundesliga 1986/7, to a complicated ending in which White's initiative and kingside majority triumphed.

9 ♘e4 de

9 ... h6 10 ♗f4 (10 ed is much less clear.) 10 ... d5 (10 ... de!? 11 ♗xe5 ♗xe5 12 de is a type of position where Black would prefer the queens exchanged.) 11 ♘f6+ (11 ♘g3 c5 12 c3 ♘c6 13 ♘e2 and Ornstein's 11 ♘c5 should both suffice for an advantage.) 11 ... ♗xf6 12 ef ♕xf6 and now instead of 13 ♕e3?! ♘c6 14 c3 ♕e7! 15 ♗xh6 e5!∓ A. Rodriguez–Alburt, Thessaloniki ol 1984, Rodriguez recommends 13 ♕g3! ♕xd4 14 ♘c3 when Black is in trouble.

10 ♗g5 ♕b4+
11 c3 ♕a5
12 ♘f6+ ♔f8
13 d5 e4

The only move, e.g. 13 ... h6? 14 de hg 15 ♘d7+ with a massacre.

14 ♕g3

After **14 ♕xe4??** h6 15 de ♗xe6, White suffers a decisive material loss: 16 ♗xe6 ♕xg5 or 16 ♗h4 g5 17 ♗xe6 ♗xf6 Gallagher–Blees, Tel Aviv 1988.

More interesting is **14 ♕f4?!**,

when Black must find some 'only' moves:

(a) **14 ... ♘a6** 15 ♗h6! (Threatens 16 ♗xg7+ ♔xg7 17 ♕e5!) 15 ... ♘c5 16 ♗c2 ♕b5 17 b4 ♘d3+ 18 ♗xd3 ♕xd3 19 ♗xg7+ ♔xg7 20 ♕e5 ♖d8 21 ♘a3 is analysis by Schüssler. White intends 22 ♖d1; it is not clear how Black can defend.

(b) **14 ... ♘xd5!** 15 ♗xd5 h6! 16 ♕xe4 hg! 17 ♗xb7 ♖h4! 18 g4 (18 ♘h7+? ♔g8; 18 ♕d3 ♗xf6 19 ♗xa8 ♗a6 20 ♕e3 ♘d7! and Black plans to attack the white king, caught in the centre, with such moves as ... ♘e5–d3+ and ... ♗d4.) 18 ... ♗xb7 (18 ... ♕b6) 19 ♕xb7 ♗xf6 20 ♕xa8 ♕e5+ 21 ♔d1 (21 ♔f1 ♕b5+ wins.) 21 ... c6! (White's king and queen are both under threat.) 22 ♘d2 (22 ♕xa7 ♕d5+ 23 ♔xc2 ♕e4+! 24 ♔b3 ♕xh1 25 ♕xb8+ ♔g7 leaves White in rather a dreadful state; 22 ♖e1 ♕c7 23 ♖e4 is better, but White's kingside pawns are a mess.) 22 ... ♕c7!–+ 23 a4 ♔g7 24 ♖a3 ♘d7! 25 ♖b3 ♘b6 26 ♖xb6 ♕xb6 27 a5 ♕xb2 28 ♕xc6 ♗xc3 0–1 Mnatsakanian–Khmelnitsky, Šibenik Open 1989.

14 ... ♘a6

Short–Alburt, Foxboro (1) 1985 saw **14 ... ♘6d7?!** 15 ♘xd7+ ♘xd7 16 de ♘c5 (16 ... fe?! 17 ♗xe6±) 17 e7+ ♔e8 18 0–0! h6 (Grabbing the rook is fatal: 18 ... ♘xb3 19 ab ♕xa1 20 ♕xc7 f6 21 ♖d1 ♔f7 22 e8♕++) and now White's best was 19 ♗e3! since 19 ... ♘xb3 20 ab ♕xa1 again fails to 21 ♕xc7. Instead after 19 ♗f4?! ♘xb3 20 ♗xc7 ♕g5! 21 ab ♕xg3 22 hg ♔xe7 23 ♘d2, White's chances were only marginally better.

Here, with the queen on g3, **14 ... ♘xd5?** fails rather drastically: 15 ♗xd5 ed 16 ♕e5 ♕b5 17 ♕xc7 ♗d7 18 ♕d8+ ♗e8 19 ♘xe8 ♕xe8 20 ♗e7+ (SDO).

15   de *(88)*

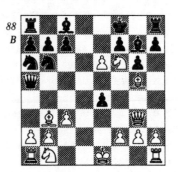

88
B

15   ...   h6

15...♗xe6 16 ♗xe6 h6 17 ♕f4! fe (17...hg?? 18 ♘h7+) 18 ♘d5+! ♔g8! (18 ... ♔e8 19 ♘xc7+ ♘xc7 20 ♕xc7 ♕xg5 21 ♕xg7 ♕c1+ 22 ♔e2 ♕xh1 23 ♕xh8+ ♔f7 24 ♕h7+ ♔f6± is given by London, with the amusing sequel 25 ♘d2 ♕xa1 26 ♘xe4+ ♔e5 27 ♕e7 ♘d5 28 ♕d6+ ♔xe4 29 ♕xe6+ ♔f4 30 g3+ ♔g5 31 h4+ ♔h5 32 ♕xd5+ and now 32 ... g5 33 ♕f3+ ♔g6 34 h5+ ♔g7 35 ♕xb7+ or 32 ... ♔g4 33 ♕e6+ ♔h5 34 f3 ♕xb2+ 35 ♔f1 ♕b1+ 36 ♔g2 ♕c2+ 37 ♔h3 ♕f5+ 38 g4+.) 19 ♘e7+ ♔h7 20 h4! (20 ♗xh6? ♕h5!) 20 ... ♘d5 21 ♕xe4

♘xe7 22 ♗xe7 ♖he8 23 ♗a3 ♕d5 24 ♘d2 h5 25 0-0-0 ♗h6 26 ♔c2 and now in London–Alburt, New York Open 1989, after 26 ... ♕f5?! 27 f3 ♖ad8 28 ♖he1 ♔g7 29 g4 hg 30 fg ♖xd2+ 31 ♖xd2 ♕xe4+ 32 ♖xe4 ♗xd2 33 ♔xd2 e5 34 ♖e1! there resulted an ending offering White excellent winning chances. London gives 26 ... ♗xd2± as Black's best.

Short's suggestion **15 ... ♕f5** has been analysed quite extensively. **16 e7+ ♔xe7** and now:

(a) **17 ♘h5+??** f6–+.

(b) **17 ♘d5++ ♔f8** 18 ♘e3 (18 ♘xc7?? ♗e5–+) 18 ... ♕d7 intending ... f6 and ... g5 gives Black slightly the better chances according to Short.

(c) **17 ♘g8++!? ♔e8** 18 ♘h6 ♗xh6 19 ♗xh6 ♗e6 20 0-0 ♗xb3 21 ab f6 (SDO) gives White very reasonable compensation for the pawn.

Blees' move, 15 ... h6, is condemned by King as a clear blunder. However, as it was surely prepared beforehand, and Black obtains very interesting play for the pawn, this criticism may be unfounded.

16	**e7+**	**♔xe7**
17	**♘d5++**	**♔e8**
18	**♘xc7+**	**♘xc7**
19	**♕xc7**	**♕xg5**
20	**♕xf7+**	**♔d8**
21	**♕xg7**	**♖e8** *(89)*

The end of a forced sequence. Black's king is surprisingly safe, while ... e3 is in the air, as are ...

89
W

♗h3 ideas should White castle.

22	♘d2	♗g4
23	♕d4+	♔c7
24	♕e3	♕xe3+
25	fe	♖ad8

The exchange of queens has not lessened the awkwardness of White's position.

26	h3	♗e6
27	♔e2	♗d7
28	♖hf1	h5
29	♖f7	♔b8
30	♖g1	♖e5
31	♖f6	♗b5+
32	c4	♖ed5!

This clever piece of tactics brings Black fully into the game. 33 ♘xe4 ♘xc4 34 a4 ♖d3 35 ♖d1 ♘xb2 36 ♖xd3 ♗xd3+ 37 ♔f3 a5 38 ♘c5 ♗c4 39 ♗c2 g5 40 ♖b6 ♗d5+ 41 e4 ♘c4 42 ♖h6 ♗f7 43 ♖h7 ♘e5+ 44 ♔e3 ♘c4+ 45 ♔f2 ♖d2+ 46 ♔g1 ♘e3. The tactics now begin to fizzle out, and an ending results in which White is just able to hold a draw: 47 ♗b3 ♗xb3 48 ♖xb7+ ♔c8 49 ♖xb3 ♖xg2+ 50 ♔h1 ♖e2 51 ♘e6 g4 52 ♘f4 ♖e1+ 53 ♔h2 ♘f1+ 54 ♔g2 ♘d2 55 ♖c3+

♔b7 56 ♖d3 gh+ 57 ♖xh3 ♖xe4 58 ♘d3 ♖g4+ 59 ♔f2 h4 60 ♔e2 ♘c4 61 ♔f3 ♖d4 62 ♘f4 ♘d2+ 63 ♔g4 ♖xa4 64 ♖xh4 ♔b6 65 ♔g3 ♔b5 66 ♔f2 ♘e4+ 67 ♔e3 ♘c5 68 ♘g6 ♖a2 69 ♘e5 ♖c2 70 ♖h8 ♘a6 71 ♘d3 ♖c6 72 ♖h5+ ♔b6 73 ♘e5 ♖c8 74 ♘d7+ ½–½.

Timman–Albert
Taxco/Montetaxco IZ 1985

1 e4 ♘f6 2 e5 ♘d5 3 d4 d6 4 ♘f3 g6 5 ♗c4 ♘b6 6 ♗b3 ♗g7 7 ♘g5 e6 8 ♕f3 ♕e7 9 ♘e4 de 10 ♗g5 ♕b4+ 11 c3 ♕a5

| 12 | ♗f6 | ♗xf6 |

12 ... 0–0 13 ♗xg7 ♔xg7 14 ♕f6+ ♔g8 15 ♕xe5 affects the move-number, but not the position.

| 13 | ♕xf6 | 0–0 |
| 14 | ♕xe5 | ♕xe5 |

The more ambitious **14 ... ♘c6** has been condemned on the basis of the game Ljubojević–Albert, New York Open 1985, in which Black was routed by a mating attack. However, Khmelnitsky has continued to play the move, but none of his opponents have been curious enough to see his improvement.

(a) **15 ♕xc7 ♘xd4 16 0–0!?** ♘xb3 17 ab ♕xa1 (Dunworth suggests 17 ... ♕f5 18 ♘bd2 ♘d5, which is certainly better than being mated, but queenside development remains a problem.) 18 ♘f6+. Now Ljubojević–Albert continued with **18 ... ♔g7** which

lost quite trivially: 19 ♕e5 ♖d8
20 ♘d2 ♕xb2 21 ♘de4 ♕e2 and
now 22 ♘e8++ ♔f8 23 ♕c5+
♔g8 24 ♘4f6+ ♔h8 25 ♕f8#
was quickest. Ljubojević analysed
18 ... ♔h8 19 ♕e5! ♕xb2 20 g4
(20 ♖d1 ♗d7! 21 ♘xd7+ f6 22
♘xf6 ♖f7) 20 ... ♕c2 (20 ... ♕xb3
21 ♘d2 ♕a3 22 ♘de4 ♕e7 23 ♖d1
♘c4 24 ♕g5 ♖g8 25 ♕h6 ♖g7
26 ♘g5 ♘e5 27 ♘gxh7 ♘xg4 28
♕h4+−) 21 c4 (Threatens c5; 21
♔g2?! f5!) 21 ... ♕xb3 22 ♘d2
♕a2 23 ♘de4 ♘xc4 24 ♕g5+−.

(b) **15 ♘f6+ ♔h8 16 ♕f4 ♔g7**
and now:

(b1) **17 g4!?** h6 18 ♘e4?! (18
g5!?; 18 h4) 18 ... f5!∞ Frolov–
Khmelnitsky, Simferopol 1989.

(b2) **17 ♘g4?!** f5! (17 ... ♕f5?!
18 ♕h6+! ♔g8 19 f3± Kruppa–
Khmelnitsky, Kiev 1989) 18 ♘e5
(18 ♘e3?! e5!) 18 ... ♘xe5 19 ♕xe5
♕xe5 20 de a5 21 ♘a3 ♗d7 22
0-0-0 ♗c6 23 f3 a4 24 ♗c2 ♖a5
25 ♖he1 ♖c5 26 ♖d4 ♖a8 27 ♖e2
g5! 28 f4 ♖aa5 29 g3 gf 30 gf ♖d5
31 ♖b4 ♖ac5 32 ♖e3 ♖d7 33
♗d1 ♔f8! 34 ♖g3 ♖cd5 35 ♗e2
♖d2 36 ♖e3 and now 36 ... ♘d5
37 ♔xd2 ♘xb4+ 38 ♔c1 ♘d5
39 ♖f3 ♖g7 would have given
Black a won ending in Kruppa–
Khmelnitsky, Ukrainian Ch
(Kherson) 1989.

15   de   ♘c6
15 ... ♗d7 is an important
alternative. 16 0-0 ♗b5 (16 ...
♗c6) 17 ♖e1 ♘8d7 18 f4 ♘a4
posed Black no problems in
Ornstein–Alburt, Thessaloniki ol

1984, so White has preferred **16
♘bd2 ♗c6** *(90)*:

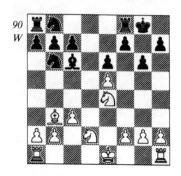

(a) **17 0-0-0** ♘8d7 (17 ... a5 18
f4 ♔g7 19 h4 ½-½ Fedorowicz–
Benjamin, San Francisco 1991) 18
f4 a5 (Meshkov–Dzhalilov, Penza
1985 continued 18 ... ♘a4 19
♗xa4 ♗xa4 20 b3 ♗c6 21 ♖he1
♖fd8 and now Meshkov gives 22
g4! ♘b6 23 c4±) 19 ♖he1 a4 20
♗c2 ♖fd8 21 g3 ♔f8 22 ♘f3
♗d5 23 ♔b1 ♘c4 24 ♘d4 ♔e7
25 ♘b5 ♖dc8 26 b3 ab 27 ab
♘a3+ 28 ♘xa3 ♖xa3 29 ♔b2
♖a6 30 ♖a1 ♖b6 31 ♘d2 h6 32
c4 ♗c6 33 ♔c3 ♘b8 gave Black
a position which, although rather
passive, was quite well organised,
in W. Watson–Alburt, New York
Open 1987. In these lines Black
always has long-term prospects of
counterplay against White's kingside pawns.

(b) **17 f4** was met by **17 ... ♘6d7**
in Khalifman–Fedorowicz, Wijk
aan Zee 1991, though it is not
clear that White has anything
better than transposing to the
above lines after 17 ... ♘8d7. The

game continued 18 ♗c2 a5 19
0–0–0 ♔g7 20 ♖he1 a4 21 b4 ab
22 ab ♘a6 23 b4 ♘b6 24 ♔b2
♖ad8 25 g3 ♗b5 26 ♗b3 ♗a4
27 ♗xa4 ♘xa4+ 28 ♔b3 b5 29
♘f3 c5 30 ♖xd8 ♖xd8 31 ♘d6
and Black had serious problems.

| 16 | f4 | ♘a5 |
| 17 | ♘bd2 | ♘xb3 |

17 ... ♗d7 18 h4 h5 19 ♘f6+
♔g7 20 ♘xd7 ♘xd7 21 ♗c2 ♘b6
22 ♗e4 c5 23 ♘b3 ♘xb3 24 ab
♘d5 25 g3± Mariasin–Meshkov,
USSR 1988.

| 18 | ab | ♘d5 |
| 19 | 0–0 | |

In Sisniega–Alburt, Taxco/
Montetaxco IZ 1985, White kept
his king in touch with the open
file with 19 g3 ♔g7 (19 ... b6!? 20
♔f2 ♗b7 21 b4 ♔g7= Oll–
Bagirov, Valka 1987.) 20 ♔e2 b6
21 h4 h5 22 ♘f3 a5 23 ♖hd1 ♗b7
24 ♘fg5 ♖fd8 25 ♖d4 ♘e7 26
♖ad1 ♖xd4 27 ♖xd4 ♗c6 28
♔f2 ♖c8, but Black's position
was comfortable.

| 19 | ... | ♖d8 |

Alburt proposed alternatively
19 ... b6, with the possible continuation 20 ♘f6+ ♔g7!? (20 ... ♘xf6
21 ef ♗b7 22 ♗c4 ♗d5 gives a
tenable ending following the
exchange on c4.) 21 ♘xd5 ed 22
b4 whereupon a somewhat unbalanced ending results.

| 20 | c4 | ♘e3 |

The position after **20 ... ♘b4** 21
♖fd1 ♗d7 22 ♘f3 ♗c6 23 ♘f6+
♔g7 arose in Qi Jingxuan–
Alburt, Taxco/Montetaxco IZ

1985 (via the move order 19 ...
♔g7 20 c4 ♘b4 21 ♘f3 ♖d8 22
♖fd1 ♗d7 23 ♘f6 ♗c6). After **24
♔f2** a6 25 ♘d4 h5 26 ♖d2 ♖xd4
27 ♖xd4 ♘c2 28 ♖ad1 ♘xd4 29
♖xd4 a5 Black had comfortably
equalised, whilst **24 ♖xd8 ♖xd8
25 ♖xa7 ♘d3** is dangerous only
for White.

21	♖fc1!	♔g7
22	♔f2	♘g4+
23	♔e2	h5

Alburt rejected the pawn grab
23 ... ♘xh2 due to the dangerous
opening of the h-file after 24 ♘f6
h5 25 ♖h1.

24	h3	♘h6
25	♘f6	♗d7
26	♖d1	♗c6
27	♘f3	♖xd1
28	♖xd1	♘g8
29	♘xg8	♔xg8
30	g3	♗xf3+

A safe alternative is 30 ... ♔f8 31
♘d4 ♗e8.

31	♔xf3	a5
32	♔e4	♔f8
33	♖a1	♖a6?!

Now Alburt begins to go astray.
A fully adequate answer to White's
threat of b4 was 33 ... c5 34 ♖d1
♔e7 35 ♖d6 ♖a6, since the pawn
ending is a draw. The text is a
little too clever (34 b4? ab 35 ♖xa6
ba 36 ♔d4 a5 37 ♔c5 c6!–+),
as Timman's reply shows it to be
a loss of time:

34 ♔d4 ♖b6 35 ♔c3 ♖a6 36
c5! b5 37 cb cb? (Black could still
hope for a successful defence with
37 ... ♖xb6. As played, Black's

rook has no reasonable prospects of activity.) 38 ♔c4 ♖a8 39 ♔b5 ♖d8 40 ♖a3 h4 41 gh ♖b8?! (Black can only hope to cause White technical difficulties; to this end ... ♔g7–h6–h5 was more suitable.) 42 ♖a4 ♔e7 43 ♖c4 ♔d7 44 ♖c3 f6 45 ef ♖f8 46 ♔xb6 ♖xf6 47 ♔xa5. Black can now

do little but watch the b-pawn advance. The game concluded: 47 ... ♖f5+ 48 ♔a4 ♖xf4+ 49 b4 ♖f2 50 b3 ♖a2+ 51 ♔b5 ♖a8 52 ♖c4 ♖a3 53 ♔b6 ♖xb3 54 b5 e5 55 ♔a6 ♖a3+ 56 ♔b7 ♖b3 57 b6 ♖g3 58 ♔a7 g5 59 hg ♖xg5 60 b7 ♖g8 61 ♖c5 ♖e8 62 b8♕ ♖xb8 63 ♔xb8 1–0.

10 4 ... ♝g4: Introduction and Old Main Line

The pin with 4 ... ♝g4 is Black's most natural reply to 4 ♞f3. White generally breaks the pin immediately with the equally natural 5 ♝e2. The alternatives can lead to interesting play, but are not especially harmful.

After 5 ♝e2, Black generally chooses between 5 ... c6 and 5 ... e6. The former is the subject of the next chapter.

5 ... e6 intends simple development. The popularity of the move has been waning due to atrocious results in practice. The main problem is the line 6 0–0 ♝e7 7 c4 ♞b6 8 ♞c3 0–0 9 ♝e3 d5 10 c5 ♝xf3 11 gf! (or the same line with h3 ♝h5 inserted, though this somewhat reduces White's attacking possibilities) when in addition to plans of swamping Black on the queenside, White has ideas of sacrificing on d5, liberating a large pawn mass, and possibilities of a vicious kingside attack using the open g-file and/or the f5 pawn break. Maybe Black's position ought to be playable, but only Bagirov seems at all capable of surviving in these lines. Anyone wishing to follow in his footsteps should be armed with a lot of new ideas.

There are a number of attempts to vary at move 9 (or 10, with h3 ♝h5), but White keeps at least a small advantage against these.

Vitolinš–Bagirov
Jurmala 1985

1 e4 ♞f6 2 e5 ♞d5 3 d4 d6 4 ♞f3
4 ...   ♝g4 *(91)*

91
W

5   c4
5 ♝c4 e6 6 h3 (6 0–0 ♝e7 7 h3 ♝h5 8 ♛d3?! ♝g6 9 ♛b3 ♞b6

10 ♖e1 ♘xc4 11 ♕xc4 d5∓) 6 ...
♗h5 7 ♕e2 ♘b6 8 ♗b3 ♘c6 9
g4 ♗g6 10 ♘c3 de 11 de ♘d4 12
♘xd4 ♕xd4 13 ♗e3 ♕d7 14 ♖d1
♕c6 15 f3 ♗b4∓ Akopian–
Alburt, Kiev 1970.

5 ...   ♘b6
6 d5!?

6 ♗e2 is an old recommendation of Alekhine's. Black can
respond with 6 ... c6, transposing
to the Flohr–Agzamov variation,
6 ... e6 with an Old Main Line,
or 6 ... ♘c6 with the line 5 ♗e2
♘c6 6 c4 ♘b6 having side-stepped
6 0–0, White's strongest option.
Instead, Black can try to punish
this move order with **6 ... de**.
White then has two options:

(a) **7 ♘xe5** ♗xe2 8 ♕xe2 ♕xd4
9 0–0 (9 ♘a3!? ♘8d7 10 ♘f3) 9
... ♘8d7 10 ♘xd7 ♕xd7! (10 ...
♘xd7? 11 ♘c3 c6 12 ♗e3 ♕e5
13 ♖ad1 e6 14 ♕f3!± Alekhine–
Reshevsky, Kemeri 1937) 11 a4!
(11 ♘c3 e6 12 ♗e3 ♗e7 13 ♖ad1
♕c6 14 ♕g4 0–0 15 b3 f5∓
Thomas–Flohr, London 1932) 11
... ♕c6 12 ♘a3 e6 13 a5 ♘d7 14
♘b5 and Alekhine liked White's
compensation.

(b) **7 c5** e4 (7 ... ♘6d7 8 ♕b3!±)
8 cb (8 ♘g5 ♗xe2 9 ♕xe2 ♘d5
and now 10 ♕b5+?! ♘c6 11
♕xb7? ♘db4 fails, so White must
settle for 10 0–0 ♘c6 11 ♖d1 e6=)
8 ... ef 9 ♗xf3 ♗xf3 10 ♕xf3
♘c6 (10 ... ab 11 ♕xb7 ♘d7 12
♗f4 e5! 13 ♗xe5 ♘xe5 14 de
♗b4+ 15 ♘c3 ♗xc3+ 16 bc 0–0
17 0–0 ♕e7 18 ♖fe1 ♕c5 19 ♖e3

♖a3 20 ♕f3 was Alekhine–Euwe,
Amsterdam World Ch 1935. 20 ...
♕c4 would have equalised.) 11 0–0
(11 d5 ♘b4 12 ♕b3 ♘xd5 13 bc
♕xc7!; 11 bc?! ♕xc7 12 ♗e3 ♖d8
13 ♕d1? e5 14 d5 ♕a5+ 15 ♘c3
♗b4 16 0–0 ♗xc3 17 bc ♕xd5
18 ♕g4 f6!∓ Parfenëv–Bagirov,
Baku 1966) and now Black's best
is **11 ... g6!?**, since 11 ... e6 12
♘c3 ab 13 d5! ed 14 ♘xd5 ♖a5
15 ♖e1+ ♗e7 16 ♘xe7 ♘xe7 17
♗g5! ♖xg5 18 ♖ad1 ♕c8 19 ♕e3
1–0 Ciocaltea–Sutiman, Romanian Ch (Bucharest) 1952 was a
rout, and **11 ... ♘xd4** 12 ♕xb7 ab
13 ♘c3! gives an overwhelming
attack in view of the threats of
♖d1 and ♘b5.

6 ed gives White no more
options than does playing 5 ♗e2
followed by 6 c4 ♘b6 7 ed, except
in the positioning of the king's
bishop, which is unlikely to find a
better square than e2. Black must
only be careful to avoid a line of
the Exchange Variation with the
bishop prematurely committed to
g4.

(a) **6 ... cd 7** ♘c3 g6 8 h3 ♗xf3
9 ♕xf3 ♘c6 10 ♗e3 ♗g7 11 ♖d1
(11 ♕d1?! 0–0 12 ♗e2 d5 13
c5 ♘c4∓ Torfasen–Solmundsen,
Reykjavik 1970) 11 ... 0–0 12 ♗e2
and now 12 ... e6 preparing ... d5
should be given preference over 12
... e5? 13 de ♘xe5 14 ♕f4 when
White threatened c5 in Filipowicz–
Liliedahl, Poland 1973. After **7
♗e2**, Black must choose between
7 ... e6, transposing to the

exchange variation of the Old Main Line, and **7 ... g6** 8 0-0 &g7 9 &e3 0-0 10 ♘bd2 with a line of the Exchange Variation where Black would prefer the bishop not committed to g4: 10 ... ♘c6 11 d5 secures a solid space advantage.

(b) **6 ... ed** is considered under the move order 4 c4 ♘b6 5 ed ed 6 ♘f3 &g4, though note that 7 &e2 c6 transposes to Yudasin–Timoshenko in the Flohr–Agzamov Variation, and 7 &e2 ♘c6 to 5 &e2 ♘c6 6 c4 ♘b6 7 ed ed.

6 ... e6

6 ... de 7 h3 &xf3 8 ♕xf3 is untried, since White's compensation is very reasonable. A major alternative is **6 ... ♘8d7 7 e6!?** (7 ed is harmless) **7 ... fe** when White has two approaches, both leading to unclear play:

(a) **8 &e2** ed 9 cd ♘f6 10 ♘c3 c6 11 0-0 ♘bxd5 12 ♘g5 &xe2 13 ♕xe2 ♕d7 14 f4 g6 15 f5 Vitolinš–Palatnik, Jurmala 1981.

(b) **8 h3** &xf3 9 ♕xf3 ♘e5 (9 ... ed 10 cd c6!? 11 ♘c3 ♘e5 12 ♕e4 ♕d7 13 f4 cd 14 ♘xd5 ♘xd5 15 fe e6 16 &e2 de 17 0-0 0-0-0 18 &g5 &e7 19 ♖ac1+ ♔b8∞ Campora–Palatnik, San Nikolas 1988) 10 ♕b3 ed 11 cd g6 12 ♘c3 &g7 and now **13 f4!?** ♘ed7 (13 ... ♘f7 14 &b5+) 14 &e3 0-0 15 0-0-0 a5 16 a3 a4 17 ♕c2 Hartmann–Grün, Bamberg 1984 is more promising than **13 &e3** c5! 14 dc (14 0-0-0 c4 15 ♕c2 ♙c8) 14 ... bc 15 f4 ♘f7 16 f5 gf

17 &d3 ♖b8! 18 ♕e6 ♕d7 19 &xf5 ♕xe6 20 &xe6 ♘d8 21 &b3 d5 22 0-0 Vitolinš–Bagirov, Riga 1981, when 22 ... ♖b7! 23 ♖ad1 ♖f8 was the simplest way to consolidate.

7 ed &xd6

7 ... ♕xd6 has been played in three games between Vitolinš and Kengis. Though less natural than capturing with the bishop, it has the merit of keeping g7 defended, and seems viable. After **8 ♘c3 ed 9 cd c6**, Vitolinš has tried two moves:

(a) **10 h3 &h5!?** (10 ... &xf3 11 ♕xf3 ♕e5+ 12 ♕e3 &d6 13 f4! ♕xe3+ 14 &xe3 0-0?! 15 0-0-0± led to trouble in an earlier game Vitolinš–Kengis, Riga 1984, though Kengis suggests the improvements 11 ... cd!? and 14 ... ♘xd5 15 ♘xd5 cd 16 0-0-0 ♘c6 17 ♖xd5 0-0-0 18 &b5 ♖he8 19 &d2 ♖e4!± .) 11 g4 &g6 12 &g2 ♘xd5 13 ♘xd5 cd 14 0-0 &e7 (14 ... ♘c6) 15 ♕d4!? ♘c6!? (Kengis analysed 15 ... 0-0 16 &f4 ♕a6! 17 ♕xd5 ♘c6 18 ♘e5 ♖ad8! 19 ♘xc6! bc 20 ♕xc6 ♕xc6 21 &xc6 &f6 22 ♖ad1 &xb2! 23 &d6 &c2 24 ♖d2 &e5 with equality.) 16 ♕xg7 0-0-0 17 ♕h6 ♖he8! 18 &f4 ♕b4 19 a3 (19 &g3 &f8 20 ♕c1 &g7 21 a3 ♕c4!∓) 19 ... ♕xb2 20 ♖ac1 &xa3! 21 &e3 ♖e4 and now 22 &xa7 ♖c4 would have given very messy play. Instead, in Vitolinš–Kengis, Riga 1984, Black took over after 22 &g5? ♕h8!.

(b) **10 ♗e2!** ♘xd5 **11 ♘d4 ♗e6**
(11 ... ♗d7 12 ♘db5! and 11 ...
♗xe2 12 ♕xe2+ ♕e7 13 ♘xd5
♕xe2+ 14 ♔xe2 cd 15 ♘b5 are
both good for White.) **12 0–0 ♗e7
13 ♘xe6 fe 14 ♗h5+ g6 15 ♗g4
♘xc3!** (15 ... 0–0 16 ♘e4±) **16 bc
♕xd1 17 ♖xd1 ♘a6 18 ♗xe6 ♘c5
19 ♗c4 b5 20 ♖e1 ♔d7! 21 ♗a3
♗f8!** led to a survivable ending
for Black in Vitoliņš–Kengis,
Jurmala 1985.

8	♕d4	♗xf3
9	♕xg7	♖f8
10	gf	♘8d7
11	♗g5	♗e7
12	♖g1!	

Though these moves are not
all forced, sensible alternatives are
not apparent. For example, 12 h4
ed 13 ♘c3 ♗f6!

12	...	ed
13	♘c3	♗xg5

This exchange cannot be delayed, as after 13 ... dc 14 0–0–0!
♗xg5+ 15 ♖xg5, Black has no
check on e7; after the text 14 ♖xg5
would be met by 14 ... ♕e7+.

14	♕xg5	♕xg5
15	♖xg5	dc
16	0–0–0 *(92)*	

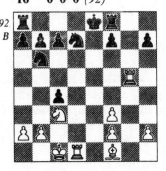

A highly unbalanced ending has
arisen. The attempt to compromise Black's queenside with 16 a4
also weakens b3: 16 ... a5 17
0–0–0 f6 18 ♖g7 (18 ♖h5 ♖f7) 18
... 0–0–0 19 ♖xh7 ♘c5!∓.

16	...	0–0–0
17	a4	

17 ♗h3 c6 (The weakness of d6
is not serious.) 18 ♘e4 ♔c7 19
♖g7 ♘d5 20 ♘g5 ♖g8!∓ 21 ♖xg8
♖xg8 22 ♘xf7 ♖f8 23 ♘g5 ♘c5
24 ♖d4 h6 25 ♘e4 ♘d3+ 26 ♔b1
♖xf3 27 ♗g2 ♖f4–+ 28 ♖xc4
♘xf2 29 b3 ♘e3 30 ♘xf2 ♘xc4 31
♘d3 ♖d4 32 ♘c5 ♖d1+ 33 ♔c2
♘e3+ 0–1 Down–Burgess, Keyn-
sham 1989.

17	...	f6

17 ... ♘f6 18 ♖xd8+ ♔xd8 19
a5 ♘bd7 20 ♗xc4 ♔e7 is roughly
balanced.

18	♖h5	

18 ♖g7 ♘c5! again seizes on the
weakness of White's queenside.

18	...	♘e5
19	♖xd8+	♖xd8
20	♖xh7	♘d3+
21	♔b1	

Bagirov assesses 21 ♗xd3
♖xd3 22 ♖h3 ♘d5 as equal.

21	...	♖e8
22	♗h3+	♔b8
23	a5	♘c8
24	♘e4	a6
25	♗d7!	♖f8
26	♗e6	b5
27	ab	♘xb6
28	h4	♖e8
29	♗f7	♖e5

The h-pawn is a potent force,

but Black finds counterplay against b2.

30	♖h5	f5
31	♘c3	♖e1+
32	♔c2	♖h1

This is adequate to hold, but **32 ... ♖f1** was more ambitious and consistent. The game concluded: 33 ♖h8+ ♔a7 34 h5 ♘e1+ 35 ♔d2 ♘xf3+ 36 ♔e3 ♘e5 37 ♗e8 ♖h4 38 ♖f8 ♘c8! 39 ♖xf5 ♘g4+ 40 ♔f3 ♘d6 41 ♖f8 ♘xe8 ½-½.

Bagirov analysed 42 ♔g3 ♖xh5 43 ♔xg4 ♖e5 44 f4 ♖e1 45 f5 ♘d6= and 42 ♖xe8 ♘f6! (42 ... ♘h2+? 43 ♔g3 ♖xh5 44 ♖e1!+ −) 43 ♖f8 ♘xh5= as the basis for the peaceful conclusion.

De Amarel–R. Fernandes
Correspondence 1985

1 e4 ♘f6 2 e5 ♘d5 3 d4 d6 4 ♘f3 ♗g4

5	h3	♗xf3
6	♕xf3	de
7	de	e6

This line was originally investigated by Panov and Boleslavsky. Crucial in determining how well White's idea will work are how effectively Black's queen's knight can be placed, and whether the white queen can exert useful pressure or simply be kicked around. Black has worked out good plans over the years, so consequently most of the games in this variation are rather old.

8 a3

8 ♗d3 ♘c6 9 ♕g3 ♘db4 10 ♗e4 ♕d4 11 ♘c3 0-0-0 (11 ... ♕xe5? 12 ♗f4 ♕c5 13 0-0-0 ♘d4 14 ♖d2 0-0-0 15 ♖hd1± Schmittdiel–Kindl, Wiesbaden Open 1986) 12 0-0 (Dunworth pointed out that 12 ♗f4? ♕xe4+! 13 ♘xe4 ♘xc2+ gives Black excellent compensation.) 12 ... ♕xe5 13 ♗f4 ♕a5 14 a3 ♘d5= Krauss–Kindl, Landau 1988.

8 ♗d2 ♘d7 (8 ... ♘c6?! 9 ♗b5) 9 ♕g3 ♘e7! (9 ... ♘c5!? 10 ♘c3 ♘xc3 11 ♗xc3 ♘e4 12 ♕e3 ♘xc3 13 ♕xc3 ♕d5! 14 ♗e2 ♕c5= Mikenas) 10 ♘c3 ♘f5 11 ♕f4 g6 12 0-0-0 ♗g7∓ Seifert–Bagirov, Wroclaw 1976.

8 ♕e4 ♘d7 9 ♗c4 (9 ♗e2 c6 10 0-0 ♕c7 11 f4 0-0-0!) and now Black has tried three moves:

(a) **9 ... c6** has been played a number of times. The best attempt at justification was Mark Tseitlin–Klochko, Leningrad 1970: 10 0-0 ♕c7 11 ♖e1 ♗c5 12 ♘d2 ♕b6 13 ♖f1 0-0-0 14 ♘f3 h6 15 a3 f5∞ 16 ef ♘5xf6 17 ♕g6?! (17 ♕e2 e5 18 b4!?) 17 ... e5 18 ♗e6 ♖he8 19 ♗xd7+ ♖xd7 20 ♕f5 e4! 21 ♘e5 ♗xf2+ 22 ♖xf2 ♖xe5−+.

(b) **9 ... ♘5b6** 10 ♗e2 (10 0-0 ♘c5 11 ♕e2 ♘xc4 12 ♕xc4 ♕d5 13 ♕e2 ♕e4= Pavlenko–Bagirov, Sumgait 1972) 10 ... ♘c5 11 ♕f4 ♘d5 12 ♕c4 (12 ♕g3) 12 ... c6 13 ♗d2 ♕c7 14 f4 0-0-0 15 ♗f3 g5!?∓ Paoli–Bagirov, Baja 1971.

(c) **9 ... ♘c5** 10 ♕e2 ♘b6 11 ♗b3 (11 ♘c3; 11 0-0 ♘xc4 12 ♕xc4 ♕d5=) 11 ... a5 12 a3 ♘xb3 13 cb ♗e7 14 0-0 0-0 15 ♘c3

♘d5 16 ♘e4 c6 17 ♗d2 ♕b6 18
♕g4 ♔h8∓ Kupreichik–Bagirov,
Vitebsk 1970.

8 ♗c4 ♘c6 9 ♕e4 ♘de7 (9 ...
♘d6?! 10 ♗b5 11 ♘c3± Suetin–
Mikenas, Tallinn 1965) and now
White has tried two moves, neither
of which poses Black any great
problems.

(a) **10 c3** ♘g6 11 ♗f4 (11 ♗b5
♕d5 12 ♕xd5 ed 13 f4 f6=) 11 ...
♘xf4 12 ♕xf4 g5!? 13 ♕f6 (13 ♕e3?
♗g7 14 ♗b5 ♕d5∓ Gipslis–
Mikenas, Riga 1963.) 13 ... ♖g8
14 ♘d2 ♗g7 15 ♕f3 ♘xe5 16
♕xb7 ♖b8 and now 17 ♕xa7
♖xb2 18 0–0–0 ♘d3+ 19 ♗xd3
♕xd3 20 ♕a4+ ♔d8 21 ♕a8+
♔d7 22 ♕a4+ is a draw. Instead,
Õim–Mikenas, Palanga 1965 continued 17 ♕e4? ♖xb2 18 0–0–0
♖b8 19 ♘f3 ♕f6!∓.

(b) **10 ♗e3** ♘f5 (Playable,
though less ambitious, is 10 ... a6
11 f4 ♘a5 12 ♗d3 ♘d5 13 ♗f2
♘b4 14 0–0 ♘xd3 15 ♖d1 ♕e7
16 ♖xd3 ♕b4 17 ♘c3 ♘c6 18
a3 ♕xe4 19 ♘xe4± Zhuravlev–
Simonov, USSR Spartakiad 1978.)
11 0–0 (11 ♘c3 ♗b4∓) 11 ...
♕h4! 12 ♕xh4 (12 f4? ♘g3 13 ♗f2
♗c5!; 12 ♗f4?! 0–0–0 13 c3 g5∓)
12 ... ♘xh4 13 ♗b5 ♘f5 14
♗xc6+ bc 15 ♘d2 (15 ♗f4?
♘d4–+; 15 ♖e1 0–0–0 16 ♘c3
♗b4) 15 ... ♘xe3 16 fe ♖d8 17
♘c4 g6 18 ♔f2 ♖d5 19 ♔f3 ♗g7
20 ♔e4 ♔e7 gave Black a very
good ending in Zhuravlev–Alburt,
Odessa 1974.

Although 8 ... ♘c6 is logical

with the bishop already posted on
c4, **8 ... ♘d7** is also reasonable:

(a) **9 ♕e2!?** c6 (9 ... ♘5b6 leaves
Black a tempo down on the
equivalent line following 8 ♕e4.)
10 0–0 ♕c7 11 ♖e1 occurred in
Nun–Landenbergue, Prague 1990
(by transposition from 4 ♗c4 c6
5 ♘f3 ♗g4 6 0–0 de 7 de e6 8
♖e1 ♘d7 9 h3 ♗xf3 10 ♕xf3 ♕c7
11 ♕e2). 11 ... ♗c5 12 ♘d2 0–0–0
13 ♘f3 h6 14 a3 g5 15 ♗d3 ♖dg8
16 c4 ♘5b6 17 b4 ♗e7 gave Black
good play.

(b) **9 ♕g3** ♘e7 10 0–0 c6 (10 ...
♘f5 11 ♕f4 ♗c5 12 ♘d2 ♕h4
13 ♘f3 ♕xf4 14 ♗xf4 ♘d4∓
Zhuravlev–Alburt, Daugavpils
1974.) 11 ♘d2 ♕c7 12 ♘f3 ♘f5 13
♕f4 h6 14 ♖e1 ♗c5 15 ♗d3 g5
16 ♕c4 ♕b6! 17 ♗xf5 ♗xf2+ 18
♔h2 0–0–0!∓ Schandorff–
Hansen, Groningen 1983.

8   ...   ♘d7

8 ... c6 9 ♕g3 ♘d7 and 9 ♘d2
♘d7 10 ♕g3 are considered in the
note to Black's ninth, but **8 ...
♘c6?** 9 ♗b5 ♕d7 10 c4 ♘de7 11
0–0 ♖d8 12 ♘c3 left Black in
difficulties in Boleslavsky–
Khavin, Moscow 1944.

9   ♕g3

9 c4?! ♘e7! 10 ♕xb7?! c6! 11 b4
a5 12 ♗b2 ♘c5!∓ Khachaturov–
Mikenas, Moscow 1943.

9   ...   h5! *(93)*

This surprising thrust is one of
Black's most important resources
in this variation. The further
advance of this pawn will gain
time on the white queen and gain

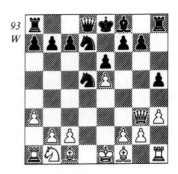

93
W

h5 for the rook; should White play 10 h4, then f5 will be an excellent post for a knight (10 ... ♘e7 11 ♗d3 ♘c5). Also viable is **9 ... c6 10 ♘d2 ♘e7** whereupon White has tried:

(a) **11 ♘e4 ♘g6!?** (11 ... ♘f5 12 ♕c3 ♕c7 13 ♗f4 ♗e7 14 0-0-0 0-0 15 g4 ♘h4 16 ♗g3 ♘b6? 17 ♘f6+! Panov–Mikenas, Moscow 1942) 12 f4 (12 ♘d6+ ♗xd6 13 ed ♕h4) 12 ... ♘c5 13 ♘xc5 ♗xc5 14 ♗d2 ♕h4∓ Banas–Bagirov, Stary Smokovec 1981.

(b) **11 ♘c4 ♘f5** 12 ♕c3 ♘b6 13 ♘xb6 ab 14 ♗d3 ♕d5 15 ♖g1 ♗c5 16 ♗xf5 ef 17 ♗e3 ♖d8 18 ♔e2 ♗xe3 19 fe 0-0 20 ♖ad1 ♕e4∓ Sandkamp–Graf, Bundesliga 1987/8.

(c) **11 ♘f3 ♘g6** (Threatens 12 ... ♘xe5) 12 ♗d2 ♘c5 13 ♕g4 (13 ♗e3? ♘e4 14 ♕h2 ♕a5+ 15 c3 0-0-0∓ Steiner–Koblents, 1937) 13 ... h5 14 ♕c4=.

10   ♗e2

10 ♘d2 h4 11 ♕b3 ♖h5! 12 ♘f3 ♘xe5 was good for Black in Panov–Mikenas, Moscow 1943.

10   ...   c6!

10 ... h4 is less satisfactory. Nemet–Segal, USSR 1967, continued 11 ♕b3 ♖b8 (11 ... ♘xe5!?) 12 0-0 ♘xe5 13 c4 ♘b6 14 ♗e3 ♘c6 (14 ... ♕f6) 15 ♖d1 ♕f6 16 ♘c3 ♗e7 17 ♖d2 0-0 18 c5 and White was better. The text prepares a more comfortable way of defending b7.

11	♘d2	h4
12	♕b3	♕c7

Thus Black is able to cover b7 and pressure e5.

13	♘c4	♖b8
14	f4	b5!
15	♘d6+	♗xd6
16	ed	♕xd6
17	0-0	♘e7!

Having forced the win of a pawn, Black must play a little carefully. For example, 17 ... ♘7f6 18 f5! gives White counterplay.

18	♗e3	a6
19	a4	♘f6
20	ab	ab
21	♖fd1	♘fd5
22	♗f2	0-0!

Having consolidated the extra pawn, Black must avoid being greedy: 22 ... ♕xf4 23 ♖d4!∞.

23	♗xh4	♘f5!
24	♗f2	♕xf4
25	♖a6	

25 c4 bc 26 ♕xc4 ♕xc4 27 ♗xc4 ♘fe3 is clearly miserable for White.

| 25 | ... | ♖fd8! |
| 26 | ♖xc6 | |

26 ♖d3 e5 27 ♖f3 ♕g5 28 ♗d3 (28 ♖a7 e4–+; 28 ♖xc6 ♘f4 29 ♗f1 ♖d1–+) 28 ... ♘f4 29 ♗f1

e4 30 ♖c3 ♖d1—+.

26 ... **♘de3**

27 ♖xd8+

27 ♖d3 ♖xd3! 28 ♕xd3 ♖a8 29 ♗xe3 ♘xe3 30 ♗f3 ♕g3!—+; 27 ♖e1 ♖d2 28 ♖c3 (28 ♗f3 ♖xf2!; 28 c3 ♘xg2!; 28 ♗xe3 ♘xe3 29 ♗f3 ♘xg2!; 28 ♖c5 ♖bd8! 29 c3 ♖xe2 30 ♖xe2 ♖d1+) 28 ... ♘xg2! (analysis by Fernandes).

27 ... **♖xd8**

28 ♕xb5

28 ♗f3 ♖d2 29 ♗xe3 ♘xe3; 28 ♗xe3 ♘xe3 29 ♕xb5 (29 ♗f3 ♕g3!) 29 ... ♕g3 30 ♗f1 ♘xg2!

28 ... **♘d4**

29 ♕d3 **♕e4!!**

30 ♗xe3

30 ♕xe4 ♘xe2+ 31 ♔h2 ♘f1+ 32 ♔h1 ♘fg3+.

30 ... **♘xe2+**

31 ♕xe2 **♕xc6**

32 b4 **♕e4**

0–1

Vogt–Bagirov
Tallinn 1981

1 e4 ♘f6 2 e5 ♘d5 3 d4 d6 4 ♘f3 ♗g4

5 ♗e2 **e6**

5 ... ♘c6 is a move which appears very logical. **6 h3 ♗xf3 7 ♗xf3 de 8 de e6 9 0–0 ♘db4** equalises comfortably, whilst **6 e6 fe 7 ♘g5 ♗xe2 8 ♕xe2 ♘xd4 9 ♕d1** (9 ♕e4 c5 10 ♘xh7 ♘f6) 9 ... h6 10 ♘xe6 ♘xe6 11 ♕xd5 ♕c8 12 ♕h5+ ♔d8 13 0–0 ♘d4 (13 ... g5) 14 ♕d1 ♘c6 15 f4 ♕f5 16 ♘c3 e6 17 ♗e3 ♗e7 18 ♕f3 ♗f6 19 ♘e4 ♔e7 was no more than

unclear for White in Mukhin–Grigorian, Kiev 1970.

6 c4 ♘b6 7 ed ed (7 ... cd?! 8 d5! ♗xf3 9 ♗xf3 ♘e5 10 ♗e2 g6 11 ♗e3 ♗g7 12 ♗d4 0–0 13 ♘c3±♔ Sokolov–Vaganian, Minsk Candidates 1986) may give White nothing better than transposing to the Exchange Variation, since 8 d5 ♗xf3 9 ♗xf3 ♘e5 10 ♗e2 is not especially threatening, e.g. 10 ... ♗e7 11 f4 ♘g6 12 0–0 0–0 13 ♘c3 ♗f6 14 ♘e4 ♖e8 15 ♕d3 ♘d7 16 ♖b1 ♘c5= Gavrikov–Kaunas, Vilnius 1983, or 10 ... g6 11 ♗e3 (11 f4) 11 ... ♗g7 12 0–0 0–0 13 ♘d2 ♖e8 14 ♕c2 ♕h4∞ Maxion–Clara, Bundesliga 1989/90.

However, the simple **6 0–0!** leaves Black rather stuck for a purposeful reply:

(a) **6 ... g6** 7 e6 fe 8 ♘g5± Zita–Vidmar, 1946. ... ♗g4 and ... g6 don't generally mix well.

(b) **6 ... ♗xf3** 7 ♗xf3 de 8 de e6 9 c4 ♘de7 10 ♕a4 ♕d4 11 ♗g5!± Kirilov–Zukhovitsky, USSR 1946.

(c) **6 ... de** 7 ♘xe5 ♗xe2 8 ♕xe2 ♘xe5 (8 ... ♕d6 9 ♕b5±; 8 ... ♘xd4? 9 ♕c4! c5 10 ♗e3 a6 11 ♘c3 e6 12 ♗xd4 ♘b6 13 ♕b3 cd 14 ♘a4! ♘xa4 15 ♕xb7! ♕d5 16 ♕xf7+ ♔d8 17 ♖fe1 ♘c5 18 ♖ad1 ♔c8 19 c3 d3 20 b3 d2 21 ♖e2 ♘d7 22 ♘f3! 1–0 Thorsteins–C. Hansen, Reykjavik 1985) 9 de ♕d7 10 ♖d1 ♖d8 11 ♔h1! e6 (11 ... ♕c8 12 c4 ♘b6 13 ♖xd8+ ♕xd8 14 e6) 12 c4 ♘f4 13 ♖xd7

♘xe2 14 ♖xd8+ ♔xd8 15 ♗e3 left Black's knight in great trouble in Ulybin–Nosenko, Jurmala 1985.

(d) **6 ... e6** transposes to 5 ... e6 6 0–0 ♘c6 — see below.

(e) **6 ... ♘b6** 7 h3 (7 a4; 7 ed) 7 ... ♗xf3 8 ♗xf3 de (8 ... e6 9 ed gives Black an unpleasant choice between 9 ... ♕xd6 10 c3 intending ♘d2–e4, and 9 ... ♗xd6 10 ♗xc6+ bc 11 ♘c3 0–0 12 ♘e4± Listengarten–Mikenas, Riga 1962.) 9 de ♕xd1 10 ♖xd1 e6 11 b3 (11 ♗xc6+) 11 ... ♗e7 (11 ... ♘xe5?! 12 ♗xb7 ♖b8 13 ♗a6 ♘d5 14 ♗b2 ♗d6 15 ♗f1 f6 16 c4 ♘b4 17 ♘c3 ♗e7 18 ♖d2± Novopashin–Mikenas, Erevan 1962) 12 ♗b2 leads to a very pleasant endgame for White.

5 ... ♗xf3?! 6 ♗xf3 c6 7 c4 ♘c7 8 ♕b3! gave Black great difficulties in Ghinda–Mozes, Romania 1987. 8 ... ♕c8 (8 ... ed? 9 ♕xb7 ed 10 ♗f4+ –; 8 ... b6±) 9 ed ed 10 0–0 ♗e7 11 ♖e1 ♘d7 (11 ... h6 12 ♗f4 ♘e6 13 ♗xd6!) 12 ♗g5 ♘f6 13 ♗xf6 gf 14 ♘d2 f5 15 d5 c5 16 ♕c3!+ – was the grizzly continuation.

6 0–0 ♗e7

6 ... ♘c6 allows White to seize the advantage by forceful means. **7 c4** and now:

(a) **7 ... ♘de7** 8 ed ♕xd6 (8 ... cd 9 d5) 9 ♘c3 ♗xf3 (9 ... 0–0–0 10 ♘g5! ♗xe2 11 ♘xe2 ♘xd4 12 ♘c3!±; 9 ... ♘g6 10 d5! ed 11 cd ♗xf3 12 gf! ♘ce5 13 ♘b5 ♕d7 14 f4 ♘h4 15 fe ♕h3 16 ♘xc7+

♔d8 17 ♘e6+! 1–0 Aronin–Mikenas, Yaroslavl 1951) 10 ♗xf3 ♘xd4 (10 ... 0–0–0 11 ♘b5! ♕d7 12 ♕b3! a6 13 ♘a7+ ♔b8 14 ♘xc6+ ♘xc6 15 ♗e3 ♖e8 16 ♖fd1 ♘d8 17 d5! gave White an enormous attack in Matulović–Knežević, Bajmok 1975) 11 ♗xb7 ♖b8 12 ♗e4 (12 ♕a4+ ♕d7 13 ♕xa7±) 12 ... f5 13 ♗d3 ♔f7 14 ♗e3 ♖d8?! (14 ... c5±) was Ciocaltea–Knežević, Vrnjacka Banja 1975. 15 c5! ♕d7 (15 ... ♕xc5? 16 ♘b5!) 16 b4 ♘dc6 17 ♕b3! ♕xd3 18 ♖ad1 ♕a6 19 b5 (Ciocaltea) would then have been thoroughly unpleasant for Black.

(b) **7 ... ♘b6** 8 ed cd 9 d5 ed (9 ... ♗xf3 10 gf ♘e5? 11 f4 ♘ed7 12 de) 10 cd ♗xf3 (10 ... ♘e7? can be met by 11 ♖e1 or 11 ♘c3 g6?? 12 ♕d4 ♗xf3 13 ♗b5+ 1–0 Ernst–Storland, Gausdal 1987) 11 gf! ♘e5 12 ♗b5+ ♘ed7 (12 ... ♘bd7? 13 f4 ♘g6 14 f5 ♘e5 15 ♕e2 a6 16 ♗xd7+ 1–0 Wahls–Ostl, Bundesliga 1989/90) 13 ♕d4 ♕f6 14 ♖e1+ ♗e7 (14 ... ♔d8 15 ♕d1! ♕f5 16 ♘c3 ♘e5 17 f4 ♕g4+ 18 ♕xg4 ♘xg4 19 ♘a4! ♔c7 20 ♘xb6 ♔xb6 21 ♗e8! Boleslavsky) 15 ♕xf6 gf 16 ♘c3 a6 (16 ... ♔d8 17 f4 f5 18 ♗d3 ♗f6 19 ♗xf5 ♗xc3 20 bc ♘xd5 21 ♗a3± Bagirov) 17 ♗e2 ♘e5 18 f4 ♖g8+ 19 ♔f1 ♘g4 20 ♗d3! f5 21 ♗xf5± Vogt–Uddenfeldt, Skopje ol 1972.

6 ... a6 is quite a clever idea, as Black then intends 7 ... ♗xf3 8 ♗xf3 de, with the point 9 c4 ♘b6

10 ♗xb7 ♖a7. However, 7 c4 ♞b6 8 ed cd 9 ♞c3 ♗e7 10 ♗e3 exposes the artificial nature of Black's plan — see 6 ... ♗e7 7 c4 ♞b6 8 ♞c3 0–0 9 ♗e3 a6.

7 c4 ♞b6
8 ed cd *(94)*

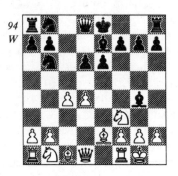

94
W

9 ♞bd2

9 ♞c3 is considered in the context of the game Short–Bagirov.

9 a4 d5 10 c5 ♗xf3 11 ♗xf3 ♞6d7 12 b4 is given as unclear by Hort. Black can seek immediate counterplay with 12 ... ♗f6 or 12 ... ♞c6.

9 b3 is a related idea to the text, but retains more flexibility with the queenside pieces. After **9 ... ♞c6**, 10 h3?! ♗xf3 11 ♗xf3 ♗f6 12 ♗e3 d5 13 c5 ♞d7!∓ threatened 14 ... ♞xc5 in Vitkovsky–Mikenas, Riga 1960, whilst 10 ♗b2 gives Black the choice between 10 ... d5 11 c5 ♞d7 12 a3 0–0 13 b4 a6 14 ♞bd2 ♗f6 15 h3 ♗h5 16 ♖e1 b6!? with decent play in Durão–Hecht, Málaga 1972, Hort's 10 ... ♗f6 11 ♞bd2 d5 12 c5 ♞d7, and transposing to

the main line below with 10 ... 0–0 11 ♞bd2. Therefore, White generally plays **10 ♞c3**:

(a) **10 ... ♗f6!?** 11 ♗e3 d5 12 c5 ♞d7 13 b4 ♗xf3 (13 ... ♞xb4 14 ♖b1 ♞c6 15 ♖xb7 ♞a5 16 ♖b5 a6 17 ♖b1 0–0 18 ♞a4 ♞c4 19 ♗xc4 dc 20 c6 ♞b8 21 ♞b6±) 14 ♗xf3 ♞xb4 15 ♖b1 ♞c6 16 ♖xb7 0–0! 17 ♛a4 ♛c8 18 ♖b3 was judged ± by Mikenas, e.g. 18 ... ♖d8 19 ♞b5?! (19 ♖fb1; 19 ♖c1) 19 ... ♞b6! 20 ♛a3 ♞c4 21 ♛a4 ♞b6 22 ♛a3 ♞c4 23 ♛a4 ½–½ Pogats–Cherenkov, USSR 1959, or 18 ... a6 19 ♞xd5! ed 20 ♗xd5 ♞d4 Szabo–Mikenas, Majus 1955.

(b) **10 ... 0–0 11 ♗e3 d5** (11 ... ♗f6 12 ♞e4 ♗e7 13 d5± Tal–Bagirov, Moscow 1979) **12 c5** and then can follow:

(b1) **12 ... ♞d7!?** 13 b4 ♞xb4 14 ♖b1 ♞c6 15 ♖xb7 ♖b8! 16 ♖xb8 ♞dxb8 17 h3 (17 ♛a4 ♛a5) 17 ... ♗xf3 ♛a5! (18 ... ♗xc5?? 19 dc d4 20 ♛a4+–) 19 ♛d3 ♗f6 20 ♖b1 ♞a6 21 ♖b5 ♞ab4! 22 ♛d2 ♛a3= Tal–Vasiukov, USSR Ch (Kharkov) 1967.

(b2) with h3 ♗h5, this variation is more difficult for Black, since the advance of White's g-pawn can cause problems. Therefore, it makes sense for Black to take on f3 immediately. After **13 ... ♗xf3 14 ♗xf3 ♞c8**:

(b21) **15 b4 ♗f6** (15 ... a6 16 ♖b1 ♗f6 17 a4 ♞8e7 18 b5 ab 19 ab ♞a5 20 ♗e2 ♞f5 21 ♗d3 g6. Black plans ... b6.) 16 b5 ♞a5 17

♗e2 b6 18 ♕c2 ♘e7 19 ♖ad1 ♘f5 20 c6 g6 21 ♕c1 ♗g7 22 g4 ♘xe3 23 ♕xe3 a6 24 a4 ♕d6 gave Black superb play in Zolnierowicz–Palatnik, Baku 1988.

(b22) **15 ♕d2 ♗f6 16 g4!?** g6 and now White should play 17 ♖ac1 b6 18 ♘a4±. Instead 17 ♗g2? b6 18 ♘a4 bc 19 ♘xc5 ♘d6 20 ♖ac1 ♖ac8 21 a4 (else 21 ... ♘b5) 21 ... ♕e7! was good for Black in Adorjan–Timman, Amsterdam 1971.

9	...	♘c6
10	b3	0-0
11	♗b2	♗f5

11 ... ♕b8!? 12 ♘e1 ♗xe2 13 ♕xe2 d5 14 c5 ♘d7 15 ♘d3 ♗f6 16 ♘f3 b6 17 b4 cb 18 cb ♕b5 gave Black excellent play in Pacl–Bagirov, Wroclaw 1976.

With h3 ♗h5 inserted, **12 ... ♕b8** is equally viable, e.g. 13 ♗c3 a5 14 a3 ♖c8 15 ♖c1 (15 b4? ♘a4) 15 ... ♗g6 16 ♖e1 ♗f6 17 ♗f1 d5$\overline{\overline{=}}$ Bertok–Kovačević, Vinkovci 1976.

Also with h3 ♗h5, **12 ... ♗g6** is analogous to the text. 13 a3 a5 14 ♖e1 (14 ♗c3 ♗f6 15 ♖e1 e5 16 ♘f1 e4 17 ♘3h2= Tal–Bagirov, Leningrad 1977) 14 ... ♗f6 15 ♖c1 (15 ♘f1 ♖c8 16 ♘e3 ♗h5 17 ♘g4 ♗xg4 18 hg g6 19 ♕d2 ♗g7= Tseshkovsky–Alburt, Leningrad 1974) 15 ... d5 16 c5 ♘d7 17 ♗c3 b6 18 b4 (18 ♗b5 ♘db8 19 b4 ab 20 ab bc 21 bc ♕c7=) 18 ... ab 19 ab bc 20 bc ♕c7= (20 ... ♖a3!? 21 ♘f1 ♕a8! 22 ♘e3 ♖b8 23 ♘g4 ♗d8$\overline{=}$ Bagi-

rov) 21 ♘f1 ♖fb8 22 ♘e3 ♕b7 23 ♘g4 ♗d8 24 ♗d3 ♕b3 gave Black excellent play in Kudrin–Bagirov, Belgrade GMA 1988.

Black should probably delay the ... d5 advance, e.g. **11 ... d5** 12 c5 ♘d7 13 b4 b6 14 ♕b3 ♕c7 (Kagan–Birnboim, Netanya 1977) 15 ♖fc1±, or, with h3 ♗h5, **12 ... d5** 13 c5 ♘d7 14 ♗c3!? b6 15 b4 bc 16 bc ♕c7 17 ♕a4 ♗g6 (17 ... ♗xf3 18 ♘xf3 e5 19 ♗b5 ed 20 ♗xc6 ♘xc5 21 ♕xd4± Kapengut) 18 ♘b3 e5?! (18 ... a6 19 ♘a5 ♘db8±) 19 ♗b5 ♘b6 20 ♗a5!! won material in Kapengut–M. Ivanov, Yalta 1976.

12	a3	a5
13	♖e1	(95)

13 b4 ab 14 ab ♖xa1 15 ♗xa1 ♘xb4 16 ♕b3 ♘a6! 17 ♗c3 ♘d7 18 ♕xb7 ♕c8 19 ♕xc8 ½-½ Frois–Bagirov, Cascais 1986.

13 ♗c3 ♕b8 14 b4? ♘a4! is an idea worth noting.

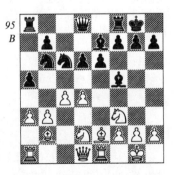

95
B

13	...	♗f6

13 ... d5 may well be better. 14 c5 ♘d7 15 ♘f1 (15 ♗b5 ♕c7 16 ♗c3 b6) 15 ... e5 16 ♘e3 ♗e6

17 ♘xe5 (17 de ♗xc5 18 ♘xd5
♘dxe5 19 ♘xe5 ♘xe5 20 ♗xe5
♕xd5=) 17 ... ♘dxe5 18 de ♗xc5
19 ♗d3 ♕b6 20 ♖c1 g6 21 h4
♗xe3 22 ♖xe3 d4= led to a draw
in Matulović–Vukić, Uljma 1976.
Minić also proposed **13 ... ♕b8**
14 ♘f1 d5 as possibly superior.

14   ♖c1

14 ♗f1 d5 15 c5 ♘d7 16 ♖c1
♕b8 17 ♗b5 ♖c8 18 b4 ab 19 ab
b6 20 ♕e2 bc 21 bc ♖a5 22 ♗xc6
♖xc6 23 ♖a1 ♖axc5!∓ was a good
exchange sacrifice in Benjamin–
Alburt, US Ch (Jacksonville) 1981.

14 ♘f1 is logical with the bishop
a little exposed on f5: 14 ... d5 15
c5 ♘d7 16 ♕d2 b6 17 b4 ab 18 ab
♕c7 19 ♘e3 ♗e4 20 ♘g4± ♗e7
21 ♗c3 ♖fd8 22 b5 ♖xa1 23 ♖xa1
♗xf3 was Matulović–Kovačević,
Rovinj–Zagreb 1975. 24 gf?! ♘a7
25 c6 ♘f8 26 ♖a6 ♘c8 27 ♖a8
♗d6 28 h3 ♕e7 gave Black
counterplay, but Minić suggested
that the natural 24 ♗xf3 ♘a7 25
♕b2 should maintain an advantage.

14	...	d5
15	c5	♘d7
16	♘f1	b6
17	♗b5	♖c8
18	♕d2	♗e4!
19	cb	

Ftačnik recommends 19 b4±,
as after the text White's extra
pawn cannot be maintained.

19	...	♕xb6
20	♗xc6	♖xc6
21	♖xc6	♕xc6
22	♕xa5	♕c2

23	♕c3	♖c8!
24	♕xc2	♖xc2
25	♗a1	♗e7
26	a4	♗b4
27	♘e3	½–½

In view of 27 ... ♗xe1 28 ♘xc2
♗xc2 29 ♘xe1 ♗xb3.

Short–Bagirov
Baku 1989

1 e4 ♘f6 2 e5 ♘d5 3 d4 d6 4 ♘f3
♗g4 5 ♗e2 e6 6 0–0 ♗e7

7	h3	♗h5
8	c4	♘b6

White may now exchange
immediately on d6, whereafter 10
♘bd2 and 10 b3 are considered in
the context of the game Vogt–
Bagirov.

9   ♘c3

9 ♗e3 0–0 **10 ♘bd2 ♘c6 11 ed
cd 12 ♖c1** *(96)* is a relatively
recent idea. Note that the move-
order is important, since 9 ed cd
10 ♗e3 d5 strikes at c4 before it
has been reinforced by White's
knight. Now:

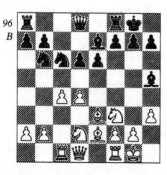

(a) **12 ... e5?** 13 de de 14 ♘xe5
♗xe2 15 ♘xc6 ♗xd1 16 ♘xd8±
Przewoznik.

(b) **12 ... a5** 13 ♖e1 d5 14 c5 ♘d7 15 ♕a4 ♗g6 16 ♗b5 ♕c7 17 ♘b1!? ♘f6 (17 ... ♗e4 can be met by 18 ♗e2 and ♘c3–b5.) 18 ♗xc6 bc 19 ♘e5 ♖fc8 20 ♘c3 ♘d7 21 ♘xd7 ♕xd7 22 ♕d1! ♖cb8 23 ♘a4 ♗d8 24 ♗f4 ♖b7 25 ♕d2 ♖aa7 26 b3 ♖b4 27 ♕e3 h6 28 ♖cd1 ♔h7 29 g4 condemned Black to a difficult defence in Rodriguez–Marinković, Amsterdam 1987. White won by means of a prolonged kingside attack.

(c) **12 ... d5** 13 c5 ♘c8 (Without h3 ♗h5, 12 ... ♘d7 13 b4 a6 14 a3 f5 15 ♘b5 g5 gave Black counterplay in Lein–Peters, US Ch 1980.) 14 b4 (After 14 a3 a5 15 ♕a4 f5!? 16 ♗f4 g5, Przewoznik considers Black's counterplay reasonable.) 14 ... a6 (14 ... h6 15 b5 ♘a5 15 ♗f4±; 14 ... ♘xb4 15 ♕b3 a5 16 a3 ♘c6 17 ♕xb7 ♘8a7 18 ♗d3! ♖b8 19 ♕a6 ♖b2?! 20 ♖b1 ♕b8? 21 ♗f4!±) 15 ♕b3 ♗f6 16 a4 a5 (16 ... e5 17 de ♘xe5 18 ♖fe1±; 16 ... h6!?) 17 b5 ♘b4 18 ♗f4! h6 (18 ... ♘e7? walks into g4–g5+ −.) 19 ♖fe1 ♘e7 20 ♗d6! ♖e8 21 ♘e5 ♗xe2 22 ♗xe7! ♖xe7 23 ♖xe2 ♗xe5 24 ♖xe5 ♕c7 (24 ... f6 25 ♖e3 e5 26 ♖ce1) 25 ♖ce1 ♖ae8 26 ♕c3 f6 27 ♖5e3 e5 28 ♘b3 e4 29 b6 ♕d7 30 ♘xa5 ♘d3 (30 ... ♕xa4 31 ♖a1 ♕b5 32 ♘xb7 ♖xb7 33 ♖b1+ −) 31 ♖a1 ♖e6 32 c6! gave White two unstoppable passed pawns in Przewoznik–Solozhenkin, Naleczow 1988.

9 ...   0-0

10 ed   cd
11 ♗e3

11 ♖e1 hopes to gain a tempo over normal lines, by accomplishing b2–b4 in one move, while not allowing ... ♘c4, e.g. 11 ... d5?! 12 c5 ♘6d7 13 b4 ♗xf3 14 ♗xf3 ♗f6 15 ♖b1 ♘c6 16 ♗e3± Lobron–Hammer, Biel 1981. Black's best reply is **11 ... a6!**, threatening ... ♗xf3 by freeing a7 for the rook. After **12 b3 ♘c6**:

(a) without h3 ♗h5, **12 ♗b2** de 13 ♘e5?! (13 c5 ♗xf3 14 ♗xf3 ♘c8=) 13 ... ♗xe2 14 ♕xe2 ♘xe5 15 de dc was promising for Black in Planinc–Vukić, Yugoslav Ch 1975.

(b) **13 ♗e3** d5 14 c5 ♗xf3 15 ♗xf3 ♘c8 16 ♖b1 ♗f6 17 b4 ♘8e7 18 ♗g4 g6 19 a4 h5 20 b5!± Smyslov–Schmidt, Moscow–Warsaw 1980.

(c) **13 d5?!** ♗f6! (13 ... ed 14 ♘xd5 ♘xd5 15 ♕xd5 ♗f6 16 ♕xh5 was Kupreichik–Palatnik, Lvov 1986. Black should have settled for 16 ... ♗xa1 17 ♗g5 ♗f6 18 ♗d3 g6 19 ♕h4 ♔g7 20 ♗h6+ ♔g8 21 ♗g5 with a draw.) 14 dc ♗xc3 15 cb ♖b8 16 c5 ♗xa1 17 ♗g5 ♗f6 18 ♗xf6 ♕xf6 19 c6 ♘c3! 20 ♕c1 ♕a5 21 a3 ♘d5 22 b4 ♕b6 23 ♖d1 ♘e7 24 ♖xd6 ♗xf3 25 ♗xf3 ♖xb7 26 cb ♕xd6 27 ♕e3 ♖b8 28 ♕a7 ♕c7 29 a4 ♘d5 0–1 Djurić–Palatnik, Tallinn 1986.

11 ♗f4 can be met by 11 ... ♘c6 12 d5 ed 13 ♘xd5 ♗xf3 14 ♗xf3 ♘xc4 15 ♕b3 ♘b6.

11	...	d5
12	c5	♗xf3
13	♗xf3	♘c4
14	♗f4	

14 ♗c1 ♘c6 15 b3 ♘4a5. Now:

(a) **16 ♗e3** b6 17 ♘a4 (17 cb ♕xb6 18 ♘a4 ♕b4=) 17 ... ♗f6 is given as unclear by Alburt.

(b) **16 ♖b1** ♗f6 17 ♘e2 a6 18 a4!? (18 b4 ♘c4 19 a4 b5!=). Now 18 ... b6? 19 b4 ♘c4 20 b5 was good for White in Mednis–Martz, US Ch 1972. Mednis recommends 18 ... ♘b4! 19 ♗a3 ♘ac6=.

(c) **16 ♗b2** ♗f6 17 ♘a4 g6 (Sergeev suggests saving two tempi with 17 ... ♕c7, ... ♖ad8 and ... e5.) 18 ♗e2 ♗g7 19 ♕d2 ♕c7 20 ♖ac1 ♖ad8 21 ♗c3!? e5 22 de ♗xe5 23 f4! ♗xc3 24 ♘xc3± Savon–Sergeev, USSR 1990.

14	...	♘c6

14 ... ♗g5!? 15 ♗xg5 ♕xg5 16 ♗e2 ♘c6 17 b3?? (17 ♗xc4 dc 18 ♘e2 ♖fd8 19 ♖c1 ♕d5 20 ♕c2= Bagirov) 17 ... ♘e3! 0–1 Short–Gil, World Junior (Glostrup) 1982.

15	b3	♘4a5
16	♖c1	b6
17	cb	

17 ♘a4 ♗f6 18 ♗e3 b5!? 19 ♘c3 b4 20 ♘e2 ♘e7 followed by ... ♘ac6, grants Black equality.

17	...	♕xb6
18	♗e3	♖ac8

18 ... ♗f6 19 ♘a4 ♕b4 20 ♖c5 ♗xd4 21 ♗d2 ♗xc5 was reasonable for Black in Short–Wiemer, Bundesliga 1983. Bagirov proposes **20 ♕d3!** since Black can-not take on d4: 20 ... ♗xd4 21 a3! or 20 ... ♘xd4 21 ♗d2! ♘xf3+ 22 gf.

19	♘a4	♕b8
20	♘c5	♗xc5
21	♖xc5	

After 21 dc ♖fd8 Black's central pawns are a considerable force.

21	...	♘b7
22	♖c3	♘e7

22 ... ♘d6 allows White to control the c-file with 23 ♕d2 and ♖fc1.

23	♖xc8	♖xc8
24	♕d3	♘d6
25	♖c1	♘df5
26	♖xc8+	♕xc8
27	♗d2	♘c6
28	♗c3	a5
29	♗d1	♕b7
30	g4	♘d6
31	a4!	*(97)*

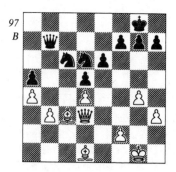

Black's accurate play has succeeded in limiting White's queen-side ambitions, but full equality is still some way off. The following semi-ending is of an important type for the opening as a whole.

31	...	g6
32	f3	♕b6
33	♔g2	♘b4
34	♕d2	♘c6
35	♕f4	♘b4
36	h4	♔f8
37	h5	♘e8
38	h6	♔e7
39	♗e1	♘d3
40	♗h4+	f6
41	♕e3	♘b4
42	f4	

42 ♕c3!? ♘d6 43 ♗e2 ♕c6! (43 ... ♘c6? 44 ♕c5!) **44 ♕c5!** (44 ♗e1? ♘f7!) **44 ... ♕xc5 45 dc ♘b7!** (45 ... ♘f7? 46 ♗b5 ♘xh6 47 g5!) **46 ♗f2 e5 47 ♗b5 d4** (47 ... ♘d8? 48 ♗e1 ♘e6 49 ♗xb4 ab 50 ♗c6!!±) **48 c6 ♘d6 49 c7 ♘d5 50 ♗e1 ♘xc7 51 ♗c6 ♘f7 52 ♗xa5 ♔d6 53 ♗b7 ♘xh6 54 ♗b4+** is Bagirov's analysis. White retains marginally the better chances.

42	...	♘c6!

Else 43 f5 is strong.

43	♗f2	♘d6
44	♗c2	

44 f5 gf 45 g5 ♘e4 46 gf+ ♔xf6 47 ♗h4+ ♔f7 48 ♗h5+ ♔f8∞ Bagirov.

44	...	♔f7
45	f5	ef
46	gf	♘xf5
47	♗xf5	gf
48	♕g3	♕a7!!

The only defence to White's threats. The game concluded: 49 ♕g7+ (49 ♕d6 ♘b4) 49 ... ♔e6 50 ♕g8+ ♕f7 51 ♕c8+ ♕d7 52 ♕g8+ ♕f7 53 ♕a8 ♕c7! 54 ♗g3

♕d7 (54 ... f4!? 55 ♕g8+ ♔f5 56 ♕xd5+ ♔g4 57 ♕f3+ ♔g5∞) 55 ♕g8+ ♕f7 56 ♕c8+ ♕d7 57 ♕g8+ ♕f7 58 ♕a8 ♕d7 59 ♗f4 ♔f7! 60 ♕h8 ♔g6! 61 ♕g8+ ♔h5 62 ♕g3 ½-½ (62 ... ♘xd4 63 ♕d3 ♘c6 64 ♕h3+ ♔g6=).

Kokkila–Biehler
Groningen 1986

1 e4 ♘f6 2 e5 ♘d5 3 d4 d6 4 ♘f3 ♗g4 5 ♗e2 e6 6 0-0 ♗e7 7 c4 ♘b6 8 ♘c3 0-0

9	♗e3	d5

Black can try to profit from White's omission of h3 ♗h5 by playing **9 ... ♘c6!? 10 ed cd 11 d5 ed**:

(a) **12 ♗xb6 ♕xb6 13 ♘xd5 ♕xb2 14 ♖b1 ♕xa2 15 ♘xe7+ ♘xe7 16 ♖xb7=** Bagirov.

(b) **12 cd ♗xf3 13 ♗xf3 ♘e5 14 ♗e2** (14 ♗d4 ♗f6 15 ♗e2 ♘ec4 16 ♘e4 ♗xd4 17 ♕xd4 ♘e5 18 f4 ♘ed7 19 ♘xd6 ♘f6= Nasibullin–Baburin, Novosibirsk 1989) **14 ... ♘bc4** (14 ... ♖c8; 14 ... ♘ed7 15 ♗f4!? and now 15 ... ♖c8 is better than 15 ... ♖e8?! 16 a4 ♖c8 17 a5! ♘c4 18 ♕b3! ♘xa5 19 ♕b4± Ciocaltea–Schmidt, Malta ol 1980.) **15 ♗d4 ♖c8 16 b3 ♘b6= 17 a4 a6 18 a5 ♘bd7 19 f4 ♘g6 20 b4 ♖e8 21 ♕d3 ♗f6 22 ♗g4** (Sahović–Schmidt, Sombor 1978) **22 ... ♖c7!.**

(c) **12 ♘xd5 ♘xd5 13 ♕xd5** (13 cd?! ♗xf3 14 ♗xf3 ♘e5= 15 ♗e2 f5! 16 f4 ♘d7 17 ♕b3 ♗f6 18 ♗f3 ♖e8 19 ♖fe1 ♕a5 20 ♔f1 ♘b6 ½-½ Short–Hort, Dortmund

1986) **13 ... &f6** *(98)* (13 ... ♛c8
14 b3 ♛e6 15 ♛d2±; 13 ... &e6
14 ♛d2±) and now:

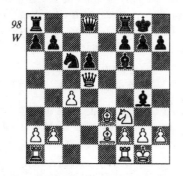

(c1) **14 ♛d2** ♛a5 15 ♖fd1 ♖fd8!?
16 ♛c2?! d5!∓ Hort.

(c2) **14 ♖ad1** &xb2 15 ♛b5 (15
♖b1 &e6! 16 ♛b5 &f6 17 ♛xb7
♖c8 18 ♛a6 ½–½ Tukmakov–
Olafsson, Moscow 1971.) 15 ...
&a3 16 ♛xb7 Kurajica.

(c3) **14 ♖ab1** &e6 (14 ... ♛c8!?
Hort) 15 ♛b5 d5!? 16 ♖bd1 d4 17
♛xb7 ♛d6 18 ♛a6 ♛c5 19 ♛b5
(19 &f4 ♖ad8!) 19 ... ♛xb5 20 cb
de 21 bc ef+!? 22 ♖xf2 ♖ab8!? 23
♘d4 &xa2 24 ♖xf6!? gf 25 &g4
♖xb2! was promising for Black in
Matanović–Ghizdavu, Bath 1973.

(c4) **14 ♖fd1** ♖c8 (14 ... &e6 15
♛d2 ♛a5 16 ♘d4± Sax; 14 ...
♛c8?! 15 ♖d2 ♘e5 16 ♖c1 b6 17
b3 ♖d8 18 ♖cd1± Georgadze–
Grigorian, Vilnius 1971) 15 ♖d2
(15 ♛d2; 15 ♛xd6? ♛xd6 16 ♖xd6
&xb2 17 ♖b1 &a3 18 ♖d3 &f5!)
15 ... ♛a5! 16 ♛xa5 (16 ♛xd6?
&xf3 17 &xf3 ♖cd8! 18 ♛f4
&e5!∓   Browne–Hort,   San
Antonio 1972) 16 ... ♘xa5 17

♖c1 and now Black can try for
counterplay with 17 ... &xf3 or
17 ... b5.

Note   that   with   h3   &h5
inserted, **10 ... ♘c6** is dubious: 11
ed cd 12 d5 ed 13 ♘xd5 &xf3
(13 ... ♘xd5 14 ♛xd5 &g5 15
♖ad1±) 14 &xb6 ab 15 &xf3
&f6 16 ♘xf6+ ♛xf6 17 ♛d2 ♖fe8
(17 ... ♖a5?! 18 &d5 ♖fa8 19
♖fe1± Nunn–M. Kuijf, Lugano
1987) 18 ♖fe1 ♖e5 19 ♖e4 ♖ae8
20 ♖ae1 is considered by Nunn to
give White only a small advantage,
but it is a very clear one.

9 ... a5 is more playable than
with h3 &h5, but still holds little
prospect of equality.

(a) **10 ed** cd offers White some
advantage after 11 ♘b5 ♘a6 12
♖c1 a4 13 h3 &h5 14 ♛d2
Chandler–Wiemer,   Bundesliga
1983/4, or 11 d5 &xf3 12 &xf3
♘xc4 13 de fe.

(b) **10 b3**

(b1) **10 ... ♘a6** appears to have
been   rendered   unplayable   by
Dorfman's energetic treatment: 11
h3 &f5 (11 ... &h5 12 g4) 12 g4!
&g6 13 h4! de?! (13 ... &xh4? 14
g5 traps the bishop; 13 ... h5 14
g5 &f5 15 ed cd 16 d5 e5 17 ♘d2
g6 18 ♘de4 with f4 to follow,
opening   lines   towards   Black's
king; 13 ... h6!? 14 g5 hg 15 hg
&h5 might be Black's best, but
still leaves White with a powerful
kingside initiative.) 14 h5 &b4 15
hg &xc3 16 gf+ ♖xf7 (16 ... ♔h8
17 ♘xe5 &xa1 18 ♔g2!+−) 17
♘xe5 &xa1 18 ♘xf7 ♔xf7 19

♕xa1 left Black with weak pawns and hopelessly uncoordinated pieces in Dorfman–Bagirov, Moscow GMA 1989.

(b2) **10 ... d5** 11 c5 ♘6d7 (11 ... ♗xf3 12 ♗xf3 ♘6d7 13 ♗e2 b6 14 cb ♘xb6 15 ♖c1 c6 16 f4 f5 17 ef ♗xf6 and White's plan of ♕c2, ♗d3, ♘e2 and a kingside pawn storm proved effective in Wahls–Wiemer, Bundesliga 1986/7.) 12 ♘e1 (12 a3 f6 13 ef ♗xf6 14 ♕d2 ♗xf3 15 ♗xf3 c6± P. Littlewood–Alburt, Hastings 1980/1; 12 ♖c1 c6?! 13 ♘d2 ♗xe2 14 ♕xe2 b6 15 cb ♕xb6 16 ♕g4 ♔h8 17 ♘f3 ♘a6 18 ♗g5 ♕d8 19 ♘e2 c5 20 ♖fd1 ♖c8 21 ♘f4 h6 22 ♗xe7 ♕xe7 23 ♘h5 ♖g8 24 ♖c3 ♔h7 25 h4 g6? 26 ♘f6+ ♘xf6 27 ef ♕xf6 28 ♘g5+! hg 29 hg ♕h8 30 ♖h3+ ♔g7 31 dc 1–0 Mainka–Graf, Bundesliga 1990/1) 12 ... ♗xe2 13 ♕xe2 b6 14 cb c5? (14 ... ♘xb6 15 f4 g6 16 ♘d3±) 15 ♘a4! cd 16 ♗xd4± Illescas–Fernandez Garcia, Las Palmas 1987.

9 ... a6 gives Black little hope of equal play, whether White resorts to forceful measures or not, e.g. **10 ed** cd 11 d5 ♗xf3 12 ♗xf3 ♘xc4 13 de fe 14 ♗g4 ♕d7 15 ♕e2 ♘e5 16 ♗h3 ♘bc6 17 f4 ♘f7 18 ♗b6 ♘fd8 19 ♘d5± Ulybin–Kengis, Pinsk 1986, or **10 b3** ♘8d7 11 h3 ♗f5 12 ed cd 13 ♖e1 h6 14 ♗d3± Chandler–Hort, Surakarta 1982. Most incisive, with h3 ♗h5, is **11 ed** (11 ♕b3!?) 11 ... cd 12 c5! ♘c8 (12 ... dc 13 dc ♘6d7 14 b4; 12 ... ♘6d7 13 ♕b3 b6 14

♖fd1) 13 ♕b3 ♕c7 (13 ... b6 14 d5!?) 14 cd! ♗xd6 15 ♖ac1 ♘c6?! (15 ... ♕e7) 16 d5! ed 17 ♘xd5± Mestel–Kovačević, Plovdiv 1983. Note that **8 ... a6** (instead of 8 ... 0–0) changes nothing, since 9 ♗e3 ♗xf3?! 10 ♗xf3 ♘xc4? (10 ... de±) 11 ♕a4+ b5 12 ♘xb5! wins.

	10	**c5**	♗xf3
	11	**gf!**	

The capture with the bishop, 11 ♗xf3, is naturally feasible here, but in this case the omission of h3 can hardly help White.

	11	**...**	♘c8

11 ... ♘6d7 rather neglects the d5 square. A good example of the importance of this was Bjelalac–Vukić, Yugoslav Ch 1977: 12 b4 a6 (12 ... f6 13 f4 f5 14 ♔h1 ♔h8 15 ♖g1 ♖g8 16 b5!±) 13 f4 ♘c6 14 ♖b1 ♔h8 15 a4 f5 16 ♔h1 ♖g8 17 ♖g1 ♕f8 18 ♗f3! ♕f7 19 ♕b3! ♖gd8 20 ♘xd5 ed 21 ♗xd5 ♕h5 22 ♖g3 ♗h4 23 ♗f3 ♕e8 24 ♖g2 ♖ab8 25 ♖bg1 ♕f8 26 ♕c3 ♖e8 27 b5 ab 28 ab ♘e7 29 d5 ♘g6 30 ♗h5 ♕g8 31 ♕d3 ♘xc5!? 32 ♕xf5 ♖f8 33 ♕g4 ♘xf4 and now 34 ♗xc5! ♘xg2 35 ♖xg2 would have won easily.

	12	**♔h1**	

This is a very direct approach. White intends to kill Black down the g-file, or, by threatening to do so, cause so much inconvenience that Black will never be able to organize much of a position.

Another aggressive move is **12 f4**. Then **12 ... ♘c6** is considered in the game Aseev–Bagirov. It is difficult to recommend the alternatives:

12 ... c6 13 ♗d3 (13 f5!? ef 14 ♗d3) 13 ... g6 14 b4± Gurgenidze–Suba, Varna 1975.

12 ... a5 13 f5 ♗g5 14 f4 ♗h6 15 fe fe 16 ♗g4± Shamkovich–Vukić, New York 1976.

12 ... g6 13 f5 (13 ♔h1 ♔h8 14 f5 gf?! 15 ♖g1 ♘c6 16 ♕d2 and White simply walked into Black's kingside in Kiik–Jänes, Tartu 1986.) 13 ... ef (13 ... gf 14 ♗h6) 14 ♕b3± b6? 15 ♗h6 ♖e8 16 ♕xd5 c6? 17 ♕xf7+!+− Dietrich–Kindl, Böblingen 1989.

12 ... ♗h4 13 ♗d3 g6 (13 ... ♘e7!? 14 ♗xh7+; 13 ... f5?! 14 ef g6 15 f7+! ♖xf7 16 ♘g4 ♕e7?! 17 ♘xd5+−) 14 f5! (14 ♕g4!? h5 15 ♕h3±) 14 ... ef 15 ♕f3! c6 16 ♔h1 ♔h8 17 ♖g1 ♘e7 18 ♕h3! (An example of White's access to the h3 square being tremendously important.) 18 ... ♘g8 19 ♗xf5!+− ♗e7 (19 ... gf 20 ♕g2 ♗f6 21 ef ♕xf6 22 ♘e2! with ♗f4 to follow.) 20 ♘e2 ♘a6 21 ♘f4 ♔g7 22 ♗xg6! 1–0 Pokojowczyk–Schmidt, Poland 1976.

12 ... f5 13 ♔h1 (13 ef!? ♗xf6 14 f5 ef 15 ♘xd5 c6?! 16 ♘xf6+ ♕xf6 17 ♕b3+ ♔h8 18 ♕xb7+− Düster–Christ, Wiesbaden Open 1988.) Black has a hard time defending the kingside:

(a) **13 ... ♖f7** 14 ♖g1 g6 15 b4 ♘c6 16 b5 (A more measured queenside advance may cause Black more problems — compare Georgiev–Popov below.) 16 ...

♘a5 17 ♕a4 b6 18 ♖ac1 ♗h4 19 ♘b1 ♕e8 20 ♕b4 ♖g7 21 ♘d2 ♗d8 22 ♘f3 was Hjartarson–Milos, Szirak IZ 1987. Black's position is solid but passive.

(b) **13 ... g6** 14 b4 ♘c6 15 ♖g1 ♔h8 (15 ... ♖f7) 16 ♖g2 ♖g8 17 a3 ♗h4 18 ♗f3 ♘8e7 19 ♕d2 a6 20 ♘e2 ♖g7 21 ♘c1 ♘g8 22 ♘d3 gave White very pleasant prospects on both sides of the board in Kir. Georgiev–Popov, Bulgarian Ch (Sofia) 1986.

(c) **13 ... ♔h8** 14 ♖g1 ♗h4? (14 ... g6) 15 ♗h5 ♕e7?! (15 ... g6? 16 ♗xg6!; 15 ... ♘e7 16 ♕f3 g6 17 ♕h3!) 16 ♗g6! gave White an overwhelming attack in Kharitonov–Dautov, Kaliningrad 1986: after 16 ... hg 17 ♖xg6 ♕f7 18 ♕h5+ ♔g8 19 ♕h6! ♘e7 20 ♖g2 g5, 21 ♖ag1! would have been immediately decisive.

(d) **13 ... ♘c6** 14 b4 a6 15 ♖b1 ♔h8 16 a4 a5 17 b5 ♘b4 18 ♖g1 ♖f7? (18 ... ♖g8) 19 ♗h5 g6 (19 ... ♖f8 20 ♕f3) 20 ♖xg6!+− Bjelajac–Popov, Novi Sad 1981.

12 ...   f5

12 ... ♘c6 13 ♖g1 f5 (13 ... ♔h8 14 f4 ♗xc5 15 f5 ♗e7 16 f6! ♗xf6 17 ef ♕xf6 18 ♖g4 ♕e7 19 ♗d3 ♘d6 20 ♕f3 f5 21 ♕h3 ♖f7 22 ♖ag1 ♘e8 23 ♘e2 ♘f6 24 ♘f4 ♔g8 25 ♖h4 ♕d6 26 ♘xe6+− Korneev–Bagirov, Moscow 1990) 14 ♗h6 ♖f7 15 f4 ♔h8 16 ♗h5 g6 17 ♖xg6! hg 18 ♗xg6 ♕g8 19 ♕h5 ♖h7 20 ♗xh7 ♕g4 (20 ... ♕xh7 21 ♕e8+ ♕g8 22 ♗g7+!) 21 ♗g7+ ♕xg7 22

♖g1 ♗f8 23 ♖xg7 ♗xg7 24 ♗xf5+ 1-0 Guillen–Urday, Asunción 1987.

12 ... ♗h4 13 ♖g1 (In Ciocaltea–Bagirov, Tbilisi 1974, Black was allowed time to organise a position: 13 ♗d3 ♘e7 14 f4?! g6 15 ♕g4 ♘f5 16 ♗xf5 ef 17 ♕f3 c6=) 13 ... ♘e7 (13 ... f6 14 f4 fe 15 fe ♗xf2 16 ♗xf2 ♖xf2 17 ♖xg7+! ♔xg7 18 ♕g1+ ♔h8 19 ♕xf2 ♘d7 20 ♖g1 ♕f8 21 ♕g3 ♘e7 22 ♗g4 ♖d8 23 ♗xe6 ♘b8 24 ♕g2 ♘bc6 25 ♘xd5 ♘xd4 25 ♖f1 ♕h6 27 ♗f7 ♘xd5 28 ♗xd5 ♘e6 29 ♖g1 ♘g7 30 ♕f3 c6 31 ♗b3 ♘e6 32 ♕g3 ♘g7 33 ♗f7 ♖d2 34 ♖f1 ♖d8 35 e6 1-0 Shemagonov–Khramov, Moscow 1987) 14 ♗d3 f5 (14 ... g6 15 ♕f1 ♘f5 16 ♗xf5 ef 17 ♕h3± Elliott–Cawte, Middlesex League 1988) 15 f4 ♘bc6 16 a3 ♘g6 17 ♘g6 ♖f7 18 ♘e2! ♔h8 19 ♘c1! ♔g8 20 ♘b3 ♘f8 21 ♕h5! g6 22 b5 ♖g7 23 ♕h6 ♘b8 24 a4 ♗e7 25 ♕h3! c6 26 ♕f3 ♕e8?! 27 ♕e2 ♗d8 28 ♘d2! h6 29 ♘f3 ♘h7 30 ♕d2 ♔h8 31 ♖g3! (Threatening ♖h3) 31 ... ♘f8 32 h4 ♘h7 33 ♖ag1+– Ciocaltea–Bondoc, Romania 1976.

13	♖g1	f4
14	♗d3	fe
15	fe	♕e8 *(99)*

A variation illustrating the full power of White's conception is 15 ... ♗g5 16 f4 ♗h6 17 ♕h5 ♔h8 18 ♖xg7! ♔xg7 19 ♖g1+ ♔h8 20 ♕xh6 ♖f7 21 ♕xe6 ♕d7 22 ♕h6 ♖g7 23 ♕f6 ♕e7 (23 ... ♔g8

24 ♖xg7+ ♕xg7 25 ♕d8+ ♕f8 26 ♕xd5+) 24 ♖xg7 ♕xg7 25 ♕d8+ ♕g8 26 ♕xg8+ ♔xg8 27 ♘xd5 ♘a6 (27 ... ♘d7 28 ♗f5+–) 28 ♗xa6 ba 29 ♘xc7 ♖b8 30 d5 when the swathe of pawns is unstoppable.

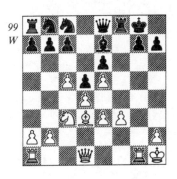

99
W

16	f4	♕f7
17	♕g4	♗d8
18	f5	♘e7

Since 18 ... ef fails trivially to 19 ♗xf5, Black must let the f-pawn do its worst. The rest is slaughter.

19	f6	♘g6
20	♕h5	♗xf6
21	♖af1	♘d7
22	♖xg6	♖fd8
23	♕xh7+	1-0

Aseev–Bagirov
Berlin 1990

1 e4 ♘f6 2 e5 ♘d5 3 d4 d6 4 ♘f3 ♗g4 5 ♗e2 e6 6 0-0 ♗e7 7 c4 ♘b6 8 h3 ♗h5 9 ♘c3 0-0 10 ♗e3

| 10 | ... | d5 |

10 ... a5 has a serious disadvantage compared to 9 ... a5 (without h3 ♗h5): 11 ed cd 12 ♕b3! ♘8d7

(12 ... a4 13 ♕b5 hits the bishop of h5. After it retreats, both 14 c5 and 14 d5 give White a solid plus.) 13 ♕b5 (13 c5 ♘c8 14 ♖ac1!? ♕c7? 15 ♗f4 led to a quick win in Svensson–Sandström, Sweden 1990, but Black should play 14 ... dc 15 dc ♕c7.) 13 ... ♗g6 14 c5! (14 ♖fd1 ♕c7∞) 14 ... ♘c8 15 ♖fd1! ♕c7 (15 ... d5 16 ♕xb7±) 16 ♗f4! gave Black serious problems in Glek–Shabalov, Belgorod 1989. 16 ... b6 17 cd ♗xd6 (17 ... ♘xd6 18 ♕a4) 18 ♗e3!? (Glek suggests 18 ♘e5!? with such ideas as 18 ... ♖d8 19 ♗f3 ♘a7 20 ♕a6!± and 18 ... ♗xe5 19 de ♘c5 20 ♕c4! ♘a7 21 ♖d6±.) 18 ... a4 (18 ... ♘a7 19 ♕b3! b5 20 ♖dc1! a4 21 ♘xa4!) 19 ♖ac1 ♖a5 20 ♕c4 ♕xc4 21 ♗xc4 ♘a7 22 ♗e2 f5?! (22 ... a3 23 b3±) 23 ♘e5!+− ♘xe5 24 de ♗c5 25 ♗xc5 ♖xc5 26 ♘xa4 ♖xe5 27 ♗f1 ♘c8 28 ♗a6 set up an ending in which White's two connected passed pawns on the queenside proved decisive.

11   c5

11   cd

(a) **11 ... ♘xd5** 12 ♕b3 ♘b6 (12 ... ♘c6? 13 ♕xb7 ♘db4 14 ♕b5 ♖b8 15 ♕a4 ♗xf3 16 ♗xf3 ♘xd4 17 ♗xd4 ♕xd4 18 a3+− Kasparov–Gitsin, USSR 1977; 12 ... ♘xe3 13 fe± b6?! 14 d5! ♗c5 15 de± Georgadze–Alburt, Tbilisi 1977) 13 d5!? (13 ♖fd1 c6 14 a4 a5 15 d5 ♘xd5 16 ♕xb7 ♘d7 17 g4 ♗g6 18 ♕xc6 ♖c8∞ Lobron–Alburt, New York 1983) 13 ... ed (13 ... ♘xd5 14 ♖fd1 c6 15 ♕xb7

♘d7 16 g4 ♗g6 17 ♕xc6 ♖c8 18 ♕a4± illustrates an advantage of omitting a4.) 14 ♗xb6 ab 15 ♘xd5 ♗c5 16 ♖ad1 ♕c8 and now White can choose between 17 a3!? ♘c6 18 ♕c3 ♖e8 19 ♖fe1± (Kremenietsky) and 17 ♘f4 ♗xf3 18 ♗xf3 ♘c6 19 e6! ♘d4 20 ♖xd4 ♗xd4 21 ef+ ♖xf7 22 ♗g4 ♕d8 23 ♗e6 ♕f6 24 ♗xf7+ ♕xf7 25 ♘e6 ♗f6 26 ♖e1± Kremenietsky–Kolev, Ruse 1987.

(b) **11 ... ed.** Now White's most ambitious idea is 12 g4!? ♗g6 13 ♘e1. Then 13 ... f5 14 ♘d3 c6 15 ♘f4 ♕d7 16 ♔h2 ♘a6 17 ♘xg6 hg 18 gf gf 19 ♗xa6 ba 20 ♖g1± f4?! 21 ♖xg7+! ♔xg7 22 ♕h5 gave Black grave problems in Ornstein–Alburt, Reykjavik Open 1984, so a better try may be 13 ... ♗b4 14 ♖c1 ♘c6 15 ♘g2 f6 16 e6 ♕e7 17 ♘f4 ♗xc3 18 ♖xc3 ♘d8 19 ♕b3 c6 20 a4 ♗e8 21 a5 ♘c8 22 ♗f3 ♘d6 23 ♕b4 g5, though in Hebden–Bricard, Clermont-Ferrand 1989, 24 ♗xd5!? gave White interesting play.

11 b3 can be comfortably met by 11 ... dc 12 bc ♘c6 13 ♖b1 (13 g4 ♗g6 14 ♕b3 ♘a5!? 15 ♕b5 ♘bxc4! 16 ♗xc4 c6) 13 ... ♖b8!.

11   ...   ♗xf3

12   gf

12 ♗xf3 is rather unfashionable, though mainly due to the strength of capturing with the pawn rather than any defect of this very natural move. After **12 ... ♘c4:**

(a) **13 b3** ♘xe3 14 fe ♘c6 15

♖b1 (15 b4 a6) 15 ... f6 (15 ... a5 16 a3 b6 17 b4 ab 18 ab bc 19 bc ♖a3 was recommended by Petrosian.) 16 ef ♗xf6 17 b4 ♘e7 18 ♗g4 ♕d7 19 ♔h1 ♖ad8 20 e4 de 21 ♕b3 ♔h8 22 ♘xe4 ♘f5= Olafsson–Andersson, Nice ol 1974.

(b) **13 b4** saves a tempo over 13 b3, but Black need be in no hurry to capture on e3 and can choose between Alburt's **13 ... ♘c6** 14 b5 (14 ♖b1 a5!?) 14 ... ♘xe3 15 fe ♘xe5 16 de ♗xc5 with ... ♕g5 to follow, and Gipslis' **13 ... b6** 14 ♖c1 c6 15 ♗e2 a5 16 ♗xc4 ab!? 17 ♘a4 dc 18 ♘xb6 ♖xa2 19 ♖xc4 ♘a6 20 ♕b3 ♖a5∞.

(c) **13 ♗c1** poses few problems: 13 ... b6 14 b3 ♘a5 15 b4 (15 ♘a4 ♘b7! 16 ♕c2?! ♘c6 17 cb ♘xd4∓ Matanović–Vukić, Umag 1972) 15 ... ♘c4 16 ♗e2 a5! 17 ♗xc4 ab∓ Gufeld–Alburt, Baku 1972.

(d) **13 ♗f4 ♘c6** (13 ... b6 14 b3 ♘a5 15 ♖c1 bc 16 dc ♘ac6 17 ♖e1 ♗g5 18 ♘xd5!? ed 19 ♗xg5 ♕xg5 20 ♗xd5 was rather a promising sacrifice in Kavalek–Schmid, Nice ol 1974. After 20 ... ♔h8, White should have tried 21 ♕e2 a5 22 ♕e4 ♖a6 23 f4.) **14 b3 ♘4a5.** Now **15 ♕d2** b6 (15 ... ♕d7) 16 ♖ac1 (16 ♘a4 f6) 16 ... bc 17 dc ♖b8! 18 ♗xd5 (18 ♘e2!?) 18 ... ed 19 ♘xd5 ♖b5 20 b4 ♘xb4 21 ♘xb4 ♕xd2 22 ♗xd2 ♖d8 23 ♗c3 ♖xc5 was equal in Geller–Timman, Wijk aan Zee 1975. A more common move is **15 ♖c1** (100):

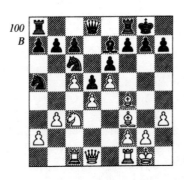

(d1) **15 ... b6** 16 ♘a4! ♗g5 (16 ... f6 17 ef ♗xf6 18 cb ab 19 b4! ♘xb4 20 ♕e1! ♘d3 21 ♕xe6+ ♔h8 22 ♗xc7!± Tseshkovsky–Alburt, Odessa 1974) 17 ♗xg5 ♕xg5 18 ♕d3! was Geller–Timman, Teesside 1975. 18 ... f6 should then have been tried.

(d2) **15 ... ♗g5!?** 16 ♘e2 ♗xf4 17 ♘xf4 ♘e7! 18 ♗g4 ♘ac6 19 ♕d2 (19 ♗xe6∞) 19 ... ♔h8! 20 ♖c3 ♘g8 21 ♗d1 ♕h4 22 ♗c2 ♕h6 23 ♖g3! ♖ae8 (23 ... f6? 24 ♖g6!+ −) 24 ♖d1 ♘ge7 25 b4 a6 and now 26 a3 ♘g6! 27 ♘e2 (27 ♘xg6+ fg) 27 ... ♕xd2 28 ♖xd2 ♘ge7 29 ♘f4 g6 30 h4 h6 gave Black equal play in Hübner–Hort, Biel 1984. Hort suggests that 26 ♗a4!? may pose more problems.

(d3) **15 ... ♕d7** 16 ♗e3 (16 ♕d3 b6 17 ♘a4 f6 18 ♗d1 fe 19 ♗xe5 ♘xe5 20 de ♗g5 21 ♗c2 g6 22 ♖ce1 ♘b7 gave Black good play in Hermlin–Palatnik, Tallinn 1985. 16 ♖e1 f6 17 ef ♗xf6 gives White nothing better than 18 ♗e3 since 18 ♖xe6? ♘xd4∓ and 18 ♘e2?! ♘e7 19 ♕d2 ♘ac6 20 ♗g4 ♘f5 21 ♗xf5 ef∓ Beliavsky–

Alburt, Kiev 1978 can hardly be recommended.) 16 ... f6! 17 ef _xf6 18 ♕d2 b6 19 ♘a4 ♘e7 20 _e2 ♘f5= Geller–Bagirov, Tbilisi 1978.

| 12 | ... | ♘c8 |
| 13 | f4 | ♘c6 *(101)* |

13 ... _h4 is playable, with White's pawn on h3. 14 _d3 g6 15 ♕g4 (Pointless is 15 f5 ef 16 ♕f3 c6 17 ♔h1 ♔h8 18 ♖g1 ♘e7, since 19 ♕h3 is not possible.) 15 ... ♔h8 (Agzamov's suggestion 15 ... h5 16 ♕f3 ♘e7 is logical.) 16 b4 ♘c6 17 a3 (17 ♖ab1 h5! 18 ♕f3 ♘8e7 19 b5 ♘a5 20 ♔h2 b6 21 f5 failed in Diesen–Vaganian, Hastings 1974/5 after 21 ... ef 22 ♕f4 ♘g8 23 ♖g1 ♘c4!∓ 24 e6 ♔h7! 25 ef ♖xf7 26 ♕f3 ♘xe3 27 fe bc 28 dc ♘e7! 29 ♘e2 ♕h8! 30 ♘f4 ♕e5 31 ♔h1 ♖f6 32 ♖b4 g5!∓.) 17 ... f5 18 ♕d1. Now Black could try 18 ... g5, since in Psakhis–Agzamov, USSR Ch (Moscow) 1983, 18 ... a6 19 ♔h1 ♘8e7 20 ♘e2 ♘g8 21 ♘g1 ♘h6 22 ♘f3 (A standard manoeuvre against a bishop on h4.) 22 ... ♘f7 23 _d2 _e7 (23 ... ♖g8!?) 24 a4 ♘b8 25 b5 ab 26 ab ♘d7 27 ♕c2 c6 28 ♕b2 ♖b8 29 ♖a7 g5 ought not to have given Black quite enough counterplay. In Solozhenkin–Bagirov, Sevastopol 1986, the same position after 18 moves arose. There followed 19 ♔h2 ♘8e7 20 ♘e2 ♘g8 21 ♘g1 ♘h6 22 ♘f3 ♘f7 23 _d2 ♖g8 24 a4 ♕e7 25 b5 ab (25 ... ♘b8 26 c6!±) 26 ab ♖xa1 27 ♕xa1 ♘cd8 28

♕a5 (28 c6!? bc 29 ♕a5 g5!? 30 _b4 ♕d7∞ Bagirov) 28 ... c6 29 ♕b6 g5! 30 ♘xh4 gh 31 ♖g1 ♖g6 32 _e2 ♔g7 33 _h5 ♖xg1 34 ♔xg1 cb! and Black, with two good knights, was fine.

13 ... f5 is a good deal more playable than without the inclusion of h3 _h5: 14 b4 _h4 (14 ... b6 15 a3 c6 16 ♔h2 ♖f7 17 ♘a4 _f8 18 ♖c1 ♖b7 19 _d2!± Byrne–Vukić, Bugojno 1978) 15 ♔h2 ♔h8 16 ♖g1 ♖g8 17 b5 ♘e7 18 a4 ♕e8 19 _d3 ♘d7 20 ♖g2 ♘f8 21 ♘e2 ♘eg6 22 ♘g1 _d8 23 ♕h5 ♕f7 24 ♕e2 ♘h4 25 ♖g3 h6 26 ♘f3 ♘xf3+ 27 ♕xf3 ♘g6 28 ♖ag1 ♘h4 gave Black a reliable position in Khmelnitsky–A. G. Panchenko, Pula 1990. Instead 14 ♔h2 ♘c6 15 ♖g1 ♕e8 16 ♖g2 _d8 17 ♖b1 ♔h8 18 b4 ♘8e7 19 _h5 g6 20 _e2 ♘g8 21 ♕b3 left Black rather passive in Listengarten–Bagirov, Baku 1975.

Agzamov's suggestion 13 ... f6 14 _g4 (14 f5 fe 15 fe ed 16 ♕xd4 c6∞) 14 ... ♕d7 15 ♘xd5 f5! 16 ♘xe7+ ♘xe7 17 _f3 ♘d5 is well worth considering.

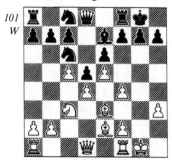

101
W

14 f5
14 b4:

(a) **14 ... ♗h4 15 ♖b1** (15 b5 ♘a5 16 ♗d3 g6 17 ♕g4 (Dorfman–Bagirov, Ordzhonikidze 1978) 17 ... ♔h8! with ... ♖g8 and ... c6 to follow.) **15 ... a6** (15 ... ♘8e7 16 ♗d3 f5 17 ♕h5 ♘g6 18 ♔h2 ♗e7 19 ♖g1 ♘h4 Bagirov; 15 ... ♔h8 16 ♗d3 g6 17 ♕g4 ♖g8 18 ♔h2 h5 19 ♕f3 ♘8e7 20 a3± Wolff–Alburt, US Ch [Estes Park] 1985) **16 ♗d3 f5 17 ♔h2 ♕e8 18 ♖g1 ♘8e7 19 ♗e2 ♔h8 20 ♖b2 ♕d7** (Kuzmin–Bagirov, USSR Ch 1978) **21 ♘b1±.**

(b) **13 ... a6**, without h3 ♗h5, was condemned by Alburt on the basis of **14 f5 ef 15 f4! ♘b8** and now Van Riemsdijk's suggestion **16 ♗f3 c6 17 ♕b3** intending ♘xd5, liberating a colossal pawn phalanx. However, he played 13 ... a6 against Short (Foxboro [5] 1985). Perhaps his intention was **14 ... f6!?**. The game itself proceeded **14 ♖b1 f6!? 15 ♗d3 ♕e8 16 ♕g4 f5 17 ♕h3 a5?! 18 b5 ♘b4 19 ♗e2 ♘c2 20 ♔h1 g6 21 ♖g1 ♖f7 22 ♗f3 ♗f8 23 ♖b2 ♘a3 24 ♗c1 ♘a7 25 ♗e2 ♕d7 26 ♖d1! ♖d8 27 ♕f1** and Black had great difficulties due to the a3 knight.

(c) **13 ... f6**, without h3 ♗h5, has been tried by Palatnik: **14 ♗g4?! ♕d7 15 f5 fe! 16 fe ♕d8 17 ♘e2 ♗f6 18 f4 ed 19 ♘xd4 ♘xd4 20 ♗xd4 ♗xd4+ 21 ♕xd4 ♕h4!∓** (note that this works due to the pawn being on h2 here) was Lanc–Palatnik, Trnava 1987, but a better approach was **14 b5 ♘a5 15 ♗d3 f5 16 ♖c1 b6 17 ♘e2 ♖f7 18 ♗d2 ♘b7 19 c6 ♘a5 20 ♕a4 ♗f8 21 ♗xa5 ba 22 ♕xa5 g6 23 ♕d2 ♕h4 24 ♔h1 ♘b6 25 ♖a1 ♘c4! 26 ♗xc4 dc 27 ♕c3 ♗h6 28 ♕f3?! ♕g4 29 ♕xg4 fg ½-½** Jansa–Palatnik, Trnava 1987.

14 ♗d3 is a tough move to meet. **14 ... g6** (14 ... ♗xc5? 15 dc d4 16 ♗xh7+! ♔xh7 17 ♕h5+ ♔g8 18 ♘e4!) **15 f5!? ef** (15 ... gf? 16 ♔h2 ♔h8 17 ♖g1 ♖g8 18 ♖xg8+ ♕xg8 19 ♕f3) **16 ♕f3 ♗xc5 17 dc d4** (17 ... ♘xe5 18 ♕xd5 ♘xd3 19 ♖fd1±) **18 ♗h6 dc 19 e6! ♘d4** (19 ... ♘e5 20 ♕xb7! is strong: 20 ... ♘e7 21 ef+ ♖xf7 22 ♖ad1 ♖b8 23 ♗c4! or 20 ... ♕xd3 21 ef+ ♔h8 22 ♗f4! ♘xf7 23 ♕xa8 ♕xh3 24 ♕d5 ♕g4+ 25 ♗g3 h5 26 ♖ad1) **20 ef+ ♖xf7 21 ♕xb7 ♘e7 22 bc ♘dc6 23 ♗c4 ♖b8 24 ♕a6 ♘e5 25 ♖ad1 ♕e8 26 ♖fe1 ♘7c6 27 f4 ♘f3+ 28 ♔f1 ♘xe1 29 ♗xe1 ♕d7 30 ♗e6 ♕d2 31 ♗xf7+ ♔xf7 32 ♕c4+ 1-0** Sokolov–Veingold, Tallinn 1981.

13 ♖b1, without h3 ♗h5, has been played with success. Like b4, this move envisages queenside activity, but without giving Black a target for counterplay (e.g. White will not be inconvenienced by having to attend to the threat of ... ♘xb4 at some point.)

(a) **13 ... ♗xc5?!** is a logical attempt to exploit the lack of support for c5, but only succeeds in highlighting White's space advantage: 14 dc d4 15 ♘e4 de 16 fe ♛xd1 17 ♖fxd1 ♘8e7 18 ♔f2 ♖fd8 19 ♘c3 ♔f8 (19 ... ♖xd1?! 20 ♖xd1 ♖d8 21 ♖xd8+ ♘xd8 22 ♘b5) 20 ♗f3 ♔e8 21 ♔e2 ♖xd1 22 ♖xd1 ♖d8 23 ♖g1! (Very instructive: White makes the most of the rook's mobility before returning to contest the open file.) 23 ... ♔f8 24 ♖b1 ♖d7 25 b4 h6 26 b5 ♘a5 27 ♖b4 b6 28 c6 ♖d8 29 ♖d4 and Black was soon pushed off the board in Abramović–Alburt, New York Open 1988.

(b) 13 ... ♗h4 was tried in Zsofia Polgar–Palatnik, Rome 1989. White succeeded in making good use of the h3 square: 14 ♔h1 ♘8e7 15 ♗d3! g6 (15 ... ♘f5? 16 ♗xf5 ef 17 ♛f3! ♘e7 18 ♛h3+ −) 16 ♛g4 ♘f5 17 ♗xf5 ef 18 ♛f3 ♘e7 19 ♛h3 ♘c8 (19 ... ♘c6 20 b4±) 20 ♖g1 ♔h8 21 b4 a6 22 a4 c6 and now 23 ♖b3, preparing b5, would have made Black's position very difficult. Instead after 23 b5?! ab 24 ab ♖a3 25 ♖gc1 (25 ♘e2?? ♗xf2) 25 ... ♗e7, the ... ♗xc5 threat gave Black serious counterplay.

14 ... ef

Without h3 ♗h5, 13 ... ♗h4 14 ♗d3 ef 15 ♛f3 ♘b4?! (15 ... ♘8e7 16 ♛h5 ♘g6 17 ♗xf5 ♘ce7 18 ♗d3 ♛d7 19 ♔g2 f5 20 f4 followed by a transfer of a rook to h3 gives White the advantage, while 15 ... ♘xe5!? 16 de d4 17 ♛xf5 g6 18 ♛e4 is also pleasant for White.) 16 ♗xf5 g6 17 ♗h6!

♘e7 18 ♗b1 ♖e8 19 ♛g4 ♘c8 20 a3 ♘a6 21 ♘xd5+ − was Zvonitsky–Stefanishin, USSR 1989.

15 ♗f3

Without h3 ♗h5, **14 ♛b3** f4 (14 ... ♗g5 15 ♛xb7 ♗xe3) 15 ♛xb7 fe 16 ♛xc6 ef+?! (16 ... ♖b8!?) 17 ♖xf2 ♖b8 18 ♛xd5 ♖xb2 19 ♛e4 g6 20 ♖af1 ♖d2 21 ♗d3 ♖xf2 22 ♖xf2 c6 23 ♗c4 gave White slightly the better prospects in Ulybin–Palatnik, Uzhgorod 1988.

Naturally, **15 f4?** fails to 15 ... ♗xc5.

15 ... ♗g5

15 ... ♗h4?! 16 ♗xd5! ♘8e7 (16 ... ♛d7 17 f4 ♘8e7 18 ♗g2±) 17 ♗xc6 bc 18 ♛h5± Lukin–Yuneev, Daugavpils 1989.

15 ... f4 16 ♗xf4 ♗g5 17 ♗g3 ♘8e7 18 ♗g4 f5 19 ef ♖xf6 20 f4 ♗h6 (102)

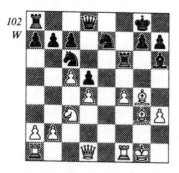

(a) **21 ♗h4 ♖xf4 22 ♗e6+ ♔h8 23 ♖xf4 ♗xf4 24 ♘xd5 ♗g3!** (note that this is only possible with the pawn on h3) and now Ivanchuk analysed:

(a1) **25 ♗g5 ♛f8 26 ♛d2 ♘xd5 27 ♗xd5 ♛f5 28 ♗xc6 bc 29**

♔g2 h6 30 ♖f1 (30 ♗xh6 ♗h4)
30 ... ♕d5+ 31 ♔xg3 hg∞.

(a2) **25 ♗xg3** ♘xd5 26 ♕f3
♘f6! 27 ♖d1 ♘xd4 28 ♕e3 (28
♕xb7?! ♖b8 29 ♕xc7?? ♘f3+) 28
... ♕e7 29 ♖xd4 ♖e8 30 ♗h4 (30
♖a4 h6! 31 ♖xa7 ♘d5!∞) 30 ...
♕xe6 31 ♕xe6 ♖xe6 32 ♗xf6 gf
33 ♖d8+ ♔g7 34 ♖d7+ ♔g6 35
♖xc7 ♖c6 36 ♖xb7 ♖xc5=.

(b) **21 ♕d3** was played in Sax–
Ivanchuk, Tilburg 1989. Ivanchuk
recommends 21 ... ♘b4! 22 ♕e2
♘f5 23 ♗xf5 ♖xf5 24 a3 ♘c6 25
♕e6+ ♖f7 26 ♖ad1 ♕d7∞, since
in the game 21 ... ♔h8 22 f5 ♗g5
23 h4 ♗h6 24 ♘b5!? ♖c8 25 ♗e5
♘g8! 26 ♖ae1 ♕d7 27 ♗h3 ♕f7
28 ♕g3 a6 29 ♘c3 ♘ge7 30 ♗xf6
(30 ♔h1! ♖f8 31 ♗xf6 ♕xf6 32
♕g4+ −) 30 ... ♕xf6 would have
been insufficient after 31 ♔h1!
♘xd4 32 ♖xe7 ♕xe7 33 f6+ −.

16 ♘xd5 f4
17 ♗xf4

It is less potent to take with the
knight. Without h3 ♗h5, Tseshkovsky–Alburt, Daugavpils 1978
continued **16 ♘xf4** ♗xf4 17 ♗xf4
♕xd4 18 ♗g3 ♘8e7 19 ♕c2 ♕d7
20 ♕e4 ♕e6 21 b4 ♘f5 (21 ...
a6!?∞) 22 ♖fe1 ♖fe8 23 ♕f4 ♘fd4
24 ♗g4! ♕g6 25 b5 ♘xe5? (25 ...
♘xb5±) 26 ♗d1! ♘ec6 27 ♖xe8+
♖xe8 28 bc ♖e1+ 29 ♔g2 ♕d3
30 ♗e2!! ♖xe2 31 cb ♖b2 33
c6!+ −.

17 ♗c1!? ♕d7 (17 ... ♘8e7 18
♘xe7+ ♘xe7 19 d5±) 18 b4 ♘8e7
19 ♘xe7+ ♗xe7 (19 ... ♘xe7 20
d5 ♕xh3 21 ♖e1 ♘g6 22 ♖b1

♘h4 23 ♖b3) 20 ♗b2 ♖ad8 (20
... ♘xb4 21 ♕b3) 21 d5 ♘xb4 22
d6 ♗g5 (22 ... cd 23 cd ♕xh3 24
de! ♖xd1 25 ♖fxd1 ♕xf3 26 ♖d8
♕g4+ 27 ♔f1 ♕h3+ 28 ♔e1+ −
Copié) 23 ♔h2 cd (23 ... ♕b5
24 ♕d4! ♘c2 25 ♕c3 ♘xa1 26
e6!+ −) 24 cd ♕f5 25 ♖g1 ♗h6
(25 ... h6 26 e6) 26 e6 fe 27 ♕d4
♘d5 28 ♗xd5 1-0 Copié–Pena
Gomez, corres. 1987.

17 ... ♗xf4
18 ♘xf4 ♘8e7!*(103)*

18 ... ♕xd4 19 ♕xd4 ♘xd4 20
♗xb7 ♖b8 21 ♗xc8 ♖fxc8 22
♘d3±.

After **18 ... ♕h4** 19 ♘g2 ♕xh3
20 ♗g4 ♕h6 21 f4, Sax prefers
White's chances based on pushing
the d-pawn.

Without h3 ♗h5, **17 ... ♘xd4**
18 ♗xb7 ♖b8 19 ♗g2! ♖xb2 20
♕g4! ♕e7 (20 ... f5 21 ♕h5! g6 22
♕d1! ♘e7 23 ♕a4+ −) 21 ♖ae1
♘e6 22 ♘d5 ♕g5 23 ♕xg5 ♘xg5
24 ♘xc7 ♖xa2 25 f4 led to a
won ending for White in Popović–
Bagirov, Moscow GMA 1989.

Bagirov's 18 ... ♘8e7 is based
on the point that Black need not
recapture the pawn immediately,
but may secure the queenside first.

19 b3

19 ♕d2 ♕d7.

19 ... ♖b8
20 ♗e4

20 ♘e2 ♕d7 21 ♗g4 ♕d5 22
f4 ♖fd8 23 ♗f3 ♕d7 24 ♗g4
♕d5=.

20 ... ♕xd4

20 ... ♘xd4 fails to 21 ♕g4!±.

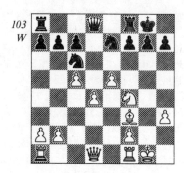

103
W

21	♕xd4	♘xd4
22	♖fd1	♖fd8
23	♖d3?	

Bagirov recommends 23 ♘d5 ♘e2+ 24 ♔f1 ♘xd5 25 ♖xd5 ♖xd5 26 ♗xd5 ♘f4! 27 ♗g2 ♔f8 28 ♖d1 ♔e7 as a way for White to avoid serious problems, though Black is for preference.

| 23 | ... | ♘dc6 |

| 24 | e6? | |

24 ♗xc6 ♖xd3 25 ♘xd3 ♘xc6∓.

24	...	f5!
25	♗g2	♖xd3
26	♘xd3	♖d8
27	♘f4	g6!

The simple plan of activating the king shows White's play to have been over-optimistic. 28 ♖e1 ♔g7 29 ♗xc6 bc! (29 ... ♘xc6? 30 e7!) 30 ♔g2 (30 h4 ♖d4−+) 30 ... g5! 31 ♘e2 ♔f6 32 h4 gh! 33 ♘f4 ♖d4?! (33 ... ♘g6!) 34 ♔f3 ♖e4 35 ♖xe4 fe+ 36 ♔xe4 ♘d5 (36 ... ♘g6!) 37 ♘e2 ♘e7 38 ♘d4 h3! 39 ♘f3 (39 ♔f3!?) 39 ... ♘d5 40 e7 ♔xe7 41 ♔f5 ♘f6! 42 ♔f4 ♔e6 43 ♔g3 ♘e4+ 44 ♔xh3 ♘xf2+ 45 ♔h4 ♔d5 46 ♔g5 0−1.

11 Flohr–Agzamov Variation: 5 ... c6

5 ... c6 is a logical and direct way to attack White's pawn centre. Having blocked the h1–a8 diagonal, Black is ready to play ... ♗xf3 and ... de, giving White a weak pawn on e5. Often White pre-empts this in some way, but this may break up White's pawns without Black needing to do anything.

The line has been attracting an increasing following for the last ten years thanks particularly to the efforts of Kovačević, Knežević, Dreev, Fernandez Garcia and the late Tashkent grandmaster Georgy Agzamov. A particularly appealing feature of the Flohr–Agzamov Variation is that it is possible for Black to win almost automatically against inaccurate play by means of a kingside pawn storm, winning the e5 pawn, or both.

6 0–0 allows Black's idea. This line has a poor reputation, but this is largely undeserved. With accurate play White can pose problems.

6 ♘g5 is best met by 6 ... ♗f5. White then has a number of sharp attempts, but Black's resources seem adequate.

After 6 c4 ♘b6, White can reasonably hope for a normal white advantage with 7 ed, 7 ♘g5 or 7 ♘bd2, though Black's game is perfectly playable.

Zsofia Polgar–Fernandez Garcia
Benidorm Open 1989

1 e4 ♘f6 2 e5 ♘d5 3 d4 d6 4 ♘f3 ♗g4 5 ♗e2

5   ...   c6 *(104)*

6   0–0

Since Black intends to exchange on f3 at the first opportunity, **6**

h3? is clearly a very illogical use of a tempo. After **6 … ♗xf3 7 ♗xf3 de 8 de e6** the only attempt at justification is **9 c4 ♘e7 10 ♕xd8+ ♔xd8** when the white king is centrally placed for the ending, though Black is still comfortable. Black can disrupt this plan with 9 … ♘b4 or 9 … ♗b4+ 10 ♗d2 ♘f4 11 ♗xb4 ♘d3+ 12 ♔e2 ♘xb4 13 ♕xd8+ ♔xd8 14 ♗e4 ♘d7 15 f4 ♘c5 16 ♘c3 ♔c7. In Malaniuk–Kengis, Odessa 1982, after **9 0–0**, Black used the free tempo well: 9 … ♘d7 10 ♕e2 ♕c7 11 ♖e1 ♗c5 12 c3 (12 ♘d2 0–0 13 ♘b3 ♗b6 14 c4 ♘e7 15 ♗d2 a5 16 ♗c3 a4∓ Janošević–Knežević, Majdanpek 1975) 12 … a5 13 a4 ♘e7 14 ♗f4 ♘g6 15 ♗g3 0–0 16 ♔h1 ♖ad8 17 ♘d2 ♗a7 18 ♘c4 ♘c5 19 h4 ♕e7 20 h5 ♘h4 21 ♗g4 ♘c5 22 ♗xf5 ef 23 ♘d6 ♕g5 24 ♕f3 g6 25 ♔g1 ♘e6 26 ♖ad1 ♖d7 27 ♔f1 ♖fd8 28 ♘e8 ♖xd1 29 ♘f6+ ♔g7 30 ♖xd1 ♖xd1+ 31 ♕xd1 f4 32 ♘e8+ ♔h8 33 ♘d6 ♔g8 34 ♗h2 ♕xe5 35 ♘xb7 ♕c7 36 ♘d6 ♕d8 37 hg hg 38 ♕d2 ♕h4+ 39 ♔g1 f3 40 gf ♘g5 41 ♔h1 ♕xh2+0–1.

6 ♘bd2? is met by the irritating 6 … ♘f4. **6 ed ed** is liable to transpose to the line 6 c4 ♘b6 7 ed ed (see Yudasin–Timoshenko), but Black may well try 6 … ♕xd6 after which knight invasions on b4 or f4 are a possibility.

6	…	♗xf3
7	♗xf3	de
8	de	e6

9   ♗h5?!

An interesting idea, aiming to secure c4 for the knight, was tried in Howell–Lutz, Groningen 1984: **9 a4 ♘d7 10 ♕e2 ♕c7 11 ♖e1 ♗c5 (11 … ♖d8!?** prepares to remove a knight from a3 without loss of tempi, and to meet 12 c3 with 12 … ♘c5, when b3 and d3 are a little sensitive. After 12 ♗g5 ♗e7 13 ♗xe7 ♘xe7 14 ♘a3 ♘g6 15 ♘c4 0–0 Black has ideas of … b5. Another idea is 11 … a5 12 ♘a3 ♗b4 13 c3 and now 13 … ♗xa3 14 ♖xa3∞, rather than 13 … ♗e7? 14 ♗xd5 cd 16 ♘b5 ♕b8 17 ♕g4± Kalegin–Baburin, USSR 1987.) 12 ♘a3 0–0 (12 … ♗d4? 13 ♘c4; 12 … ♗xa3 removes the knight, but how is Black then to generate counterplay?) 13 c3 (13 ♘c4!? ♘7b6) 13 … a5 (Black should now take the knight, as the rook is then rather inactive on a3.) 14 h4±.

Another rare move is **9 ♘d2**. Black secured counterplay in Arnason–Agzamov, 1983: 9 … ♘d7 10 ♖e1 ♕c7 11 ♘c4 (11 ♕e2!? ♗c5 12 ♘b3 ♗b6 13 c4?! ♘e7 14 ♗f4 a5! gave Black the advantage in Cullip–Burgess, Hastings Challengers 1990/1, but White has better with 13 ♗g5 h6 14 ♗d2 0–0–0 15 a4 a5∞) 11 … ♘7b6 ♕d4 ♘xc4 13 ♕xc4 0–0–0 14 a3 ♗e7 15 ♕e2 h6 16 c4 ♘b6 17 b4 ♖d7 18 ♖b1 ♖hd8.

9 b3 ♘d7 10 ♗b2 ♗b4! (There is little point waiting for ♖e1 before playing this: 10 … ♕g5 11

♜e1 ♝b4 12 ♜e4± Plachetka–
Popov, Stara Pazova 1988. In
Loginov–Donchenko, USSR
1988, 10 ... ♛c7 11 ♜e1 a5 12 a3
♜d8 13 g3 ♞e7 14 ♛e2 ♞g6 15
h5 ♝c5 16 ♜a2! 0–0 17 ♞d2 ♝a7
18 ♞f1 ♝b8 won the e-pawn, but
for rather good compensation: 19
h5! ♞gxe5 20 ♝g2 c5 21 ♞e3 ♞c6
22 h6 g6 23 ♝g7!±. Would the
king have been safer after 12 ...
0–0–0 ?) 11 a3 ½–½ Dončević–
Paulsen, Bundesliga 1989/90.
White cannot develop without giving the bishop tempi to attack the
e5 pawn.

9 c4 ♞e7 10 ♛xd8+ (10 ♝e4?!
♞d7 11 f4 ♞c5 12 ♝c2 ♞f5 13 b4
♛d4+ 14 ♛xd4 ♞xd4 15 ♝d1
♞d3∓ Voronov–Kopylov, Kiev
1970) **10 ... ♚xd8** leaves White
somewhat tied down to defending
e5. **11 ♝e4** (11 ♝h5 g6 or 11 ...
♞g6; 11 ♝d2 ♞d7 12 ♝c3 ♞g6
13 ♜e1= Panov–Kopylov,
Moscow 1958; 11 ♝e2?! ♞d7 12
f4 ♞f5 13 ♞c3 ♝c5+ 14 ♚h1
h5∓ Ramirez–Westerinen, Haifa
1976; 11 ♝g5?! ♞d7 12 ♜e1 ♚c7
13 ♝h5?! g6 14 ♝g4 h6∓ Per-
nishky–Ghinda, Pernik 1978; 11
♝f4 ♞d7 12 ♜e1 ♚c7 13 ♞c3
♞g6 14 ♝g3 ♝b4 15 ♜ac1 ♜ad8
16 a3 ♝xc3 17 ♜xc3 ♞c5 18 b4
♞a4 19 ♜ce3 ♜d4∓ Zurakhov–
Kopylov, Leningrad 1955) **11 ...
♞d7** *(105)* (11 ... ♞g6 is also
playable and can be met by 12 f4
♝c5+ 13 ♚h1 ♞d7 14 ♞d2 ♚c7
15 ♞f3 ♝e7 16 ♝e3 ♜ad8=
Hess–Siebenhaar, Mainz 1985 or

12 ♝xg6 hg 13 ♝e3 ♞d7 14 f4
♝b4 15 ♜d1 ♚e7 16 ♞d2 ♝xd2
17 ♜xd2 ½–½ Noyce–Burgess,
Birmingham 1990.) and White has
now tried:

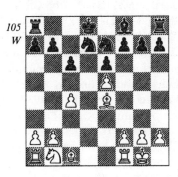

(a) **12 ♜d1 ♚c7** 13 ♝f4 g6! 14
♞d2 ♝g7 15 ♞f3 ♜ad8 16 ♚f1
♞b6 17 b3 ♜xd1+ 18 ♜xd1 ♜d8
½–½ Vuković–Puc, Yugoslav Ch
(Belgrade) 1945.

(b) **12 f4 ♞f5** 13 g4?! (13 ♞c3 h5
14 ♝xf5 ♝c5+ 15 ♚h1 ef 16 ♜e1
♚c7= Fatalibekova–Semënova,
Bad Kissingen 1982) 13 ... ♝c5+
14 ♚g2 ♞e3+ 15 ♝xe3 ♝xe3
16 g5 (16 h4 ♚c7 17 ♞c3 ♝d4 18
♜ac1 ♞c5 19 ♝b1 a5∓ Bajković–
Popov, Plovdiv 1982) 16 ... ♝d4
17 ♞d2 ♚c7 18 ♜ab1 ♞c5 19
♝c2 ♜ad8 20 ♞e4 ♞xe4 21 ♝xe4
h6∓ Živković–Knežević, Yugo-
slavia 1981.

(c) **12 ♝f4 ♞g6** 13 ♝xg6 hg 14
♞c3 ♚e8! (14 ... ♜h5 15 ♜ad1
♚e8 16 g4 ♜h4 17 f3± Rozentalis–Landenbergue, Geneva
1987) 15 ♜ad1 ♝e7 16 ♞e4 (16
♜fe1) 16 ... ♜h5 17 g4 (17 ♞d6+
♝xd6 18 ed should not be a

problem, though in O'Donnell–
Fernandez Garcia, Thessaloniki
ol 1988, Black trapped his own
rook: 18 … ♖a5 19 ♖d3 f6 20 a3
♖a4 21 ♖c1 c5 22 h4 ♖d8 23
♖b3! b6 24 ♖bc3 ♘b8 25 ♖d1
♘c6 26 ♗c1 ♘d4 27 ♔f1) 17 …
♖xe5! 18 ♗xe5 ♘xe5 19 b3 ♘xg4
20 ♖fe1 g5 21 ♖d3 ♘e5 was
a very good exchange sacrifice;
Black went on to win in
Kaidanov–Dreev, Lvov 1987.

9	…	♘d7
10	f4	♗c5+
11	♔h1	0–0
12	♕e2	b5
13	♖f3?	

Black now has a cunning way
of shutting White's bishop out of
play. Better was **13 a4**, though
Black is very comfortable.

13	…	f6!
14	♗g4	

14 ef ♘7xf6 15 ♕xe6+ ♔h8 16
♕h3 ♘xh5 17 ♕xh5 ♕e8! highlights the deficiencies of White's
first rank, while **14 ♘d2?** fe 15 fe
♘f4 loses material.

14	…	f5
15	♗h3	♗b6 *(106)*

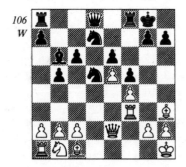

106
W

White can now do little to
oppose … ♘c5–e4.

16	♘c3	♘c5
17	g3	♘xc3
18	bc	

After 18 ♖xc3 ♘e4 19 ♖f3 ♕d4!
White's position falls apart.

18	…	♘e4
19	♗g2	♖f7!
20	♕e1	♖d7
21	♗e3	♗a5!

Black's positional plusses are
sufficient to ensure decisive
material gains. The game concluded 22 ♗g1 ♖d2 23 ♖f1 ♖xg2!
24 ♔xg2 ♗xc3 25 ♕e2 ♗xa1 26
♖xa1 ♕a5 27 g4 ♖d8 28 ♖d1 ♘c3
29 ♖xd8+ ♕xd8 30 ♕f3 ♕d2+
31 ♔h3 ♘d5 32 gf ef 33 ♔g3
♕xc2 34 e6 ♕c3 35 ♗xa7 ♕xf3+
36 ♔xf3 ♘c7 37 e7 ♔f7 38 ♔e3
♘e6 0–1.

Ivanović–Kovačević
Yugoslav Ch (Subotica) 1984

**1 e4 ♘f6 2 e5 ♘d5 3 d4 d6 4 ♘f3
♗g4 5 ♗e2 c6 6 0–0 ♗xf3 7
♗xf3 de 8 de e6**

9	♕e2

After **9 ♖e1** ♘d7, 10 ♕e2 is
considered in the note to White's
tenth move, as is 10 a3 after either
10 … a5 11 ♕e2 ♕c7 (the order
used in Bogdanović–Kovačević)
or 10 … ♕c7 11 ♕e2 ♗c5.

9	…	♘d7

9 … ♗c5 has been tried by the
postal player Diepstraten. Transpositions to normal lines are quite
possible, but an independent
option is 10 c4 ♘e7 11 ♖e1 ♕c7

12 ♗d2 ♘g6 13 ♗c3 ♕b6 14 ♘d2 ♘f4 15 ♕f1 0–0 16 b4 ♗d4= Groffen–Diepstraten, corres. 1979.

10 g3

10 ♖e1 ♕c7 *(107)* is a more usual move order, whereupon 11 g3 transposes to the game. Other attempts:

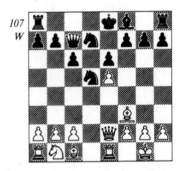

107
W

(a) **11 ♘d2!? ♗c5** (11 ... ♘f4 12 ♕e4 ♘g6 — compare [c].) 12 ♘b3 ♗b6 13 ♗g5 h6 14 ♗d2 0–0–0 15 a4 a5∞ 16 ♘c1 ♘e7 17 ♘d3 ♘g6 18 ♗c3 Dolmatov–Böhm, Amsterdam 1979.

(b) **11 ♗d2 ♗c5** 12 c4 (12 ♘c3 ♗d4 13 ♗xd5 cd 14 ♘b5 ♕b6 and now 15 ♘xd4 ♕xd4 16 ♗c3 ♕b6 is equal, while 15 ♘d6+? ♔f8 simply drops the e-pawn.) 12 ... ♘e7 13 ♗c3 a5 (A standard idea in these lines, intending ... ♗a7–b8 according to circumstances.) 14 ♘d2 (14 a3 ♘g6 15 g3 ♗a7 16 ♘d2 ♖d8!∓ Matanović–Knežević, Yugoslav Ch 1972) 14 ... ♗b4 (14 ... ♘g6) 15 ♗h5! ♗xc3 16 bc ♘c5 17 ♘f3 ♖d8 18 ♘d4 0–0∞ Bashnev–Sergeev, USSR 1982.

(c) **11 a3 a5** (11 ... ♗c5 12 c3 a5 13 b3 0–0 14 ♖a2 ♖fd8 15 g3 ♘e7 16 ♗h5 ♗b6= Evans–Shamkovich, Lone Pine 1978; 11 ... ♘e7 12 b3 ♘g6 13 ♗b2 0–0–0 14 g3 ♗e7∞ Kotkov–Kopylov, Volgograd 1964) 12 g3 (12 ♘d2 ♘f4 13 ♕e4 ♘g6 14 ♘c4 ♗e7 with kingside castling to follow is considered sufficient for equality by Kovačević.) 12 ... ♗c5 13 ♘d2 (13 ♗g2? ♗d4) 13 ... 0–0 14 ♗e4 (14 ♗g2 a4 followed by ... ♖fd8 gives Black very reasonable chances.) 14 ... f5!? (More ambitious than 14 ... ♕xe5 15 ♗xh7+ when a draw is likely.) 15 ef ♖xf6 16 ♘f3 ♖af8 17 ♖f1 (17 c4 ♘e5!) 17 ... b5 18 ♗e3 (18 ♗g5!? ♖6f7 19 ♗e3=) 18 ... ♗xe3 19 fe ♘c5 20 ♗d3 e5 21 ♘d2! ♕b6 gave Black rather the better chances in Bogdanović–Kovačević, Yugoslavia 1983, though White should have been able to survive.

10 b3 is a logical move which has scored badly in practice. **10 ... ♕c7 11 ♗b2** (11 ♖e1 a5 12 a4 ♗b4 13 c3 ♗e7= Bagirov) **11 ... ♘f4** (An important point: White has not used a tempo with c4 to drive the knight to its best square, g6, so it gains a tempo instead on the queen.) **12 ♕e4 ♘g6** and now White should certainly defend the e-pawn:

(a) **13 ♗h5?! ♘gxe5** 14 f4 ♘g6 15 f5 0–0–0! (When playing the tricks, one must beware of such counter-tricks!) 16 fe (16 fg?

hg−+) 16 ... fe 17 ♘d2 ♗d6∓ 18 g3 ♗xg3 19 ♘f3 ♗f4 20 ♕xe6 ♖he8 21 ♕h3 ♗e3+ 22 ♔h1 ♘f4 23 ♕h4 ♘xh5 24 ♕xh5 ♘f6 25 ♗xf6 gf 26 ♕f5+ ♕d7 27 ♕xf6 ♖f8 28 ♕c3 ♗b6 29 ♕d2 ♕e6 30 ♕e1 ♕g6 31 ♕e2 ♖g8 32 ♘e5 ♕e6 33 ♕e4 ♖d5 34 ♖ae1 ♖e8 35 ♖f5 ♗c7 36 ♘xc6 ♕xe4+ 37 ♖xe4 ♖d1+ 0–1 Hulak–Jansson, Skara 1980.

(b) 13 ♖e1. On which side will Black's king be more secure?

(b1) 13 ... ♖d8!? 14 a4 (14 g3? ♗c5 threatened ... ♘gxe5 in Antonov–Timmer, Biel 1989; 15 b4 ♕b6−+ did not help.) 14 ... a5 15 ♘a3 (15 ♘d2 ♘b6∓) 15 ... ♗b4 16 ♘c4 (16 ♖e3 ♗c5 17 ♖ee1 ♘b6∓) 16 ... ♗xe1 17 ♖xe1 (17 ♘d6+? ♔f8 18 ♖xe1 ♘dxe5) 17 ... 0–0 18 ♗a3 b5 19 ♗d6! ♕a7 20 ♘e3 ♖fe8∓ C. Hansen.

(b2) 13 ... 0–0–0 14 a4 a5 15 ♘a3 (15 ♗c3?! ♕b6!) 15 ... ♗b4 16 ♖e3 (16 ♖e2? ♗xa3 17 ♖xa3 ♘dxe5!; 16 ♘c4! ♘b6= Kuznetsov–Kopylov, Volgograd 1964) 16 ... ♘b6 17 c3 ♗c5 18 ♖e2 ♖d5! was quite pleasant for Black in Sax–Kovačević, Sarajevo 1982, but White generated counterplay: 19 c4 ♖d7 20 ♘c2 ♖hd8 21 h4 ♖d3 22 h5 ♘f8 23 ♗a3 ♖d1+ 24 ♔h2 f5 25 ♕h4 ♗xa3 26 ♖xd1 ♖xd1 27 ♘xa3 ♘bd7 28 ♕e7 ♕d8 29 ♕xd8+ ♔xd8 30 c5 ♖d3 31 ♘c4∞.

10	...	♕c7
11	♖e1	♗c5!

11 ... a5?! 12 a4 ♗b4 (12 ...

♗c5) 13 c3 ♗e7 14 ♘d2 0–0 15 ♘b3! ♖fd8 16 h4 ♘f8 17 ♗d2 ♖d7 18 h5 ♕b6 19 ♕c4 h6 20 ♖ad1 ♔h8 21 ♗c1 ♖ad8 22 ♖d4 ♕a7 23 ♖g4 ♘h7 24 ♗e4 f5!? 25 ef ♘hxf6 26 ♖g6 ♗f8 27 ♗c2 gave White rather the better of things in Tukmakov–Bagirov, Rostov 1971.

12	♘d2	0–0
13	♘b3	

13 ♗g2!? a5 14 ♔h1 ♖ae8?! 15 f4 f5?! 16 ♘f3 h6 17 ♘h4 was good for White in Conquest–D. Werner, Bad Wörishofen 1990. Black should try 14 ... a4!?, preparing ... f6.

13	...	♗b6
14	c4	

14 ♔g2 unpins the f-pawn but is rather slow. Nonhoff–Grün, Bundesliga 1982, continued 14 ... a5 15 a4 ♘e7 16 ♗d2 ♘c5 17 ♘xc5 ♗xc5 and Black was ready to use the d-file.

14	...	♘e7
15	♗d2	a5
16	♗c3	a4
17	♘d2	♗a5!

By simple means Black has achieved a very promising position. The removal of a key defender of the e-pawn forces some major structural weaknesses.

18	♗g2	♗xc3
19	bc	♖fd8
20	f4	♘c5

With a knight on d4 White's position would make some sense, so Black pre-empts this by threatening a knight invasion of his own.

After the exchange of knights, White's position will forevermore be thoroughly passive: 21 ♘e4 ♘xe4 22 ♗xe4 ♕a5 23 ♕e3 ♖d7 24 ♖ad1 ♖ad8 25 ♖xd7 ♖xd7 26 ♔g2 g6 27 ♖e2 ♕d8 28 g4 ♘c8 29 ♔g3 a3 (Prepares a route for the knight into White's position, whilst this bold pawn cannot be captured without allowing a nasty trick, as we shall see.) 30 h4 ♘b6 31 ♕c5 ♘a4 32 ♕xa3 ♖d3+! 33 ♗xd3 ♕xd3+ 34 ♔f2 ♘xc3 35 ♖e3 ♘d1+ 36 ♔f3 ♕f1+ 37 ♔e4 ♕xc4+ 38 ♔f3 ♕f1+ 39 ♔e4 ♘xe3. Black's combination has led to a queen and pawn ending with an extra pawn and by far the safer king. The game concluded 40 ♕a8+ ♔g7 41 ♔xe3 ♕e1+ 42 ♔f3 ♕d1+ 43 ♔e3 ♕e1+ 44 ♔f3 ♕xh4 45 ♕xb7 ♕h3+ 46 ♔e4 ♕xg4 47 ♔b2 ♕d1 48 ♔e3 h5 49 f5 ♕g1+ 50 ♔d3 ♕f1+ 51 ♔d4 ♕g1+ 52 ♔c4 gf 53 ♕a3 ♕g5 0–1.

Barua–Landenbergue
London (Lloyds Bank) 1986

1 e4 ♘f6 2 e5 ♘d5 3 d4 d6 4 ♘f3 ♗g4 5 ♗e2 c6 6 0–0 ♗xf3 7 ♗xf3 de 8 de e6 9 ♕e2 ♘d7
    10 c4

This is the most commonly played move, but seems rather obliging as the knight is well played on e7, ready to pressurise e5 from g6, while White has weakened d3 and deprived the queen's knight of the c4 square. In any case 10 c4 has achieved dismal practical results, which are largely responsible for the harmless reputation of 6 0–0.

  10 ...   ♘e7
  11 ♗g4

11 b3 is no more successful than on the previous move. After **11 ... ♘g6 12 ♗b2**, both 12 ... ♕c7 and 12 ... ♕g5 are promising:

(a) **12 ... ♕c7** 13 ♗h5?! (13 ♖e1? ♗b4 or 13 ... ♖d8; 13 ♗e4!? ♘gxe5 14 f4 ♘g6 15 f5 ♘f4 16 ♕f3 e5 Thorsteinsson–Westerinen, Reykjavik 1976) 13 ... ♘dxe5 14 f4 ♘d7 15 f5 0–0–0! 16 fe (16 fg? hg– +) 16 ... fe 17 ♕xe6 (17 ♗xg6? ♗c5+ 18 ♔h1 hg 19 h3 ♕g3 20 ♖f3 ♖xh3+ 0–1 Miolo–Kovačević, Surakarta 1983) 17 ... ♗d6 18 ♗xg7 ♖hg8 19 ♗h6 ♗xh2+ 20 ♔h1 ♗e5∓ Meštrović–Kovačević, Yugoslavia 1981.

(b) **12 ... ♕g5** 13 ♖e1 (13 ♘c3 ♘dxe5 14 ♔h1 ♘xf3 15 ♕xf3 ♘h4 16 ♕h3 0–0–0∓ Hardicsay–Suba, Budapest 1976; 13 g3 ♘dxe5 14 ♗g2 0–0–0∓ Manoj Kumar–Schulte, Oakham 1986) 13 ... ♗b4 14 ♕e3 ♕xe3 15 ♖xe3 0–0–0 16 g3 ♗a5 17 ♗h5 ♗c7 18 ♗xg6 hg 19 ♖e2 ♘c5 20 ♘d2?! ♘d3 21 ♗c3 ♗xe5 22 ♗xe5 ♘xe5 23 ♔g2 ♘d3 24 ♘e4 ♖h5 25 h4 f6 26 a3 g5 27 hg f5 28 ♘d2 ♖xg5 29 ♖e3 f4 30 ♖e4 ♘c5 0–1 Hernandez–G. Garcia, Granma Z 1987.

11 ♗f4 turns out to place the bishop badly, provided Black responds correctly.

(a) **11 … ♕c7** 12 ♘c3 (12 ♖e1 ♘g6 13 ♗g3 ♗b4 14 ♘c3 ♗xc3 15 bc 0–0–0 and Black is much better after either 16 ♗e4 ♘c5 17 ♗c2 ♖d7 18 ♕e3 ♕a5 19 f4 ♖hd8 20 f5 ef 21 ♗xf5 ♘e6 Chekhover–Kopylov, Leningrad 1954 or 16 h4 ♘c5 17 ♖ad1 ♕a5 18 ♕e3 ♘e7 19 ♗g4 h5 20 ♕g5 ♕c7 21 ♗xh5 ♘f5 Aronin–Furman, Odessa 1952) 12 … g5 13 ♘e4 ♗g7 14 ♘d6+ ♔f8 15 ♗g3 ♘g6 16 ♗h5 ♗xe5∓ Sherzer–Horn, Rio Gallegos 1987. White should have taken the g-pawn.

(b) **11 … ♘g6** 12 ♗g3 ♕a5! (12 … ♕c7? 13 ♗b5! and now either capture on e5 fails to an advance of the f-pawn, so Rausch–Blau, Hessen 1969 continued 13 … ♗e7 14 f4 ♗h4 15 ♘c3 ♗xg3 16 hg 0–0 17 ♘e4±. 12 … ♗c5!? pins the f-pawn and intends … ♗d4. Timmer–Böhm, Holland 1986 continued 13 ♗h5 ♕g5 14 ♗xg6 hg 15 ♘d2 ♕h5 16 ♘f3 g5 17 ♖fd1 g4 18 ♘d4 and now 18 … 0–0–0 would have been quite good for Black.) 13 ♗h5 (13 ♖e1 ♗b4 14 ♘c3 ♗xc3 15 bc 0–0 16 ♕e3 ♖fd8 17 h4 ♘c5 18 ♖ad1 ♘e7 19 ♗g4 h6 20 ♖d6 ♖d7 21 h5 ♘c8 22 ♖d4 ♘b6 23 (f4 ♕xa2 24 f5 ♘xc4 25 ♕f4 ♘b6 26 ♖xd7 ♘bxd7 27 ♖d1 ef 28 ♗xf5 ♘f8 29 ♕g4 ♘ce6–+ Findlay–Kovačević, Toronto 1989) 13 … ♘e7 (13 … ♘gxe5?! 14 f4 g6 15 fe gh 16 ♕xh5 0–0–0) 14 ♘d2 (14 f4!?) 14 … g6 15 ♘e4 ♘f5 16 ♗g4 ♘xg3 17 fg ♗e7∓ 18 ♘f6+ ♗xf6

19 ef 0–0–0 20 a3 h5 21 ♗f3 ♕e5 22 ♕f2 ♔b8 23 b4 ♕xf6 24 ♖ae1 ♘e5 25 ♖e4 ♘xf3+ 26 gf ♕c3 27 ♕e3 ♕xe3+ 28 ♖xe3 ♖d2–+ Anka–C. Horvath, Hungarian Ch (Budapest) 1989.

11 ♘c3 ♕a5 12 ♗f4 (12 ♖e1 ♘g6) 12 … ♘g6 13 ♗g3 and now Anand considered 13 … ♘gxe5 very strong since 14 ♗h5 g6 15 f4 is ineffective. Instead Sherzer–Burgess, Prestwich 1990 continued 13 … ♘dxe5 14 ♗h5 0–0–0 (14 … ♗e7!? Galliamova) 15 f4 ♕c5+? (After 15 … ♘d7 White has some compensation.) 16 ♔h1 ♘xc4 17 f5 ♖d2 18 ♕e1! ef 19 b3! ♕e3 20 bc! ♕xc3 21 ♖xf5+ – ♕d4 22 ♖d5 1–0.

11 ♗d2 ♕c7 (After 11 … ♘g6 12 ♗c3 ♕g5, 13 ♖e1 ♘h4 is equal, but in Perenyi–Popov, Berlin 1988, 13 g3 ♘gxe5 14 ♗g2 ♕g4 15 ♕c2 h5 16 ♘d2 0–0–0 17 ♖ae1 ♘d7 gave White quite reasonable compensation. Black could consider 15 … ♕xc4) **12 ♗c3** *(108)*. Black has tried three moves:

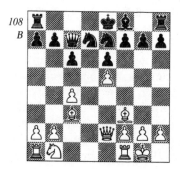

108
B

(a) **12 ... 0–0–0** 13 ♘d2? (13 b4!? c5∞) 13 ... ♘g6 14 ♖ae1 ♘dxe5! 15 ♗e4 ♘f4∓ Kostro–Maciejewski, Poland 1973.

(b) **12 ... g5** 13 ♘d2 (13 ♗h5? ♗g7 14 ♖e1 ♘g6 15 ♗xg6 hg 16 ♘d2 f5! 17 ♖ad1 ♗f8∓ Matanović–Knežević, Belgrade 1965) and rather than 13 ... ♗g7? 14 ♘e4!± Karasev–Bagirov, Riga 1970, Bagirov recommends 13 ... ♘g6! 14 ♘e4 ♗e7 15 ♘f6+ ♘xf6 16 ef ♗d6 17 g3 ♗e5.

(c) **12 ... ♘g6** 13 ♖e1 ♖d8!? (13 ... a5 14 a3 ♗c5 with ideas of placing the bishop on b8; 13 ... ♘c5 14 ♗e4 0–0–0 15 ♗xg6 hg 16 g3? ♘d3 17 ♖d1 ♘xf2! 18 ♖xd8+ ♔xd8 19 ♕xf2 ♗c5 20 ♕xc5 ♕d1+ ∓ Avshalumov–Sergeev, Leningrad 1979; 13 ... 0–0–0 14 b4 ♗e7 15 ♕b2 ♘f4 16 ♗e4 f5 17 ♗c2 c5 18 b5 g5 19 ♘d2 ♘f8 20 ♘f1 ♘8g6 21 ♘e3 ♘h4 22 a4 b6 23 a5 and now in Qwint–P. Cramling, corres. 1982, Black should have played 23 ... ♕b7∞) 14 b4 (14 ♘d2? ♘dxe5) 14 ... ♗e7 (Threatens ... ♘dxe5!) 15 ♕b2 (15 ♘a3?! a5∓) 15 ... 0–0 16 g3 ♘b6! 17 ♕b3 f6! Black embarks on an attack down the f-file, while it is not clear how White should seek counterplay. Day–Segal, Dubai ol 1986, continued 18 ef ♗xf6 19 ♗xf6 (After 19 ♗g4 ♘e5! 20 ♗xe6+ ♔h8, both 21 ♘d2 ♖xd2 22 ♗xd2 ♕d6 23 c5 ♕xd2 24 cb ♘d3–+ and 21 ♗xe5 ♗xe5 22 ♘c3 ♘a4! 23 ♘xa4 ♗xa1 24 ♖xa1 ♕e5∓ illustrate

Black's ideas well.) 19 ... ♖xf6 20 c5?! (20 ♗g2 ♘e5 21 ♘c3 ♘f3+ ∓) 20 ... ♘d5 21 ♗g2 ♖df8 22 f4 (22 ♖f1 ♕e5 23 ♘d2 ♖xf2–+; 22 ♖e2 ♘gf4!) 22 ... ♘gxf4! 23 gf ♕xf4 24 ♘a3 ♖h6!–+ 25 ♕g3 (25 h3 ♕f2+ 26 ♔h1 ♘f4) 25 ... ♕xb4 26 ♗e4 ♘c3! 27 ♘c2 ♕xc5+ 28 ♕e3 ♘xe4 0–1.

11 ...   ♕c7

The immediate **11 ... h5** is also feasible. 12 ♗xh5?! ♘f5! threatens ... ♕h4 and ... ♘d4, so Bönsch–Bagirov, Berlin 1979, proceeded instead 12 ♗h3 ♕c7 13 ♖e1 (13 f4 transposes back to the main game.) 13 ... 0–0–0 14 ♘c3 (14 ♗g5? ♕xe5!) 14 ... ♘g6 15 f4 (15 ♗g5 ♗e7 16 ♗xe7 ♘xe7 17 f4=) 15 ... ♗b4 16 ♗e3 ♗xc3 17 bc ♕a5 18 ♕f2 ♘e7 19 ♖ab1 g6! with roughly level chances.

12 f4   h5

More reserved approaches are **12 ... 0–0–0** 13 ♗e3 ♘f5 14 ♗xf5 ef 15 ♕f2 (15 ♕c2 g6 16 ♕a4 a5!∓) 15 ... b6 16 ♘d2 ♘c5 17 ♘f3 ♘e4 18 ♕c2 ♗e7 19 a3 c5∓ Gligorić–Vidmar, Yugoslav Ch (Belgrade) 1945 and **12 ... ♘f5** 13 ♘c3 0–0–0 14 ♗xf5 ef 15 ♗e3 ♗c5 16 ♘a4 ♗xe3+ 17 ♕xe3 ♘b6 ½–½ Kristiansen–Knežević, Reykjavik 1984.

13 ♗h3

13 ♗xh5?! ♘f5 threatens 14 ... ♗c5+ and 14 ... ♘d4; 14 g3 ♘d4!∓.

13 ...   0–0–0

13 ... ♘f5 14 ♗xf5 (14 ♘c3) 14 ... ef 15 e6 (15 ♗e3) 15 ... ♘c5

16 ef++ &xf7 17 ♕c2 g6 18 ♘d2
♕b6 19. &h1 &g7 20 ♖b1 ♖ae8
21 b4 ♘e4∓ Gaiduk–Chnishev,
Moscow 1950.

14 ♘c3

Botvinnik–Flohr, Nottingham
1936, one of the first few games
with the Flohr–Agzamov Variation, saw instead 14 &e3 ♘f5
(14 … g5!?) 15 &xf5 ef 16 ♕f2
♕a5 17 ♘d2 ♘b6 18 a3 (18
&h1!?∞) 18 … ♖d3∓ 19 ♖fd1
&e7 20 c5 ♘d5 21 ♘c4 ♖xd1+
22 ♖xd1 ♕a4 23 ♖c1 h4 24 b4 h3
25 g3 ♖d8 26 ♕c2 ♕xc2 27 ♖xc2
&d7 28 &f2 &e6 29 &c1 g6 30
&b2 ♖a8 31 ♘a5 ♖b8 32 &f3
&d8 33 ♘b3 &d7 34 ♘d4 ♖a8
35 ♖e2 &e7 36 ♘b3 &f8 ½–½.

14 … g5!? (109)

Rather an audacious move. The
faint-hearted may prefer 14 … ♘f5
15 &xf5 ef 16 a3 &c5+ 17 &h1
&d4 18 ♘a4 ♘f8! 19 ♖b1 ♘e6
20 b4 g6 21 c5 f6 which was
quite good for Black in Ustinov–
Bagirov, Vilnius 1960.

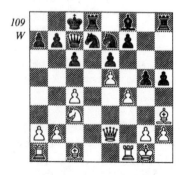

109
W

| 15 | fg | ♘xe5 |
| 16 | &h1 | ♘7g6 |

17 &e3 ♘g4
18 &g1 &c5

Even without the direct threats
to the white king, Black's exchanging manoeuvre was a very good
idea on positional grounds.

19	g3	&xg1
20	&xg1	♘4e5
21	♖ad1	♖xd1
22	♘xd1	h4!
23	g4	♖d8
24	&g2	♖d4

Black's moves flow very
smoothly. By simple means the
deficiencies of the white position
are laid bare. The game concluded
dramatically: 25 ♘e3 ♘f4 26 ♕f2
h3 27 &f3 ♕e7 28 ♕h4 ♕c5 29
b4 ♘xf3+ 30 ♖xf3 ♖d1+ 31 &f2
♖d2+ 32 &f1 ♕d4 33 g6 ♖xh2
34 ♖xf4 ♕a1+ 0–1.

Zuse–D. Paulsen
Bundesliga 1989/90

**1 e4 ♘f6 2 e5 ♘d5 3 d4 d6 4 ♘f3
&g4 5 &e2 c6**

6 ♘g5 &f5

6 … &xe2?! 7 ♕xe2 de 8 de e6
9 0–0 ♘d7 (9 … &e7 10 ♘e4 0–0
11 c4±; 9 … ♕c7 10 ♖d1 ♘d7 11
♘f3 ♘e7 12 ♘bd2 ♘g6 13 ♘c4!
b5 14 ♘d6+ &xd6 15 ed ♕b7
16 h4 gave White a devastating
initiative in Tseshkovsky–Hort,
Manila IZ 1976. Instead 11 … b5
12 c4 bc 13 ♕xc4 gives White a
solid positional advantage.) 10 c4
(10 f4 &e7 11 ♘e4 can be met by
11 … b5 12 &h1 ♘c5 13 ♘bd2
♕b6 or 11 … ♘c5 12 ♘xc5
&xc5+ 13 &h1 0–0.) 10 … ♘e7

(10 ... ♘5b6 11 ♖d1! ♕c7 12 f4
♗e7 13 ♘e4 0–0 14 ♗e3 ♘a4 15
b3 ♘ac5 16 ♘bc3± Ermenkov–
Popov, Bulgarian Ch 1985) 11
♘c3 (11 ♖d1 ♕c7!?) 11 ... ♘f5 (11
... ♕c7 12 f4 ♘f5 13 ♔h1 h5?! 14
♘ce4 ♘c5 15 ♖d1 ♘xe4 16 ♘xe4
♗e7 17 ♗e3 c5 18 ♗f2 g6 19
h3± Tseshkovsky–Maciejewski,
Bucharest 1974) 12 ♖d1 ♗e7 (12
... c5 13 ♘f3± Adamski; 12 ...
♕c7?! 13 ♘ce4! ♗e7 14 ♗f4
♘xe5 15 c5! 0–0 16 ♘xh7! ♖fd8
17 ♘hg5 ♖xd1+ 18 ♖xd1 ♖d8
19 ♘xf7!!± Novopashin–Agzamov, Riga 1976) 13 ♘ce4 c5 14 f4
(14 ♕h5?! g6 15 ♕h3 h6 16 ♘f3
♕c7 17 g4 ♘d4 18 ♘xd4 cd 19
♖xd4 ♘xe5 20 ♗f4 g5∓ Baleev–
Kopylov, Beltsy 1972) 14 ... ♕c7
(14 ... ♘d4 15 ♕f2 ♘b8 16 b4!)
15 ♗e3!± h6 16 ♘f3 0–0–0? (16
... h5) 17 ♗f2 h5 18 a3 f6? (18 ...
♖he8) 19 ♘c3! fe 20 ♘b5 ♕b8 21
♘xe5 ♘xe5 22 fe a6 23 ♘d6+ led
to a rout in Petrik–Cibulka, Stary
Smokovec 1973.

The point of the text is that if
White insists on an exchange of
bishops, Black would prefer to
leave White's queen on d3 or g4,
rather than her ideal post, e2.

7   ♗g4

7 a3 was introduced in Short–
Benjamin, World Junior Ch
(Dortmund) 1980. Black could
now try 7 ... ♕a5+!? when 8
♗d2?! ♕b6 and 8 ♘d2?! ♘b4 are
both pleasant for Black, while 8
c3 de 9 de e6 10 0–0 (10 b4? ♕c7)
10 ... ♘d7 11 c4 (11 f4?! ♗xb1 12

♖xb1 ♕b6+ 13 ♔h1 ♘xc3) 11
... ♘e7 12 f4 h6 intending 13 ...
g5!? yields interesting play. Best is
8 b4 ♕a4 9 c4 ♕xd1+ 10 ♗xd1
♗xb1 though Black should not
be worse. Instead Short–Benjamin
continued **7 ... h6** 8 ♘f3 de 9 de
e6 10 c4 (For 10 0–0 see 7 0–0
below.) 10 ... ♘e7 11 ♘d4 ♘d7
12 f4 ♕b6?! (12 ... ♗e4!?) 13 ♘c3
♘c5 14 ♗e3 ♖d8 (14 ... ♕xb2
15 ♘db5) 15 b4 ♘d3+ 16 ♗xd3
♖xd4 17 ♕e2 ♗xd3 18 ♕d2 ♘f5
19 ♗xd4 ♕xd4 20 0–0–0 ♗e7
21 g3! and a winning ending for
White resulted.

7 0–0 de (7 ... e6) 8 de h6 9 ♘f3
e6. Now **10 ♘d4 ♗h7** offers White
little, while the attempt to return
to standard lines with **10 ♗d3** is
of course met by 10 ... ♗g4!.
After **10 a3**, 10 ... a5 11 c4 ♘b6
12 ♕b3 a4 13 ♕c3 ♘8d7 14 ♘d4
♗g6 15 f4 ♗c5 held the balance
in Karpov–Klings, Bensheim
simultaneous 1983, but more purposeful play, by Black at any rate,
was seen in Sanz Alonso–Fernandez Garcia, Salamanca 1990: **10
... ♘d7** 11 c4 ♘e7 12 ♗f4 g5 13
♗g3 ♗g7 14 ♘c3 ♗g6 15 ♘d4
♗xe5 16 ♗xe5 ♘dxe5 17 g4
♗xg4 18 ♗xg4 ♘xg4 19 ♕xg4
♘e5 20 ♕g3 ♕xd4 21 ♖fe1 ♘g6
22 ♘e4 0–0 23 ♖ad1 ♕xb2 0–1.

7 f4 is less good than Maus'
idea 6 c4 ♘b6 7 ♘g5 ♗f5 8 f4,
since c4 will now be met by ...
♘b4. Krauss–Kindl, Wiesbaden
1987 continued 7 ... e6 8 0–0 ♗e7
9 ♗d3?! ♗xd3 10 ♕xd3 ♗xg5

11 fg de 12 de ♘d7 13 ♕e2 ♕c7 14 ♖e1 0–0 15 c4 ♘e7 16 ♗d2 ♘g6∓.

7 ♗h5!? is a move with a much higher pedigree. After 7 ... g6 8 ♗g4 ♗xg4 (8 ... ♕d7 9 ♗xf5 ♕xf5 10 g4 is given as ± by Marjanović, though this is far from clear.) 9 ♕xg4 it is not so easy for Black to equalise. 9 ... de (9 ... ♕d7 10 ♕e2 ♗g7 11 0–0 ♘c7 12 ed ♕xd6 13 ♖e1 h6 14 ♗f4 ♕d8 15 ♘f3 ♘e6 16 ♗e5± Matulović–Popov, Zemun 1983) 10 de h6 (10 ... ♗g7?! 11 e6±) 11 ♘e4 ♕d7! (11 ... ♗g7? 12 e6 0–0 13 ef+ ♔h8 14 h4!) 12 ♕e2 (12 e6!? ♕xe6 13 ♕xe6 fe 14 ♘c5 ♘d7! equalises: 15 ♘xb7? a5 16 ♗d2 ♗g7–+; 15 ♘xe6 ♔f7 16 ♘xf8 ♘xf8=) 12 ... ♗g7 (12 ... ♘a6 13 0–0 ♗g7 14 c4?! ♘b6 15 c5 ♘d5 16 f4 0–0–0 17 ♗d2 f5 18 ef ♘xf6 19 ♗c3 ♕d5 picked up the c5 pawn in Bednarski–Behrhorst, Berlin 1985.) 13 f4 ♘a6 14 a3 (Marjanović suggests 14 0–0!? 0–0 15 c4; Black may choose instead to castle long.) 14 ... 0–0 15 0–0 f6 16 ef ef 17 f5 ♖fe8 18 ♕d3 ♕e7 19 ♘g3 g5 20 b4 ♖ad8 was Marjanović–Kovačević, Pula 1984. Black's control of the centre files more than compensated for the inactivity of the g7 bishop.

7 ... ♗xg4

An unlikely-looking alternative is **7 ... ♕d7**, though White can only maintain a small plus:

8 ♗xf5 ♕xf5 9 0–0!? de 10 de ♕xe5?! (10 ... e6) 11 c4 ♘f6 12

♕d8+ ♔xd8 13 ♘xf7+ ♔e8 14 ♘xe5± Naumkin–Arkhangelsky, Moscow 1984.

8 ♕f3!? e6 (8 ... ♗xg4? 9 ♕xf7+ ♔d8 10 h3! ♗f5 11 e6+–) 9 ♗xf5 ef 10 0–0 (10 ♕e2 de 11 de ♘a6 12 0–0 0–0–0 13 c4 ♘db4 14 ♘c3 ♘c5 15 ♗e3 ♘bd3 16 ♖ad1 h6 17 ♗xc5 ♗xc5 18 e6 fe 19 ♘xe6 ♖de8 20 ♘xc5 ♘xc5 21 ♖xd7 ♖xe2= Kempen–Eisenmann, corres. 1990) 10 ... ♘a6 (10 ... ♗e7 11 c4 ♘b4 12 ♕e2±) 11 c4 ♘dc7 12 ed (12 ♗f4± Winsnes) 12 ... ♗xd6 13 ♖e1+ ♗e7 14 ♘c3 0–0 15 d5 cd 16 ♘xd5 ♘xd5 17 ♕xd5 ♕xd5 18 cd ♗f6= Pirrot–Werner, Saarlouis 1986.

8 ♕xg4 de

8 ... h6?! invites 9 ♘e4! when the weakness of d6 causes problems. Instead, Adams–Burgess, Prestwich 1990, continued **9 ♘f3?!** de 10 de e6 11 0–0 ♘d7 12 a3?! ♕c7 13 ♖e1 0–0–0 14 c4 ♘e7 15 b4 g5! 16 ♕d4 c5 (16 ... ♗g7 17 ♕xa7 ♘xe5 and since 18 ♕a8+? ♔d7! 19 ♖d1+ ♘d5 fails, White has nothing better than 18 ♘xe5 ♗xe5 19 ♖a2∓.) 17 ♕e4 ♘c6?! (17 ... cb 18 ab ♘c6, as suggested by Anand, gives Black a powerful initiative.) 18 ♘c3 cb 19 ♘b5! ♘c5? 20 ♕e3 ♕b6?! 21 ab ♘a6 22 ♕e2+– g4 23 ♗e3 gf 24 ♕xf3 ♘d4 25 ♗xd4 ♖xd4 26 ♘xd4 ♕xd4 27 ♖ed1 1–0. Naturally, **8 ... e6** may be considered.

9 de

9 ♕f5!? is a sharp alternative.

Note that this position can also be reached via the move order 7 ♗d3 ♗xd3 8 ♕xd3 de 9 ♕f5. The resultant play is of a rather forcing nature, though with accurate play Black's chances are reasonable. **9 ... f6 10 ♘xh7 ed 11 0–0** *(110)* (11 ♕h5+?! ♔d7 12 ♘xf6+?? ef 13 ♕xh8? ♗b4+; 11 c4!? dc 12 ♕h5+ ♔d7 13 ♘xf6+ was obscure in Rayner–Westerinen, Glasgow 1976.) and Black should opt for active defence:

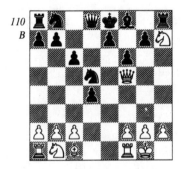

110
B

(a) **11 ... e6?!** 12 ♖e1 ♗e7 13 ♕g4!

(b) **11 ... e5?!** 12 c4 ♘c7 13 f4! and now **13 ... ♕d7** 14 ♕h5+ ♔d8 15 fe ♕e8 16 ♕xe8+ ♔xe8 17 ♘xf8 ♖xf8 would leave White only a little better. Instead Vasiukov–Bagirov, Baku 1972 continued **13 ... ♘d7?** 14 ♘g5! ♖h6 15 fe g6 16 ♕f2 ♘xe5 17 ♘e4 f5 18 ♗g5! ♘g4 19 ♕g3 ♕d7 20 ♕xg4! fg 21 ♘f6+ ♔d8 22 ♘xd7+ ♔xd7 23 ♖f7+ ♔e6 24 ♖xf8+ −.

(c) **11 ... ♕d6!** aims for counterplay against h2. 12 c4 dc 13 bc (13

♘xc3) 13 ... ♘d7 14 ♕g6+ ♔d8 15 ♖d1 ♘e5 16 ♕c2 (16 ♕e4? f5 17 ♕xf5 g6!) and rather than the dreadful 16 ... g6? 17 ♘xf8+ ♖xf8 18 ♗a3 ♕c7 19 c4+ − of Dobsa–Bullockus, corres. 1976, Black should naturally unpin with 16 ... ♔c7, when Black's chances should certainly be no worse.

9	...	**e6**
10	**0–0**	**♘d7**

10 ... ♕c7 11 ♖e1 (11 f4 ♘d7 12 c4 ♗c5+ 13 ♔h1 h5! with the rather blatant intention of ... ♘e7–f5 and ... h4) 11 ... h6 (Viable now that 12 ♘e4 drops the e-pawn.) 12 ♘f3 ♘d7 13 b3 (13 a3?! transposes to Adams–Burgess in the note to Black's 8th move, above.) 13 ... 0–0–0 14 ♗b2 g5! 15 ♘bd2 ♖g8 16 ♘e4 ♔b8 17 ♖ad1?! (17 a3) 17 ... ♗b4!∓ 18 c3 ♗e7 19 c4 ♘f4 20 ♗c3 (20 h4? ♘xg2!) 20 ... ♘c5 21 ♖xd8+ ♖xd8 22 ♘xc5 ♗xc5 23 h4 ♕b6 24 ♔h2 ♗xf2 25 ♖f1 ♕e3−+ Pavlov–Jansson, Sweden 1978.

| **11** | **c4** | **♘e7** *(111)* |

11 ... ♘b4?! 12 ♕e2 a5 13 ♘c3 ♕c7 14 a3 ♘a6 15 ♗f4! ♗e7 (15 ... h6 16 ♘ge4! ♘xe5? 17 ♕h5!+ −) 16 ♕h5 gave White a substantial advantage in Ciocaltea–Westerinen, Bucharest 1974.

| **12** | **♗f4** | |

12 ♕f4 ♘f5 is not really menacing, as 13 g4 can be met by simply 13 ... ♘h6, and 13 ♘xf7? ♔xf7 14 g4 by 14 ... g5! 15 ♕f3 ♘xe5.

| **12** | **...** | **♘g6** |
| **13** | **♖e1** | **♗e7** |

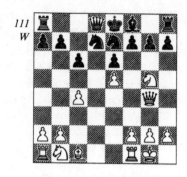

111
W

14	♘f3	♘c5
15	♗e3	h5
16	♕g3	♘e4
17	♕h3	♗b4

Already it is clear that the opening has been a complete success for Black.

18	♘bd2	♘xd2
19	♘xd2	♕d3!
20	♖ad1	0-0-0
21	a3	♗e7
22	f4	♘h4
23	♖c1	♕g6
24	♘f3	♘f5
25	♗xa7	♕g4
26	♖e4	♖d3

By original means Black is forcing open lines towards the white king.

27	♕xg4	hg
28	♘d4	g3
29	♘xf5	ef
30	♖d4	♖b3
31	hg	b6

The pressure has finally resulted in a material gain. The remainder is a largely technical matter. 32 ♗xb6 ♖xb6 33 b4 c5 34 ♖d5 cb 35 c5 ♖bh6 36 ♔f2 ba 37 c6 ♖h1 38 ♖c2 ♖b1 39 ♖a5 ♖hh1 40 ♖a8+ ♖b8 41 ♖a7 ♖b2 42 ♖a8+ ♔c7 43 ♖a7+ ♔b6 44 ♖b7+ ♔a6 45 ♖cxb2 ab 46 ♖xb2 ♗c5+ 47 ♔e2 ♗b6 48 ♔d3 ♖c1 49 g4 fg 50 f5 ♖d1+ 51 ♔c4 ♖d4+ 52 ♔b3 ♖e4 53 ♖c2 ♗c7 54 ♖d2 ♔b5 55 ♖d7 ♖e3+ 56 ♔c2 ♔xc6 57 f6 gf 0-1.

Sisniega–Fernandez Garcia
Salamanca 1987

1 e4 ♘f6 2 e5 ♘d5 3 d4 d6 4 ♘f3 ♗g4 5 ♗e2 c6 6 ♘g5 ♗f5

| 7 | e6 | fe |

7 ... ♗xe6 8 ♘xe6 fe gives White a number of promising lines.

(a) **9 c4** ♘f6 (The knight is needed on the kingside: 9 ... ♘c7?! 10 ♗d3) 10 g4!? (10 ♘c3 e5! 11 de de 12 ♕xd8+ ♔xd8 13 ♗e3 ♘bd7 14 0-0-0 ♔c7 15 g4 h6 was at least OK for Black in Velimirović–Kovačević, Vinkovci 1982.) 10 ... e5 (10 ... h6 11 f4) 11 g5 ♘fd7 12 ♗d3 g6 13 h4± Marjanović.

(b) **9 ♕d3!?** is probably best met by 9 ... ♘a6, as the alternatives are not appealing: 9 ... ♘d7?? 10 ♗h5+; 9 ... g6? 10 h4!; 9 ... ♘c7?! 10 ♘d3± (heading for f3 and g5); 9 ... ♕a5+ 10 ♗d2; 9 ... ♘f6 10 0-0 ♘bd7 11 f4 g6 (11 ... e5 12 fe de 13 de ♘xe5 14 ♕g3±) 12 ♘d2!±, again heading for g5 in Ivanović–Kovačević, Novi Sad 1984.

(c) **9 ♗g4** is the normal move, but may not be strongest.

(c1) **9 ...** ♕a5+ 10 c3 ♘c7

11 0–0 ♘d7 12 b4 ♕d5 13 ♘a3
(Threatens to trap the queen.) 13
... e5 14 ♗f3 ♕f7 (14 ... ♕e6 15
b5±; 14 ... e4 15 c4 ♕e6 16 ♗g4
♕f7 17 f3!±) 15 b5 d5 16 bc bc
17 ♗g4! ♘f6 18 ♗h3 e6 19 c4!±
exposed the black king in Smagin–
Galakhov, USSR 1983.

(c2) 9 ... ♘c7 10 ♕e2 (10 0–0
♘d7 11 ♖e1 e5 12 ♗xd7+ ♕xd7
13 de d5 is perfectly satisfactory
for Black; 10 ♕d3!? g6 11 ♗g5
♗g7 12 ♘d2 e5 13 0–0–0 ♘d7 14
♘e4 (Sinkko–Ziese, corres. 1977)
14 ... ♘f6 15 de ♘xe4 16 ♕xe4
♗xe5 17 f4 ♗g7 18 f5) 10 ... ♘d7
11 0–0 ♘f6 (11 ... e5 12 de!? ♘xe5
13 ♗h3 (Dolmatov, Smagin) gives
White a powerful initiative; one
idea is to fling the f-pawn up the
board.) 12 ♗h3 g6 13 ♘d2 ♗g7
14 ♘f3 h6 15 ♖e1 ♕d7 16 ♗d2 g5
forced White to initiate exchanges
on e6, with approximate equality,
in Hernandez–Fernandez, Thessaloniki ol 1988.

8   ♗h5+

Apart from the normal 8 g4,
White can try two other squares
for this bishop.

8 ♗g4 ♘f6 9 ♗xf5 (9 h3 ♗xg4
10 hg e5) 9 ... ef 10 0–0 ♕d7 11
♖e1 ♘a6 12 ♕f3 ♘c7 13 ♕b3 h6
14 ♕f7+ ♔d8 15 ♘h3 e6 16 ♕g6
♕e8 17 ♕g3 g5 gave Black a sound
extra pawn in Pesch–Hänisch, W.
Germany 1985, though the position needs some organising.

8 ♗d3 ♘a6 9 0–0 ♘ac7 10 c4
♘f6 11 ♘c3 g6 12 ♖e1 ♗g7 13
♗xf5 ef 14 ♕b3 (Gufeld–Bagirov,

Tbilisi 1971) 14 ... ♖b8!∓.

8   ...   g6
9   g4   ♘f6?!

Black should certainly prefer 9
... ♗xc2 10 ♕xc2 gh when the
knight has a choice of captures:

(a) 11 ♘xh7?! gives Black two
options: 11 ... ♕b6 12 ♘xf8 ♖xf8
13 ♗e3 ♘xe3 14 fe ♕a5+ 15
♘c3 ♕g5 16 0–0–0 ♔d7 17 ♕b3
♘a6∓ Wason–Zeh, corres. 1967
and 11 ... hg 12 ♕g6+ ♔d7 13
♘g5 ♘f6 14 d5!? ♕a5+ 15 ♘c3
(Perenyi–Sindik, Kecskemet 1980)
15 ... ♖g8 whereupon 16 de+?
♔c7 17 ♕f7 ♘a6 leaves the white
queen in trouble.

(b) 11 ♘xe6 *(112)*. Black has a
safe continuation and an adven-
turous one:

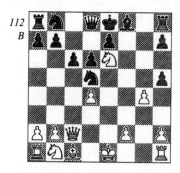

(b1) 11 ... ♕d7 12 ♕f5 ♖g8!?
(12 ... ♘f6 13 0–0!?) 13 ♘c3 ♘f6
14 g5 ♔f7 15 ♘d8+ ♔e8 16
♘e6 ♔f7 ½–½ Matsuura–Segal,
Brazilian Ch 1988.

(b2) 11 ... ♕a5+ 12 ♗d2 ♘b4
13 ♕b3 (13 ♕e4?! ♘8a6 14 a3
♕d5∓ Lorenz) 13 ... ♘8a6 14 0–0
♕d5 15 ♗xb4 ♕xb3 16 ab ♘xb4

17 ♘c7+ ♔d7 18 ♘xa8 ♘a6 gave
Black good structural compen-
sation in Bastian–Grün, Bad
Neunahr 1980.

| 10 | gf | ♘xh5 |
| 11 | fg | |

Naturally 11 fe also comes into
consideration, but the text logically exposes the black king.

11	...	hg
12	♘xe6	♛a5+
13	♘c3	♘a6
14	d5!	♘f6
15	♛d3	♖g8
16	dc	♘b4
17	♛e2	bc
18	a3	♘bd5
19	♗d2	♔d7
20	0-0-0	♘xc3
21	♗xc3	♗h6+?!

Now White's initiative becomes
overwhelming: 22 ♔b1 ♛b5 23
♖d3 ♘d5 24 ♗d4 ♘f4 25 ♘xf4
♗xf4 26 ♖e1 ♖ae8 (26 ... e5 27
♛g4+ ♔c7 28 ♛e6 ♖gd8 29 ♗e3
does not help Black.) 27 a4! ♛a5
28 ♖b3 ♔c7 29 ♗c3 ♛xa4 30
♖b4 1–0.

Deev–Agzamov
Erevan 1981

1 e4 ♘f6 2 e5 ♘d5 3 d4 d6 4 ♘f3
♗g4 5 ♗e2 c6 6 ♘g5 ♗f5 7 e6
fe

| 8 | g4 | ♗g6 |
| 9 | ♗d3 | |

9 h4 h6 10 ♘xe6 ♛d7 11 ♘f4
♘xf4 (11 ... ♗f7 12 c4 ♘b6 13
b3 ♘a6 14 ♗b2 0–0–0 15 ♘c3
♛e8 16 ♘g2 ♘c7 17 ♘e3 d5 18 c5
♘d7 19 f4 ♘xc5∞ Malaniuk–

Sergeev, Kiev 1984.) 12 ♗xf4 ♘a6
13 h5 ♗h7 14 ♛d2 e6 15 ♖h3
♗e7 16 ♘a3 0–0 17 ♗e3 ♘c7 18
c4?! b5! 19 g5 ♗xg5 20 ♗xg5 hg
21 ♛xg5 b4 22 ♘b1 e5 23 ♗g4
♗f5 24 ♖g3 ♗xg4 25 ♛xg4 ♛f7
26 ♖g2 ed 27 ♘d2 ♖ae8+ ♔f1
♖e6 29 ♛xd4 ♖h6 30 ♘e4 ♘e6
31 ♛xd6 ♛xh5 32 ♘g3 ♛h3 33
♛xc6 ♖hf6 34 ♘e4 ♛xg2+ 35
♔xg2 ♘f4+ 0–1 Ulybin–Dreev,
Sochi 1986.

9 ♘xe6 ♛d7 10 ♘f4 ♗f7 (10
... ♘xf4) 11 c4 ♘b6 12 b3 (Jasni-
kowski's 12 d5 can be met by 12
... e5 13 de ♗xe6) 12 ... e5 13 de
de 14 ♘d3 ♛c7 15 ♘c3 ♘a6 16
♗g5 ♗g6 17 ♛d2 ♘c5∓ Türn–
Keres, Estonian Ch (Tallinn) 1945.

| 9 | ... | ♗xd3 |
| 10 | ♛xd3 | ♘f6 *(113)* |

10 ... ♘a6 11 ♘xh7 ♛a5+ 12
c3 ♘f6 13 ♘g5 ♘c7?! (13 ... ♛d5)
14 f3 c5 15 0–0 cd 16 cd g6 17
♘c3 ♗h6 18 b4± Majstorović–
Kopylov, corres. 1970.

10 ... g6 has been the normal
move here, but gives White a
pleasant choice:

(a) 11 ♛f3 ♘f6 12 ♘xe6 ♛d7
13 ♛e2 ♘a6 (13 ... ♔f7 does not
work very well with a weakened
kingside.) 14 ♘c3 ♘c7 15 ♘xc7+
♛xc7 16 ♗g5 ♗g7 17 0–0–0
0–0–0 18 ♔b1 ♛d7?! 19 f3± e6?
20 ♖he1 ♖de8 21 ♖d3 ♛f7 22
♖e3± Oll–Kulinski, Yaroslavl
1983.

(b) 11 ♘c3 ♘f6 (11 ... ♘c7? 12
♛f3; 11 ... ♗h6? 12 ♘xh7!±
Frolov–Minich, Trnava 1989) 12

♘xe6 ♕d7 13 ♕e2 ♘a6 14 h3 ♘c7
15 ♘xc7+ ♕xc7 16 ♗g5 0–0–0
17 0–0–0 ♗g7 18 ♖he1 ♖de8 19
♖d3 e5 20 ♖e3 ♘d7 21 de ♖xe5
22 ♖xe5 ♗xe5 23 f4 h6 24 fe hg
26 e6 ♘e5 was reasonable for
Black in McDonald–Landen-
bergue, Zug 1989.

(c) **11 h4!?** ♘f6? (11 ... ♘a6) 12
♘xe6 ♕d7 13 ♕e2 ♘a6 (13 ...
♔f7 14 h5!) 14 h5 ♘c7 (14 ... gh
15 g5+ −) 15 ♘xc7+ ♕xc7 16 hg
♗g7 17 g5 ♕a5+ 18 ♗d2 ♕d5 19
♖h4+ − Belotti–Herndl, Mitropa
Cup 1990.

(d) **11 0–0**

(d1) **11 ... ♕d7**

(d11) **12 ♕e2** ♘a6 13 c4? (13
♘xe6 ♘ac7 14 ♘xc7+ ♘xc7 15
♖e1) 13 ... ♘dc7 14 ♕f3 (14 ♖e1
♗g7!∓) 14 ... ♗h6! 15 ♕f7+
♔d8 16 h3 (16 ♘xh7 ♗xc1 17
♖xc1 e5!∓ Dunworth) 16 ... ♘b4
17 ♘a3 ♗xg5 18 ♗xg5 ♕e8 19
♕f3 h5! was Thipsay–Agzamov,
Calcutta 1986. The white king is
in grave danger down the h-file,
while the central pawn mass pro-
tects the black king very well.

(d12) **12 ♖e1** ♘a6 13 ♕f3 ♘ac7
14 ♕f7+ ♔d8 15 ♘c3 (15 ♘xh7
♕e8 16 ♘g5 ♔d7; 15 ♘xe6+
♘xe6 16 ♕xe6 ♕xe6 17 ♖xe6
♔d7=) 15 ... ♘xc3 16 bc ♗h6
17 ♘xh7 ♕e8 18 ♘g5 ♗xg5 19
♕xe8+ ♔xe8 20 ♗xg5 ♔d7 21
♔g2 ♖h7 was about equal in
Kristoffel–Idema, corres. 1984.

(d2) **11 ... ♗h6** 12 ♘xe6 ♕d7
13 ♕e2 ♗xc1 14 ♖xc1 ♘a6 (14
... ♘c7 15 ♘xc7+ ♕xc7 16 ♖e1±

Euwe) 15 f4 ♘ac7 16 f5 ♘xe6 17
fe ♕c8 18 ♘d2 0–0 19 ♖f1 ♘f4
Pineault–Wright, corres. 1985.

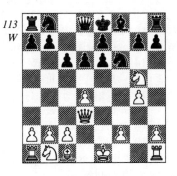

**113
W**

11   ♘xe6

11 f3 ♕d7 12 ♕e2 ♘a6 13 ♘xe6
♘c7 14 ♘xc7+ ♕xc7 15 ♘c3
0–0–0 16 ♕e6+ ♕d7 17 ♕xd7+
♘xd7 18 ♗f4 e5 19 de ♘xe5 20
♗xe5 ♖e8 21 f4 de 22 f5 ♗b4 23
♔e2 ♗xc3 24 bc e4∓ Moss–
Burgess, Hastings Challengers
1989/90.

11 ♕e2!? ♕d7 12 ♘c3 ♘a6 13
♗d2 ♘c7 14 0–0–0 h6 (14 ... g6)
15 ♘ge4 0–0–0 16 h3 g5?! (16 ...
♕e8) 17 f4 gf 18 ♗xf4 ♗g7 19
♖hf1 ♖df8 20 ♔b1 ♘fd5 21 ♗c1
♕e8 22 ♘xd5 gave White rather
the better chances due to the weakness of Black's kingside in Morris–
Burgess, Birmingham (BUCA)
1990, though a swindle was forthcoming: 22 ... cd?! 23 ♘g3 ♖xf1
24 ♕xf1 ♕a4!? 25 ♘h5? (25 ♕d3±)
25 ... ♗xd4! 26 b3 ♕b5!∓.

11	...	♕d7
12	♕e2	♔f7!
13	♘g5+	♔g8
14	h3	

14 f3 h5 (14 ... ♘a6) 15 ♕e6+
♕xe6 16 ♘xe6 ♘a6 17 g5 ♘d5 18
g6?! ♘ac7 19 ♘xc7 ♘xc7 20 ♘c3
e5 21 de ♖e8 22 ♗f4 de 23 ♗d2
♘e6 24 0–0–0 h4 25 ♗e3 a5 26
♘e4 ♖h5 27 c3 ♖f5 28 ♖hf1 ♘f4∓
Hill–Burgess, Bristol Ch 1990.

14	...	♘a6
15	f4	h5
16	♖g1	hg
17	hg	e5
18	de	de
19	f5	

19 fe ♖e8 20 e6 ♕d4 also fails
to keep lines closed.

19	...	♗c5
20	♘e3	♗xe3
21	♕xe3	♘d5
22	♕d2	♕e7
23	♘c3	♘f4
24	♘ce4	♖d8
25	♕e3	♖h2
26	♕b3+	♖d5

Black is much better, as White
has no way of exploiting the pin.
Note, for instance, 27 ♖d1??
♕b4+! 28 ♕xb4 ♖e2+ 29 ♔f1
♖xd1+ mating.

Smagin–Agzamov
USSR Ch (Riga) 1985

1 e4 ♘f6 2 e5 ♘d5 3 d4 d6 4 ♘f3
♗g4 5 ♗e2 c6 6 ♘g5 ♗f5
7 ♗d3 ♗xd3

7 ... ♕d7?! 8 ♕f3 g6 (8 ... e6) 9
ed (9 g4) 9 ... e6 10 ♗xf5 (10 ♘e4)
10 ... gf 11 c4 ♘b4 12 ♕b3 ♗xd6
13 c5 ♗xc5 14 dc ♘d3+ 15 ♔e2
♘xc1+ 16 ♖xc1 ♖g8 17 ♕e3 ♕e7
18 ♘f3 ♖xg2 19 ♘c3 ♘d7 20 ♖g1
♖xg1 21 ♖xg1 0–0–0 gave Black

interesting play in Morris–D.
Ledger, Hastings Challengers
1990/1.

8 ♕xd3 h6

8 ... de 9 de h6 generally transposes, but cuts out some of Black's
options and gives White the extra
possibilities 9 ♕f5 (see 7 ♗g4
♗xg4 8 ♕xg4 de 9 ♕f5) and 10
♘xf7 ♔xf7 11 c4 ♕a5+ 12 ♗d2
♘b4 13 ♕f5+ ♔g8 14 a3 c5∞
(Hort).

For 8 ... e6!, see the game
Winsnes–Crocker.

9 ♘f3

9 ♘e4! is the most promising
move. Then:

(a) 9 ... ♘d7? 10 ed! ed 11 ♕e2
wins a pawn.

(b) 9 ... ♕b6 10 0–0 de (10 ...
♘d7?! 11 ed ed 12 c4 ♘b4 13
♕e2± U. Nielsen–Crocker, Gausdal Peer Gynt 1990) 11 de ♘d7 12
e6±.

(c) 9 ... ♕c7?! 10 ed± or 10
♕g3.

(d) 9 ... ♘a6 10 ♕g3 (10 e6? fe;
10 ed!?) 10 ... de 11 de ♘c5 12
♘xc5 ♕a5+ 13 c3 ♕xc5 14 e6.

(e) 9 ... de 10 de and now:

(e1) 10 ... ♘c7 11 ♕e2 ♘e6 12
0–0 ♘d4 13 ♕d3 ♘f5 14 ♘f6+
gf 15 ♕xf5± Subašić–Knežević,
Sarajevo 1978.

(e2) 10 ... ♕c7 11 f4 ♘d7 12 c4
♘5b6 13 0–0 0–0–0 14 ♕e2 f5 15
♘f2 e6 16 a4 ♘c5 17 a5 ♘bd7 18
b4 ♘b3 19 ♖a4 ♘xc1 20 ♖xc1 g5
21 ♘d2 ♖g8 22 ♘d3 ♘b8 23
c5 ♕d7 13 ♖a3 gf 25 ♘c4 was
Yudasin–Landenbergue,   Bern

1989. White's attack turned out to be the stronger.

(e3) **10 ... e6** 11 0–0 ♘d7 12 ♕g3 (12 f4?! ♘c5=; 12 ♘d6+!? ♗xd6 13 ed ♘e5 14 ♕d4± Ostojić–Jäckle, Berlin 1987) 12 ... g6 (12 ... g5 13 c4 ♘b4 14 ♖d1; 12 ... ♕b6) 13 c4 (13 b3 h5 14 h4 ♗c5 15 ♖d1 ♕b6? 16 ♘bd2! ♗d4 17 ♘c4± Panchenko–D. Cramling, Hradec Kralove 1981) 13 ... ♘b4 14 ♖d1 ♘c2? (14 ... ♕a5) 15 ♖xd7! ♔xd7 16 ♕d3+ ♔c7 17 ♕xc2 ♕d4 18 b3! ♖d8 (18 ... ♕xa1 19 ♘ec3) 19 ♘bc3 ♕xe5 20 ♗b2 ♕f5 21 ♘b5+ cb 22 ♗xh8 ♗b4 23 cb+ ♔b6 24 ♖c1 ♕f4 25 g3 1–0 Roozenbeck–Blees, Apeldoorn 1987.

9 ♕h3?! de 10 de e6 11 0–0 ♘d7 12 c4 ♘e7 13 f4 ♕b6+ 14 ♔h1 hg! 15 ♕xh8 ♘g6 16 ♕h5 gf 17 ♕e2 ♕d4 gave Black at least enough compensation in Koppel–Pavlov, corres. 1978.

9 ♘h7?! ♕a5+ 10 ♗d2 ♕a6 11 c4 (11 ♕xa6 ♘xa6 12 ♘xf8 de 13 ♘e6 fe 14 de 0–0–0) 11 ... ♖xh7 12 ♕xh7 ♕xc4 13 ed (13 ♕e4 de 14 ♕xe5 ♘d7 15 ♕e2 ♕xd4) 13 ... ♘a6 14 ♕e4 ♘c5 15 ♘a3 ♕a4 16 ♕e2 ♕xd4 17 0–0 e6 was promising for Black in Schneider–D. Cramling, Sweden 1981.

9	...	e6
10	0–0	de
11	de	♘d7
12	♕e2	

12 ♖e1 ♕c7 *(114)* gives a position that can be reached via 8 ... e6 9 0–0 de 10 de ♘d7 11 ♖e1 h6

12 ♘f3 ♕c7. White has a variety of approaches:

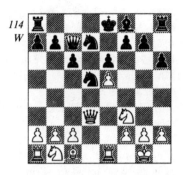

114
W

(a) **13 a3** a5 14 ♘c3 ♘xc3 15 ♕xc3 ♗e7 16 ♖e4 ♘b6 17 ♕e1 a4 18 ♗d2 c5 19 c4 ♕c6∓ Lutikov–Bagirov, Chelyabinsk 1972.

(b) **13 ♕e4** 0–0–0 (Black's play in Martinović–Tatai, Pamporovo 1982 was not really in the spirit of the position: 13 ... ♗e7?! 14 a3 b5 15 ♘bd2 c5 16 a4 b4 17 a5 ♖d8 18 ♘c4±. Only with a pair of knights exchanged can such a queenside advance be a good idea for Black.) 14 a3 g5 15 b4 ♗g7 16 ♗b2 ♔b8 17 ♘bd2 ♖dg8 18 ♘c4 ♘7b6 19 ♘xb6 ♘xb6 20 a4 ♘d5∞ Martinović–Rogulj, Vrnjacka Banja 1982.

(c) **13 c4** ♘e7 14 ♘c3 g5? (14 ... 0–0–0 15 ♕e2 g5 gives equal chances.) 15 ♘e4 ♗g7 16 ♕d6! (16 ♘d6+? ♔f8 leaves e5 weak.) 16 ... ♖c8 (16 ... ♕xd6 17 ♘xd6+ ♔f8 18 ♘xb7 ♘g6 gives White a very good ending due to the weakness of Black's queenside.) 17 ♕a3 ♖d8?! (17 ... ♖a8) 18 ♘d6+

♔f8 19 ♗xg5! hg 20 ♘xf7 ♖h6 (20 ... ♔xf7 21 ♘xg5+ ♔e8 22 ♘xe6 ♕xe5 just prolongs the suffering.) 21 ♘3xg5 ♖g6 22 ♘xd8 ♕xd8 23 ♕f3+ ♔g8 (23 ... ♘f5 24 ♘xe6+ ♖xe6 25 ♕xf5+ ♔e7 26 ♕g5+) 24 ♕f7+ ♔h8 25 ♕xg6 1–0 Adams–Burgess, London (Barbican) 1990.

(d) 13 ♘bd2 and Black has tried three moves:

(d1) 13 ... ♖d8 14 ♘f1 c5 15 b3 ♘7b6 16 a3 ♘e7 17 ♕e4 ♘f5 18 ♘g3 g6 was level in Tringov–Rogulj, Vrnjacka Banja 1982.

(d2) 13 ... 0–0–0 14 ♘c4 g5 15 h3 and now 15 ... ♗e7 16 ♘d6+ ♗xd6 17 ed ♕xd6 18 c4 ♘c5 19 ♕a3 ♘c7 20 ♕xa7 gave White the better prospects in Gufeld–Landenbergue, Biel Open 1989. Instead 15 ... ♖g8!? is Gufeld's recommendation.

(d3) 13 ... a5 14 ♘c4 b5 15 ♘e3 ♖b8 16 c4 ♘f4 17 ♕e4 ♘g6 18 cb cb (18 ... ♗b4 Bagirov) 19 ♗d2 ♗c5 20 ♖ac1 0–0 21 ♖c2 was Dvoiris–Kengis, USSR 1982. The simplest way of maintaining equality was now 21 ... ♖fc8 22 ♖ec1 ♕d8.

12 ♘bd2 ♕c7 13 ♖e1 is considered under 12 ♖e1 ♕c7 13 ♘bd2 above.

The options avoided by the 8 ... e6 move order are 12 b3 and 12 ♖d1:

(a) Chiburdanidze–Agzamov, USSR Ch (Tashkent) 1980, the stem game for 8 ... h6, continued 12 b3 ♕c7 13 ♗b2 ♗e7 14 ♘bd2

0–0 15 ♘e4 ♖fd8 16 c4 ♘f4 17 ♕e3 ♘g6 18 ♖fe1 b6 19 ♘g3 ♘c5=.

(b) 12 ♖d1 ♕c7 13 c4 ♘e7 14 ♘c3 (14 ♗f4 ♘g6 15 ♗g3 0–0–0 16 ♘c3 ♗b4!∓ Hort) and Black can choose between a calm approach and a wilder one:

(b1) 14 ... ♘g6 15 ♘e4 ♘c5 (15 ... ♘dxe5? 16 ♘xe5 ♘xe5 17 ♕g3) 16 ♕e3 (16 ♘d6+ ♗xd6 17 ♕xd6 ♖d8=) 16 ... ♘xe4 17 ♕xe4± Lane–Burgess, Hastings Challengers 1988/9.

(b2) 14 ... g5!? 15 ♘e4 ♗g7 16 ♘d6+ (16 ♕d6 is less effective than with the rook on e1: 16 ... ♕xd6 17 ♘xd6+ ♔f8 18 ♘xb7 ♘xe5 or 16 ... ♖c8 17 ♕a3 ♖d8 18 ♘d6+ ♔f8.) 16 ... ♔f8 17 ♘xb7 ♘xe5 18 ♕d6 ♕xd6 19 ♘xd6 ♘xf3+ 20 gf ♗e5 21 ♗e3 ♘g6 gave Black slightly the better of it in Sorensen–Sprenger, corres. 1985.

12 ...   ♕c7
13 ♗d2

13 c4 ♘e7 14 ♘c3 0–0–0 15 b3?! (15 ♖e1 g5 16 ♗e3) 15 ... g5 16 ♗b2 g4!? (16 ... ♗g7) 17 ♘e1 ♗g7 18 ♕xg4 (18 ♘d3 ♘g6) 18 ... ♖hg8 19 ♕d1 ♗xe5 20 ♕h3 led to disaster for White in Unzicker–Grün, Bundesliga 1982/3. Black's pieces simply piled into White's kingside: 20 ... ♖g6 21 ♔h1 ♖dg8 22 ♖g1 ♘f6 23 ♘d3 ♘g4 24 g3 ♘f5 25 ♖d2 ♗d4 26 ♘e4 ♗xb2 27 ♖xb2 h5 28 ♖e1 h4 29 f3 (29 ♖g1 ♖h6 30 ♕f1 ♘xh2!) 29 ... hg 30 fg ♖xg4 31 ♘f6 ♖h4 32 ♕xh4

♘xh4 33 ♘xg8 g2+ 34 ♖xg2 ♘xg2 35 ♔xg2 ♕d8 0–1.

13 b3 ♗c5 (A more active plan, beginning with 13 ... 0–0–0 or 13 ... g5!? could be preferred.) **14 c4 ♘e7 15 ♗b2 ♘g6 16 g3 0–0 17 ♔g2** (17 h4 f5!? and 17 ♘bd2 ♗b4! are both mentioned by Mencinger.) **17 ... ♖fd8 18 h4** gave White somewhat the better chances in Mencinger–Rogulj, Yugoslavia 1987, as it is hard for Black to create counterchances against White's kingside push.

13	...	a5
14	♖e1	♘c5
15	♘c3	♘xc3
16	♗xc3	♗e7 *(115)*

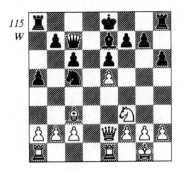

Agzamov now considered the position equal. As the further course of the game demonstrates, Black's chances are based on queenside expansion.

17	♗d4	♖d8
18	♕e3	b6
19	♖ad1	0–0
20	♖d2	♘d7
21	♖ed1	

21 c4 followed by ♖ed1 and ♗c3 was suggested by Agzamov as a way to frustrate Black's queenside ambitions.

21	...	c5!
22	♗c3	♕c6

By threatening ... a4, ... b5, ... ♘b6, Black provokes a weakness.

23	b3	a4
24	♕f4	ab
25	ab	♖fe8
26	♗b2?	

After this rather pointless move White's problems become acute. 26 h4 was better.

26	...	b5
27	h4	♘b6
28	♖xd8	♖xd8
29	♖xd8+	♗xd8
30	♕d2	♕d5
31	h5	♗c7
32	♕e2	c4!

Now 33 bc ♘xc4! with ... b4 and ... ♘a3 would give White serious problems, so there followed: 33 b4 ♘c8 34 ♗d4 ♘e7 35 c3 ♕a8 36 g4?! ♘d5 37 ♕e4 ♕a1+ 38 ♔g2 ♕c1 39 ♘g1 ♗d8! 40 ♘e2 ♕d1 41 ♘g1 ♗g5 42 ♘f3 ♗c1! 43 ♗e3 (43 ♕e1 ♘f4+ 44 ♔g3 ♕d3 wins the c-pawn, since White is powerless against ... ♗b2 and ... ♘e2+.) 43 ... ♗xe3 44 fe ♕e2+ 45 ♔g3 ♘xc3 46 ♕a8+ ♔h7 47 ♕a7 ♘e4+ 48 ♔f4 ♕g2 0–1.

Black threatens 49 ... ♕g3+ 50 ♔xe4 ♕g4 #, whilst 49 ♕xf7 ♕xf3+ 50 ♔xf3 ♘g5+ wins the knight.

Winsnes–Crocker
Gausdal International 1990

**1 e4 ♞f6 2 e5 ♞d5 3 d4 d6 4 ♞f3
♝g4 5 ♝e2 c6 6 ♞g5 ♝f5 7
♝d3 ♝xd3 8 ♛xd3**

8 ... e6!

This novelty was conceived and analysed by the Cambridge contingent at Gausdal, Summer 1990. Ideally, Black would like to play 8 ... de 9 de e6, but after 10 c4 Black must experiment with 10 ... ♛a5+ since 10 ... ♞b4? 11 ♛xd8+ ♚xd8 12 ♞xf7+ loses a pawn. Also, 8 ... h6 9 ♞f3 de 10 de e6 is desirable, but 9 ♞e4! makes it difficult, if at all possible, for Black to equalise in view of the sensitive nature of the d6 square.

8 ... e6 aims to avoid these problems. There are also a couple of 'spin-offs': firstly the messy line 8 ... de 9 ♛f5 is avoided; secondly, thanks to Black delaying ... h6, after 8 ... e6 9 0–0 de 10 de ♞d7 White is more tied down to defending e5 than after 8 ... h6 9 ♞f3 de 10 de e6.

Some novelties have to wait decades for a practical test. This one was uncorked less than two days after its invention. The theoretically knowledgeable player of the white pieces sank into nearly an hour's agonised thought before threatening mate in one.

9 ♛f3

Instead **9 0–0** de 10 de ♞d7 leads, after 11 ♛e2 h6 12 ♞f3, or 11 c4 ♞e7 12 ♛e2 ♛c7 13 ♜e1 h6 14 ♞f3, or 11 ♜e1 h6 12 ♞f3, to positions normally reached via 8 ... h6 9 ♞f3 de 10 de ♞d7. White has a number of independent options:

(a) **9 ♞xh7?!** ♝e7 leaves the knight in trouble: 10 ed ♛xd6; 10 f4? ♞b4; 10 ♛h3 ♚d7 (10 ... g6) 11 ed (11 ♛d3 ♞b4) 11 ... ♝xd6.

(b) **9 ed** ♝xd6 is a good Caro-Kann type position for Black. Note that 10 ♞xh7? fails to 10 ... ♞b4 11 ♛e4 f5 12 ♛xe6+ ♛e7.

(c) **9 ♞e4** is harmless when Black has not used a tempo on ... h6. 9 ... de 10 de ♞d7 at least equalises.

(d) **9 a3** more or less wastes a tempo: 9 ... de 10 de ♞d7.

(e) **9 c4 ♞b4 10 ♛b3** was the main line of our original analysis. It appears that Black's resources are sufficient. **10 ... de 11 a3 ♝e7!** *(116)*

116
W

(e1) **12 ♞f3?** e4.

(e2) **12 ♞e4?** ♛xd4.

(e3) **12 h4** h6 13 ♞h3 ♞4a6 is very similar to the main line.

(e4) **12 f4!?** h6 (12 ... ♛xd4 13 ab ef is perhaps a little speculative after either 14 ♘h3 ♗h4+ 15 ♔f1 g5 or 14 ♘f3 ♕e4+ 15 ♔f1 ♘a6; 12 ... ♗xg5 13 ♕xb4 ef 14 ♕xb7 ♘d7∞) 13 ♘h3 ♘4a6 13 ♕xb7 ed! — compare (e52).

(e5) 12 ♘h3 ♘4a6 13 ♕xb7 (13 de?! ♘c5) and Black has two good methods:

(e51) 13 ... ♕b6!? 14 ♕xb6 (14 ♕c8+ ♗d8; 14 ♕xa8 0–0 (threatening 15 ... ♘c7) 15 c5 ♕c7 16 de ♘d7∓) 14 ... ab 15 de with good compensation for Black: 15 ... ♘b4 16 ♔d1 (After 16 0–0 Black can take a draw with ... ♘c2–b4–c2.) 16 ... ♘d7 17 f4 ♘c5 intending ... ♘cd3 and ... ♗c5–d4, or Peter Wells' idea 15 ... ♘c5!? 16 0–0 ♘b3 17 ♖a2 ♘a6 18 ♘c3 (18 ♘d2 ♘xc1 19 ♖xc1 ♘b4 20 ♖aa1 ♘d3) 18 ... ♘ac5 19 ♗e3 ♘d3.

(e52) 13 ... ed!? (Wells) 14 ♕xa8 ♕b6 15 b4 0–0 16 c5 ♕c7 17 b5 (17 0–0 ♘d7 18 ♕xf8+ ♔xf8) 17 ... ♘xc5 to be followed by ... ♘d7–b6.

9 ...   ♕c7
10 c4

10 ed ♗xd6 11 c4 gives Black the additional options 11 ... ♗f4!? and 11 ... ♘f6.

10 ...   ♘b4
11 ed   ♗xd6
12 ♕e4

12 ♕e2 ♗f4 is comfortable for Black (13 0–0 ♗xc1 14 ♖xc1 ♕f4).

12 c5 is also best met by 12 ... ♗f4, e.g. 13 ♗xf4 ♕xf4 14 ♕xf4 ♘d3+ 15 ♔d1 ♘xf4 16 ♘e4 b6 with ... ♘a6 to follow. Note that

instead 12 ... ♗xh2? fails to 13 ♖xh2 f6 (13 ... ♕xh2 14 ♕xf7+ ♔d8 15 ♕xg7+–) 14 ♕h5+ g6 15 ♕xg6+.

12 ...   ♘d7

12 ... ♗f4?! 13 0–0!? ♗xh2+ 14 ♔h1 leaves Black's development seriously deficient.

13 a3 *(117)*

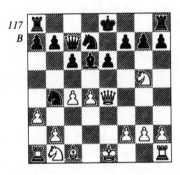

13 ...   ♘a6?!

13 ... ♘f6! equalises: 14 ♕e2 (14 ♘xe6?? fe 15 ♕xe6+ ♔f8–+) 14 ... ♗f4 15 0–0 ♗xc1 16 ♖xc1 ♕f4 17 ♕e3 (17 ♕d2 ♕xd2 (17 ... ♘d3) 18 ♘xd2 ♘d3) 17 ... ♘d3 18 ♖c2 ♘g4.

14 ♘c3   ♘f6
15 ♕e2   0–0–0?!

15 ... 0–0 is rather less hubristic.

16 ♘f3   ♖he8
17 0–0   ♘g4?

The only consistent continuation was **17 ... e5 18 d5 ♘c5!?**, when Black still has reasonable chances.

18 h3   ♘h2
19 ♖d1   ♘xf3+
20 ♕xf3

Now White has a ready-made queenside attack. The finish is somewhat agonising: 20 … e5 21 d5 ♘c5 22 ♗e3 ♘b3 23 ♖ab1 ♔b8 (23 … c5 24 ♘b5) 24 dc bc 25 ♘e4 ♘d4 26 ♗xd4 ed 27 g3 ♗e5 28 b4 g6 29 ♘c5 ♕d6 30 ♕xf7 ♖e7 31 ♕f3 ♖ee8 32 ♘a6+ ♔b7 33 b5 ♖f8 34 ♕d3 ♖f5 35 bc++ ♔xc6 36 c5 ♕f6 37 ♕b5+ ♔d5 38 ♕b3+ ♔e4 39 ♖e1# (1–0).

Yudasin–Timoshenko
Podolsk 1989

1 e4 ♘f6 2 e5 ♘d5 3 d4 d6 4 ♘f3 ♗g4 5 ♗e2 c6

6   c4   ♘b6

6 … ♘c7 is rather a solid continuation which presents White with few difficulties in maintaining some advantage.

(a) **7 ♗e3** ♗xf3 8 ♗xf3 de is probably not White's best.

(b) **7 ♘g5** ♗f5 8 ♗g4 ♗xg4 9 ♕xg4 ♕d7 10 h3 h6 11 ed ed 12 ♘f3 ♘ba6 13 ♘c3 0-0-0 14 ♕xd7+ ♖xd7 15 ♗e3 g6 16 0-0-0 ♗g7 17 ♖he1± Hübner–Hort, Bundesliga 1988/9.

(c) **7 ♕b3** de (7 … ♕c8 8 ♕e3 ♗xf3 9 ♗xf3 d5 10 b3± Sokolov–Kengis, Tallinn 1981) 8 de ♕c8 9 ♘c3 ♘d7 10 ♗f4 ♘e6 11 ♗g3 ♘dc5 12 ♕a3± Bohm–Wiiala, corres. 1984.

(d) **7 ed ed**. Practice strongly suggests that White's most promising plans involve the cramping thrust d5:

(d1) **8 d5!?** ♗e7 9 0-0 0-0 10 ♘c3 cd 11 cd ♘d7 12 ♗f4!± Ehlvest–Kengis, Tallinn 1981.

(d2) **8 ♕b3** ♕c8 9 h3 ♗h5 (9 … ♗f5) 10 ♘c3 ♗e7 11 0-0 0-0 12 d5! (12 ♖e1 ♖e8 13 ♗e3 ♘d7 14 ♘d2 ♗g6 15 ♖ac1 ♘e6 16 ♕d1 a5 17 ♗f1 ♕d8 18 g3± Hort–Kindl, Bad Wörishofen 1986) 12 … c5 (12 … ♘ba6) 13 ♗f4± h6 14 ♖fe1 g5? 15 ♘xg5!! ♗xe2 16 ♘ge4 was overwhelming for White in Rodriguez–D. Cramling, Biel Open 1988.

(d3) **8 0-0** ♗e7 9 ♘c3 0-0 (9 … ♘d7) 10 d5 (10 h3 ♗h5 11 ♕b3 ♕c8 transposes to [d2].) 10 … c5 11 ♗f4 ♘d7 12 ♘e4 ♘e8 (12 … ♘f6 and 12 … ♘b6 are both met by 13 ♘xc5) 13 ♘fd2 ♗f5 14 ♗d3 and the threat of ♘xc5 causes some awkwardness: **14 … ♗g6** 15 ♕c2 ♗f6 16 ♘xd6 ♗xd3 17 ♕xd3 ♗xb2 18 ♖ab1± ; **14 … g5** 15 ♗e3 ♗xe4 16 ♘xe4 f5 17 ♘g3! f4 18 ♕h5 ♖f7 19 ♘f5± Widenmann–Herbrechtsmeier, corres. 1984.

7   ed

A rarely played, but quite sensible idea. How useful is … c6 in an Exchange Variation?

7   …   ed

7 … ♗xf3?! can be met by either 8 ♗xf3 ♘xc4 9 de ♗xe7 10 0-0 0-0 11 ♘c3 ♗f6 12 d5± (Yudasin) or 8 de ♕xe7 9 gf ♘xc4 10 0-0 when Black has some problems on the e-file.

8   0-0

A more direct defence of c4 (against 8 … ♗xf3 9 ♗xf3 ♘xc4)

is **8 b3**, but this invites **8 ... a5!**
with immediate counterplay.
More standard methods are alsó
adequate: **8 ... ♗e7** 9 0–0 0–0 (9
... ♗xf3 10 ♗xf3 d5 11 ♖e1
0–0 Hergott–Paulsen, Graz 1981)
10 ♘c3 ♖e8 (10 ... ♘8d7 11 h3
♗h5 12 ♗f4 ♖e8 13 ♖e1 ♘f8 14
♕d2 ♗f6 15 ♘g5 ♗xe2 16 ♖xe2
♖xe2 17 ♘xe2 d5 18 c5 ♘bd7 19
♖e1 b6 20 b4 a5 21 b5 ♖c8 22
♘c3 ♘g6 secured counterplay in
Moroz–Timoshenko, Podolsk
1990.) 11 h3 ♗h5 12 ♗f4 ♗f6
13 ♕d2 d5 14 c5 ♘6d7 15 ♖ae1
♘f8= 16 ♘e5 ♗xe2 17 ♖xe2
♘bd7 18 ♖fe1 ♘xe5 19 ♗xe5
♗xe5 20 ♖xe5 ♖xe5 21 ♖xe5
♘e6 Wittmann–Bagirov, Frunze
1983.

8 ... ♗e7

9 ♘bd2!?

Thrusting forward the a-pawn
also provides counterplay in the
following lines: **9 ♕c2** 0–0 10 b3
a5! 11 a3 d5 12 c5 ♘6d7 intending
13 ... b6; **9 b3** a5! 10 ♗b2 (10 a3?
a4 undermines c4 in preparation
for 11 ... ♗xf3.) 10 ... a4 freezes
White's queenside, intending ...
♘a6–b4 and ... ♗f5.

9 ... 0–0

10 ♖e1!? *(118)*

10 ♕c2 can be met by 10 ...
♗h5, avoiding committing the b8
knight while preparing to hit
White's queen. **10 b3** again runs
into 10 ... a5, giving Black satisfactory play after either 11 ♗b2
a4 12 ♖b1 ♘a6 or 11 a4 ♘a6.

10 a4 is rather harmless at this

point: 10 ... d5 (10 ... a5) 11 c5
♘6d7 12 b4 ♗f6 13 ♕c2 ♖e8 14
♗d3 ♘f8 15 ♖b1 ♗h5 16 b5
♕c7 17 ♖b3 ½–½ Servat–Segal,
Mar del Plata 1990.

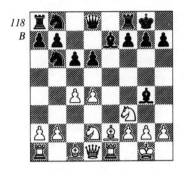

10 ... ♘8d7

After this move White demonstrates an interesting plan which
maintains some advantage. **10 ...
♖e8** 11 ♕c2 ♗h5 (11 ... ♘8d7 12
a4 is similar to the game.) 12 ♘f1
intending ♘g3, ♕b3 and h4 leaves
White with at least a pleasant
space advantage, but **10 ... ♗f6!**
puts far more pressure on White's
centre: 11 ♘e4? ♗xf3; 11 a4 d5!?
(or 11 ... a5); 11 ♕c2 ♖e8.

11 a4!

With Black's knights now a long
way from b4, this is logical. The
forthcoming ♖a3–e3 manoeuvre
is another point in favour of omitting b3.

11 ... a5

Yudasin gives this as the only
move, presumably since 11 ... d5
12 c5 ♘c8 13 b4 ♗f6 14 ♖a3
gives White slightly accelerated
play.

12   ♖a3!   ♖e8

12 ... ♗f6 is now well met by 13 ♘e4, as the rook defends f3, while **12 ... ♘f6** gives the white knights freedom of action on the kingside: 13 h3 ♗h5 14 ♘f1 with ♘g3 and ♘h4 to follow. Yudasin suggests that **12 ... ♗h5** and **12 ... ♕c7** keep White's advantage to a minimum, whilst **12 ... d5** may be considered.

13   ♖e3   ♘f8

White's control of the e-file causes some awkwardness: **13 ... ♗f6** is met by 14 ♘e4 whilst **13 ... ♗f8 14 ♗d3!?** ♖xe3 15 fe gives White a strong centre.

14   ♕b3!   ♗e6

Directed against 15 d5, though **14 ... ♕c7** is worth considering.

15   ♗d3   ♖b8
16   ♕c2!   d5

Now White's advantage becomes concrete. The structure that arises is much more palatable for Black with an unweakened queenside. Here White can make progress very quickly. 16 ... ♕c7 was still preferable, while counter-measures on the kingside tend to create extra weaknesses.

17   c5   ♘bd7
18   ♘b3!±   b6
19   ♗d2   ♖a8
20   ♖c1! *(119)*

By threatening 21 cb ♕xb6 22 ♕xc6 ♕xb3 23 ♗xh7+, Yudasin provokes a weakening of the king-side. After 20 ... ♔h8, 21 h4! prepares an assault on f7.

20   ...   g6

119 B

21   h4!   ♗g4
22   ♖ce1!

Mission accomplished, the rook resumes action on the e-file.

22   ...   ♗xf3
23   gf!

After 23 ♖xf3 bc, the h-pawn hangs. Now White intends pushing the h- and f-pawns, and will meet 23 ... bc? with 24 ♗xa5!+−.

23   ...   ♘e6
24   cb!   ♗xh4
25   b7!   ♖b8
26   ♕xc6   ♘df8!

Instead, 26 ... ♕g5+ 27 ♔f1 ♘f4 fails to 28 ♖xe8+ and ♗xf4. After the text, **27 ♖e5 ♕f6 28 ♕xd5** would leave Black bereft of chances. Instead, in mutual time trouble, the game becomes wildly unclear.

27   ♔f1?   ♗g5!
28   ♗xa5   ♕f6
29   ♘c5?!   ♗xe3
30   ♖xe3   ♕h4
31   ♘xe6   ♘xe6
32   ♔e1!   ♔g7?

32 ... ♖e7! 33 ♕c8+ (33 ♗c3? ♘f4 34 ♕c8+ ♔g7 35 ♖xe7

♕xe7+ ∓; 33 ♗a6 ♘xd4 34 ♕c8+ ∞) 33 ... ♖e8 34 ♕c6 is a peculiar draw by repetition.   `

33   ♗b4!!

By covering e7 and freeing the way for the a-pawn, White again achieves a winning position.

33   ...   ♘f4?!

33 ... ♘xd4 34 ♕xe8! ♖xe8 35 ♖xe8 and Black cannot quite stop the pawn. The best chance was **33 ... ♕h1+ 34 ♔d2 ♕g2 35 ♗d6!.** After the text the game finished **34 ♕xe8 ♘d3+ 35 ♔e2! ♘f4+ 36 ♔d1! ♖xe8 37 ♖xe8 ♕xf2 38 b8♕ ♕xf3+ 39 ♔c2 ♕d3+ 40 ♔c1 ♕f1+ 41 ♗e1 ♕c4+ 42 ♗c3 ♕f1+ 43 ♔c2 ♕d3+ 44 ♔b3 ♕d1+ 45 ♔b4 ♘d3+ 46 ♔a5 1–0.**

Brunner–Landenbergue
Biel 1990

1 e4 ♘f6 2 e5 ♘d5 3 d4 d6 4 ♘f3 ♗g4 5 ♗e2 c6 6 c4 ♘b6

7   ♘g5

One of White's best lines against the Flohr–Agzamov variation, as it is now inadvisable for Black to avoid the exchange of bishops. Note that 6 ♘g5 ♗f5 7 c4?! ♘b4 is ineffective.

7   ...   ♗xe2

After 7 ... ♗f5?! White has a very pleasant choice, as the knight on b6 is badly placed in many lines.

(a) **8 f4!?** h6 (Opening the f-file immediately leaves f7 exposed, while 8 ... e6? 9 ed fails completely.) 9 ♘f3 de 10 fe e6 11 ♘c3

♗e7 (Ideas with ... c5 leave Black a move down on lines of the Four Pawns.) 12 0–0 0–0 13 ♗e3 ♘8d7 14 c5 ♘d5 15 ♘xd5 cd 16 b4± Maus–Crocker, Gausdal Peer Gynt 1990.

(b) **8 e6!?** leaves the b6 knight poorly placed to defend the kingside after both 8 ... ♗xe6 9 ♘xe6 fe 10 ♗d3 and 8 ... fe 9 g4.

(c) **8 g4** is Wahls' idea. 8 ... ♗xb1 (8 ... ♗g6 9 e6!? f6!?) 9 ♖xb1 de 10 de ♕xd1+ 11 ♔xd1 e6 12 f4 ♘8d7 13 ♔c2 h6 14 ♘e4 ♘c5 15 ♘d6+ ♗xd6 16 ed ♘e4 17 b4 a5 18 ba ♘d7 19 ♖xb7 ♖xa5 20 ♖c7 ♘xd6 21 a3 c5 22 ♗b2 gave White supremacy in Wahls–Fleck, Bundesliga 1985/6. He polished off crisply: 22 ... f6 23 ♖d1 ♔e7 24 ♖c6 ♘f7 25 f5 ef 26 gf ♖d8 27 ♗f3 ♘de5 28 ♖c7+ ♔f8 29 ♗d5 ♘d6 30 ♗xe5 fe 31 f6 g5 32 ♖h7 1–0.

8   ♕xe2   de

8 ... h6 immediately may be a little more accurate, as then 9 ♘e4 can be met by 9 ... d5, whilst 9 ♘f3 de 10 de transposes to the game. Compared with the variation 6 ♘g5 ♗xe2 7 ♕xe2, Black's only advantage is the vulnerability of White's c- and e-pawns. Black must make the most of this by denying White's king's knight the e4 square.

9   de   h6

The attempt to kick back the knight with the bishop is rather dubious: 9 ... e6 10 0–0 ♗e7 11 ♘e4 ♕d4 12 b3 ♕xe5 (12 ... ♕xa1?

13 ②ec3 traps the queen.) 13 ♗b2.

10 ②f3

The pawn sacrifice **10 ②e4 e6** (10 ... ♕d4) 11 0–0 ♕d4 12 b3 ♕xe5 13 ♗b2 gave White reasonable compensation in Rechel–Paulsen, Bundesliga 1989/90. Play continued 13 ... ♕c7 14 f4 ②8d7 15 f5 e5 16 ♕e3 (16 f6) 16 ... ②f6?! 17 ②xf6+ gf 18 ②d2 ②d7 19 ②e4 ♕b6 20 ♖fe1 0–0–0 21 ♕xb6 ab 22 ♗c3 ♗e7 23 b4 ②b8 24 ♖e3 ②a6 25 ♖b1 ②c7 26 ♖g3 b5 27 c5 ♖d7 28 ♔f2 ♖hd8 29 ♖g7 and White went on to win.

10 ... e6
11 0–0 ②8d7 (120)

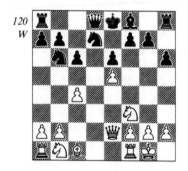

12 b3

After **12 ②c3 ♕c7 13 ♗f4**, Black has tried castling both long and short. The former seems the more satisfactory, but either way it is hard work for Black.

(a) **13 ... ②c5** 14 ♖ad1 a5 15 ♖d2 ♗e7 16 ♖fd1 0–0 17 b3 ♖fd8 18 ②d4 ②bd7 19 ♗g3 ②f8 20 h4 ♖d7 21 f4 ♖ad8 22 f5 ♕b6 23 ♔h2 a4 24 ♕f3 ②h7 25 ♕g4 ♗f8 26 ♗f4 and now the

exchange sacrifice 26 ... ♖xd4 led to an ending in Ernst–Kovačević, Thessaloniki ol 1984, in which Black should not have been losing, but actually managed to win!

(b) **13 ... 0–0–0** 14 ②e4 c5 15 ♗g3 ♔b8 16 a4 a6 17 ♖fd1 ♔a8 18 ♖d3 ♗e7 19 b3 ②c8 20 ♖ad1 ②a7 21 ♕d2 ②c6 22 ♕b2 (22 ♖xd7? ♖xd7 23 ♕xd7? ♖d8–+) 22 ... ♖hg8 23 ②f6!? ♗xf6 24 ef e5 25 fg f6 26 ♕d2 ♖xg7 27 ♕xh6 ♖dg8 28 ♔h1 ♕c8 29 ♕e3 ②d4 30 ②e1 ♕c6 31 f4 ef 32 ♕xf4 ②e5 33 ♖e3 ②g4 34 ♖ed3 ②e5 35 ♖e3 ②g4 36 ♖ed3 ②e5 ½–½ Wahls–Westerinen, Altensteig 1987.

12	...	♕c7
13	②c3	0–0–0
14	♗b2	♗e7
15	②e4	♔b8
16	♖ad1	②c8
17	♕e3	c5
18	♖d3	②db6
10	♖fd1	♖xd3
20	♖xd3	♖d8

White's back rank provides Black with a vital tempo to oppose the d-file — a familiar idea from Wahls–Westerinen.

21	②e1	♖xd3
22	②xd3	②d7
23	♕f4	♕a5

Again Black profits from White's back rank, as now 24 ♕xf7 is strongly met by 24 ... ♕xa2.

24	②c3	♕d8
25	♔f1	

25 ♕xf7 ②xe5 26 ②xe5 ♕d2 keeps Black well in the game.

After White's cautious king move, events unfolded without such drama: 25 ... ♕e8 26 ♘e4 a6 27 ♔e2 ♘a7 28 h4 ♘c6 (This manner of activating the knight is worth noting.) 29 h5 a5 30 a4 ♔a7 31 ♗c3 b6 32 g4 ♘db8 33 ♕e3 ♘a6 34 f4 ♘ab4 35 ♘xb4 ab 36 ♗b2 ♕d7 37 ♕d2 ♕xd2+ 38 ♔xd2 g6 39 g5 ♗f8 40 hg fg 41 gh ½–½.

Kovalëv–Dreev
Minsk 1986

1 e4 ♘f6 2 e5 ♘d5 3 d4 d6 4 ♘f3 ♗g4 5 ♗e2 c6 6 c4 ♘b6
7 ♘bd2
Originally advocated by Levenfish, this move, aiming to deny Black a good way to resolve the central tension, is probably the most critical test of Black's resources in the Flohr–Agzamov Variation. Black's best reply, 7 ... ♘8d7, is considered in the next game.

7 ... de?!
7 ... ♘a6?! 8 0–0 ♘d7 was tried in Nunn–Kovačević, Thessaloniki ol 1984, but simple methods proved effective: 9 ed! ed and now 10 ♖e1 ♗e7 11 d5 c5! 12 ♘g5 0–0! 13 ♗xg4! ♗xg5 14 ♗xd7 ♕xd7 15 ♘e4 ♗xc1 16 ♕xc1! ♖ad8 17 ♖e3 was sufficient for a small advantage, but better still is Nunn's suggestion 10 d5! cd (10 ... c5 11 ♘d4! ♗xe2 12 ♕xe2+ ♕e7 13 ♕xe7+ ♗xe7 14 ♘f5+) 11 ♖e1! ♗e7 (11 ... dc 12 ♘d4±) 12 ♘d4±.

8 ♘xe5 ♗f5 (121)
8 ... ♗e6 and 8 ... ♗xe2 have also been played, but White has no problems maintaining a small advantage against the former, and a large one against the latter.
(a) **8 ... ♗e6**
(a1) **9 ♘e4 f6 (9 ... h6? 10 ♘c5 ♗c8 11 ♗h5+ −) 10 ♘c5! ♗g8 11 ♘f3 ♕c7 (11 ... ♘xc4 12 ♘xb7 ♕c7 13 ♘c5) 12 b3 e5 13 ♘e4 (13 0–0?! ♗xc5 14 dc ♘d7 15 ♕d6 ♕xd6 16 cd c5!) 13 ... ♘8d7 14 de ♘xe5 (14 ... 0–0–0 15 ef ♘xf6 16 ♕c2 ♘xe4 17 ♕xe4 ♗b4+ 18 ♗d2 ♗xd2+ 19 ♘xd2 is rather a speculative pawn sacrifice.) 15 0–0 ♗f7 16 ♗b2 ♘xf3+ 17 ♗xf3 ♗e7 18 c5! ♘d5? (18 ... ♘c8 19 ♕d4 0–0 20 ♘g5 ♖d8 21 ♕c3± Bagirov) 19 ♘d6+ ♗xd6 20 cd ♕xd6 21 ♖e1+ ♔f8 22 ♕d4± Vogt–Bagirov, Riga 1981.
(a2) **9 ♘ef3 g6 (9 ... f6?! 10 0–0 ♗f7 11 ♕c2 ♘8d7 12 ♗d3 g6 13 ♖e1 ♕c7 14 a4± Scholonthier–Grzesik, W. German Ch [Bad Neuenahr] 1984) 10 b3 ♗g7 11 ♗b2 ♗f5 (11 ... 0–0 12 0–0 ♗f5 13 ♕c1 ♘8d7 14 ♘h4 e6 15 ♘xf5 ef 16 ♘f3± Nunn–Perović, Lugano 1984) 12 b4 (12 0–0 c5; 12 ♘f1 c5 13 ♕d2 cd 14 ♗xd4 ♗xd4 15 ♘xd4 ♘c6± Grosar–Horn, Zurich 1986) 12 ... a5 13 a3 ♘a6 14 ♗c3 0–0 15 0–0 ♘d7 (15 ... ab 16 ab ♘d7 17 ♕b3 ♘c7 intending ... b5.) 16 ba c5 17 ♕c1 cd 18 ♘xd4 ♗xd4 19 ♗xd4 e5 20 ♗c3 ♘ac5 gave Black reasonable play in Werner–Horn, Therwil 1986.

(b) **8 ... ♗xe2?!** 9 ♕xe2 gives Black an unprepossessing set of options.

(b1) **9 ... g6** 10 ♘df3 ♗g7 11 ♘xf7!+ –.

(b2) **9 ... e6** 10 ♕f3 ♕f6 11 ♕b3 ♕e7 12 c5 ♘d5 13 ♘e4 ♕c7 14 ♕f3! with very potent threats in Korolev–Sprenger, corres. 1985.

(b3) **9 ... ♕xd4** 10 ♘df3 ♕c5 11 0–0 f6 (Else ♗e3 and ♘g5.) 12 ♗e3 ♕a5 13 ♗d2 ♕a6 14 b3! fe 15 ♘xe5 ♘8d7 16 ♕h5+ g6 17 ♘xg6 ♘f6 18 ♕h3 ♖g8 19 ♘f4 ♕a3 20 ♖fe1! ♘bd7 21 ♘e6 ♔f7 22 ♖ad1 ♕xa2 23 ♕c3± Marczell–Krecak, corres. 1986.

(b4) **9 ... ♘8d7** 10 0–0 e6 (10 ... ♘xe5 11 de e6 12 ♘f3±) 11 b3 ♗e7 12 ♗b2 0–0 13 ♘e4 ♕c7 14 ♖ad1 ♖ae8 15 ♖fe1 ♘f6 16 ♘xf6+ ♗xf6 17 ♘g4 ♗e7 18 ♖d3 ♘d7 19 d5 cd 20 cd ♗b4 21 d6 ♕a5 22 ♘h6+ ♔h8 23 ♗xg7+ ♔xg7 24 ♕g4+ ♔h8 25 ♖g3 1–0 V. Ivanov–Donchenko, Moscow CSK 1990.

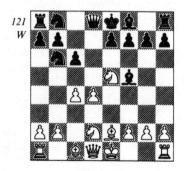

121
W

9 ♘df3

9 ♘ef3 is not very harmful. 9

... e6 10 0–0 ♗e7 11 ♖e1 0–0 12 ♕b3 c5 13 dc ♗xc5 14 ♘f1 ♘c6 15 ♗e3 ♕e7 16 ♖ed1 a6 17 ♗xc5 ♕xc5 18 ♕e3 ♘a4! 19 ♕xc5 ♘xc5 20 ♘e3 ♗e4 21 ♖d2 a5 was promising for Black in Sorokin–Dreev, Sochi 1986.

9 ♘f1 ♘8d7 10 ♗f4 (10 ♘e3 ♘xe5 11 c5 ♗g6 12 cb ♘d7=; 10 ♘f3?! ♗e4 11 ♘e3 e6 12 0–0 ♗e7 13 b3 0–0 14 ♗b2 a5!? 15 a3 ♕c7 16 ♕c1 ♖fd8 17 ♖d1 ♘f8 18 ♘d2 ♗g6 19 ♗f3 ♘bd7 preparing a central thrust, gave Black the edge in Ghinda–Agzamov, Potsdam 1985.) and now Speelman's suggestion 10 ... ♘xe5 11 ♗xe5 f6 12 ♗g3 e5!? is well worth trying. Black has compensation after either 13 de ♗b4+ 14 ♘d2 ♘a4!? or 13 ♘e3 ♗b4+ 14 ♔f1 ♗e6 15 de 0–0. Instead, Speelman–Burgess, London (Lloyds Bank) 1989 continued 10 ... e6 11 ♘e3 ♘xe5 (11 ... ♗b4+ 12 ♔f1 ♗e7 13 ♘xf5 ef 14 h4!?) 12 ♗xe5 ♗g6 13 0–0 f6 (13 ... ♘d7 14 ♗g3 ♗e7 15 ♗f3±) 14 ♗g3 ♗e7 and rather than 15 c5 ♘d5 16 ♘xd5 ed 17 ♗h5 0–0 when Black had almost equalised, 15 b4! (King) would have maintained a sizeable advantage.

9 ♕b3! is probably White's best move. 9 ... ♘8d7 10 ♘xd7 ♕xd7 11 ♘f3 ♗e4 (11 ... e6 12 ♗f4 ♗e7 13 a4 0–0 14 a5 ♘c8 15 0–0 ♗d6 16 ♘e5 ♕c7 17 c5 ♗xe5 18 ♗xe5 ♕d7 19 ♖a4 was very awkward for Black in Pesch–Schulte, Bundesliga 1985/6.) 12

♗e3 ♗xf3 13 ♗xf3 e6 14 0–0 ♗e7 15 a4 ♘c8 16 d5 (In Malaniuk–Dreev, Novosibirsk 1986, White inexplicably refrained from this thrust: 16 a5!? a6 17 ♕a4?! ♘d6 18 ♗g4?! h5 19 ♗h3 g5 20 g3 g4 21 ♗g2 ♘f5∓) 16 ... cd 17 cd ed (17 ... e5? 18 ♗g4+ −) 18 ♕xd5 ♘d6 19 ♗c5 0–0 20 ♖fe1 (20 ♖ae1!?±) 20 ... ♖fe8 21 h3 ♗f8 22 ♖xe8 ♕xe8 23 b3 ♖d8 24 ♖d1 b6 25 ♗e3 ♕e6 26 ♕xe6 fe± Reeh–Burgess, Gausdal Peer Gynt 1990.

9 ... e6?

After this, Black more or less loses by force. Black could try **9 ... ♘8d7**, though White can keep some advantage with normal moves, e.g. 10 0–0.

More challenging is **9 ... f6!?**. A move that Kovalëv recommended is **10 ♘h4?!** but this loses a pawn to 10 ... fe 11 ♘xf5 e6. Speelman considered that **10 ♘d3 ♘xc4 11 ♘f4** yields compensation, but not enough to tempt him to play it. **10 c5 ♘d5 11 ♘c4±** is given by Kovalëv, but 10 ... fe 11 cb ♘d7 is more in the spirit of things, when Black should be OK.

10 ♘g5! ♗b4+

10 ... f6 11 ♘ef7 ♕c7 12 ♘xh8 fg 13 g4 ♗e4 14 f3 ♗xf3 15 ♗xf3 ♘xc4 16 0–0–0+ −.

10 ... ♗g6 11 h4 ♗e7 12 h5 ♗c2 13 ♘gxf7 ♗xd1 14 ♘xd8 ♗xe2 15 ♘xe6 ♗xc4 16 ♘c7+ ♔d8 17 ♘xa8±.

11 ♔f1 0–0

11 ... ♗g6 12 c5! ♘6d7 (12 ...

♘d5 13 h4±) 13 ♘xg6 hg 14 ♕b3±.

12 g4! ♗g6

12 ... f6 13 gf fg 14 fe ♕f6 15 ♗e3 ♕xe6 16 ♗xg5±.

13 c5! (122)

After 13 h4?! ♗e7! Black can defend. Now 13 ... ♘d5 and 13 ... ♘6d7 are both met by 14 ♘xg6 hg 15 ♕b3 with ideas of 16 ♕h3, so Black must keep ... ♕d5 available. However, there are other ways to break open the black king's defences.

13	...	♘c8
14	h4!	f6
15	♘xg6	hg
16	♗c4!	fg
17	♗xe6	♖f7
18	♕b3	♕f6
19	♖h2!	gh
20	g5	1–0

Sion Castro–Fernandez Garcia
Salamanca 1990

1 e4 ♘f6 2 e5 ♘d5 3 d4 d6 4 ♘f3 ♗g4 5 ♗e2 c6 6 c4 ♘b6 7 ♘bd2

7 ... ♘8d7

8 ♘g5

8 h3 seems rather less logical

than castling, but the pawn on h3 can be useful in holding up the advance of Black's g-pawn. **8 ... ♗xf3 9 ♘xf3 de 10 de e6 11 0–0 ♛c7** *(123).*

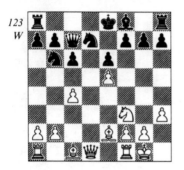

123
W

(a) **12 ♗f4 h6** (12 ... ♗c5 intends ... ♘c8–e7–g6 with reasonable play.) 13 ♛c2 g5 (Black's play in Veröci–P. Cramling, Havana IZ 1985 was inconsistent with her twelfth move: 13 ... a5 14 a3 a4 15 ♖fe1 ♗c5 16 ♖ad1 ♘c8 17 ♗d3 ♘e7 18 ♛e2 ♗b6 19 ♗c2 ♘c5 20 ♖d6 ♘c8 21 ♖ed1! ♛e7 22 ♖6d4 ♗a5 23 ♘d2 g5 24 ♗g3 ♗xd2 25 ♛xd2 ♘b6 26 ♛b4±) 14 ♗g3 0–0–0 15 ♖fd1 ♗e7 16 a3 h5 17 b4 g4 18 hg hg gave Black good counterplay in Nöcker–Hebels, corres. 1984.

(b) **12 ♛d4 h6** (Sokolov gives 12 ... 0–0–0 13 ♗g5 ♖e8 14 a4 when the tempi lost with Black's rook are more important than that which will be lost by the bishop. An important point is 14 ... ♔b8? 15 a5 ♘c8 16 ♖fd1 ♘c5 17 ♗d8+ −, though naturally 14 ... a5 comes into consideration.) **13**

♖d1 (13 b3 g5 14 ♗b2 ♘c8 15 ♗d3 ♖g8, delaying committing the king and bishop, was an interesting method of obtaining counterplay in Arnold–Miltner, Baden Württemburg 1982.) **13 ... g5** (Sokolov's 13 ... g6 14 b3 ♗g7 15 ♗b2 0–0± is one of Black's less dynamic options.) **14 b3** and now Sokolov–Kremenietsky, Moscow 1990 continued with **14 ... ♗g7**, which is surely a mistake, as it creates no real threats from g7, while blocking the g-file and giving up control of b4 and c5. Black was starved of counterplay after 15 ♗b2 0–0–0 16 ♛e3 ♔b8 17 a4 ♘c8 18 b4 ♘e7 19 ♗d3! and resorted to desperate measures: 19 ... a5 20 ba ♛xa5 21 ♖db1 ♘c5 22 ♗c2 ♘f5 23 ♗xf5 ef 24 ♘d4 f4 25 ♛a3 ♔a8 26 ♗c3! ♛a7 27 a5! ♗f8 28 a6 ♘xa6 29 ♛a5 ♖xd4 (29 ... ♖c8 30 ♘b5! cb 31 cb b6 32 ♛a4! ♖xc3 33 ♛e4+! ♛b7 34 ♖xa6+ ♔b8 35 ♛d4 ♖c5 36 e6 f6 37 ♛xf6 ♗g7 38 ♛g6 ♖hc8 39 e7+ − Sokolov) 30 ♗xd4 ♛xd4 and White had a choice of wins. Clearly Black should leave the bishop on f8 for a while at least, with **14 ... 0–0–0, 14 ... ♖g8!?** or even **14 ... ♘c8!?**.

8 0–0 ♗xf3 (8 ... de?! 9 ♘xe5 gives White the upper hand after either 9 ... ♗xe2 10 ♛xe2 ♘xe5 11 de e6 12 ♘f3± or 9 ... ♘xe5!? 10 de ♗e6 11 ♛b3 g6 12 ♘f3 ♗g7 13 ♘g5 ♛c8 14 f4 0–0 15 ♗e3 Nijboer–Landenbergue, Lucerne 1989.) **9 ♘xf3 de 10 de**

e6 11 ♗d2 ♛c7 12 ♗c3 0-0-0
(Black's position is disorganised
after 12 ... h6?! 13 a4 since 13 ...
0-0-0 14 a5 condemns the knight
to the corner, whilst 13 ... a5 14
♖e1 g5 15 ♛c2 ♗g7 16 ♖ad1
denied the black king any safety
in Altschuler–Kopylov, corres.
1970.) 13 ♛c2 h6 14 a4 (14 ♗a5
g5 15 b4 c5) 14 ... ♔b8 15 a5 ♘c8
and against White's queenside
advances Black organises counterplay on the kingside and against
e5 with ... g5, ... ♘e7–g6 and ...
♗g7.

8 ed!? ed is similar to Yudasin–
Timoshenko, and indeed 9 0-0
♗e7 10 ♖e1 0-0 transposes. If
Black wishes to avoid this, the
forthright 9 ... d5 could be tried.
A further possibility is 9 0-0 ♗e7
10 a4 a5 11 ♖a3 0-0 12 ♖e3 d5
13 c5 ♘c8 14 ♛c2 ♗h5 15 ♗d3
♗g6 16 ♗xg6 fg 17 ♖fe1 ♗f6
18 ♛b3 b6 19 ♖e6 bc 20 ♖xc6
♘e7 21 ♖d6 ♖b8 22 ♛e3 ♘f5 23
♛e6+ ♖f7 24 ♖xd5 ♛c7 when, in
Van Riemsdijk–Fernandez Garcia, Buenos Aires 1990, White's
pieces were awkwardly placed.

8 ... ♗f5

8 ... ♗xe2 9 e6 f6 10 ♛xe2 fg
(124) is also playable. White has
two fundamentally different
approaches.

(a) **11 ed+** ♛xd7 12 ♘e4 0-0-0
13 ♘xg5 e5 14 de ♖e8 15 0-0
♖xe5 16 ♛c2 h6 17 ♘f3 ♛f5= 18
♛xf5 ♖xf5 19 ♘h4 ♖f7 20 ♘g6
♖g8 21 b3 d5 22 ♘xf8 ½–½ Gola-
Landenbergue, Prague Vysehrad

124
W

1989.

(b) **11 ♘e4 ♘f6 12 ♘xg5 ♘xc4!**
(Black must be prepared to return
the piece, as shown by Nigmadzh-
anov–Kaplin, USSR 1977: 12 ...
♛c7? 13 ♘f7 ♖g8 14 g4 h6 15 h4
d5 16 c5 ♘c8 17 g5 ♘e4 18 gh gh
19 ♛h5 ♘f6 20 ♘d6++ ♔d8 21
♛e8+ ♘xe8 22 ♘f7 #.) **13 0-0** (13
♛xc4 ♛a5+ 14 ♗d2 ♛d5) **13 ...
♛a5 14 ♛xc4 h6 15 ♘f7 ♖g8 16
♛b3** (16 ♛c2, threatening 17 ♛g6,
can be met by 16 ... g5.) **16 ...
♛b5** (16 ... ♛b6 17 ♛d3 g5) **17
♛xb5 cb.** Black now intends to
capture the e6 pawn (... g5, ...
♖g6, ... ♘d5), in some lines trap-
ping the f7 knight. White must
play very actively to prevent this:
**18 ♗d2 g5 19 ♖ac1 ♘d5 20 ♖c2
♖g6 21 ♖e1 ♗g7** is inadequate.
18 h4 ♘d5 19 ♗d2 g5 20 h5! (20
hg hg is good for Black after either
21 ♗xg5 ♘c7 or 21 ♘xg5 ♗h6
22 ♘f3 ♗xd2 23 ♘xd2 ♘f4.) **20
... ♖c8! 21 ♖ac1 ♖c6 22 ♖xc6**
(22 ♗a5 ♘f4!) **22 ... bc 23 ♖c1
♘c7 24 ♖xc6 ♘xe6 25 ♘e5 de 26
♖xe6 ed 27 ♔f1** and in Vogt–
Rogulj, Balatonbereny 1986 a

draw was agreed since White's active rook constitutes just enough compensation for the extra pawn.

9   e6

In Martín–Fernandez Garcia, Spanish Ch 1978, the stem game for 8 ... ♗f5, White played the weaker 9 ♗g4?!. There followed 9 ... e6! 10 f4 de 11 ♗xf5 ef 12 de h6 13 ♘gf3 (13 ♕h5?! g6 14 ♕h3 ♘c5 15 0-0 ♘d3 leaves White in great difficulties.) 13 ... ♘c5 14 0-0 ♕d3! 15 ♕e1 ♘e6 16 ♔h1 0-0-0 17 g3 g5! and Black embarked on a vicious kingside onslaught. White succumbed as follows: 18 fg hg 19 ♘b3 f4! 20 gf g4! 21 f5 gf 22 fe ♗b4 23 ♕f2 ♖xh2+! 24 ♔xh2 ♖h8+ 25 ♔g3 ♖g8+ 26 ♔f4 fe! 27 ♕xf3 ♖f8+ 27 ♔g3 ♗e1+ 29 ♔g2 ♖xf3 30 ♖xe1 ♖g3+ 31 ♔h2 ♖h3+ 0-1.

9   ...   fe

Less logical is 9 ... ♗xe6 10 ♘xe6 fe 11 0-0 e5 12 ♘f3 e4 13 ♘g5 ♘f6 14 d5!?, as analysed by Winsnes.

10   g4

10 ♗h5+ g6 11 g4 naturally deserves consideration. 11 ... ♗d3 12 ♕f3 ♘f6 is rather unclear.

10   ...   ♗g6

11   ♕b3

11 ♘xe6 ♕c8 and now 12 f4 ♗f7!? or 12 g5!? (Crocker) 12 ... ♘e5!? 13 ♘xf8 ♘d3+ 14 ♗xd3 ♗xd3.

11	...	♕c8
12	♗d3	♗xd3
13	♕xd3	♘f6
14	♕e2	h6!

15	♘xe6	♔f7
16	g5	hg
17	♘f3	♘h7 (125)

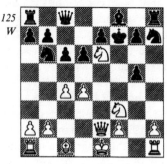

125
W

18	♘fxg5+	♘xg5
19	♘xg5+	♔g8
20	♘e6	♔f7
21	♘g5+	♔g8

Black can hardly tolerate a knight on e6, so has nothing better than repeating moves. Sion Castro decides to try for more, but Fernandez demonstrates that Black has hidden defensive and counterattacking resources.

22	♕d3	♖h6!
23	♗e3	♕g4!
24	h4	d5
25	b3	dc
26	bc	e5

Thus the f8 bishop springs into action and the white king is in grave danger. The game continued 27 c5 ♘d5 28 de ♖e8 29 ♕b3 ♖xe5 30 ♕xb7 ♖f6 31 ♕b3.

Now 31 ... ♗xc5? fails to 32 ♕b8+, but Black finds an effective method of demolition: 31 ... ♖xf2! 32 ♔xf2 ♖xe3 33 ♕xe3 ♘xe3 34 ♔xe3 ♗xc5+ 35 ♔d3 ♕d4+ 36 ♔e2 ♕e3+ 37 ♔d1 ♗b4 38 ♔c2 ♕c3+ 0-1.

Index of Variations

9 ♘f3
   9 ... ♘b4 *114*
   9 ... ♕d7 10 ♗e2
      10 ... 0–0–0 11 0–0 *115*
      10 ... ♖d8
         11 0–0 ♗g4 *117*
         11 ♕d2 *117*
   9 ... ♗g4
      10 ♗e2 ♗xf3 11 gf ♕h4+ 12 ♗f2 ♕f4 *118*
      10 ♕d2
         10 ... ♕d7 *120*
         10 ... ♗e7 *121*
         10 ... ♗b4 11 a3 (11 ♗e2 *121*) 11 ... ♗e7 *122*
   9 ... ♗b4 10 ♗e2 (10 ♖c1 *123*; 10 a3 *123*) 10 ... 0–0 *123*
   9 ... ♗e7
      10 ♗e2 0–0 11 0–0 f6 *124*
      10 d5 ♘b4
         11 ♘d4 *125*
         11 ♖c1 *126*

**2 e5 ♘d5 3 d4 d6 4 c4 ♘b6 5 f4 de 6 fe ♘c6 7 ♗e3 ♗f5 8 ♘c3 e6
9 ♘f3 ♗e7 10 d5 ed 11 cd** (11 ♗xb6 *127*) **11 ... ♘b4 12 ♘d4 ♗d7**
   13 ♘f3 *128*
   13 ♕b3 c5 14 dc bc *128*
   13 ♕f3 c5 14 dc bc *129*
   13 e6 fe 14 de ♗c6 15 ♕g4 ♗h4+ 16 g3 ♗xh1
      17 0–0–0 ♕f6 18 gh 0–0
         19 ♗h3 *131*
         19 ♗g5 *131*
         19 ♗e2 *131*
         19 ♗b5
            19 ... c6 *133*
            19 ... c5 20 ♗g5 ♕e5 *132*
      17 ♗b5+ c6 18 0–0–0 0–0 19 gh *133*

2 e5 ♘d5 3 d4 d6 4 ♘f3
   4 ... c6 *135*
   4 ... ♗f5 *136*
   4 ... ♘b6
      5 ♘c3 *136*
      5 ♗e2 *136*